Transforming Agriculture in South Asia

Debates about public expenditure in the agricultural sector have reopened in many developing and emerging economies because of high budget deficits and changes in public opinion. As a result, agricultural policy in many of these countries is beginning to take a more market-oriented approach to agrarian problems, most notably through the introduction of contract farming. This book explores the policy issues around contract farming and its transformative potential and addresses the lack of empirical research on this topic by focusing on South Asia: principally India, Bangladesh and Nepal.

The book first addresses the effects of contract farming (vertical coordination) on productivity, food security indicators (yield, consumption expenditures, prices), employment and input usage. Then it draws lessons from the South Asian case studies on the impact of institutional changes, like contract farming, on income and food security of smallholder households. The core of the book includes case study chapters on several commodities that are produced under contract farming, including vegetables and fisheries in Bangladesh, low-value crops in Nepal and coffee in India. Other chapters also explore contracts, storage, input usage and technical efficiency in these cases.

This book serves as an essential guide to academics, researchers, students, legislative liaisons and think tank groups interested in agrarian issues, agricultural economics and agricultural policy in emerging economies and particularly in South Asia.

Ashok K. Mishra is Kemper and Ethel Marley Foundation Chair, Morrison School of Agribusiness, W. P. Carey School of Business, Arizona State University, Tempe, USA.

Anjani Kumar is Senior Research Fellow, International Food Policy Research Institute, South Asia Office, New Delhi, India.

Pramod K. Joshi is former Senior Advisor to the Director General and Director–South Asia, International Food Policy Research Institute, New Delhi, India.

Routledge Studies in Agricultural Economics
Series Editor
Ashok K. Mishra
Arizona State University, USA

Public Policy in Agriculture
Impact on Labor Supply and Household Income
Edited by Ashok K. Mishra, Davide Viaggi and Sergio Gomez y Paloma

Agricultural Development in Brazil
The Rise of a Global Agro-food Power
Edited by Antonio M. Buainain, Rodrigo Lanna and Zander Navarro

The Economics of Food Loss in the Produce Industry
Edited by Travis Minor, Suzanne Thornsbury, and Ashok K. Mishra

Transforming Agriculture in South Asia
The Role of Value Chains and Contract Farming
Edited by Ashok K. Mishra, Anjani Kumar and Pramod K. Joshi

For more information about this series, please visit: www.routledge.com/Routledge-Studies-in-Agricultural-Economics/book-series/RSAG

Transforming Agriculture in South Asia

The Role of Value Chains and Contract Farming

Edited by Ashok K. Mishra, Anjani Kumar and Pramod K. Joshi

Routledge
Taylor & Francis Group
LONDON AND NEW YORK

First published 2021
by Routledge
2 Park Square, Milton Park, Abingdon, Oxon OX14 4RN

and by Routledge
52 Vanderbilt Avenue, New York, NY 10017

Routledge is an imprint of the Taylor & Francis Group, an informa business

British Library Cataloguing-in-Publication Data
A catalogue record for this book is available from the British Library

Library of Congress Cataloging-in-Publication Data
A catalog record for this book has been requested

ISBN: 978-0-367-45727-3 (hbk)
ISBN: 978-1-003-02499-6 (ebk)

Typeset in Bembo
by Apex CoVantage, LLC

Contents

Figures

Tables

Contributors

Muhammad Umer Afzal is Research Associate with International Maize and Wheat Improvement Center. He has more than five years of research and development experience. Before CIMMYT, he served at Innovative Development Strategies (IDS). He completed MSc (Honors) from the University of Arid Agriculture, Rawalpindi, Pakistan.

Akhter Ali started his professional career with the National Rural Support Program (NRSP). He then served on the Pakistan Agricultural Research Council (PARC) for more than 12 years before joining CIMMYT in 2013. He obtained his PhD in Agricultural Economics from the University of Kiel, Germany, in 2010 on the 'Impact of Land Tenure Arrangements, Bt cotton Adoption and Market Participation on the Welfare of Farm Households in Rural Pakistan.' He has also supervised several MS and PhD students. His research interest focuses on the adoption and impact of agricultural technologies, food security, poverty, climate change, gender mainstreaming, social inclusiveness, value chain etc. He has more than 70 international publications.

Seema Bathla is Professor, Centre for the Study of Regional Development, Jawaharlal Nehru University, New Delhi, India. She has previously worked in the Institute of Economic Growth, the Energy Research Institute and Delhi College of Arts and Commerce, Delhi. She was a fellow under the International Visitors Program sponsored by the U.S. government. She obtained her MPhil from Delhi School of Economics and PhD from Jawaharlal Nehru University. She has undertaken several assignments for the World Bank, IFPRI, UNCTAD, WWF-India and IASRI. She was conferred the Jawaharlal Nehru Award for Outstanding Post-Graduate Agricultural Research by the Indian Council of Agriculture Research, New Delhi in 2008; Dr. R. T. Doshi award for the best paper published in Agricultural Economics Research Review in 2014 and 2015; Dr. S. R. Sen prize for best book by the Indian Society of Agricultural Economics in 2018. During recent years, she has undertaken important research studies on public and private capital formation and subsidies in Indian agriculture, agrarian change and food security, growth performance of food processing industry, multilateral and regional trade agreements in agriculture.

Pratap S. Birthal is National Professor at the National Institute of Agricultural Economics and Policy Research, New Delhi, India. Earlier, he has served as Principal Scientist at the International Crops Research Institute for the Semi-Arid Tropics, Patancheru (Telangana) and Director, Institute of Development Studies, Jaipur. He has made notable contributions in agricultural economics and policy research. His contributions focus on the interrelationship among agricultural diversification, growth and rural poverty; market linkages and value chains in smallholder production systems; the impact of information on returns from farming; institutional and policy requirements for accelerating the adoption of technologies; the impact of climate change; and adaptations in agriculture.

Tirtha Chatterjee is Assistant Professor at the Centre for Development Studies (CDS), Kerala, India. She holds a PhD (Development Studies) from Indira Gandhi Institute of Development and Research (IGIDR), Mumbai. Her research interests include agriculture and nutrition interlinkages, agricultural marketing in India, agricultural commodity futures market and spatial econometrics.

Varun Kumar Das is a doctoral student at the Indira Gandhi Institute of Development Research (IGIDR), Mumbai, India. His doctoral research is on the determinants of farmers' income and diversification decisions. His research interests include development economics, agricultural economics and labor.

S. Mahendra Dev has been Director and Vice-Chancellor of the Indira Gandhi Institute of Development Research, Mumbai, India, since 2010. He was a member and vice chairman of the International Food Policy Research Institute. He is a consultant and adviser to many international organizations, such as the United Nations Development Programme, the World Bank, the International Labour Organization and the Food and Agriculture Organization of the United Nations. He was Chairman of the Commission for Agricultural Costs and Prices, Ministry of Agriculture, from 2008 to 2010. From 1999 to 2008, S. Mahendra was director of the Centre for Economic and Social Studies in Hyderabad, India. He was acting chairman of the National Statistical Commission. He is a member of several government committees, including the Prime Minister's Task Force on Employment and the Committee on Financial Inclusion. His work in the areas of agricultural development, poverty and public policy, food security, employment guarantee schemes, social security and farm and non-farm employment is well recognized.

Devika, C. M. is Senior Consultant at the Agricultural Development and Rural Transformation Centre, Institute for Social and Economic Change,

Bengaluru, India, and holds a doctorate in Economics and a postgraduate diploma in Environmental Law.

Madan M. Dey is Chair and Professor of Agricultural Economics at Texas State University, USA. He began his career in the economics of agricultural development focusing on rice and completed his postdoctoral research on the agricultural economy of Asia under the mentorship of Professor Robert Evenson of Yale University from 1991 to 1993. He has worked in various academic and research organizations and has researched several subsectors of agriculture and natural resources, including crop, livestock and fisheries. Over the past 30 years, he has led and implemented a number of pioneering, innovative and interdisciplinary agricultural projects in the United States, Asia and Africa.

Alwin Dsouza is a PhD candidate at Morrison School of Agribusiness, W. P. Carey School of Business, Arizona State University, Tempe, USA. He was formerly Research Associate at the International Maize and Wheat Improvement Centre (CIMMYT). He has completed his MPhil in Economics from Jawaharlal Nehru University, New Delhi, India. He was involved in qualitative and quantitative research while working at International Maize and Wheat Improvement Centre (CIMMYT) and the International Food Policy Research Institute (IFPRI). His current research is on analyzing food loss/waste in both developing and developed countries and finding feasible solutions to reduce it. His area of interest lies in social networks among farmers, technology adoption, food access and contract farming.

A. Ganesh-Kumar is Professor and Dean of Faculties at the Indira Gandhi Institute of Development Research (IGIDR), Mumbai, India. He specializes in computable general equilibrium (CGE) modeling with a focus on food and agricultural policies and issues relating to sustainable human development and economic growth. He is on the editorial board of two journals, *Agricultural Economics*, the journal of the International Association of Agricultural Economists, and *Indian Journal of Agricultural Economics*, the journal of the Indian Society of Agricultural Economics. He has undertaken several projects for the Government of India, Reserve Bank of India and various international agencies such as the Food and Agriculture Organisation, UN-ESCAP, World Bank, USDA, the Carnegie Endowment for International Peace and IDRC, among others. He has published over 90 publications, including books, monographs, journal articles, book chapters, project reports and working papers.

Ashok Gulati is Infosys Chair Professor for Agriculture at the Indian Council for Research on International Economic Relations (ICRIER). Previously, he was the chairman of the Commission for Agriculture Costs and Prices (CACP), Government of India. He also served as the director at the International Food Policy Research Institute (IFPRI) for more than ten years. He is also currently on the Central Board of Directors of the Reserve Bank of

India (RBI), National Bank for Agriculture and Rural Development (NABARD) and National Commodity and Derivatives Exchange (NCDEX). He has published 15 books and several research papers on Indian and Asian agriculture. He is a prolific writer in media on agri-policies, and for his contributions to the field, the president of India honored him with the Padma Shri award in 2015.

Jaweriah Hazrana is a researcher at the National Institute of Agricultural Economics and Policy at (NIAP) of Indian Council for Agricultural Research (ICAR). Her research focuses on climate change and its impact on agriculture in low-income and developing countries, the scope of diverse adaptation strategies in building resilience against climate change and the acroeconomic cost of natural disasters.

Stefan Hirsch is Assistant Professor of Agricultural and Food Economics at TUM School of Management, Germany. His research focuses on the competitiveness of agribusiness firms. This involves investigating the drivers of vertical and horizontal integration, production flexibility, innovation, efficiency and profitability. Furthermore, his research deals with the effect of oligopolistic market structures at different stages of the food supply chain on the performance of firms in up- and downstream sectors. His research has a strong empirical orientation and is based on a broad range of theoretical microeconomic approaches and econometric methods.

Akbar Hossain is Senior Agronomist at Bangladesh Wheat and Maize Research Institute, Bangladesh. He earned his bachelor of science in Agriculture and master of science in Agronomy from Bangladesh Agricultural University, Bangladesh, and a PhD degree in plant ecology from Astrakhan State University, Russia. He worked as a postdoctoral fellow for 'Isolation, Characterization, and Purification of Rhizobium Strain to Enrich the Productivity of Groundnut (*Arachis hypogaea* L.)' in Bidhan Chandra Krishi Viswavidyalaya, West Bengal, India, through India Science and Research Fellowship. Dr. Hossain started his career as an agronomist in Bangladesh Agricultural Research Institute, Bangladesh. His research interests and expertise are plant physiology, crop management, conservation agriculture, climate change impact assessment on field crops through modeling.

Md. Israil Hossain, Director General (in charge) of Bangladesh Wheat and Maize Research Institute (BWMRI), is a renowned Agricultural Engineer in Bangladesh. He obtained his bachelor of science in Agricultural Engineering, master of science in Farm Power and Machinery and PhD degrees from Bangladesh Agricultural University, Bangladesh. He started his career as a scientific officer in Farm Machinery and Postharvest Process Engineering Division (FMPE) of the Bangladesh Agricultural Research Institute. He is the pioneer of the development and expansion of the BARI power maize sheller and BARI wheat thresher in Bangladesh. As one of the leading agricultural engineers who has made a considerable contribution in the expansion of small machinery, expansion and conservation agriculture–(CA–) based machinery, he provides technical supports to promote local agricultural machinery manufacturers. For his contribution in the field of agricultural mechanization in Bangladesh, he has received several awards from the World Congress of Conservation Agriculture, Food for Progress, Cornell University–USA and ACIAR–Australia. He is an active member of the Technical Working Group of Centre for Sustainable Mechanization (CSAM), UN ESCAP (China).

Abu Hayat Md. Saiful Islam is Associate Professor in the Department of Agricultural Economics, Bangladesh Agricultural University, Mymensingh, Bangladesh. He holds a PhD in Agricultural Economics from the University of Bonn, Germany. His research interests focus on adoption and impact assessment of different technology, policy and institutional innovation with particular focus on developing country agriculture by using a range of cross-sectional and panel microeconometric techniques including experimental and quasi-experimental methods.

Abhishek Jha is pursuing his PhD in Economics at the Centre for the Study of Regional Development, Jawaharlal Nehru University, New Delhi, India. He is also a visiting consultant at the Trade Promotion Council of India engaged in research on agricultural trade, regional trade agreements and trade policies. He has published several research papers in refereed journals and edited books.

Pramod K. Joshi is a former director for South Asia, International Food Policy Research Institute, New Delhi, India. Previously, he held the positions of the director of the National Academy of Agricultural Research Management, Hyderabad, India, and the director of the National Centre for Agricultural Economics and Policy Research, New Delhi. Earlier, Dr. Joshi has received several important awards, including the Dr. MS Randhawa Memorial Award of the National Academy of Agricultural Sciences (2009–2011), Dr. RC Agarwal Life Time Achievement Award of the Indian Society of Agricultural Economics (2012–2013) for his outstanding contribution in social science and agricultural economics research. He is Fellow of the National Academy of Agricultural Sciences and the Indian Society of Agricultural Economics. Dr. Joshi was president-elect of the Indian Society of Agricultural Economics (2014), conference president of the Indian Society of Agricultural Marketing (2014) and Conference President of Agricultural Economics Research Association–India (2015). He is presently the president of the Agricultural Economics Research Association–India and the secretary of the National Academy of Agricultural Sciences. Dr. Joshi has served as the chairman of the SAARC Agricultural Centre's governing board in Dhaka, Bangladesh (2006–2008); chairman of the UN–CAPSA governing board in Bogor (2007); and member of the intergovernmental panel on the World Bank's International Assessment of Agricultural Science and Technology for

Development (2007–2008). His areas of research include technology policy, agricultural markets and institutional economics.

Elumalai Kannan is Associate Professor in the Centre for the Study of Regional Development (CSRD), School of Social Sciences (SSS)-III, Jawaharlal Nehru University (JNU), New Delhi, India. He works in the area of agricultural economics, natural resource management, institutional economics, non-farm sector and rural development. He has worked at various reputed institutions such as International Maize and Wheat Improvement Centre, New Delhi Office, National Council of Applied Economic Research, Madras School of Economics, Chennai, and the Institute for Social and Economic Change, Bangalore. During recent years, he has undertaken important research studies on inclusive agricultural growth, agricultural productivity, agrarian change and farm sector distress, agricultural market reforms, peri-urban agriculture and trade in agricultural products.

Anjani Kumar is a Senior Research Fellow at International Food Policy Research Institute (IFPRI) South Asia office. Previously, he was Principal Scientist (Agricultural Economics) at the International Crops Research Institute for the Semi-Arid Tropics (ICRISAT), Hyderabad. Earlier, he served as Principal Scientist at the National Centre for Agricultural Economics and Policy Research (NCAP), New Delhi, and as Senior Agricultural Economist in the Asia Office of International Livestock Research Institute (ILRI), Nairobi. He has also worked as a consultant for several national and international institutions, including FAO, World Bank, National Agricultural Cooperative Marketing Federation of India (NAFED) and Department of Science and Technology (DST), Government of India. He has made significant contributions to agricultural economics and policy research. His contributions have been well recognized, and he is a Fellow of the National Academy of Agricultural Sciences (NAAS) of India. He has won a number of awards from national and international institutions. To list a few, he was awarded the prestigious Rafi Ahmad Kidwai Award (2017), Lal Bahadur Young Scientist Award (2005) and NAAS Young Scientist Award (2003).

Parmod Kumar is Professor of Agricultural Development and Rural Transformation Centre, Institute for Social and Economic Change, Bengaluru, India. He obtained his postdoctorate as Sir Ratan Tata Fellow from the Institute of Economic Growth and doctorate from Jawaharlal Nehru University, New Delhi. He was fellow under the International Visitors Leadership Program (IVLP) sponsored by the US government. He was Visiting Scholar to Glasgow University, OECD-FAO Paris and Zurich University of Applied Sciences (ZHAW), Institute of Natural Resource Sciences, Switzerland. He was managing editor of the *Journal of Social and Economic Development* for three years and is on the editorial board of *Agricultural Situation in India* and the *Indian Journal of Agricultural Marketing*. Professor Kumar was empaneled as Visiting Professor in Economics for deputation to the ICCR

Chair Abroad by the Indian Council for Cultural Relations (ICCR), New Delhi. He has been conferred the IDRC India Social Science Research Award for his work on the public distribution system. His major areas of research are in Agricultural Economics, Environment Economics, Rural Development and Development Economics.

Manjunatha, A. V. is Assistant Professor in the Centre for Ecological Economics and Natural Resources of the Institute for Social and Economic Change, Bengaluru, Karnataka. India. He obtained his MSc degree in Agricultural Economics from the University of Agricultural Sciences, Bengaluru, and an International MSc degree in Rural Development (Erasmus Mundus Fellow) from the University of Ghent, Belgium. He holds a doctoral degree in Agricultural Economics (DAAD Fellow) from Justus Liebig University, Giessen, Germany. He has worked in several national and international projects and has been involved in drafting policy documents for state and central governments. His main research areas include NRM, agricultural water management, agricultural markets, value chains, the impact analysis of developmental programs, technology adoption, international trade, energy and climate change in agriculture.

Ashok K. Mishra is Kemper and Ethel Marley Foundation Chair in Food Management, Morrison School of Agribusiness, W. P. Carey School of Business, at the Arizona State University, USA, where he conducts research and teaching activities in public policy, finance, agribusiness and food security. He has published more than 170 papers in peer-reviewed journals, 15 book chapters and more than 230 presentations at national and international conferences. The quality of his research output has been recognized through several awards, most notably, the Outstanding Journal Article award, in the agricultural economics profession's premier journal, the *American Journal of Agricultural Economics*. It also includes the Outstanding Journal Article award in the prestigious *Journal of Agricultural and Applied Economics*. He assumed a leadership role in the agricultural economics profession by serving as editor and/or associate editor for six journals in addition to service work for the American Agricultural Economics Association (AAEA). He has presented his work to non-academics such as USDA Secretary, OECD, National Public Policy Education Committee, the National Agricultural Research, Extension, Education, and Economics Advisory Board and key policymakers from the Office of Management and Budget, Council of Economic Advisors. Mishra received a PhD in Economics at North Carolina State University in 1996. Previously he has held positions at Louisiana State University and the Economic Research Service of the USDA. His international work is in collaboration with IFPRI, IRRI, CIMMYT and ICRISAT.

Khondoker Abdul Mottaleb is a scientist (agricultural economist) at the Socioeconomics Program, International Maize and Wheat Improvement Center (CIMMYT), El Batan Texcoco, Mexico. He earned his BSS (Honors) and

MSS degrees in Economics from Rajshahi University, Bangladesh, and MA and PhD degrees in International Development Studies from the National Graduate Institute for Policy Studies (GRIPS), Tokyo, Japan. He started his career as a research officer in the Bangladesh Public Administration Training Center (BPATC), Savar, Dhaka. Later, he worked as a postdoctoral fellow in GRIPS, Tokyo, Japan, under the JSPS Fellowship Program; as a Postdoctoral Research Fellow at Social Sciences Division, International Rice Research Institute (IRRI), Philippines. His research interests include the complex interaction between a household's decision making and utility maximization, choice under risk and uncertainty and ex-ante impact assessment of promising technologies.

Ghanshyam Pandey is Assistant Professor in the Department of Economics at SRM University, Amravati, Andhra Pradesh, India. His work focuses on development economics, climate change and agriculture.

Vijay Laxmi Pandey is Professor at Indira Gandhi Institute of Development Research (IGIDR), Mumbai, India. She is an agricultural economist by training and has over 25 years of experience working in the field of agriculture and its relations with the environment, nutrition and rural economy. She has vast experience in conducting the household level survey. She has completed many national and international research and consultancy projects. Recently she has completed studies on 'System of Promoting Appropriate National Dynamism for Agriculture and Nutrition (SPANDAN),' a Bill and Melinda Gates initiative, and 'Comprehensive Study of Impact of Investment in Watershed Development Project,' sponsored by NIRD, Hyderabad. She has a large number of research publications, which include research papers in peer-reviewed journals, edited books and policy reports.

Raghav Raghunathan began his professional career working and living in the Central Indian Tribal belt building RamRahim, an agricultural value chain enterprise owned by 3,000 women farmers. In three years, he helped grow this enterprise into one of India's largest and most profitable enterprises where he pioneered the use of futures contracts to be directly used by farmers to sell/hedge prices on a national level electronic platform—the first in the country. After this, he worked directly with the commodities exchange, as principal, to scale this initiative across India.

Devesh Roy is Senior Research Fellow in the CGIAR Research Program on Agriculture for Nutrition and Health (A4NH) at the International Food Policy Research Institute. He holds a PhD in Economics from the University of Maryland at College Park and a master's degree from Delhi School of Economics. His areas of expertise include international trade, environment, firm farm linkages and food safety. He has recently been involved in research related to economics of animal disease outbreaks. Further, he has been conducting research on issues relating to food safety in developing countries particularly from the demand side.

Tariq Saleem is Senior Impact Evaluation Specialist with the Government of Khyber Pakhtunkhwa, Pakistan, and has over 18 years of research and development experience in agriculture, local governance, community-driven development and microfinance. He has worked as Research Associate in CIMMYT, Research Fellow in the Pakistan Agricultural Research Council (PARC) and research and M&E professional in private sector development organizations. He has authored a dozen technical reports, a research article and several programs' assessment and evaluation reports.

Madhuri Saripalle is Associate professor at the IFMR Graduate School of Business, KREA University, India, and teaches postgraduate courses on microeconomics, applied industrial organization and game theory. She received her doctorate in Agriculture and Resource Economics from the University of Connecticut, USA. Her research explores the role of technology, trade and supply chain management in industry and the agricultural markets. She has worked on projects related to the agricultural value chain, environment-friendly industrial policies for industries and employment-oriented industrialization and has published in various journals.

Sunil Saroj is Research Analyst at the IFPRI South Asia office. Before joining IFPRI, he worked with IPE Global Pvt. Ltd., Micro Insurance Academy (MIA) and Collaborative Research and Dissemination (CORD). He has worked on various issues like public health and nutrition, education, micro insurance, economic development, livelihood, poverty, gender, equity, public finance/public expenditure etc. He has an exposure to different verticals of development consultancy/socio-economic research: monitoring and evaluation, impact evaluation studies, client interaction and negotiation, sampling and field survey, literature review, data collection and analysis, report writing, presentation and dissemination, liaison with development partners.

Vinay K. Sonkar is a Research Analyst-II with the International Food Policy Research Institute. He received his master's degree in Economics in 2012 from the Indian Institute of Technology–Kanpur (IIT K). His research interests lie in food safety, agricultural credit, adoption of improved varieties and livelihood.

Suman Kumar Sourav is Junior Researcher at the Faculty of Organic Agricultural Sciences, University of Kassel, Germany. Currently, he is engaged in a megacity project stationed in Bengaluru to estimate the impact of socioecological interaction on soil nutrient flux in the peri-urban space of Bengaluru city, while pursuing his PhD on the topic. He received an International Masters in Rural Development (IMRD) degree from Ghent University, Belgium, during 2012–2014. He was awarded Erasmus Mundus scholarship to pursue his master's degree. After his master's, he worked through different international, national and sub-national organizations at different research positions. He has worked with other organizations, including the

International Water Management Institute (IWMI); United Nations Economic and Social Commission for Asia and the Pacific (UNESCAP); Indian Council for Research on International Economic Relations (ICRIER); Institute for Social and Economic Change (ISEC); Precision Agriculture for Development (PAD).

D. Suganthi is a Research Officer at the Reserve Bank of India. Earlier, she worked as a research associate in System of Promoting Appropriate National Dynamism for Agriculture and Nutrition (SPANDAN), funded by Bill and Melinda Gates Foundation placed at IGIDR. Her research interests include agriculture markets, agro-food supply chains and nutrition. Her current research work involves commodity supply management and its implications on commodity inflation and agriculture–nutrition disconnect in India.

Prasanna Surathkal is Research Associate at the Department of Agriculture of Texas State University, San Marcos, Texas, USA. He has MS degrees in Aquaculture/Fisheries and Agricultural Economics. His research interests are applied econometrics, including price analysis, demand and choice modeling and benchmarking.

Hiroyuki Takeshima is a Senior Research Fellow of IFPRI and based in Japan. He obtained a PhD in Agriculture & Consumer Economics from the University of Illinois at Urbana–Champaign, USA. He has authored 30 peer-reviewed journal articles, as well as an edited book and numerous book chapters, focusing on various developing regions, including Africa, Central Asia, South Asia, as well as Southeast Asia such as Vietnam. He also authored the chapter 'Agricultural Modernization in South Asia' in the book of *Agricultural Development* being edited by Keijiro Otsuka and Shenggen Fan, the Director-General of IFPRI, and is currently editing a book on *Agricultural Mechanization* based on experiences in 13 African and Asian countries. Hiroyuki is also the 2018 recipient of the Nils Westermack Award of the International Association of Agricultural Economist (IAAE). His areas of research include agricultural and rural transformation, public and private investment, agricultural technology adoption, economic geography and, finally, agriculture–nutrition linkages.

Ganesh Thapa is a freelance agricultural economist and has a PhD in Agricultural Economics from Purdue University. His doctoral study was supported by Feed the Future Nutrition Innovation Lab. He has previously worked as a fisheries development officer with the Ministry of Agriculture and Livestock Development and as an economist for the World Bank based in Nepal. He has also worked as a consultant for several reputed international institutions such as IFPRI, CIMMYT, ILO, WFP and the World Bank. His research interests include food security, agricultural development, child nutrition, value chains, impact evaluation, technology adoption and diffusion, poverty alleviation, agricultural price analysis, marketing, food safety and child labor.

Gaurav Tripathi is Senior Research Analyst in the South Asia Regional Office of the International Food Policy Research Institute, New Delhi, India. He has a master of business administration (MBA) degree from the University of Lucknow. His interests are contract farming, food safety and adoption of agricultural technologies.

Kedar Vishnu is an Assistant Professor in the Department of Economics at Christ University, India. He teaches Applied Macro Economics and Institutional Economics to undergraduates and graduates. Previously he taught economics at the Bengaluru Dr. B. R. Ambedkar School of Economics (BASE), Bangalore, India. He is working towards getting his PhD in Economics from the Institute for Social and Economic Change (ISEC), India. He is an alumnus of Ronald Coase Institute, USA. His research interests are production economics, institutional economics and contract farming. He has presented his research in China, Russia, Germany, Slovakia and USA.

Foreword

The food system in South Asia has been undergoing a structural transformation, and the emergence of an integrated food supply chain is one of the most visible phenomena in the region. This transformation is driven by the region's increasing income, growing urbanization, expanding female employment and gradual integration with the global economy. These developments led the dietary transition, and the share of high-value commodities such as fruits, vegetables, livestock, marine food and processed products has been increasing in the consumption basket. This dietary transition has put additional pressure on supply chain integration, and contract farming has emerged as one of the most viable innovative institutional arrangements to facilitate integration among different stakeholders along the agricultural value chain.

The role and impact of contract farming in developing countries have prompted extensive debate, but there is still no substantial evidence for confirming whether contract farming improves farmers' welfare. This issue is paramount in South Asia, where smallholders dominate the rural landscape and produce several commodities, including high-value products.

Transforming Agriculture in South Asia: The Role of Value Chains and Contract Farming is a rich source of analytical information on various aspects of agricultural transformation and on the role of contract farming in South Asia. It contains a number of insightful articles based on rigorous analysis and written by selected experts of the theme. The book covers a wide range of issues and provides policy options for the government and other stakeholders to address the emerging challenges and to harness the benefits of new opportunities.

This book is divided into three parts. The first part discusses the role of agriculture in South Asia, the agricultural sector in various South Asian countries and the transformation of agriculture via vertical coordination in these countries. The chapters also present cases on how and why contract farming plays a vital role in modern food retail chains. The second part presents results from several case studies on contract farming at the farm level in various commodities in Bangladesh, India and Nepal. The third part draws out and distills the impact of contract farming on commodity storage, input usage and technical productivity.

Editors Ashok K. Mishra, Anjani Ku mar and P. K. Joshi have worked hard to bring together eminent experts for this timely publication. I believe that this book will be useful to policy makers, academia, development partners, civil society and those interested in economic and agricultural development in South Asia. I congratulate the authors and the editors for bringing out this useful publication.

M. S. Swaminathan
Founder Chairman
Ex-Member of Parliament (Rajya Sabha)

Acknowledgements

Any large project involves an equally large number of individuals, and this book is no exception. As editors of this volume, we are grateful to a significant number of people who collaborated with us, supported us and assisted us in the preparation of these chapters of the book, as well as all the underlying activities. First, the idea of this book came several years ago (at the 29th International Conference of Agricultural Economists in Milan, Italy, 2015) when Ashok first met with Anjani and Pramod. Since then, a series of research activities and joint research projects have been undertaken and completed with number of scientists in India, Bangladesh and the IFPRI South Asia Office. Over the years, the editors, with similar educational attainments, backgrounds and research interests, became excellent friends though a continent apart. Second, we would like to thank the chapter writers themselves who willingly and efficiently revised or prepared materials so that they could be utilized in this form. Third, country research teams organized and conducted studies in Nepal, Bangladesh and Pakistan.

We wish to thank the Marley Foundation and the International Food Policy Research Institute for supporting and encouraging us to bring out this book. The funding support provided by the Indian Council of Agricultural Research, New Delhi, India, by the Regional Strategic Analysis and Knowledge Support System for Asia (ReSAKSS-Asia) and by the United States Agency for International Development–Nepal Mission for undertaking some of the studies covered in this book is gratefully acknowledged. We sincerely appreciate the sacrifices made by our families, since the time spent putting this edited book was a time that would have otherwise been spent at home and with family members. Their sacrifice and understanding enabled the editors to spend the time required for this volume to become a reality.

Finally, the views expressed here are solely those of the authors and may not in any circumstances be regarded as stating an official position of the International Food Policy Research Institute and/or any other institution with which they are associated.

1 Introduction and overview

Ashok K. Mishra, Anjani Kumar and Pramod K. Joshi

The food system in South Asia has been undergoing a paradigm shift, and one of the most visible market phenomena in India is the emergence of an integrated food supply chain. This paradigm change is attributed to the region's increasing income, growing urbanization, expanding female employment and gradual integration with the global economy. These developments, in addition to food security goals, have led the dietary transition from food grains to high-value commodities such as fruits, vegetables, livestock, marine foods and processed products. However, this dietary transition has put additional pressure on supply chain integration. In this context, contract farming (CF) has emerged as one of the most viable instruments to facilitate integration among different stakeholders along the agricultural value chain. In contract farming, agribusiness firms contract with external farmers to receive goods at a fixed price with the certainty of delivery of a specified quality and quantity at a specified time. Rather than owning farms themselves, the firms rely on these smallholders to produce and provide their goods.

Some 70% of South Asia's population (70%) is rural and engaged in agriculture, and crop failure assistance and rural livelihood support programs are significant national expenses. For example, the Government of India's National Agricultural Policy 2000 and National Policy for Farmers 2007 both emphasized and promoted contract farming as a way to accelerate technology transfer, to secure capital inflow and to ensure markets for agricultural products, especially horticultural crops. Contract farming is evolving quickly as a mechanism of alternative marketing in India. To further promote contract farming in the country, the Government of India enacted an ordinance called the Farmers (Empowerment and Protection) Agreement on Price Assurance and Farm Services Ordinance. This legislation, enacted in June 2020, is a comprehensive, promotional and facilitative contract farming act that is expected to enable large-scale adoption of contract farming. According to Chand, Raju and Pandey (2007), contract farming's benefits for smallholders go beyond access to credit, inputs and extension services. Contract farming can help improve the links between these smallholders and international markets by organizing the production of high-value food crops. Additionally, contract farming mutually benefits smallholders and agribusiness firms by significantly reducing imperfections in the spot market and reducing costs arising from uncertainty over quantity and prices. For more on contract farming in the broader context of supply chain management issues, see Bellemare (2018). Contract farming offers numerous opportunities for farmers, including access to stable markets and pricing, inputs, information and marketing services (Otsuka, Nakano and Kazushi, 2016; Mishra et al., 2018; Bellemare and Lim, 2018).

The rationale for vertical coordination in developing and emerging economies

Contract farming has been used for a long time in different forms, such as sharecropping contracts, which initially were regarded as a feudal form of agriculture because of the dominant nature of absent or underdeveloped markets (Eswaran and Kotwal, 1985). Today, farmers and buyers commonly use contract farming to make advance agreements on volume, specific requirements, delivery and price. Initially, contract farming was a common practice in developed countries, principally driven by concerns about food safety and quality (Otsuka, Nakano and Kazushi, 2016; Mishra et al., 2018; Bellemare and Bloem, 2018). Glover (1984) describes contract farming as institutional arrangements that have advantages of both plantations and smallholder production. Over the past five decades, Indian agriculture has undergone significant changes, including in its production capacity and institutional reforms (Asokan and Singh, 2003). However, the rural and agricultural landscape still is dominated by smallholders with less than two hectares of land. Contract farming is viewed as a way to overcome the credit, input and extension constraints that these smallholders face. The role and impact of contract farming in developing countries have been fertile ground for controversy and debate (see Masakure and Henson, 2005; Winters, Simmons and Patrick 2005; Oya, 2012; Prowse, 2012; Otsuka, Nakano and Kazushi, 2016; Mishra et al., 2018; Bellemare and Bloem, 2018).

A growing body of the recent empirical literature, based on case studies from around the world, documents contract farming's positive effects on welfare. However, a second strand of research on contract farming in developing countries highlights the dangers that it can pose for smallholder households (see Simmons, 2017; Singh, 2002; Little and Watts, 1994). These studies argue that contractors gain more from contracts than the farmers with whom they contract; the farmers, by contrast, end up with debt, skewed income distribution, food insecurity and family tensions. Looking specifically at developing economies, earlier work by Minot (1986) found that contract farming improved participants' incomes but noted that contract farming schemes had very high failure rates.[1] However, it should be pointed out that Little and Watts (1994) found that participants in contract farming increased their incomes between 30% and 60% compared to non-participants. In another study in Africa, Porter and Phillips-Howard (1997) concluded that although there were social problems related to contract farming, farmers who participated in it generally were better off than those who did not. The strand of literature that focuses on positive outcomes of smallholders' participation in contract farming (Govereh and Jayne, 2003) has investigated farmers' decisions to contract (Zhu and Wang, 2007) and has studied contract farming's impact on the welfare of more impoverished farmers (Simmons, Winters and Patrick, 2005). Most of these studies show that contract farming can improve the marketing of crops, enhance poor farmers' access to technology and lower the costs of other inputs and extension services.

With looming budget deficits, losses in agricultural productivity and increased food security goals, the governments in South Asia's developing countries have encouraged private-sector investments through contract farming.[2] Contract farming can help accelerate technology transfer, secure capital inflow and ensure markets for crop production, especially for high-value horticultural crops like baby corn. Contract farming also may reduce cultivation costs, as it can provide access to better inputs and more efficient production methods. Contract farming benefits smallholders by lowering production and marketing risks (Allen and Lueck, 1995) through the provision of inputs, access to credit and technical assistance. Through contract farming, contractors or corporations can overcome land size constraints and achieve reliability and consistency in production (Eaton and Shepherd, 2001). Contract farming is common in developed countries, principally driven by concerns about food safety and quality. The role and impact of contract farming in developing countries have prompted extensive debate (see Simmons, Winters and Patrick, 2005). Recent studies by Mishra et al. (2018) and Bellemare and Bloem (2018) provide an extensive literature review and examples of contract farming in general and contract farming in developing countries in particular. But Bellemare and Bloem (2018) concluded that there is still no substantial evidence for confirming whether contract farming improves farmers' welfare. This issue is paramount in South Asia, where smallholders dominate the rural landscape and produce several commodities, including high-value products. Specifically, the literature lacks a common source of information assessing contract farming's impacts on food security indicators (yield, income and prices), employment, resource use, productivity and the welfare of smallholder farm families as it relates to developing and emerging economies.

A structured discussion around contract farming

This book is a rich source of analytical information on various aspects of agricultural transformation and the role of contract farming in South Asia. It covers a wide range of issues and provides policy options for the government and other stakeholders to address the emerging challenges and to harness the benefits of new opportunities. The importance of vertical coordination and its impact on rural smallholders in South Asia is not underestimated, but a more concise book was thought to be more attractive to the readership. We hope this book will be useful to policymakers, academia, development partners, civil society and those interested in economic and agricultural development in South Asia.

This book is divided into three parts. The first part discusses the role of agriculture in South Asia, the agricultural sector in various South Asian countries and the transformation of agriculture via vertical coordination in these countries. These chapters present cases on how and why contract farming plays a vital role in modern food retail chains. The second part presents results from case studies on contract farming at the farm level in various commodities in Nepal, India and Bangladesh. The third part draws out and distills contract farming's impact on commodity storage, input usage and technical productivity.

Understanding the agricultural sector, transformation, value chains and contract farming

The first part of this book presents an expansive view of the agricultural sector in Nepal, Bangladesh and India. It illustrates the transformation taking place in the farming sector, the role of vertical coordination, the development of value chains and the financing of the value chains.

Chapter 2 reviews the recent trends in and prospects for South Asia's agricultural sector. In particular, the chapter sheds light on the critical patterns of agricultural production growth, modernization, diversification and trade over the past few decades. In doing so, the chapter also highlights the relatively unique aspects of South Asia, compared to other regions in Asia, including Eastern and Southeastern Asia. The chapter also reviews the critical studies offering projections on demand, production, trade growth and the impacts of climate change for South Asian agriculture. The chapter concludes that South Asia's agricultural sector has evolved steadily over several decades. The industry has experienced unique diversification in terms of its set of commodity groups. Domestic markets remain dominant, but trade within South Asia and outside South Asian regions has expanded. The potential can be substantial in terms of geography and commodity and in the scope for agricultural business produced by contract farming in South Asia. The economic stakes remain high for further agricultural modernization in South Asia, including contract farming, and the productivity growth to realize such potential can be significant if continuous investments are made to sustain past productivity growth.

Chapter 3 highlights the value chain patterns of three major crops—wheat, maize and rice—in Bangladesh. The wheat value chain is highly segmented between the smallholder and '*chakki*' mill owners' value chain and the large wheat- and flour-importing companies' value chain. To ensure benefits to smallholder farmers, smallholders must generate a market surplus to connect to the growing wheat value chain. For this, enhancing wheat yield is imperative. In comparison, maize farmers are strongly linked to maize value chains, but there is still scope to provide more significant benefits to those farmers. In Bangladesh, smallholder rice farmers produce rice mostly for self-consumption. However, they apply modern inputs, such as fertilizer and pesticides, extensively. Thus, although they are strongly linked with the backward-linkage value chain, they mostly are disconnected from the forward-linkage progressive value chains. This chapter highlights pathways for the development of Bangladesh's agricultural sector, which can generate valuable lessons for other emerging nations in sub-Saharan Africa and South Asia.

Chapter 4 deals with the structural transformation and sources of growth in South Asian agriculture. The primary focus of this chapter is to understand paths to agricultural transformation in the countries in South Asia in a broader context of economy-wide changes in domestic and international markets. The chapter tracks trajectories of agricultural growth and factors underlying the trajectories and decomposes agricultural growth due to technological change, area expansion, diversification and price increases. The chapter also identifies crops or crop groups that potentially can influence the pace of agricultural transformation.

Chapter 5 assesses agricultural performance in Nepal, emphasizing the importance of agriculture in the country's economy, and presents the challenges and problems of the farming sector. The chapter also illustrates the scope and significance of high-value crops and examines the status and importance of value chain linkages and contract farming, both of which are required for the promotion of high-value crops and agricultural commercialization in Nepal. The agricultural policies that aim to promote agricultural commercialization in the country and the program activities of development agencies on value chain development and agribusiness promotion also are discussed in this chapter with an illustration of some case studies. The chapter concludes with policy implications for promoting contract farming, value chain development and commercial agriculture in Nepal.

Chapter 6 explores the prospects of the value chain approach in improving the interface between financial institutions and product markets. The chapter discusses opportunities for value chain development in South Asia and provides the conceptual framework of value chain finance. The chapter also provides a brief review of a few successful value chain models, focusing on their financing mechanisms, their efficiency and inclusiveness and their economic impacts. Lessons drawn from these models are presented and discussed in this chapter.

Chapter 7 attempts to quantify the impact of opportunistic behavior and asymmetric information on chili farmers in India. The authors measure the magnitude of transaction costs and their components (such as bargaining costs, information costs and enforcement costs) in production and marketing contracts, compared to transaction costs incurred by independent farmers in traditional marketing channels (TMCs). The study also measures the impact of transaction costs on profits earned by marginal and small farmers. The findings from this chapter can help in implementing policies aimed at reducing transaction costs, given that they may constitute a significant proportion of expenses of small and marginal growers.

Case studies in contract farming

With a better understanding of the role of contract farming, the second section of this book adds to the discussion of vertical coordination by examining a set of commodity- and country-specific case studies. The viewpoints gained from these case studies of vertical coordination in commodities and countries are critical to understanding contract farming, its success and its failure in raising the welfare of smallholders in developing and emerging economies. Because products, farmers and markets have unique attributes that influence the adoption of contract farming, this section explores the similarities and differences between commodities and countries by investigating case-specific commodities to identify the advantages and disadvantages that contract farming has for the welfare of smallholders.

Chapter 8 examines whether contract farming could provide a pathway to incentivize low-value crop farmers to pursue commercial agriculture. In particular, the authors test whether contract farming can increase yields, revenues and profits, and they examine whether the benefits are distributed homogeneously among various sizes of smallholder farms. Chapter 9 evaluates formal and informal milk value chains and their implications for price realization and compliance with food safety measures. It identifies the factors influencing dairy farmers' choice of formal and informal outlets. The chapter concludes that both formal and informal value chains exist but that informal chains dominate the milk market in Bangladesh. This chapter's findings further shed light on the trade-off between food safety and price realization.

The main goal of Chapter 10 is to identify potential value chain actors and awareness of contract farming among various actors in Pakistan's durum wheat value chain, as well as critical constraints in that value chain. Findings in this chapter provide recommendations for the smooth operation of the durum wheat value chain in Pakistan.

Chapter 11 examines the impact of contract farming in brinjal cultivation in Bangladesh. The chapter also identifies the drivers for participation in contract farming. The chapter shows that contract farming has a significant positive impact on farmers' profits in brinjal cultivation and that contract farming positively influences food safety measures at the farm level. The chapter argues that contract farming should be promoted to improve smallholder farmers' economic welfare and to improve compliance with food safety measures in Bangladesh.

Chapter 12 analyzes value chains in aquaculture and fisheries in Bangladesh and highlights the rapid growth and transformation of the country's fish value chains. The authors indicate several gaps in the proper understanding of the value chain's transformation in Bangladesh. The authors conclude that the fish value chains in Bangladesh present tremendous opportunities for research into the production, distribution and socio-economics of changes in food value chains.

Chapter 13 presents and discusses mango value chains in India. The chapter includes a description of the broad trends in mango production and a typology of mango value chains in the country. It also discusses some of the factors influencing the contract choice and identifies the determinants of farmers' choice between modes of contracts. The chapter highlights that, although the government-managed cooperative value chains provide better prices and market linkages than traditional markets, their limited scale of operations and stringent quality requirements constrain resource-poor farmers from participating and investing in quality-enhancing activities.

Chapter 14 on coffee value chains looks at the dominant trends in India's coffee production and markets, the emergence of specialty and sustainably certified value chains and the key actors involved. The first part of the chapter briefly reviews theoretical literature on the Food and Agriculture Organization's (FAO) global value chain framework, and the subsequent section analyzes the sustainability standards prevalent in global value chains, with particular reference to the coffee industry. The last section discusses the coffee value chain in the context of India, supplemented by a primary comparative analysis at the micro level. The authors evaluate the sustainability of India's coffee value chains from the perspective of a producer country.

Contract farming, storage and technical efficiency

Having formed an empirical framework, coupled with a synthesis of the literature and results collected for individual commodities and countries, we move forward to a better understanding of contract farming's role in storage, input usage and productivity. The final section of this book details contract farming's impact on these issues, using farm-level studies of smallholders from India and Pakistan.

Chapter 15 briefly explains the functioning of global value chains and outlines the methodology used to estimate the integration of exports into global value chains. It also presents trends in agricultural exports, bifurcated into primary categories (raw products that undergo minimal processing) and secondary categories (products that undergo value addition in the industry), from 2001 to 2017. This is followed by empirical estimates of the production (output) linkages between primary and processed agricultural products and the integration of exports of agricultural, processed food and beverage and allied sectors into the global value chains. The chapter finds that there is little integration of India's agriculture, allied industries and processed-food exports into global value chains and calls for accelerating agricultural reforms and investment to gain from the world's growing trade in agriculture.

The primary purpose of Chapter 16 is to assess the role of value chain actors in the maize value chain in Pakistan and how they can contribute to enhancing and strengthening the value chain business.

Chapter 17 examines several objectives. The authors assess farmers' decisions to participate in the output market and the degree of their participation in output markets in terms of the number of products they sell, the number of output market transactions they undertake and the diversity of marketing agencies they use. This chapter's findings show that, apart from farm- and household-level factors, several structural or location-specific variables affect farmers' marketing decisions.

Chapter 18 identifies constraints on the participation of farmers and farmer groups in futures markets and how best to resolve these constraints. It also looks at some selected case studies in India and the experiences of other smallholder economies, such as China, to learn best practices. The chapter looks at linking futures to value chains through two interim steps: linking farmers to farmer-producer organizations (FPOs) and linking these organizations to futures markets. The chapter concludes that farmers' participation in the futures trade is meager in India, and institutional and policy measures are needed to increase smallholders' involvement in farmer-producer organizations.

Chapter 19 presents and studies contract farming's impact on the productivity, irrigation costs and fertilizer costs of baby corn producers in India. The authors use a farm-level survey of smallholders in two states of India, Punjab and Haryana, which are considered at the forefront of the Green Revolution but now face significant productivity, soil and environmental problems. This chapter highlights that private market intervention, like contract farming, can increase yield, decrease irrigation costs and decrease fertilizer usage. Thus contract farming bodes well for both farmers and policymakers when it comes to food security, and it provides environmental benefits for society at large.

Chapter 20 provides valuable information on the farm efficiency of contracted farmers and independent farmers using data from Punjab and Haryana, India. The findings show significant differences in the farming efficiency of contract and non-contract farmers for barley, wheat, potato, mustard, tomato, green chili and baby corn. The chapter highlights substantial policy implications for improving the farms' efficiency.

Chapter 21 examines the drivers of initial inclusion and retention of farmers in the Aditya Birla More Collection Centre (ABM CC) supply chain, conditional on spatial characteristics. Further, the authors examine the dynamic elements and how a farmer's perception of risk shapes the transactional relationship in smallholders' choice of supplying ABM's collection center or raditional markets. It also probes the factors influencing the firm's decisions on procurement. Even though the analysis is based on cross-sectional data, the experience of discontinued suppliers provides insights into the dynamic aspect of the transactional relationship between farmers and the ABM supply chain.

Future discussion and explorations

Contract farming provides an opportunity to empower smallholders and improve their livelihood. There are ample examples of different models of the successes of contract farming. However, despite enormous benefits to both farms and firms, these models are not taking root in South Asian countries. Bulk buyers, big retailers and processors often procure food and related commodities from the wholesale markets and avoid the route of contract farming.

One possible reason for this may be the high transaction costs to the firms in contracting for and collecting farm produce due to the tiny marketable surpluses of multiple smallholders. This important issue needs to be studied and explored. The other reasons may be the firms' regular demand for farm produce compared to the farmers' limited supply. The farmers, however, gain significantly through a contractual arrangement that reduces their transaction costs, assures a market and minimizes risk. Another issue that may be important to explore is how to align the interests and optimize the profits of both smallholders and firms.

Contract farming's success will rely on how farmers can ensure regular, bulk and quality supplies to firms. Aggregating farmers can overcome this hurdle, through either farmer-producer organizations or cooperative farming. On top of this, federating farmer-producer organizations and cooperatives will further reduce firms' transaction costs. However, in the absence of an enabling agribusiness environment, firms (or the corporate sector) are not expected to engage in contract farming. Two recent ordinances promulgated in India are expected to change the product portfolio in favor of high-value commodities and to promote contract farming. Government support through creating appropriate infrastructure and eliminating bureaucratic obstructions will attract the corporate sector in promoting contract farming. The success of contract farming in South Asian countries is expected to contribute to accelerating the pace of agricultural transformation.

Notes

1 In sub-Saharan Africa, Little and Watts (1994) report several cases in which disagreement between smallholders and the contractors led to a failure of contract farming.

2 Contract farming is a system for producing and supplying agricultural/horticultural produce under forward contracts between producers/suppliers and buyers. It has different names for different variants, such as the centralized model (a company–farmer arrangement) and out-grower schemes (a government/public sector/joint venture). Contract farming varies depending on the nature and type of contracting agency, the technology used, the nature of the crop/produced and the local and national context.

References

Allen, D., and Lueck, D. 1995. Risk Preferences and the Economics of Contracts. *The American Economic Review* 85 (2): 447–451.

Asokan, S. R., and Singh, G. 2003. Role and Constraints of Contract Farming in Agro-Processing Industry. *Indian Journal of Agricultural Economics* 58 (3): 566–576.

Bellemare, M., and Bloem, J. 2018. Does Contract Farming Improve Welfare? A Review. *World Development* 112: 259–271.

Bellemare, M., and Lim, S. 2018. In All Shapes and Colors: Varieties of Contract Farming. *Applied Economic Perspectives and Policy* 40 (3): 379–401.

Chand, R., Raju, S. S., and Pandey, L. M. 2007. Growth Crisis in Agriculture: Severity and Options at National State Levels. *Economic and Political Weekly* 42 (26): 2528–2533.

Eaton, C., and Shepherd, A. W. 2001. Contract Farming Partnership for Growth. *FAO Agricultural Services Bulletin* 145. Rome.

Eswaran, E., and Kotwal, A. 1985. A Theory of Contractual Structure in Agriculture. *The American Economic Review* 75 (3): 352–367.

Glover, D. 1984. Contract Farming and Smallholders Outgrower Schemes in Less-Developed Countries. *World Development* 12 (11/12): 1143–1157.

Govereh, J., and Jayne, T. 2003. Cash Cropping and Food Crop Productivity: Synergies or Trade-Offs? *Agricultural Economics* 28 (1): 39–50.

Little, P., and Watts, M. (Eds.). 1994. *Living Under Contract: Contract Farming and Agrarian Transformation in Sub-Saharan Africa*. Madison: University of Wisconsin Press.

Masakure, O., and Henson, S. 2005. Why Do Small-Scale Producers Choose to Produce Under Contract? Lessons From Nontraditional Vegetable Exports From Zimbabwe. *World Development* 33 (10): 1721–133.

Minot, N. 1986. Contract Farming and Its Effect on Small Farmers in Less-Developed Countries. Working Paper No. 31. Michigan State University, East Lansing.

Mishra, A. K., Kumar, A., Joshi, P. K., and D'Souza, A. (2018). Production Risks, Risk Preference and Contract Farming: Impact on Food Security in India. *Applied Economic Perspectives and Policy* 40 (3): 110–121.

Otsuka, K., Nakano, Y., and Kazushi, T. 2016. Contract Farming in Developed and Developing Countries. *Annual Review of Resource Economics* 8 (1): 353–376.

Oya, C. 2012. Contract Farming in Sub-Saharan Africa: A Survey of Approaches, Debates and Issues. *Journal of Agrarian Change* 12 (1): 1–33.

Porter, G., and Phillips-Howard, K. 1997. Comparing Contracts: An Evaluation of Contract Farming Schemes in Africa. *World Development* 25 (2): 227–238.

Prowse, M. 2012. *Contract Farming in Developing Countries: A Review*. Paris: Agence Française de Développement a Savoir.

Simmons, P. 2017. Overview of Smallholder Contract Farming in Developing Countries. ESA Working Paper No. 02–04. Agricultural and Development Economics Division, FAO, Rome.

Simmons, P., Winters, P. and Patrick, I. 2005. An Analysis of Contract Farming in East Java, Bali, and Lombok, Indonesia. *Agricultural Economics* 33 (s3): 513–525.

Singh, S. 2002. Contracting Out Solutions: Political Economy of Contract Farming in the Indian Punjab. *World Development* 30 (9): 1621–1638.

Winters, P., Simmons, P., and Patrick, I. 2005. Evaluation of a Hybrid Seed Contract between Smallholders and a Multinational Company in East Java, Indonesia. *The Journal of Development Studies* 41 (1): 62–89.

Zhu, H., and Wang, X. 2007. An Analysis on the Influencing Factors of Tomato Growers' Participation in Contract Farming in Xinjiang Autonomous Region. *Chinese Rural Economy* 7: 67–75.

Part I

Understanding the agricultural sector, transformation, value chains and contract farming

2 Agriculture in South Asia

Trends and prospects

Hiroyuki Takeshima

The agricultural sector remains an important source of income and food security in South Asia. The sector has experienced significant transformation in recent decades, but the region still has lagged behind other parts of Asia, including East Asia and Southeast Asia, in pace with labor leaving farming for employment in other sectors (Takeshima et al. 2020). Despite the gradual modernization of South Asia's agricultural sector, significant scope remains for further sophistication of the sector, including contract farming. Some of the important aspects of such modernization are the overall growth of the sector's size; the sector's gaps in, patterns of and potentials for diversification; and its integration with outside regions through trade.

This chapter reviews the recent trends and prospects of South Asia's agricultural sector. In particular, the chapter sheds light on the key patterns of agricultural production growth, modernization, diversification and trade over the past few decades. In doing so, the chapter also highlights South Asia's relatively unique aspects compared to other regions in Asia, including East and Southeast Asia. The chapter also reviews the key studies offering projections of demand, production, trade growth and climate change impacts for South Asian agriculture.

Detailed reviews of recent trends in the agricultural sector have been conducted for various countries within South Asia, including India (Brouwer & Joshi 2016), Nepal (Thapa et al. 2019) and Pakistan (Spielman et al. 2017), as well as for South Asia as a whole (e.g., Takeshima et al. 2020). This chapter focuses on aspects that complement these earlier studies. This chapter also complements Takeshima et al. (2020), which provides overviews of related aspects of agricultural modernization in South Asia, including productivity growth, dietary transformation and general patterns of agricultural modernization. Unlike Takeshima et al. (2020), however, the chapter provides more detailed and focused descriptions of the changing diversification patterns of food commodities, trade and the outlook for production growth of various commodities in the region.

Agricultural production, diversification and trade growth in South Asia

Overall production growth, intensifications

According to the Food and Agriculture Organization (FAO) of the United Nations (2020), the net production value of South Asia's agriculture and livestock sector increased by 2.9% annually between the 1960s and 2010s (decadal averages in international dollars) and by 3.4% between the 1990s and 2010s. The growth rates have been slower than in East Asia (3.9% and 3.7%) and in Southeast Asia (3.5% and 3.4%) but faster than at the global level (2.4% and 2.5%). In particular, annual net production values in South Asia grew faster for milk (3.8% and 3.7%), vegetables (3.7% and 3.8%) and fruits (3.0% and 3.6%) than for most other commodity groups. Such production growth in South Asia has corresponded with production intensification, characterized by increased land-use intensity and labor uses and the increased adoption of modern inputs. During this period, agricultural land in rain-fed cropland equivalent increased by 0.7% per year, and economically active labor in agriculture increased by 1.8% per year (USDA-ERS 2020). The increase in agricultural land in rain-fed equivalent has been primarily due to the growing share of irrigated area.

Extent of modern inputs use

The share of cultivated areas equipped with irrigation in South Asia increased from 24% in 1973 to 34% in 1993 and to 46% in 2013 (AQUASTAT). The share of irrigated area has grown more quickly than in East Asia (which grew from 46% in 1973 to 56% in 2013) or in mainland Southeast Asia (which grew from 13% in 1973 to 28% in 2013) and has been one of the fastest-growing in the world.

Farmers in South Asia have continued to adopt improved, newer varieties since the introduction of well known Green Revolution varieties for staple crops (Evenson & Gollin 2003). In recent decades, the public and the private sectors have also developed hybrid varieties, including hybrid maize, hybrid rice, hybrid wheat (Matuschke et al. 2007) and pearl-millet (Matuschke & Qaim 2008). The adoption of hybrid maize has grown considerably, and hybrid rice has gradually started to spread in countries like India and Bangladesh (Spielman et al. 2012). Biotechnologies (including genetic engineering) have been applied gradually to varietal development, including Bt cotton and Bt eggplant. The adoption of modern varieties also has been observed in fishery sectors, such as modern varieties of fish in aquaculture in Bangladesh (Rashid & Zhang 2019) and the application of modern breeding technologies like genetic modification (ADB 2005). The private sector increasingly has played key roles in varietal development, particularly through the advancement of hybrid technologies and other modern biotechnologies, as well as the strengthening of intellectual property rights and the deregulation of the seed sector that started in the 1990s (Kolady et al. 2012; Pray & Nagarajan 2014).

The use of chemical fertilizer and agrochemicals also has risen considerably. The intensity of chemical fertilizer use grew substantially by the 1980s and kept growing afterward. By the 2000s, most South Asian countries exceeded the intensity of 100 kg of nutrients per hectare (FAOSTAT). The use of agrochemicals (pesticides and herbicides) also has gradually intensified. In India, herbicide use grew 2.5 times between 2005–2006 and 2015–2016 and reached 1kg/ha (Das Gupta et al. 2017). This is still considerably lower than in countries like Japan but is comparable to levels in the United States.

Growing modernization of agriculture in South Asia also has included the gradual growth of certain frontier technologies, including protected farming, precision farming and vertical farming. In India, various precision-agriculture technologies have been adopted, including drip and sprinkler irrigation, which have been growing steadily but still account for only a fraction of irrigated areas (Kalubhai 2015), and laser-land-leveling technologies, including those in the states of Western Uttar Pradesh and Haryana (Tiwari and Jaga 2012). Shruthi et al. (2018a) examines the differences among pigeon-pea growers in India using precision agriculture and non-users and finds lower chemical fertilizer use and higher incomes of 10,536.34 Rs/ha. Similarly, Shruthi et al. (2018b) find similar differences among paddy growers who use precision agriculture and those who do not in Karnataka. In Kerala, precision farming has been adopted for banana cultivation, particularly among larger farms with more educated owners (Franco et al. 2018).

Agricultural mechanization, returns to scale and farm size

Farm size has continued to decline in many South Asian countries, similar to the rest of Asia. According to the World Census of Agriculture, between the 1970s and the 2010s, the average holding size declined by almost half in most South Asian countries. However, mechanization adoption grew considerably during this period. In particular, the share of cultivated area prepared by tractors increased considerably within a few decades in Bangladesh (20% in the 1990s to almost 90% in the 2010s), India (30% in the 1990s to almost 90% in the 2010s), lowland Nepal (10% in the 1990s to 50% in 2010) and in the rice area of Sri Lanka (less than 50% in the 1980s to almost 100% in the 2010s) (Diao et al. 2021). Such growth in mechanization was realized primarily through the expansion of custom-hiring services offered by the private sector, including tractor-owning medium- to large-scale farmers. The growth in mechanization has been associated with and has sometimes directly caused the rise in returns to scale among smallholders (e.g., Takeshima 2017). A swift reversal of the declining trend of farm size in South Asian countries may be unlikely, as such changes have not occurred in the rest of Asia, except in Japan. However, technology-driven changes in returns to scale (such as through mechanization) may have somewhat complex effects when interacted with institutional changes in production systems, including contract farming. The recent trend in South Asian countries suggests that closer investigations of such interactive effects of technology advancement and contract farming are likely to be important in future studies.

Value chain development

Modernization at the post-harvesting stage also has been significant during the past few decades. Market institutions have evolved, particularly through the private sector's greater participation in both processing and marketing. Some examples include staple crops like rice and potato (Reardon et al. 2012) and non-staple crops (Fafchamps et al. 2008), as well as the development of vertical integration for crops like sugarcane in India (Patlolla et al. 2015). Markets for minor crops also have expanded, and producers' increased participation has been positively associated with greater on-farm crop diversity (e.g., minor millet in India; Takeshima and Nagarajan 2012). However, further development of agricultural value chains in South Asia still has significant scope. For both staple and non-staple crops, post-harvest quality enhancement has been confined mostly to the crops' observable quality. Efforts to enhance unobservable quality, such as food safety or greater use of organic inputs, have been limited due to buyers' inability to validate such quality and the resulting low premiums (Fafchamps et al. 2008; Minten et al. 2012). Premiums could be sufficiently raised, however, as incomes rise and consumer demands further evolve (Vandeplas and Minten 2015), potentially creating room for further institutional innovations, including contract farming, that could lead to greater quality enhancement of commodities. More recent studies suggest that marketing institutions, including contract farming and cooperatives, have grown more important for production and marketing of high-value vegetables and fruits, poultry or higher-quality milk, for which the demand for improved food safety practices has been rising (Joshi et al. 2007; Kumar et al. 2018). Similarly, even where increased demand for quality has modernized post-harvest activities, it had relatively limited effects on on-farm activities or productivity (e.g., Minten et al. 2012, 2013). On-farm productivity enhancement, therefore, continues to be important and must be part of the transformation of South Asia's whole food system.

Production diversification

Despite the growing cross-regional trade of agricultural commodities, food consumption in South Asia and in many other regions still relies considerably on production within each region. The patterns of production diversification within the region are therefore one of the important yardsticks of its food security and dietary diversity. Although production diversification in South Asian agriculture has been recognized (Joshi et al. 2007; Takeshima et al. 2020), information has been relatively limited regarding its extent, and gaining a comparative perspective of how it has differed across regions is needed using the standard definitions of commodity groups. This section briefly highlights these aspects.

Unique aspects of overall production diversification, compared to other Asian regions and the world

Figure 2.1 illustrates the shares of different food groups with respect to total production values based on decadal averages since the 1960s, along with their trends up to the 2010s, for South Asia, Southeast Asia, East Asia and the whole world (including South Asia). The figure shows South Asia's uniqueness compared to these other regions. The declining share of cereals in South Asia is consistent with the patterns in Southeast Asia and East Asia and seems to converge to its lower share at the global level. However, the food groups emerging in South Asia are somewhat different: primarily milk, fruits and vegetables and root crops (albeit from a low level). The share of milk is rising particularly quickly, exceeding 20% of total production values. These patterns are more similar to those in East Asia than in Southeast Asia, but the increase in share is much greater for milk, much lower for meat, and the share is increasing for root crops, unlike the rest of Asia. The patterns in Southeast Asia and East Asia also differ from each other. Figure 2.1 suggests, therefore, that South Asia's diversification pattern is just as unique as those in other regions and is likely to continue in such a way in the future. All in all, the food groups with higher shares in South Asia than in other regions are naturally important in South Asia. At the same time, food groups with lower shares in South Asia could

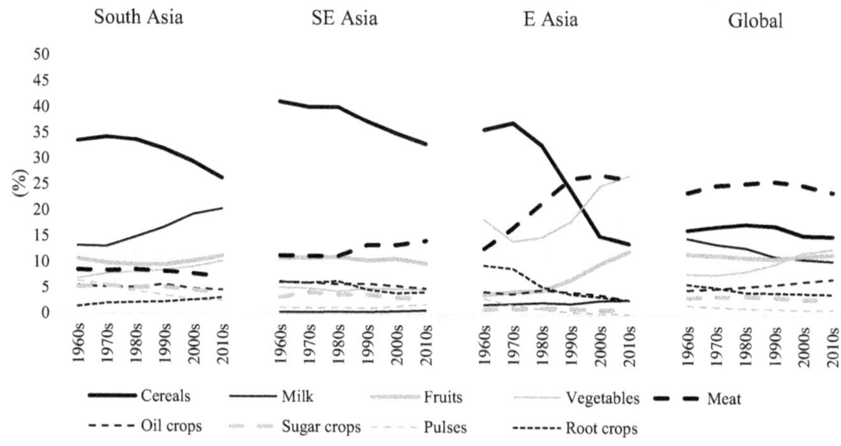

Figure 2.1 Production value shares (%) of major commodities groups among total agricultural production values, by regions (%)

Source: FAO, 2019.

indicate that there is potential for expansion by transferring available technologies from other regions.

Diversification within major food groups

Figure 2.2 illustrates further disaggregated shares within each of the major food commodity groups in order to show the major crops within each group, how their relative importance changed and how South Asia has differed from other regions. Here we show figures for groups whose relative shares have been growing or have been higher than in most other regions, based on Figure 2.1, namely vegetables, fruits, milk, oil crops, pulses and root crops.

For vegetables, categories 'fresh vegetables, nes [not elsewhere specified]' are excluded due to the potential changes in their definitions over time.

Overall, South Asia has been unique in various ways. Among vegetables, the shares of tomato (and, to some extent, onions since the 1990s) have increased rapidly, but the share of okra, which had been the major vegetable (another unique aspect of South Asia), has declined in relative terms. The shares of cauliflower and eggplant have remained much higher than in other regions. Among fruits, mangoes and bananas have historically dominated in South Asia, similar to Southeast Asia. However, declining shares of mangoes and rising shares of bananas in South Asia are unique, even compared to Southeast Asia, where the patterns have been somewhat reversed. Shares of apples and grapes, important fruits in East Asia and globally, have remained low in South Asia.

Among milks, the share of buffalo milk has remained persistently high in South Asia, still accounting for more than half of all milk in the region. That is unlike elsewhere, where cow milk now dominates. Such persistence is also different from Southeast Asia, where another type of non-cow milk, goat/sheep milk, has declined and cow milk's share has increased over time. Among oil crops, patterns in South Asia are unique in terms of a declining share of groundnuts and a rising share of soybeans (particularly given their near absence in the 1960s and 1970s in the region). Unlike in Southeast Asia, with a similarly tropical climate, the share of coconuts has been lower. Pulses have accounted for relatively greater shares in South Asia than elsewhere. Among pulses, shares of other crops than beans, such as chickpeas or pigeon peas, have been relatively higher in South Asia, unlike elsewhere, where beans have dominated. Such relative diversity among pulses has persisted in South Asia during the last six decades.

Lastly, among root crops, the share of potato increased significantly in South Asia during the last five decades, becoming the dominant root crop. The pattern is relatively similar to that in East Asia or globally but very different from that in Southeast Asia, where cassava has remained the dominant root crop. Overall, although agricultural diversification has existed and continued in South Asia as elsewhere, this has been with a highly unique set of crops. To the extent that certain technologies and institutional issues are crop specific, South Asia's unique patterns give rise to the importance of investigating the

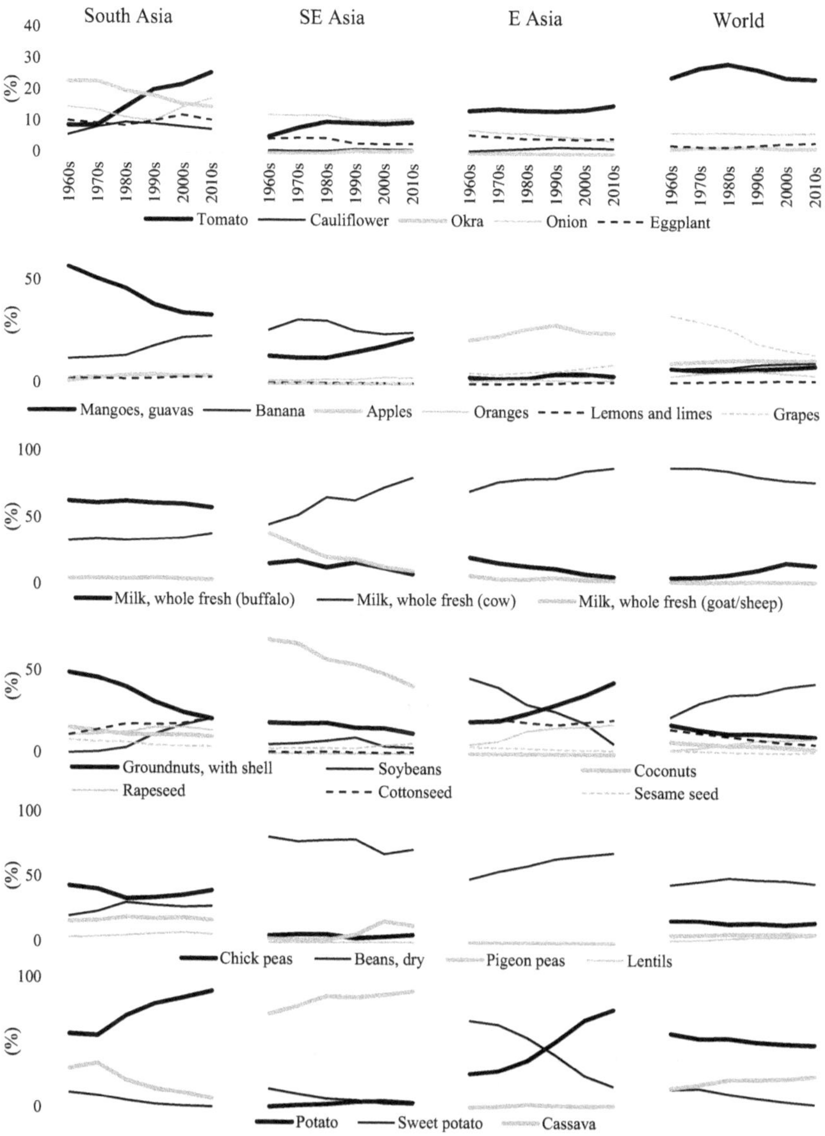

Figure 2.2 Share of major commodities among total production of each major food group in South Asia and other regions (vegetables, fruits, milk, oil crops, pulses, root crops)

Source: FAO, 2019.

agricultural sector issues, including those of contract farming, with a significant within the region.

Trade patterns: origins and destinations by agricultural commodities

The share of agricultural commodities traded has remained modest compared to the amount domestically produced and consumed, in terms of values. In 2011–2013, the shares of net exports (negative if net imports) to total consumption within the South Asia region have been between −10% and 10% for major food groups that account for a large share of total production values, including cereals, root crops, vegetables, fruits, sugar crops and milk (Takeshima et al. 2020). Nevertheless, the shares of traded amounts have been somewhat higher for pulses, oil crops, meat, spices and vegetable oils than some of the other commodities, and South Asia's trade of agricultural commodities has grown in absolute terms over time. Importantly, sets of trade partners have varied and continue to vary substantially across commodity groups. Here, we briefly highlight the key figures of trade origins and destinations for South Asia by commodity groups.

Table 2.1 summarizes the percentages of each group of agricultural commodities that South Asia countries export to and are imported by other South Asia countries and commodities that South Asia countries export to and are imported by regions outside South Asia, based on FAOSTAT's Trade Matrix (FAO 2019). Certain commodities have been increasingly traded among South Asia countries rather than with outside regions. These commodities include cereals, root crops, fiber, milk and cotton. For example, between 1986 and 2000, 17% of cereals exported by South Asian countries were imported by other South Asian countries, and only 1% of cereals imported by South Asian countries had been exported by other South Asian countries. These figures grew to 31% and 19%, respectively, for 2010–2016. In contrast, commodities including pulses and fruits have been increasingly traded with regions outside South Asia.

Outside South Asia, Southeast Asia and West Asia generally have emerged as major export destinations, particularly for commodities including cereals, root crops, vegetables, beverage, egg, meat and non-milk dairy products. However, diverse trade partners also have emerged in terms of relative shares. Regions like East Asia, East and North Africa, North America, and Eastern and Western Europe have remained important partners in both exports and imports. Some regions are particularly important partners for certain commodities, including export destinations like Northern Europe (hide and skin) and North Africa (milk) and import origins like Australia and New Zealand (milk and other dairy products) or West Africa (nuts and cotton). Furthermore, historically, the South Asia market has been the major destination for exports of commodity groups originating elsewhere in South Asia, including root crops, milk, dairy (other) and pulses (often accounting for more than 50%). South Asia also has been the major destination for imports originating elsewhere in South Asia for

Table 2.1 Share of trade partner regions for agricultural commodities exported to and imported by South Asian countries[a] (%)

Commodity groups	*Share (%) of SA countries among all trade partners (1986–2000, 2001–2010, 2011–2016)*						*Major trade partner regions outside South Asia (2011–2016)*	
	Export			*Import*				
	86–00	*01–10*	*11–16*	*86–00*	*01–10*	*11–16*	*Export destination*	*Import origin*
Cereals	17	33	31	1	11	19	SE Asia (28), W Asia (16)	N America (28), E Europe (17)
Root crop	52	66	65	28	45	60	W Asia (14), SE Asia (5)	W Europe (15), E Europe (10)
Sugar crop	23	38	22	10	18	18	W Asia (24), E Africa (17)	S America (64), SE Asia (6)
Pulse	29	56	37	8	6	2	W Asia (26), N Africa (20)	N America (41), SE Asia (18)
Nuts	0	2	4	2	5	7	W Asia (27), N America (26)	W Africa (62), E Africa (13)
Oil crop	5	7	6	45	7	9	SE Asia (43), W Asia (12)	N America (40), E Europe (17)
Vegetable	20	29	27	52	50	67	W Asia (21), SE Asia (14)	E Asia (24), W Asia (3)
Fruits	22	23	24	51	38	35	W Asia (32), W Europe (14)	W Asia (15), E Asia (15)
Fiber	9	24	30	13	16	30	E Asia (53), SE Asia (12)	N America (13), AU/NZ (11)
Spice	11	21	16	42	44	40	SE Asia (23), W Asia (16)	SE Asia (28), E Africa (14)
Fodder	4	16	22	41	56	37	SE Asia (26), E Asia (22)	S America (17), SE Asia (15)
Stimulants	2	3	3	13	13	11	W Asia (32), E Europe (16)	E Africa (37), SE Asia (22)
Oil (vegetable/ animal)	8	5	3	1	1	0	E Asia (38), W Europe (24)	SE Asia (70), S America (17)
Beverage	8	26	12	1	21	21	W Asia (37), SE Asia (15)	N Europe (45), W Europe (13)
Egg	29	13	22	26	66	64	W Asia (33), SE Asia (12)	N America (11), W Europe (11)
Meat	2	2	2	0	11	12	W Asia (95), SE Asia (3)	S America (30), N America (20)
Milk	49	42	56	0	6	6	W Asia (19), N Africa (12)	AU / NZ (64), W Europe (10)
Dairy (other)	46	29	25	1	6	8	W Asia (38), SE Asia (20)	W Europe (33), AU / NZ (25)
Hide skin	20	10	25	4	3	4	N Europe (20), E Asia (20)	W Asia (36), E Africa (13)
Cotton	9	24	31	23	15	32	E Asia (54), SE Asia (13)	N America (17), W Africa (11)

Source: Author's calculations based on FAOSTAT.

Notes:
AU/NZ = Australia and New Zealand.
[a] Figures are based on the nominal, period-total trade values.

vegetables, spice (over 40%), eggs, as well as fruits and fodder (albeit at declining rates).

The shares of trade to total production or consumption in South Asian countries remain modest, and the domestic market will remain the dominant source of demand in the future (as also described in the next section). However, South Asia still has some potential to expand the trade of various agricultural commodities both within and outside the region by growing exports of certain commodities and substituting imports of certain commodities by developing domestic value chains. Both of these can offer opportunities for contract farming.

Outlook for agriculture in South Asia

We have observed the gradual, steady and unique trends of the agricultural sector's growth in South Asia over the last several decades. What are the prospects for the sector's growth, and what might they imply in terms of challenges and opportunities? Such prospects can offer a useful context for discussions on contract farming in this book. Although full examinations of such prospects are beyond this chapter's scope, this section briefly reviews studies providing some analytical projections of demand, production and trade in South Asia. Different aspects are covered for different countries, and therefore we show collective insights for South Asia instead of comparisons between countries.

Outlook for demand and production

South Asia's agriculture by 2030 and 2050 is projected to grow steadily but also to face continuous challenges, primarily due to climate change and the degradation of natural resources. Successful contract farming in the region may require partly addressing the productivity and risk constraints arising from these challenges. Demand for and production of agricultural commodities generally are expected to grow in South Asia by 2030 and 2050, in response to a growing population and possible shifts in food preferences.

According to projections based on the Global Food and Water System (GFWS) platform, a number of South Asian countries are expected to experience greater food deficits by 2050 (Grafton et al. 2015). Depending on different assumptions of projected yield growth, food deficits are expected to grow between 700,000 kcal and 1.2 million kcal in India and by about 200,000 kcal in Pakistan, while Bangladesh is expected to experience a reduced food surplus or a greater food deficit (Grafton et al. 2015). The projected deficits in South Asian countries often are greater than in other major countries in Asia and elsewhere (Grafton et al. 2015). Similar prospects for widening deficits in South Asia by 2030 and 2050 also are provided for particular commodities. For example, South Asia is projected to face a deficit in pulses of 9 million tons by 2050 (6 million tons by 2030), based on IMPACT models and a business-as-usual scenario, that is, a continuation of historical trends in the area and yield growth (Joshi and Rao 2017).

Another study, focusing specifically on India, offers slightly more optimistic scenarios at least until 2030, according to projections based on household-level data on dietary patterns and consumer expenditures and on primary and secondary estimates of demand and supply elasticities (Kumar et al. 2016). According to that study, India could reduce its deficit for rice (from 3 million tons in 2010 to 0.3 million tons in 2030), increase its surplus for overall cereals (1.4 million tons to 30.9 million tons) and achieve a surplus for milk (from a deficit of 1.3 million tons in 2010 to a surplus of 8.8 million tons in 2030). The study, however, still projects deficits (often expanding) for most non-grains in 2030, including edible oils (a deficit of 2.1 million tons in 2030), pulses (0.2 million tons), vegetables (32.0 million tons), fruits (9.9 million tons) and poultry and bovine meat (1.2 million tons). Similarly, Scott et al. (2019) suggest that potato production could potentially increase by 24–37 million tons by 2030 in India (depending on climate change scenarios and population and economic growth scenarios), compared to the production of 46.4 million tons in 2014, based on IMPACT models. Although per capita potato consumption in South Asia has increased considerably, from 3.5 kg in 1962 to 24 kg in 2013, it is still less than in other Asian countries, and therefore there is room for further increases in consumption.

In Bangladesh, Mainuddin and Kirby (2015) provide relatively more optimistic scenarios for rice and wheat for meeting national food consumption requirements by 2050, under the assumption that past production and yield growth can be sustained through continued technological development, including varietal development. They project that if yields can reach 80% of the potential by 2050 (i.e., 4.0, 5.2 and 6.0 tons/ha, respectively, for *aus*, *aman* and *boro* rice, and 4.0 tons/ha for wheat), domestic production can meet 100% of rice consumption, and self-sufficiency for wheat can increase to between 26% and 48%. These projections are qualitatively similar to more recent studies for Bangladesh (e.g., Timsina et al. 2018), which also show the prospects for maize similar to those for wheat. Between 2010 and 2030, demand in India is expected to grow about 1.5% per year for cereals; 2.0% or more for pulses, edible oils, vegetables, fruits and milk; and close to 3.0% per year for poultry and bovine meat (Kumar et al. 2016). Similarly, in Nepal, demand for food is expected to grow between 2015 and 2035 by 1.4% to 1.9% per year for cereals; 2% to 3% for pulses, vegetables, edible oils, sugar, milk and meat/fish/eggs; and 2.9% to 3.6% for fruits, based on assumptions of future growth in population and incomes and on estimated demand elasticities (Kumar et al. 2019).

Kumar et al. (2016) projects that production in India may grow by 2030 by 1.8% per year for cereals; 2% to 3% per year for pulses, vegetables, fruits and milk; and 3% to 4% per year for edible oils and meat. In Pakistan, using variants of a computable general equilibrium model, Spielman et al. (2017) estimate that overall agricultural production may grow at a rate similar to projected economic growth, i.e., 3% per year in Punjab province, which accounted for 63%

of the country's production in 2008, and at slightly faster rates in other provinces, although deviations of up to 1% per year are expected, depending on different climate change scenarios and investments in irrigation infrastructure.

Livestock and fishery production also are expected to grow significantly in terms of consumption and production. Beef, dairy and poultry production are expected to more than double in South Asia between 2010 and 2050 in response to increased global demand (Enahoro et al. 2019). Between 2010 and 2050, the number of livestock animals is expected to grow: dairy cattle at 0.6% per year, beef cattle at 0.9% per year and poultry at 1.8% per year. Among livestock products, South Asia may change from a net importer of 5.1 million tons in 2010 to a net exporter of 27.1 million tons in 2050, which is also consistent with the preceding projection for India (Kumar et al. 2016). In contrast, net imports of poultry and beef may expand by 2050, to 9.5 million tons and 1.8 million tons, respectively. Demand for livestock feeds within South Asia is expected to grow by 2.9% per year, and cereals are expected to meet 54% of all feed demand in 2050. South Asia's producer income from livestock-derived foods (LDF) production is expected to increase by 2.6% per year, from 103.1 billion US$ in 2010 to 284.5 billion US$ in 2050.

Within two decades, the production of fish is expected to more than double in India, and aquaculture in other South Asia countries also is projected to grow more than 90% (Kobayashi et al. 2015). The growth of aquaculture production is expected to be particularly robust in Bangladesh. Between 2015 and 2030, total fish production is expected to increase by 2.6% per year for a total of 47% during this period (most of it from aquaculture rather than inland capture or marine/mixed systems). Fish consumption per capita may increase by 27%, given the reasonable estimates of productivity growth, population growth, income growth, multimarket models and demand systems estimated through modified QUAIDS (Quadratic Almost Ideal Demand System) (Rashid and Zhang 2019, Chapter 6).

Changing climate conditions are expected to further affect these outlooks for South Asian agriculture. Reported projections of climatic change in South Asia include temperature increases of between 0.88°C and 3.16°C by 2050 and between 1.56°C and 5.44°C by 2080, with particularly greater increases during post-monsoon and winter seasons, increased frequency of floods during the monsoon, increased precipitation in most months except winter season and fewer rainy days (Jat et al. 2016). However, there would be significant variations and uncertainty across subregions within the country, including in the maximum and minimum temperatures, the incidence of drought and floods, among other conditions.

Projections of the effects of climate change on South Asia's agriculture remain challenging. However, the consensus is that without appropriate mitigation efforts, the effects are overall negative and substantial. In particular, negative effects on cereal yields due to rising temperatures are widely reported for South Asia, often in the range of 5% to 10% for wheat and rice, 10% to 30% for maize and 20% for sorghum in India and of up to 30% for rice and 60% or more for wheat in Bangladesh (Aryal et al. 2019). In Pakistan, wheat yield may decrease by 5% to 7% with a temperature change of 3°C, while in Sri Lanka, rice outputs may drop by 6%, and yield may drop by 1% to 5%, with less than a 1°C increase in temperature (Aryal et al. 2019). Yields sometimes may increase in higher elevations like the hills and mountains in Nepal (Aryal et al. 2019), but these regions face a different set of challenges, like landslides—due to the increased frequency of monsoonal storms and flooding in the Himalayas—as well as glacier meltdown (Jat et al. 2016). The resulting effects on outputs are also substantial. In India, a 10% to 40% loss in crop production can occur by 2080–2100 due to rising temperatures, including the loss of 4–5 million tons of wheat for every 1°C increase in temperature (Jat et al. 2016 p. 149). A temperature increase of 2°C–2.5°C would leave 63 million people unable to meet their caloric demand by production in the Indus, Ganges and Brahmaputra basins (Vinke et al. 2017). For the whole of South Asia, climate change will reduce rice production by about 2% to 6.5% annually from 2005 to 2050, depending on the scenario (Vinke et al. 2017).

Outlook for trade

Projected trade growth patterns for South Asia also offer useful insights for the future of contract farming in the region. Table 2.2 summarizes sectors' shares of national exports and imports in 2007 and projections for 2030 for South Asia, for all developing countries and for the world.

Compared to other regions in the world, South Asia's trade is characterized by a greater share of services among exports and of other primary goods among imports. By 2030, these patterns are projected to become stronger. Importantly, paralleling this growth, the shares of agriculture and food commodities are projected to decline to 2.3% among exports and to increase to 12.0% among imports. These patterns are much sharper than those in other regions.

Table 2.2 Sectoral shares of national exports and imports, 2007 and 2030 (%)

Exports/ imports	*Region*	*2007*				*2030 (Projection)*			
		Agriculture and food	*Other primary*	*Manu-factures*	*Services*	*Agriculture and food*	*Other primary*	*Manu-factures*	*Services*
Exports	South Asia	7.9	4.2	60.0	27.8	2.3	4.5	59.7	33.4
	All developing	5.9	18.5	61.9	13.7	5.0	16.1	65.3	13.6
	World	6.1	9.8	65.8	18.2	7.4	12.9	62.4	17.2
Imports	South Asia	5.6	25.8	52.3	16.3	12.0	31.8	44.6	11.6
	All developing	6.5	11.4	66.4	15.7	9.7	16.8	60.1	13.5
	World	6.4	10.2	65.9	17.6	7.7	13.4	62.5	16.4

Source: Author's extraction from Anderson and Strutt (2016, Table 3, Table 5).

Table 2.3 Share of South Asia's trade to the world trade, agricultural and food products, 2007 and 2030 (projection)

Region	*Exports*		*Imports*	
	2007	*2030*	*2007*	*2030 (projection)*
South Asia	2.4	1.0–1.5	2.1	5.5–6.6
East Asia	12.1	9.0–11.7	18.2	30.0–40.5
All developing	34.8	35.4–41.8	32.0	53.5–59.0

Source: Author's extraction from Anderson and Strutt (2016, Table 8).

Imports of agricultural and food commodities in South Asia are projected to rise overall, not only in terms of the sector's share but also in terms of its share in the global market. Table 2.3 summarizes South Asia's trade of agricultural and food products as a share of world trade in 2007 and 2030 (projection). South Asia's share of global imports is projected to almost triple from 2.1% in 2007 to between 5.5% and 6.6% in 2030. The projected growth rate is relatively greater than those of East Asia or all developing countries. At the same time, South Asia's projected share in 2030 is still small compared to East Asia's (30.0%–40.5%), despite the two regions' similar population sizes. This pattern suggests that developing the domestic agricultural sector, through contract farming and overall productivity improvement, will remain crucial in South Asia in the near future.

More rigorous assessments are needed in further studies to distinguish the nature of these projected trade growth patterns. However, growth in trade is expected to reflect not simply the growing domestic demand for quantity (due to population growth) but also the potential growing domestic demand for quality. These projections imply that the domestic market, rather than foreign markets, may hold the greatest potential for output markets for contract farming in South Asia. The domestic market also remains important because it accounts for a significant share of the destinations for most agricultural commodities. Productivity growth also continues to be critical for the expansion of export-oriented contract farming.

Conclusions

This chapter has attempted to provide some context for how South Asia's agricultural sector has been and will be evolving, in terms of overall production, diversification and trade with outside regions. The chapter also attempted to provide more comparative figures across commodities and regions to highlight, where relevant, South Asia's uniqueness. The agricultural sector in South Asia has continued to evolve over the last few decades. Agricultural production has grown steadily, although at a somewhat slower pace than the impressive growth rates in East and Southeast Asia. This growth has been associated with significant modernization in terms of the use of modern inputs and value chain development. South Asia's agricultural sector also has experienced significant diversification. The diversification pattern has been unique in terms of the set of commodity groups and in terms of the emergence and decline of a particular set of crops within each group, including milk, vegetables, fruits and root crops, for which contract farming is likely to be significantly relevant. Although domestic markets continue to account for the dominant outlets for production in South Asia, trade within and outside the region also has expanded. A brief review of trading patterns revealed a significant growth of integration within and outside the region, characterized by diverse trading partners (in terms of partner regions) that vary depending on commodity groups, directions (exports or imports) and the relative importance of trade within South Asia compared to trade with the outside region. For trade-involved contract farming in South Asia, the potential is substantial in terms of geography and commodity scope.

The review of the outlook for South Asia's agricultural sector generally revealed that production growth, diversification and modernization continue to remain critical for food security in the region, where demand is expected to grow with relative shifts toward more diverse non-staple food groups, in response to population growth and economic growth that are faster than in many other regions of the world. The projections of food deficits and trade suggest that the economic stakes are high for further agricultural modernization, including contract farming, and that the productivity growth needed to realize such potential is significant but achievable as long as countries make continuous investments to sustain past productivity growth.

References

Anderson, K., & A. Strutt. (2016). "Impacts of Emerging Asia on African and Latin American Trade: Projections to 2030," *The World Economy* **39** (2), 172–194.

Aryal, J. P., T. B. Sapkota, R. Khurana, A. Khatri-Chhetri, D. B. Rahut, & M. L. Lat. (2019). "Climate Change and Agriculture in South Asia: Adaptation Options in Smallholder Production Systems." *Environment, Development and Sustainability* **22**.

Asian Development Bank (ADB). (2005). *An Impact Evaluation on the Development of Genetically Improved Farmed Tilapia and Their Dissemination in Selected Countries*. Impact Evaluation Studies IES: REG 2004–20, ADB, Manila, ISBN:971-561-584-8.

Brouwer, F., & P. K. Joshi. (2016). *International Trade and Food Security: The future of Indian Agriculture*. Wallingford, UK and Boston. CABI.

Das Gupta, S., B. Minten, N. C. Rao, & T. Reardon. (2017). "The Rapid Diffusion of Herbicides in Farming in India: Patterns, Determinants, and Effects on Labor Productivity," *European Journal of Development Research* **29**(3), 596–613.

Diao, X., H. Takeshima, & X. Zhang. (2021). *A New Paradigm of Agricultural Mechanization Development: How Much Can Africa Learn from Asia?* Washington, DC. IFPRI.

Enahoro, D., D. Mason-D'Croz, M. Mul, K. M. Rich, T. P. Robinson, P. Thornton, & S. S. Staal. (2019). "Supporting Sustainable Expansion of Livestock Production in South Asia and Sub-Saharan Africa: Scenario Analysis of Investment Options," *Global Food Security* **20**, 114–121.

Evenson, R., & D. Gollin. (2003). *Crop Variety Improvement and Its Effect on Productivity: The Impact of International Agricultural Research*. Wallingford, UK. CABI.

Fafchamps, M., R. V. Hill, & B. Minten. (2008). "Quality Control in Nonstaple Food Markets: Evidence from India," *Agricultural Economics* **38** (3), 251–266.

FAO. (2019). *FAOSTAT*. Rome, Italy: FAO.

Franco, D., D. R. Singh, & K. V. Praveen. (2018). "Evaluation of Adoption of Precision Farming and Its Profitability in Banana Crop," *Indian Journal of Economics and Development* **14** (2), 225–234.

Grafton, Q., J. Williams, & Q. Jiang. (2015). "Food and Water Gaps to 2050: Preliminary Results from the Global Food and Water System (GFWS) Platform," *Food Security* **7**, 209–220.

Jat, M. L. et al. (2016). "Chapter 3: Climate Change and Agriculture: Adaptation Strategies and Mitigation Opportunities for Food Security in South Asia and Latin America," *Advances in Agronomy* **137**, 127–235.

Joshi, P. K., A. Gulati, & R. W. Cummings (Eds.). (2007). *Agricultural Diversification and Smallholders in South Asia*. New Delhi, India. Academic Foundation.

Joshi, P. K., & P. P. Rao. (2017). "Global Pulses Scenario: Status and Outlook," *Annals of the New York Academy of Sciences* **1392** (1), 6–17.

Kalubhai, P. (2015). *Present Status and Prospects of Micro Irrigation System in Mahisagar District of Gujarat*. Doctoral dissertation, Anand Agricultural University, Anand, India.

Kobayashi, M., S. Msangi, M. Batka, S. Vannuccini, M. M. Dey, & J. L. Anderson. (2015). "Fish to 2030: The Role and Opportunity for Aquaculture," *Aquaculture Economics & Management* **19** (3), 282–300.

Kolady, D. E., D. Spielman, & A. Cavalieri. (2012). "The Impact of Seed Policy Reforms and Intellectual Property Rights on Crop Productivity in India," *Journal of Agricultural Economics* **63** (2), 361–384.

Kumar, A., S. Saroj, P. K. Joshi, & H. Takeshima. (2018). "Does Cooperative Membership Improve Household Welfare? Evidence from a Panel Data Analysis of Smallholder Dairy Farmers in Bihar, India," *Food Policy* **75**, 24–36.

Kumar, P., P. K. Joshi, & S. Mittal. (2016). "Demand vs Supply of Food in India-Futuristic Projection," *Proceedings of the Indian National Science Academy* **82** (5), 1579–1586.

Kumar, P., A. Kumar, & P. K. Joshi. (2019). Food Demand System and Projections to 2035: Nepal, in *Agricultural Transformation in Nepal: Trends, Prospects, and Policy Options*, G. Thapa, A. Kumar, & P. K. Joshi (eds). Singapore. Springer.

Mainuddin, M., & M. Kirby. (2015). "National Food Security in Bangladesh to 2050," *Food Security* **7** (3), 633–646.

Matuschke, I., R. Mishra, & M. Qaim. (2007). "Adoption and Impact of Hybrid Wheat in India," *World Development* **35** (8), 1422–1435.

Matuschke, I., & M. Qaim. (2008). "Seed Market Privatisation and Farmers' Access to Crop Technologies: The Case of Hybrid Pearl Millet Adoption in India," *Journal of Agricultural Economics* **59** (3), 498–515.

Minten, B., K. A. S. Murshid, & T. Reardon. (2013). "Food Quality Changes and Implications: Evidence from the Rice Value Chain of Bangladesh," *World Development* **42**, 100–113.

Minten, B., A. Vandeplas, & J. Swinnen. (2012). "Regulations, Brokers, and Interlinkages: The Institutional Organization of Wholesale Markets in India," *Journal of Development Studies* **48** (7), 864–886.

Patlolla, S., R. Goodhue, & R. Sexton. (2015). "Managing Quantity, Quality, and Timing in Indian Cane Sugar Production: Ex Post Marketing Permits or Ex Ante Production Contracts?" *World Bank Economic Review* **29** (3), 606–630.

Pray, C., & L. Nagarajan. (2014). "The Transformation of the Indian Agricultural Input Industry: Has It Increased Agricultural R&D?" *Agricultural Economics* **45** (S1), 145–156.

Rashid, S., & X. Zhang (Eds.). (2019). *The Making of a Blue Revolution in Bangladesh: Enablers, Impacts, and the Path Ahead for Aquaculture*. Washington, DC. International Food Policy Research Institute.

Reardon, T., K. Chen, B. Minten, & L. Adriano. (2012). *The Quiet Revolution in Staple Food Value Chains in Asia: Enter the Dragon, the Elephant, and the Tiger*. Mandaluyong City, Philippines, and Washington, DC. Asian Development Bank and IFPRI.

Scott, G. J., A. Petsakos, & H. Juarez. (2019). "Climate Change, Food Security, and Future Scenarios for Potato Production in India to 2030," *Food Security* **11** (1), 43–56.

Shruthi, K., G. M. Hiremath, A. T. Joshi, & S. S. Patil. (2018a). "An Application of Precision Farming Techniques in Production of Pigeonpea—An Economic Analysis," *Progressive Agriculture* **18** (1), 15–19.

Shruthi, K., G. M. Hiremath, A. T. Joshi, & S. S. Patil. (2018b). "An Economic Analysis of Precision Agriculture—A Case Study of Paddy in North Eastern Karnataka," *Indian Journal of Economics and Development* **14** (2), 274–280.

Spielman, D. J., D. Kolady, P. Ward, H. A. Rashid, & K. Gulati. (2012). *Public Expenditures, Private Incentives, and Technology Adoption: The Economics of Hybrid Rice in South Asia*. IFPRI Discussion Paper 01233.

Spielman, D. J., S. J. Malik, P. Dorosh, & N. Ahmad. (Eds.). (2017). *Agriculture and the Rural Economy in Pakistan: Issues, Outlooks, and Policy Priorities*. Philadelphia, PA. University of Pennsylvania Press.

Takeshima, H. (2017). "Custom-Hired Tractor Services and Returns to Scale in Smallholder Agriculture: A Production Function Approach," *Agricultural Economics* **48** (3), 363–372.

Takeshima, H., A. Kumar, A. Akhter, & P. K. Joshi. (2020). Agricultural Development and Modernization in South Asia, in *Agricultural Development: New Perspectives in a Changing World*, K Otsuka & S Fan (eds). In Progress.

Takeshima, H., & L. Nagarajan. (2012). "Minor Millets in Tamil Nadu, India: Local Market Participation, On-farm Diversity and Farmer Welfare," *Environment and Development Economics* **17** (5), 603–632.

Thapa, G., A. Kumar, & P. K. Joshi. (2019). *Agricultural Transformation in Nepal: Trends, Prospects, and Policy Options*. Singapore. Springer.

Timsina, J., J. Wolf, N. Guilpart, L. G. J. Van Bussel, P. Grassini, J. Van Wart, . . . M. K. Van Ittersum. (2018). "Can Bangladesh Produce Enough Cereals to Meet Future Demand?" *Agricultural Systems* **163**, 36–44.

Tiwari, A., & P. K. Jaga. (2012). "Precision Farming in India—A Review," *Outlook on Agriculture* **41** (2), 139–143.

Vandeplas, A., & B. Minten. (2015). "Food Quality in Domestic Markets of Developing Economies: A Comparative Study of Two Countries," *Agricultural Economics* **46** (5), 617–628.

Vinke, K. et al. (2017). "Climatic Risks and Impacts in South Asia: Extremes of Water Scarcity and Excess," *Regional Environmental Change* **17**, 1569–1583.

USDA-ERS. (2020). *USDA Economic Research Service Agricultural Productivity Project*. Washington, DC. USDA.

3 Agriculture on the rise in Bangladesh

The future role of value chains

Khondoker Abdul Mottaleb, Akbar Hossain and Md. Israil Hossain

Bangladesh is 147,570 km^2 (Government of Bangladesh, 2019), smaller than the U.S. state of Georgia (153,910 km^2). Yet Bangladesh hosts 163.7 million people (Government of Bangladesh, 2019), which is half the total population of the United States (327.2 million) (World Bank, 2020). Due to the enormous population pressure, the average farm size in Bangladesh has decreased to 0.68 ha. Nonetheless, Bangladesh has moved from being a country of chronic food shortages in the 1970s to one of food self-sufficiency now (Ahmed et al., 2000; Dorosh, 2000; Hossain, 2009; Hossain et al., 2007, 1994; Mottaleb et al., 2015). This chapter highlights the success of Bangladesh's agriculture sector via a value chain analysis.

In 1971, just after independence, Bangladesh produced 0.74 million metric tons (MMT) of fish and seafood. By 1995, it had increased production to 1.1 MMT (FAOSTAT, 2020). By 2013, the total supply of fish and seafood had increased to 3.2 MMT, of which 2.6 MMT was harvested only from inland freshwater sources (FAOSTAT, 2020). As Bangladesh is one of the major exporters of frozen fish, crab and shrimp, local producers are linked with the global value chain. Bangladesh is now the third-largest producer of inland water fish in the world and the fifth-largest in the world in total aquaculture production (Government of Bangladesh, 2019). Bangladesh is the fourth-largest tilapia producer in the world, and in Asia, it is ranked third in tilapia production (Government of Bangladesh, 2019). In Bangladesh, fish contributes 50% of the per capita daily protein intake (FAO, 2018). In addition, Bangladesh is a net exporter of frozen fish and seafood products. For instance, in 2011–2013, Bangladesh exported about 107,000 metric tons (MT) of fish and seafood. Thus, local producers in Bangladesh are linked to the global fish and seafood value chains.

In terms of vegetable production, Bangladesh produced 16.4 MMT in 2018, which was five times higher than in 1971 (The Asian Age, 2018). In 2018, more than 16 million farmers produced 156 types of vegetables, and the country exported about US$ 83 million worth of vegetables to 50 countries (The Asian Age, 2018). Bangladesh now ranks third in the world in vegetable production.

Bangladesh's most significant success, however, is becoming self-sufficient in cereal food production. From 1971 to 1995, the annual average yield of the major cereals, namely rice, wheat and maize, were 2.1 MT/ha, 1.7 MT/ha and 0.90 MT/ha, respectively (FAO, 2019a). In the early 1970s, with a population of less than 70 million, Bangladesh faced massive food shortages and famine (Dorosh, 2000; Hossain, 2009), but despite the population growing to nearly 164 million, the country is now almost self-sufficient in staple food production. The annual average yield of rice, wheat and maize has increased to 3.9 MT/ha, 2.3 MT/ha and 4.8 MT/ha, respectively (FAO, 2019a). In 2017, Bangladesh ranked as the fourth-largest paddy-rice-producing country (49.5 MMT) in the world after China (214 MMT), India (169 MMT) and Indonesia (81.4 MMT) (FAO, 2019a). Importantly, Bangladesh also ranks as the top rice-consuming country, at 268.5 kg yearly per capita (FAO, 2019b). In the 1990–1992 triennium average, the per capita dietary energy intake rate was 2,112 kcal/daily, which increased to 2,574 kcal/daily in 2015–2017. In 2019, Bangladesh ranked 88th out of 117 countries on the Global Hunger Index (Grebmer et al., 2019), compared to 2006, when it ranked 102nd out of 119 countries (Wiesmann et al., 2006).

Interestingly, the agriculture sector's contribution to gross domestic product (GDP) and the share of employment in Bangladesh have typically followed Petty's law (e.g., Murata, 2008). According to Petty's law, with the economic progress of a country, the agricultural sector's relative contribution to GDP and its share of employment gradually decline compared to the contributions of industry and service sectors. This is because households' expenditures on food gradually fall compared to their expenditures on non-food items, such as manufactured goods or services. This economic transition from an agriculture-based economy to an industry and service sector–based one has been observed repeatedly in many countries around the world.

In line with this, in 1994–1995, the agriculture sector's contribution to Bangladesh's GDP was US$9.5 billion (World Bank, 2020), or nearly 21% of GDP (Government of Bangladesh, 2005). In 1994–1995, agriculture and forestry value-added US$84 per capita/year. In 2015–2017, the agriculture sector's contribution to GDP was US$31.1 billion (World Bank, 2020), or 11.7% of GDP (Government of Bangladesh, 2019), with an added value of US$197 per capita/year (World Bank, 2020). Similarly, the agriculture sector's share of employment in Bangladesh decreased from 69.5% in 1991 to 40.1% in 2017 (World Bank, 2020). However, from 2004–2005 to 2018–2019, the agriculture and forestry sector of Bangladesh maintained a growth rate of 3.5% per year, and the fishery sector achieved a growth of 6.3% per year (Government of Bangladesh, 2019). Thus Bangladesh's economy has been gradually reducing its reliance on the agriculture sector while achieving steady growth in absolute contribution in the form of value added to GDP.

This chapter examines the development of the value chains for wheat, maize and rice, the three major cereal crops of Bangladesh. This chapter mainly relies on information from FAOSTAT (online data of the Food and Agriculture Organization of the United Nations [FAO]), World Development Indicators

(World Bank, 2020), the Bangladesh Rice Research Institute (BRRI) and information available online from the government of Bangladesh.

Wheat

To ensure basic food security for the country after independence, the Bangladesh government mainly underscored the extension of rice cultivation, as rice is the major staple of Bangladesh. At the same time, wheat cultivation was discouraged, given that eating bread was part of Pakistani culture (Ahmed and Meisner, 1996). This anti-wheat attitude, however, was altered by a 1974 visit to Bangladesh from the chief breeder and top scientists of the Centro Internacional de Mejoramiento de Maiz y Trigo (CIMMYT), or the International Maize and Wheat Improvement Center. The CIMMYT scientists successfully convinced the government of Bangladesh that crop diversification could reduce climate-related risks and thereby ensure food security for the country. Moreover, the scientists stressed that without hampering rice production, Bangladesh could produce more than 1 million MT of wheat as an alternative winter crop. As high-yielding wheat seed was in short supply, in 1975 the government imported 4,000 tons of Sonalika and Kalyansona wheat seed from India and Mexico. The national government also trained agriculture extension officers ahead of the wheat season. Ahmed and Meisner (1996) stressed that it was the first major, well organized and successful government initiative to expand wheat production in Bangladesh.

Until recently, Bangladesh's national agricultural program focused on attaining self-sufficiency in rice production because of its strategic importance. However, with growing food demand for wheat in food security, the government now is keen to also expand wheat cultivation in Bangladesh (Figure 3.1). In 1971, wheat research in Bangladesh was initiated under a scheme named the Accelerated Wheat Research Program for Bangladesh. This program continued until the Wheat Research Center (WRC) was established in 1980. In 2017, a bill was passed to create a separate research institute for wheat and maize, the Bangladesh Wheat and Maize Research Institute (BWMRI) (Daily Sun, 2017).

Although wheat production in Bangladesh has increased dramatically in yield, production failed to keep pace with increasing consumption by the growing population (Figure 3.1). Thus the self-sufficiency ratio in wheat, calculated as the total domestic production divided by total domestic supply, where domestic supply includes domestic production plus imports and wheat food aid from abroad, has declined over the years (Figure 3.1). For example, in 1990–1992, the self-sufficiency ratio in the wheat supply was more than 39%, which means domestic production supplied 39% of the total wheat supply of Bangladesh. In 2017–2019, domestic wheat production was 1.2 MMT, and total supply was 8.5 MMT; thus the self-sufficiency ratio had declined to 13%. Thus, in 2017–2019, domestic wheat production provided less than

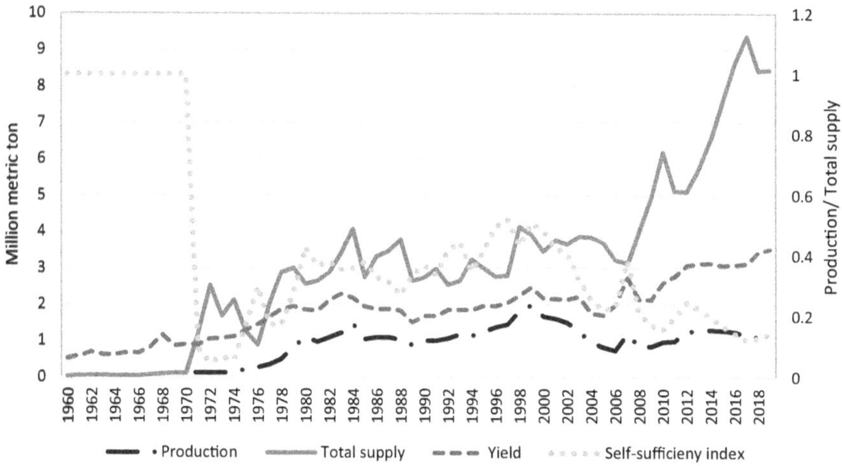

Figure 3.1 Temporal changes in wheat yield, production, total supply and self-sufficiency ratio (domestic production/total domestic supply) during 1960–2019

Source: Authors, based on USDA (2019).

20% of the total wheat supply in Bangladesh, with 80% being supplied by imports. During 2000–2002, Bangladesh imported 1.9 MMT of wheat, worth US$205 million, whereas during 2015–2017, it imported 5.4 MMT of wheat, worth US$1.1 billion (FAOSTAT, 2020).

Wheat is used mainly as a food product in Bangladesh. In 2015–2017, more than 55% of the total wheat in Bangladesh was used as food, and use as animal feed was only 17% (FAOSTAT, 2020). In Bangladesh, for a long time, yearly rice consumption has oscillated around 170 kg per capita, whereas wheat consumption has fluctuated over the decades but steadied in the early 2000s at around 17 kg per capita (Figure 3.2). Recent studies conclude that growth in per capita income (GDP), speedy urbanization and population growth are the forces driving increased wheat consumption in Bangladesh (Mottaleb et al., 2018a, 2018b).

The wheat flour value chain in Bangladesh is segmented into two distinct types: large imported-wheat-based commercial companies and local smallholder producers and millers. Local wheat farmers of Bangladesh are generally smallholder farmers who produce wheat mostly for self-consumption. These farmers typically use the services of the *chakki* system flour mills to produce whole wheat flour (*atta*). *Chakki* mills are stone-wheeled mills mostly imported from India and operated by a small horse-powered motor or diesel engine with a milling capacity of 300–800 kg a day (Hussain and Leishman, 2013). These mills are mostly located in rural areas, where there is no electricity or poor access to it.

Figure 3.2 Wheat and rice consumption trends in Bangladesh (yearly/per capita/kg)

Source: Authors, based on FAOSTAT, 2020.

The large imported-wheat-based companies' use of roller mills has diminished the importance of the *chakki* system of traditional flour mills. Nonetheless, until 2013, there were 2,000 traditional *chakki* system flour mills providing services to smallholder farmers (Hussain and Leishman, 2013). Currently, the wheat import market of Bangladesh is worth more than 1 billion US$ (FAOSTAT, 2020). Until 1990, all wheat imports were regulated by the government under procurement or food aid from foreign donors. However, 75% of wheat imported to Bangladesh now is controlled by large private importers (Hussain and Leishman, 2013). These private companies, using large-capacity modern roller mills, supplied more than 93% of the total commercial wheat flour in the market. In 2013, 20 large roller mills, 120 medium roller mills, and 200 small roller mills were operating in Bangladesh (Hussain and Leishman, 2013). Several large groups of companies, such as ACI Limited, Ifad Group, Bashundhara Group and Meghna Group, supply brand-name wheat products mainly targeting urban consumers (Figure 3.3).

Generally, flour mills in Bangladesh produce a single grade of flour known as *atta*, which is commonly used to make flatbreads such as *chapati* and *roti*. However, modern rolling mills, using sophisticated technology, are producing different grades of flour for bread, biscuits, pasta, noodles and crackers. The expansion of fast-food restaurants, the emergence of supermarket culture and the rise of Bangladesh as a middle-income nation have been expanding the frontiers of the high-protein wheat value chain.

(a)

(b)

Figure 3.3 Open wheat flour (a) and branded 1-kg wheat flour packet for sale (b) in Savar market, Dhaka, Bangladesh

Source: Authors.

Maize

Maize is used mainly as feed in the poultry and aquaculture sectors of Bangladesh. The dramatic expansion of the poultry and aquaculture sectors since the 1990s contributed to expanding maize cultivation (Ali et al., 2008; Bober and Mittal, 2015). In 1991–1992, the total poultry population in Bangladesh was 110.5 million (Government of Bangladesh, 2006), more than tripling to 344.0 million in 2018–2019 (Government of Bangladesh, 2019). In 1996–1997, the total area under aquaculture (pond, shrimp/prawn farms, semi-closed water bodies, baors) was 0.34 million ha, and total production was 0.49 MMT (Government of Bangladesh, 2006). In 2015–2016, the aquaculture area more than doubled, to 0.79 million ha, and production increased to 3.25 MMT (Government of Bangladesh, 2016). Bangladesh now is the third-largest inland water fish producer in the world and fifth-largest in total aquaculture production (Government of Bangladesh, 2019). In addition, Bangladesh is the third-largest tilapia producer in Asia and fourth in the world (Government of Bangladesh, 2019). The growing demand for maize feed in the poultry and aquaculture sectors has contributed tremendously to maize cultivation. Currently, 61 private feed mills link maize farmers with the maize value chain and supply feed for the poultry and fishery sector (Bangladesh Business Directory, 2018).

Seeing the growing demand for feed, private seed companies imported and introduced high-yielding and hybrid maize to Bangladesh (Bober and Mittal, 2015). The involvement of non-governmental organizations (NGOs) in maize cultivation contributed to expanding maize cultivation in Bangladesh (Lynamm et al., 2010). For example, since 1994, the Bangladesh Rural Advancement Committee (BRAC)—the world's largest NGO—has been marketing hybrid maize seeds in Bangladesh. With 7,000 contract farmers and 22 production centers, BRAC is the largest producer of hybrid maize seed in Bangladesh (BRAC, 2016) and now markets 14 hybrids of maize seed. Government initiatives to expand maize cultivation are also highly visible. By 2018, the Bangladesh Agricultural Research Institute (BARI) reported the dissemination of 25 maize varieties, of which 17 were hybrid maize (Table 3.1).

Given all these efforts, land allocation to maize production has increased to 400,000 ha, and with a yield of 8.2 MT/ha, total maize production has increased to 3.3 MMT from 3,350 MT on 3,300 ha in 1990 (FAO, 2019a) (Figure 3.4). Until 2015, a total of 86 maize varieties, including improved and hybrid maize, were available in Bangladesh, of which *Dekalb981*, *Miracle*, *NK40* and *Pioneer 30V92* were the most popular varieties (Bober and Mittal, 2015). Note that with a 8.2-MT/ha maize yield, Bangladesh's maize yield is the highest in South Asia, the 29th highest in the world and 10th highest in Asia (FAO, 2019a). Nearly 91% of the total maize area is under hybrid maize cultivation (Bober and Mittal, 2015).

Table 3.1 Varietal release of maize by the Bangladesh Agriculture Research Institute (BRRI) up to 2016

Year	*Number of variety released*	*Name of the variety*	*Yield range (tons/ha)*	*Major characteristics*
Up to 2000	7	BARI hybrid *Bhutta*-1, BARI *Bhutta*-6, BARI *Bhutta*-5, Khoibhutta, Mohar, Barnali, Shuvra	4.0–5.6	Large cobs; golden yellow color grain; high popping quality (95%); medium pigmentation Almost resistant to diseases and pests
2001–2004	6	BARI Hybrid *Bhutta*-5, BARI top cross hybrid *Bhutta*-1, BARI Hybrid *Bhutta*-2; BARI Hybrid *Bhutta*-3; BARI *Bhutta*-7; BARI Misty *Bhutta*-1;	5.5–10.5	Orange yellow; short and long duration; open pollinated and hybrid Susceptible to leaf blight disease
2005–2009	6	BARI hybrid maize 6, BARI hybrid maize 7, BARI hybrid maize 8, BARI hybrid maize 9, BARI hybrid maize 10, BARI hybrid maize 11,		
2010–2018	6	BARI baby corn-1; BARI hybrid *Bhutta* (Maize)-12, BARI Hybrid *Bhutta* (maize)-13, BARI hybrid *Bhutta* (maize)-14, BARI hybrid *Bhutta* (maize)-15, BARI Hybrid *Bhutta* (maize)-16	1.3–11.6	Short and long duration; open pollinated and hybrid Yield range: 1.2–11.5T/ha Susceptible to leaf blight disease

Source: BARI, 2020a.

Due to suitable agroclimatic conditions, maize in Bangladesh is cultivated almost year-round under different cropping systems (Table 3.2). Winter (October–March) is the main maize season in Bangladesh (Rahman et al., 2009), but summer (March–June) maize also is cultivated under maize-transplanted *aman* rice and a maize-fallow-wheat cropping system. The high return from maize cultivation, a cash crop, is widely acknowledged (Ali et al., 2008; Dewan et al., 1998; Fischer et al., 2014). Maize also requires less water than the major competing winter crops, *boro* rice or wheat (Fischer et al., 2014) and has the highest relative yields. Thus the lower resource requirements and the potential for higher farm incomes are driving maize cultivation in Bangladesh.

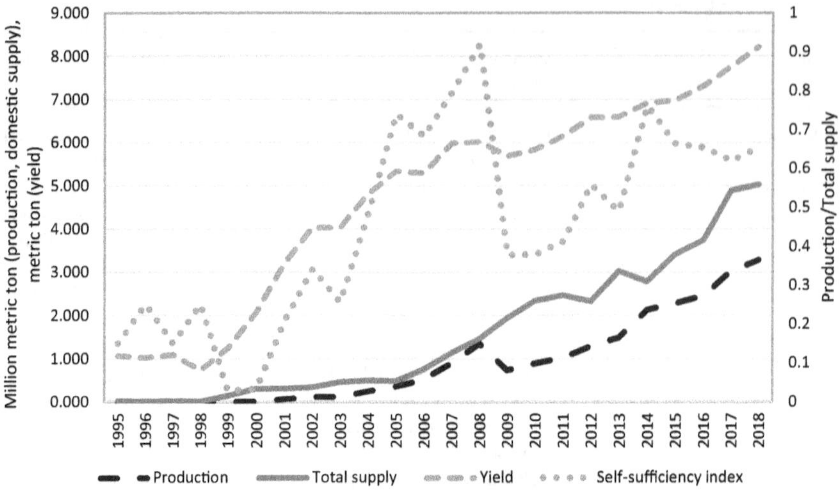

Figure 3.4 Temporal changes in maize yield, production, total supply and self-sufficiency ratio (domestic production/total domestic supply) during 1960–2018

Sources: Authors, based on FAOSTAT (2020) and USDA (2019).

Note: Data on total supply collected from USDA (2019).

Table 3.2 Wheat, maize, *aus*, *aman* and *boro* rice suitability in ha (%), Bangladesh

			Rice		
Suitability	*Wheat*	*Maize*	*Aus*	*Aman*	*Boro*
Very suitable	1.3 (13.5)	2.3 (66.8)	1.4 (14.3)	3.7 (37.7)	3.5 (35.5)
Suitable	3.5 (35.8)	2.0 (74.9)	2.7 (27.5)	0.19 (1.9)	2.7 (28.7)
Moderately suitable	1.4 (13.8)	1.5 (14.1)	2.6 (26.5)	1.51 (15.4)	1.1 (11.0)
Marginally suitable	1.1 (11.0)	0.9 (63.7)	1.74 (17.7)	0.50 (5.1)	1.4 (13.8)
Not suitable	2.5 (25.9)	3.1 (2.6)	1.42 (14.5)	2.2 (22.4)	1.2 (11.9)
Total crop area of Bangladesh	9.81				

Source: BARI, 2020b.

Note: Values in parentheses are percentages.

Interestingly, although maize is used mainly as animal feed in Bangladesh; a few studies reported that several wheat flour mills mix maize with wheat in various proportions without mentioning it (Quasem, 1999). By revealing the information on the packaging and examining consumer preferences, it is possible to formalize such mixing in a legal way. The government could train and sensitize mill operators to use a preferred mixture of wheat and maize and to disclose the information on the packages. In addition to the general consumer, various relief and development programs of the government, such as food for work and education programs, could use this mixed flour. Also, there is an increasing demand in the urban market for corn flakes as a breakfast item and for corn oil. Breeding specific types of maize for producing corn flakes and corn oil not only could meet the growing demand of affluent consumers but could ensure higher profits for maize farmers. Both public and private initiatives are necessary to strengthen the value chain of maize, which ultimately can benefit resource-poor maize farmers.

Rice

Rice is the major staple grain of Bangladesh. There are three rice seasons in Bangladesh: *aus*, the summer season rice, grown during mid-March to early August; *aman*, the rainy season rice, grown June through January; and dry season *boro* rice, grown mid-November to June (BBS, 2018). In Bangladesh, of the total crop area, nearly 42% is very suitable or suitable for *aus*, nearly 40% for *aman* and more than 64% for *boro* rice (Table 3.2). In 2017, Bangladesh ranked as the world's fourth-largest paddy-rice-producing country (49.5 MMT), after China (214 MMT), India (169 MMT) and Indonesia (81.4 MMT) (FAO, 2019a). With 268.5 kg of rice consumed yearly per capita, Bangladesh is the world's top rice-consuming country (FAO, 2019b). The expansion of irrigation facilities dramatically accelerated the expansion of *boro* rice areas, mostly by replacing the summer season rain-fed *aus* rice areas (Figure 3.5). Note that *aus* and *aman* rice are mostly rain-fed and consequently are more prone to yield loss due to climate-related disasters (Mottaleb et al., 2015). In contrast, *boro* rice is almost 100% irrigated, and thus water-related stress is almost absent in *boro* cultivation. For example, in the 1990–1991 financial year, *aus* rice was grown on 2.25 million ha, *aman* on 5.77 million ha and *boro* on 5.48 million ha (Figure 3.5). In 2018–2019, the area growing *aus* rice declined to 1.14 million ha, and the *aman* area declined to 5.62 million ha, whereas the *boro* area increased to 4.9 million ha (Figure 3.5). Since 1990, irrigated *boro* rice has undermined the domination of *aus* rice in the sector.

In addition to the expansion of irrigated *boro* area, the adoption of modern varieties (MV) of rice in Bangladesh in all three seasons has expanded significantly. For example, during the 1990–1991 financial year, the modern-variety adoption rate was 17% in *aus* rice, 29% in *aman* rice and 89% in *boro* rice BRRI (2020). Now, the modern-variety adoption rate is 89% in *aus* rice, 78% in *aman* rice and nearly 100% in *boro* rice.

Due to the rapid proliferation of small irrigation facilities, rapid scaling of modern-variety rice and the expansion of *boro* rice, the overall rice yield also has increased significantly. For example, in 1990–1991, *aus* yield was 1.1 MT/ha, *aman* yield was 1.6 MT/ha, and *boro* yield was 2.5 MT/ha (BRRI, 2020). In contrast, in 2018–2019, *aus* yield increased to 2.6 MT/ha, *aman* yield to

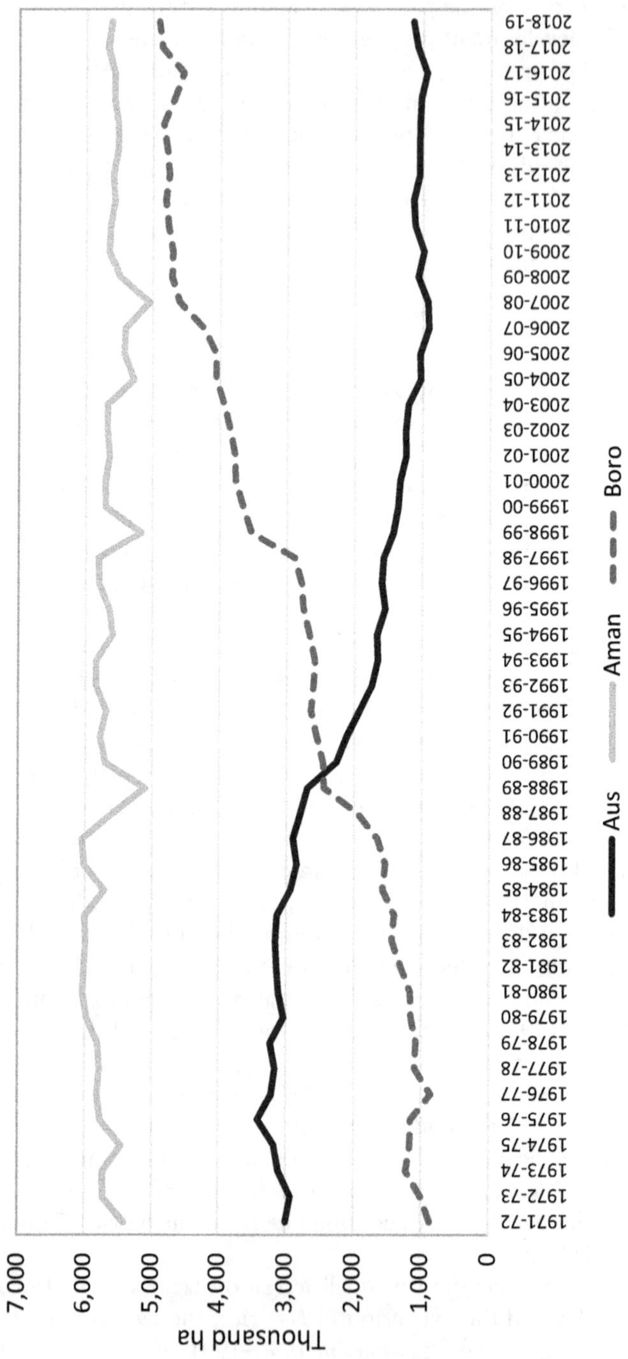

Figure 3.5 Temporal changes in the land allocation to *aus*, *aman* and *boro* rice in Bangladesh during 1971–2019

Source: Authors, based on BRRI, 2020.

2.5 MTha and *boro* rice yield to 4.2 MT/ha (BRRI, 2020). The government also developed new high-yielding, stress-tolerant and protein-, iron- and zinc-enriched rice varieties (Table 3.3), and the Bangladesh Rice Research Institute (BRRI) developed and disseminated six hybrid rice varieties targeting *aman* and *boro* rice seasons (Table 3.3).

Table 3.3 Varietal release of rice by the Bangladesh Rice Research Institute (BRRI), 1971–2019

Year	*Number released*	*Name of the variety*	*Yield range (tons/ha)*	*Major characteristics*
Aus				
Up to 1990	10	BR1, BR2, BR6–9, BR12, BR15, BR20, BR21	3.0–5.0	Short-medium slender and bold grain Duration: 110–130 days
1991–2000	3	BR24, BR26, BRRI 27	3.5–4.0	Long, slender and white grain Duration: 105–115 days Protein content: 7%–8.9%
2005–2009	3	BRRI 42, BRRI 43, BRRI 48	3.5–5.5	Medium to slender grain and white color Duration: 98–110 days Long and medium grain Protein content: 7.6%–8.5%
2010–2018	5	BRRI 55, BRRI 65, BRRI 82, BRRI 83, BRRI 85	3.5–5.5	Medium to slender grain and white color Duration: 98–110 days Drought tolerant Protein content: 7.6%–8.3%
Aman				
Up to 1990	6	BR 4–5, BR 10–11, BR22, BR23,	5.0–5.5	Short-medium, bold and white grain Duration: 145–150 days
1991–2000	11	BR25, BRR30–34, BRRI 37–41	3.5–.5.0	Short and bold grain, aromatic and small grain Duration: 118–148 days
2005–2009	3	BRRI 44, BRRI 46, BRRI 49	4.5–6.5	Short-medium-long, bold and slender grain Duration: 125–150 days Less nitrogen required Protein content: 8.5% Submergence tolerant

(*Continued*)

Table 3.3 (Continued)

Year	*Number released*	*Name of the variety*	*Yield range (tons/ha)*	*Major characteristics*
2010–2018	24	BRRI 51–54, BRRI56–57, BRRI 62, BRRI 66, BRRI 70–73, BRRI 75–80, BRRI 87, BRRI 90, BRRI 91, BRRI 93, BRRI 94, BRRI 95	3.5–7.5	Short-medium-long, bold and slender grain Duration: 100–156 days Less nitrogen required Protein content: 7.0%–8.9% Zinc: 19–22.8 mg/kg Salinity tolerant, drought and submergence tolerant
	2	BRRI Hybrid 4, BRRI Hybrid 6	6.5	Long slender grain Duration: 110–118 days
Boro				
Up to 1990	14	BR1–3, BR6–9, BR 12, BR14–19	5.5–6.5	Short and bold grain /long and slender grain Duration: 140–170 days Protein content: 7.8%–8.1% Zinc: 19–22.8 mg/kg
1991–2000	4	BRRI 28–29, BRRI 35–36	5.0–7.5	Short-medium and bold grain Duration: 140–152 days Protein content: 7.2–8.1%
2005–2009	3	BRRI 45, BRRI 47, BRRI 50	6.0–6.5	Short-medium and bold grain, aromatic grain, long and slender grain Duration: 140–155 days Protein content: 8.3% Salinity tolerant
2010–2019	21	BRRI *dhan* 55, BRRI *dhan* 58–61, BRRI *dhan* 63–64, BRRI *dhan* 67–69, BRRI *dhan* 74, BRRI *dhan* 81, BRRI *dhan* 84, BRRI *dhan* 86, BRRI *dhan* 88, BRRI *dhan* 89, BRRI *dhan* 92, BRRI Hybrid *dhan* 1, Hybrid *dhan* 2, Hybrid *dhan* 3, BRRI Hybrid *dhan* 5	7.0–9.7	Short-medium and bold grain, aromatic grain, long and slender grain Duration: 144–160 days Protein content: 7.8%–10.1% Zinc content: 27.6 mg/kg Iron content: 10.1 mg/kg Salinity tolerant

Source: BRRI, 2019.

For all these combined efforts, rice production has increased dramatically. In 1990–1991, *aus* production was 2.3 MMT, *aman* production was 9.2 MMT and *boro* production was 6.4 MMT (BRRI, 2020). In 2018–2019, *aus* production increased to 2.9 MMT, *aman* production to 14.1 MMT and *boro* production to 20.4 MMT (BRRI, 2020). Consequently, the rice self-sufficiency ratio, calculated as the domestic production divided by the total rice supply (domestic production plus imports), reached more than 0.96 (Figure 3.6), meaning that domestic rice production met 96% of Bangladesh's total rice demand.

However, the expansion of *boro* rice has generated some severe sustainability issues. *Boro* rice is 100% irrigated, and for that, farmers in Bangladesh generally rely on underground water reserves. Because of overextraction in several places, the level of underground water has been declining (Mottaleb et al., 2019). *Boro* rice also relies intensively on chemical fertilizer and pesticides. The overuse of highly subsidized chemical fertilizer and pesticides has generated severe threats to the overall ecological system (Mottaleb et al., 2019a). As farmers are predominantly producing modern-variety rice, which is highly irrigated and chemical fertilizer and pesticide intensive, part of this value chain is harmful and non-sustainable.

In addition, Bangladesh has been exporting rice since 2014 (USDA, 2019), yet many farmers still do not reap the benefits of this value chain. Although most of the smallholders produce rice for self-consumption, the rice millers, using their brokers and networks, collect, mill and market paddy rice. As a result, rice millers mostly enjoy the market premium, and smallholders and marginal farmers are mostly deprived of such benefits. Moreover, wheat

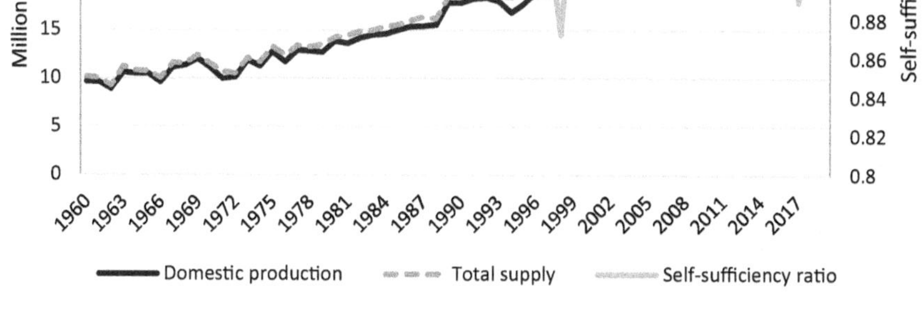

Figure 3.6 Domestic milled rice production, total supply and rice self-sufficiency ratio (domestic production/ total supply) during 1971–2019

Source: Authors, based on USDA, 2019.

production is more profitable than *boro* rice in some places, as wheat requires less water and fewer inputs like chemical fertilizer and insecticides (Mottaleb et al., 2019b, 2018c). *Boro* rice farmers incur a loss as the price at harvest time is lower than at the planting season. In addition, studies have found a mismatch between consumer demand and rice supply in Bangladesh (Mottaleb et al., 2017; Mottaleb and Mishra, 2016). It is found that with increases in income and rapid urbanization, educated households in Bangladesh prefer to consume more slender and long grain rice compared to bold grain rice (Figure 3.7).

(a): 1 kg packet of branded aromatic and small grain high-quality '*chini gura*' rice

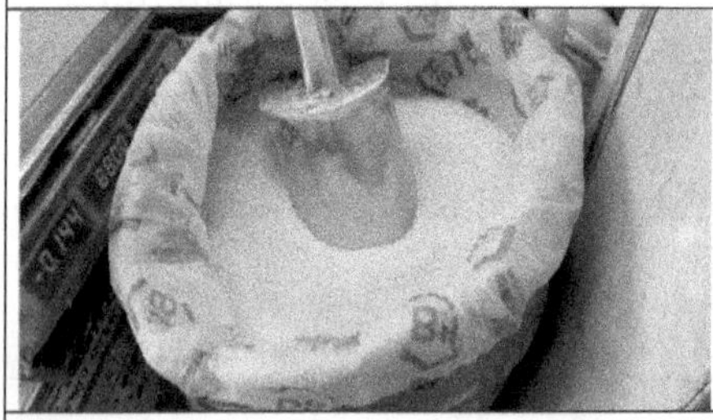

(b): Non-branded ordinary rice grain

(c): Long and slender grain rice

Figure 3.7 1 kg packet of branded aromatic and small grain high-quality *chini gura* rice (a); non-branded ordinary rice grain (b); and long and slender grain rice (c) for sale in Savar market, Dhaka, Bangladesh

Source: Authors.

Because of the shortage in supply, rice millers in Bangladesh polish short- and bold-grain rice, make it slender and long grain rice and supply it to the market under a popular rice variety named Minikit. However, there is no actual rice variety released in Bangladesh called Minikit. To meet demand, it is imperative to develop and disseminate not only high-yielding rice but also rice with better grain quality, such as long and slender grain rice. In addition, as Bangladesh has progressed toward becoming a middle-income nation, it is crucial to find innovative uses for rice and rice by-products. For example, due to its low cholesterol, rice bran oil is in high demand in urban markets, which currently meet that demand with imports. Breeders in Bangladesh should develop rice varieties targeted for rice bran oil. Such innovative use of rice can ensure higher returns for resource-poor rice farmers by linking them to multiple sectors in the rice value chain.

Conclusion and policy implications

Despite significant achievements in rice self-sufficiency, Bangladesh is still a major importer of wheat and maize. The wheat market of Bangladesh is worth US$1 billion. It is projected that due to rapid urbanization and increases in per capita GDP, with the respective changes they bring to the population's lifestyle, wheat consumption will increase further. Thus without significant action from the government, wheat imports will continue to grow (Mottaleb et al., 2018a). Similarly, despite a tremendous expansion in maize production, 30% of the total maize demand is met by imports. As the poultry and aquaculture sectors expand to meet the demand of the rising middle class, the demand for maize feed in Bangladesh also will continue to increase. Previously, almost all government efforts were targeted at the rice sector to achieve self-sufficiency. It is now time to focus on wheat and maize.

This chapter highlights the value chain patterns of three major crops in Bangladesh: wheat, maize and rice. The wheat value chain is highly segmented: the smallholder and *chakki* mill owners' value chain and the large wheat- and flour-importing companies' value chain. To ensure benefits to smallholder farmers, it is vital that smallholders generate a market surplus to connect to the growing wheat value chain. For this, enhancing wheat yield is imperative.

Compared to wheat, although maize farmers are strongly connected to maize value chains, there is still scope to provide greater benefits to farmers. First, the government can provide credit facilities to feed mill owners at the time of planting and harvesting, so farmers can get a good price for their products. Second, several wheat flour mills mix maize with wheat without proper labeling (Quasem, 1999). By printing accurate labels, it is possible to improve the maize value chain from feed to food, potentially increasing demand and ensuring a fairer price for maize farmers.

In Bangladesh, smallholder rice farmers produce rice mostly for self-consumption, but they apply modern inputs such as fertilizer and pesticides extensively. Thus, although they are strongly linked with the backward-linkage value chain, they are mostly disconnected from the forward-linkage progressive value chains. Moreover, large rice millers use their brokers and networks to collect paddy rice, thereby depriving small farmers of getting a fair price at harvest time. The government may vigorously implement the price support system by strengthening public procurement, particularly at harvest time. Also, a market mismatch exists between consumer demand and rice supply in Bangladesh in terms of grain quality (Mottaleb et al., 2017; Mottaleb and Mishra, 2016). To mitigate the market mismatch problem, it is imperative to develop and disseminate not only high-yielding rice but also rice with better grain quality, such as the long and slender grain rice that consumers highly prefer. This chapter highlights pathways for the development of Bangladesh's agriculture sector, which can generate valuable lessons for other emerging nations of sub-Saharan Africa and South Asia.

References

Ahmed, R., Haggblade, S., Chowdhury, T.-E. (Eds.), 2000. *Out of the Shadow of Famine: Evolving Food Markets and Food Policy in Bangladesh.* The Johns Hopkins University Press, Baltimore and London.

Ahmed, S.M., Meisner, C.A., 1996. *Wheat Research and Development in Bangladesh.* Bangladesh Australia Wheat Improvement Project and CIMMYT-Bangladesh, Dhaka.

Ali, M.Y., Waddington, S.R., Timsina, J., Hodson, D.P., Dixon, J., 2008. Maize-Rice Cropping Systems in Bangladesh: Status and Research Opportunities. *Agricultural Economics* 3, 35–53.

The Asian Age, 2018. BD Produces Over 16m MT Vegetables Annually. *News Desk* 1–9.

BARI, 2020a. Search Variety (Commodity) [WWW Document]. Bangladesh Agricultural Research Institute (BARI). URL http://baritechnology.org/en/home/tech_commodity#result (accessed 31.03.2020).

BARI, 2020b. Land Suitability Assesment and Crop Zoning of Bangladesh [WWW Document]. Ministry of Agriculture, Government of the People's Republic of Bangladesh. URL http://cropzoning.barcapps.gov.bd/ (accessed 2.17.2020).

Bangladesh Business Directory, 2018. Feed Mills in Bangladesh Full List [WWW Document]. Feed mills Incl. Poult. Feed. Sink. fish Feed. Float. fish Feed. shrimp Feed TMR Feed Co. Bangladesh. URL https://bangladeshbusinessdir.com/feed-mills-in-bangladesh-full-list/ (accessed 2.18.20).

BBS, 2018. *Yearbook of Agricultural Statistics-2017, 29th Series.* Bangladesh Bureau of Statistics (BBS), Statistics and Informatics Division (SID), Ministry of Planning, Dhaka.

Bober, C., Mittal, S., 2015. *SIAC Activity 2.1: Organize the Collection of Crop Germplasm Improvement Research Related Direct Outcomes in South, Southeast and East Asia-Maize.* Final Technical Report, Texcoco (Mexico).

BRAC, 2016. BRAC Seed and Agro Enterprise [WWW Document]. BRAC Nursery, Bangladesh Rural Adv. Comm. URL www.brac.net/brac-enterprises/item/899-brac-seed-and-agro-enterprise (accessed 2.19.20).

BRRI, 2020. Total Rice (Aus, Aman and Boro) Area (000' ha), Production (000' ton) and Yield (ton/ha) of Bangladesh [WWW Document]. Rice Database, Bangladesh Rice Res. Inst. (BRRI), Gazipur, Bangladesh. URL http://brri.portal.gov.bd/sites/default/files/files/brri.portal.gov.bd/page/b6531346_66a5_45e7_9cb0_d00c7c7009dc/2020-02-05-15-30-48171b6000b3d2981cf24a51216b6656.pdf (accessed 2.21.20).

Daily Sun, 2017. Bill Placed to Establish Wheat. Maize Research Institute 16–18.

Dewan, S.F.K., Salam, M.A., Mondal, A.A., 1998. *Prospects and Challenges o Expanding Maize Production in Bangladesh*. International Maize and Wheat Improvement Center (CIMMYT), Texcoco (Mexico).

Dorosh, P., 2000. Food Grain Production and Imports: Toward Self-Sufficiency in Rice? In: Ahmed, R., Haggblade, S., Chowdhury, T.-E. (Eds.), *Out of the Shadows of Famine: Evolving Food Markets and Food Policy in Bangladesh*. International Food Policy Research Institute (IFPR1), Washington, DC, pp. 1–17.

FAO, 2018. The State of World Fisheries and Aquaculture 2018: Meeting the Sustainable Devleopment Goals. *Journal of Applied Poultry Research*. Rome. https://doi.org/10.1093/japr/3.1.101.

FAO, 2019a. Data: Production [WWW Document]. Online Database Crop Prod. Harvest. Area. URL www.fao.org/faostat/en/#data/QC (accessed 4.26.19).

FAO, 2019b. Food Balance Sheets: Report [WWW Document]. Online Database Food Balanc. Sheets. URL www.fao.org/faostat/en/#data/FBS (accessed 8.19.19).

FAOSTAT, 2020. Commodity Balances—Livestock and Fish Primary Equivalent [WWW Document]. Online database Commod. Balanc. Food and Agriculture Organization. United Nations (FAO). URL www.fao.org/faostat/en/#data/BL (accessed 2.3.20).

Fischer, R.A., Derek, B., Edmeades, G.O., 2014. Crop Yields and Global Food Security: Will Yield Increase Continue to Feed the World? ACIAR Monograph No. 158, Australian Centre for International Agricultural Research, Canberra. Food Secur. 634. https://doi.org/10.1007/s12571-014-0392-y.

Government of Bangladesh, 2005. Bangladesh Economi Review 2005. Dhaka.

Government of Bangladesh, 2006. Bangladesh Economic Review 2005. Dhaka.

Government of Bangladesh, 2016. Bangladesh Economic Review 2016. Economic Adviser's Wing, Finance Division, Ministry of Finance, Government of Bangladesh, Dhaka.

Government of Bangladesh, 2019. Bangladesh Economic Review 2019. Dhaka.

Grebmer, K. von, Bernstein, J., Mukerji, R., Patterson, F., Wiemers, M., Chéilleachair, R.N., Foley, C., Gitter, S., Ekstrom, K., Fritschel, H., 2019. *2019 Global Hunger Index: The Challenge of Hunger and Climate Change*. Welthungerhilfe, Bonn and Dublin.

Hossain, M., 2009. *Shallow Tubewells, Boro Rice, and Their Impact on Food Security in Bangladesh (No. 00917)*. 2020 Vision Initiative, Washington, DC.

Hossain, M., Lewis, D., Bose, M.L., Chowdhury, A., 2007. Rice Research, Technological Progress, and the Impact on the Rural Economy: The Bangladesh Case. In: *Agricultural Research, Livelihoods and Poverty: Studies of Economic and Social Impacts in Six Countries*. International Food Policy Research Institute (IFPR1), and The Johns Hopkins University Press, Washington, DC and Baltimore, pp. 56–102.

Hossain, M., Quasem, M.A., Jabbar, M.A., Akash, M., 1994. Production Environment, Modern Variety Adoption, and Income Distribution in Bangladesh. In: David, C.C., Otsuka, K. (Eds.), *Modern Rice Technology and Income Distribution in Asia*. Lynne Rienner Publishers and International Rice Research Institute (IRRI), Philippines, Boulder, London and Manila, pp. 221–279.

Hussain, S.S., Leishman, D., 2013. *Wheat Milling in Bangladesh. United States Department of Agriculture*. Foreign Agricultural Service, Dhaka.

Lynamm, J., Chowdhury, M., Sattar, M., Habib, M.A., 2010. *Plant Breeding and Seed Systems for Rice, Vegetables, Maize and Pulses in Bangladesh*. A Report for the Global Partnership Initiative for Plant Breeding Capacity Building, Rome.

Mottaleb, K.A., Gumma, M.K., Mishra, A.K., Mohanty, S., 2015. Quantifying Production Losses Due to Drought and Submergence of Rainfed Rice at the Household Level Using

Remotely Sensed MODIS Data. *Agricultural Systems* 137. https://doi.org/10.1016/j.agsy.2014.08.014.

Mottaleb, K.A., Krupnik, T.J., Keil, A., Erenstein, O., 2019. Understanding Clients, Providers and the Institutional Dimensions of Irrigation Services in Developing Countries: A Study of Water Markets in Bangladesh. *Agricultural Water Management* 222, 242–253. https://doi.org/10.1016/j.agwat.2019.05.038.

Mottaleb, K.A., Mishra, A.K., 2016. Rice Consumption and Grain-Type Preferene by Household: A Bangladesh Case. *Journal of Agricultural and Applied Economics* 48, 298–319. https://doi.org/10.1017/aae.2016.18.

Mottaleb, K.A., Rahut, D.B., Erenstein, O., 2019a. Small Businesses, Potentially Large Impacts. *The Journal of Agribusiness in Developing and Emerging Economies* 9, 109–124. https://doi.org/10.1108/JADEE-08-2017-0078.

Mottaleb, K.A., Rahut, D.B., Kruseman, G., Erenstein, O., 2018a. Evolving Food Consumption Patterns of Rural and Urban Households in Developing Countries. *British Food Journal* 120, 392–408. https://doi.org/10.1108/BFJ-12-2016-0620.

Mottaleb, K.A., Rahut, D.B., Kruseman, G., Erenstein, O., 2018b. Changing Food Consumption of Households in Developing Countries: A Bangladesh Case. *Journal of International Food and Agribusiness Marketing* 30, 156–174. https://doi.org/10.1080/08974438.2017.1402727.

Mottaleb, K.A., Rahut, D.B., Kruseman, G., Erenstein, O., 2018c. Wheat Production and Consumption Dynamics in an Asian Rice Economy: The Bangladesh Case. *The European Journal of Development Research* 30, 252–275. https://doi.org/10.1057/s41287-017-0096-1.

Mottaleb, K.A., Rahut, D.B., Mishra, A.K., 2017. Modeling Rice Grain-Type Preferences in Bangladesh. *British Food Journal* 119, 2049–2061. https://doi.org/10.1108/BFJ-10-2016-0485.

Mottaleb, K.A., Singh, P.K., He, X., Hossain, A., Kruseman, G., Erenstein, O., 2019b. Alternative Use of Wheat Land to Implement a Potential Wheat Holiday as Wheat Blast Control: In Search of Feasible Crops in Bangladesh. *Land Use Policy* 82, 1–12. https://doi.org/10.1016/j.landusepol.2018.11.046.

Murata, Y., 2008. Engel's Law, Petty's Law, and Agglomeration ☆. *Journal of Development Economics* 87, 161–177. https://doi.org/10.1016/j.jdeveco.2007.06.001.

Quasem, M.A., 2011. Conversion of Agricultural Land to Non-agricultural Uses in Bangladesh: Extent and Determinants. *The Bangladesh Development Studies* 34, 59–85.

Quasem, M.A., 1999. Maize Production and Marketing in Bangladesh: An Indicative Exercise. FMRSP Working Paper No. 14. Dhaka.

Rahman, M.M., Mondal, M.R.I., Rahman, K., Barma, N.C., Selimuddin, M., 2009. *Agricultural Research Priority: Vision-2030 and Beyond*. Crops: Cereals Other Than Rice, Sugarcane and Jute, Dhaka.

USDA, 2019. USDA Foreign Agricultural Service [WWW Document]. United States Department of Agriculture (USDA), The Foreign Agricultural Service. URL https://apps.fas.usda.gov/psdonline/app/index.html#/app/advQuery (accessed 8.29.19).

Wiesmann, D.D., Weingärtner, D.L., Schöninger, D.I., 2006. *The Challenge of Hunger Global Hunger Index: Facts, Determinants, and Trends*. Deutsche Welthungerhilfe (DWHH), and International Food Policy Research Institute (IFPRI), Bonn and Washington, DC.

World Bank, 2020. World Development Indicators [WWW Document]. Data Bank, World Development Indicators. URL https://databank.worldbank.org/data/reports.aspx?source=world-development-indicators# (accessed 2.7.19).

4 Structural transformation and sources of growth in South Asian agriculture

Pratap S. Birthal and Ghanshyam Pandey

One of the stylized facts of the economic development process is the structural transformation of a low-income economy from subsistence-oriented, low-productivity agriculture into a higher-income and more diversified economy with an agricultural sector that is more productive and smaller in terms of its share of gross domestic product and the workforce. In this process, agriculture releases surplus labor and provides raw material to other economic sectors. Rapid growth in agriculture is thus a precursor to the process of structural transformation.

Of late, South Asia has experienced robust economic growth. Since the beginning of the 21st century, driven by the manufacturing and services sectors, the region's GDP grew at an annual rate of 5.8%, making it one of the fastest-growing regions in the world. However, the pace of structural transformation has not been as robust as in developed countries. South Asia's agricultural sector grew slowly, at an annual rate of about 3.2%, and its share of GDP declined, from around 21% in 2000 to around 14% in 2015. This outcome is notwithstanding the continued employment pressure—agriculture's share of the workforce during this period declined from 49% to 38%. Agriculture, therefore, remains important to the livelihood of a majority of the rural population and to the food security and poverty reduction.

Nevertheless, there are marked intercountry differences in the structural and agricultural transformations in South Asia because of differences in resource endowments, technological changes, supporting infrastructure, institutions and policies. The main aim of this chapter is to understand paths to agricultural transformation in the countries of South Asia in a broader context of economy-wide changes in domestic and international markets. The chapter tracks the trajectories of agricultural growth and factors underlying the growth trajectories. Toward this end, we decompose agricultural growth due to technological change, area expansion, diversification and price increases. This chapter also identifies crops or crop groups that could influence the pace of agricultural transformation.

An understanding of past sources of growth is important in prioritizing efforts and investments to cope with emerging challenges to the future growth of agriculture and agriculture-based livelihoods. Such an analysis will provide evidence-based feedback to policymakers, research managers, development organizations and financial institutions to design and implement technically feasible, economically viable and environmentally sound strategies for the faster, efficient, sustainable and inclusive growth of agriculture.

The next section of this chapter briefly discusses the data sources and analytical approach used to decompose agricultural growth. The third section discusses the nature, extent and speed of agricultural transformation in South Asian countries. The fourth section discusses the relative contributions of different sources of growth, and the fifth section discusses factors that explain differences in these sources' contributions within and across the countries of South Asia. We discuss conclusions and implications in the last section.

Data and empirical approach

Data sources

The data on sectoral gross domestic product (GDP) for each country in South Asia have been extracted from the FAOSTAT (www.fao.org/faostat) and the data on workforce engaged in different economic sectors from the Asian Productivity Organization (APO) (www.apo-tokyo.org/wedo/measurement).

The FAOSTAT is also a rich source of information on area allocations to different crops and their yields, prices and value of output. However, it lacks a time series on producer prices for all the crops and all the countries in South Asia. Nevertheless, it contains a time series on the value of output of most crops, which we use to derive the time series on their producer prices. The nominal data on all the economic variables have been converted into their real equivalents by deflating these by the GDP deflator (US$ at 2010 constant prices).

The time series on agricultural variables, especially prices, is often noisy or shows a random walk. An analysis based on a noisy data set may result in erroneous estimates and misleading conclusions. We therefore smoothen the time series of all the variables, including sectoral GDP, cropped area, production and value of output of crops, by applying the Hodrick—Prescott (HP) filter.

Decomposition of growth

Growth in agriculture may result from any or all of the following sources: an increase in the cultivated area or area expansion, yield improvements or technological change, an increase in producer prices and a reallocation of area from lower-value to higher-value crops or crop diversification. To know their relative shares in the overall growth of agriculture, we employ the 'growth accounting' approach as in Minot et al. (2006), Joshi, Birthal and Minot (2006) and Birthal et al. (2014). The change in revenue for a single crop between two points in time or over a period of time can be explained by a change in its area under cultivation, a change in its yield, a change in its real prices or all of these.

Let A_i be the area under crop i, Y_i its yield and P_i its real price. Then revenue R_i can be written as:

$$R_i = A_i Y_i P_i \tag{4.1}$$

If there are n crops, then summing the revenues of individual crops provides the total revenue:

$$R = \sum_{i=1}^{n} A_i Y_i P_i \tag{4.2}$$

Cropping systems are dynamic and are influenced by several demand- and supply-side factors. Given the scarcity of resources, a producer will choose a combination of crops that maximizes his or her utility. In other words, he or she will (re)allocate land from lower-value to higher-value or from higher-risk to lower-risk crops. Thus we have area reallocation or crop diversification as an additional source of change in total revenue or agricultural growth. To internalize this in the growth accounting approach, we write area under crop i as a proportion of total cropped area, i.e., $a_i = \left(\frac{A_i}{\sum_i A_i}\right)$, and substitute this in Equation (4.2):

$$R = \left(\sum_{i=1}^{n} a_i Y_i P_i\right) \sum_{i=1}^{n} A_i \tag{4.3}$$

Total derivative of both sides of Equation (4.3) provides the contribution of each component of change to the change in total revenue:

$$\partial R \cong \left(\sum_{i=1}^{n} a_i Y_i P_i\right) \partial\left(\sum_{i=1}^{n} A_i\right) + \left(\sum_{i=1}^{n} A_i\right) \partial\left(\sum_{i=1}^{n} a_i Y_i P_i\right) \tag{4.4}$$

The change in total revenue in Equation (4.4) is just an approximation, as it excludes the effect of interactions among different components of change in the total revenue.

We decompose the second term on the right-hand side of Equation (4.4) from a change in sums to the sum of changes and rewrite it as:

$$\partial R \cong \left(\sum_{i=1}^{n} a_i Y_i P_i\right) \partial\left(\sum_{i=1}^{n} A_i\right) + \sum_{i=1}^{n} \partial\left(a_i Y_i P_i\right) \tag{4.5}$$

Expanding the second term in Equation (4.5) and rearranging the terms provide us with the following expression:

$$\begin{aligned}\partial R \cong & \left(\sum_{i}^{n} a_i Y_i P_i\right) \partial \sum_{i=1}^{n} A_i + \sum_{i=1}^{n} A_i \sum_{i=1}^{n}\left(a_i P_i \partial Y_i\right) \\ & + \sum_{i=1}^{n} A_i \sum_{i=1}^{n}\left(a_i Y_i \partial P_i\right) + \sum_{i=1}^{n} A_i \sum_{i=1}^{n}\left(P_i Y_i \partial a_i\right)\end{aligned} \tag{4.6}$$

Equation (4.6) decomposes the change in total revenue due to a change in total cropped area, crop yields, real producer prices and crop diversification. The first term on the right-hand side of Equation (4.6) provides us with an estimate of the change in total revenue due to a change in the total cropped area or area expansion. The second term provides the effect of a change in real producer prices on the total revenue. The third term measures the effect of changes in crop yields or technological change. The fourth term quantifies the contribution of crop diversification. A positive value on the fourth term implies a reallocation of area from lower-value to higher-value crops, and a negative value implies the reverse. Dividing both sides of Equation (4.6) by the sum of changes in the total revenue from all crops provides us with each source's share in the overall growth of agriculture. The growth accounting method leaves a small, unexplained residual term due to the intractable interactions among different components of growth, which has no ready explanation, hence it is ignored in the discussion.

Agriculture and structural transformation

South Asia consists of eight countries: Afghanistan, Bangladesh, Bhutan, India, Maldives, Nepal, Pakistan and Sri Lanka. We restrict our analysis of structural and agricultural transformations to six countries, leaving out Afghanistan and Maldives because of the lack of consistent data series, especially on crop production variables. Elsewhere in the region, agriculture is an important economic sector in terms of its share of GDP and the workforce.

However, there are significant intercountry differences in economic structures, income levels, technological capabilities, infrastructures and institutions that define the path of structural transformation of different countries. We begin by looking into income levels. There are significant disparities in per capita incomes among South Asian countries. Sri Lanka had the highest per capita income in 2016, followed by Bhutan, India, Pakistan, Bangladesh and Nepal (Table 4.1). Over time, per capita incomes have risen everywhere in the region. Sri Lanka, Bhutan and India experienced rapid increases. Per capita income in Pakistan also improved, but not to the extent of other countries in the region. Notwithstanding, growth in per capita income has accelerated in all the South Asian countries. A significant acceleration in income growth in Sri Lanka, Bhutan and India is partly due to the base effect.

Table 4.1 Changes in per capita income (US$ at 2010 prices)

	Per capita income			*% annual growth*	
	1991	*2000*	*2016*	*1991–2000*	*2001–2016*
Nepal	367	455	729	2.4	3.4
Bangladesh	436	524	1062	2.5	4.6
Pakistan	758	826	1119	0.7	1.9
India	575	826	1874	4.3	5.4
Bhutan	790	1165	3036	4.4	6.3
Sri Lanka	513	870	3886	6.5	12.6

Source: Authors' estimate using data from APO.

Further, we see how the agricultural sector has performed in relation to the overall economy. Most countries in the region have experienced robust economic growth in the past two and one-half decades (Table 4.2). Except for Nepal, all countries in the region saw an acceleration in their economic growth. The annual rate of economic growth during 2001–2016 was more than 6% in Bangladesh, India, Bhutan and Sri Lanka. It remained muted at around 4% in Pakistan, and it decelerated in Nepal from 4.9% during 1991–2000 to 4.2% during 2001–2016.

By comparison, the performance of the agricultural sector has been modest. The sector grew slowly in Bhutan—1.9% during the 1990s and 1.7% during 2001–2016. In almost all other countries, the sector grew between 3% and 4% annually during the past two and one-half decades. Agricultural growth accelerated significantly in Sri Lanka and modestly in Bangladesh and India, remained almost muted in Nepal and Bhutan, and decelerated in Pakistan.

Although there are important differences in economic performance across countries in South Asia, agriculture's share of GDP declined throughout the region, except in Pakistan, where it has remained about one-fourth of GDP since 1991. Agriculture's share declined drastically in Bhutan, from 44.5% in 1991 to 14.8% in 2015, and in Bangladesh, from 23.5% to 14.8%. It also declined in India, Sri Lanka and Nepal but not as drastically. In 2015, the agricultural sector's share of GDP was 31.3% in Nepal, 14.2% in India and 7.7% in Sri Lanka.

Table 4.2 Annual growth in GDP and agricultural GDP (%)

	Overall GDP		*Agricultural GDP*	
	1991–2000	*2001–2016*	*1991–2000*	*2001–2016*
Nepal	4.9	4.2	3.1	3.1
Bangladesh	4.7	6.1	3.0	4.1
Pakistan	3.8	4.1	4.4	3.1
India	6.0	6.9	3.3	3.7
Bhutan	5.5	7.7	1.9	1.7
Sri Lanka	5.3	6.2	2.3	4.2

Source: Authors' estimates using data from FAOSTAT.

Table 4.3 Trends in share of agriculture in GDP and workforce

	% share in GDP			*% share in workforce*		
	1991	*2000*	*2015*	*1991*	*2000*	*2015*
Nepal	43.4	35.2	31.3	79.5	61.4	67.9
Bangladesh	23.5	20.5	14.8	47.8	46.5	37.3
Pakistan	25.9	27.2	21.7	47.5	48.4	42.4
India	32.5	24.8	14.2	64.0	56.4	48.0
Bhutan	44.5	31.4	14.8	77.4	69.0	53.6
Sri Lanka	13.7	10.6	7.7	44.6	37.2	24.3

Source: Authors' estimate: GDP data from FAOSTAT and workforce from APO.

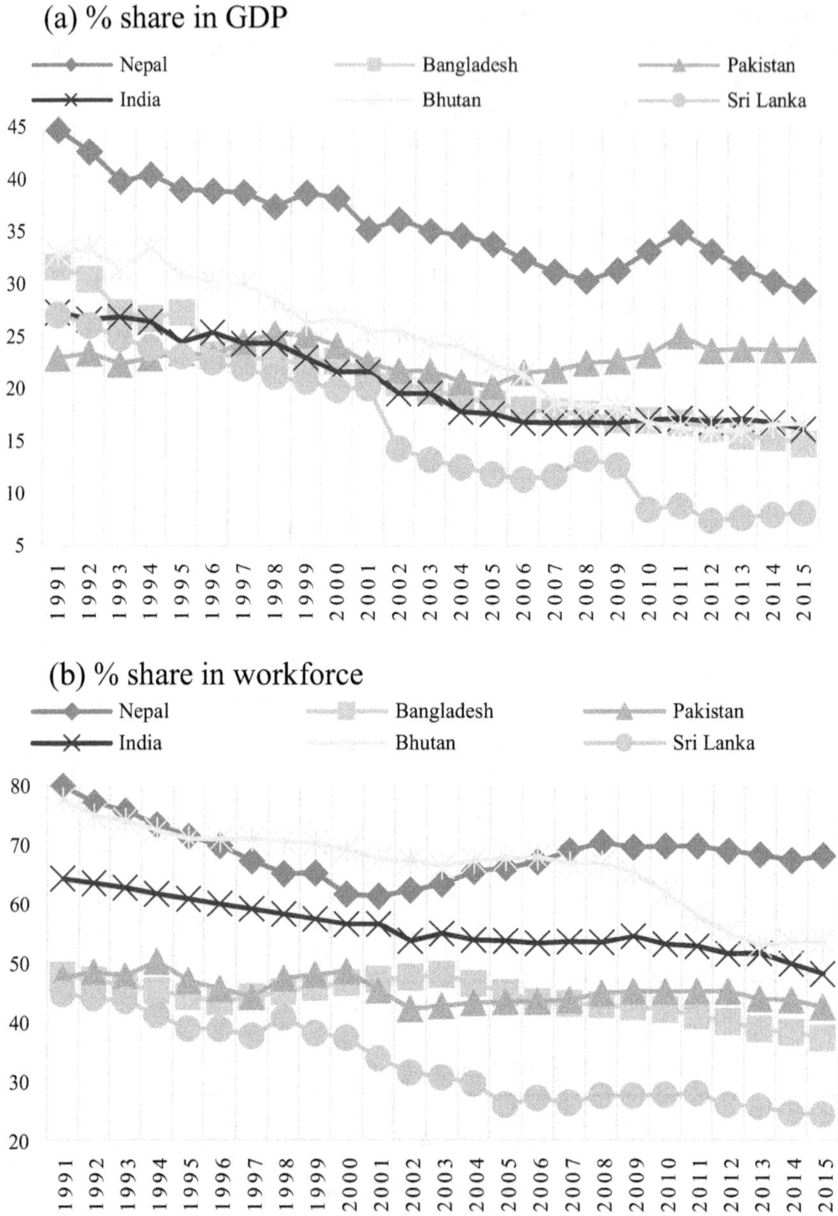

Figure 4.1 Trends in share of agriculture in GDP and workforce

Source: Authors' estimate: GDP data from FAOSTAT and workforce from APO.

The share of agriculture in the workforce has fallen, too, but not as drastically as its share of GDP (Table 4.3, Figure 4.1). Throughout the region, the pace of the transfer of labor from agriculture to non-agricultural sectors has been tardy, keeping the sector under excessive employment pressure. In 2015, agriculture still engaged as much as 68% of the total workforce in Nepal, 53% in Bhutan, 48% in India, 42% in Pakistan, 37% in Bangladesh and 24% in Sri Lanka.

These findings show that South Asian economies have undergone a structural transformation but at different paces. Nonetheless, this transformation has helped improve labor productivity in agriculture. Labor productivity, measured as agricultural GDP per worker in agriculture, has increased in all the countries (Table 4.4). Yet, at any point of time, it has been lower in Nepal and Bangladesh. Sri Lanka, on the other hand, has had the highest labor productivity.

Dynamics of labor productivity differ across South Asian countries. During the 1990s, growth in labor productivity was higher in Nepal and India than in the other countries. Subsequently, it accelerated in India to 3% but decelerated drastically in Nepal, falling to a low of 0.3% during 2001–2015 from 3.2% during the 1990s. During the latter period, growth in labor productivity in Pakistan turned negative but at margin. Labor productivity growth in Bhutan also decelerated, from 0.7% in the 1990s to 0.2% during 2001–2015. Bangladesh and Sri Lanka, on the other hand, experienced significant acceleration in labor productivity growth.

In Nepal, Bhutan and Pakistan, an extremely slow transfer of labor from agriculture is one of the main causes of slow growth in their labor productivity. Further, agriculture in South Asia is dominated by small landholdings, and these have been fragmenting unabatingly, which is also one of the main causes of slow growth in labor productivity in agriculture. To summarize, the pace of structural transformation varies across South Asian countries. It is advanced in Sri Lanka, remains muted in Pakistan and is slow in other countries. The cross-country differences in structural transformation could be due to several factors, including differences in resource endowments (land, labor and capital),

Table 4.4 Trend in labor productivity in agriculture (US$ at 2010 prices)

	AgGDP per worker			*Growth in AgGDP per worker (%)*	
	1991	*2000*	*2015*	*1991–2000*	*2001–2015*
Nepal	572	743	785	3.2	0.3
Bangladesh	519	577	877	0.9	3.3
Pakistan	1,511	1,740	1,878	1.9	−0.2
India	720	925	1,390	2.5	3.0
Bhutan	1,252	1,425	1,419	0.7	0.2
Sri Lanka	1,326	1,553	2,639	1.4	3.9

Source: Authors' estimate: GDP data from FAOSTAT and workforce from APO.

agroclimatic conditions, technological capabilities, extent of diversification and commercialization of agriculture, investments, infrastructures and institutions.

Sources of agricultural growth

Crops comprise the main segment of the agricultural sector in South Asia, in terms of both land use and economic contribution.[1] In this section, we analyze changes in agricultural production systems and factors responsible for these or, alternatively, the sources of growth in the crop subsector.

Changes in crop composition

Rice is the main staple food in most South Asian countries, except in Pakistan, and it dominates their cropping patterns (Figure 4.2). Rice occupies as much as 73% of the total cropped area in Bangladesh, 44% in Sri Lanka, 30% in Nepal, 22% in India and in Bhutan and 13% in Pakistan. Since the early 1990s, rice's share of cropped area has remained almost unchanged in Bangladesh and Bhutan, declined in Nepal and India and increased in Sri Lanka and Pakistan. Wheat, with a share of 43% in gross cropped area, is the most important crop in Pakistan. It is also important in Nepal (16%) and India (15%).

Together the oilseeds (soybean, groundnuts, coconuts, rapeseeds and mustard) occupy the largest share of gross cropped area after rice. Oilseeds are

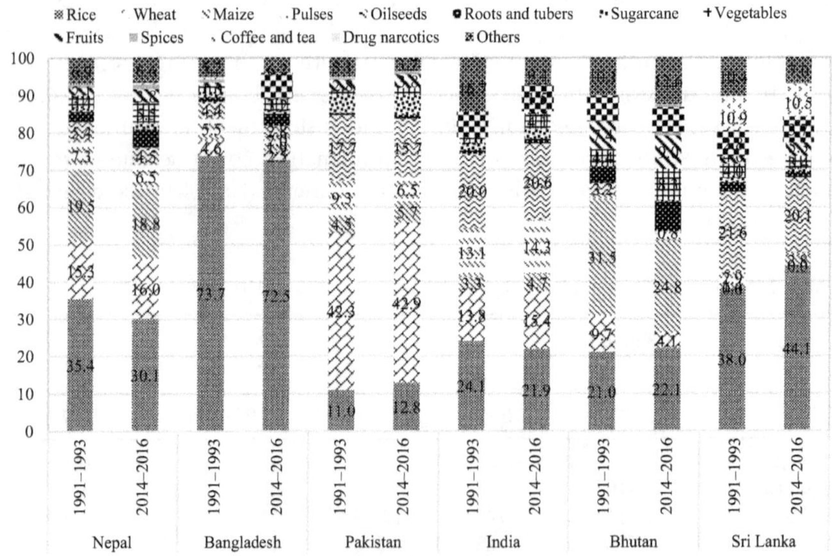

Figure 4.2 Share of crops in gross cropped area, 1991–1993 and 2014–2016 (%)

Source: Authors' estimates using data from FAOSTAT.

prominent in India, Sri Lanka and Pakistan, where they are cultivated on about one one-fifth of the cropland. Their area shares in Nepal, Bangladesh and Bhutan have rarely exceeded 5% of the total cropped area. Horticultural crops, including vegetables, roots and tubers, fruits and spices, have the highest share of gross cropped area (about one-fourth) in Bhutan, followed by Nepal (14%), Sri Lanka (10%), Bangladesh (9.4%) and India (8.9%). Over time, horticultural crops have gained in their area shares: roots and tubers in Nepal, Bangladesh, India and Bhutan; vegetables throughout the subcontinent, except in Sri Lanka; and fruits in all the countries. Spices are also important crops in Bhutan and Sri Lanka.

Plantation crops, including coffee, tea and rubber, are important in Sri Lanka, and together they occupy more than 16% of the country's total cropped area. Rubber, however, has lost its area share by 3 percentage points since 1991–1993. The value shares of crops closely correspond to their area shares. Except in India and Pakistan, rice's share of the total value of the crop sector's output is less than its area share (Figure 4.3). Horticultural and plantation crops, which generate higher returns per unit of land compared to the widely grown cereals or other such crops, have a relatively larger share in value than in area. Value shares of horticultural crops have improved throughout the subcontinent, except in Pakistan and Sri Lanka. Roots and tubers have gained considerably

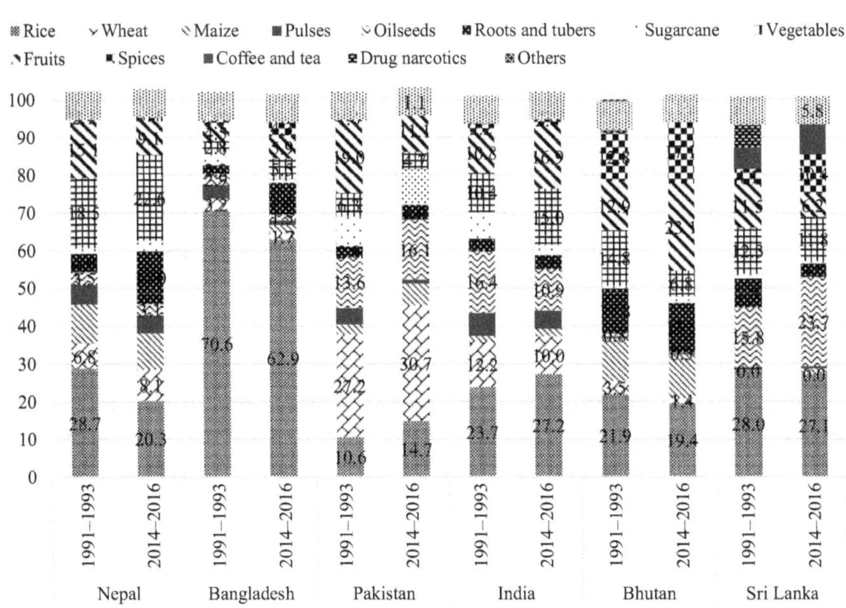

Figure 4.3 Share of crops in the total value of output, 1991–1993 and 2014–2016 (%)

Source: Authors' estimates using data from FAOSTAT.

in Nepal and Bangladesh; coffee in Sri Lanka; and spices in Bhutan. However, fruits have lost their value shares in Nepal, Pakistan and Sri Lanka.

These findings show that cropping systems in South Asian countries are dynamic and respond to emerging changes in domestic and global markets, changing food preferences, infrastructures, institutions and policies. In the following subsection, we look at the sources of change in production systems in South Asian countries.

Decomposition of growth

Table 4.5 shows the contributions of area expansion, yield improvements, diversification and price increases to the growth of the crop subsector. Yield increases have been the main source of agriculture growth in the subcontinent but with significant cross-country differences. Agriculture growth in Bangladesh, Sri Lanka and Bhutan has been fueled by technological change. Area expansion has been the second-largest contributor to growth in Bangladesh and Sri Lanka. The price effect on output growth is also quite large in Bhutan, as high as that of technological change. On the other hand, the price effect is substantially negative in Bangladesh and positive but small in Sri Lanka. Growth sources in India, Pakistan and Nepal are diverse. In these countries, technological change has been the main source of growth. In Nepal, diversification comprises the second-largest source of growth, closely followed by area expansion. The growth effects of diversification and prices are almost similar (23%) in India. In Pakistan, area expansion, diversification and prices have almost similar shares of growth (18% to 19%).

These sources of growth are expected to vary over time depending on changes in infrastructure, markets, institutions, policies etc. To know how growth sources have evolved, in Figures 4.4 (a–f) we plot year-on-year changes in each source's contribution to growth. There is a discernible trend in the annual changes in the value of output of crops in Nepal; it kept declining but at margin until 1997, then increased significantly, reached a peak in 2010 and declined afterward. Technological change has remained the most important

Table 4.5 Contribution of different sources to output growth during 1991–2016 (%)

Countries	*Area expansion*	*Yield improvements*	*Price increases*	*Diversification*	*Interaction*	*Total*
Nepal	23.4	54.6	−5.7	27.2	0.5	100
Bangladesh	24.1	83.1	−22.5	15.4	−0.1	100
Pakistan	18.4	42.9	19.7	18.8	0.3	100
India	16.9	35.1	23.6	23.2	1.2	100
Bhutan	−39.3	60.2	61.4	18.6	−0.8	100
Sri Lanka	22.9	79.8	5.7	−9.1	0.8	100

Source: Authors' estimates using data from FAOSTAT.

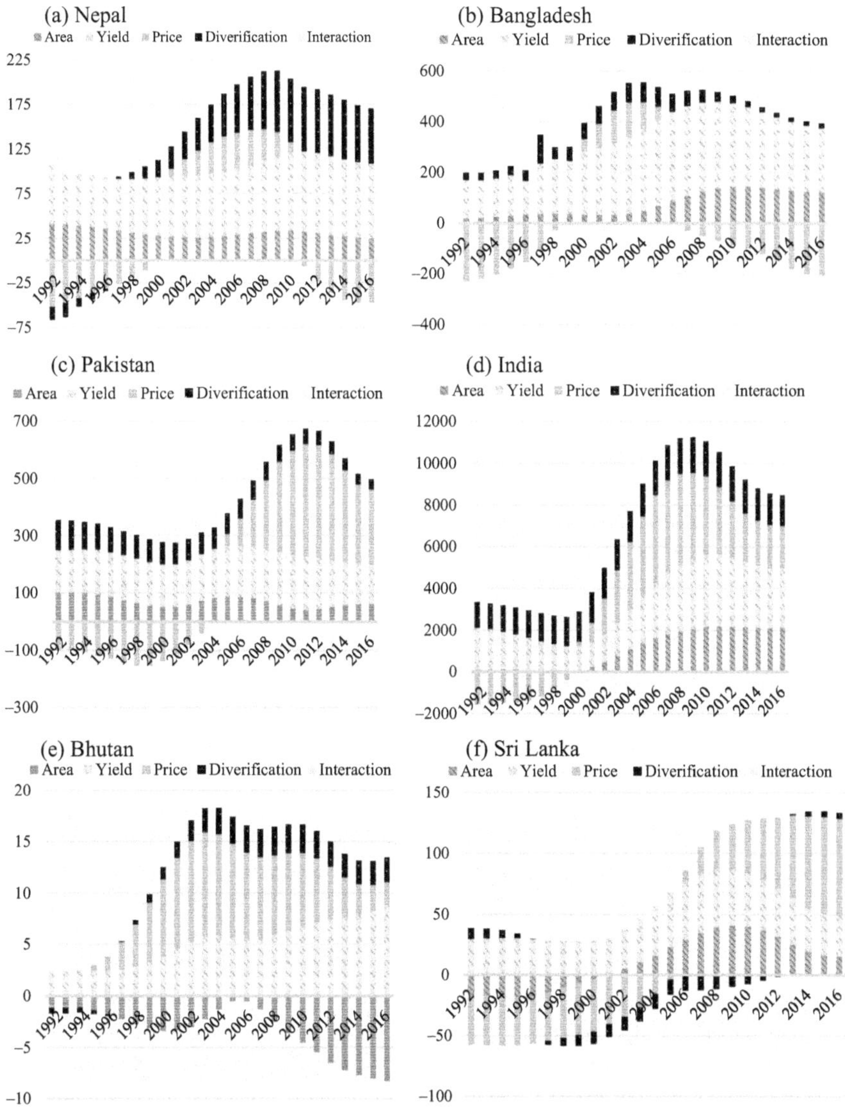

Figure 4.4 Year-on-year changes in sources of growth (US$ million)

Source: Authors' estimates using data from FAOSTAT.

and consistent source of growth throughout. Likewise, the contribution of area expansion has been consistent. Diversification emerged as a source of growth from 2004 onward and turned out to be the second-largest source after technological change in the recent period. Prices rarely have been an important source of growth in the country.

Spurred by technological change, agriculture in Bangladesh has grown consistently over the past two and one-half decades. Area expansion has been the second-largest source of growth throughout. However, diversification never has been an important source of growth, primarily because of a greater policy emphasis on achieving self-sufficiency in rice, the country's main staple food. The price effect has remained negative most of the time. Growth in India and Pakistan is almost similar: a marginal decline in the value of output until 2001 and a rapid increase thereafter, reaching a peak around 2010. Afterward, agriculture growth started showing signs of fatigue. Technological change and diversification have remained sustainable sources of agricultural growth in both countries. The price effect, which was negative until the early 2000s, started becoming stronger afterward but weakened in recent years. The contribution of area expansion has remained positive in Pakistan throughout the past two decades, but in India it started emerging as a source of growth after 2001.

Growth in Bhutanese agriculture accelerated during the 1990s but started decelerating afterward. Over time, technological change consolidated its share of growth and emerged as the largest component of growth in recent years. Diversification has emerged as a sustainable source of growth since 2000. Beginning in 1995, the contribution of prices increased until 2005 but slowed down afterward. Area's effect on growth has remained negative throughout the past two and one-half decades but turned out stronger in the recent period. As elsewhere in South Asia, technological change has been a sustainable source of growth in Sri Lankan agriculture. Behavior of other sources, however, is erratic. For instance, price effect, which was negative until 2005, emerged as the largest source of growth in recent years. Diversification never has been an important source of growth in the country.

These findings lead us to conclude that technological change has been the main and sustainable source of agricultural growth in South Asia but with significant intercountry differences. Diversification also has contributed to agricultural growth in some countries, but the contributions of area expansion and prices have been erratic in most countries. There are significant differences in technological progress across crops and countries. Therefore, we examine the contribution of crops or crop groups to the overall growth in agriculture, and results are presented in Table 4.6. Agriculture growth in Bangladesh and Pakistan has been largely cereal-centric. In Bangladesh, rice, due to its dominant position in the cropping pattern, accounts for about half of the growth. Horticulture (roots, tubers, vegetables, fruits and spices) accounts for approximately 40% of agriculture's growth in Bangladesh. Likewise, about two-third of the growth in Pakistan's agriculture has come from cereals—wheat (34%), rice (20%) and maize (10%). Horticulture's contribution, on the other hand, is miniscule.

In India, horticultural crops, mainly fruits and vegetables, have contributed more than 48% to the growth in agriculture. Rice, with a 30% share,

Table 4.6 Share of crops in overall growth of crop sector (%)

Crops	*Nepal*	*Bangladesh*	*Pakistan*	*India*	*Bhutan*	*Sri Lanka*
Rice	13.0	52.5	19.8	29.6	17.4	23.7
Wheat	9.4	0.6	34.1	8.3	0.8	
Maize	9.6	5.5	9.9	2.5	13.6	5.4
Pulses	4.2	−1.3	−3.4	3.8	0.2	-0.5
Oilseeds	2.8	0.0	19.9	5.8	0.0	46.7
Roots and tubers	22.0	15.4	5.6	3.9	13.5	−8.2
Sugarcane	4.0	−2.0	11.9	-0.7	2.4	−1.3
Vegetables	25.7	8.6	2.7	19.2	2.8	10.8
Fruits	3.4	7.2	0.7	22.6	26.2	−7.5
Spices	4.7	7.5	0.8	2.9	20.0	28.8
Coffee and tea	0.3	−0.2	0.0	0.5	0.0	14.0
Drug and narcotics	−0.3	0.5	−0.1	0.3	0.5	−15.3
Others	1.14	5.71	−1.70	1.37	2.60	3.4
Total	100	100	100	100	100	100

Source: Authors' estimates using data from FAOSTAT.

is the second-largest contributor, and the rest comes from wheat, pulses and oilseeds. In the similar way, more than 55% of the growth in Nepalese agriculture has come from horticulture, including vegetables (26%) and roots and tubers (22%). Cereals, including rice, wheat and maize, account for more than one-third of the growth. In Bhutan, too, horticulture, mainly fruits, spices, roots and tubers, have contributed more than 60% to agriculture's growth. Rice and maize share 17% and 14%, respectively, of the growth. In contrast, nearly half the growth in Sri Lankan agriculture has come from oilseeds (47%), followed by horticultural crops, mainly spices (29%) and vegetables (11%), and plantation crops (14%). Rice contributes about one-fourth to the growth.

Factors influencing sources of growth

Intercountry variation in growth sources can be explained by several economic, institutional and policy factors that influence demand and supply of food and non-food commodities, directly or indirectly. Laborde et al. (2018) and Vos (2018) explain variations in agricultural transformation across developing-country regions and over different periods of time through the differences in price incentives, public spending and priorities for investment in research and development, infrastructure, education and institutional reforms. In this section, we try to correlate some of these factors with the sources of agriculture's growth in South Asian countries.

Input use and crop yields

Seed, water and fertilizer are important factors in productivity growth. South Asia has one of the highest rates of irrigated agriculture—estimated at around 40% of the total cultivated area. The share of irrigated area has been rising, facilitating the use of chemical fertilizers (Figure 4.5). Fertilizer consumption per hectare of cropland is the highest in Pakistan, followed by Sri Lanka, Bangladesh and India, and the lowest in Bhutan, followed by Nepal. Nonetheless, the intensity of fertilizer use has been increasing in all countries in the region. Moreover, capital intensity has increased significantly in some of the countries (e.g., India), which is reflected in the increased use of mechanization and decreased use of labor. Dawe (2015) finds the uptake of machine use in agriculture (for soil preparation, sowing and harvesting) among small and larger farms alike.

Among other things, the rising rates of fertilizer use and mechanization of cropping activities have led to significant improvements in crop yields (Figure 4.6 a–d). During 1991–2016, rice yield grew at an annual rate of 4.9% in Bhutan, 2.7% in Bangladesh, 1.8% in Pakistan, 1.6% in Nepal, 1.4% in India and about 1% in Sri Lanka (Figure 4.6 (a–d), and Table A4.1 in the appendix). Maize yield has risen very significantly in Bangladesh (11%), Sri Lanka (6.2%) and Pakistan (5.7%). Trends in yields of pulses and oilseeds (i.e., mustard and rapeseed) are not encouraging in most countries in the region.

Total factor productivity

Several studies (e.g., Fuglie 2015; Vos, 2018) have shown that growth in total factor productivity (TFP) has become the main driver of agricultural growth in

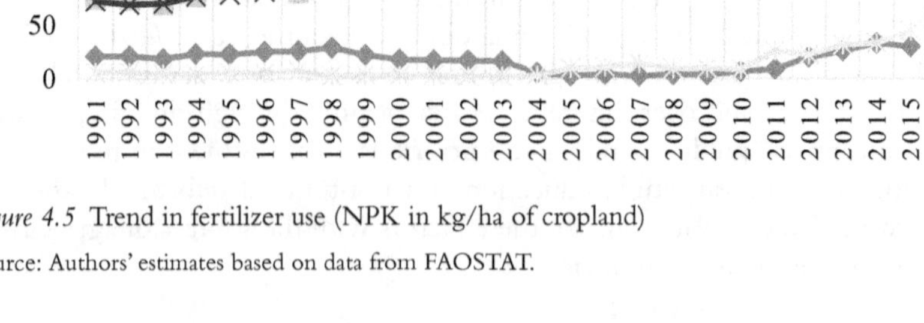

Figure 4.5 Trend in fertilizer use (NPK in kg/ha of cropland)

Source: Authors' estimates based on data from FAOSTAT.

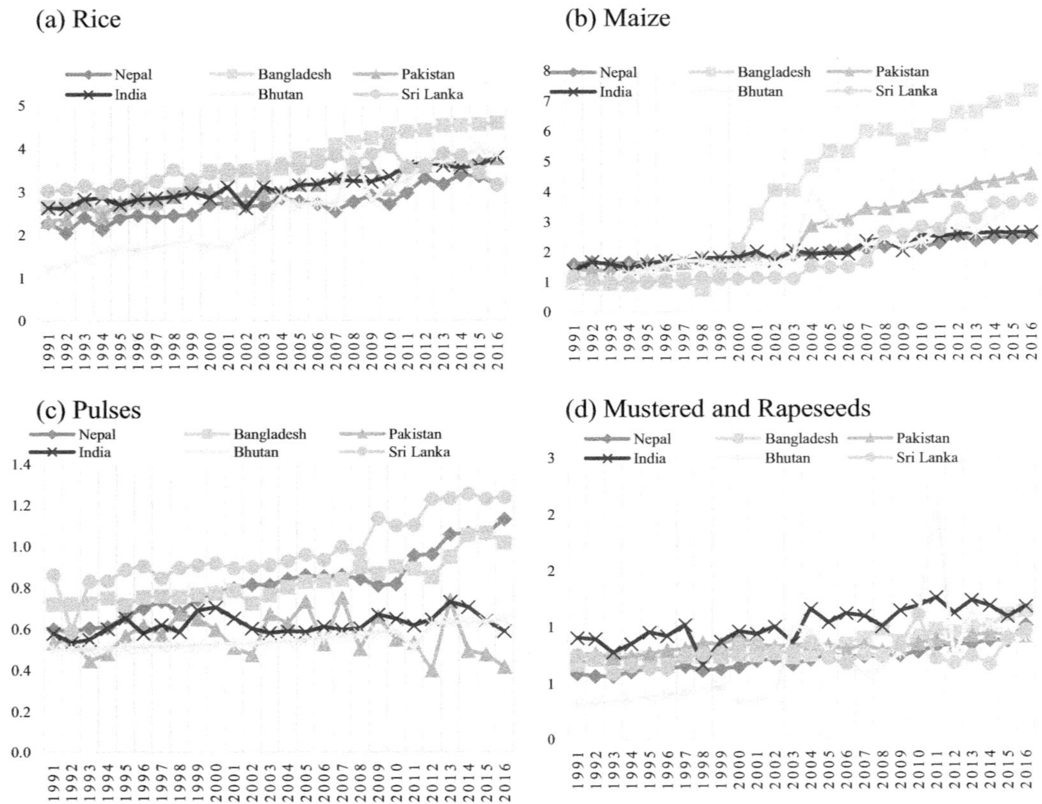

Figure 4.6 Trend in yields of important crops (tons/ha)

Source: Authors' estimates using data from FAOSTAT.

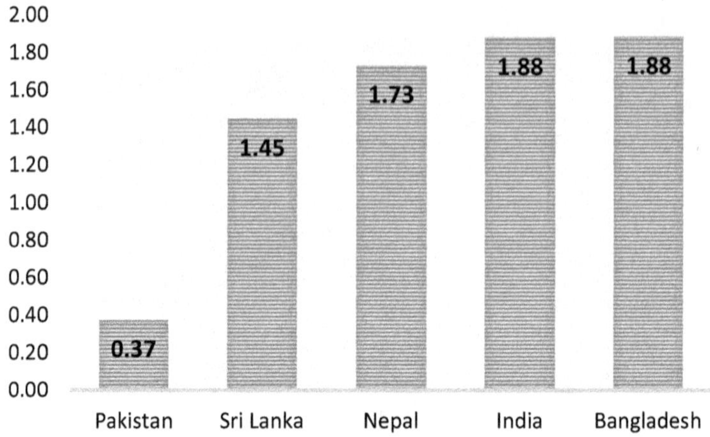

Figure 4.7 TFP growth in South Asian agriculture (% per annum)

Source: Authors' estimates using data from USDA.

much of Asia in recent years. Figure 4.7 shows growth in TFP in agriculture. During 1991–2016, TFP grew at an annual rate of close to 1.9% in India and Bangladesh, 1.7% in Nepal and 1.5% in Sri Lanka (Figure 4.7). On the other hand, performance of TFP has been dismal in Pakistan, where it grew at a rate of less than 0.4% a year.

Increase in cultivated area and cropping intensity

Area expansion surfaced as one of the important sources of agricultural growth in some of the South Asian countries. The additional area brought under cultivation could be due to an increase in cropping intensity, utilization of previously waste and fallow lands, diversion of land from non-agricultural activities, e.g., forests, or all of the these. A quantitative assessment of their exact shares of area expansion under crops is out of this chapter's scope. Nonetheless, a comparison of the changes in land use can help us understand the causes of area expansion (Table 4.7).

Gross cropped area shows a significant positive trend in all the South Asian countries except Bhutan. During 1991–2016, the area expanded at an annual rate of less than 1% in all the countries but contracted in Bhutan at an annual rate of 1.8%. Part of the additional area brought under cultivation in the rest of the countries probably has come from clearing forests, as indicated by negative growth rates in forest land. The spread of cultivation on marginal lands and the intensification of existing cropland also have contributed to area expansion. This is indicated by a slower rate of growth in arable land than in the gross cropped

Table 4.7 Percentage annual growth in the land use, 1991–2016

	Gross cropped area	*Cropland*	*Arable land*	*Forest land*
Nepal	0.81	−0.14	−0.51	−1.18
Bangladesh	0.61	−0.27	−0.65	−0.19
Pakistan	0.48	0.05	0.00	−2.37
India	0.54	−0.02	−0.20	0.50
Bhutan	−1.75	−1.76	−1.64	0.41
Sri Lanka	0.58	1.01	2.04	−0.45

Source: Authors' estimates based on data from FAOSTAT.

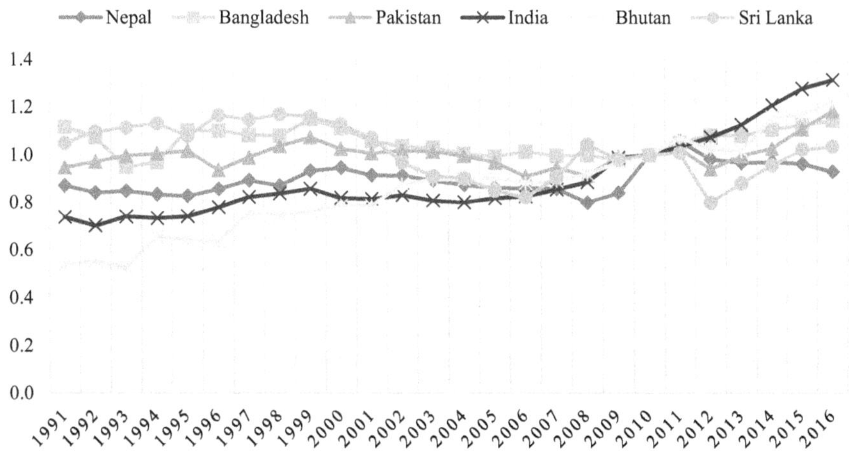

Figure 4.8 Trend in terms of trade

Source: Authors' estimates based on data from FAOSTAT.

area in most countries. A stronger positive trend in the gross cropped area than in the arable land or cropland indicates a rise in cropping intensity, i.e., multiple cropping on the same piece of land, facilitated by increasing availability of water for irrigation.

Terms of trade

The temporal variation in price's effect on agriculture growth across countries could be due to several factors, including the degree of protection accorded to agriculture through price policy. Figure 4.8 shows terms of trade, measured as a ratio of the agricultural GDP deflator to the manufacturing GDP deflator. There is a huge variation in terms of trade across countries and over time. Until 2009, terms of trade were not favorable to agriculture (except in Bangladesh, Sri Lanka and Pakistan), but these have been improving continuously. Bangladesh is a net importer of rice, and to achieve self-sufficiency in rice it has insulated its domestic market from global price hikes. Lately, terms of trade have improved considerably in India and Bhutan. India fixes minimum support prices for 24 commodities and assures their procurement if prices in the open market fall below predetermined prices. This policy, however, is effective for rice and wheat that are procured in large quantities for safety-net programs and buffer stocking.

Changes in consumer preferences

Sustained increases in per capita incomes and fast-growing urban populations have led to expanding food markets and changes in food baskets. With higher incomes, the share of food in total expenditure falls, but in absolute terms, food expenditure continues to rise as households substitute dietary energy and protein from cheaper cereals with that from more expensive fruits, vegetables and animal-source foods. South Asia's food baskets have been shifting in favor of high-value food commodities (Table 4.8). The changes in consumer preferences are not similar across the countries. Consumption of fruits and vegetables is higher in Nepal and India than in other countries in the region, and it has increased considerably since 1990. Fruit and vegetable consumption is low in Pakistan and Sri Lanka and has not changed much. Their consumption is also low in Bangladesh but has increased rapidly. Consumption of starchy roots has increased in all the countries. In Pakistan, consumption of meat and milk is very high compared to the other countries, and thus animal-based nutrients substitute for plant-based nutrients. On the other hand, cereal consumption

Table 4.8 Food consumption (kg/capita/annum)

	Nepal		*Bangladesh*		*Pakistan*		*India*		*Sri Lanka*	
	1990	*2013*	*1990*	*2013*	*1990*	*2013*	*1990*	*2013*	*1990*	*2013*
Cereals	180.8	193.2	181.1	190.1	151.5	141.9	151.3	148.5	140.8	152.3
Starchy Roots	35.5	85.4	12.4	48.0	8.7	18.1	19.1	30.8	22.1	19.9
Sugar	23.8	39.8	3.5	1.9	25.7	18.5	10.4	9.5	17.0	30.1
Pulses	8.1	12.7	6.1	6.6	8.0	6.6	13.1	14.4	4.9	9.3
Edible oils	0.1	0.9	0.3	0.7	0.6	1.8	6.4	7.8	66.7	72.4
Vegetables	50.0	114.1	12.2	27.3	27.4	26.3	52.1	88.7	31.3	46.2
Fruits	23.2	61.2	11.5	23.3	33.3	29.4	27.7	56.4	37.2	36.2
Meat	10.3	12.2	3.0	4.1	11.9	16.4	4.1	3.7	3.2	6.5
Eggs	1.0	1.4	0.6	2.1	1.7	3.0	1.1	2.6	2.5	4.6
Milk	40.5	52.1	13.9	21.9	113.0	183.1	52.6	84.5	28.2	35.0
Fish	0.8	2.2	7.6	19.2	2.1	1.9	3.8	5.0	15.2	25.7
Percentage of urban population	8.9	17.8	19.8	32.7	30.5	35.6	25.5	32.0	18.5	18.1

Source: Authors' estimates based on data from FAOSTAT.

has increased in Nepal, Bangladesh and Sri Lanka, while it has decreased in India and Pakistan.

Demand is driving these changes in food baskets. Rapid increases in per capita incomes and advancements in urbanization have been the main factors changing food baskets in favor of high-value food commodities. Urbanization is relatively higher in India, Bangladesh and Pakistan than in the other countries. In Nepal, although the rate of urbanization is low, the urban population's share of the total population has grown rapidly, from 9% in 1990 to 17.8% in 2013. The share of urban population in Sri Lanka has remained stable, around 18% during this period. In general, factors underlying changes in consumer preferences have been robust recently and are unlikely to subside in the near future, implying further changes in consumption and demand, which in turn will trigger changes in food production systems.

Conclusions and implications

South Asian economies have been undergoing transformation but at different paces. In general, the pace of structural transformation has remained low, except in Sri Lanka. Agriculture's share of GDP declined in most countries, but it was not accompanied by a commensurate decline in its share of workforce. As a result, labor productivity in agriculture in most South Asian countries remains low. Enhancing agricultural growth thus remains important to the livelihood of millions of smallholders who are a force to reckon with in this region. The subcontinent's agricultural sector also has undergone transformation. In the past two and one-half decades, driven by technological change and demand-driven diversification, the agricultural sector experienced fairly robust growth throughout South Asia. Other sources of growth, i.e., area expansion and prices, however, are erratic across countries and over time. These findings have some important implications for the future growth of South Asian agriculture.

Given the fixed supply of land and increasing demand for non-agricultural uses, the prospects for bringing additional land under cultivation are extremely limited. In addition, farm sizes are small and have been declining throughout South Asia. About 60% of farms are less than or equal to 2 ha (Vos, 2018). Therefore, the recourse has to be with exploiting land at its intensive margin through raising the cropping intensity. This, however, will put additional pressure on natural resources, leading to deterioration in their quantity and quality. There is sufficient evidence regarding the degradation of land and water resources due to the intensification of agriculture in the post–Green Revolution period. In several of the countries, the best potential of agricultural technologies has been exploited to a large extent. Yield growth of important crops like rice and wheat has decelerated (Birthal, 2019), indicating diminishing returns to additional input use. To compensate farmers for income lost due to a slowdown in yield growth, governments have resorted to providing higher producer prices. The price-driven growth, however, is unlikely to be sustained in the long run. Poor consumers will suffer more from price-driven growth, and within the farm sector, only those who have larger marketable surplus will benefit from higher prices.

To enhance agricultural growth and farmers' livelihoods, recourse has to be with technological change and crop diversification in favor of high-value crops that have been the sustainable sources of growth in the past. Lately, though, the growth effects of technological change have started diminishing, which is a matter of concern. This could be due to several factors, including a lack of investment in agricultural research, inefficiency of agricultural research, poor linkages between research and extension systems and a lack of supporting infrastructure essential to harnessing potential gains from investment in research. In much of South Asia, investment in agricultural research is miniscule. For example, the expenditure on agricultural research in India is hardly 0.6% of the agricultural gross domestic product, much less than the more than 2% in developed countries (Stads, 2016).

Increased investment in agricultural research is essential to increase yields and to reduce the cost of production for the efficient and sustainable growth of agriculture. Another implication is that the agricultural research agenda needs to be revisited and prioritized given the emerging challenges of climate change, rising prices of agricultural commodities and energy inputs, increasing cost of production, labor shortages, degradation of natural resources and, above all, changing demand patterns. For food security reasons, the focus of agricultural research will remain on breeding for higher yields, but research on management of biotic and abiotic stresses need not be undermined. Research on horticultural crops merits special attention, as these have realized fewer yield gains. Finally, to benefit from the investment in research, the countries need to develop information systems and to invest in infrastructure, such as irrigation and electricity.

Diversification toward high-value crops not only enhances agricultural growth and reduces production risk but creates opportunities for smallholders to enhance their incomes, escape poverty and participate in global value chains. Domestic and global demand for high-value food commodities has been increasing due to sustained income growth, urbanization and the globalization of agri-food markets. Harnessing potentials of diversification would require increased investment in public infrastructure (roads, electricity and communication) to reduce transportation and transaction costs and attract private investment in agro-processing, cold storages, refrigerated transportation and retail chains; greater access to technology for farmers, credit, inputs, information and extension services; and appropriate policies that facilitate institutional arrangements, like contract farming, producers' organizations and cooperatives that provide farmers with easy access to markets, reduce marketing and transaction costs and mitigate market price risks.

Note

1 In monetary terms, crops comprise the largest subsector of agriculture in South Asia. Their value of output is at least three times that of the value of livestock production.

References

Birthal, P.S. (2019). "From food security to farmers' prosperity: Challenges, prospects and way forward," *Indian Journal of Agricultural Economics* 74(1): 78–95.

Birthal, P.S., P.K. Joshi, D.S. Negi, and S. Agarwal. (2014). "Changing sources of growth in Indian agriculture: Implications for regional priorities for accelerating agricultural growth," IFPRI Discussion Paper No. 1325. Wasington, DC: International Food Policy Research Institute.

Dawe, D. (2015). "Agricultural transformation of middle-income Asian economies: Diversification, farm size and mechanization," ESA Working Paper 15–04. Rome: Food and Agriculture Organization of the United Nations.

Fuglie, K.O. (2015). "Accounting for growth in global agriculture," *Bio-Based and Applied Economics* 4(3): 221–254.

Joshi, P.K., P.S. Birthal, and N. Minot. (2006). "Sources of agricultural growth in India: Role of diversification toward high-value crops," MTID Discussion Paper No. 85. Washington, DC: International Food Policy Research Institute.

Laborde, D., T. Lallemant, K. McDougall, C. Smaller, and F. Traoré. (2018). *Transforming Agriculture in Africa and Asia. The Role of Policies and Public Investment*. Washington, DC and Geneva: IFPRI and IISD.

Minot, N., M. Epprecht, T.T. Tram Anh, and L.Q. Trung. (2006). "Income diversification and poverty in Northern Uplands of Vietnam," Research Report 145. Washington, DC: International Food Policy Research Institute.

Stads, Gert-Jan. (2016). "A snapshot of agricultural research investment and capacity in Asia," Available at: www.asti.cgiar.org/sites/default/files/pdf/APAARI-HLPD-Synthesis.pdf.

Vos, R. (2018). "Agricultural and rural transformations in Asian development: Past trends and future challenges: Past trends and future challenges," WIDER Working Paper 2018/87. United Nations University World Institute for Development Economics Research.

Appendix

Table 4A.1 Annual growth in yield of major crops, 1990–2016 (%)

Crops	*Nepal*	*Bangladesh*	*Pakistan*	*India*	*Bhutan*	*Sri Lanka*
Rice	1.61	2.68	1.75	1.40	4.92	0.84
Wheat	2.65	1.91	1.71	1.07	2.76	—
Maize	2.01	10.94	5.76	2.51	4.62	6.73
Millets	0.18	−1.30	1.96	2.42	4.36	2.52
Other coarse cereals	0.88	4.73	−0.18	0.82	2.26	2.56
Total cereals	1.76	2.80	2.14	1.69	4.79	0.97
Total pulses	2.41	1.51	−0.18	0.47	1.02	2.07
Soybean	2.90	—	−1.65	0.55	0.57	2.75
Groundnuts	—	2.43	−0.88	1.76	—	6.33
Coconuts	—	−1.93	1.86	0.22	—	1.72
Rapeseeds	1.90	1.91	0.70	1.59	6.29	0.94
Others Oilseeds	0.76	3.52	0.93	4.17	—	2.64
Total oilseeds	2.04	1.88	0.98	1.92	5.71	1.62
Nuts	0.96	−0.93	−2.26	1.13	0.26	0.17
Fibers	0.82	1.05	0.55	1.68	0.12	—
Roots and tubers	2.53	3.08	2.14	1.44	1.51	1.87
Sugarcane	1.45	−0.06	1.19	0.16	0.07	0.26
Vegetables	2.44	1.82	−0.26	1.29	2.09	2.45
Banana	−0.39	0.11	0.76	2.11	—	−0.76
Mangoes	−0.27	4.58	0.26	-0.76	7.61	−1.86
Pineapple	−1.74	1.61	—	0.66	—	−1.09
Citrus fruits	−1.52	0.95	0.76	-0.30	1.03	−6.39
Other fruits	−0.63	1.10	−1.62	0.31	1.97	−0.11
Total fruits	−0.50	0.62	−0.66	0.48	0.34	−1.20
Spices	5.09	4.24	1.22	3.20	4.23	1.47
Coffee and tea	−0.35	0.30	—	0.14	—	1.22
Drug and narcotics	1.49	2.80	1.22	0.94	0.25	2.49
Rubber	—	−0.08	—	2.52	—	3.43

Source: Authors' estimates using data from FAOSTAT.

5 The agricultural sector in Nepal

Scope of improvement and value chains

Ganesh Thapa

Rapid urbanization, rising parity in purchasing power, increased diversity in consumers' diets and recent transformations in food and agricultural systems have increased the demand for high-value and differentiated food products in Nepal (NADS 2016). Due to increasing food safety and health consciousness, consumers gradually have shifted their market outlet choices from the traditional open markets to supermarkets and modern domestic urban markets (Reardon and Berdegué 2002). As a result, supermarkets and modern outlets are burgeoning in urban and peri-urban areas. This has presented income-enhancing opportunities for smallholders by catering to unique consumer preferences and tastes. Connecting poor smallholders to the markets has been important to supermarkets and agri-processors to sustainably address and meet the demands of high-end consumers (Narrod et al. 2009). However, literature suggests smallholders have been unable to meet stringent requirements such as those for food safety and freshness (Reardon and Berdegué, 2002; Ghezán et al., 2002). Therefore, new institutional arrangements and value chain (VC) linkages are required to enable smallholders to remain competitive. Integrating smallholder farmers with modern value chains has been found to address food safety issues and deliver quality produce (Narrod et al. 2009).

Nepalese agriculture is dominated by subsistence farmers with average per capita landholdings of less than 0.8 ha (NADS 2016). Such small landholdings are not enough to meet food needs, improve nutrition and meet household expenditures. Therefore, how to raise productivity for such farms has been a huge challenge in addressing rural poverty and food insecurity. Given that a household has only land as a productive capital asset, increasing land productivity is important to boost household income (Deninger 2003). There is a high potential for the development of several value chains that have good market prospects in international markets.[1] Agricultural diversification toward high-value crops has been found to increase agricultural productivity and household welfare of the poor rural populace in several developing countries (Thapa et al. 2018; Bellora et al. 2017). Although high-value crops realize significantly higher returns than cereal crops, the high-value products are perishable, their production process is cost-intensive, prices are volatile, and they require reliable market access (Birthal et al. 2013). In the absence of effective value chain linkages (vertical coordination) and contract farming (CF) schemes, post-harvest losses are high, output prices are highly variable and net returns are unpredictable (Meemken and Bellemare 2020).

Furthermore, smallholders are scattered and isolated, and they face problems in procuring inputs and in accessing credits, technology and markets. They usually sell meager quantities of produce, which is of low quality, during the peak harvest season. However, the agro-processing industry and supermarkets prefer to buy produce in large amounts and expect a year-round supply of quality products. Therefore, both the processors/supermarkets and farmers benefit if the value chain is developed. Contract farming and the development of value chain linkages have been considered the means of spurring the development of an agribusiness sector, reducing poverty and food insecurity (Swinnen and Maertens 2007; Diao et al. 2012) and launching structural transformation in the developing country.

The government of Nepal has promoted competitive and commercial agriculture and put a strong emphasis on expanding vertical linkages. The Agriculture Development Strategy (ADS), which is the principal guiding document for Nepal's agricultural development in the next 20 years, has identified a value chain development program as one of four flagship programs for agribusiness development (NADS 2016). Various national and international agencies have launched projects with objectives to promote value chain linkages, contract farming and cooperatives and to improve smallholders' welfare. Some empirical studies have assessed the impact of contract farming (Khanal and Mishra 2018; Mishra et al. 2018b; Kumar et al. 2016, 2019), value chain linkages (Singh et al. 2013; Basnett and Pandey 2014; Gurung et al. 2015) and cooperatives (Mishra et al. 2018a) on agricultural performance and the welfare of farmers in the country. However, there is a lack of study that rigorously examines agricultural performance and its scope for improvement in the context of contract farming and value chain development. This chapter aims to fill that gap.

First, the chapter assesses agricultural performance, emphasizing the importance of agriculture in Nepal's economy. Second, we present the challenges and problems the agricultural sector faces. Third, we illustrate the scope and importance of high-value crops.[2] Fourth, we examine the status and importance of value chain linkages and contract farming required for the promotion of high-value crops and agricultural commercialization in Nepal. Fifth, we examine the agricultural policies that aim to promote agricultural commercialization in the country. Sixth, we discuss the program activities of development agencies on value chain development and agribusiness promotion. Seventh, we illustrate the case studies of a successful poultry firm that engages in contract farming and is vertically integrated. Finally, the study provides policy implications for promoting contract farming, value chain development and commercial agriculture in Nepal.

Methodology

This study is based primarily on a literature review of studies related to contract farming and value chain studies from Nepal. Agricultural policy documents and agricultural statistics are reviewed to assess agricultural performance and to identify challenges and problems in the country's agricultural development. A key informant interview (KII) was conducted with the executive directors (Mr. Shree Krishna Ghimire and Mr. Hari Rawal) of the Valley Group, a private company that is engaged in contract farming and vertical integration of poultry production activities. Challenges and opportunities for value chain development and contract farming are explored.

Agricultural performance

About 80% of Nepal's population lives in rural areas. Most of the poor are from the same areas where agriculture is the vital means of subsistence. Therefore, agricultural growth is the main engine for reducing poverty (Haggblade et al. 2007; Christiaensen et al. 2011). The World Development Report 2008 indicated that GDP growth originating in agriculture is more effective in benefiting the poorest segment of the country's population than is growth generated in the non-agricultural sector (WB 2007). Agricultural development is the basis for promoting off-farm and on-farm employment opportunities, stabilizing agricultural prices, narrowing the trade deficit, alleviating poverty and improving food security in the country. Next, we discuss four indicators of agricultural performance: agricultural GDP growth, agricultural productivity, labor productivity and agricultural trade. All these indicators reveal that Nepalese agriculture has performed unsatisfactorily.

Agricultural GDP

Agriculture is the backbone of Nepal's national economy, contributing 28.2% to GDP in 2017 (NMOF 2018). Figure 5.1 shows that the country's agricultural growth rate since 1966 has been sluggish and erratic. During the last five decades, agriculture grew at 2.74% (AGDP), slightly higher than the population growth rate of 2% per year. Although the agricultural growth rate averaged about 4.52% per year between 1981 and 1989, it averaged only 2.9% per year during 2010–2018. The subsistence nature of the sector, the dominance of rain-fed agriculture, and the limited arable land per capita are some of the reasons for the low performance of Nepal's agricultural sector (NADS 2016).

Agricultural production

Agricultural production is not satisfactory in the country. Nepal lags many South Asian countries in terms of productivity of the main cereal crops (Table 5.1). The average paddy yield in China is 6.91 metric tons (MT)/ha, but Nepal's

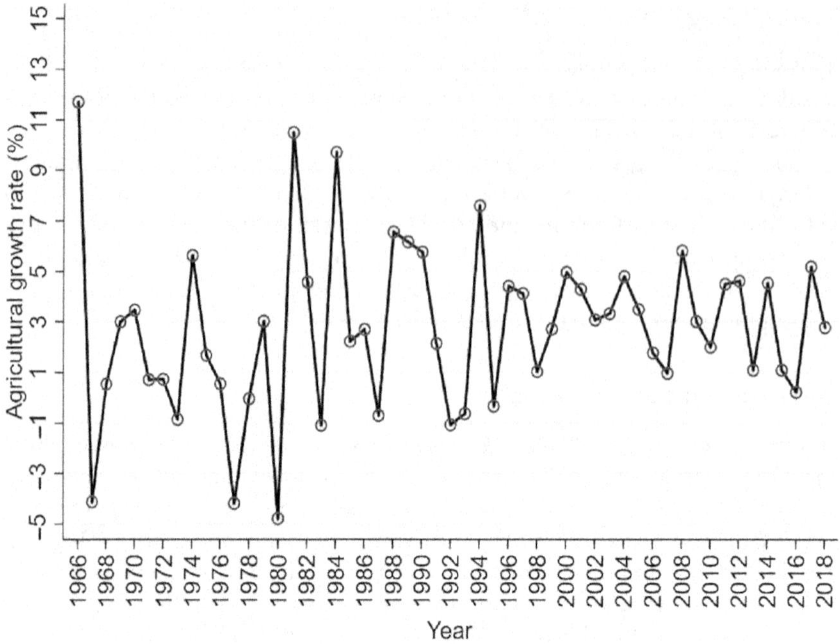

Figure 5.1 Annual agricultural growth rate of Nepal, 1966–2018

Source: WDI (2018).

Table 5.1 Productivity of main cereal crops and potato (MT/ha), 2017

Countries	*Paddy*	*Maize*	*Wheat*	*Potato*
Afghanistan	3.09	1.29	2.03	15.98
Bangladesh	4.35	7.76	3.16	20.44
Bhutan	4.15	3.38	1.79	11.02
China	6.91	6.11	5.48	17.20
India	3.85	3.12	3.22	22.31
Nepal	3.37	2.55	2.55	13.86
Pakistan	3.85	4.64	2.97	22.52
Sri Lanka	2.05	3.73	—	16.46

Source: FAOSTAT (2017).

agricultural productivity in paddy is about half that (3.37 MT/ha). Similarly, Nepal's performance for maize and wheat is not satisfactory and is ahead of only Afghanistan in maize and ahead of Afghanistan and Bhutan in wheat. Maize yields in Bangladesh are more than three times those in Nepal. In the case of potato, Nepal's productivity is among the lowest among the South Asian countries. Such high yield gaps (the difference between potential and actual yields) suggest that Nepal has a huge potential to boost its agricultural production.

Table 5.2 shows the area share allocated to the cultivation of different crops in Nepal. Although cereal crops yield low net returns and do not have a competitive edge, the major share of area is allocated to paddy, followed by maize and wheat. A higher proportion of area is allocated to rice, but 70% is for subsistence. However, the area share of cereal crops is declining over time, and the area shares of high-value crops such as fruits, vegetables, spices and condiments and potato are increasing. Figure 5.2 shows that agricultural production

Table 5.2 Area share of different crops in Nepal (%)

Crops	*1995*	*2004*	*2010*
Paddy	44.32	38.32	34.65
Maize	23.44	21.12	20.98
Wheat	19.35	16.80	17.77
Oilseed rape	5.48	4.67	4.95
Potato	3.14	3.65	4.23
Vegetables	4.27	4.49	5.65
Spices/condiments	—	0.85	1.16
Fruits	—	2.22	2.73
Pulses	—	7.87	7.74

Source: MOAD (2011).

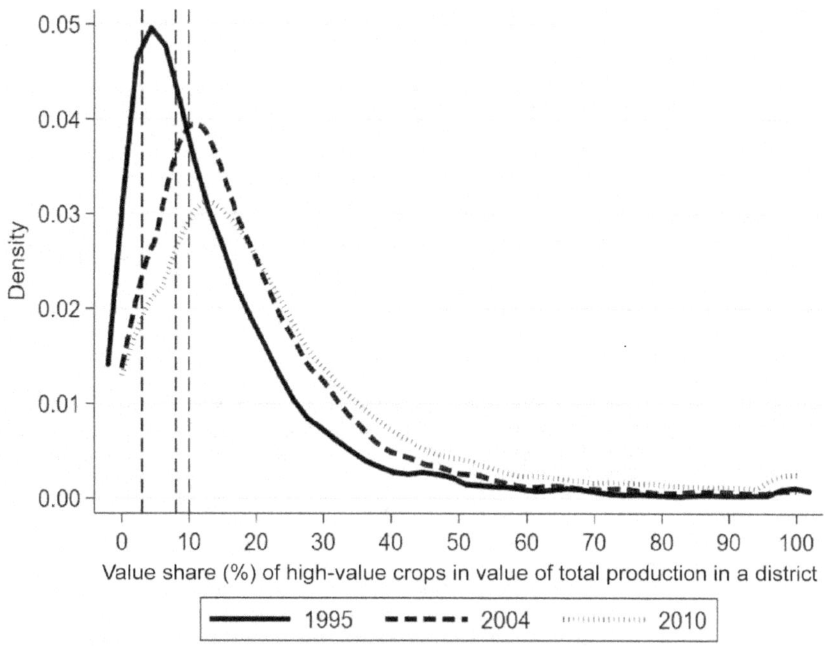

Figure 5.2 Value share of high-value crops in total HH production value in 1995, 2004 and 2010 in Nepal (%)

Source: CBS (2011).

has shifted toward high-value crops in 2011. This shows that Nepal is gradually diversifying its agricultural production toward high-value crops—a positive sign of agricultural development in the country.

Labor productivity

Agriculture is the major source of livelihood, providing employment for about 70% of the economically active population (ILO 2019). Although the share of agricultural GDP fell from two-thirds in 1980 to less than one-third in 2017, the economically active population in the agriculture sector fell less dramatically from 80% to 70%, in the same period. Despite the slightly positive growth rate, Nepal's labor productivity has been stagnant and lags behind that of its South Asian peers (Figure 5.3). This is mainly because of the subsistence farming still practiced by the majority of farming households and the high population growth rates.

Agricultural trade deficit

Nepal's trade situation has been deteriorating over the last two decades. Domestic production is not keeping pace with rising demand. Although the country was a net exporter and self-sufficient in food production before the 1990s, food

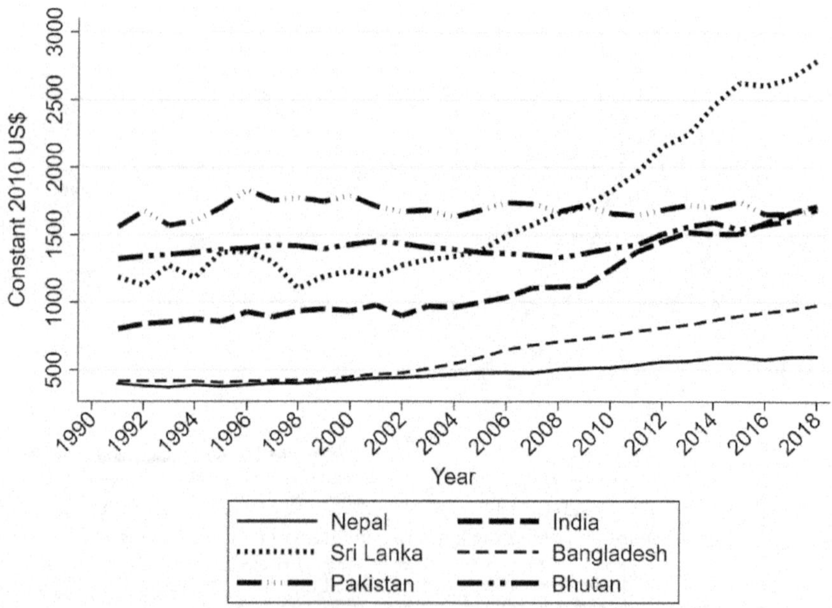

Figure 5.3 Labor productivity of Nepal, 1991–2018

Source: WDI (2018), Value Added per Worker Is a Measure of Labour Productivity.

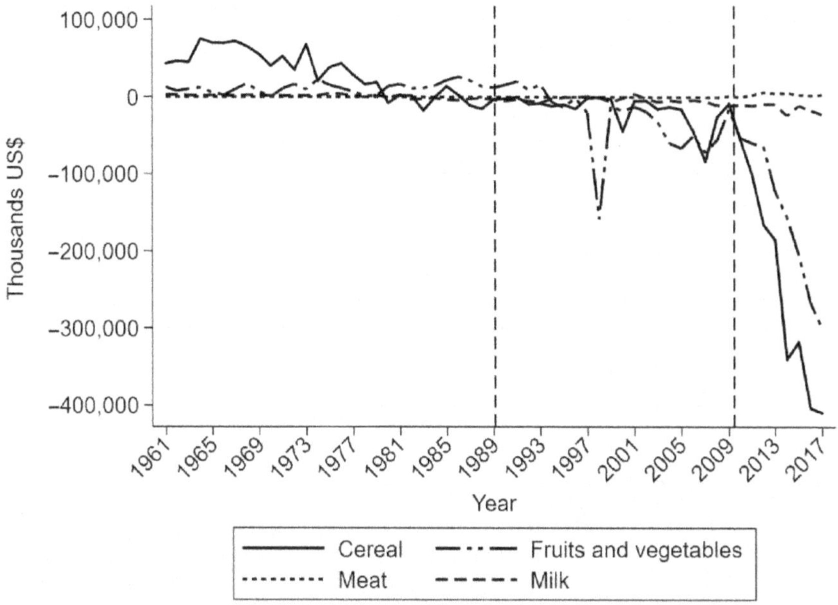

Figure 5.4 Balance of trade of the agricultural commodities of Nepal, 1961–2017

Source: FAOSTAT (2017).

imports have increased exponentially, especially after 2010 (Figure 5.4). This has posed huge challenges to the country's food security situation. Despite the large share of land allocated for cereal production, cereal imports have increased dramatically. Imports of fruits and vegetables also have increased relative to exports. Agricultural performance in the livestock sector, however, is relatively better. Nepal is a net importer of milk but a net exporter of meat items. Overall, the trade situation reflects the low competitiveness of Nepalese agriculture.

Agricultural problems and challenges

This section discusses the major problems and challenges that Nepal's agricultural sector faces.

Subsistence agriculture

Nepalese agriculture is dominated by a subsistence production system (NADS 2016). Such a system conducts farming at a small scale; employs low levels of technology adoption, inputs and managerial skills; and produces poor-quality products, diminishing agricultural competitiveness. In addition, households practicing subsistence farming have a low capacity to bear risks, and they rely on low-value staple crops and obtain low incomes.

Land in Nepal has been gradually fragmented, mainly as parents' land is inherited by multiple children and as plotting of land increases, particularly in urban and peri-urban areas. Most of the fertile cultivated lands are used for residential purposes. All these factors have led to a decrease in the average farm size and an increase in the number of farms. Based on census data, the average landholding size in Nepal declined from 1.13 ha in 1981 to 0.79 ha in 2001 and to 0.68 ha in 2011 (CBS 2013). Since landholding size and household-level food self-sufficiency are positively correlated, about 40% of households with landholdings of less than 0.50 ha are food self-insufficient (CBS 2013). Smaller and fragmented farms will have problems realizing economics of scale and generating income above the poverty level. The government launched a land use policy in 2012 and proposed a land use bill to promote the optimal use of land for agricultural production.

Low agricultural investment

The agricultural sector has been continuously underinvested in Nepal. Despite its huge potential to generate employment and stop the forced migration of labor, agricultural investment has declined compared to investment in the manufacturing sector. Although the Nepal government plans to be self-reliant in agriculture by 2021 and to double agricultural production by the end of 2022/2023, the budget allocated to the agricultural sector is not satisfactory. Only 1.8% (NRs 34.80 billion) of the country's total budget (NRs 1.53 trillion) was allocated for the agricultural sector in 2019 (NMOF 2019). The budget mainly emphasized modernization, commercialization, mechanization and expansion of the value chain in agriculture. However, agricultural policymakers say at least about 5% of the total budget is required for the country to promote agricultural commercialization, reduce trade deficits and reduce food insecurity in the country. Nepal's public investment in the agricultural sector is poor and low compared to the investments of its South Asian neighbors.

The Nepal government has prioritized private investment in the agricultural sector. However, given the risk of political instability and the high cost of doing business, returns on investment are low in the country. Due to the large number of smallholders, transaction costs to secure farm outputs are high. As agriculture depends primarily on weather, and as input supply uncertainty is high and infrastructure is weak, the agricultural sector has failed to attract much foreign direct investment (Pant 2010). As of 2010, foreign investment in Nepal's agricultural sector is less than 1% of the total foreign investment (DOI 2011).

Out-migration, labor scarcity and feminization in agriculture

Unemployment and low agricultural incomes are the main drivers of out-migration in Nepal (Ciacci et al. 2018). Increasing out-migration by a productive youth labor force has changed the labor market dynamics and influenced agriculture's transformation in the country (Lokshin et al. 2010). Due to the labor scarcity, the agricultural wage rate has increased, which has led to increased costs of production. The real labor wage grew 9% per year between 2008 and 2015 (Pokharel 2019). Labor shortages are strongly felt during the planting and harvesting seasons of major crops such as rice. Planting has been delayed, intercultural operations have been neglected and land has been abandoned. Several cases have been reported in which households are forced to abandon their land or land productivity is not satisfactory (Khanal 2018). As men migrate, more women, elderly people and children are left at home. An increasing share of the workload has shifted toward women, leading to feminization in agriculture (Tamang et al. 2014; Ciacci et al. 2018). In 2013, 71% of women were found to work in agriculture, while only 54% of men did. Women usually face problems in accessing land and inputs, and they produce lower yields than men (Basnett et al. 2014).

Although remittances are likely to help farmers purchase costly inputs and hire agricultural machinery, evidence indicates that such remittances are used largely for consumption and loan repayment than for capital formation and investment (Wasti 2017). Increasing out-migration and remittances in the country have led to surges in imports and have widened the trade deficit (Bhatta 2013).

Low agricultural competitiveness

Nepalese farmers incur higher costs of production than farmers in China and India. This is because India and China subsidize several inputs (like fertilizers, seeds, electricity etc.), making Chinese and Indian agricultural products highly cost-competitive in Nepalese markets. Consumers purchase cheap products irrespective of the source of origin, which discourages Nepalese farmers from being involved in agriculture. As a result, agriculture has become a less profitable, neglected profession among younger generations. Many of them have boycotted farming and headed abroad for better jobs and decent incomes. Farm income's share of total household income fell from 61% to 28% between 1995/1996 and 2010/2011 (CBS 2011).

Moreover, Nepal's agricultural and non-agricultural trade situation is unhealthy, with increasing imports and decreasing exports, high product concentration of exports (carpets, ready-made garments, pashmina, handicrafts, pulses, jute goods and vegetable ghee), concentration of trade with few partners (India and the United States) and low value addition of the exported products (Sharma 2019). In absence of a third-party certification system that attests to compliance with quality standards and good agricultural practices (GAPs), the agricultural products from Nepal are either rejected at the border or fetch lower prices in the international market. Nepal lacks the modern laboratory infrastructure to assess quality standards of imported and exported products. Training of quality inspectors also is required to ensure that products exported from Nepal meet quality standards in their destination markets (NADS 2016).

Input availability, technology adoption and agricultural extension services

Timely availability of agricultural inputs has been a huge challenge for Nepal's farmers. Specifically, access to inputs is highly problematic in the remote areas of hilly and high mountainous districts. Due to the remoteness, agricultural inputs are not available when required or will be very costly in such areas due to the added transportation costs.

There is a huge scarcity of chemical fertilizers every year during the paddy planting season, and Nepal depends on India for the fertilizers. Although the government allocated about NRs 9 billion as a subsidy grant in 2019, only 350,000 MT of fertilizers can be purchased to meet current demand for about 600,000 MT in the country. If we compare fertilizer use among South Asian countries, Nepal lags many other countries (Table 5.3). Recently, the government, in collaboration with cooperatives and the private sector, has prioritized establishing factories to produce chemical fertilizer to facilitate the timely supply, increase the use of agricultural inputs and sustainably meet the demand for chemical fertilizers in Nepal.

Most farmers in Nepal still practice traditional farming. Although several high-yield varieties and hybrid varieties with high-yield potential have been released, farmers continue to grow local varieties despite their poor performance. Because smallholders have no additional income sources to buffer themselves from crop failures, they flinch at taking the risk of adopting the non-traditional varieties. Demonstration and extension services for such farmers are inadequate to motivate the adoption and diffusion of technologies. Furthermore, seed replacement rates are low, and farmers are unaware of modern agricultural practices. Although the desirable seed replacement rate for crops is about 25% to 30%, the seed replacement rate is about 6% for wheat, followed by 4.4% for rice, 3.8% for maize and 1.6% for pulses (NADS 2016). One of the main reasons behind the low technology adoption is the problematic access to public-sector agricultural services. Only 15% of farm households have received public-sector agricultural services (Joshi 2018). Due to the low number of extension agents and the remote nature of the country, providing effective extension services to individual farmers is challenging. The Nepal Agricultural

Table 5.3 Fertilizer used (kg/hectare of arable land)

Country	*2005*	*2010*	*2016*
Afghanistan	4.24	4.25	12.18
Bangladesh	197.75	212.96	289.40
Bhutan	7.56	10.04	13.25
China	423.41	515.41	503.32
India	127.61	179.04	165.85
Nepal	3.57	25.09	74.08
Pakistan	123.48	138.30	144.33
Sri Lanka	255.29	229.05	131.92

Source: WDI (2018).

Research Council (NARC) was established in 1991 to conduct agricultural research in the country, but the organization has limited resources and can conduct research on only selective and prioritized issues. Less than 0.3% of AGDP is allocated to research, and less than 0.4% is allocated to extension services in Nepal (NMOF 2018).

As agriculture is largely rain fed, Nepal's national production depends on whether the monsoon is good or bad. Although the amount of irrigated land has expanded significantly, rising from 27.4% in 2001 to about 51.7% in 2016, a perennial source of irrigation is available to only about 36% of the cultivated land (MOAD 2017).

Access to credit has become a problem for smallholders. Although farmers are willing to borrow, about 42% did not have access to credit (CBS 2013). Without credit at affordable interest rates, farmers are unable to expand their agribusiness or purchase inputs. Agricultural insurance and access to credits are confined to Nepal's urban and peri-urban areas. Commercial farmers and entrepreneurs face difficulty accessing longer-term credits as commercial banks lend only micro-credit. The insurance system in agriculture is still at the embryonic stage. Agricultural production insured is just 0.9% of AGDP (Pokharel 2019). Its coverage is low and limited to a few commodities. The lack of risk-related data systems, difficulty in fixing price premiums, farmers' inability to understand the insurance systems and weak promotion activities are the major constraints that agricultural insurance faces (NADS 2016).

Infrastructure

Nepal's poor transportation infrastructure has been a challenge for agricultural development. This has increased transportation and transaction costs and made farmers' involvement in the markets expensive (Shively and Thapa 2017). Reliable connectivity of rural roads to urban centers, establishment of collection centers, cold storage facilities and rural electrifications are vital to support agricultural commercialization and to reap economies of scale. In several locations in the remote hills and mountains of Nepal, not all agriculture products enter the market because of the lack of access to roads, markets and post-harvest facilities (Thapa and Shively 2018).

Political stability and good governance

Political instability and lack of good governance have been challenges for Nepal's agricultural development. The country faced a disastrous civil war from 1996 to 2006 that adversely affected agricultural growth and development. Although a peace accord was signed in 2006 and a new constitution promulgated in 2015, leadership and government staffs have changed repeatedly. The change of visionary and motivated agriculture leaders within the short period will result in the poor implementation of policies, plans and programs.

For example, the continuation and cessation of input subsidies over the past 15 years have led farmers to chaos. Microfinance institution withdrew services during the civil war. When such uncertainty occurs, private investors hesitate to take risk and do not invest in the agricultural sector. Due to the lack of good governance, not all the subsidies allocated for fertilizer procurement and other extension services reach farmers. Lack of strict monitoring of fertilizer and seed procurement, lack of strict monitoring of the distribution system and the absence of government staffs' accountability have led to the distribution of poor-quality fertilizers and unimproved seeds and have resulted in huge losses for farmers (Bista et al. 2016).

Scope and importance of high-value crops

Nepal has limited cultivable land of about 17%. Although cereal crops have a low level of agriculture productivity, about 80% of the land is covered by cereal crops such as paddy, maize, millet, wheat and barley (MOAD 2017). This strictly undermines the country's structural transformation process. Relative to cereal crops, high-value crops have a high potential for agricultural commercialization and provide higher returns. Nepal's major agricultural exports are high-value commodities such as cardamom, ginger, herbs, ayurvedic medicine, tanned skin, woolen carpet, garments and pashmina. These products offer good opportunities for expansion and fetch premium prices in the international market. Nepal's government has underscored the promotion of high-value crops and has encouraged farmers and cooperatives to comply with phytosanitary measures to increase exports (NADS 2016). Moreover, high-value crops have high potential for generating employment opportunities (Paudel and Wagle 2019) and can reduce the forced migration of labor in Nepal. Diversification from traditional agriculture to commercial agriculture and high-value crops has been considered a viable pathway for reducing poverty (Thapa et al. 2018).

Demand for high-value agricultural commodities has been increasing (Kumar et al. 2020). Households have gradually shifted their consumption toward high-quality staples (such as long grain and fine rice instead of coarse rice) and high-value processed products. As a result, imports of high-value crops have been surging in Nepal. The increasing demand for high-value crops has been reflected in farm-gate prices, which have increased 6%–17% per annum (MOAD 2017). Specifically, domestic producers have huge opportunities to export vegetables to India in the off season to India, when supplies are low and prices are high. Although there has been some progress in the production of high-value agricultural commodities such as tea, coffee, cardamom, dairy processing, vegetable seeds, poultry and fisheries, Nepal needs to establish more agriculture-based industries and to facilitate the value chain linkages. Strengthening these linkages will ensure markets for local producers and realize price premiums for high-value commodities.

Value chain and contract farming in Nepal

Previous sections of this chapter have discussed the challenges and problems of agricultural growth and development in Nepal, with emphasis on the scope and importance of high-value commodities. Although high-value crops can lead to better agricultural productivity, smallholders face several challenges and risks without effective value chain linkages and contract farming. This section examines the status and importance of value chain linkages and contract farming and discusses their role in promoting high-value crops and agricultural commercialization in Nepal.

Although high-value commodities (HVCs) performed well over the last decade, value addition remains low. Due to the perishable nature of these commodities, there is a huge potential to process them by adding value, extending shelf life, packaging them properly and storing them to minimize distress selling. However, smallholders lack enough resources to add value and undertake potential risks. By establishing linkages between smallholders and agri-processors, the processors can purchase the fresh products, process them and transport them to the market centers. Contract farming can be a suitable institutional mechanism benefiting both parties (farmers and contractors/buyers). Although the government has promoted contract farming, its growth is not satisfactory. As of 2011, only about 11% of land was under contract farming in Nepal, up from about 8% in 2001. (CBS 2013).

Smallholders produce high-value commodities on a small scale at a disaggregated level. During the production, harvesting and marketing process, such farmers face several problems. First, they may not find the chemical fertilizers and improved seed varieties during the peak planting season. Second, they are less aware of modern agricultural practices important for enhancing product quality and increasing yields (NADS 2016). Third, they lack market information and may not receive competitive market prices. Moreover, high-end consumers demand high-quality fresh or processed products. Smallholders are less likely to respond to these requirements due to their small quantities of production, limited resources and isolated operations. For the high-value commodities to compete with agricultural products in the global markets, they need to meet designated international standards. Such challenges and opportunities have incentivized stakeholders to follow the whole-of-chain development and management perspectives (Swinnen and Maertens 2007), increasingly being referred to as value chain approaches (Fearne et al. 2012). The value chain approach has been regarded as a successful way to enhance smallholders' access to markets and to bring all value chain actors together as an integrated whole close to consumers (Henderson and Isaac 2017).

Nepalese farmers suffer from imperfections in both input and output markets. This seriously constrains the welfare and productivity of marginal farmers. Value chain development has been a popular policy instrument to help farmers overcome market imperfections. Except for a few commodities (such as tea, coffee and sugarcane), agro-industries are not integrated with agricultural producers in Nepal (NADS 2016). Bhattarai et al. (2013) assessed the competitive market opportunities for Nepali agricultural products and identified 11 key value chains (tea, coffee, honey, ginger, large cardamom, lentil, potato, milk and dairy, meat, fish and non-timber forest products). Accessing domestic and international markets and reaching the growing high-value markets has been a challenge for the smallholders growing high-value commodities.

Agricultural cooperatives and contract farming have been promoted as potential policy instruments to address several problems smallholders face (Di Falco et al. 2008; Francesconi and Wouterse 2015; Valentinov 2007). Agro-processors or contractors prefer to be linked with cooperatives rather than individual farmers in order to minimize transaction costs. Cooperatives not only help reduce the cost of the farming business but also provide farmers with more bargaining power (Coulter et al. 1999; Baumann 2000). This results in higher profits to the farmers. In the context of increasing globalization and the free-trade regime, the development of cooperatives and contract farming schemes will lead to the vertical coordination of small farms with processors and exporters. Contract farming is likely to make agriculture remunerative to farmers. Special contracts will be made between growers/farmers and buyers/contractors. The growers commit to deliver a specific quantity and quality of products in a certain period of time, and the buyers agree to supply inputs and technical advice and commit to pay the output prices or guarantee the market. Farmers take the production risks, and the buyers/contractors take the marketing risk.

Contract farming provides an impetus for agricultural commercialization (Dolan and Humphrey 2000; Masakure and Henson 2005) and agricultural modernization (WB 2007). It boosts farm profitability (Briones 2015; Huddleston and Tonts 2007; Mishra et al. 2016), enables processors to procure and supply quality inputs at the right time with the least cost (Kirsten and Sartorius 2002), enhances access to technology for poor farmers and provides extension services at a lower cost (Bellemare 2012; Simmons et al. 2005). Similarly, contract farming has led to improved household welfare (Kalamkar 2012; WB 2007), reduced food insecurity (Bellemare and Novak 2017) and increased households' asset holdings (Michelson 2013).

Although contract farming has several advantages, the net effects may be ambiguous. Contracts are likely to favor larger growers (Little and Watts 1994) and lead to inequalities in rural income (Key and Runsten 1999). Large contractors may exercise monopsonic power over smallholders. In many instances, contractors gain more from contracts than do farmers. In the absence of legal settings and regulatory mechanisms to strictly enforce contract agreements, contract farming is likely to fail in developing countries (Prowse 2012).

The Policy Reform Initiatives Project (PRIP), supported by the U.S. Agency for International Development (USAID) and implemented by the International Food Policy Research Institute (IFPRI), commissioned several studies on contract farming in Nepal. Some published studies focused on high-value commodities such as ginger, lentil, tomatoes and paddy seed production. Ginger producers engaged in contract farming received 58% higher net returns than independent producers (Kumar et al. 2016). Major factors attributed to increasing the net returns are higher price realization, training received on practices and provision of quality seeds. Among different forms of contract farming decisions, farmers who engaged in contract farming with output conditions generated higher revenue, and farmers who engaged in contract farming with input and output conditions generated higher profit, than farmers not engaged in contract farming (Khanal and Mishra 2018). Paddy seed cultivators engaged in contract farming received 23% higher profits than farmers not engaged in contract farming (Kumar et al. 2019). This is mainly due to the higher seed yield and better prices received by farmers participating in contract farming. Contract farming through cooperatives has positive and significant impacts on profit and yield for tomato producers (Mishra et al. 2018a) but a negative effect on employment. Lentil producers with 0.01 to 0.05 ha of land obtained higher revenues, profits and yield from contract farming in Nepal than producers with more than 0.05 ha of land (Mishra et al. 2018b).

Although the Hill Maize Research Project (HMRP), supported by the Centro Internacional de Mejoramiento de Maize y Trigo, or the International Maize and Wheat Improvement Center, initiated the seed multiplication program through a community-based seed production (CBSP) approach, not all maize seed produced was sold due to a lack of understanding of the market demand for desired variety and quantity (CIMMYT 2014). The project initiated a pre-sowing seed contract (PSSC) with private organizations (agrovets, cooperatives, seed banks and seed companies) and signed a formal agreement on the variety and quantity to be delivered. Such contracts have led to better seed prices and ensured a market for community-based production.

Remote areas of the hills and high mountains of Nepal offer good opportunities for contract farming. Although marketing and transaction costs are high, several advantages stem from contract farming in such places. First, buyers do not have to worry about side selling—selling to a third party, breaching contract—due to the absence of local markets. Second, contract farmers in remote areas are more likely to stay longer with buyers than farmers living near highways (Cai 2008). Third, the land in remote areas is more organic and is free from contamination such as pesticides; therefore, food produced from such land is wholesome and safe. In such remote places where government fails to coordinate the input and output markets, contract farming is likely to reduce transaction costs and correct market failure (Singh 2002). Contract farming serves as an intermediate institution that provides necessary services to farmers who have no access to credit institutions and who lack non-farm job opportunities (Kulkarni and Grethe 2009). Despite the potential benefits, Nepal has yet to have an act on contract farming. Although contract farming is practiced in the country, contracts are made based on trust and oral agreement in the absence of laws.

Projects focused on value chains in Nepal

Value chain development and contract farming have attracted the attention of development agencies and government in Nepal. Several donor-supported programs and projects, jointly implemented with Nepal's government, have focused on value chains and agribusiness. We briefly summarize the activities and outcomes of some of the promising projects that focus on value chain development.

The Asian Development Bank (ADB) supported a few projects focusing on agricultural commercialization and value chain development. The bank implemented a commercial agricultural development project in 11 districts of the eastern development region from 2007 to 2013.[3] The project aimed to reduce rural poverty through equitable and sustainable commercialization and to improve efficiency in marketing and processing high-value commodities. The major activities included helping smallholders develop or participate in income-generating agricultural activities and strengthening stakeholders (farmers, traders and processors). The project resulted in increased farm production, generated employment opportunities and improved access to technology, markets, credit and information (ADB 2016).

The Ministry of Agriculture and Livestock Development (MOALD) implemented the High Mountain Agribusiness and Livelihood Improvement (HIMALI) project from 2011 to 2018 with financial support from the Asian Development Bank. The project's objective is to increase the incomes and employment of people living in the high mountain areas of Nepal through commercialization of agribusinesses and development of value chains for niche agricultural products, livestock, medicinal and aromatic plants (MAPs) and non-timber forest (NTF) products. The project was expected to generate \$20 million of gross production value per year of agricultural products, create 7,500 jobs and generate \$6.4 million in wages by 2017. The HIMALI project provided complete packages to the beneficiaries—grants, business management training, knowledge and access to improved production technologies and value addition—and it organized several workshops and tours and facilitated market linkages. Under the value chain capacity development component, government infrastructure such as offices, service centers, sheds, residential buildings (quarters), boundary walls and apple- and seed-processing centers were either rehabilitated or constructed. The project also provided necessary technology support and improved breed to the research/technology centers, and it supported the construction of livestock trails and two ayurvedic medicine processing facilities (DOL 2018).

The Asian Development Bank also supported the Raising Incomes of Small and Medium Farmers (RISM) project, implemented between 2011 and 2017. The project aimed to reduce market and business risks for small and medium-sized farmers who diversify into high-value commodities in ten districts of the mid- and far-western development regions of Nepal. The project aims to enhance supply chain links to buyers and markets, improve post-harvest facilities and provide agribusiness support. The project's outcome is to boost the production of high-value commodities and increase the profitability of small and medium-sized farmers. The project is expected to benefit about 18,700 farm households (ADB 2010).

The World Bank supported the Project for Agriculture Commercialization and Trade (PACT) from 2009 to 2018 with the goal of improving the competitiveness of smallholder farmers and the agribusiness sector in selected commodity value chains in 25 districts. The value chains focused on were seeds, vegetables, coffee, ginger, potato, floriculture, honey, mushroom, oilseed (mustard and ground nuts), fruits (citrus, banana, papaya and mango), lentil, herbs, fish, feed, milk processing, dairy processing and poultry. The project aimed to help farmer groups and cooperatives engage in profitable market-oriented production, strengthen linkages with industry along the value chains and reduce obstacles to agricultural and food trade. Results from the project's impact assessment indicate that agricultural output per unit of production for horticulture crops (fresh produce) and dairy cows (milk) increased more than 25% and that farm productivity for cereal crops increased about 23%. Agribusiness productivity, measured by the increase in the volume of commodities sold for processing, increased at least 40% (WB 2019).

The Ministry of Agriculture and Livestock Development, with the Korea International Cooperation Agency (KOICA) and the United Nations Development Programme (UNDP), has been implementing the Value Chain Development of Fruit and Vegetables Project in Bagmati and Gandaki provinces. The project began in 2018 and is expected to end in 2022. Its objective is to increase smallholders' income through increased production, reduced post-harvest losses and better market linkage for selected fruit and vegetables. The project targets agricultural producer organizations (such as cooperatives, farmers group associations and market centers) for sustainable value chain development. The expectation is that such producer organizations will provide agribusiness development services based on their members' immediate needs (UNDP 2018).

The High Value Agriculture Project in Hill and Mountain Areas (HVAP) is a collaboration between the government of Nepal and the International Fund for Agricultural Development (IFAD). The project was executed from 2012 to 2018 by the Ministry of Agricultural and Livestock Development (MoAD) and was focused on promoting fruits, medicinal and aromatic plants, non-timber forest products and livestock. The project's main goal was to reduce poverty, improve food security and reduce social inequality in the rural hilly areas of Nepal by developing inclusive value chains and strengthening service markets. The project documented increased productivity and revenue from market-driven value chains with improved commercial relations and a 45% reduction in post-harvest loss (IFAD 2018).

The USAID launched Nepal Economic Agriculture and Trade (NEAT) activity from 2010 to 2013 to foster the economic growth and competitiveness of Nepal's high-value agricultural products in national and international markets. The project also aims to address deficiencies in the legal framework for businesses and trade and to facilitate important regulatory and administrative reforms to attract agricultural investment and increase exports. NEAT has supported the government of Nepal in drafting a new Agribusiness Promotion Act, which includes a legal framework for contract farming. The high-value commodities focused on were lentils, vegetables, ginger and orthodox tea. USAID supported the establishment of Annapurna Organic Agriculture Industries, the first ginger processing plant in Nepal, to ensure a market for local farmers and strengthen the value chain for ginger. The industry has contracted with 3,000 ginger farmers in western Nepal to guarantee a year-round supply of ginger for the factory (Chemonics International Inc. 2013).

Nepal's government launched the Prime Minister Agriculture Modernization Project (PMAMP) in 2016, prioritizing agricultural commercialization and mechanization to achieve food self-sufficiency in the country. The government classified the agricultural production sector into pockets (10 ha of land), blocks (100 ha), zones (500 ha), and super zones (1,000 ha). The project allocated about Rs 5.75 billion, with subsidy distribution the major priority. Subsidies of about 50% are provided on urea, 25% on other fertilizers, 75% on livestock insurance premiums, 50% on farm machinery and 85% on processing and marketing. Cooperatives and organized groups have priority in receiving subsidies.

Policies on agricultural commercialization and value chain development

Several policy formulations have been undertaken to support and guide agricultural development in Nepal. Some of the pertinent policies discussed in this section relate to value chain development and agricultural commercialization. We also briefly discuss the Agriculture Perspective Plan (APP) (1995–2014) and the Agriculture Development Strategy (2015–2034), which have been the main mantras guiding agricultural development in the country since the 1990s.

Agriculture received the highest priority in national development planning in the fifth five-year plan (1975–1980). The government initiated structural reforms to move toward a more market-oriented economy during the 1990s. The Agriculture Perspective Plan provided the development framework, and its formulation was focused on a Green Revolution perspective. In the eighth five-year plan (1992–1997), agricultural intensification and income diversification were prioritized to increase food production. The ninth and tenth five-year plans prioritized the agricultural sector based on the strategies outlined in the Agriculture Perspective Plan. The tenth five-year plan (2007–2010) emphasized agricultural commercialization and diversification. In its three-year interim plan (2010–2012), the government underscored transforming subsistence farming into commercial farming, increasing vertical linkages and boosting agricultural production and productivity. The Agriculture Perspective Plan underscored the diversification of agricultural production based on geographic location and agro-products commercialization. The policy's main aim is to transform the current system of subsistence-oriented farming into commercial and competitive farming.

Building on lessons learned from the Agricultural Perspective Plan, Nepal has approved a long-term Agriculture Development Strategy (2015–2034). Its goal is to create a self-reliant, sustainable, competitive and inclusive agricultural sector that drives economic growth and contributes to improved livelihoods and food and nutrition security. The strategy plans to accelerate agricultural sector growth through four strategic components related to governance, productivity, profitable commercialization and competitiveness.

The strategy takes into account the conceptual framework of agricultural transformation in Nepal from a society based primarily on agriculture to a society that derives most of its income from services and industry sectors. Therefore, the strategy considers not only the production sectors (crops, livestock, fisheries and forestry) but also the processing sector, trade and other services (storage, transportation and logistics, finance, marketing, research and extension). One promising target of the strategy is to increase agricultural land productivity (AGDP/ha) from $1,804 in 2010 to $4,787 in 2030 and lead the country toward structural transformation.

We briefly discuss the National Agriculture Policy (NAP) 2004, the Agri Business Promotion Policy 2006 and the National Cooperative Policy 2012, which have played vital roles in value chain development and agriculture commercialization in Nepal. The National Agriculture Policy 2004 is formulated to transform subsistence-oriented farming into commercial and competitive agriculture, contribute to food security and alleviate poverty. The policy's objectives are to increase agricultural productivity, expand commercial agricultural production and promote sustainable natural resource management. One of the policy's key strategies is to promote low-volume and high-value commodity production in remote areas. The policy proposes promotion of market-based, high-value commercial agricultural production along major highways and north–south road corridors; advancement of export-based organic farming; and support for cooperative farming and marketing of agricultural products. The policy aims to create an enabling environment for agriculture-led rural development and includes guidelines for the promotion of contract farming. The policy broadly classified farmers into two groups—resource-poor (those with less than 4 ha) and resource non-poor (those with 4 ha or more) and aims to provide proportionately more resources to the resource-poor farmers.

The Agri Business Promotion Policy 2006 was formulated to transform subsistence-oriented agricultural production systems into modern, sustainable, competitive and commercial production systems. The policy complements the National Agriculture Policy 2004, which emphasizes the establishment of business service centers to facilitate farmers' sustainable access to quality agriculture inputs and services. The Agri Business Promotion Policy 2006 emphasizes agricultural diversification, commercialization and promotion of the agriculture sector, encouraging the private sector's involvement in commercial farming. The policy encourages production of competitive and market-oriented agro-products and improvements in linkages with domestic and global markets. Further, the government formulated the Agribusiness Promotion Act 2017 with the goal of promoting agriculture by strengthening linkages between farmers and agribusiness persons. In this act, municipalities or professional organizations related to agriculture can establish agricultural markets in any suitable place, thus improving market access to local producers.

The National Cooperatives Policy 2012 was formulated to positively transform the society through an efficient cooperative system leading to sustainable and equitable economic development in Nepal. The cooperative sector has been recognized in the new constitution of Nepal 2015 as one of the national economy's three pillars. Accordingly, a new cooperative act and regulations were enacted in 2018 and 2019. Several cooperative societies related to dairy, fruits and vegetables, beekeeping, tea, coffee etc. now operate in Nepal.

Successful poultry value chain in Nepal

We illustrate with the case study of the Valley Group, a successful agribusiness in the poultry sector that has functioned well in the value chain approach. This is the only private company in the poultry industry that is vertically integrated from feed to food production and marketing. It has its own poultry feed industry, hatcheries, poultry farm, processing center, cold store, veterinary service center, breeding and research center, restaurant and market outlet. Such integration has reduced production costs by coordinating the capacity of each stage of production. By combining production stages into large vertically integrated firms, the company has been able to take advantage of rapidly changing technology.

Meat produced by the Valley Group is certified to ISO 22000:2005 and halal-certified. Meat products go through rigorous examination in Valley Group's own lab before distribution to market. Because of the quality meat production, Kentucky Fried Chicken (KFC) and modern market outlets are Valley Group's prime customers. It now produces 150 tons of feed and processes about 6,000 kg of meat per day. The company has progressed constantly since its establishment. It has been able to manage the value system and address supply chain problems of Nepal's scattered poultry-keeping activities, integrating several elements into its value chain system. Today, it is one of Nepal's five largest poultry feed industry and hatchery businesses.

The Valley Group started business in backyard farming, selling about 13 kg of broilers' meat in 1981. During those days, about 95% of the chicken was consumed by hotels and restaurants that mainly served tourists. Only 5% was consumed by domestic consumers as they were not used to consuming broilers' meat. The company made efforts to build consumer preferences and tastes and to create a market for broilers' meat. Over time, it learned that consumers prefer tender meat with high protein and much flesh. It also found that the meat quality was governed by the quality of the feed. To deliver quality meat to consumers, the company built its own feed industry in 1991 and recruited a feed specialist to formulate a balanced diet.

As time elapsed, the company learned that meat quality also is determined by the type of breeds. In 2001, it established its own breeding and hatchery farm by importing parent day-old chicks of improved and high-performance breeds (such as Cobbs 500). After the success of its feed industry and hatcheries, the company established its own poultry farm in 2003. Its own production meets 30% of the requirement, and it buys the rest from farmers under a contract farming scheme such that feed, chicks, veterinary services, technical advice, managerial expertise and market knowledge are provided to the farmers, and prices are fixed in advance. However, contract farming with fixed prices in advance did not work due to the high fluctuation of chicken meat prices. Side selling by growers was a huge problem when chicken meat prices became higher than what had been negotiated in the contract process. As a result, the company started a buyback scheme, buying live broilers at prevailing market prices and supplying the inputs and management care. The company has been working in this way to ensure the steady supply of broilers for its processing unit and its industrial customers (hotels and food processing firms).

After learning consumers' preferences for differentiated meat products such as boneless chicken, breasts, wings, drumsticks etc., in 2011 the Valley Group established a processing unit well equipped with a modern slaughterhouse. Taking into account increasing food safety and health consciousness, the company also obtained ISO 22000:2005 certification, complying with quality standards. In the last few years, the company established its own restaurant as well. The executive director of the company mentioned that companies that are limited to hatcheries, feed production or marketing are less likely to be sustained as they have no other means of diversifying their risks. For example, many hatcheries collapsed when chick prices plummeted last year. Several broiler production farms were shut down a few years ago due to rumors of the possible spread of bird flu. Today, the Valley Group's cold store has succeeded in developing a sustained network of reciprocal interdependence to ensure the quality and regularity of poultry products and services through well developed backward and forward linkages among value chain players.

Figure 5.5 depicts the supply channel of the Valley Group. The poultry value system includes the foundation stock, parent stock, hatcheries, poultry farm, slaughter and processing houses, cold store and market distribution. Depending on the breed types, the Valley Group either imports parent stocks from overseas or purchases them from a domestic company. At the breeding farm, the primary breeder produces breeder eggs and hatches them into breeder chicks. At company-owned hatcheries, the day-old commercial chicks are hatched, vaccinated and delivered to the farms of growers under contract. The company has a special agreement with suppliers, dealers and retailers who interact with and supply the necessary inputs, medicines, vaccines and technical services to the farmers. After five to seven weeks, the chicks reach marketable size. The live broilers are transported to and processed in the slaughterhouses, then packed

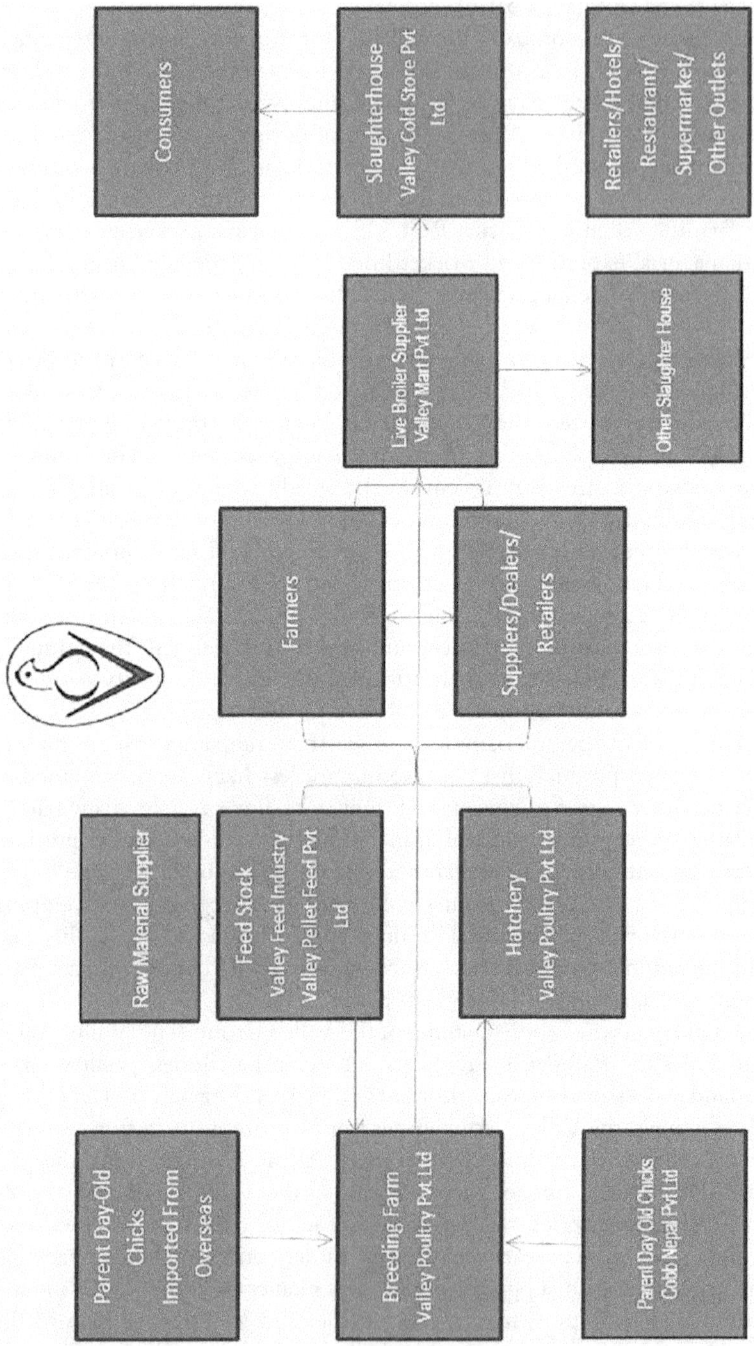

Figure 5.5 Supply chain of the Valley Group, Nepal

Source: Nepal Valley Group Pvt. Ltd.

and distributed to the market outlets. Figure 5.6 shows the Valley Group's cold store, poultry farm, slaughterhouse and retail outlet.

The Valley Group established Valley Feed to consistently supply quality feeds to the poultry farmers, and it established Valley Poultry to consistently supply chicks to the farmers. The company also established the Valley Mart to ensure a market for live broilers. The Valley Mart buys live broilers from farmers throughout the year. These live broilers are processed mainly at the company-owned slaughterhouse, although some firms may buy live broilers, slaughter them at their own facilities and sell them directly to consumers. The Valley Group processes the chicken and sells the processed, differentiated, packed and labeled products to consumers from its outlets or sells them to retailers, hotels, supermarkets and other market outlets. Due to the gradual

Figure 5.6 Glimpses of the Valley Group showing the valley cold store, poultry farm, slaughterhouse and retail outlet

Source: Nepal Valley Group Pvt. Ltd.

adoption of technological innovation, vertical integration and understanding and responding to market demands, the company has been a market leader in the poultry industry.

Conclusion and policy implications

Agricultural policies in Nepal have emphasized the transformation from subsistence-based farming to modern, sustainable, competitive and commercial-based production. However, the country's agricultural performance has not matched the policies' strategies and guidelines. Despite the poor performance of the agricultural sector, the absolute poverty rate and nutrition outcomes in Nepal have improved over time thanks to increasing remittances, which have raised household incomes and living standards for the Nepalese people. Remittances' share of the national economy has outpaced agriculture's share in recent years. Although the country may do fine with increasing remittances in the short run, remittances that the migrant-originating country receives can be highly vulnerable to shocks in the host country. As the major share of remittances is used for paying debts and buying food instead of creating productive assets, Nepal may face huge consequences if Middle Eastern countries alter their labor policy or go through an economic recession. Therefore, Nepal needs to revive its domestic agricultural sector to create job employment, alleviate poverty and increase net exports. The emergence and expansion of supermarkets and modern outlets during the last five years have revealed consumers' preferences for high-value, fresh and processed food products. This implies a huge market potential for smallholders in Nepal. Value chain development and contract farming can be suitable instruments to help these smallholders exploit the untapped market potential. This chapter examines the agricultural performance and assesses the scope for improvement considering the role of value chains and contract farming in the country.

Agricultural performance is not satisfactory in Nepal. The trade deficit has increased exponentially, but agricultural GDP growth is erratic and sluggish. Agricultural productivity is lower than in other South Asian countries. Public and private investment in agriculture is not promising. Agricultural commercialization is still at the embryonic stage due to the dominance of subsistence farming. Although the share of area in high-value crops has increased over time, cereal still dominates the total area and production in the country. Given the unique agro-climatic variability in Nepal, there is a huge potential for the country to expand its high-value crops. The increasing numbers of supermarkets and modern outlets and the rising incomes of urban consumers have increased demand for high-value crops. Contract farming and value chain development can be suitable instruments to help smallholders organize, to provide technological support including key inputs and to insure them against marketing risks.

Nepal has not yet enacted the contract farming act into law. Evidence shows that contract farming may fail in developing countries in the absence of legal settings and regulatory mechanisms to enforce contract agreements. Therefore, policy and legislation related to contract farming needs to be formulated and implemented urgently to enhance development of the agricultural sector. Many farmers in Nepal may not be aware of the importance and scope of contract farming. Such farmers should be taught about its potential benefit. Although the investment in high-value crops by agribusiness has been increasing in Nepal, technical assistance packages are required to increase the net returns on these investments. A limited number of agri-processors exist in specific value chains. Their numbers should be increased to address the increasing market demand and to achieve economies of scale of the value chain. Enterprises such as input providers (agrovets and the seed industry), agro-processors, marketing cooperatives, logistic companies, importers and exporters of agricultural products, distributors, traders and agricultural service providers play a crucial role in strengthening backward and forward linkages among value chain players. Therefore, promoting agro-enterprises is key for successful agricultural commercialization.

Given the Nepal's entry into the World Trade Organization (WTO), a developing market network and infrastructure is required for agricultural commercialization. The country has been importing inferior-quality agro-related goods due to the absence of modern food testing labs and trained inspectors. Absence of such facilities also has affected the quality of exports. Nepal has not fully developed the capacity to comply with the growing number of quality standards, which has restricted exports. For export promotion, Nepal needs to develop adequate capacity (trained inspectors) and infrastructure (food testing labs); develop collaborative participation among farmers, non-governmental organizations and private sectors; and make several agreements on food safety, quality standards, phytosanitary measures and quarantines.

In the new federal transition, the government has set up 51 Agriculture Knowledge Centers (AKC) across the country, instead of 75 District Agriculture Offices, and has deployed agricultural manpower at the new centers. Agriculture technicians employed in the service centers need to be well trained to support farmers on the technology and knowledge required for commercial farming. Shortages of key inputs such as fertilizer, a lack of perennial irrigation, high seed replacement rates, continuous use of traditional varieties and problematic market access have hindered agricultural commercialization in Nepal. Remote households suffer from high market transaction costs that significantly reduce their farms' profitability. Factors increasing farmers' transaction costs should be assessed, and necessary interventions should be made to reduce these costs. Commercial banks need to think beyond micro-credit when addressing the needs of commercial farmers and agribusinesses. Expanded road connectivity and improved road infrastructure should be given top priority. Infrastructure like rural electrification, irrigation and collection centers should be developed.

The country needs to expand agriculture insurance by providing adequate subsidies for insurance premiums in agriculture, livestock and fisheries. The current coverage of agriculture insurance is low and is limited to the few commodities. Due to weak promotion activities, farmers are not aware of the potential benefits of the insurance system. Government should modify the loan procedure related to investment in commercial agriculture and livestock by providing subsidies in interest on all types of bank loans. Government needs to promote the cooperatives by providing adequate subsidies for the purchase of equipment for the milk-, meat-, fruit- and vegetable-processing industries. Necessary arrangements should be made to help them purchase quality agricultural inputs at affordable prices. Sustainable farming, good agricultural practices and good veterinary animal husbandry practices need to be established and adopted.

Overall, Nepal's agricultural sector will attract more investment only when it is transformed to a more commercial and competitive industry. Only then can the sector support skilled and high-paid employment. The country needs to enable an environment that reduces the cost of domestic production and that makes its agricultural products highly competitive in the domestic and international markets.

Notes

1 Nepal ranges from 60 m to 8,848 m in altitude from the sea level. Such a high variation in altitude results in a wealth of micro agro-ecological conditions suitable for growing a variety of niche products (such as hill-grown tea, ayurvedic medicines, herbs, apple and high-altitude yak cheese).
2 The high-value commodities focused on were banana, cardamom, ginger, mango, orange, potato, tea and vegetables (tomato, onion and cabbage).
3 The project targeted population from ten high mountain districts (Dolakha, Dolpa, Humla, Jumla, Manang, Mugu, Mustang, Rasuwa, Sankhasabha and Solukhambu).

References

ADB. (2010). *Proposed Grant Nepal: Raising Incomes of Small and Medium Farmers Project.* Accessed via www.adb.org/sites/default/files/project-document/62354/38423-02-nep-rrp.pdf on 1/26/2020.

ADB. (2016). *Nepal: Commercial Agriculture Development Project.* Validation Report. Asian Development Bank. Accessed via www.adb.org/sites/default/files/evaluation-document/189247/files/pvr-448.pdf on 1/26/2020.

Basnett, Y., Henley, G., Howell, J., Jones, H., Lemma, A., & Pandey, P. R. (2014). *Structural Economic Transformation in Nepal.* Kathmandu, Nepal: A Diagnostic Study Submitted to DFID Nepal.

Basnett, Y., & Pandey, P. R. (2014). *Industrialization and Global Value Chain Participation: An Examination of Constraints Faced by the Private Sector in Nepal.* Asian Development Bank Economics Working Paper Series, (410).

Baumann, P. (2000). *Equity and Efficiency in Contract Farming Schemes: The experience of Agricultural Tree Crops.* ODI working paper 139.

Bellemare, M. F. (2012). As you sow, so shall you reap: The welfare impacts of contract farming. *World Development*, *40*(7), 1418–1434.

Bellemare, M. F., & Novak, L. (2017). Contract farming and food security. *American Journal of Agricultural Economics*, *99*(2), 357–378.

Bellora, C., Blanc, É., Bourgeon, J. M., & Strobl, E. (2017). *Estimating the Impact of Crop Diversity on Agricultural Productivity in South Africa* (No. w23496). National Bureau of Economic Research.

Bhatta, G. R. (2013). Remittance and trade deficit nexus in Nepal: A VECM approach. *NRB Economic Review*, *37*.

Bhattarai, S., Nepali, N., Thaller, J., Thewarapperuma, A., & Webb, J. (2013). *Promoting Agribusiness Innovation in Nepal, Feasibility Assessment for an Agribusiness Innovation Center.* Washington, DC: The World Bank.

Birthal, P. S., Joshi, P. K., Roy, D., & Thorat, A. (2013). Diversification in Indian agriculture toward high-value crops: The role of small farmers. *Canadian Journal of Agricultural Economics/Revue Canadienne D'agroeconomie*, *61*(1), 61–91.

Bista, D. R., Dhungel, S., & Adhikari, S. (2016). Status of fertilizer and seed subsidy in Nepal: Review and Recommendation. *Journal of Agriculture and Environment*, *17*, 1–10.

Briones, R. M. (2015). Small farmers in high-values chains: Binding or relaxing constraints to inclusive growth? *World Development*, *72*, 43–52.

Cai, J., Ung, L., Setboonsarng, S., & Leung, P. (2008). *Rice Contract Farming in Cambodia: Empowering Farmers to Move Beyond the Contract toward Independence.* Discussion Paper 109. Tokyo: Asian Development Bank Institute.

CBS. (2011). *Nepal Living Standard Survey*. Kathmandu, Nepal: Central Bureau of Statistics.

CBS. (2013). *National Sample Census of Agriculture Nepal, 2011/12*. Kathmandu, Nepal: Central Bureau of Statistics (CBS), National Planning Commission, Government of Nepal.

Chemonics International Inc. (2013). *Strengthening the Foundations for Inclusive Economic Growth*. Nepal Economic, Agriculture, and Trade (NEAT) Activity: Final Report. Submitted to the United States Agency for International Development (USAID). Accessed via www.chemonics.com/wp-content/uploads/2017/10/Nepal-NEAT-Final-Report.pdf on 1/26/2020.

Christiaensen, L., Demery, L., & Kuhl, J. (2011). The (evolving) role of agriculture in poverty reduction—An empirical perspective. *Journal of Development Economics*, *96*(2), 239–254.

Ciacci, R., Kaaria, S., Slavcheska, V., Townsend, R., Kar, A., & Mane, E. (2018). *Male Outmigration and Women's Work and Empowerment in Agriculture*. Washington, DC: World Bank Publications.

CIMMYT. (2014). Contract maize seed production started in Nepal. *Hill Maize Research Project, The International Maize and Wheat Improvement Center (CIMMYT)*. Accessed via http://hmrp.cimmyt.org/index.php/newsroom/51-contract-maize-seed-production-started-in-nepal on 1/25/2020.

Coulter, J., Goodland, A., Tallontire, A., & Stringfellow, R. (1999). Marrying farmer cooperation and contract farming for service provision in a liberalising sub-Saharan Africa. *Natural Resource Perspectives*, *48*, 1–4.

Deininger, K. W. (2003). *Land Policies for Growth and Poverty Reduction*. Washington, DC: World Bank Publications.

Di Falco, S., Smale, M., & Perrings, C. (2008). The role of agricultural cooperatives in sustaining the wheat diversity and productivity: The case of southern Italy. *Environmental and Resource Economics*, *39*(2), 161–174.

Diao, X., Thurlow, J., Benin, S., & Fan, S. (Eds.). (2012). *Strategies and Priorities for African Agriculture: Economywide Perspectives from Country Studies*. Washington, DC: The International Food Policy Research Institute.

DOI. (2011). *Industry Statistics*. Department of Industry, Ministry of Industry, Commerce and Supplies, Nepal Government.

DOL. (2018). *High Mountain Agribusiness and Livelihood Project (HIMALI)*. Project Completion Report. Submitted by the Government of Nepal, Ministry of Livestock Development, Department of Livestock Services.

Dolan, C., & Humphrey, J. (2000). Governance and trade in fresh vegetables: The impact of UK supermarkets on the African horticulture industry. *Journal of Development Studies*, *37*(2), 147–176.

FAOSTAT. (2017). *Food and Agriculture Organization (FAO) of the United Nation*. Rome, Italy: United Nation.

Fearne, A., Martinez, M. G., & Dent, B. (2012). Dimensions of sustainable value chains: implications for value chain analysis. *Supply Chain Management: An International Journal*, *17*(6), 575–581.

Francesconi, G. N., & Wouterse, F. (2015). Promoting the role of farmer-based organizations for value chain integration: The tension between a program's targeting and an organization's investment strategy. *Agricultural Economics*, *46*(4), 527–536.

Ghezán, G., Mateos, M., & Viteri, L. (2002). Impact of supermarkets and fast—food chains on horticulture supply chains in Argentina. *Development Policy Review*, *20*(4), 389–408.

Gurung, M. B., Partap, U., & Choudhary, D. (2015). Empowering mountain women through community-based high value product value chain promotion in Nepal. *International Journal of Agricultural Resources, Governance and Ecology*, *11*(3–4), 330–345.

Haggblade, S., Hazell, P. B., & Dorosh, P. A. (2007). Sectoral growth linkages between agriculture and the rural nonfarm economy. *Transforming the Rural Nonfarm Economy: Opportunities and Threats in the Developing World*, 141–182.

Henderson, H., & Isaac, A. G. (2017). Modern value chains and the organization of Agrarian production. *American Journal of Agricultural Economics*, *99*(2), 379–400.

Huddleston, P., & Tonts, M. (2007). Agricultural development, contract farming and Ghana's oil palm industry. *Geography*, *92*(3), 266–278.

IFAD. (2018). *High-Value Agriculture Project in Hill and Mountain Areas Supervision Report*. International Fund for Agricultural Development. Accessed via https://operations.ifad.org/documents/654016/24c3d9a7-8cb5-4ee0-8a61-71230397e664 on 1/26/2020.

ILO. (2019). *ILO Stats*. International Labour Organization. Retrieved January 26, 2020.

Joshi, G. R. (2018). *Agricultural Economy of Nepal: Development Challenges & Opportunities*. Kathmandu: Sustainable Research & Development Center.

Kalamkar, S. S. (2012). Inputs and services delivery system under contract farming: A case of broiler farming §. *Agricultural Economics Research Review*, *25*(conf), 515–521.

Key, N., & Runsten, D. (1999). Contract farming, smallholders, and rural development in Latin America: The organization of agroprocessing firms and the scale of outgrower production. *World Development*, *27*(2), 381–401.

Khanal, A. R., & Mishra, A. K. (2018). *Impacts of Contract Farming Decisions on High Value Crop Production of Smallholder Nepalese Farmers: A Multinomial Endogenous Switching Regression Approach*. Washington, DC: Agricultural & Applied Economics Association Annual Meeting, August 5–August 7.

Khanal, U. (2018). Why are farmers keeping cultivatable lands fallow even though there is food scarcity in Nepal? *Food Security*, *10*(3), 603–614.

Kirsten, J., & Sartorius, K. (2002). Linking agribusiness and small-scale farmers in developing countries: Is there a new role for contract farming? *Development Southern Africa, 19*(4), 503–529.

Kulkarni, S., & Grethe, H. (2009). *Does Vertical Integration Benefit Farming Community? A Comparative Study of Contract and Noncontract Farmers in India*. Leuven: Katholic University of Leuven.

Kumar, A., Roy, D., Joshi, P. K., Tripathi, G., & Adhikari, R. P. (2019). Impact of contract farming of paddy seed on smallholder farm profits: evidence from Nepal. *Agricultural Economics Research Review, 32*(1), 25–39.

Kumar, A., Roy, D., Trapathi, G., Joshi, P. K., & Adhikari, R. P. (2016). *Can Contract Farming Increase Farmers' Income and Enhance Adoption of Food Safety Practices? Evidence from Remote Areas of Nepal* (Vol. 1524). Washington, DC: The International Food Policy Research Institute.

Kumar, A., Thapa, G., Mishra, A. K., & Joshi, P. K. (2020). Assessing food and nutrition security in Nepal: Evidence from diet diversity and food expenditure patterns. *Food Security*, 1–28.

Little, P. D., & Watts, M. (Eds.). (1994). *Living Under Contract: Contract Farming and Agrarian Transformation in Sub-Saharan Africa*. Wisconsin: University of Wisconsin Press.

Lokshin, M., Bontch-Osmolovski, M., & Glinskaya, E. (2010). Work-related migration and poverty reduction in Nepal. *Review of Development Economics, 14*(2), 323–332.

Masakure, O., & Henson, S. (2005). Why do small-scale producers choose to produce under contract? Lessons from nontraditional vegetable exports from Zimbabwe. *World Development, 33*(10), 1721–1733.

Meemken, E. M., & Bellemare, M. F. (2020). Smallholder farmers and contract farming in developing countries. *Proceedings of the National Academy of Sciences, 117*(1), 259–264.

Michelson, H. C. (2013). Small farmers, NGOs, and a Walmart world: Welfare effects of supermarkets operating in Nicaragua. *American Journal of Agricultural Economics, 95*(3), 628–649.

Mishra, A. K., Kumar, A., Joshi, P. K., & D'souza, A. (2016). Impact of contracts in high yielding varieties seed production on profits and yield: The case of Nepal. *Food Policy, 62*, 110–121.

Mishra, A. K., Kumar, A., Joshi, P. K., & D'Souza, A. (2018a). Cooperatives, contract farming, and farm size: The case of tomato producers in Nepal. *Agribusiness, 34*(4), 865–886.

Mishra, A. K., Kumar, A., Joshi, P. K., & D'Souza, A. (2018b). Impact of contract farming on yield, costs and profitability in low-value crop: Evidence from a low-income country. *Australian Journal of Agricultural and Resource Economics, 62*(4), 589–607.

MOAD. (2011). *Statistical Information on Nepalese Agriculture. Ministry of Agricultural Development*. Singha Durbar, Kathmandu, Nepal: Monitoring, Evaluation and Statistics Division Agri Statistics Section.

MOAD. (2017). *Statistical Information on Nepalese Agriculture. Ministry of Agricultural Development*. Singha Durbar, Kathmandu, Nepal: Monitoring, Evaluation and Statistics Division Agri Statistics Section.

NADS. (2016). *Final Report*. Kathmandu, Nepal: Agriculture Development Strategy.

Narrod, C., Roy, D., Okello, J., Avendaño, B., Rich, K., & Thorat, A. (2009). Public—private partnerships and collective action in high value fruit and vegetable supply chains. *Food Policy, 34*(1), 8–15.

NMOF. (2018). *Economic Survey: Fiscal Year 2017/18*. Kathmandu, Nepal: Ministry of Finance.

NMOF. (2019). *Economic Survey: Fiscal Year 2018/19*. Kathmandu, Nepal: Ministry of Finance.

Pant, B. (2010). Enhancing foreign development investment flows to Nepal during the period of post-conflict transition and global recession. *NRB Economic Review*, *22*, 19–39.

Paudel, R., & Waglé, S. (2019). Structural transformation and growth: Whither agriculture in Nepal? In *Agricultural Transformation in Nepal* (pp. 11–25). Singapore: Springer.

Pokharel, C. (2019). Agricultural diversification in Nepal. In *Agricultural Transformation in Nepal* (pp. 323–384). Singapore: Springer.

Prowse, M. (2012). *Contract Farming in Developing Countries: A Review*. In (A Savoir 12). Paris: Agence Française de Développement.

Reardon, T., & Berdegué, J. A. (2002). The rapid rise of supermarkets in Latin America: challenges and opportunities for development. *Development Policy Review*, *20*(4), 371–388.

Sharma, R. (2019). Trends, structure and drivers of Nepal's agricultural trade. In *Agricultural Transformation in Nepal* (pp. 443–474). Singapore: Springer.

Shively, G., & Thapa, G. (2017). Markets, transportation infrastructure, and food prices in Nepal. *American Journal of Agricultural Economics*, *99*(3), 660–682.

Simmons, P., Winters, P., & Patrick, I. (2005). An analysis of contract farming in East Java, Bali, and Lombok, Indonesia. *Agricultural Economics*, *33*, 513–525.

Singh, O. P., Singh, P. K., Singh, H. P., Singh, R., & Regmi, K. R. (2013). A value chain analysis of vegetables: A case study of Palpa District, Nepal. *Economic Affairs*, *58*(2), 135–146.

Singh, S. (2002). Contracting out solutions: Political economy of contract farming in the Indian Punjab. *World Development*, *30*(9), 1621–1638.

Swinnen, J. F., & Maertens, M. (2007). Globalization, privatization, and vertical coordination in food value chains in developing and transition countries. *Agricultural Economics*, *37*, 89–102.

Tamang, S., Paudel, K. P., & Shrestha, K. K. (2014). Feminization of agriculture and its implications for food security in rural Nepal. *Journal of Forest and Livelihood*, *12*(1), 20–32.

Thapa, G., & Shively, G. (2018). A dose-response model of road development and child nutrition in Nepal. *Research in Transportation Economics*, *70*, 112–124.

Thapa, G., Kumar, A., Roy, D., & Joshi, P. K. (2018). Impact of crop diversification on rural poverty in Nepal. *Canadian Journal of Agricultural Economics/Revue Canadienne D'agroeconomie*, *66*(3), 379–413.

UNDP. (2018). *Value Chain Development of Fruit and Vegetables in Nepal (2018–2022 / USD 5,500,000)*. Project Document. United Nations Development Programme. Access via www.np.undp.org/content/dam/nepal/docs/projects/ProDoc_value%20chain%20project2018.pdf on 1/26/2020.

Valentinov, V. (2007). Why are cooperatives important in agriculture? An organizational economics perspective. *Journal of Institutional Economics*, *3*(1), 55–69.

Wasti, K. (2017). Remittances and long-term livelihood security in the Mountains of Nepa 155. *International Labor Migration and Livelihood Security in Nepal: Considering the Household Level*, *22*, 113.

WB. (2007). *World Development Report 2008: Agriculture for Development*. New York: Oxford University Press.

WB. (2019). Implementation completion and results report. Project for Agriculture Commercialization and Trade (PACT). Assessed via http://documents.worldbank.org/curated/en/796931552077915059/pdf/ icr00004552-03052019-636875928851271059.pdf on 1/26/2020.

WDI. (2018). *World Development Indicators*. Washington, DC: World Bank.

6 Financing agricultural value chains

Pratap S. Birthal, Pramod K. Joshi and Jaweriah Hazrana

Among other things, imperfections in product and credit markets are important constraints on the diversification and commercialization of agriculture in smallholder-dominated agrarian economies (Meenakshi and Benerjei, 2005; Pingali et al., 2005; Negi et al., 2018). In South Asia, landholdings measuring less than or equal to 1 ha comprise about 63% of total landholdings but account for less than one-fifth of the agricultural land (Lowder et al., 2016). A majority of smallholder farmers remain stuck in subsistence production, despite the expanding market opportunities for diversification of agriculture toward high-value food commodities, i.e., fruits, vegetables, milk, meat, fish and eggs.

The agri-food markets in South Asia are fragmented (Chand, 2012). Food supply chains are long, dominated by a number of intermediaries from production to end consumption, leading to high market costs and margins, and a low share for producers in the final price that consumers pay. Market constraint is more binding on the farmers who cultivate small pieces of land and produce small surpluses for the market. Rural markets, especially for high-value food commodities, are thin, and trading the small quantities in distant urban markets is not remunerative because of the higher transaction costs (Pingali et al., 2005; Birthal et al., 2005). Most of these farmers sell their produce to local traders, who often exploit them by paying less than the market price (Negi et al., 2018). There is evidence that even in the organized or government-regulated markets, farmers receive less than the prevailing market prices because of their poor bargaining power vis-à-vis large traders or commission agents (Negi et al., 2018) and because of the cartelization of traders and commission agents (Meenakshi and Benerjei, 2005).

Leaving aside imperfections in the output market, the transformation of smallholder agriculture is severely constrained by farmers' poor access to financial resources for the adoption of market-driven production portfolios and investment in land improvement, irrigation, farm mechanization etc. Enterprises like horticulture, floriculture, plantation and animal husbandry require substantial initial investment, have longer gestation periods and are more prone to production and price risks, all discouraging smallholders from undertaking or scaling up such enterprises.

Although smallholder farmers do not have big financial requirements, commercial banks and other such financial institutions rarely prefer lending to them because of the higher transaction costs and lending risks associated with small loans. Smallholder farmers have limited physical assets, often undocumented, to offer as collateral for securing loans from the financial institutions, and the financial institutions confront asymmetric information on the potential borrowers. Policy-induced distortions (e.g., subsidies and loan waivers) also discourage financial institutions from lending to smallholder farmers. However, there is an increasing realization among policymakers, agricultural industry and other stakeholders that some of the marketing and financial constraints on the transformation of smallholder subsistence agriculture can be alleviated by following a value chain approach that links flows of goods and services between different stakeholders, including farmers, aggregators, traders and processors (Meyer, 2007; Trienekens, 2011).

For financial institutions, a value chain is an entry point for integrating their financial products and services along the chain. Financial institutions often confront the problem of information asymmetry on potential borrowers, leading to higher search and information costs and lending risks. The chain actors, on the other hand, being from the same sociocultural environment, possess ample information on one another's activities and attributes, which financial institutions can acquire at negligible cost (Meyer, 2007; Casuga et al., 2008; Miller and Jones, 2010; Miller, 2012) for evaluating the creditworthiness of the chain actors, analyzing the business risks and assessing the competitiveness of the entire value chain. More importantly, a value chain, because of its product market orientation, can serve as a guarantee or collateral to advance loans to the chain actors.

Based on a review of empirical literature, this chapter explores prospects for improving the interface between financial institutions and product markets through a value chain approach. The following section discusses opportunities for value chain development in South Asia. The conceptual framework of value chain finance is discussed in the third section. The fourth section provides a brief review of a few successful value chain models, focusing on their financing mechanisms, efficiency and inclusiveness, and the fifth section discusses their economic impacts. The sixth section discusses lessons drawn from this review.

Opportunities for agribusiness and value chain development

Opportunities for the development of agribusiness in South Asia are vast. Over the past few decades, South Asian countries have experienced robust positive trends in per capita income, urbanization and information and communication technology that have caused a perceptible shift in consumers' dietary patterns away from staple food grains toward nutrient-rich food commodities such as fruits, vegetables, milk, meat, fish and eggs (Pingali, 2005; Minten et al., 2012; Joshi and Kumar, 2016). Consumers also are becoming increasingly aware of the health benefits of safe and quality foods. The trends in these factors have been quite robust recently and are unlikely to subside soon, implying a faster growth in the demand for these commodities. Global demand for high-value commodities also has been expanding quickly, especially in developing countries. The growing demand for high-value food commodities offers considerable scope for processors, traders, exporters and retailers to expand their business by integrating their 'front-end' activities of wholesaling, processing, logistics and retailing with the 'back-end' activities of production (procurement of outputs, provision of inputs and services) through institutional arrangements like contract farming, cooperatives and producers' associations.

On the supply side, although smallholder farmers operate on a tiny scale, they make a substantial contribution to agricultural production. They have larger endowments of labor in relation to land and thus possess a comparative advantage over large farmers in labor-intensive, high-value agricultural activities (Chand et al., 2011; Birthal et al., 2014, 2015), in terms of yield as well as the cost of production. Smallholder production systems therefore have better prospects for the diversification-led growth of agriculture and the development of efficient and inclusive value chains.

To harness growth opportunities in the high-value segment of agriculture, most countries in South Asia have begun reforming agricultural markets. The process includes liberalizing domestic markets for greater participation by the private sector, allowing foreign direct investment (FDI) in food processing and retailing and rationalizing taxes and duties on processed food products and manufacturing machinery. Reforms also have been undertaken in the financial sector to accelerate the flow of institutional credit to agriculture and agriculture-based industries: for example, group lending and the provision of credit cards to farmers in India. These reforms, to an extent, have succeeded in achieving their objective of attracting private investment in the procurement, processing and retailing of agricultural commodities. This is visible from a rapid rise in supermarkets and organized food retail sales, accompanied by the emergence of institutions such as contract farming and producers' associations that link farmers to remunerative markets (Reardon et al., 2012).

Conceptual framework for value chain finance

A value chain refers to 'the organized links between the groups of producers, traders, processors and service providers, including non-government organizations, that join together to improve productivity and the value added from their activities' (ADB, 2013). Value chains differ in their governance structure; therefore, the mechanisms of financing value chains may differ depending on the business model these are built upon. A value chain could be producer driven, buyer driven or facilitator driven. A producer-driven value chain represents the collective strength of producers and is developed to improve producers' access to remunerative markets, reduce transaction costs and improve their bargaining power with buyers. Examples include producers' associations, cooperatives and self-help groups. Notwithstanding these benefits, participants in producer-driven value chains may face difficulties in understanding market dynamics that are becoming complex in view of the increasing globalization of agri-food markets (Miller, 2012).

Buyers—traders, processors, retailers and exporters—also develop value chains to gain control over the production process and optimally utilize their resources, infrastructure and manpower; to consolidate their market position; and to reduce the costs of aggregating scattered marketable surplus. Such a value chain is termed a buyer-driven value chain, of which contract farming is a common form. Buyer-driven value chains often face criticism. Sponsors of these chains often exclude smallholder farmers and small-scale entrepreneurs because of the higher costs of contracting with a large number of them. Another criticism is that buyer-driven value chains confer monopsonistic power on the sponsors to extract rent from the producers. Therefore, to facilitate participation of smallholder farmers in the value chains, civil society organizations and government agencies help producers form cooperatives and/or producers' associations to improve their bargaining power with buyers. Sometimes, the buyers also promote collective action to avoid the marketing and transaction costs of contracting with a large number of producers. Such value chains are termed facilitator-driven value chains.

Irrespective of the type of value chain, one motive for different stakeholders to participate in value chains is to gain access to finance (Maertens et al., 2007; Minten et al., 2009; Reardon and Minten, 2011). Finances can be accessed from within the value chain or from outside the value chain. In the case of within-chain finance, the lender may be a trader, a processor or a retailer, and he or she extends financial support to producers against the commitment of sale of produce. External financing refers to lending by financial institutions to chain actors with or without facilitation by the chain sponsor. Chain actors can gain access to credit from financial institutions using product market orientation of the value chain as collateral or guarantee. On the other hand, for financial institutions, a value chain can reduce the transaction costs and lending risks associated with small loans (Miller and Jones, 2010). Figure 6.1 demonstrates the interface between financial institutions and value chain actors.

Casuga et al. (2008) argue that internal chain financing plays an important role in the initial phases of value chain development. However, as value chains consolidate and improve their efficiency and market position, financial institutions face lower transaction costs and lending risks, and external financing may overtake internal financing.

Mechanisms of financing value chains

Smallholder farmers in South Asia have traditionally relied on informal markets both for selling their outputs and for securing financial requirements. Farmers often obtain their financial requirements (cash or inputs) from the lenders (e.g., moneylenders, traders, commission agents and input dealers), supposedly

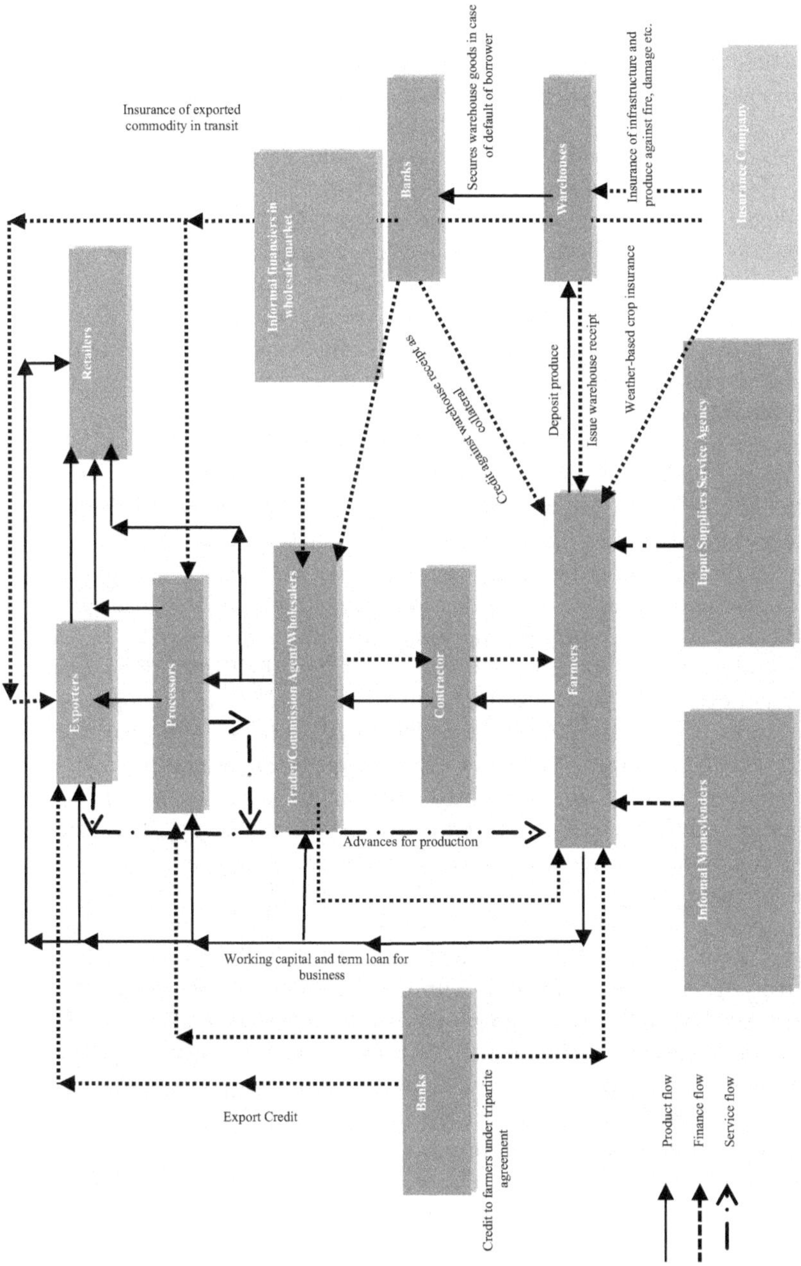

Figure 6.1 Flow of credit along the value chain

Source: Adapted from Chen et al. (2015) and Birthal and Joshi (2017).

against a commitment of the sale of their produce after harvest (Mitra, 1982; Gill, 2004; Negi et al., 2018). Such interlinked transactions have been shown to exploit farmers in terms of exorbitantly higher interest rates and underpriced produce (Gill, 2004).

Nonetheless, with reforms in product and financial markets, the incidence of such uncontrolled buyer–seller relationships has been declining. For example, in India, with the increasing outreach of financial institutions, farmers' financial dependence on informal money lenders, including traders, has declined considerably in the past four decades (GoI, 2014). This is expected as product markets move from uncontrolled buyer–seller relationships toward vertical coordination and as prospects for financing chain activities both from within and outside the chain become brighter (Miller, 2012). In South Asia, the agricultural value chains and their financing mechanisms have yet to develop, but there is evidence that the value chains in some commodities have built-in financing mechanisms. A few such evidences, mostly from India, are discussed next (Table 6.1).

India's dairy cooperative model, a form of producer-driven value chains, is acclaimed globally for its success in linking small-scale dairy producers to remunerative markets. Upstream, the dairy farmers are organized into village-level dairy cooperative societies, which are federated into district-level milk unions, which in turn are federated into milk unions at the state level. A key factor in dairy cooperatives' success has been their integration with financial institutions. Initial financial support for developing cooperatives came from the World Bank under a project called Operation Flood, implemented by the National Dairy Development Board (NDDB) from 1970 to 1996. The bank recently provided financial support for developing integrated dairy value chains. The village dairy cooperatives also facilitate farmers' access to credit from financial institutions for the purchase of dairy animals and the construction of cattle sheds. Financing happens through a quadripartite agreement involving farmers, dairy cooperatives, commercial banks and insurance providers. Dairy cooperatives also provide finance in terms of cattle feed and breeding and health services.

Contract farming is a common form of buyer-driven value chains in broilers, where chain-based financing is quite prominent. Production activities are financed using resources from both within the chain and outside the chain. Internal financing is done through provision of inputs—day-old chicks, feed and medicines—by chain sponsors or lead firms. These inputs account for about three-fourths of the total cost of broiler production. Risk sharing is another important feature of contract farming of broilers: sponsors share production and market risks. Sharing of production risk is limited to 5% of the mortality rate (Birthal et al., 2005). The lead firm absorbs market risk through its pricing mechanism. Producers are offered fixed growing charges (based on the average body weight of broilers) irrespective of the prevailing market prices. Thus, besides performing the market function, contract farming also assumes the roles of banking and insurance. A few sponsors also facilitate the financing of back end activities from commercial banks through a tripartite agreement.

Table 6.1 Value chain models and their financing mechanisms

Value chain	*Type value chain*	*Main features*	*Location*	*Financing*	*Source*
AMUL Dairy Cooperatives	Producer driven	Initially producer driven, later supported by government to develop market	All India	Internal External	Gandhi and Jain (2011) www.amul.com; www.nddb.org.
Mahagrapes	Facilitator driven	Aims mainly exporting grapes, facilitates food safety compliance	Maharashtra	Internal	Roy and Thorat (2008)
Mother Dairy Fruits and Vegetable Ltd.	Facilitator driven	Informal producer organizations, provided technical guidance on crop planning, standards	Northern India	Internal	Birthal et al. (2005)
Kesla Poultry Cooperative	Facilitator driven	Promoted by non-governmental organization to scale up subsistence poultry	Madhya Pradesh	Internal	SA PPLPP (2009) http://mpwpcl.org/kesla.htm.
Koutla-B Mutually Aided Cooperative Society (MACS)	Facilitator driven	Promoted by micro-finance company to reduce farmers' exploitation in input and output markets	Andhra Pradesh	External	Amarnath (2007)
Agrocel Pure and Fair Cotton Growers' Association	Facilitator driven	Promoted by the lead firm to produce organic cotton for export markets	Gujarat	Internal	Neslon and Smith (2011), www.fairtrade.org.uk
Sunstar Organic Basmati Rice Growers' Association	Facilitator driven	Promoted by the lead firm to produce organic Basmati rice for export	Uttarakhand	Internal	www.sunstaroverseas.com
Farmer-producer Organization (FPO)	Facilitator driven	A holistic approach to develop backward and forward linkages followed by the government of India	All India	External	GoI (2013); www.sfacindia.com

(*Continued*)

Table 6.1 (Continued)

Value chain	*Type value chain*	*Main features*	*Location*	*Financing*	*Source*
Contract farming in broilers	Buyer driven	A number of firms engaged in contract farming of broilers Written contracts Risk sharing	Southern and western India	Internal	Birthal et al. (2005); Ramaswami et al. (2009), www.venkys.com. www.sugunapoultry.com
Contract farming of milk by Nestle India Ltd.	Buyer driven	Promoted by lead firm to source milk from small producers through village collection centers Mutual trust between buyer and sellers	Punjab, Haryana	Internal External	Birthal et al. (2005), Gandhi and Jain (2011)
Contract farming of milk by Heritage Foods (India) Ltd.	Buyer driven	Promoted by lead firm to source milk from small producers through village collection centers Provides loans	Andhra Pradesh, Karnataka, Maharashtra	Internal External	Gandhi and Jain (2011) www.heritagefoods.co.in.
Dairy lease model of Samridhi Agri Products Pvt. Ltd.	Buyer driven	Unique model to improve asset base of farmers	Uttar Pradesh	External	www.samridhiindia.com.
Contract farming of potatoes by PepsiCo	Buyer driven	Third-party facilitated contract with small producers with provision of finance, insurance and services	Jharkhand	Internal	Amarnath (2007)
Contract farming of seaweed by PepsiCo.	Buyer driven	Third-party facilitated contract with small producers with provision of finance, insurance and services	Tamil Nadu	Internal External	Casuga et al. (2008)

Source: Extracted from Chen et al. (2015).

Many dairy processors (e.g., the global dairy giant Nestle S.A.) also procure milk through contracts, but the contract mechanism is different than for broilers. Generally, the lead firms enter a contract agreement with large dairy farmers, but milk from small farmers is sourced through the village collection centers managed by local agents for a fee (Birthal et al., 2005). The lead firms provide cattle feed and animal health and breeding services. Lead firms purchase cattle feed in bulk at wholesale price and, after adjusting for transport and other costs, sell it to producers at a price lower than the retail price. Some lead firms also provide direct finance to farmers and their milk collection agents (e.g., Heritage Foods Ltd. in Andhra Pradesh, India), and they facilitate financing from commercial banks through a tripartite agreement. Milk prices are determined based on fat and solid non-fat contents but are competitive.

An innovative model of integrating a credit market with a product market was conceptualized and implemented by Samridhi Agri Products Pvt. Ltd. in Uttar Pradesh, India (www.samridhiindia.com). The firm purchases in-milk dairy animals and, after getting them insured, leases them to poor households against their commitment of the sale of milk and proper management of the animals. The firm also provides cattle feed and health and breeding services. On completion of the lease, the firm takes back the animals, leaving their offspring for the farmers (at no cost). This helps build up productive assets, essential for escaping poverty.

A similar value chain was developed by PRADAN (Professional Assistance for Development Action), a non-governmental organization, for transforming backyard poultry into a marketed-oriented activity in the tribal-dominated Kesla block of Hoshangabad District in Madhya Pradesh, India. PRADAN organized households into Self-Help Groups (SHGs) to enable them to obtain funds from commercial banks and government-run rural development and poverty alleviation programs (http://sapplpp.org/goodpractices/small-holder-poultry/SAGP03-making-modern-poultry-markets-work-for-the-poor/#.UxmXJU1WEdU). It facilitated self-help groups' linkages with hatcheries and feed manufacturers. Later, the self-help groups were federated to form a cooperative society, known as the Kesla Poultry Cooperative Society. Initially, the society sold its produce in neighboring towns, but it later set up its own retail outlets in larger cities. The society is now a producer company named the Madhya Pradesh Women Poultry Producers Company Pvt. Ltd. It has its own hatcheries and feed manufacturing units, and it maintains reserves to protect farmers from production and price risks.

Cotton is highly prone to pest risks. Before the introduction of Bt cotton in India, cotton farmers often bought pesticides from input dealers-cum-commission agents against their commitment of the sale of produce. Such an interlinked arrangement exploited farmers. BASIX, a microfinance and livelihood promotion institution, saw an opportunity in such unscrupulous practices to expand its lending base. It started providing crop loans to farmers in Koutla-B village in the Adilabad District of Andhra Pradesh, India, through joint liability groups that could buy pesticides and inputs in bulk at wholesale prices (Amarnath, 2007). Encouraged by its initial success, BASIX facilitated formation of a mutually aided cooperative society named Koutla-B MACS and linked it to spinning mills for selling their produce. Price is determined based on the daily market prices prevailing in major cotton markets. Koutla-B MACS is now a producers' company.

Following the joint liability approach, BASIX also facilitated contract farming of potatoes on behalf of PepsiCo Inc. in the Indian states of Bihar and Jharkhand (Amarnath, 2007). Under this agreement, PepsiCo provided seeds and a package of practices, and BASIX provided financial support for farmers' purchase of fertilizers and pesticides and trained them in good production practices. In a similar way, PepsiCo promoted contract farming of seaweeds in Tamil Nadu, India. It encouraged farmers to form self-help groups to access financial support from commercial banks (Casuga et al., 2008).

Several export-oriented agribusiness firms (e.g., Agrocel Industries Ltd. and Sunstar Overseas Ltd.) rely on growers' associations for their requirements of organic produce (Nelson and Smith, 2011). Agrocel promotes organic cotton and Sunstar organic rice, conforming to fair-trade standards in the Indian states of Gujarat and Uttarakhand, respectively. The cost of organic certification is quite high for individual farmers, and these firms facilitate group certification for the produce. They provide inputs and extension services and interest-free loans to their clients, and they help them access credit from financial institutions. The pricing strategy is linked with international market prices. Fair trade pays an additional premium of 5%–10%, a part of which the farmers share, and the rest is invested in community development projects. Likewise, Mahagrapes, an apex organization of grape growers' cooperatives in Maharashtra, India, helps farmers participate in export-oriented value chains and provides them with quality inputs, services and on-farm storage facilities (Roy and Thorat, 2008).

Mother Dairy Fruits and Vegetables Ltd. (MDFVL), a subsidiary of the National Dairy Development Board, procures its requirements of fruits and vegetables from informal producers' associations for retailing in metropolitan Delhi (Birthal and Joshi, 2007). It supports farmers in their agricultural land allocation decisions based on its demand forecasts for different fruits and vegetables, provides them technical support and links them to input dealers. The firm's pricing strategy is based on the open market price. It offers a small premium on the modal price prevailing in the Delhi market.

Recently, India has started a mega-program of linking farmers to markets through farmer-producer organizations (FPOs). These organizations blend the spirit of cooperation and the principles of sustainable business (GoI, 2013). Interest groups are formed at the village level, then federated into a producer organization. Farmer producer organizations facilitate market linkages with processors, traders and retailers and coordinate supply and demand. They also facilitate the access of farmers' interest groups to input suppliers, research institutions and commercial banks. Funding support for these organizations comes from India's premier financial institution, the National Bank for Agriculture and Rural Development (NABARD).

Economic impacts

Several recent studies have shown that producers gain from participation in value chains irrespective of the business models the chains are built upon. Kumar (2006) estimated net revenue from contract farming of several crops was almost twice that from independent farming. Similar findings are reported in Birthal et al. (2005), Birthal and Joshi (2007), Gupta and Roy (2011) and Vandeplas et al. (2013) in the case of dairying.

The question is how do participants gain from value chains? The gains accrue from (1) reductions in marketing and transaction costs because of the assured purchase of produce and supply of inputs and services by the firms, (2) adoption of improved technologies and practices, resulting in higher yields and lower production costs, (3) better output price realization and (4) reduction in production and market risks.

In their analysis of milk and vegetable value chains, Birthal et al. (2005) found that producers benefit from participating in value chains mainly because of lower marketing and transaction costs. Such costs guzzle 15%–20% of the producer price, but contracts reduce those by 66%–90%. They also find that chain sponsors' provision of inputs, technologies, information and services contributes to higher profit realization via increases in yields and reductions in production cost. Singh and Singla (2011) also provide similar evidence. Kumar (2006), on the other hand, attribute most gains to higher yields.

Risk transfer and financing are the mains function of contract farming in commodities like broilers. Ramaswami et al. (2009) have shown that lead firms' provision of inputs and services reduces farmers' dependence on financial institutions for their capital requirements. Further, through income contracts, the producers shift as much as 88% of the market or price risk to the sponsors. In case of contract farming of milk, lead firms bear the entire risk if machines fail at the collection centers (Birthal et al., 2005). Some cooperative societies (e.g., Kesla Poultry Cooperative Society) maintain reserves to protect farmers from market and production risks.

Lessons learned

The increasing commercialization of agriculture creates scope for the development of value chains and chain-based financing. From a review of some successful models, we find that a value chain approach has the potential to improve small farmers' access to inputs, output markets and credit; reduce marketing and transaction costs; and mitigate supply and market risks. Nonetheless, agricultural value chains in South Asia have yet to develop. Developing value chains and their financing mechanisms are a challenge, but the challenge is not insurmountable if value chain sponsors, financial institutions and policymakers adopt innovative approaches. A few important lessons that we draw from the existing studies on value chains in South Asia are as follows:

- Poor economies of scale deter the evolution of agricultural value chains in South Asia. This implies the need for a collective approach at the farm level to overcome the scale limitations. However, to operationalize the collective action, some non-governmental or governmental organizations have to mediate it. The government should encourage producer organizations to aggregate outputs for marketing and to source and distribute inputs and financial and non-financial services. Such organizations should be empowered to identify market opportunities and develop linkages upstream and downstream within the chain and in agricultural laws, food safety compliance procedures, financial systems, conflict management etc. Agribusiness firms also can promote collective action by collaborating with non-governmental organizations.
- Breach of contract is an important issue for sellers and buyers. It happens primarily because of prefixed prices. When the market price is less than the prefixed price, the agribusiness firms tend to buy from the market, and when the market price is higher than the agreed price, the sellers engage in extra-contractual sales. Evidence from successful value chains suggests that agribusiness firms should consider open-market prices as the base of their pricing strategy, allowing a premium as an incentive for sellers to discourage them from extra-contractual sales. Further, institutional mechanisms need to evolve to facilitate the formalization of contracts and the resolution of conflicts and disputes.
- In the case of input supplies, the value chain sponsors, who often buy in bulk at wholesale prices, should transfer part of their price margin to their clients in order to strengthen buyer–seller relationships.
- Value chains are an important entry point for financial institutions to integrate their financial products with product markets. Financial institutions should recognize the value chains' product market orientation in their lending decisions. Toward this, financial institutions should improve their capacity to better understand agriculture and agricultural risks, market opportunities and challenges for identifying bankable projects and developing financial products and services.
- Group lending is an important means of improving farmers' access to institutional credit. For financial institutions, it is also a means of reducing lending costs and the risks associated with small loans. The government can facilitate group lending by commercial banks and other financial institutions and by building alliances among financial institutions, lead firms and farmers.
- Risk management is reassurance to financial institutions to integrate their products in the value chain. This can be done through lead firms or facilitators providing inputs and technical services. Producer organizations

(e.g., cooperatives) can use surpluses and savings to protect farmers from production and price risks.

- Finally, a generic lesson is that investment in public infrastructure is crucial to attract private investment in value chains. The government may identify niche areas and commodities for value chain development and develop public infrastructure (roads, electricity, communication etc.) accordingly to attract private investment in storage, processing and cold chains. A stable policy environment is important for the private sector's sustained interest in agribusiness.

References

ADB-Asian Development Bank. (2013). *Agricultural Value Chains for Development*. Asian Development Bank, Manila, Philippines.

Amarnath, S. (2007). "Financing the agricultural value chain: BASIX experiences", www.ruralfinance.org.

Birthal, P.S., and Joshi, P.K. (2007). "Institutional innovations for improving smallholder participation in high-value agriculture: A case of fruit and vegetable growers' associations", *Quarterly Journal of International Agriculture* 46(1), 49–68.

Birthal, P.S., and Joshi, P.K. (2017). "Agricultural value chain finance in India: Issues and implications", *Journal of Responsible Finance*, 4 (July).

Birthal, P.S., Joshi, P.K., and Gulati, A. (2005). "Vertical Coordination In High-Value Food Commodities: Implications for smallholders", Markets, Trade, and Institutions Division Discussion Paper No. 85, International Food Policy Research Institute, Washington, DC.

Birthal, P.S., Joshi, P.K., Negi, D.S., and Agarwal, S. (2014). "Changing sources of growth in Indian agriculture: Implications for regional priorities for accelerating agricultural growth", Discussion Paper 01325, International Food Policy Research Institute, Washington, DC.

Birthal, P.S., Roy, D., and Negi, D.S. (2015). "Assessing the impact of crop diversification on farm poverty in India", *World Development* 72, 70–92.

Casuga, M.S., Paguia, F.L., Garabiag, K.A., Santos, M.T.J., Atienza, C.S., Garay, A.R., Fernandez, R.A., and Guce, G.M. (2008). "Financial Access and Inclusion in the Agricultural Value Chain", APRACA FinPower Publication: 2008/1. Asia-Pacific Rural and Agricultural Credit Association (APRACA), Thailand.

Chand, R. (2012). "Development policies and agricultural markets", *Economic and Political Weekly* 47 (52), 53–63.

Chand, R., Prasanna, P.A.L., and Singh, A. (2011). "Farm size and productivity: Understanding the strengths of smallholders and improving their livelihoods," *Economic and Political Weekly* 46 (26/27), 5–11.

Chen, K., Joshi, P.K., Cheng, E., and Birthal, P.S. (2015). "Innovations in financing of agri-food value chains in China and India: Lessons and policies for inclusive financing", *China Agricultural Economic Review* 7 (4), 1–27.

Gandhi, V.P., and Jain, D. (2011). "Institutional innovations and models in the development of agro-food industries in India: Strengths, weaknesses and lessons", Working Paper No. 2011–04–03, Indian Institute of Management, Ahmedabad.

Gill, A. (2004). "Interlinked agrarian credit markets: Case study of Punjab", *Economic and Political Weekly* 39 (33), 3741–3751.

GoI-Government of India. (2013). *Policy and Process Guidelines for Farmer Producer Organizations*. Ministry of Agriculture, New Delhi.

GoI-Government of India. (2014). *All India Debt and Investment Survey*. National Sample Survey Office, Ministry of Statistics and Program Implementation, New Delhi.

Gupta, K., and Roy, D. (2011). "Gains from coordination in Milkfed Dairy in Punjab", *Journal of Agribusiness in Developing and Emerging Economies* 2 (2), 92–114.

Joshi, P.K., and Kumar, P. (2016). "Food demand and supply projections for India", in: *International Trade and Food Security—The Future of Indian Agriculture* (Eds: F. Brower and P.K. Joshi). CAB International, Wallingford, UK.

Kumar, P. (2006). "Contract farming through agribusiness firms and state corporation", *Economic and Political Weekly* 41 (52), 5367–5375.

Lowder, S.K., Skoet, J., and Raney, T. (2016). "The number, size, and distribution of farms, smallholder farms, and family farms worldwide", *World Development* 87, 16–29.

Maertens, M., Dries, L., Dedehouanou, F.A. and Swinnen, J.F.M. (2007). "High-value supply chains, food standards and rural households in Senegal", in *Global Supply Chains. Standards and the Poor: How the Globalization of Food Systems and Standards Affects Rural Development and Poverty* (Ed: J.F.M. Swinnen). CABI, Wellington.

Meenakshi, J.V., and Banerji, A. (2005). "The unsupportable support price: An analysis of collusion and government intervention in paddy auction markets in North India", *Journal of Development Economics* 76 (2), 377–403.

Meyer, R.L. (2007). "Analysing and financing value chains: Cutting edge developments in value chain analysis", Paper Presented at the 3rd African Microfinance Conference: New Options for Rural and Urban Africa, Uganda.

Miller, C. (2012). *Agricultural Value Chain Finance Strategy and Design*. International Fund for Agricultural Development (IFAD), Rome.

Miller, C., and Jones, L. (2010). *Agricultural Value Chain Finance: Tools and Lessons*. Food and Agriculture Organization of the United Nations and Practical Action Publishing, Warwickshire, UK.

Minten, B., Randrianarison, L., and Swinnen, J. (2009). "Global retail chains and poor farmers: Evidence from Madagascar", *World Development* 37 (11), 1728–1741.

Minten, B., Singh, K.M., and Sutradhar, R. (2012). "Branding and agricultural value chains in developing countries: Insights from Bihar, India", IFPRI Discussion Paper 1207, International Food Policy Research Institute (IFPRI), Washington, DC.

Mitra, P. (1982). "A theory of interlinked rural transactions", Development Research Department Discussion Paper no. DRD 33. World Bank, Washington, DC.

Negi, D.S., Birthal, P.S., Roy, D., and Khan, M.T. (2018). "Farmers' choice of market channels and producer prices in India: Role of transportation and communication networks", *Food Policy* 81, 106–121.

Nelson, V., and Smith, S. (2011). *Fairtrade Cotton: Assessing Impact in Mali, Senegal, Cameroon and India*. National Research Institute, University of Greenwich, and Institute of Development Studies, Sussex.

Pingali, P. (2005). "Westernization of Asian diets and the transformation of food systems: Implications for research and policy", *Food Policy* 32, 281–298.

Pingali, P., Khwaja, Y., and Meijer, M. (2005). "Commercializing small farms: Reducing transaction costs", ESA Working Paper No. 05–08, Agricultural and Development Economics Division, Food and Agriculture Organization, Rome.

Ramaswami, B., Birthal, P.S., and Joshi, P.K. (2009). "Grower heterogeneity and the gains from contract farming: the case of Indian poultry", *India Growth and Development Review* 2 (1), 56–74.

Reardon, T., and Minten, B. (2011). "The quiet revolution in India's food supply chains", Discussion Paper No. 1115, International Food Policy Research Institute, Washington, DC.

Reardon, T., Timmer, C.P., and Minten, B. (2012). "Supermarket revolution in Asia and emerging development strategies to include small farmers", *PNAS* 109 (31), 12332–12337.

Roy, D., and Thorat, A. (2008). "Success in high value horticultural export markets for the small farmers: The case of Mahagrapes in India", *World Development* 36 (10), 1874–1890.

Singh, S., and Singla, N. (2011). *Fresh Food Retail Chains in India: Organization and Impacts.* Allied Publishers, New Delhi.

South Asian Pro Poor Livestock Policy Programme. (2009). *Making Modern Poultry Markets Work for the Poor: An example of Cooperative Development from Madhya Pradesh: SAGP03 Good Practice Note.* South Asian Pro Poor Livestock Policy Programme, New Delhi.

Trienekens, J.H. (2011). "Agricultural value Chains in developing countries a framework for analysis", *International Food and Agribusiness Management Review* 14 (2), 51–83.

Vandeplas, A., Minten, B., and Swinnen, J. (2013). "Multinationals vs. cooperatives: The income and efficiency effects of supply chain governance in India", *Journal of Agricultural Economics* 64 (1), 217–244.

7 Role of transaction costs in modern food retail chains

Empirical evidence from India

Kedar Vishnu and Alwin Dsouza

Modern food retail chains (MFRC) have attracted attention recently due to growth in the number of private players and stores and in sales of fruits and vegetables over the last two decades (Reardon et al., 2005). Since the 2000s, India, China and Vietnam have been among the emerging economies experiencing significant transformation in their retail food chains. In India, for example, the total number of supermarket outlets rose from 1,391 in 2007 to 3,259 in 2017 (Vishnu & Kumar, 2019). The surge in popularity of modern food retail chains has provided farmers with opportunities to increase their incomes (Reardon & Berdegué, 2002). Modern food retail chains used to procure fruits and vegetables from the retail markets, but now they are becoming an alternative market supplier of fruits and vegetables. Since the early 2000s, most food retail chains started modernizing through investments in existing supply chains and enforcement of quality standards (Trebbin, 2014a). These changes have brought both opportunities and challenges for small and marginal farmers.

Modernization of food retail chains has led to lower production risks and higher profits for small and marginal farmers (Mishra et al., 2016, 2018). However, contractors in these chains have been reported to behave opportunistically (Allen & Lueck, 1993; Escobal & Cavero, 2012). Farmers are exposed to risks through contracts, mainly when the contractors are either monopsonist or oligopolist (Sivramkrishna & Jyotishi, 2008). Risks of an incomplete agreement or contract and asymmetric information regarding quality, quantity and price give the chains opportunities to exploit small and marginal farmers (Hobbs, 1997). This has led to an increase in the 'costs of running the economic system' (Arrow, 1969). Most of these costs are associated with uncertainty, concentration of input suppliers, asset specificity and internalization costs (Frank & Henderson, 1992). In literature, these costs are defined as transaction costs (TCs). Broadly, transaction costs have three components: information costs, monitoring costs and bargaining costs. Of these, information-related expenses have been found to be as high as 70% of transaction costs in the case of fruits and vegetables (De Silva & Ratnadiwakara, 2008). An increase in transaction costs may have implications for the profits that small and marginal farmers earn in emerging economies. Transaction costs have adversely affected the profits of small and marginal farmers, particularly those involved in modern food retail chains (Singh, 2002). Transaction costs create a gap between achievable profits and earned profits—a gap that, in developing countries, may be significant. Previous studies did not incorporate transaction costs in their estimations, which may lead to overestimation of farmers' profits (Mishra et al., 2016, 2018).

In this contextual role of the institution, an arrangement may be necessary to reduce uncertainty and production costs, hence leading to lower transaction costs. Through effective legal systems, laws, property rights, norms and codes of conduct, institutions can reduce transaction costs. Good institutions enhance growth and improve efficiency. However, due to the reduced effectiveness of the institutional framework in emerging economies, transaction costs have increased and have impacted the profits of small and marginal farmers (Otsuka et al., 2016). Therefore, it is important to measure the magnitude of transaction costs in order to analyze its impact on profits and costs of small and marginal farmers.

This chapter attempts to quantify the impact of opportunistic behavior and asymmetric information on chili farmers in India. We measure the magnitude of transaction costs and their components in production and marketing contracts compared to the transaction costs for independent farmers in traditional marketing channels (TMC). Production contracts and marketing contracts are systematically different. Production contracts are characterized by fixed prices and the provision of input supplies. In contrast, marketing contracts are characterized by prices higher than those in traditional markets and by the provision of technical guidance on chemicals and fertilizers. In traditional marketing channels, farmers sell any quantity and any quality of produce at spot market prices. Farmers pay fixed commissions to intermediaries for the role they play between the farmers and the fruit and vegetable purchasers. This chapter also measures transaction costs' impact on small and marginal farmers' profits. Our results would help in implementing policies aimed at reducing transaction costs, given that they may constitute a significant proportion of small and marginal farmers' profits.

Modern food retail chains and transaction costs

Modern food retail chains (MFRCs) have become popular in emerging economies, but empirical evidence on the degree of smallholders' participation in such chains is mixed. Empirical studies on fruit and vegetable chains in India have confirmed the relative advantage for farmers connected with modern chains. Farmers contracted by these chains receive higher prices and have better access to inputs and technology (Dhananjaya & Rao, 2009; Singh & Singla, 2010), generate higher net profits (Mangala & Chengappa, 2008; Birthal et al., 2005; Mishra et al., 2016) and incur lower transaction costs (Joseph et al., 2008) than farmers in traditional markets. Other studies, however, highlight the modern retail chains' adverse impact on producers and consumers, arguing that these chains reduce land productivity and food security. The chains also adversely affect price stability, credit and employment (Gopalakrishnan & Sreenivasa, 2009).

Modern chains may shift production decisions from farmers to corporate contractors, and farmers may have to make additional investments to meet quality standards and avoid rejections (Reardon et al., 2012). A recent study (Singh & Singla, 2010) revealed that lower acceptance rates and higher rejection rates from modern chains remain significant problems for the majority of small and marginal farmers. Furthermore, lack of credit, lower prices for low-quality produce and less time allowed for harvest, eventually increasing labor costs, were other challenges that small and marginal farmers commonly faced (Singh & Singla, 2010). In practice, modern food retail chains believe that small farmers might not be able to produce fruits and vegetables that meet higher quality standards (Vishnu & Kumar, 2014). These challenges limit small and marginal farmers' participation in the chains. Existing studies have not investigated the reasons behind the lack of participation or the increasing number of exits by small and marginal farmers from farming in emerging economies.

The role of risk and uncertainty associated with modern food retail chains in general may be relevant in understanding farmers' lack of participation. Modern chains involve a significant amount of risk (Pingali et al. 2005). Other studies have put more emphasis on studying transaction costs and their impacts on supplier selection (Stanton, 2000; Reardon & Barrett, 2000). They found that supermarkets prefer to procure from larger farmers to reduce the transaction costs associated with dealing with smallholders. Key and Runsten (1999) show that modern food retail chains put more emphasis on quality and output, mainly because of the need for stability in supply and better quality but, more importantly, to reduce transaction costs. Other studies also show that supermarkets prefer to procure from large farmers due to the administrative costs associated with monitoring (Reardon & Barrett, 2000).

A few empirical studies focused on asymmetric information and the transaction costs farmers incur. De Silva and Ratnadiwakara's (2008) findings show that information-related costs accounted for 70% of total transaction costs. Furthermore, the study shows that information costs accounted for 15% of total production costs incurred by vegetable farmers in Sri Lanka who sell to wholesale agricultural markets. The search for price information was the reason farmers incurred information costs in the market. Studies from sub-Saharan African countries found that having proper information in the market helped maize farmers receive 12.7% higher prices and groundnut farmers receive 9.7% higher prices from traders (Courtois & Subervie, 2014). These studies have highlighted the prevalence of asymmetric information of prices in the open market and the transaction costs the incurred by farmers. Hobbs (1996) found that economic agents face costs in searching for information about products, prices, inputs and buyers or sellers. Matungul et al. (2001) and Alene et al. (2007) found that smallholders in Africa frequently face high transaction costs in the production and marketing of agricultural outputs due to the perishable nature of fruit and vegetables and due to the lack of a proper institutional environment. Dorward et al. (1998) put more emphasis on the importance of an institutional framework for reducing famers' uncertainty about selling to a supermarket. Other studies stress the importance of capturing institutional arrangements in contract farming and show that it helps farmers reduce price and marketing uncertainty (Trebbin, 2014b; Mishra et al., 2016).

Further, Masakure and Henson (2005) studied the motivations behind smallholders' decision to grow vegetables under contract in Zimbabwe. The result shows that farmers engage in contract farming mainly to reduce uncertainty about prices in the open markets. However, there is a paucity of studies that properly explain farmers' motivation to join modern food retail chains. Furthermore, one study revealed that due to the lack of institutional framework in developing countries, specifically India, farmers face more uncertainty with modern food retail chains (Trebbin, 2014b). Similar results have been found for potato farmers in Ethiopia (Abebe et al., 2013).

The institutional economics framework is responsible for creating an atmosphere for the successful emergence of modern food retail chains. The new institutional economics (NIE) framework provides a way in which market failures related to uncertainty, risk sharing and coordination failure in contracting can be overcome (Grosh, 1994). In the context of farming, institutions are expected to have a positive impact on income, risk and yield (Grosh, 1994). However, due to the lack of a proper legal system, enforcement mechanisms and awareness, institutions are unable to play a significant role in contract farming. Coase (1937) put more emphasis on the cost associated with searches for price information, arguing that transaction costs have an essential role in the organization of firms and contracts. Alchian (1965) introduced the role of property rights and enforcement as new dimensions of transaction costs, putting more emphasis on enforcement than on asymmetric information. Studies by Williamson put more emphasis on a firm's opportunity behavior and the role of bounded rationality. According to Williamson, transaction costs are incurred due to bounded rationality, opportunism and asymmetric information problems. (Kedar, 2018) found that a lack of proper institutional frameworks in most developing countries was responsible for higher transaction costs.

In reviewing the contract farming literature, we noted several gaps. First, although many authors discussed the importance of transaction costs, surprisingly little attention has been paid to measure the relative importance of these costs from the farmers' perspective (Kedar, 2018). In India, about 84% of farmers are small or marginal, so connecting them with modern food retail chains is vital for boosting their income. Therefore, understanding the role of transaction costs in farmers' participation in the chains is quite important. There are very limited studies from developing countries that capture transaction costs appropriately, as they are not easily accountable (Ning, 2003).

Recall that transaction costs can be divided into three classes: information costs, negotiation or bargaining costs and monitoring or enforcement costs. Information costs result when economic agents incur costs searching for information about prices, inputs, products and contractor reputations. Furthermore, negotiation costs result from the physical act of the transaction, such as opportunistic behavior by the modern food retail chain in setting procurement prices and the quantity rejected. Negotiation costs are expected to be higher when contracts are incomplete and enforcement is lacking. Due to lower bargaining powers, farmers face delayed payments, higher rejection rates of fruits and vegetables than decided and lower procurement prices than agreed upon. Farmers also may incur monitoring or enforcement costs when selling fruits and vegetables to modern food retail chains. These costs may be related to supervision of the farmers, verification of produce quality and costs associated with ensuring that all contractual terms are met. They may include costs associated with compensation to stakeholders in case of disputes (Hobbs, 2004).

One important question that the existing literature does not address is why smallholders are unable to participate; that is, what are the current barriers to smallholders' participation in modern food retail chains. Limited studies on this subject stress the lack of capacity (Birthal et al., 2005). This includes scarcity of resources, lack of investment and lack of ability to produce quality products, which prevents smallholders from participating in modern chains that require better quality (Schipmann & Qaim, 2011; Mishra et al., 2018). Williamson (1985) suggested three sources of transaction costs: uncertainty, frequency of transactions and asset specificity. These three sources can raise the potential for opportunistic behavior and therefore determine the level and nature of transaction costs. Uncertainty can be driven by costly and asymmetric information. Infrequent transactions face more uncertainty and can create a non-trusting environment among economic agents, but higher frequency always lowers the risk of opportunistic behavior (Williamson, 1985; Key & Runsten, 1999). Asset specificity refers to the level at which physical assets are tied to particular transactions specified by contracts or other commitments. Transaction costs emerge when a power imbalance exists between farmers and modern food retail chains due to asset specificity.

According to Coase (1960), high transaction costs may result in inefficient allocation of resources. High transaction costs may make contracts expensive and infeasible for poor and marginal farmers. This may impact their adoption of contracts with modern food retail chains and may explain the slow adoption rates, particularly in emerging economies. The new institutional economics framework provides tools for addressing barriers to fair contracting. Some of these tools may involve regulating the terms of contracts, defining the rule of contracts and enforcing the terms of contracts. A limitation of transaction costs analysis is that a large number of the associated costs are not readily observable and relevant information is not accessible, particularly in emerging markets. The empirical applications of the transaction cost analysis have not kept pace with theoretical development partly due to data limitations; therefore, there have been few applications of transaction cost analysis in agricultural marketing (Hobbs, 1997). This chapter emphasizes empirically measuring the transaction costs that farmers incur in different sets of modern food retail chain arrangements. We have used proxy variables for measuring transaction costs (Table 7.1).

Table 7.1 Variables used for measuring transaction costs (TCs) incurred by farmers

	Variable	*Individual Transaction costs*	*Nature of the measurement*	*Measurement details*
01	Information costs: • Arise prior to an exchange • Are incurred due to uncertainty and asymmetric information	Search for buyers and reliability of potential buyers	Actual	1 Opportunity cost of time (Rs/acre)[a] 2 Travel expenses (Rs/acre) 3 Phone call charges (Rs/acre)
		Price uncertainty (search cost associated with incurring the offered prices by MFRCs and price uncertainty)	Actual	
		Quality standard/product quality uncertainty	Actual	
		Other information required on (seeds type + packaging materials etc.)	Actual	
02	Bargaining/negotiation costs (during exchange)	Lack of control over sale order	Relative	Is the lack of control over the sale order in which products are sold at MFRCs[b]
		Unequal bargaining power	Relative	Do you have to take whatever prices are offered by the MFRCs?[b]
		Frequency of sale	Actual	Number of sales in week
		Cost and time spent on negotiating the prices and quality of the product with the company	Actual	1 Opportunity cost of time (Rs/acre) 2 Travel expenses in (Rs/acre) 3 Phone call charges (Rs/acre)
		Monetary value due to opportunist behavior	Actual	1 Transportation costs associated with sale of rejected product by MFRCs into other market (Rs/acre) 2 Monetary value of the wastage (Rs/acre)[c] if the rejected product is not sold
03	Monitoring costs (incurred to ensure that the conditions of an exchange are met)	Product quality (supervision cost to fulfill the MFRCs' quality, extra effort spent by the owner-farmers)	Actual	1 Opportunity cost of time (Rs/acre) 2 Travel expenses in (Rs/acre) 3 Phone call charges (Rs/acre)
		Grade uncertainty (ensuring that the product is graded as per contract in the field as well as at the collection centers)	Actual	

Source: Authors' primary survey (2017).

Notes:

[a] Number of visits × Time spent (hr) × Wage rate (per hr).

[b] Possible responses were 1, not a problem; 2, minor problem; 3, a problem; 4, relatively significant problem; 5, major problem.

[c] Mostly applicable for the quality that would have been accepted by MFRCs.

Empirical framework

We use a quasi-experimental framework for this study to compare the treatment and control groups. This method is used to retrieve the counterfactuals for suggesting policies. We also need to address self-selection bias (Stefanides & Tauer, 1999). Ideally, farmers should be assigned randomly between the two groups (those contracting with modern food retail chains and those who are independent farmers), but they self-select into one of the two groups. Let us consider the relationship between the choice of modern food retail chains and outcome variables (like profit per acre, yield per acre, cost of cultivation per acre etc.) Specifically:

$$\begin{aligned} MFRC^{*}{}_{i} &= \beta Z_i + \xi_i \\ MFRC_i &= 1 \text{ if } MFRC_i^{*} > 0 \end{aligned} \tag{7.1}$$

MFRC is a binary variable that equals 1 if a farmer adopts production and marketing contracts, and it equals zero otherwise. β is a vector of parameters to be estimated; Z is a vector of explanatory variable, and ξ_i is the error term. As previously mentioned, MFRC participation helps farmers increase chili yields per acre and profit per acre and hence helps improve the welfare of the farmers' household. Assume that total costs, yield and profits are a linear function of a dummy variable for *MFRC*:

$$Y_i = \lambda X_i + \phi MFRC_i + \xi_i \tag{7.2}$$

where Y_i represents outcome variables (like profit per acre), $MFRC_i$ is an indicator variable for participation in either production contracts or marketing contracts as defined, λ and θ are vectors of parameters to be estimated, and ξ is an error term. Here, note that the impact of *MFRC* adoption on outcome variables is measured by ϕ as noted, and $\varepsilon_i \epsilon N\left(0,\sigma^2\right)$. The self-selection bias arises if unobservable factors influence both error terms of the *MFRC* choice. The adoption decision may depend on some other unobservable variables such as skills, innovation and land fertility, which may be correlated with the outcome variables. Hence, the estimation of Equation (7.2) might lead to biased results. Mishra et al. (2018) argued that estimation using the ordinary least squares (OLS) method would lead to biased results. Several estimation techniques are available for overcoming selection bias; Greene (2012) argued that Heckman two-step methods and the instrumental variables approach might be useful. But these techniques impose linear functional form, and finding appropriate instrument variables is quite difficult (Mishra et al., 2016). A few recent studies (Dehejia & Wahba, 2002; Rao et al., 2012; Fischer & Qaim, 2012) used statistical matching to overcome selection bias. Several studies on agricultural economics (Tauer, 2009; Liu & Lynch, 2007) have used propensity score matching (PSM) to compare treated and non-treated farmers. Hence, we follow Rosenbaum and Rubin (1985) PSM and focus our analysis on the average treatment effect on treated (ATT). Becker and Ichino (2002) argued that ATT could be considered the main parameter. Hence, the ATT for the individual can be defined as the difference between the expected outcome variable (like profits per acre, yield per acre and costs per acre) with and without *MFRC* adoption for individuals who have access to *MFRC*. Specifically:

$$\begin{aligned} ATT &= E\left[Y(1)-Y(0)\,|\,T=1\right] \\ ATT &= E\left[Y(1)\,|\,T=1\right]-E\left[Y(0)\,|\,T=1\right] \end{aligned} \tag{7.3}$$

Estimation of Equation (7.3) is possible only when we control for a vector of observable variables like education, age and infrastructure-related variables. Caliendo and Kopeinig (2008) argued that, given X (variables that are not affected by the treatment), potential outcomes are independent of the treatment assignment. Specifically:

$$\begin{aligned} ATE(X) &= E\left[Y(1)-Y(0)\,|\,X\right] \\ ATE &= E\left[Y(1)\,|\,T=1,X\right]-E\left[Y(0)\,|\,T=1,X\right] \end{aligned} \tag{7.4}$$

However, Smith and Todd (2005) and Mishra et al. (2018) argued that we could not control for unobservable heterogeneity in Equation (7.4), and it may influence both the adoption of *MFRC* and the outcome variables (like profit and yield in this study). Mishra et al. (2018) argued that we first need to estimate a probability model to calculate the probability of each smallholder adopting MFRC, which is essentially a propensity score, and then need to calculate the ATT as follows:

$$T_{ATT}^{PSM}(X) = E\left[Y(1)\,|\,T=1,P(X)\right]-E\left[Y(0)\,|\,T=1,P(X)\right] \tag{7.5}$$

Existing studies have discussed various techniques for matching the propensity scores of participating farmers and independent farmers. Wooldridge (2010) and Cameron and Trivedi (2005) argue that the PSM estimation technique could be considered non-parametric. The most commonly used methods are nearest neighbor matching (NNM) and kernel-based matching (KBM). This study applies an NNM matching estimator. The NNM method picks each treated unit (MFRC farmers) and searches for the control unit (independent farmers) that has the closest propensity matching score. NMM's main attractive characteristic is that all the treated groups find a match (Mishra et al., 2016).

PSM's primary purpose is to balance the observable distribution of covariates across the two farmer groups (MFRC farmers and independent farmers). The balancing test is done to ensure that the differences in the covariates between the MFRC and independent farmers are eliminated. Thereafter, the matched comparison group can be considered a counterfactual. Rosenbaum and Rubin (1985) suggests measuring the mean absolute standardized bias (MASB) between MFRC farmers and independent farmers and recommends that if a substantial large standardized difference (greater than 20%) still exists, then the matching process would be considered to have failed.

Data and descriptive statistics of MFRC and independent farmers

The primary survey was conducted in 2017 in the District of Kolar of the Indian state of Karnataka. Kolar is known for being India's largest producer of chili. We interviewed 300 chili households: 100 under MFRC with production contracts, 100 under MFRC with marketing contracts and 100 under traditional market channels. Chili farmers were sampled using stratified sampling. The questionnaires were designed to obtain socio-economic variables and input variables, and, to help calculate transaction costs, we asked questions about opportunistic behavior, asymmetric information, asset specificity and price and grading standards uncertainty. Earlier studies failed to provide a proxy variable for transaction costs, so our questionnaire was designed to obtain information on a wide range of potential transaction cost variables.

Table 7.2 reports descriptive statistics for selected MFRC farmers and independent farmers. At the 10% level of significance, independent farmers have a higher average age, a higher land area, a household member (HH) with less education and smaller loan amounts than the MFRC farmers. Hence, there exists a negative selection bias by independent farmers in MFRC because better-off farmers within these parameters are more likely to join the MFRC. The farming experience of the household head was higher for those with production contracts than for independent farmers, but the difference was not statistically significant. Our findings show that MFRC farmers had shorter distances to input markets ($p < 0.01\%$) and shorter distances between their houses and their fields ($p < 0.01\%$) compared to independent farmers. Farmers associated with MFRC had advantages in easy access to infrastructure variables compared to independent farmers. Nonetheless, MFRC and independent farmers were similar with respect to land area and the household's farming experience.

Regarding perceptions of production risk and financial risk, the study finds that production-contract and marketing-contract farmers' perceive higher production risk (significance < 0.01%). This indicates that chili farmers contracting with the chains were more willing to take risks than were independent farmers, which might give them an advantage in meeting the chains' higher quality standards. It can be observed from Table 7.2 that the share of farmers perceiving high risk was 32% of those with marketing contracts, followed by 23% of those with production contracts and 10% of independent farmers. The share of farmers perceiving medium risk was 73% ($p < 001\%$) of those with production contracts, significantly higher than the 48% of independent farmers. These findings indicate that risk-averse farmers were less likely to participate in modern food retail chains. We present household member education status in Table 7.2 and found that a higher share of independent farmers were illiterate or had primary education compared to farmers in the modern chains. This finding indicates that modern food retail chains prefer to associate with educated farmers to procure better-quality produce.

Table 7.2 Characteristics of contract and independent chili producers, India, 2017–2018

Variable	*IFs*	*PCs*	*MCs*
Land area (acre)	3.84	4.76	3.44
Age of head of household (HH, in years)	48.12	41.45**	44.32**
Farming experience of HH (years)	13.86	16.08	14.08
Household size (number)	4.00	5.00	4.00**
Loan amount (Lakhs per HH)	0.77	3.09**	1.78***
Distance to input market (km)	12.80	6.98***	7.00***
Nearby road distance from agricultural field (km)	1.06	1.11	0.93***
Distance of HH agricultural field from home (km)	1.01	0.81*	0.9***
Near other collection centers (km)	13.52	16.82**	10.44*
HH member, perceiving high risk (%)	10.00	23.00*	32.00***
HH member, perceiving medium risk (%)	48.00	73.00***	36
HH member, lower medium risk (%)	34.00	4.0***	14.00**
HH member, perceiving no risk (%)	8.00	4.00	18.00
HH member, education (years)	2.66	9.12***	7.7***
HH member, illiterate (%)	26.00	1.00***	4.00***
HH member, primary education (%)	48.00	26.00***	44.00
HH member, secondary school education (%)	26.00	43.0**	26.00
HH member, tertiary education (%)	0.00	30.0***	26.00***
Area under chili per acre	1.55	1.22***	1.15***
Total labor cost acre (Rs)	3,154	16,264	15,746
Total input per acre (Rs)	18,778	3,305	12,869
Total variable costs[a] per acre (Rs)	26,522	58,349	54,310
Total cost per acre (Rs)	48,454	77,918***	82,925***
Total revenue per acre (Rs)	82,810	135,228***	123,328***
Total profit per acre (Rs)	34288	57,310**	40,403*
Procurement Prices (Rs/kg)	18.38	21.41***	20.20*
Yield (kg per acre)	4.92	7.95***	7.39***
Total cost per quintal (Rs)	985	980	1,122
Net profit per quintal (NPR)	698	721	547
Number of observations	*100*	*100*	*100*

Source: Authors' primary survey (2017).

Notes: a Also known as operation costs, includes seeds, seed treatment, fertilizer (urea, potash, DAP), micronutrients, manure, pesticides and miscellaneous.

* Significant at the 10% level.

** Significant at the 5%.

*** Significant at the 1% level.

Finally, Table 7.2 compares independent farmers with production-contract and marketing-contract farmers. We found that the procurement price of chili from farmers with production contracts is significantly higher, about Rs 21.41 per kg ($p < 0.01\%$), than from independent farmers, about Rs 18.38 per kg, meaning production contract (PC) farmers received prices 16.49% higher than independent farmers received. Table 7.2 also shows that farmers with marketing contracts received a significantly higher ($p < 0.1\%$) price, Rs 20.20 per kg, than independent farmers (IFs) received. These findings suggest that farmers may prefer production contracts in modern food retail chains to get more income. The table also shows that, compared to independent farmers, farmers with production and marketing contracts reported significantly higher yields per acre of chili, higher revenue per acre of chili and higher total costs ($p < 0.01\%$). Specifically, the costs of chili cultivation per acre were 60.81% higher for production-contract farmers and 71.14% higher for marketing-contract (MC) farmers than for independent farmers. This finding indicates that procurement prices were higher mostly due to the contract farmers providing better quality, which was responsible for the higher production costs.

The production and marketing-contract farmers reported a significantly lower area under chili cultivation than independent farmers. Production-contract farmers grew chili on 1.22 acres while marketing contract farmers grew on 1.15 acres of land. From our primary survey, it became clear that production-contract farmers prefer to have areas of mostly one acre under chili. The farmers then can utilize their maximum labor for grading and harvesting. Interestingly, Table 7.2 shows that production-contract farmers have significantly higher ($p < 0.05\%$) profit (Rs 57,310 per acre), followed by marketing-contract farmers (Rs 40,403 per acre), than independent farmers (Rs 34,288 per acre). Put another way, we found that production-contract farmers received 67.14% higher profit and marketing-contract farmers received 17.83% higher profit than independent farmers. We can conclude that farmers in the modern food retail chain reported significantly higher profit than independent farmers did, mainly due to higher yield and to the higher procurement prices offered by the chains. However, participating in these chains is associated with higher transaction costs. We consider such costs in the next section.

Results and discussion

The empirical result of the probit model is presented in Tables 7.3 and 7.4. Table 7.3 shows the result of Model I, and Model II, to be discussed in detail, consists of infrastructure variables included to check for robustness. The observation with the same propensity score must have the same allocation of observable characteristics. Furthermore, Model II is chosen because of the higher pseudo R-square. The probit model controls for socio-economic variables like age, education, net sown area and risk preference, along with infrastructure variables such as distance to collection centers, input markets and roads.

Table 7.3 Propensity score for PC MFRC farmers vs. IF for chili (probit estimation)

Variable	*Model I*		*Model II*	
	Coefficient	*Standard error*	*Coefficient*	*Standard error*
ln age (years)	−0.750	(1.452)	−0.849	(1.347)
HHs, illiterate[a] (dummy)	−1.960	(262.3)	−1.870	(262.3)
HHs, primary education[a] (dummy)	−9.184	(262.3)	−8.604	(262.3)
HHs, secondary education[a] (dummy)	−7.235	(262.3)	−6.635	(262.3)
High-risk HH[b] (dummy)	5.987**	(2.727)	6.757***	(2.558)
Medium-risk HH[b] (dummy)	3.923**	(1.587)	6.202***	(2.385)
Low-risk HH[b] (dummy)	2.019	(1.593)	4.726**	(2.201)
ln net sown area (acre)	0.905	(0.800)	1.351**	(0.550)
Household size (number)	0.0459	(0.115)	−0.208	(0.566)
ln price received (Rs/kg)	3.692**	(1.454)	2.648**	(1.150)
ln plots (number)	−1.152	(0.730)	−2.888***	(1.101)
ln loan borrowed (Rs)	−0.0269	(0.0513)	−0.0469	(0.0313)
Preference for fixed price [c] (dummy)	−0.606	(0.502)	−0.853	(0.612)
Aware of MFRC contractors (dummy)	0.470	(0.629)	0.774	(0.625)
ln distance to collection center (km)	—	—	1.019**	(0.451)
ln distance of Input Market (km)	—	—	−2.440***	(0.864)
ln distance of nearest road from farm (km)	—	—	−0.449	(0.657)
Constant	−6.184	(4.737)	1.841	(262.4)
Pseudo-R^2	0.7233		0.7595	
Number of observations	*100*	*100*	*100*	

Source: Authors' primary survey (2017).

Notes:
[a] Base is farmers with primary/illiterate/secondary/(tertiary or other education).
[b] Base is farmers with no risk.
[c] Base household will not prefer fixed prices in advance.
Standard errors in parentheses: *** $p < 0.01$, ** $p < 0.05$, * $p < 0.1$.

The probit estimates state that households with high-risk appetites are more likely to adopt production contracts or marketing contracts over independent farming. Other studies show similar results (Mishra et al. 2018). The net sown area is positive and significant in both tables, indicating that an increase in the net sown area increases the likelihood that farmers will adopt production or marketing contracts. A higher expected price seems to be one of the motivations for adopting either type of contract. Our findings are similar to those of other studies in Kenya (Rao et al. 2012), China (Miyata et al., 2009) and

Table 7.4 Propensity score for MC MFRC farmers vs. IF for chili (probit estimation)

Variable	*Model I*		*Model II*	
	Coefficient	*Standard error*	*Coefficient*	*Standard error*
ln Age (years)	−1.447	(2.494)	−0.195*	(0.108)
HHs, illiterate[a] (dummy)	−9.525	(0.628)	−8.585	(0.752)
HHs, primary education[a] (dummy)	−11.26	(595.9)	−10.26	(595.9)
HHs, secondary education[a] (dummy)	−12.00	(595.9)	−10.00	(595.9)
High Risk HH[a] (dummy)	5.698**	(2.336)	8.253**	(4.208)
Medium Risk HH[a] (dummy)	0.691	(1.164)	1.347	(1.736)
Low Risk HH[a] (dummy)	−3.010*	(1.772)	−0.873	(1.178)
ln net sown area (acre)	3.574**	(1.666)	3.244**	(1.456)
Household size (number)	0.025	(0.408)	1.035*	(0.608)
ln price received (Rs/kg)	6.542*	(2.263)	7.888**	(3.912)
ln plots (number)	−7.409***	(2.626)	−3.652*	(2.024)
ln loan borrowed (Rs)	0.635***	(0.1567)	0.253***	(0.0867)
Preference for fixed price[c] (dummy)	0.300	(0.654)	−0.573	(1.095)
Aware of MFRC contractors (dummy)	6.381***	(2.355)	2.945**	(1.447)
ln distance to collection center (km)	–		−0.665	(0.659)
ln distance of input market (km)	–		−0.892	(1.083)
ln distance of nearest road from farm (*km*)	–		−7.835**	(3.850)
Constant	2.956	(11.93)	−6.469	(596.0)
Pseudo-R^2	0.7602		0.825	
Number of observations	*200*		*200*	

Source: Authors' primary survey (2017).

Notes:

[a] Base is farmers with primary/illiterate/secondary/(tertiary or other education).

[b] Base is farmers with no risk.

[c] Base household will not prefer fixed prices in advance.

Standard errors in parentheses *** $p < 0.01$, ** $p < 0.05$, * $p < 0.1$.

Ghana (Boahene et al., 1999). A lower number of plots seems to increase the likelihood of farmers' adopting production and marketing contracts. This may be the criterion for selecting farmers. A large number of plots may increase inefficiency in managing daily operations and harvesting and make the process more tedious. This is also the case when the produce needs to be lifted before it is delivered to the contractor. Among the infrastructure variables, production-contract farmers' distance to collection centers is positive and significant, but distance to input markets is negative and significant. This is because farmers are more likely to adopt production contracts when a marketing contractor's collection center is far. In production contracts, the contractor's employees come to the field to lift the produce. Production-contract farmers also would prefer closer input markets because these farmers receive constant information from the contractor's employees and therefore need to visit the input market often. However, for marketing-contract farmers, the closeness of roads to their farms is important because they need to deliver the produce to the contractor's collection center. The closeness of the collection center is important but was not statistically significant.

Transaction costs were significantly higher for farmers in modern food retail chains than for independent farmers. Such costs accounted for 14.5% of total costs for production-contract farmers and for 9.6% of total costs for marketing-contract farmers but for less than 6% of total costs in the traditional marketing channel. This indicates that transaction costs are significantly higher for contract farmers than for independent farmers. Table 7.5 shows that transaction costs were Rs 9,178 ($p < 0.01\%$) higher for production-contract farmers and Rs 5,394 ($p < 0.01\%$) higher for marketing-contract farmers than for independent farmers. This finding is in line with previous studies (Pingali et al., 2005; De Silva & Ratnadiwakara, 2008).

Now we analyze the different components of transaction costs, that is, information costs, monitoring costs and bargaining costs. Among the transaction costs, monitoring costs constituted the major component for all farmers. Information costs, though insignificant, were 22.6% higher for production-contract farmers compared to independent farmers. However, information costs were 79.5 higher ($p < 0.01\%$) for marketing-contract farmers than for independent farmers, mainly due to the uncertainty associated with price volatility and more frequently changing quality standards. Modern food retail chains give farmers a flexible price option, so price volatility and uncertainty about chili quality would affect to a large extent smallholders' decisions on whether to participate in a chain. Monitoring costs were 5.3% higher ($p < 0.01\%$) for production-contract farmers and 2.6% higher ($p < 0.01\%$) for marketing-contract farmers compared to independent farmers due to the supervision needed to produce higher-quality products. Our discussion with farmers during the primary survey revealed that monitoring costs were higher due to uncertainty about standard grading. Most of the time, managers in modern food retail chains do not grade products appropriately. Farmers therefore must be present during the grading to ensure that it is done appropriately; consequently, they report huge enforcement costs. Modern food retail chains also expect contractors to provide better quality than independent farmers provide, so farmers have to put extra effort into monitoring at various stages of chili production. Our finding is consistent with Furubotn and Richter (1997).

Bargaining costs were twice as high ($p < 0.01\%$) for production-contract farmers and 1.5 times higher ($p < 0.01\%$) for marketing-contract farmers relative to independent farmers. Bargaining costs include the cost of and time spent negotiating the product's price and quality with the modern food retail chains. Bargaining costs were higher for production-contract farmers, followed

Table 7.5 Average treatment effects and results of sensitivity analysis, MFRC, chili

Matching algorithm	*Outcome (Rs per acre)*	*Treated*	*Controls*	*Difference*	*t-stats*	*Critical level of hidden bias* Γ	*Number treated*	*Number of controls*
(1) PC vs. IF	Information costs per acre	819	668	151	0.57	1.3–1.35	100	100
Nearest neighbor	Monitoring costs per acre	8,465	1,335	7,131	6.61	5–5.05	100	100
matching (NNM)	Bargaining costs per acre	3,740	1,844	1,896	3.43	1.6–1.65	100	100
	Total Transaction costs per acre	13,025	3,846	9,178	6.00	5–5.05	100	100
	Cost per acre (C1) (including TCs)	89,820	63,070	26,750	3.92	3.3–3.35	100	100
	Profits per acre (P1) (including TCs)	40,331	17,649	22,682	2.54	1.55–1.6	100	100
	Revenue per acre	1,30,151	80,719	49,432	4.4	2.1–2.15	100	100
	Cost per acre (C2) (excluding TCs)	76,453	60,522	15,930	2.41	1.35–1.40	100	100
	Profits per acre (P2) (excluding TCs)	53,699	20,346	33,353	3.74	2.25–2.3	100	100
	Difference in Cost (C1–C2)	*13,367*	*2,548*	*10,820*				
	Difference in Profits (P1–P2)	*−13,368*	*−2,697*	*−10,671*				
(2) MC vs. IF	Information costs per acre	1,228	684	545	2.86	2.35–2.4	100	100
Nearest neighbor	Monitoring costs per acre	4,784	1,336	3,447	4.75	5.0–5.05	100	100
matching (NNM)	Bargaining costs per acre	2,364	963	1,402	4.51	2.85–2.90	100	100
	Total Transaction costs per acre	8,376	2,982	5,394	5.08	4.75–4.80	100	100
	Cost per acre (C1) (including TCs)	87,498	49,846	37,652	4.36	3–3.05	100	100
	Profits per acre (P1) (including TCs)	31,197	31,901	−704	−0.08	1.45–1.5	100	100
	Revenue per acre	1,18,695	81,747	36,948	2.77	1.75–1.8	100	100
	Cost per acre (C2) (excluding TCs)	79,122	46,864	32,258	3.88	2.45–2.5	100	100
	Profits per acre (P2) (excluding TCs)	39,573	35,357	4,216	0.50	1.7–1.75	100	100
	Difference in cost (C1−C2)	*8,376*	*2,982*	*5,394*				
	Difference in profits (P1−P2)	*−8,376*	*−3,456*	*−4,920*				

Source: Authors primary survey (2017).

by marketing-contract farmers, than for independent farmers. Table 7.5 shows that bargaining costs accounted for the second-highest share of transaction costs. This is due mainly to opportunistic behavior by the chains. Existing studies argue that farmers' bargaining power would increase with unity or with the increased availability of chains. We feel that collective efforts can help farmers reach scale and gain bargaining power to negotiate with the chains. Our finding is consistent with Holloway et al. (2000) and Lyon (2003).

Now we compare profits and costs per acre before and after including transaction costs. The difference in cost is higher by 17.4%, and profits are lower by 24.9% for production-contract farmers when transaction costs are included in the calculation. Similarly, the difference in cost is higher by 10.6% and profits lower by 21% for marketing-contract farmers when transaction costs are included in the estimate. The proportions were significantly lower for independent farmers. However, with the inclusion of transaction costs, production-contract farmers still earn profits that are more than twice higher ($p < 0.01\%$) than what independent farmers earn. But marketing-contract farmers' profits are 2% lower (statistically insignificant) than independent farmers' profits, indicating that marketing-contract farmers incur losses when transaction costs are considered. This also suggests that studies that do not incorporate transaction costs in their calculations may have overestimated or underestimated profits and costs of production-contract, marketing-contract and independent farming, and therefore transaction costs should be incorporated in cost and profit calculations.

Conclusions and policy implications

The details of institutional arrangements between modern food retail chains and farmers have not received significant attention in existing studies. The institutional framework provides a way in which contracting with modern food retail chains overcomes market failures related to uncertainty, risk sharing and coordination failure. However, due to the lack of a proper legal system, enforcement mechanisms and awareness, institutions are not able to play a significant role in contract farming. Evidence from existing studies reveals that modern food retail chains tend to behave opportunistically toward farmers. Studies from developing countries have discussed the problems that smallholders face in participating in such chains. However, little attention has been paid to capturing how the lack of institutional arrangements in modern food retail chains is responsible for smallholders' lower participation in these chains. Existing studies have not quantitatively measured the impact of the chains' opportunistic behavior and asymmetric information on smallholders' profit and welfare. This chapter attempts to quantify the effects of opportunistic behavior and asymmetric information on chili farmers in India. We measure the magnitude of transaction costs and their components of bargaining costs, information costs and enforcement costs across the chains' production and marketing contracts compared to independent farmers.

This study used the propensity score matching to estimate the profit and transaction cost variables for farmers contracting with modern food retail chains and for independent farmers. The major advantage of this method is that it eliminates selection bias on observable differences between farmers contracting with the chains and independent farmers. We found that production-contract farmers have significantly higher (1% of level of significance) profits (Rs 57,310/acre) than independent farmers have (Rs 34,288/acre) and that marketing-contract farmers have higher profits (Rs 40,403/acre) than independent farmers. However, transaction costs were significantly higher for contract farmers than for farmers in traditional markets. Transaction costs accounted for 14.5% of total costs for production-contract farmers and for 9.60% of total costs for marketing-contract farmers, whereas transaction costs were less than 6% for independent farmers. Transaction costs were almost Rs 9,178 higher ($p < 0.01\%$) for production-contract farmers and Rs 5,394 higher ($p < 0.01\%$) for marketing-contract farmers than for independent farmers. We argue that the existing studies on modern food retail chains overestimated the farmers' profit from such chains.

Our results suggest that opportunistic behavior by the chains imposes significant transaction costs on chili farmers. Asymmetric information on price and grading uncertainty also significantly increased farmers' transaction costs. This has implications for farmers' participation in modern food retail chains. We suggest that governments need to introduce proper institutional setups in written and oral contracts between the chains and farmers. The institutional structure should focus first on controlling chains' opportunistic behavior, which is the most effective way to reduce transaction costs. We also suggest a strict enforcement mechanism, which would make the cost associated with opportunistic behavior less critical for farmers and might increase farmers' participation. Further, we suggest that problems of asymmetric information can be solved with cooperation and collective efforts to get information on prices and quality standards. We strongly feel that farmers' cooperatives would significantly reduce uncertainty about prices and product quality standards.

References

Abebe, Gumataw K., Jos Bijman, Ron Kemp, Onno Omta, and Admasu Tsegaye. (2013). "Contract Farming Configuration: Smallholders' Preferences for Contract Design Attributes," *Food Policy* 40: 14–24. https://doi.org/10.1016/j.foodpol.2013.01.002.

Alchian, A. A. (1965). "Some Economics of Property Rights," *Il Politico, Rubbettino Editore* 30: 816–829.

Alene, A. D., V. M. Manyong, G. Omanya, H. D. Mignouna, M. Bokanga, and G. Odhiambo. (2007). "Smallholder Market Participation Under Transactions Costs: Maize Supply and Fertilizer Demand in Kenya," *Food Policy* 33 (2008): 318–328.

Allen, D. W., and D. Lueck. (1993). "Transaction Costs and the Design of Cropshare Contracts," *The RAND Journal of Economics* 24 (1): 78–100.

Arrow, K. (1969). "The Organisation of Economic Activity: Issues Pertinent to the Choice of Market Versus Non-Market Allocation", *The Analysis of and Evaluation of Public*

Expenditure: The PPB System, Volume 1. US Joint Economic Committee, 1st Session, pp. 59–73.

Becker, S. O., and A. Ichino. (2002). "Estimation of Average Treatment Effects Based on Propensity Scores," *Stata Journal* 2 (4): 358–377.

Birthal, P. S., P. K. Joshi, and A. Gulati. (2005). "Vertical Coordination in High-Value Food Commodities: Implications for Smallholders," MTID Discussion Paper No. 85. International Food Policy Research Institute, Washington, DC, USA.

Boahene, K., T. A. B. Snijders, and H. Folmer. (1999). "An Integrated Socioeconomic Analysis of Innovation Adoption: The Case of Hybrid Cocoa in Ghana," *Journal of Policy Modeling* 21 (2): 167–184.

Caliendo, M., and S. Kopeinig. (2008). "Some Practical Guidance for the Implementation of Propensity Score Matching," *Journal of Economic Surveys* 22: 31–72.

Cameron, A. C., and P. K. Trivedi. (2005). *Microeconometrics: Methods and Applications*. Cambridge: Cambridge University Press.

Coase, R. H. (1937). "The Nature of the Firm," *Economica* 4: 386–405.

Coase, R. H. (1960). "The Problem of Social Cost," *The Journal of Law and Economics* 3: 1–44.

Courtois, P., and J. Subervie. (2014). "Farmer Bargaining Power and Market Information Services," *American Journal of Agricultural Economics* 97 (3): 953–977.

De Silva, H., and D. Ratnadiwakara. (2008). "Using ICT to Reduce Transaction Costs in Agriculture Through Better Communication: A Case-study from Sri Lanka". Accessed on March 14, 2009. http://lirneasia.net/wp-content/uploads/2008/11/ transactioncosts.pdf.

Dehejia, R. H., and S. Wahba. (2002). "Propensity Score Matching Methods for Nonexperimental Causal Studies," *Review of Economics and Statistics* 84 (1): 151–161.

Dhananjaya, B. N., and A. U. Rao. (2009). "Namdhari Fresh Limited, In: Inclusive Value Chains in India—Linking the Smallest Producers at Modern Markets", Ed: M. Harper. World Scientific, Singapore, Case study 1, Chapter 3, pp. 26–41.

Dorward, Andrew, Kydd Jonathan, and Poulton Colin. (1998). *Smallholder Cash Crop Production under Market Liberalisation: A New Institutional Economics Perspective*. Wallingford: CAB International, pp. 240–265.

Escobal, J. A., and D. Cavero. (2012). "Transaction Costs, Institutional Arrangements and Inequality Outcomes : Potato Marketing by Small Producers in Rural Peru," *World Development*. Elsevier Ltd. 40 (2): 329–341. doi: 10.1016/j.worlddev.2011.07.016.

Fischer, Elisabeth, and Matin Qaim. (2012). "Linking Smallholders to Markets: Determinants and Impacts of Farmer Collective Action in Kenya," *World Development* 40 (6): 1255–1268. https://doi.org/10.1016/j.worlddev.2011.11.018.

Frank, S., and D. Henderson. (1992). "Transaction Costs as Determinants of Vertical Coordination in the US Food Industries," *American Journal of Agricultural Economics* 74: 941–950.

Furubotn, E. G., and R. Richter. (1997). *Institutions and Economics Theory: The Contribution of the New Institutional Economics*. Ann Arbor, MI: The University of Michigan Press.

Gopalakrishnan, Shankar, and Priya Sreenivasa. (2009). "Corporate Retail: Dangerous Implications for India's Economy," *Economic and Political Weekly* 44 (32): 48–55. https://doi.org/10.2307/25663422.

Greene, W. (2012). *Econometric Analysis*, eighth ed. Upper Saddle River, River, NJ: Prentice Hall.

Grosh, B. (1994). "Contract Farming in Africa: An Application of the New Institutional Economics," *Journal of African Economies* 3: 231–261.

Hobbs, J. E. (1996). "A Transaction Cost Approach to Supply Chain Management," *Supply Chain Management* 1 (2): 15–27.

Hobbs, J. E. (1997). "Measuring the Importance of Transaction Costs in Cattle Marketing," *American Journal of Agricultural Economics* 79 (4): 1083–1095.

Hobbs, J. E. (2004). "Information Asymmetry and the Role of Traceability Systems In." *Agribusiness* 20 (4): 397–415. https://doi.org/10.1002/agr.20020.

Holloway, G., C. Nicholson, C. Delgado, S. Staal, and S. Ehui. (2000). "Agroindustrialization Through Institutional Innovation: Transaction Costs, Cooperatives and Milk-Market Development in East-African Highlands," *Agricultural Economics* 23: 279–288.

Joseph, M., N. Soundararajan, M. Gupta, and S. Sahu. (2008). "Impact of Organized Retailing on the Unorganized Sector," Technical Report, Indian Council for Research on International Economic Relations (ICRIER), New Delhi.

Kedar, Vishnu. (2018). "Magnitude of Transaction Costs in Vegetable Markets? Empirical Findings from India," Ronald Coase Institute. www.coase.org/2018bratislavaabstracts.htm#kedar.

Key, N., and D. Runsten. (1999). "Contract Farming, Smallholders, and Rural Development in Latin America: The Organization of Agroprocessing Firms and the Scale of Outgrower Production," *World Development* 27 (2): 381–401.

Liu, X., and L. Lynch. (2007). "Do Agricultural Preservation Programs Affect Farmland Conversion?" Selected Paper Prepared for Presentation at the Agricultural and Applied Economics Association Annual Meeting, Portland, OR, July 29–August 1.

Lyon, F. (2003). "Community Groups and Livelihoods in Remote Rural Areas of Ghana: How Small-Scale Farmers Sustain Collective Action," *Community Development Journal* 38 (4): 323–331.

Mangala, K. P., and P. G. Chengappa. (2008). "A Novel Agribusiness Model for Backward Linkages with Farmers : A Case of Food Retail Chain," *Agricultural Economics Research Review* 21: 363–370.

Masakure, Oliver, and Spencer Henson. (2005). "Why Do Small-Scale Producers Choose to Produce Under Contract ? Lessons from Nontraditional Vegetable Exports from Zimbabwe," *World Development* 33 (10): 1721–1733. https://doi.org/10.1016/j.worlddev.2005.04.016.

Matungul, P. M., M. C. Lyne, and G. F. Ortmann. (2001). "Transaction Costs and Crop Marketing in the Communal Areas of Impendle and Swayimana," KwaZulu Natal. *Development Southern Africa* 18 (3): 347–363.

Mishra, Ashok K., Anjani Kumar, Pramod K. Joshi, and Alwin D'Souza. (2016). "Impact of Contracts in High Yielding Varieties Seed Production on Profits and Yield: The Case of Nepal," *Food Policy* 62: 110–121. https://doi.org/10.1016/j.foodpol.2016.05.005.

Mishra, Ashok K., Anjani Kumar, Pramod K. Joshi, Alwin D'Souza, and Gaurav Tripathi. (2018). "How Can Organic Rice Be a Boon to Smallholders? Evidence from Contract Farming in India." *Food Policy* 75 (February): 147–157. https://doi.org/10.1016/j.foodpol.2018.01.007.

Miyata, S., N. Minot, and D. Hu. (2009). "Impact of Contract Farming on Income: Linking Small Farmers, Packers, and Supermarkets in China," *World Development* 37 (11): 1781–1790.

Ning, Wang. (2003). "Measuring Transaction Costs : An Incomplete Survey," Working Papers, Number 2, Ronald Coase Institute. http://www.coase.org/workingpapers/wp-2.pdf.

Otsuka, K., Y. Liu, and F. Yamauchi. (2016). "Growing Advantage of Large Farms in Asia and Its Implications for Global Food Security," *Global Food Security*: 1–6.

Pingali, Prabhu, Yasmeen Khwaja, and Madelon Meijer. (2005). "Commercializing Small Farms : Reducing Transaction Costs," ESA Working Paper No. 05–08, Agricultural and Development Economics Division, The Food and Agriculture Organization of the United Nations.

Rao, Elizaphan J.O., Bernhard Brümmer, and Matin Qaim. (2012). "Farmer Participation in Supermarket Channels, Production Technology, and Efficiency: The Case of Vegetables in Kenya," *American Journal of Agricultural Economics* 94 (4): 891–912. https://doi.org/10.1093/ajae/aas024.

Reardon, T., and C. B. Barrett. (2000). "Agroindustrialization, Globalization, and International Development: An Overview of Issues, Patters, and Determinants," *Agricultural Economics* 23: 195–205.

Reardon, T., and J. A. Berdegué. (2002). "The Rapid Rise of Supermarkets in Latin America: Challenges and Opportunities for Development," *Development Policy Review* 20 (4): 371–388. https://doi.org/10.1111/1467-7679.00183.

Reardon, T., J. A. Berdegué, and C. Peter Timmer. (2005). "Supermarketization of the Emerging Markets of the Pacific Rim: Development and Trade Implications," *Journal of Food Distribution Research* 36 (1): 3–12. http://ageconsearch.umn.edu/bitstream/26754/1/36010003.pdf.

Reardon, T., K. Chen, B. Minten, and L. Adriano. (2012). *The Quiet Revolution in Staple Food Value Chains: Enter the Dragon, the Elephant and the Tiger.* Mandaluyong City, Philippines: Asian Development Bank.

Rosenbaum, P. R., and D. B. Rubin. (1985). "Constructing a Control Group Using Multivariate Matched Sampling Methods That Incorporate the Propensity Score," *The American Statistician* 39: 33–38.

Schipmann, C., and M. Qaim. (2011). "Supply Chain Differentiation, Contract Agriculture, and Farmers' Marketing Preferences: The Case of Sweet Pepper in Thailand," *Food Policy* 36: 657–677.

Singh, Sukhpal. (2002). "Contracting Out Solutions: Political Economy of Contract Farming in the Indian Punjab," *World Development* 30 (9): 1621–1638. https://doi.org/10.1016/S0305-750X(02)00059-1.

Singh, Sukhpal, and Naresh Singla. (2010). "Fresh Food Retail Chains in India : Organisation and Impacts," *Centre for Management in Agriculture, IIMA* 238: 1–20.

Sivramkrishna, S., and A. Jyotishi. (2008). "Monopsonistic Exploitation in Contract Farming: Articulating a Strategy for Grower Cooperation," *Journal of International Development* 20 (3): 280–296.

Smith, J. A., and P. E. Todd. (2005). "Does Matching Overcome LaLonde's Critique of Non- Experimental Estimators"? *Journal of Economics* 125: 305–353.

Stanton, J. V. (2000). "The Role of Agribusiness Development: Replacing the Diminished Role of the Government in Raising Rural Incomes," *Journal of Agribusiness* 18 (2): 173–187.

Stefanides, A., and L. Tauer. (1999). "The empirical impact of bovine somatropin on a group of New York dairy farms," *American Journal of Agricultural Economics* 81 (1): 95–102.

Tauer, L. W. (2009). "Estimation of treatment effects of recombinant bovine somatotropin using matching samples," *Applied Economic Perspectives and Policy* 31 (3): 411–423.

Trebbin, A. (2014a). "Linking Small Farmers to Modern Retail Through Producer Organizations—Experiences with Producer Companies in India," *Food Policy* 45: 35–44. doi: 10.1016/j.foodpol.2013.12.007.

Trebbin, A. (2014b). "Linking Small Farmers to Modern Retail through Producer Organizations—Experiences with Producer Companies in India." *Journal of food policy* 45: 35–44. https://doi.org/10.1016/j.foodpol.2013.12.007.

Vishnu, Kedar, and Parmod Kumar. (2014). "Food Retail Chain as an Alternate Marketing Channel in India," *Indian Journal of Agricultural Marketing* 28 (3): 34–42.

Vishnu, Kedar, and Parmod Kumar. (2019). "Structure and Strategy of Supermarkets of Fruits and Vegetables Retailing in Karnataka," ISECWorking Paper, 438, Bangalore.

Williamson, O. E. (1985). *The Economic Institutions of Capitalism: Firms, Markets, Relational Contracting*. New York: The Free Press.

Wooldridge, J. M. (2010). *Econometric Analysis of Cross Section and Panel Data*. Cambridge, MA, London, England: MIT Press, pp. 453–550.

Part II

Case studies in contract farming

8 Contract farming in lentils and rice seed production

Case studies from Nepal

Ashok K. Mishra, Anjani Kumar and Stefan Hirsch

In developing countries, the agricultural sector has strong links to the rural economy and constitutes the core economic activity accounting for a major share of employment. Any shock to the agricultural sector can therefore significantly affect livelihoods, quality of life and consumption behaviors in the rural sector of these countries. Any initiative that may help smallholder farmers to overcome income risks related to inputs and outputs would therefore significantly improve the livelihood and incomes of a majority of the population in developing countries. Additionally, it is widely recognized that significant growth in developing countries' agricultural sector can reduce rural poverty levels more significantly than growth in any other sector of the economy (Christiaensen and Demery, 2007; Ravallion and Chen, 2007; Suryahadi, Suryadarma and Sumarto, 2008).

Production agriculture is a risky business (Huirne et al., 2000; Hardaker et al., 2004) caused by uncertainty about the output price and sometimes the price of inputs[1] at the time production decisions are made. Smallholders in developing and emerging countries are potentially vulnerable to these farming risks. As a consequence of these risks, smallholders with limited resources are in some cases pushed deeper into poverty. Risk management strategies are geared toward the set of produced outputs; inputs including land allocation, production techniques, such as irrigation; but also include diversification strategies related to on- and off-farm activities. In addition, farmers can use risk management strategies based on market instruments such as insurances, futures markets or contract farming (Robison and Barry, 1987; OECD, 2009). However, in developing countries, not all risks can be insured through market instruments, given their systemic nature and the lack of knowledge on the likelihood of these risks, as well as information asymmetry related to those probabilities (OECD, 2009). The latter is very true for smallholder farms in developing countries. In developed countries, contract farming (CF) has been established as a market activity to manage farming risk. Contract farming is a market-based mechanism that could be considered a risk management strategy (Robison and Barry, 1987) with potentially far-reaching implications for increasing and stabilizing the incomes of smallholder farms in developing countries. Thus contract farming can support food security and reduce poverty in developing countries (World Bank, 2007; Mishra et al., 2016, 2018b, 2018c).

Through contract farming, smallholder farm households can make agreements with contractors with appropriate terms that benefit both parties—the smallholder farm families and the companies/cooperatives. In developing countries, where formal markets for credit and inputs may be missing, contract farming would provide smallholder farmers with several advantages. These include the provision of inputs, better access to credit and technology, expertise transfers, assured- and fixed-pricing mechanisms and access to output markets and contractors (Eaton and Shepherd, 2001), given that certain preconditions are met. Through contract farming, farmers could also gain access to high-yielding varieties or stress-tolerant seeds (Gulati et al., 2005) or could indemnify themselves against supply shocks caused by nature, such as floods or droughts, or loan defaults (Eaton and Shepherd, 2001).[2] Lastly, contract farming is expected to help smallholder farm households specialize in the cultivation of high-value crops and is crucial for the process of vertical integration. This may help farmers achieve economies of scale and earn higher and more stable incomes. On the other hand, contract farming could also help in attaining so-called 'pro-poor agricultural growth'[3] (Dorward et al., 2004). In contrast, for staple crops, characterized by low values and high storability, Swinnen, Vandeplas and Maertens (2010) argue that contract farming is less obvious and introduces the possibility of contract breaches.

A large number of studies have analyzed the relevance of contract farming in the production of high-value crops (see, e.g., Oya, 2012; Wang, Wang and Delgado, 2014; Otsuka, Nakano and Kazushi, 2016; Mishra et al., 2018a); however, the number of studies focusing on low-value crops particularly in poor countries like Nepal is as yet limited (Mishra et al., 2016, 2018b, 2018c). In this chapter we therefore investigate the effect that contract farming has on Nepalese smallholders' profits and yield (or productivity), focusing on the low-value production of lentils and rice seed as a case study.

In Nepal, known as the home of Mount Everest, the agricultural sector is the core of the nation's economy, with a contribution of around 35% to the gross domestic product and providing employment for a larger number of people than the manufacturing, service and tourism industries together (Khanal and Mishra, 2018). After decades of political instability, low-income growth, natural disasters and out-migration, Nepal's agricultural sector has suffered significantly. Poor storage and transportation infrastructure, reduced credit availability and budget deficits (Sharma, 2006) also have detracted from the sector's growth. Besides these limitations, a lack of irrigation facilities has made Nepal's agriculture susceptible to the consequences of climate change. Additionally, a report by Yadav, Otsuka and David (1992) notes that formal credit institutions excluded smallholder farms from their services and catered only to large farmers. Consequently, falling agricultural output and higher input prices, along with fluctuations in the prices Nepalese farmers receive, have seriously affected the incomes of smallholder farm households. Moreover, there has been no provision for crop insurance (Manandhar et al., 2011), leaving farmers at the risk of uncertainties in the global market. A study by Pokhrel and Thapa (2007) of mandarin farmers in Nepal notes that intermediaries like banks were actually 'cheating and harassing' farmers. They would delay payment, manipulate prices and take away a major share of profits.

In this chapter, we test whether contract farming could provide a pathway to incentivize low-value crop farmers to pursue commercial agriculture. In particular, we test whether contract farming can increase yields and profits. Further, we examine whether the benefits are distributed homogeneously among smallholder farms of various sizes. As a case study, we focus on the production of lentils and rice seed. Legumes, such as lentils, are beneficial from a nutritional point of view when jointly consumed with cereal grains through amino acid complementation of proteins. However, note that global per capita production of lentils is decreasing (Vandenberg, 2009; Mishra et al., 2018b). In addition, they are favorable for the environment through nitrogen fixation.[4] Crop rotation schemes that include legumes, such as lentils, leads to increases in the amount of soil nitrogen (N) if residues are incorporated in the soil (Sainju et al., 2007). It is effective to grow lentils in rotation with sorghum/maize, although in Nepal, lentils are usually rotated with rice as a relay crop (zero tilled) or directly subsequent to the rice harvest and soil cultivation (post-rice system) (Campbell et al., 1992; Swinnen and Maertens, 2007). Alternatively, lentils can be used as a mixed crop with barley, wheat, linseed or mustard (Shrestha et al., 2005; Mishra, 2018b). Finally, producing high-yielding varieties of rice seed under contract farming can lead to an increased supply of superior crop varieties[5] and high-quality seeds, which constitute the most feasible approach of persistently enhancing agricultural production, productivity and finally food security (Ram et al., 2016).

Data and methodology

The analysis is based on primary data from a survey of Nepalese households that cultivate lentils and rice seeds. Data are collected at the household level using a structured questionnaire.[6] The survey included information on farmer characteristics, applied cropping patterns, cultivation economics, as well as marketing channels and good agricultural practices applied by the farmer. In February and March 2015, farmers in districts of the central, western and midwestern regions of Nepal were surveyed. The selection of these districts was based on the high relevance of contract farming for the production of lentils and rice seeds in these regions where private companies and/or cooperatives conclude formal, written contracts with smallholder households related to the supply of these low-value crops. From the three sample districts, smallholder households were randomly selected from 28 wards under seven Village Development Councils (VDCs). The councils within the districts were also chosen based on the prevalence of contract farmers specializing in lentil and rice seeds production. Investigating the population of farmers under contract and non-contract farmers in the regions in Nepal, a survey sample of 602 farmers were rated as suitable for lentils and a sample of 604 farmers for rice seed production. Of those farmers, 300 and 306 operated under lentil and rise seed contract farming, respectively. Non-contract farmers were also randomly selected from the same or adjacent wards under the respective councils in each of the three sample districts.

We compare two groups—one with contracts (contract farmers) and one without contracts (non-contract farmers). Note that it is possible that smallholders may self-select into one of these groups, resulting in a correlation between their unobservable attributes and their adoption decisions. This would potentially result in biased estimation. Comparing the two groups and controlling for similar observable attributes through propensity score matching could resolve the problem of selection bias (Mendola, 2007; MEDEP/UNDP, 2007). Several matching algorithms are available, with the most common methods being kernel-based matching (KBM) and radius-based matching (RBM). We used RBM to estimate outcome variables (profits and yield). Further, some hidden bias may be present as some unobservable variables might affect both the treatment (in our case, the adoption of contract farming) and the outcome variables (profits and yield). To address this issue, Rosenbaum (2002) suggests a bounding approach, which we have included in our analysis.

In the next section, we present the descriptive statistics of the sampled farmers separately for commodities and contract/non-contract farmers followed by the analysis of the outcome variables based on RBM estimation.

Descriptive statistics

Table 8.1 reports that, on average, farmers engaged in lentil cultivation operate somewhat larger farms than rice seed producers. Moreover, contract farmers involved in cultivating rice seeds (1.00 ha) and lentils (0.99 ha) operated significantly larger holdings than did non-contract farmers of those two crops. Regarding the educational attainment of smallholders, we observe a common pattern for both commodities with the majorities of farmers in contract and non-contract farming having attained high school or higher levels of education (intermediate, or 12th grade). However, for both crops, the proportion of farmers with higher education did not vary significantly between farmers under contract and non-contract farmers. Regarding farm size, almost 22% of contract farmers involved in rice seed production and 25% involved in lentil production were small farms, while the majority of farms in this category are large (43% and 46%, respectively). Nevertheless, the data suggest that a relevant share of small farms is involved in contract farming in these low-value crops. This may signal that small-sized farming households in Nepal may be benefiting from contract farming with higher income and yields. Table 8.1 reveals that profits per hectare for contract smallholder farmers were consistently higher for both commodities than profits per hectare for non-contract producers. For example, contract farmers cultivating high-yielding-variety rice seeds received

Table 8.1 Attributes of contract and non-contract producers of rice seeds and lentils, Nepal, 2014–2015

Commodities	*Rice seeds*		*Lentils*	
Variable	*Non-contract farmers*	*Contract farmers*	*Non-contract farmers*	*Contract farmers*
Total land operated (hectare)	0.60	1.00***	0.64	0.99**
Age, operator (years)	45.35	45.38	42.84	44.20
Farming experience, operator (years)	26.30	26.31	25.00	24.13**
Household size (number)	6.16	6.58	6.23	6.73**
HH member, primary education (%)	5	1***	18	17
HH member, middle school education (%)	12	09	20	25
HH member, high school education (%)	51	54	50	44
HH member, intermediate education (%)	32	36	10	12
Total profit per hectare (NPR)	9,079	24,964***	20,593	29,099***
Yield (kg per hectare)	4,296	4,669***	1,022	1,137***
Small farm[a] (%)	46	22***	49	25***
Medium farm (%)	33	35	32	28
Large farm (%)	21	43***	18	46***
District_1 (%)	32	35	29	37**
District_2 (%)	17	16	48	51
District_3 (%)	50	49	23	12***
Number of observations	*298*	*306*	*298*	*306*

Source: Mishra et al., 2016, 2018b.

Notes:

Nepali rupee; exchange rate was US$ 1 = 107 Nepali rupee at the time of the survey. All monetary variables are rounded to full Nepali rupee.

[a] The smallholder farmers are defined differently under different agricultural commodities. This is done to account for the relative sizes of land considered 'small' under different cropping regime. For paddy, small (≤0.43), medium (>0.43–≤0.73), large (> 0.73); for lentils small (≤0.51), medium (>0.54–≤ 0.85), large (>0.85).

* Significant at the 10% level.

** Significant at the 5%.

*** Significant at the 1% level.

2.7 times higher profits per hectare, and those cultivating lentils received 1.4 times higher profits per hectare, than non-contract farmers. Table 8.1 also reveals that the yield per hectare for contract smallholder farmers was consistently higher for both commodities than yield per hectare for non-contract producers. Contract farmers cultivating rice seeds recorded 9% more in yields than non-contract farmers, while contract farmers cultivating lentils recorded

11% more in yields than non-contract farmers. Note that most of the mean comparisons in the variables of interest were calculated without controlling for the attributes of smallholder farm families and therefore might provide biased results. In the following section, we control for the attributes of farm, family and operator and report the average treatment effect (ATT) of smallholders using contract farming. We also control for sample selection bias.

Results and discussion

Do smallholders of low-value crops benefit from contract farming?

For the balancing property, attributes such as age, size of land operated, educational attainment, household size, farming experience, the proportion of male households, the proportion of households with migrated members, phone ownership, castes, type of soil, districts and wealth owned were considered. The propensity score distributions of contract and non-contract farmers of rice seeds and lentils show substantial overlap, which implies that the common support assumption indicating proper matching holds. Tables 8.2 and 8.3 present the average treatment effects (ATT) estimated using the RBM method for rice seeds and lentils producers, respectively. First, Table 8.2 reports that rice seed contract producers significantly increased their profits and yield compared to what non-contract farmers received. Specifically, contract rice seed producers increased profits by about NRs 13,061 per hectare and their yield by about 358 kg/ha compared to non-contract farmers. The difference for all outcome variables was statistically significant at the 1% level of significance. In addition, the critical level of hidden bias ranged from 1.45–1.50 to 2.30–2.35, from which it can be concluded that the implications derived from the estimated effects will not change even if a significant level of unobserved heterogeneity was present (Mendola, 2007). For smallholder lentil producers, Table 8.2 shows that contract producers earned higher profits and yield than non-contract producers. Profits per hectare increased by NRs 12,146 and yields increased by 88 kg/ha through contract farming. All outcome variables were statistically significant at the 1% level of significance, and the critical level of bias ranged from 1.50–1.55 to 2.20–2.25.

A natural question that arises from this study is which of the two commodity benefits more from contract farming? In other words, which low-value commodity is economically superior for smallholders in Nepal? Table 8.3 shows the average treatment effects estimated using the RBM method for contract farmers producing lentils compared to contract farmers producing rice seeds. The table indicates that the adaptation of contract farming in lentils has a positive and statistically significant effect on profits per hectare compared to contract farming rice seed production. Specifically, results show that profits of smallholder contract farmers in lentils exceed profits of contract farmers in rice seeds by about NRs 14,266 per hectare.

Table 8.2 Average treatment effects for contract vs. non-contract rice seed and lentil producers, Nepal

Matching algorithm	*Outcome (per hectare)*	*ATT (NRs)*	t-*stats*
Rice seeds			
Radius-based matching (RBM)	Total profits	13,061	3.74
	Yield (kg)	358	2.83
Lentils			
	Total profits	12,146	4.29
	Yield (kg)	80	2.54

Source: Authors' estimation.

Notes:
Nepali rupee (NR); exchange rate was US$ 1 = 107 Nepali rupee at the time of the survey. ATT is the average treatment effect for the treated.
** Significant at the 5%; ***Significant at the 1% level.

Table 8.3 Average treatment effects of CF lentils vs. CF rice seed producers

Matching algorithm	*Outcome (per hectare)*	*ATT (NRs)*	t-*stats*
Radius-based matching (RBM)	Total profits	14,266	3.15

Source: Authors' estimation

Notes:
Nepali rupee (NR); exchange rate was US$ 1 = 107 Nepali rupee at the time of the survey. ATT is the average treatment effect for the treated.
** Significant at the 5%.
*** Significant at the 1% level.

These findings show that, even after controlling for a number of attributes including districts, contract farmers generated higher profits and yields per hectare than non-contract farmers. These results are consistent and robust for both rice seed and lentil smallholder farm households and confirm previous findings by Mishra et al. (2016, 2018b). A plausible reason is that contract farming provides a mechanism through which farmers can eliminate price risk and can have access to credit (relaxing liquidity constraint), better quality of inputs, new production technologies, fertilizers and pesticides, better irrigation systems, lower transaction costs, better quality of produce and access to extended markets, both domestic and international (Bellemare, 2015).

Do small-size producers of low-value crops benefit from contract farming?

An interesting question is whether contract farming affects large farms and small farms equally or whether a heterogeneous effect exists. To answer this, in Tables 8.4 and 8.5, we categorized smallholder farms in our sample into relatively small, medium-sized and large farms. Note that size differentiation was done separately for each commodity.[7] We then compared farmers with and without contracts in each size category.

For rice seed production, Table 8.4 reveals that small farms (≤0.43 ha) under contract benefitted with respect to profits and yield per hectare in comparison to small farms without contracts. For example, profit per hectare increased by NRs 13,793, and yields increased by about 424 kg/ha compared to small farms without contracts. Medium-size farms (>0.43–≤0.73 ha) and large farms (>0.73 ha) under contract also experienced significant increases in profit per hectare in comparison to medium-sized and large farms without contracts. However, the effect on yield among medium-sized and large farms was statistically insignificant. *This finding demonstrates that contract farming has positive implications for the welfare of relatively small farms involved in rice seed cultivation, not only with respect to yield but also with respect to profits per hectare.*

We perform a similar exercise for cultivators of the other low-value crop, lentils. Table 8.5 reveals that relatively small farms with less than 0.51 ha that operate under contracts tend to gain by about NRs 9,427 in profits per hectare and 83 kg/ha in yield compared to small-farm lentil producers without contracts. The differences were statistically significant at the 1% level. For medium-sized lentil farms (>0.54–≤0.85 ha), those with contracts generated higher profits (17,327 NPR per hectare) than non-contract smallholder farms.

Table 8.4 Average treatment effects, contract vs. non-contract rice seed producers by farm size category

Farming category (ha)	*Outcome* (ha)	*ATT* (NRs)	t-*stat*
Small (0.01–0.43 ha)	Total profits	13,793	2.35
	Yield (kg)	424	1.76
Medium (>0.43–0.73 ha)	Total profits	13,576	2.49
	Yield (kg)	445	1.29
Large (>0.73 ha)	Total profits	12,624	1.96
	Yield (kg)	345	1.64

Source: Authors' estimation.

Notes:
Nepali rupee (NR); exchange rate was US$ 1 = 107 Nepali rupee at the time of the survey. ATT is the average treatment effect for the treated.

* Significant at the 10%.

** Significant at the 5%.

*** Significant at the 1% level.

Table 8.5 Average treatment effects of contract vs. non-contract lentil producers, by farm size category, Nepal

Farming category (ha)	*Outcome* (per ha)	*ATT* (NRs)	t-*stat*
Small (0.01–0.51 ha)	Total profits	9,427	2.23
	Yield (kg)	83	1.97
Medium (>0.51–≤0.85 ha)	Total profits	17,327	2.89
	Yield (kg)	9	0.18
Large (>0.85 ha)	Total profits	7,049	1.03
	Yield (kg)	104	1.46

Source: Authors' estimation.

Notes:
Nepali rupee (NR); exchange rate was US$ 1 = 107 Nepali rupee at the time of the survey. ATT is the average treatment effect for the treated.
* Significant at the 10%.
** Significant at the 5%.
*** Significant at the 1% level.

Finally, for large lentil farms (>0.85 has), we fail to detect any statistical difference in yields and profits, between farms with contracts and those without contracts. *This finding again suggests that, compared to small non-contract farms, relatively small farms engaged in contract farming of low-value agricultural products, such as lentils and rice seeds, stand to gain in profit and yields per hectare.*

Conclusions

Evidence regarding contract farming in low-value crops is with few exceptions (e.g., Mishra et al., 2016, 2018b) as yet scarce. Proponents of contract farming have argued that it can improve vertical linkages, increase revenue and profitability and enhance food security. We test whether contract farming can attain these multiple objectives in Nepal, a poverty-ridden country, in the context of low-value crops like lentils and rice seeds. Contrary to claims by Swinnen, Vandeplas and Maertens (2010), our results show that contract farming in low-value crops like lentils and rice seeds is beneficial for smallholder farms.

We found that, compared to small non-contract producers, contract farming in low-value crops indeed improves profits and yields of smallholder farmers. The results are robust across the two commodities. Our study provides evidence that contract farming is a valuable instrument and a market-based solution that smallholder farm households growing staple foods can use to increase profits, livelihoods and economic well-being. We also found that smallholder farms engaged in contract lentil farming have higher profits than smallholder farms engaged in contract rice seed farming. Additionally, we found that, within the smallholder category, relatively small farms with contracts tend to receive higher profit and yields per hectare for rice seed and lentil cultivation than do small farms without contracts. Medium-sized farms with contracts also benefited with respect to profits compared to medium-sized non-contract farms; however, the effect on yields was insignificant within this size class. Finally, large rice farms with contracts received significantly higher profit per hectare than their non-contract counterparts. However, for both commodities, no significant change in yields between contract and non-contract farms could be detected. It is likely that the majority of large farms already engages in commercial farming and utilize better inputs. This implies, that there is likely to be no differences in the yield through contract farming, while the significantly higher profit per hectare could be explained by the contractors providing better market access and information.

Agriculture is the main economic activity in developing economies. Given that a major share of the rural population works in agriculture, any shock to this sector has a significant effect on the rural economy. However, the agricultural sector is not immune to risks, which originate mainly from fluctuations in prices, weather or yields, from imperfect input and output markets and from asymmetric information. Risks to agriculture in developing countries seem to be rising, particularly those related to climate change. The increasing frequency of droughts and the variability in production have adversely affected the livelihoods of smallholder farmers and in some cases have pushed them into deeper poverty. Various popular risk management strategies such as diversification, off-farm activities and market instruments such as insurance, contract farming and future markets have become popular choices for farmers in developed countries. Whether these market mechanisms work in developing countries is an important question. The non-insurability of systemic risks, a lack of information on the probabilities of these risks and asymmetric information may cause the failure of insurance and futures markets.

This suggests that increasing opportunities for contract farming in low-value crops (or staple foods) through private companies and/or cooperatives may be an effective way to improve income and yields and thereby the economic well-being of smallholder households in developing countries. Contract farming also would help Nepal increase production of rice seeds and exploit the comparative advantage the nation has in lentil production. Agro-processing units could be possible outlets for such high-value, better-quality and homogeneous produce. Lentils are an ideal crop to promote the consumption of nutritious whole foods, so increasing lentil production could lead to improved nutrition globally. Increased lentil production also could lead to potential improvements in the environment by encouraging environmentally sustainable cropping systems. Crop rotation with lentils can increase soil nitrogen (N) rates and is effective in rotation with sorghum/maize and rice. Via zero tillage, crop rotation that includes lentils can result in sustainable and environmentally friendly production systems.

These results suggest that private companies, cooperatives and policy leaders seeking to improve the agricultural sector's economic well-being should focus their efforts on supporting the smallest of small farm holders in both commodities in the adoption of contract farming. This could increase these farmers' profits and yields, which improves their economic well-being and ultimately leads to growth in the agricultural sector and the nation's economy. Therefore, policy recommendations on these fronts include increasing the role of market forces, like contract farming, in solving income and food security issues of smallholder farm households producing staple food crops in poor countries. While factors such as access to technology and infrastructure have not been accounted for in our study, future studies may want to analyze the scope of these factors.

Notes

1 Input-related risks mainly deal with limited accessibility to risk-reducing inputs, such as better irrigation systems, better seeds and advanced machines, fertilizers and pesticides, including fluctuations in input quality and prices.
2 However, for contract farming to be successful, governments should ensure that legal frameworks for contracts are well established (Eaton and Shepherd, 2001).
3 Pro-poor agricultural growth policies include enhancing understanding of the role of institutional, microeconomic, macroeconomic and international factors; identifying appropriate policy initiatives to address related constraints; and developing policy tools.
4 Note that soil and crop management practices potentially affect the quantity, quality and distribution of plant residues in the soil, which influence soil carbon and nitrogen fractions (Mishra et al., 2018b).
5 The government of Nepal has issued the National Seed Vision (2013–2025) report. This Seed Vision suggests that enhanced seed production increases by a factor of three; that seed replacement by farmers increases 25% for cereal crops such as rice, wheat and maize; and that rice yield increases to 3.8 metric tons (e.g., Mishra et al., 2016). The presence of certified and high-yielding seeds from the formal sector has been relatively low. Along with this, there has been a huge gap between the seed required and the seed supplied or replaced, calling for an increase in improved seed production.
6 See Mishra et al. (2016, 2018b, 2019) for other applications of data from this survey.
7 Smallholder farmers are defined differently under various agricultural commodities. This is done to account for the relative sizes of land considered 'small' under different cropping regimes. For instance, in the case of rice seeds, small (≤0.43 ha), medium (>0.43–≤0.73 ha), large (>0.73 ha); and for lentils, small (≤0.51 ha), medium (>0.54–≤0.85 ha), large (>0.85 hea).

References

Bellemare, M.F. (2015). Contract farming: What's in it for smallholder farmers in developing countries. In *Choices: The Magazine of Food, Farm, and Resource Issues.*

Campbell, C.A., R.P. Zentner, F. Selles, V.O. Biederbeck and A.J. Leyshon. (1992). Comparative effects of grain lentil—wheat and monoculture wheat on crop production, N economy and N fertility in a Brown Chernozem. *Canadian Journal of Plant Science* 72: 1091–1107.

Christiaensen, L. and L. Demery. (2007). *Down to Earth: Agriculture and Poverty Reduction in Africa*. The World Bank, Washington, DC.

Dorward, A., J. Kydd, J. Morrison and I. Urey. (2004). A policy agenda for pro-poor agricultural growth. *World Development*: 73–89.

Eaton, C. and A. Shepherd. (2001). *Contract Farming Partnerships for Growth*. FAO Agricultural Services Bulletin, Rome, p. 145.

Gulati, A., N. Minot, C. Delgado and S. Bora. (2005). Growth in high-value agriculture in Asia and the emergence of vertical links with farmers. In *Linking Small-Scale Producers to Markets: Old and New Challenges*. The World Bank, Washington, DC.

Hardaker, J.B., R. Huirne, J.R. Anderson and G. Lien. (2004). *Coping with Risk in Agriculture*. CABI Publishing, London, England.

Huirne, R.B.M., M. Meuwissen, J.B. Hardacker and J.R. Anderson. (2000). Risk and risk management in agriculture: An overview and empirical results. *International Journal of Risk Assessment and Management* 1: 125–136.

Khanal, A.R. and A.K. Mishra. (2018). Impacts of contract farming decisions on high value crop production of smallholder Nepalese farmers: A multinomial endogenous switching regression approach. Selected Paper prepared for presentation at the 2018 Agricultural & Applied Economics Association Annual Meeting.

Manandhar, S., D.S. Vogt, S. Perret and F. Kazama. (2011). Adapting cropping systems to climate change in Nepal: A cross regional study of farmer's perception and practices. *Regional Environment Change*: 335–348.

Mendola, M. (2007). Agricultural technology adoption and poverty reduction: A propensity-score matching analysis for rural Bangladesh. *Food Policy* 32: 372–393.

MEDEP/UNDP. (2007). *Mirco-Enterprises Development for Poverty Alleviation*. Mirco-Enterprises Development Programme, Ministry of Industry, UNDP, Kathmandu.

Mishra, A.K., A. Kumar, P.K. Joshi and A. D'Souza. (2016). Impact of contracts in high yielding varieties seed production on profits and yield: The case of Nepal. *Food Policy* 62 (July): 110–121.

Mishra, A.K., A. Kumar, P.K. Joshi and A. D'Souza. (2018a). Production risks, risk preference, and contract farming: Impact on food security in India. *Applied Economics Perspectives and Policy* 40(3): 353–378.

Mishra, A.K., A. Kumar, P.K. Joshi and A. D'Souza. (2018b). Impact of contract farming on yield, costs, and profitability in low-value crop: Evidence from a low-income country. *Australian Journal of Agricultural and Resource Economics* 62(4): 589–607.

Mishra, A.K., A. Kumar, P.K. Joshi and A. D'Souza. (2018c). Cooperatives, contract farming, and farm size: The case of tomato producers in Nepal. *Agribusiness: An International Journal* 34: 865–886.

Mishra, A.K., A.N. Rezitis and M.G. Tsionas. (2020). Production under input endogeneity and farm-specific risk aversion: Evidence from contract farming and Bayesian method. *European Review of Agricultural Economics* 47(2): 591–618.

OECD. (2009). *Managing Risk in Agriculture: A Holistic Approach*. OECD Publishing, Paris, https://doi.org/10.1787/9789264075313-en.

Otsuka, K., Y. Nakano and T. Kazushi. (2016). Contract farming in developed and developing countries. *Annual Review of Resource Economics* 8(1): 353–376.

Oya, C. (2012). Contract farming in Sub-Saharan Africa: A survey of approaches, debates, and issues. *Journal of Agrarian Change* 12(1): 1–33.

Pokhrel, D. and G. Thapa. (2007). Are marketing intermediaries exploiting mountain farmers in Nepal? A study based on market price, market margin, and income distribution analyses. *Agricultural Systems*: 151–164.

Ram, B.K.C., D. Singh, C.P. Lalchan and B.K. Joshi. (2016). Participatory F1 Hybrid seed production of tomato and its economic benefit. *The Journal of Agriculture and Environment* 17: 46–55.

Ravallion, M. and S. Chen. (2007). China's (Uneven) progress against poverty. *Journal of Development Economics* 82(1): 1–42.

Robison, L.J. and P.J. Barry. (1987). *The Competitive Firm's Response to Risk*. Macmillan Publishing Company, New York.

Rosenbaum, P.R. (2002). *Observational Studies*, second ed. Springer, New York.

Sainju, U.P., A. Lenssen, T. Caesar-Thonthat and J. Waddell. (2007). Dryland plant biomass and soil carbon and nitrogen fractions on transient land as influenced by tillage and crop rotation. *Soil & Tillage Research* 93: 452–461.

Sharma, K. (2006). The political economy of civil war in Nepal. *World Development*: 1237–1253.

Shrestha, R., K.H.M. Siddique, N.C. Turner, D.W. Turner and J. Berger. (2005). Growth and seed yield of lentil (*Lens culinaris* Medikus) genotypes of West Asian and South Asian origin and crossbreds between the two under rainfed conditions in Nepal. *Australian Journal of Agricultural Research* 56: 971–981.

Suryahadi, A., D. Suryadarma and S. Sumarto. (2008). The effects of location and sectoral components of economic growth on poverty: Evidence from Indonesia. *Journal of Development Economics* 89(1): 109–117.

Swinnen, J. and M. Maertens. (2007). Globalization, privatization, and vertical coordination in food value chains in developing and transition countries. *Agricultural Economics* 37: 89–102.

Swinnen, J., A. Vandeplas and M. Maertens. (2010). Governance and surplus distribution in commodity value chains in Africa. In A. Sarris and J. Morrison (Eds.), *Food Security in Africa: Market and Trade Policy for Staple Foods in Eastern and Southern Africa*. Edwards Elgar, Cheltenham, UK, pp. 77–88.

Vandenberg, A. (2009). Expansion of lentil in Canada. In A. Masood and S. Kumar (Eds.), *Milestones in Food Legumes Research*. IIPR, Ottawa, Canada, pp. 58–72.

Wang, H.H., Y. Wang, M.S. Delgado. (2014). The transition to modern agriculture: Contract farming in developing economies. *American Journal of Agricultural Economics* 96(5): 1257–1271.

World Bank. (2007). *World Development Report 2008: Agriculture for Development*. The World Bank, Washington, DC.

Yadav, S., K. Otsuka and C. David. (1992). Segmentation in rural financial markets: The case of Nepal. *World Development*: 423–436.

9 Formal versus informal milk value chains in Bangladesh

Trade-offs between price and food safety

Anjani Kumar, Vinay K. Sonkar and Sunil Saroj

Historically, dairying has been part of a mixed farming system in Bangladesh, where most rural households rear cows for draft power and to produce milk for family consumption (Saadullah, 2002; Zaedi et al., 2009; Mian et al., 2007). Dairy animals in Bangladesh include cows, buffaloes and goats. Bangladesh has one of South Asia's highest cattle densities (Karim, 1997). There are about 24 million cattle, 1.46 million buffaloes and 25.44 million goats in the country. Of the total cattle population, nearly 6 million are milch cattle, of which about 85%–90% are indigenous, and the remaining 10%–15% are crossbred. Indigenous animals consist of Nondescript Deshi, Red Chittagong, Pabna, North Bengal Gray and Munshigonj White cattle (DLS, 2012).

Over the years, milk production has increased Bangladesh, tripling from 1.82 million metric tons (MMT) in 2002–2003 to 6.09 MMT in 2015–2016, with an annual growth rate of about 9%. However, the growth rate has fluctuated considerably over the years, mainly because of natural disasters, regular flooding, the severity of the monsoon, *Sidr* (like a tsunami) and the prevalence of diseases such as anthrax (Hemme and Uddin, 2010). The average annual consumption of liquid milk in Bangladesh hovers around 10 to 12 liters per capita. It remains low compared to regional levels (for example, about 60 liters per capita in India). However, during the last three decades or so, significant changes have unfolded in the production, procurement, supply, processing and distribution of milk and milk products (Jabbar et al., 2005; Islam et al., 2015).

Until the 1990s, the Bangladesh Milk Producers' Cooperative Union Ltd. (BMPCUL) was the only formal sector that processed and marketed milk from the cooperative producers of Bangladesh. Market reforms of the 1990s, in conjunction with increases in per capita income, population, infrastructure and urbanization, led to a surge in demand for the animal products and dairy sector in Bangladesh and attracted several private-sector players. Pran, the Bangladesh Rural Advancement Committee (BRAC) Dairy known as Aarong, Amo milk and Aftab dairy, are some of the prominent formal channels in Bangladesh's milk market (World Bank, 2008; Jabbar et al., 2005; Hafez, 2004; Shamsuddin, 2011; Raha, 2009).

Formal and informal milk marketing channels coexist in Bangladesh. The formal channel includes public- and private-sector milk processing units and cooperatives such as BMPCUL. The informal channels include sales of milk directly to consumers, milk vendors, small teashops, restaurants etc. Figure 9.1 shows how milk passes from household dairy producers to consumers in both channels. In the informal channel, smallholders typically sell their milk to nearby markets, directly to neighboring consumers or to a local trader, who sells it to the local market or sometimes to the formal channel if it is available in the surrounding area. Sometimes in the informal channel, smallholders sell their milk to local processors who make dairy products such as sweetmeats and ghee, which are the leading dairy products produced in the informal sector (Hemme et al., 2004).

The integration of dairy farmers with organized and formal and informal milk marketing channel outlets remains a major policy discussion in Bangladesh. However, literature provides little or no evidence on the choice of formal and informal milk marketing channels by Bangladeshi smallholder dairy farmers and on whether participants in the marketing outlets are reaping the benefits. Therefore, this chapter's study accomplishes two objectives. First is to

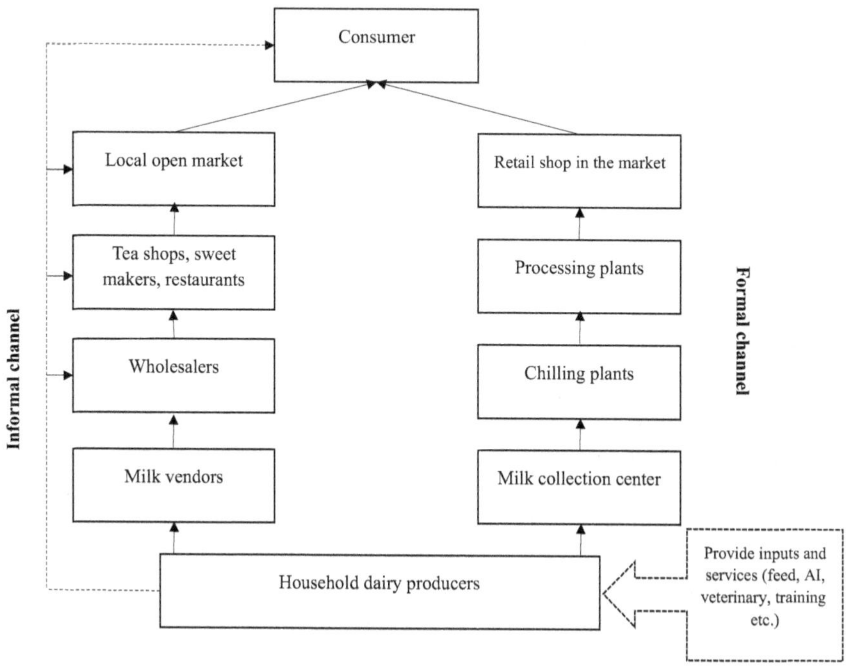

Figure 9.1 Milk marketing channel in Bangladesh

Source: Authors.

identify the factors influencing dairy farmers' choice of formal and informal outlets. Second is to estimate the impact of a farmer's choice of formal and informal outlets on price realization and the adoption of food safety measures (FSM). The study uses survey data from 1,004 dairy farmers in Bangladesh, propensity score matching and Lewbel instrumental variable (IV) models to account for sample selection bias and endogeneity.

Data

The study is based on primary data of 1,004 dairy farmers from five divisions[1] (Chittagong, Dhaka, Khulna, Rangpur and Rajshahi) in Bangladesh. We collected data in 2016–2017. We identified two districts from each division and three upazilas[2] from each district after consultation with livestock officers. These divisions, districts and upazilas have a high prevalence of commercial dairy farming in Bangladesh. The number of households in a selected upazila was allocated in proportion to the rural population. We then identified a cluster of two to five villages and interviewed the allocated number of sample households from these clusters of villages. We collected data on socio-economic and demographic characteristics. These included (1) labor endowment; (2) household assets, including livestock inventory and amount and value of equipment; (3) food safety measures practiced; (4) animal health management; (5) expenditure on food safety practices; (6) milk marketing; (7) labor uses and cost; (8) animal feed types and cost; (9) animal breeding types and cost; and (10) social networking.

Empirical methods

To address the issues of selection bias and endogeneity, we use Lewbel instrumental variable regression models in combination with propensity score matching (PSM).

Propensity score matching

We use the PSM method to construct the counterfactual and reduce problems arising from selection biases in the sample. The purpose of using this method is to find a group of farmers in the informal channel similar to farmers in the formal channel in all relevant observable characteristics. The primary modality is intended to find the 'neighbors' value (propensity score) of the non-treated group, which is close to the values of the treated group. The primary purpose of the propensity score estimation is to balance the observed distribution of covariates across the treatment and control groups. The balancing test generally is required after matching to ascertain whether the differences in covariates in the two groups in the matched sample have been eliminated, in which case the matched comparison group can be considered a plausible counterfactual (Ali and Abdulai, 2010). Although several versions of balancing tests exist in the literature, the most widely used is the standardized mean difference (bias) between treatment and control groups suggested by Rosenbaum and Rubin (1985). In principle, after matching, there should be no systematic differences in the distribution of covariates between the groups. We have eliminated about 170 observations from the total sample and used only those matched samples and controlled selection bias in the estimation. However, the PSM estimators do not account for unobservable factors. Hence, we employed the Lewbel instrumental variable method to control for the endogeneity issue.

Instrumental variable approach

The empirical model to be estimated and the identification strategy used to establish the causal impact of marketing channels (formal versus informal) on price realization and food safety measures (FSM) is given in Equation (9.1):

$$Y_{1i} = \alpha_{1i} + \beta_{1i} MKT + \gamma_{1i} X_i + \varepsilon 1_i \tag{9.1}$$

where Y denotes a column vector of dependent variable (price realized and food safety measures). MKT denotes the marketing channels and is a dummy variable that takes the value of 1 if farmers sell milk through the formal channel and 0 if they sell through the informal channel, X is a vector of control variables, and ε is an error term with mean zero. If MKT is exogenous to the outcome variables, then the coefficient β_i represents the average treatment effects of marketing channels on the dependent variable of interest. However, the marketing channels cannot be assigned randomly to the households, and there may be omitted variables that are likely to influence both the marketing channels and the dependent variable (i.e., price realized and food safety measures). For example, omitted variables related to habit formation (i.e., number of years of dairy consumption, local food safety standards related to dairy products, exposure to food safety awareness programs conducted by the government or consumer organizations) are likely to influence farmers' selection of milk marketing channels, the price realized and food safety measures. In our case, the endogeneity problem is possible due to omitted variable bias rather than simultaneous causality.

The identification strategy relies on the use of instrumental variables. There are two critical assumptions of the IV method. First, the instruments must be correlated with the endogenous (treatment) variable, which can be tested with 'first-stage *F*-statistics' in first-stage regression. Small values (less than 10) of first-stage *F*-statistics imply failure of the first assumption. The null hypothesis that the marketing channel (*MKT*) is exogenous was rejected (at the 1% level of significance). Second, the instruments must be uncorrelated with the error, which can be tested only if there are more instruments than treatments. For the identification strategy, we have used 'number of households selling milk to the formal channel at the upazila level.' We call this the network variable. This instrumental variable establishes the causal relationship between marketing channels and outcome indicators. Thus the identifying assumption is that the instrumental variable is uncorrelated with ε_2 in Equation (9.2).

$$Y_{2i} = \alpha_{2i} + \beta_{2i}\widehat{MKT} + \gamma_{2i}X_i + \varepsilon_{2i} \tag{9.2}$$

$\widehat{MKT}$ is the predicted value of MKT obtained from the first-stage regression of MKT on instrumental variables and all the control variables (X) in Equation (9.3) can be shown:

$$MKT = \alpha_3 + \beta_{3d}P + \gamma_3 X + \epsilon \tag{9.3}$$

where P is the dummy variable for the practices that fetch higher prices for milk, and ϵ is an error term with mean zero. If our instrument (P) is valid, then the coefficient β_{2i} is the main effect (i.e., local average treatment effects [LATE]) of MKT on the outcome variable.[3] Further, the standard IV regression assumes that the instrumental variables are not correlated with the error term. Thus the presence of heteroscedasticity in the data does away with the standard IV assumption, resulting in an inefficient outcome. The Lewbel (2012) technique takes care of heteroscedasticity by generating instrumental variables from the data that are not correlated with the heteroscedastic error. It gives three sets of estimates: (1) estimates based on standard IV, (2) estimates based on generated IVs and (3) estimates based on both standard IVs and generated IVs. In this method, instruments form as simple functions from the model's data. This approach can be followed when no external instruments are available, or it can be used to supplement external instruments to improve the efficiency of the IV estimator. The estimators customarily use appropriate lagged values of endogenous regressors to identify the model (Lewbel, 2012). To determine the factors affecting marketing channels, we have used the first stage of the two-stage least squares (2SLS) model.

Results and discussion

Table 9.1 shows the distribution of dairy farmers by herd size and land size. A large number of farmers (44%) have herds of five to nine milch animals. About 39% of farmers have fewer than four milch animals, and 16% of farmers are rearing more than nine milk animals. The land size distribution of sample households reveals that the majority of the dairy farmers (69%) have small landholdings, 24% belong to the medium-sized land category, and about 5% have large holdings of more than 4 ha. A tiny share (2%) of dairy farmers are landless. In our study, herd size and land size are positively correlated but not high, as we expected during the field survey.

Table 9.1 also presents the production and sale of milk by the dairy farmers' herd size and land size. On average, a dairy farmer produces 49.4 L of milk per day, of which 48.1 L are sold, and the rest is retained for household

Table 9.1 Structure of milk production and marketed surplus

	Number of households	*Average number of animals*	*Production (household/ day) (L)*	*Marketed surplus (household/ day) (L)*	*Marketed surplus as % share of production*	*% share of production*	*% share of marketed surplus*
Herd size							
<4 animals	327 (39.2)	3.2	19.1	18.1	94.4	15.2	14.7
5–9 animals	370 (44.4)	6.4	56.3	54.8	97.4	50.5	50.6
>9 animals	137 (16.4)	14.8	103.2	101.5	98.4	34.3	34.7
Land size							
Landless	17 (2.0)	4.0	15.7	14.7	94.0	0.6	0.6
Small	577 (69.2)	6.1	43.8	42.5	97.1	61.3	61.1
Medium	201 (24.1)	7.6	64.8	63.3	97.7	31.6	31.7
Large	39 (4.7)	7.7	68.9	67.4	97.7	6.5	6.6
All	834	6.5	49.4	48.1	97.3	100.0	100.0

Source: Authors.

Note: Percentage values are in parentheses.

consumption. Milk production in our sample households is predominantly a commercial activity. Across all categories of farmers, 97% of the milk produced is sold.

Choice of milk value chains and participation of small dairy farmers in milk value chains

Farmers have multiple options for selling their milk through formal and informal value chains. Formal value chains consist of dairy cooperatives and organized private processors (both domestic and multinationals). Informal value chains are represented by milk vendors or local traders, consumer households and small-scale processors. Table 9.2 presents the pattern of milk sales to formal and informal channels in terms of the number of farmers associated with different market chains, the distribution of milk sales within value chains and the distribution of milk sales across value chains. About 80% of farmers, accounting for approximately 80% of the total marketed surplus, are associated with informal milk value chains (Table 9.2). Milk vendors comprise the most preferred milk marketing outlet: 53% of the dairy farmers accounting for 44% of the total milk sales are associated with cooperatives. Hotels/tea shops (i.e., Hotel Restaurant Institutional (HRI)) and cooperatives share about 25% and 19% of milk sales, respectively. The presence of private-sector formal dairies in the milk market is negligible.

Our findings indicate that irrespective of the scale of production, most farmers are selling their milk to informal value chains. However, a positive correlation appears between herd size/land size and association with formal chains.

Table 9.2 Farmer-wise distribution of milk sales across value chains

	Formal channels			*Informal channels*			
	Dairy co-operative	*Formal dairy*	*Total*	*Milk vendor*	*Households*	*HRI*[a]	*Total*
Farmer-wise distribution of milk sales within value chains							
Herd size							
<4 animals	9.8	1.8	11.6	58.1	26.9	0.9	85.9
5–9 animals	18.9	1.6	20.5	51.9	14.1	9.5	75.4
>9 animals	18.3	0.7	19.0	44.5	8.0	26.3	78.8
Land size							
Landless	0.0	0.0	0.0	58.8	35.3	5.9	100.0
Small	11.3	1.9	13.2	54.1	20.1	8.5	82.7
Medium	25.9	1.0	26.9	50.3	11.9	9.0	71.2
Large	25.6	0.0	25.6	51.3	12.8	15.4	79.5
All	15.2	1.6	16.8	53.1	18.1	8.9	80.1
Quantity-wise distribution of milk sales within value chains							
Herd size							
<4 animals	8.5	53.0	10.5	17.8	37.1	0.7	15.8
5–9 animals	53.0	35.4	52.2	48.7	40.2	59.5	50.2
>9 animals	38.5	11.6	37.3	33.5	22.7	39.8	34.0
Land size							
Landless	0.0	0.0	0.0	0.8	1.8	0.3	0.8
Small	42.7	80.5	44.0	69.2	71.2	51.4	65.3
Medium	42.9	19.5	41.9	26.9	24.3	38.9	29.2
Large	14.3	0	14.1	3.1	2.7	9.4	4.7
All	100.0	100.0	100.0	100.0	100.0	100.0	100.0
Quantity-wise distribution of milk sale across value chains							
Herd size							
< 4 animals	11.6	2.9	14.5	55.6	28.8	1.2	85.5
5–9 animals	19.9	0.5	20.4	41.7	8.5	29.3	79.6
> 9 animals	21.3	0.3	21.5	42.4	7.1	29.0	78.5
Land size							
Landless	0.0	0.0	0.0	53.7	32.0	14.3	100.0
Small	13.7	1.0	14.7	50.7	12.9	21.7	85.3
Medium	25.2	0.5	25.7	36.2	8.1	30.1	74.3
Large	40.4	0.0	40.4	20.3	4.3	34.9	59.6
All	19.2	0.8	19.9	43.9	10.9	25.3	80.1

Source: Authors.

Note: [a]HRI stands for Hotel Restaurant Institutional.

For instance, 19% of large farmers (>9 animals) are associated with formal value chains, but only about 12% of small dairy farmers are related to formal value chains.

Price realization and food safety measures under different value chains

We have taken price realized and food safety measures as the two critical indicators of the efficiency of a milk value chain at its upstream. Price and food

Table 9.3 Distribution of price realization and FSM across different channels

	Price (Taka/L)			*Food safety measures (values between 0 to 1)*		
	Formal	*Informal*	*All*	*Formal*	*Informal*	*All*
Herd size						
< 4 animals	36.2	42.2	41.5	0.61	0.57	0.58
5–9 animals	35.5	43.9	42.2	0.62	0.61	0.61
> 9 animals	38.8	48.2	46.5	0.65	0.66	0.66
Land size						
Landless		44.1	44.1		0.58	0.58
Small	36.8	44.2	43.2	0.62	0.60	0.60
Medium	35.8	43.2	41.3	0.63	0.62	0.62
Large	36.9	41.3	40.0	0.64	0.63	0.63
All	36.4	43.9	42.6	0.62	0.60	0.61

Source: Authors

safety measures represent production and economic efficiency, respectively. In Table 9.3, we compare these two indicators across the different milk value chains. The comparison is fascinating as the food safety measures' value is higher for farmers associated with formal chains, and the reverse is true in the case of prices. On average, a dairy farmer receives Bangladesh Taka 42.6 from the sale of one liter of milk. Large dairy farmers, who have more than nine animals, receive a slightly higher price than other farmers receive, but the difference is not statistically significant. A comparison of milk prices across value chains shows that dairy farmers associated with informal chains realize significantly higher prices than farmers associated with formal chains. In food safety measures, we found that the formal channel has adopted better food safety practices than the informal channel. This also corroborates our results finding better adoption of food safety measures in the formal channel, which lead to increase in the dairy farmers' efficiency.

Descriptive analysis

Table 9.4 reports the descriptive statistics of the key variables, which can influence farmers' choice of the formal channel. Price realization is higher for the informal channel than for the formal channels, and the difference is statistically significant. However, the food safety measure is higher for the formal channel than for the informal channel, and the difference is statistically significant. We also found positive statistical differences in the case of household size and in the case of Katcha animal sheds. Dairy farmers who sell milk to the formal channel have larger households but have fewer resources for concrete animal sheds. However, in terms of land size, we found a greater share of smallholder dairy farmers (74.75%) were from informal channels, compared to the share (53.9%) from formal channels. For the rest of the variables, we found no statistical

Table 9.4 Descriptive statistics of key variables

	Formal	*Informal*	*Difference*	*All*
Outcome indicators				
Price realized (Taka/L)	36.43	43.87	−7.44***	42.61
Food safety measures (%)	64.12	61.04	3.15**	61.58
Other socio-economic variables				
Household head age (years)	49.89	49.29	0.60	49.39
Age square (number)	2,612.55	2,540.89	71.67	2,553.00
Household size (number)	6.53	5.45	1.08***	5.64
Household head education (years)	7.84	7.43	0.42	7.50
Belongs to small farmer (<1 ha) (%)	53.90	74.75	−20.85***	71.22
Income classification (%)				
Poor	34.75	30.88	3.87	31.53
Middle	29.08	34.49	−5.41	33.57
Rich	36.17	34.63	1.54	34.89
Katcha animal shed (%)	69.50	51.23	18.28***	54.32
Proportion of crossbred cattle (%)	98.98	91.98	7.00***	93.16
Observations	141	693		834

Source: Authors.

Notes:
* $p < 0.1$
** $p < 0.05$.
*** $p < 0.01$.

significant difference between households that sell through formal channels and those that sell through informal channels.

Determinants of farmers' choice of marketing chains

Table 9.5 presents the parameter estimates of the factors affecting dairy farmers' choice of the formal channel in Bangladesh. The first stage of the two-stage least squares (2SLS) model gives us the determinants that affect the choice of the formal channel in Bangladesh. The dependent variable is the marketing channel, which takes the value of 1 if farmers sell their milk through formal channels and 0 if they sell through informal channels. We controlled for division-fixed effects to accounting for unobserved characteristics influencing farmers to sell their milk through formal and informal channels. The household size is positively associated with farmers selling their milk through formal channels and is significant at the 1% level of significance. The proportion of crossbred cattle also is positive and significantly associated with the formal channels. In dairy farming, having crossbred cattle leads to animal productivity (Janssen and Swinnen, 2019). Farmers who have Katcha animal sheds also are more likely to sell milk to the formal channel than farmers who do not have such sheds.

Table 9.5 Determinants of the formal channel (1st stage of 2SLS)

Dependent variable: Formal channel = 1, Otherwise = 0	*Coef.*	*SE*
Age of household head (years)	−0.007	(0.008)
Square of age of household head (number)	0.000	(0.000)
Household size (number)	0.022***	(0.005)
Education completed (year)	0.006*	(0.004)
Belongs to small farmer (<1 ha)	−0.124***	(0.029)
Income class (Base: Poor)		
Middle	−0.074**	(0.032)
Rich	−0.066*	(0.036)
Katcha shed	0.127***	(0.029)
Proportion of crossbreed cattle	0.002***	(0.001)
Instrumental variable		
Number of households sell milk to the formal agency (log)	0.037***	(0.004)
Division fixed effect	Yes	
Constant	−0.116	(0.214)
R^2	0.266	
Observations	749	

Source: Authors.

Notes:
Standard errors in parentheses.
* $p < 0.1$.
** $p < 0.05$.
*** $p < 0.01$.

Since farmers who have such sheds are generally poor, this finding is in line with farmers' perceptions that associating with a formal channel would lead to higher economic status. However, farmers are unaware of the sheds' effect on efficiency parameters.

As expected, smallholding dairy farmers (<1 ha) are less likely to choose the formal channel than the informal channel. These farmers have less opportunity to negotiate milk prices with the formal channel (Kumar et al., 2019) and therefore choose not to sell milk in that channel. In our sample, we also have three categories of dairy farmers based on income. We found that middle-class and affluent dairy farmers chose to sell milk to informal channels because they get higher prices, and poor farmers chose the formal channel to get constant prices.

Impact of formal channel on price realization and food safety measures

In this section, we are interested in assessing the effects of formal channels on price realization and food safety measures in Bangladesh. We started with the OLS model with and without covariates to see the formal channel's impact on outcome indicators. Further, we employed the Lewbel instrumental variable method to look at the effects of formal channels on outcome indicators on the matched sample and controlled for endogeneity issues. In Tables 9.6 and 9.7, Columns 1 and 2 show parameters estimated from the OLS model, and columns 3–5 show parameters estimated through the Lewbel IV method. Column 3 of the Lewbel IV method gives the standard IV estimates, which are nothing but estimates from the 2SLS model; Column 4 gives estimates obtained through generated IV, and Column 5 gives estimates obtained through standard and generated IV. In all models, we have controlled for division-fixed effects to account for unobserved characteristics influencing farmers to sell their milk through formal and informal channels.

Price realization

As previously discussed, Table 9.6 reports the parameter estimates of our empirical model. The *t*-statistic is significant at the 1% level of significance, rejecting the null hypothesis of exogeneity of the formal channel in explaining variations in the prices dairy farmers realize in Bangladesh. In the OLS model, as expected, we found significant negative impact of a formal channel on the prices that dairy farmers realize in Bangladesh. Similarly, the coefficient is negative and statistically significant when we controlled for other covariates like socio-economic indicators. This motivates us to look beyond what factors most affect price and whether there are any omitted variables that we have not controlled for in the estimation. We then employed the Lewbel IV method. We find that the formal channel has a negative impact on prices that dairy farmers realize in Bangladesh. In columns 3–5, the coefficients are negative and statistically significant, ranging from about 8% to 22%. Households with Katcha animal sheds also are correlated with lower price realization. Generally, such households are poor, have relatively lower levels of bargaining power in price realization and have high input costs. We also found that the higher the farmers' proportion of crossbred cattle, the higher the bargaining power. Several studies found that crossbred cattle lead to an increase in higher prices for dairy farmers.

Food safety measures

Table 9.7 reports the parameter estimates of our empirical model. As previously mentioned, the *t*-statistic is significant at the 1% level of significance, rejecting the null hypothesis of exogeneity of the formal channel in explaining variations in the food safety measures of dairy farmers in Bangladesh. In the OLS model, we find a statistically significant impact of the formal channel on the food safety measures of dairy farmers in Bangladesh. The coefficient of the formal channel in the OLS model (Columns 1 and 2) is positive and statistically significant. However, this estimate is biased and is not controlled by omitted variables. We then employed the Lewbel IV method and found that the formal channel has a positive impact on the food safety measures of dairy farmers in Bangladesh.

Table 9.6 Impact of the formal channel on price realization

Dependent variable: Price (Taka/L) (log)	*OLS Model*		*Lewbel IV method*		
			Standard IV	*Both standard and generated IV*	
	Coef	*Coef*	*Coef*	*Coef*	*Coef*
Col→	*1*	*2*	*3*	*4*	*5*
Formal channel	−0.093***	−0.095***	−0.221***	−0.076***	−0.086***
	(0.014)	(0.014)	(0.040)	(0.017)	(0.017)
Age of household head (years)		−0.004	−0.005	−0.004	−0.004
		(0.003)	(0.003)	(0.003)	(0.003)
Age squared		0.000	0.000	0.000	0.000
		(0.000)	(0.000)	(0.000)	(0.000)
Household size (number)		0.003	0.006**	0.002	0.002
		(0.002)	(0.002)	(0.002)	(0.002)
Education completed (year)		0.000	0.001	−0.000	0.000
		(0.001)	(0.002)	(0.001)	(0.001)
Belongs to small farmer (<1 ha)		0.008	−0.007	0.010	0.009
		(0.012)	(0.013)	(0.012)	(0.012)
Income class (Base: Poor)					
Middle		0.011	0.005	0.011	0.011
		(0.014)	(0.015)	(0.014)	(0.014)
Rich		−0.001	−0.003	−0.001	−0.001
		(0.015)	(0.015)	(0.015)	(0.015)
Katcha shed		−0.022*	−0.004	−0.025**	−0.024*
		(0.012)	(0.014)	(0.012)	(0.012)
Proportion of crossbred cattle		0.001***	0.001***	0.001***	0.001***
		(0.000)	(0.000)	(0.000)	(0.000)
Constant	3.932***	3.953***	3.936***	3.956***	3.954***
	(0.016)	(0.083)	(0.088)	(0.082)	(0.083)
Instrumental variable	No	No	Yes		
Division fixed effect	Yes	Yes	Yes		
Observations	834	834	834	834	834
R^2	0.543	0.560	0.518	0.559	0.560

Source: Authors.

Notes:
Robust standard errors in parentheses.
* $p < 0.1$.
** $p < 0.05$.
*** $p < 0.01$.

Table 9.7 Impact of formal channel on food safety

Dependent variable: Food safety (log)	*OLS model*		*Lewbel IV method*		
			Standard IV	*Generated IV*	*Both standard and generated IV*
	Coef	*Coef*	*Coef*	*Coef*	*Coef*
Col→	*1*	*2*	*3*	*4*	*5*
Formal channel^	0.091***	0.052**	0.031	0.082***	0.071***
	(0.024)	(0.023)	(0.032)	(0.025)	(0.024)
Age of household head (years)		−0.006	−0.007	−0.006	−0.006
		(0.005)	(0.005)	(0.005)	(0.005)
Square of age of household head (number)		0.000	0.000	0.000	0.000
		(0.000)	(0.000)	(0.000)	(0.000)
Household size (number)		0.002	0.003	0.002	0.002
		(0.004)	(0.004)	(0.004)	(0.004)
Education completed (year)		0.007**	0.007**	0.006**	0.006**
		(0.003)	(0.003)	(0.003)	(0.003)
Belongs to small farmer (<1 ha)		−0.036	−0.039	−0.033	−0.034
		(0.024)	(0.024)	(0.023)	(0.023)
Income class (Base: Poor)					
Middle		0.014	0.014	0.016	0.015
		(0.021)	(0.021)	(0.021)	(0.021)
Rich		0.063***	0.063***	0.064***	0.063***
		(0.021)	(0.021)	(0.021)	(0.021)
Katcha shed		−0.080***	−0.076***	−0.084***	−0.082***
		(0.018)	(0.018)	(0.017)	(0.017)
Proportion of crossbreed cattle		0.006***	0.006***	0.006***	0.006***
		(0.001)	(0.001)	(0.001)	(0.001)
Constant	4.094***	3.772***	3.769***	3.776***	3.775***
	(0.030)	(0.134)	(0.133)	(0.133)	(0.133)
Instrumental variable	No	No	Yes		
Division fixed effect	Yes	Yes	Yes		
Observations	834	834	834	834	834
R^2	0.026	0.346	0.346	0.345	0.346

Source: Authors.

Notes:
Robust standard errors in parentheses.
* $p < 0.1$.
** $p < 0.05$.
*** $p < 0.01$.

In Columns 3–5, the coefficients are positive and statistically significant, ranging from 3% to 8%. As already discussed, we have chosen Column 5 estimates for an explanation. The education of household heads plays an important role in the adoption of food safety measures. Practicing these measures requires a little bit of knowledge and technique. In our model, we found that dairy farmers who are better educated have higher adoption of food safety measures than farmers who are less educated. However, households with Katcha animal sheds are correlated with lower adoption of food safety measures than households without such sheds. Generally, such households are poor and have relatively fewer resources and techniques for handling milk production. Also, the higher the proportion is of crossbred cattle, the higher the adoption of food safety measures as a way to maintain the wellness and general hygiene of the crossbred cattle.

Conclusions

This chapter evaluated formal and informal value chains for their implications on efficiency and price realization. We find that both formal and informal value chains exist but that informal chains dominate the milk market in Bangladesh. The findings of our study further shed light on the trade-off between food safety and price realization. Association with formal chains encourages better compliance with food safety measures at the farm level, which is critical to ensure milk safety at subsequent levels of the milk value chain, but formal chains are only a small share of the milk market in Bangladesh. This contradiction in the milk market has important implications and suggests some linkage between the two sectors (formal and informal chains). Efforts should be made to improve efficiency in the formal milk value chain, and, at the same time, enhancing the adoption of food safety measures should be adequately emphasized in the informal milk value chain. Our econometric results show that dairy farmers in the formal value chain realize lower prices but have higher food safety measures than their counterparts in the informal chains. Having crossbred cattle leads to higher prices and better food safety measures, which implies dairy farmers can gain bargaining power in the milk marketing value chain.

Notes

1 The administration of Bangladesh is divided into eight major regions called divisions, and these five divisions are important for dairy farming.

2 The upazilas are the third tier of regional administration in Bangladesh, after divisions and districts. They function as subunits of districts. Bangladesh has 492 upazilas.

3 For the details on LATE, see Angrist and Pischke (2008).

References

Ali, A., & Abdulai, A. (2010). The adoption of genetically modified cotton and poverty reduction in Pakistan. *Journal of Agricultural Economics, Wiley Blackwell*, 61(1), 175–192, February.

Angrist, J. D., & Pischke, J.-S. (2008). *Mostly Harmless Econometrics: An Empiricist's Companion*. Princeton: Princeton University Press.

DLS. (2012). *Annual report on livestock*. Department of Livestock Services. Ministry of Fisheries and Livestock, Government People's Republic of Bangladesh.

Hafez, M. R. (2004). *Small-scale dairying in Bangladesh*. Report of the Twenty-Eighth Session of the Animal Production and Health Commission for Asia and the Pacific, 27 September—1 October, Chiangmai, Thailand.

Hemme, T., Garcia, O., & Khan, A. R. (2004). *A Review of Milk Production in Bangladesh with Particular Emphasis on Small-Scale Producers*. Rome, Italy: FAO. Accessed on April 7, 2017. http://ageconsearch.umn.edu/bitstream/23774/1/wp030007.pdf.

Hemme, T., & Uddin, M. M. (2010). *Dairy policy impacts on Bangladesh and EU 15 dairy farmers' livelihoods: Dairy case study*. International Farm Comparison Network (IFCN) Dairy Research Center, Kiel, Germany.

Islam, A. H. M. S., Barman, B. K., & Murshed-e-Jahan, K. (2015). Adoption and impact of integrated rice—fish farming system in Bangladesh. *Aquaculture*, 447, 76–85.

Jabbar, M. A., Islam, S. M. E., Delgado, C., Ehui, S., Akanda, M. A. I., Khan, M. I., & Kamruzzaman, M. M. (2005). *Policy and Scale Factors Influencing Efficiency in Dairy and Poultry Producers in Bangladesh*. Joint working paper by ILRI/SLP/BSMRAU.

Janssen, E., & Swinnen, J. F. M. (2019). Technology adoption and value chains in developing countries: Evidence from dairy in India. *Food Policy*, 83, 327–336.

Karim, Z. (1997). *Agriculture for 21st century in Bangladesh*. A Final Draft Policy Report on National Livestock Development Policy, Ministry of Fisheries and Livestock, Dhaka, Bangladesh.

Kumar, A., Mishra, A. K., Saroj, S., & Joshi, P. K. (2019). Impact of traditional versus modern dairy value chains on food security: Evidence from India's dairy sector. *Food Policy*, 83, 260–270.

Lewbel, A. (2012). Using heteroscedasticity to identify and estimate mismeasured and endogenous regressor models. *Journal of Business & Economic Statistics*, 30(1), 67–80.

Mian, M. R. U., Fatema, J., & Rahman, M. H. (2007). Impact of dairy farming on livelihood of participating women under Grameen bank in a selected area of Rangpur district in Bangaldesh. *Indian Journal of Agricultural Economics*, 62(2), 259.

Paul, R. R., & Rubin, Donald B. (1985). Constructing a control group using multivariate matched sampling methods that incorporate the propensity score. *The American Statistician*, 39(1), 33–38. DOI: 10.1080/00031305.1985.10479383.

Raha, S. K. (2009). Status of dairy production and marketing in Bangladesh—Milk marketing system. In *Handbook of Dairy Nutrition-Bangladesh*, edited by Peter H. Robinson & U. Krishnamoorthy. Published by American Soybean Association (ASA). New Delhi, India: International Marketing.

Saadullah, M. (2002). *Smallholder Dairy Production and Marketing in Bangladesh. Smallholder Dairy Production and Marketing-Opportunities and Constraints*. Nairobi, Kenya: NDDB (National Dairy Development Board) and ILRI (International Livestock Research Institute), 7–21.

Shamsuddin, A. (2011). *SAARC dairy outlook SAARC Agriculture Centre (SAC)*. BARC, Bangladesh.

World Bank. (2008). *World Development Report 2008: Agriculture for Development*. Washington, DC: World Bank.

Zaedi, M., Demura, K., Yamamoto, Y., Sawauchi, D., Masuda, K., & Nakatani, T. (2009). Dairy industry in Bangladesh and structures of milk vita. *The Review of Agricultural Economics, Hokkaido University*, 64, 169–180.

10 Durum wheat value chain in Pakistan

Scanning the current picture and exploring future potential

Akhter Ali and Tariq Saleem

Agriculture contributes about 18.4% to Pakistan's gross domestic product and employs 38% of the total labor force. Wheat is an important crop for food security, occupying about 40% of the total cropped area during *Rabi* season and contributing about 10.1% to value-added products and 2.1% to overall GDP (Economic Survey of Pakistan, 2018–2019). Like other cereals, wheat possesses a high protein content, along with significant amounts of starch and sugar. A majority of rural households in Pakistan consume wheat as a complete diet, with a tiny proportion of supplemental food (Ahmad and Azkar, 1998; Amin et al., 2014; Iqbal et al., 2001; Janjua et al., 2010).

Bread wheat (*Triticum aestivum*), durum wheat (*Triticum turgidum*) and emmer wheat (*Triticum dicoccoides*) are the three major types of wheat being grown in different ecological zones of the world. Bread wheat is a well known type, commonly used for making bread (*chapati*) in much of the world. Farmers and other players involved in wheat production, trade, processing, marketing and consumption in Pakistan are not very much familiar with durum and emmer wheat. Durum wheat grain is a hard, bold, yellow grain with high protein content. It is suitable for making pasta products (noodles, spaghetti, macaroni, lasagna, shells, fettuccine and vermicelli), bulgur, couscous, bread etc. Emmer wheat is used for baking and in preparation of pastries, muesli and other processed products (Bux et al., 2012; Bakhsh et al., 2005; Sarwar and Ahmad, 2003).

Wheat value chain in Pakistan

Value addition is the process of increasing an agricultural commodity's economic value and consumer appeal. It is a production and marketing strategy driven by customer needs and preferences. The term 'value-added' is used to characterize food products that are converted from raw materials through processes that give the resulting product an incremental value in the marketplace, either through higher prices or expanded markets. Examples of value-added wheat products are bakery and pasta products. The purpose of value addition in agricultural commodities is to make more money, satisfy consumers' changing tastes and preferences and compete by differentiating a product in a highly competitive market.

Preproduction steps of the wheat value chain include seed research and distribution. Public-sector research organizations and private seed companies play lead roles in this process. The basic components of the wheat value chain are inputs, production, trade, processing and marketing. The major actors in the wheat value chain can be put into three main categories: value chain supporters, value chain players and value chain influencers. Value chain supporters are entities that provide services and add values to the product—for example, business advice, training and trade promotion; technical services (training, research and development, management services and logistics); and financial services (credit and leasing services). Value chain players are those who deal directly with and own the product: producers, dealers, processors, wholesalers/retailers and consumers. Value chain influencers include regulatory frameworks, policies and infrastructure at the local, national and international levels—affecting the businesses positively or negatively. Regulatory and administrative policies, laws and regulations, quality and quarantine measures, customs and taxes, incentives and free-trade agreements also affect value chains.

The governance structure is a value chain to determine the power dynamics of different players. Each value chain is different and depends on its length, the transformation process involved, the organization of the chain players, the competence of its actors etc. Details of the wheat value chain in Pakistan are presented in Figure 10.1.

In Pakistan's existing wheat supply chain, market-oriented players like the Pakistan Agricultural Storage and Supplies Corporation (PASSCO) and provincial food departments, as well as sales-oriented small businesses, are involved. They set quotas for wheat supply based on milling capacity, they license flour mills, and they impose bans on interdistrict wheat mobility to minimize illegal exports, particularly to Afghanistan, Iran, India and other central Asian countries. The Trading Corporation of Pakistan (TCP) imports wheat during shortages. The food industry is the second-largest industry in Pakistan, accounting for 27% of value-added production and 16% of total employment in the manufacturing sector. With a population of more than 210 million, Pakistan is the sixth-largest market in the world. About 75% of rural-based food manufacturers are in the informal sector (with difficulty in accessing raw material, skills, education and management). Pakistan's food sector is changing significantly as major shifts occur in lifestyles and traditional eating habits. Average consumers in Pakistan spend 42% of their income on food. Retail sales of processed foods are expanding by 10% per year and are estimated at US$ 1.4 billion, with imports constituting about US$ 325 million. Supermarkets are gaining popularity and account for 10% of total retail sales. Pakistan also hosts several western-style food chains, reflecting demand in the country.

Pakistan is blessed with diversified ecological zones, from high humid regions (>1,000 mm average annual rainfall) to semiarid and dry regions (<250 mm

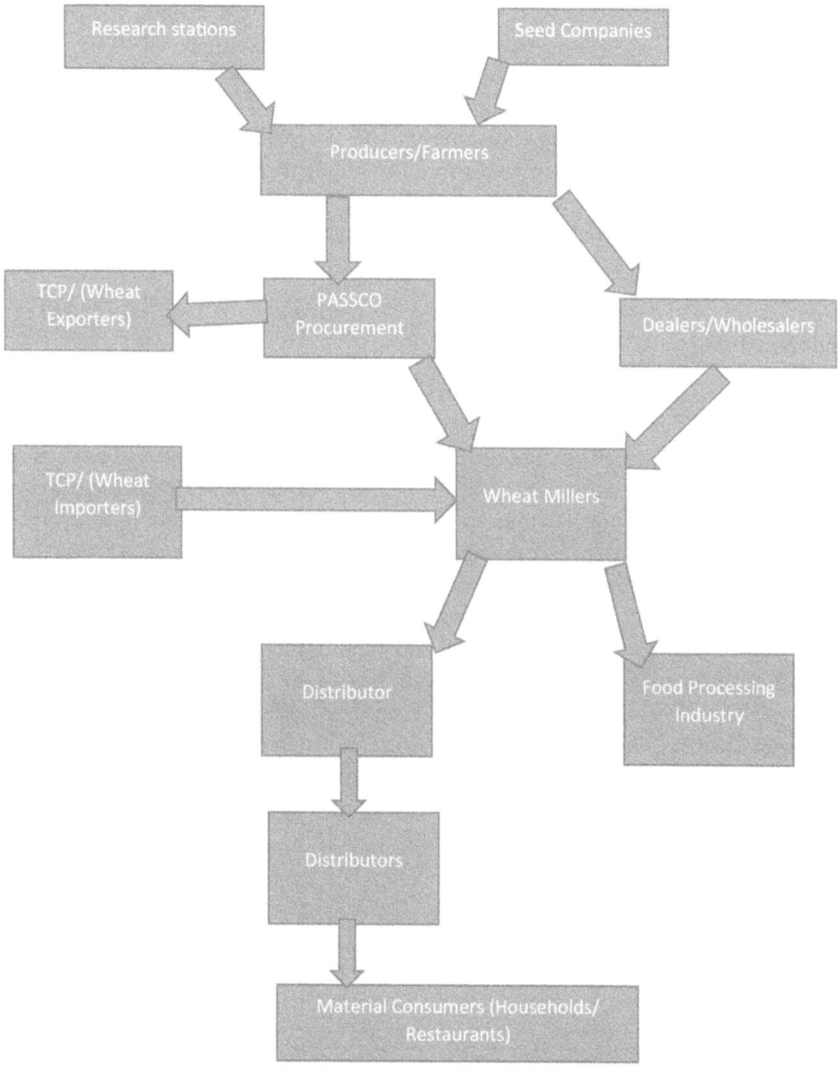

Figure 10.1 Possibility of durum wheat value chain in Pakistan

Source: Authors.

annual rainfall). Farmers are well versed in wheat production technology across the country. Changing lifestyles and tastes of the population, backed by secondary research, have led to increasing demand for pasta products over the last six to seven years in Pakistan. The international food processing industry, which is involved in pasta products, uses durum wheat flour for making quality products. The agro-ecological suitability of and huge market potential (domestic and foreign demand, mostly from Middle Eastern countries) for pasta foods lends support to the need for a comprehensive study on Pakistan's durum wheat value chain. We are interested in looking at the current scenario, identifying value chain actors, finding missing links in the value chain, assessing potential and exploring possible program interventions.

This chapter's main goal is to identify the potential value chain actors and their awareness of the durum wheat value chain in Pakistan. We also aim to point out critical constraints in the functioning of the durum wheat value chain in Pakistan. Findings will provide recommendations for the smooth operation of the country's durum wheat value chain.

Methodology

Through rigorous secondary research review, seven potential stakeholder groups in the durum wheat value chain were identified. These actors are seed companies, dealers, producers, millers, food processing industries, restaurants and consumers. A separate set of questionnaires for each stakeholder group was developed. The sampling details are presented in Table 10.1 Few food processing industries engage in processing pasta products. Therefore, two firms from Rawalpindi and three from Karachi were visited to get relevant information. In-depth interviews were conducted with wheat value chain actors to assess their awareness of, understanding of and willingness to engage in the durum wheat business. The data were analyzed using SPSS and STATA software. The analysis of each actor primarily focused on understanding their functioning mechanism, comprehending the nature of their roles and studying power dynamics in the chain. The study was conducted in seven districts of Punjab and Sindh: Faisalabad, Lahore, Sahiwal, Multan, Rahim Yar Khan, Rawalpindi and Karachi.

Table 10.1 Sampling of various stakeholders

Stakeholders	*Locations*					*Total*
	Faisalabad	*Lahore*	*Sahiwal*	*Multan*	*Rahim Yar Khan*	
Producers	04	04	04	06	04	**22**
Consumers	04	02	05	0	02	**13**
Dealers	01	01	01	01	01	**5**
Wheat millers	01	01	01	01	01	**5**
Restaurant	01	01	01	01	01	**5**
Seed companies	06	06	06	06	06	**30**
Food processing industry[a]	5					**5**
Total	**17**	**15**	**18**	**15**	**16**	**85**

Source: Authors' calculations.

Note: [a]Two from Rawalpindi and three from Karachi.

Empirical results

Seed companies

The majority of seed companies engaged in the large-scale seed business are mostly located in the Rahim Yar Khan and Jhang Districts. The companies have established proper processing and storage infrastructure and have developed an impressive number of registered growers. Most of these firms market seed through dealer networks. All seed companies depend on public-sector organizations for provision of pre-basic and basic seed with limited quantity. Most of the leading seed companies (in terms of business volume and outreach) have limited shares of their business in wheat seed because of the smaller profit margins on wheat seeds. Some seed companies also milled wheat; such seed companies could be the best option for taking on board while designing the durum wheat value chain programmatic framework. Most (60%) seed company representatives said they had never heard about durum wheat. This lack of awareness, coupled with the unavailability of durum wheat seed, are the leading reasons durum wheat is not grown in Pakistan. When told of durum wheat's features (bold grain, yellow color, hardness and suitability for pasta products), the majority of the seed companies (67%) said they were interested in engaging in the durum wheat business. According to the seed companies, possible constraints for a durum wheat market and business development were the adoption time by farmers, durum wheat crop duration as compared to bread wheat, susceptibility of durum wheat to disease, yield potential and marketability of durum wheat grain. Durum's marketability was cited as a leading constraint, followed by yield potential, by 50% and 27% of respondents, respectively. According to the seed companies, contract farming can be the best option for the establishment and smooth functioning of a durum wheat value chain. The government needs to create enabling business environments through the provision of inputs, especially seed. The government also can offer premium prices to durum producers as an incentive to cultivate durum. The government also can include all relevant stakeholders in developing a program for a durum wheat value chain.

Wheat producers

Producers are the key actors in the wheat value chain. Knowledge of farmers' priorities and parameters in adopting new technology or innovation is essential for the successful and sustainable adoption of the technology. The research team endeavored to collect information about farmers' prevailing wheat production practices and widely adopted wheat varieties. The information was collected from small, medium-sized and large producers. The area allocated to wheat averaged 19.2 acres. About 82% of the farmers have cultivated more than two varieties. The average yield obtained by the wheat farmers was 1720 kg/acre. There was a difference in the actual and potential yield obtained by the farmers. Most of the farmers (>77%) reported an increase in wheat yield as compared to the previous season, mainly due to the availability of improved inputs. About 54% of the wheat growers had never been involved in contract farming, but 80% have shown interest in it. This is quite encouraging, as it offers an opportunity for the success of the durum wheat value chain in Pakistan. About 41% of the farmers made vermicelli at home, usually through a handmade machine, and they required no specific wheat flour to make it. Only 32% of the farmers were aware of the durum wheat value chain. In Pakistan, Jalandhar Seed Company (a local seed company) distributed durum seed named Rustam on a trial basis to contract growers during 2012–2013. The average price of the durum seed was very high (Pakistani rupees 6,700 per bag). However, farmers reported heavy stem rust on the durum wheat varieties and observed crop lodging, suggesting that plant breeders need to develop high-yield, rust-resistant varieties. An overwhelming majority (77%) of the farmers were willing to cultivate durum wheat on their plots as long as subsidized seed is provided. Possible constraints the farmers pointed out included lower yields, changing climatic conditions and grain marketing suitability.

Consumers

The success of introducing a new product in a market ultimately depends on the purchasing power, eating habits, tastes and preferences of the target customers. Getting information from consumers, we can draw inference about the fate of newly introduced products. In the case of pasta products, we observed a significant difference in consumers' sources of information. Consumers from big cities and peri-urban areas were more aware of pasta products than were people living in villages. Television advertisements were the foremost source of their information about pasta foods. No difference between genders was found in preference for pasta products. Among the available range of pasta products, noodles were the items most frequently cooked at home, followed by vermicelli, macaroni and spaghetti, as reported by 100%, 73%, 64% and 55% of consumers, respectively.

Consumers said the main advantages of pasta products include ease of cooking and delicious taste. An extensive media campaign and expert chefs' regular presentations of different recipes on TV cooking channels have increased the demand for pasta foods. About 82% of the households reported rising demand for pasta products. During the last decade, demand for pasta products has increased, and the demand is greater among youths and children than among older people. About 73% of consumers were not aware of durum wheat and its uses. Consumers reported several constraints to the consumption of pasta products (Table 10.2). Lack of awareness was the major constraint, followed by a lack of cooking methods, unaffordability and undevelopment of tastes for pasta foods. Consumers said the unavailability of pasta products was the leading barrier to scaling sales of pasta food among all segments of society.

Table 10.2 Constraints in the consumption of pasta products

Constraints	*Percentage response*
Awareness	27.3
Accessibility	4.5
Taste and fashion	13.6
Quality	13.6
Durability	4.5
Cooking methods	22.7
Total	100

Source: Authors' calculations.

Restaurants

In the development of a durum wheat value chain in Pakistan, restaurants are considered quite important as ultimate users of value-added wheat products. However, their role as active stakeholders in the value chain is insignificant. A small number of traditional restaurants (only ones in big cities) have included noodles, macaroni, spaghetti and shells in their menu cards. However, Chinese and Italian restaurants in big cities have included noodles, macaroni, spaghetti and shell pasta on their menus. These restaurants make noodles on their own, and most of these restaurants use imported semolina that is available only in megastores. In response to a question about the most demanded pasta foods, half (50%) of the respondents reported that noodles were the leading pasta dish demanded by all age groups of customers. Fettuccine and macaroni were the second- and third-most demanded pasta foods at their restaurants. All multinational food chains mostly offer noodle dishes prepared by their experts. Regarding trends, the demand for pasta products is increasing daily, and men and women equally like pasta. The local restaurants use local pasta brands, and the international restaurants use imported semolina.

Seed dealers

Dealers in the wheat value chain play a significant role both in seed distribution and grain markets. From a seed distribution perspective, the dealers' role is supply oriented rather than demand oriented, as they are ready to sell whatever the seed companies distribute to them. Almost all the dealers functioned as sales agents for different national and multinational seed companies. They always are looking for good margins from the seed companies. According to seed dealers, the overall volume of the seed business is increasing. About 80% of the dealers reported that they are dealing in the certified seed business. None of the seed dealers had any information about durum wheat. However, they were ready to sell durum wheat seed if a reputable seed company provided it. Usually, seed dealers are offered a 5%–15% profit margin on new varieties and less on traditional varieties. According to dealers, farmers like high-yielding varieties the most, followed by disease-resistant varieties and price of seed. Some dealers suggested that durum wheat needs to be introduced on a trial basis at selected locations and can be upscaled later.

Wheat millers

The survey findings indicated that milling is the most critical and challenging component in the development of the value chain for durum wheat. The survey findings indicated that wholesalers are linked to millers, who then are linked to the food processing industry. The wholesalers purchase fine wheat flour (semolina) and supply the millers. A few millers have established their own food processing units. Due to better profit margins, the millers prefer to sell their products to retailers and the food processing industry. According to wheat millers, Pakistan needs to adopt a balanced approach and a premium price in introducing durum wheat in the country.

Food processing industry

Pakistan's food processing industries are mostly concentrated in the city of Karachi, where the best-known processing units are Bake Parlour and Krispo. These processing industries meet more than 80% of the national demand. A nominal proportion of their products are exported to the Middle East, the United Kingdom, the United Arab Emirates, Sri Lanka, Canada, Afghanistan and South African countries. Only two pasta processing firms, Taste Cuisine and Golden Pasta, are located in the city of Islamabad.

The food processing industries purchase refined maida (white flour) from private mills/wholesale dealers or have their own milling units. About 20% of the milling units are interested in investing in additional milling units. Most of the food processing firms visited also are involved in manufacturing bakery products, which require high-gluten wheat flours. To reach the necessary levels of gluten, some of the industries buy gluten in powder form from importers/suppliers and add it to the white flour. Out of the five food processing industries visited, four were well aware of durum wheat and showed a sincere interest in its domestic development. The price of imported semolina was \$680–\$700 per ton, and that of bread wheat flour was \$380 per ton. The processing industries said local production of durum wheat would make pasta products more competitive in the international market because the industries could get good-quality semolina at low prices.

Pasta products business trends

Vermicelli, macaroni, noodles and spaghetti were reported as the most demanded products. All pasta products are being sold in dried form, primarily to wholesale distributors, and 10%–30% of the total production is sold in the international market. However, there is vast potential for pasta products in the global market. In Pakistan, imports meet about 5%–10% of the total domestic consumption of pasta. Most of the pasta processing industries were adopting innovative market development techniques, such as sales promotion through electronic and print media, establishing display counters at super malls and conducting cooking demonstrations at exhibitions and cultural shows. Other firms promoted pasta sales through their distributors. An enabling business environment can help increase the business volume by 8%–10% per year. The food processing industries found that local production of durum wheat can boost the industry and help make the products competitive both domestically and internationally. The research and development process needs to include all the relevant stakeholders as the processing industry also creates employment for other stakeholders, including distributors.

Conclusions

The study in this chapter is based on information collected from seven potential stakeholder groups: seed companies, producers, dealers, consumers, restaurants, millers and the food processing industry. The study's findings help to understand the stakeholders' awareness of and willingness to be part of the value chain. The survey results indicated that private seed companies have established proper processing and storage infrastructure, along with an impressive number of registered growers. Some of these seed companies also engaged in milling. Most of these seed companies were interested in being part of the durum wheat seed business.

Based on study findings, the project of designing a durum wheat value chain may include the private-sector seed companies to multiply and distribute seed and even to buy back the grain to use in their own mills or supply it to wheat millers and food processing industries. Seed companies with additional milling functions could help in efficiently designing the value chain program framework for durum wheat. The murky business situation of durum wheat in Pakistan signals great potential to develop its market without competition. The durum wheat breeder should ensure yield potentials competitive with those of bread wheat varieties already being cultivated in target locations, along with ensuring disease resistance.

For producers, a comprehensive durum wheat awareness program would contain a complete production technology package and information on nutritional composition, prospective markets and expected prices for durum wheat. Contract farming can persuade the farming community to cultivate durum wheat as part of value chain. The project of designing a durum wheat value chain needs to introduce durum varieties that have proven to be rust resistant in Pakistan. In the beginning, the government needs to subsidize durum seed and other inputs to incentivize farmers and other stakeholders in the development of the durum wheat value chain. Among Pakistani consumers, the demand for pasta products is rising, more so among young people and children than among older people. Measures including print and electronic media can further enhance consumers' awareness. Value chain actors are not well connected now; hence, the government needs to provide an enabling environment for the proper connectivity. The export possibilities of pasta products will generate significant foreign exchange and employment, which will spur economic growth in Pakistan. The role of restaurants as value chain actors is insignificant as the pasta products are consumed mostly at household levels. Wheat dealers also have a negligible role as they are more supply oriented than demand oriented.

Milling units are the key and most vital component in the development of the durum wheat value chain. The milling unit is not well connected with the food processing industry, and a few millers have established their own food processing units. However, the milling units used for bread wheat are not suitable for hard durum wheat, so the milling group would need substantial investment in new units that cost about $100,000. The study findings indicated that seed companies, millers and food processing industries are the most critical stakeholders in the power dynamics of the durum wheat value chain. Coordination among these stakeholders will lead to success and sustainability. Alternatively, Pakistan could follow the Australian model by producing the durum wheat locally and exporting it for processing.

References

Ahmad, M., & Ahmad, A. (1998). An analysis of the sources of wheat output growth in the barani area of the Punjab. *The Pakistan Development Review*, 231–249.

Amin, M., Amanullah, M., & Akbar, A. (2014). Time series modeling for forecasting wheat production of Pakistan. *Japs, Journal of Animal and Plant Sciences*, 24(5), 1444–1451.

Economic Survey of Pakistan. (2018–19). *Ministry of Finance, Government of Pakistan*. Islamabad, Pakistan: Economic Survey of Pakistan.

Iqbal, M., Khan, M. A., Ahmad, M., & Ahmad, B. (2001). Determinants of higher wheat productivity in irrigated Pakistan [with Comments]. *The Pakistan Development Review*, 753–766.

Janjua, P. Z., Samad, G., Khan, N. U., & Nasir, M. (2010). Impact of climate change on wheat production: A case study of Pakistan [with Comments]. *The Pakistan Development Review*, 799–822.

Bux, H., Rasheed, A., Siyal, M. A., Kazi, A. G., Napar, A. A., & Mujeeb-Kazi, A. (2012). An overview of stripe rust of wheat (*Puccinia striiformis f. sp. tritici*) in Pakistan. *Archives of Phytopathology and Plant Protection*, 45(19), 2278–2289.

Bakhsh, K., Hassan, I., & Maqbool, A. (2005). Impact assessment of zero-tillage technology in rice-wheat system: A case study from Pakistani Punjab. *Electronic Journal of Environmental, Agricultural and Food Chemistry*, 4(6), 1132–1137.

Sarwar, G., & Ahmad, M. (2003). Development of a new high yielding mung-bean variety "AEM96" Through induced mutations. *SAARC Journal of Agriculture*, 1, 173–180.

11 Contract farming and farm performance

Evidence from brinjal cultivation in Bangladesh

Anjani Kumar, Gaurav Tripathi, Devesh Roy and Abu Hayat Md. Saiful Islam

Agriculture and allied sectors comprise a 13.3% share of gross domestic product (GDP) and contribute 40.6% of the overall employment in Bangladesh (BBS, 2019, 2020). This highlights the importance of growth in the agricultural sector for employment and for poverty reduction in Bangladesh. Further, the crops and horticulture subsector accounts for 53.5% of the country's agricultural GDP and is an important part of furthering growth in agriculture and allied sectors. Crops and horticulture subsector, with a 7.1% share in overall GDP, has the potential to boost growth in the agricultural sector, facilitated by increasing demand and better returns to smallholders engaged in vegetable cultivation. The average farm size in Bangladesh is 0.6 ha, and 84.3% of farm holdings belong to the small land class (<1 ha). Smallholders can augment their incomes substantially by cultivating vegetables. Besides households' demand for the consumption of fresh vegetables, agribusiness firms also demand vegetables for use as raw materials in processing produce products like chips, puree, pulp, pickles etc.

As the market for processed and packaged food products grows in Bangladesh with increasing urbanization, the agribusiness firms are showing interest in procuring farm produce by contracting with farmers in addition to buying produce on the open market. Despite the immense potential benefits of contract farming (CF), some policymakers in developing countries are apprehensive about issues like barriers to smallholders' participation in contract farming, the probability of large processing firms exploiting smallholders, increased instability for non-participants etc. Earlier studies have shown both positive and negative outcomes of contract farming (Glover, 1984; Goldsmith, 1985; Glover and Kusterer, 1990; Little and Watts, 1994; Morvaridi, 1995; Porter and Howard, 1997; Key and Rusten, 1999; Baumann, 2000; Opondo, 2000; Simmons et al., 2005). Many studies pertaining to contract farming's impact on income and employment reveal that contract farming contributes to enhancing farmers' income and generating employment (Glover, 1984; Goldsmith, 1985; Glover and Kusterer, 1990; Key and Rusten, 1999; Singh, 2002; Warning and Key, 2002; Birthal et al., 2005; Simmons et al., 2005; Tripathi et al., 2005; Ramaswami et al., 2006; Zhu, 2007; Setboonsarng et al., 2008; Miyata et al.,

2009; Xu and Wang, 2009; Wainaina et al., 2012; Kalamkar, 2012; Bellemare, 2012; Michelson, 2013). However, other studies depict contract farming's negative impact on the environment and on farmers' economic welfare (see Little and Watts, 1994; Morvaridi,1995; Key and Runsten, 1999; Opondo, 2000; Singh, 2002). For example, Little and Watts (1994) deny contract farming's positive impact on farmers' income, and Singh (2002) underscores that firms' monopsonistic power makes contract farming exploitative in nature. Similarly, Key and Rusten (1999) opine that inequalities in rural income are a negative outcome of contract farming.

Studies on the drivers and impact of contract farming in high-value crops like vegetables in Bangladesh are scarce. We attempt to bridge this research gap by examining the drivers of participation in contract farming and its impact on smallholders' income and compliance with good agricultural practices (GAP) by a case study of smallholder brinjal farmers in Bangladesh. Vegetables occupied about a 383,912 hectare (ha) area in Bangladesh during the triennium ending in 2019, comprising 2.5% of the gross cropped area (GCA). Brinjal, a key vegetable in Bangladesh that is known as eggplant or aubergine in other parts of the world, shared 13.4% in area under vegetables. Some 518,016 tons of brinjal were produced in an area of 51,484 ha, with a yield of 100.6 quintal (q) per ha (BBS, 2020).

The rest of this chapter is organized as follows. In the second section, we describe the survey data and methodological approach. Estimation results are presented and discussed in the third section, and the fourth section concludes and provide some policy implications.

Data and methodology

Data

This study is based on a primary survey of 259 farm households engaged in cultivating brinjal in Bangladesh. The survey was conducted from June through August 2016 in the Jessore District of the Khulna division, located in southwestern Bangladesh. Jessore is a leading brinjal-producing district in Bangladesh where contract farming of brinjal takes place on a large scale. We surveyed 259 brinjal farmers, comprising 109 contract producers and 150 independent producers, chosen randomly from 13 villages under four unions of a subdistrict (upazila) in Jessore, following a multistage sampling procedure. We randomly identified one subdistrict from Jessore: Manirampur. Then we randomly identified four union councils in Manirampur. Then we randomly selected two sample villages from each union council. Finally, we randomly selected 15 to 20 brinjal-cultivating households from each sample village, comprising both contract and independent growers.

Two distinct contractors work with the sample brinjal cultivators in Bangladesh. They are SAFAL (Sustainable Agriculture, Food Security and Linkages), which is a joint program initiative of a non-governmental organization named

Solidaridad Asia Network Ltd. and the Embassy of the Netherlands in Bangladesh, and the Jagorani Chakra Foundation, which is another non-governmental organization. The SAFAL program connects with vegetable growers, creates their farmer groups and provides them training in better cultivation and good agricultural practices. SAFAL procures brinjal from these farmers through an informal contract, providing a marketing channel that ensures better prices for them. SAFAL provides conveyances for transporting brinjal to the supermarket chains and wholesalers in Dhaka and other big markets. The Jagorani Chakra Foundation, based in the Jessore District, also contracts informally with farmers to procure brinjal. It also provides training support to farmers on cultivation and good agricultural practices. The produce is sold through the Jagorani Chakra Foundation to wholesalers and supermarket chains in big cities.

Using a structured questionnaire, we gathered data on farmers' characteristics, cropping patterns, economics of vegetable production, marketing channels, good agricultural practices, assets, social networks and risk tolerance.

Methodology

We attempt to identify the factors that motivate farmers to enter contractual arrangements with the produce buyer and assess contract farming's impact on farmers' profits and adoption of food safety measures (FSM) in brinjal cultivation. To assess the adoption of food safety measures at the farm level, we developed a food safety adoption index (FSI) comprising 45 distinct food safety practices, including record keeping and site management, propagation material, nutrition management, water management, plant protection and post-harvest management (Kumar et al., 2016).

The empirical literature on these two aspects of contract farming is extensive. Several researchers have estimated the probability of a farmer's decision to contract as the first step in a two-step econometric process to analyze contract farming's impact on farmer welfare (for example, Katchova and Miranda, 2004; Simmons et al., 2005; Miyata et al., 2009; Wang et al., 2011; Bellemare, 2012; Gupta and Roy, 2012; Ito et al., 2012). Other studies focus exclusively on the decision to participate in contract farming (Birthal et al., 2005; Guo et al., 2005; Masakure and Henson, 2005; Zhu and Wang, 2007; Fischer and Qaim, 2012; Kumar et al., 2013).

To try to address the non-random nature of participation in contract farming, several papers have used a two-step procedure (for example, Katchova and Miranda, 2004; Simmons et al., 2005; Miyata et al., 2009; Wang et al., 2011; Bellemare, 2012; Ito et al., 2012; Gupta and Roy, 2012) in assessing contract farming's impact on farm returns. Following suit, we also use a two-step procedure with instrumental variables to address the issue of endogeneity of the contracting variable.

In the first stage, the dependent variable is binary (farmer participates in a contract = 1, otherwise = 0), and the independent variables are a mix of qualitative and quantitative variables. In the second stage, to assess the impact of contract farming on farmers' profits and their food safety adoption index, the outcome function can be represented as:

$$\pi_i = \alpha + \delta d_i + \gamma X_i + \varepsilon_i \tag{11.1}$$

where π_i is the net profit per kilogram or the food safety adoption index for a farm household from the cultivation of brinjal, d_i is a dummy variable (= 1 if farmer is under contract, = 0 otherwise), X_i is a vector of farm and operator characteristics and ε_i is an error term.

Estimation of Equation (11.1) using a simple ordinary least squares (OLS) regression may result in biased estimates of the impact of contracting on farm profits or food safety adoption index. This is because farmers are not randomly chosen in contracts. Farmers are either selected for a contract by the contractor, or they decide to participate in a contract of their own accord. Both possibilities signify non-random selection. Hence, unobserved factors could be guiding farmers' decisions to enter contracts. Thus, d_i, the variable representing participation in a contract, is likely to be endogenous and could be correlated with the error term, ε_i.

Without the benefit of a randomized assignment of brinjal farmers into contracts and given that unobserved characteristics such as hidden entrepreneurial ability can play a role in the decision to participate in a contract, we rely on instrumental variable (IV) techniques to try to get unbiased estimates of contract farming's impact on farm profits. An ideal instrumental variable should not correlate with the dependent variable in Equation (11.1); however, it should be correlated with d_i, the variable representing participation in contract farming. Additionally, the variable should not be from the vector of farm and operator characteristics, X_i. It is indeed hard to find an ideal instrument in this setting.

To assess contract farming's impact on farmers' profits (in Equation [11.1]) in brinjal cultivation, we identified a specification of instrumental variables: 'range of price in last two years,' 'prefers taking risk,' 'information intensity of farmer organization' and 'information intensity of parent neighbor.' The instrumental variable 'range of price in last two years' represented the difference between the maximum and minimum prices brinjal cultivators received in the last two years. The contractual arrangement was expected to control fluctuations in brinjal prices for the farmer, and therefore the range of prices for the contract brinjal grower was expected to be less than for the independent farmer. Accordingly, the instrumental variable 'range of price in last two years' was inversely correlated with variable d_i (representing participation in contract farming). Further, farmers who liked to take risk were disinclined to participate in contracts. The instrumental variables 'information intensity of farmer organization' and 'information intensity of parent neighbor' indicate the intensity of agricultural information farmers received from a farmer organization and from a parent who is also a neighbor. An interaction of a variable symbolizing the source of information (bivariate dummy variable) and the time farmers spent with it gives the intensity of information from that source.

Farmers' intensive interaction with social networks on farming issues (including contracting) enhanced their likelihood of participating in contracts. We followed a similar approach to estimate contract farming's impact on the adoption of food safety measures. In the two-stage least squares (2SLS) regression for the food safety equation (Equation [11.1]), we used the same instrumental variables that we identified for the profit equation.

We use Hausman's test for endogeneity to detect endogeneity in variable d_i (the variable representing participation in contracts in Equation [11.1]). Endogeneity in d_i means that the presence of unobserved factors that guide farmers' participation in contracts also influences the profits or food safety adoption index, and thus contracting's effects on profits or food safety adoption index can be biased (Equation [11.1]). In such a situation, 2SLS regression is more consistent than the OLS and therefore is preferred. Alternatively, the absence of endogeneity in d_i means OLS gives an efficient outcome and is a better choice than 2SLS regression. As a first step in Hausman's test, we regress d_i on the instrumental variables used in Equation 11.1 and derive the predicted residual (say *ehat*). In the second step, we include the predicted variable derived in the first step as an independent variable in the main regression equation (Equation [11.1]) and do OLS regression. In the regression output, if the coefficient of the predicted variable (*ehat*) is significant based on the *t* test, it indicates endogeneity in d_i. Otherwise, it is exogenous. However, the outcome of the Hausman's test for endogeneity may vary with the different types of instrumental variables used. We also assess the validity of instruments (when more than one instrumental variable is used) using the Sargan test for overidentification (Table 11A.4). The instruments are valid if the Sargan test's outcome is statistically insignificant and invalid if the outcome is statistically significant.

Results and discussion

Characteristics of contract and independent farmers

Table 11.1 gives average values for variables representing key socio-demographic characteristics of brinjal-cultivating sample households. About 42% of brinjal growers participate in contract farming. The farmers' average age is 42. The average years of education for family heads is about six years, and for the highest educated person in household is about 11 years. Families average 4.4 members. The dependency ratio of farm households is 0.6. Farms average 0.5 ha in size and have an average of seven plots. Some 91% of brinjal farmers consider farming their main occupation. The farmers have an average of 12 years of experience in vegetable cultivation. About 65% of brinjal growers have access to institutional credit, about 26% belong to a cooperative, about 15% have their own agricultural transport facility and about 62% have access to electricity. Farmers received an average of eight extension visits a year from private companies and about 12 a year from government officials. Brinjal farmers' yields average 641.1 q/ ha, and prices average Taka 1,909.3/q. The gross

Table 11.1 Characteristics of contract and independent farmers of brinjal in Bangladesh

Characteristics	*All*	*Contract*	*Independent*	*Difference*	*t-test value*
Number of observations	259	109	150		
Age of household head (HH) (years)	42.1	42.3	42.0	0.2	0.1524
Education HH (years)	5.9	5.7	6.0	−0.3	0.6143
Education highest educated person in HH (years)	10.6	10.4	10.7	−0.3	0.6101
Household size (number)	4.4	4.2	4.5	−0.3	1.2809
Dependency ratio	0.6	0.5	0.6	−0.1	1.5409
Operational land (ha)	0.5	0.5	0.6	−0.1	1.5049
Number of plots	7.0	7.3	6.7	0.6	0.8298
% farmers with farming as main occupation (%)	91.1	91.7	90.7	1.1	0.2996
Experience in vegetable farming (years)	11.8	12.9	11.1	1.8*	1.9264
Access to institutional credit (%)	64.9	62.4	66.7	−4.3	0.7105
Membership of cooperative or other organization (%)	25.5	32.1	20.7	11.4**	2.0961
Own means of agricultural transport (%)	15.4	15.6	15.3	0.3	0.0576
Access to electricity (%)	61.8	64.2	60.0	4.2	0.6880
Number of extension visits per annum by private companies	8.4	9.4	7.7	1.7	1.6103
No of extension visits per annum by government official	11.6	11.3	11.8	−0.5	0.3520
Yield (q/ha)	641.1	652.4	632.8	19.7	0.4371
Price (Taka/q)	1,909.3	1,912.4	1,907.0	5.4	0.0582
Revenue by-product (Taka/q)	99.2	127.0	79.1	−47.9	1.5
Gross revenue (Taka/q)	2,008.5	2,039.4	1,986.1	−53.3	0.6
Cost of production (Taka/q)	888.3	777.2	969.0	−191.9***	3.0934
Gross Profit (Taka/q)	1,120.2	1,262.2	1,017.0	245.1**	2.3570
Food Safety Adoption Index (FSI)	43.4	49.0	39.3	9.7***	3.9587

Source: Field survey (2016).

Note: ***, ** and * represent significance at 1%, 5% and 10% levels, respectively.

revenue, adding by-product revenue, is Taka 2,008.5/q. Their average cost of production is Taka 888.3/q, and their average profit is Taka 1,120.2/q. Brinjal farmers follow about 43% of the suggested food safety measures.

Table 11.1 also gives the mean differences in the characteristics of contract and independent farmers. The farmers differ significantly in only a few characteristics. The average experience in vegetable cultivation is about 13 years for contract cultivators compared to 11 years for their independent counterparts. About 32% of contract farmers are members of a cooperative, but only 21% of independent farmers are. The average cost of production for contract growers (Taka 777.2/q) is significantly lower than that for the independent producers (Taka 969.0/q), which contributed to higher average profits for contract growers (Taka 1,262.2/q) than for independent producers (Taka 1,017.0/q). Furthermore, contract farmers follow 49% of the prescribed food safety measures at farm level, compared to independent farmers, who follow about 39% of such measures. The contract farmers in the marginal and small farm size class are significantly higher adopters of food safety practices at farm level than the independent farmers (Table 11A.1). Around 37% of the contract farmers and 20% of the independent farmers are adopters of over 60% of the prescribed food safety practices at farm level (Table 11A.2). Further, the contract farmers are significantly higher adopters of food safety practices than the independent farmers with respect to post-harvest management, plant protection, plant nutrition management and water management components of the overall food safety practices (Table 11A.3).

Determinants of farmers' decision to participate in contract farming, its impact on profit and adoption of food safety measures at the farm level

Table 11.2 depicts the determinants of brinjal farmers' participation in contract farming and the estimates of contract farming's impact on brinjal farmers' profit and adoption of food safety measures at the farm level. The first stage of the 2SLS regression in Column 3 gives estimation results for determinants of the farmers' decision to participate in contract farming in brinjal. Here, the dependent variable is participation in contract farming, and the independent variables are the farmers' socio-demographic and economic characteristics. Farmer characteristics included are the age of the farmer, education, experience in vegetable farming, economically active family members, out-migration, number of agricultural plots, farm size, ownership of agricultural transport, main occupation, access to institutional credit, membership in a cooperative, extension visits by government and private officials and visits by the farmer for extension services. We are guided in our choice of explanatory variables for analysis by the empirical literature on the subject (e.g., Miyata et al., 2007; Roy and Thorat, 2008; Bellemare, 2012; Fischer and Qaim, 2012; Kumar et al., 2013). The regression results reveal that membership in a cooperative has a significant positive impact on farmers' participation in contract farming but that farm size and access to institutional credit negatively influence participation. This means

Table 11.2 Determinants for participation in contract and its impact on profit and adoption of food safety practices (FSI) for brinjal farmers in Bangladesh

Dependent variable	*Unit profit in brinjal production (Taka/kg)*			*Food Safety Adoption Index (FSI)*	
Variable	*Coefficients*			*Coefficients*	
	OLS	*2SLS regression*		*OLS*	*2SLS regression*
		First stage	*Second stage*		*Second stage*
(1)	*(2)*	*(3)*	*(4)*	*(5)*	*(6)*
Contract farming (yes = 1, 0 otherwise)	3.275*** (0.563)		8.107*** (2.314)	4.408* (2.151)	15.72** (6.186)
Socio-demographic variables					
Ln(age of the household head) (years)	−38.54 (49.41)	2.734 (3.037)	−54.41 (52.41)	34.39 (112.9)	−2.757 (105.6)
Square of ln (age of the household head)	5.438 (6.765)	−0.379 (0.413)	7.625 (7.219)	−3.006 (14.89)	2.114 (13.99)
Ln (years of education of the household head)	−0.873 (1.542)	0.159 (0.0972)	−1.553 (1.544)	−7.370* (3.851)	−8.961 (5.947)
Square of ln (years of education of the household head)	0.563 (0.706)	−0.0505 (0.0377)	0.801 (0.785)	3.487** (1.481)	4.042* (2.267)
Ln (experience in vegetable farming)	0.464 (0.840)	0.0444 (0.0459)	0.156 (0.727)	−3.060 (2.329)	−3.781 (2.617)
Ln (number of economically active family members)	−1.321 (1.534)	0.0934 (0.0791)	−1.707 (1.924)	−1.119 (2.034)	−2.023 (1.884)
Migration (yes = 1, 0 otherwise)	0.545 (1.335)	0.102 (0.127)	0.370 (1.304)	5.526** (2.413)	5.114* (2.594)
Ln (number of plots)	−1.898** (0.729)	0.0782 (0.0494)	−2.351** (0.878)	−0.356 (1.640)	−1.418 (1.511)
Ln (operational land) (ha)	1.250* (0.635)	−0.0942* (0.0544)	1.850* (0.923)	−0.957 (1.674)	0.449 (1.932)
Own agricultural transport (yes=1, 0 otherwise)	−1.904 (1.318)	0.0162 (0.0740)	−2.126 (1.454)	−1.118 (3.056)	−1.638 (3.350)
Economic variables					
Main occupation (farming = 1, other = 0)	1.323 (2.297)	0.00763 (0.100)	1.253 (2.502)	−2.654 (1.928)	−2.818** (1.277)
Access to institutional credit (yes = 1, 0 otherwise)	−2.455 (1.798)	−0.212*** (0.0706)	−1.288 (1.762)	5.813*** (1.377)	8.544*** (2.663)

Dependent variable	*Unit profit in brinjal production (Taka/kg)*			*Food Safety Adoption Index (FSI)*	
Variable	*Coefficients*			*Coefficients*	
	OLS	*2SLS regression*		*OLS*	*2SLS regression*
		First stage	*Second stage*		*Second stage*
(1)	*(2)*	*(3)*	*(4)*	*(5)*	*(6)*
Formal source of finance in village (yes=1, 0 otherwise)	0.167 (1.414)	−0.141 (0.101)	0.681 (1.307)	−11.56*** (3.610)	−10.36** (3.571)
Member of cooperative (yes=1, 0 otherwise)	−1.653 (1.297)	0.115* (0.0695)	−2.170 (1.347)	−1.343 (2.353)	−2.553 (3.026)
Ln (number of visits by government extension officer)	−0.445 (0.509)	0.0439 (0.0303)	−0.703 (0.586)	4.302** (1.513)	3.699** (1.352)
Ln(number of visits by private extension officer)	0.587 (0.609)	0.0284 (0.0274)	0.450 (0.623)	4.692*** (1.383)	4.370*** (1.314)
Ln (number of visits by farmer for extension)	0.306 (0.716)	−0.0275 (0.0373)	0.484 (0.591)	3.618** (1.352)	4.036*** (1.266)
Household access to electricity (yes = 1, 0 otherwise)	0.460 (1.034)	0.0765 (0.0649)	0.0520 (1.787)	5.340** (2.275)	4.384*** (1.209)
Instrumental variables					
Range of price in last two years		−0.0034** (0.00168)			
Prefers taking risk (yes = 1, 0 otherwise)		−0.124* (0.0723)			
Information intensity of farmer organization		0.0138*** (0.00265)			
Information intensity parent neighbor		0.00693 (0.0142)			
Constant	80.48 (90.80)	−5.069 (5.577)	111.6 (96.31)	−54.03 (218.4)	18.76 (203.2)
Number of observations	259	259	259	259	259
R^2	0.250	0.310	0.189	0.555	0.496
Root MSE	7.5474	0.4322	7.8503	13.918	14.809
Union Fixed Effect	Yes	Yes	Yes	Yes	Yes

Source: Authors' analysis based on field survey (2016).

Notes: Standard errors in parentheses; ***, ** and * represent significance at 1%, 5% and 10% levels, respectively. Standard errors are clustered at the village level.

that farmers who have small farms and lack institutional loans prefer to join contract farming to overcome their vulnerability. Membership in a cooperative also motivates them to join contract farming.

It should be noted that the literature fails to find a consensus on the sign and significance of most of the socio-economic and demographic variables in participation in contract farming. For instance, educational attainment has been associated with participating in contract farming. Many studies support the positive relationship between education and contract farming (see Zhu and Wang, 2007; Arumugam et al., 2011; Hu, 2012; Kumar et al., 2016), but other studies have found a negative or an insignificant relationship between educational attainment and participation in contract farming (Guo et al., 2005; Ramaswami et al., 2006; Miyata et al., 2009; Wang et al., 2011; Bellemare, 2012; Ito et al., 2012; Wainaina et al., 2012; Wang et al., 2013).

The OLS model (Column 2) and the second stage of 2SLS regression (Column 4) show contract farming's impact on unit profit from brinjal cultivation. Both OLS and 2SLS regressions indicate contract farming has a significant positive impact on farmers' profit. The 2SLS regression, unlike the OLS model, takes care of the unobserved factors and thus gives contract farming's true impact on profits. The specification of instrumental variables used in the 2SLS model includes the instrumental variables 'range of price in last two years,' 'prefers taking risk,' 'information intensity of farmer organization' and 'information intensity of parent neighbor.' The Hausman test confirms the presence of endogeneity in the model for given specifications of instrumental variables. Hence, we prefer the 2SLS results to report profit. Participation in contract farming enhances brinjal cultivators' profit by Taka 8.11/kg over independent farmers. Other variables that impact profit in brinjal farming are the number of agricultural plots and farm size. Fragmentation of land into many plots reduces profit, and an increase in farm size enhances it. Having contiguous and large farms helps farmers attain efficiency in cultivation. The regressions include union fixed effect, and standards errors are clustered at the village level. Further, the Sargan test for overidentification of instrumental variables in the 2SLS regression gives an insignificant outcome, which affirms the validity of the instrumental variables (Table 11A.4).

Various studies pertaining to contract farming in developing countries have mentioned a significant positive impact of contract farming on gross margins, crop income or total household income. These include studies on Kenya (Wainaina et al., 2012), India (Singh, 2002; Birthal et al., 2005; Tripathi et al., 2005; Ramaswami et al., 2006; Kalamkar, 2012), Senegal (Warning and Key, 2002), Laos (Setboonsarng et al., 2008), Madagascar (Bellemare, 2012), Nicaragua (Michelson, 2013), China (Zhu, 2007; Miyata et al., 2009; Xu and Wang, 2009) and Indonesia (Simmons et al., 2005).

Contract farming's impact on adoption of food safety practices (FSI) at the farm level in brinjal cultivation is depicted in Column 5 (OLS model) and Column 6 (second stage of the 2SLS model). In the 2SLS model, we identify the same specification of instrumental variables for the food safety equation as we used in the profit equation (mentioned earlier). Both OLS and 2SLS estimates show that contract farming has a significant positive impact on the adoption of food safety measures at the farm level. As the Hausman test indicates, endogeneity in the food safety equation for the stated instrumental variables, we prefer to report the 2SLS estimates over the OLS. The 2SLS model shows that brinjal farmers' participation in contract farming enhances adoption of food safety measures at the farm level by 15.72%. Other variables that positively influence the adoption of food safety measures are the square of years of education, out-migration, access to institutional credit, the number of extension visits by government and private officials, the number of visits by farmers for extension services and access to electricity. High education prompts farmers to join contract farming in brinjal. Migrating household members get exposure outside the domestic environment and increase their awareness of food safety practices at the farm level. Access to institutional credit facilitates affordable implementation of food safety measures. Extension visits enhance farmers' awareness and understanding of prescribed food safety practices. Access to electricity allows farmers to use electronic media and the Internet for information on food safety measures and helps them implement food safety practices at the farm level. The variables that negatively influence adoption of food safety measures are whether farming is the main occupation and whether there is a formal source of finance in the village. A non-farm main occupation covers farmers' risk and makes implementing food safety measures more affordable. The mere presence of a formal finance source within the village does not help in adoption of food safety measures. In general, contract farming may help transfer innovative knowledge and skills, reduce compliance costs and ensure higher returns to the farmers. Similar relationships have been reported by Roy and Thorat, 2008; Narrod et al., 2009; Kumar et al., 2013. Further, the Sargan test testifies to the validity of the instrumental variables in all the specifications (Table 11A.4).

Robustness in profit and in adoption of food safety measures

To validate the robustness of results, we use propensity score matching to see the impact of contract farming on unit profit and on adoption of food safety measures for brinjal cultivators in Bangladesh. The variables involved in satisfying the balancing property and common support of the propensity score are (1) age of the household head, (2) years of education of the household head, (3) experience in vegetable farming, (4) number of economically active family members, (5) migration, (6) number of plots, (7) operational land, (8) own agricultural transport, (9) main occupation, (10) access to institutional credit, (11) formal source of finance in village, (12) member of cooperative, (13) number of visits by government extension officer, (14) number of visits by private extension officer, (15) number of visits by farmer for extension and (16) access to electricity. Table 11.3 gives outcomes of the nearest neighbor matching estimation with analytical standard errors as in Abadie and Imbens (2006) and kernel-based matching with bootstrap standard errors, respectively.

Table 11.3 Impact of CF on profit and FSM for brinjal cultivators in Bangladesh: outcomes of the nearest neighbor matching and bootstrap standard errors (kernel-based matching)

Number of matches (m)	*Variable*	*Profit (Taka/kg)*		
		All	*Marginal (<0.4 ha)*	*Small, medium-sized and large (≥0.4 ha)*
$m = 1$	Average Treatment Effect on Treated	2.237	2.028	1.620
		(1.448)	(2.142)	(1.638)
$m = 3$		3.386***	3.354*	2.014
		(1.164)	(1.771)	(1.336)
$m = 5$		3.180***	4.010**	2.335*
		(1.089)	(1.802)	(1.321)
Observations		259	119	140
Bootstrap standard errors (kernel-based matching)		2.025	8.126***	1.695
		(1.468)	(2.685)	(1.642)
Observations		259	119	140
Number of matches (m)	*Variable*	*FSI*		
		All	*Marginal (<0.4 ha)*	*Small, medium-sized and large (≥0.4 ha)*
$m = 1$	Average Treatment Effect on Treated	7.110**	7.222*	3.909
		(2.835)	(4.385)	(3.082)
$m = 3$		9.047***	8.367**	8.025***
		(2.465)	(3.691)	(2.969)
$m = 5$		9.618***	8.263**	7.860**
		(2.457)	(3.684)	(3.073)
Observations		259	119	140
Bootstrap standard errors (kernel-based matching)		8.478***	6.326	9.195**
		(2.794)	(4.742)	(4.274)
Observations		259	119	140

Source: Authors' analysis based on field survey (2016).

Notes: Standard errors in parentheses; ***, ** and * represent significance at 1%, 5% and 10% levels, respectively; m = 1, 3 and 5, indicating 1,3 and 5 neighbors, respectively.

The unit profit for contract farmers is significantly higher than that for independent farmers, in the range of Taka 3.18/kg (nearest neighbor matching with number of matches = 5) to Taka 3.39/kg (nearest neighbor matching with number of matches = 3). Farmers with marginal-sized farms performed better in profit per unit by participating in contract farming than did farmers with small, medium-sized and large farms. Similarly, contract farming has a significant positive impact on adoption of food safety measures at the farm level. Contract farmers are better adopters of food safety measures, in the range of 7.11% (nearest neighbor matching with number of matches = 1) to 9.62% (nearest neighbor matching with number of matches = 5). Contract farmers with marginal-sized farms and those with small, medium-sized and large farms are better adopters of food safety measures than independent farmers.

Conclusions

This chapter's study, based on a primary survey of brinjal-cultivating households in Bangladesh during 2016, identifies the determinants of participating in contract farming and the impact of contract farming on farmers' profit and adoption of food safety measures at the farm level in the cultivation of brinjal. The key factors influencing farmers' participation in contract farming are membership in a cooperative, farm size and access to institutional credit. Brinjal cultivators from the vulnerable class of marginal-sized and small farms who lack institutional credit participate in contract farming. Participation in contract farming has a significant positive impact on farmers' profit in brinjal cultivation. Further, contract farmers are better adopters of food safety measures at the farm level than independent farmers are.

In developing countries, farmers and policymakers look upon the institution of contract farming with suspicion and perceive it as exploiting There also is literature that supports the view that large firms benefit from contract farming at the cost of unorganized and weak farmers (Singh, 2002; Ghosh, 2003; Sivramkrishna and Jyotishi, 2008). However, researchers also consider contract farming as a way to promote agricultural commercialization (Warning and Key, 2002; Simmons et al., 2005; Birthal et al., 2005; Pomareda, 2006; Miyata et al., 2007). Findings from our study suggest that contract farming can substantially increase income for vegetable-cultivating households and significantly improve compliance with food safety measures at the farm level. Thus encouraging farm households to participate in contract farming may help alleviate poverty in Bangladesh. Policymakers also should design appropriate strategies and mechanisms to promote contract farming in other agricultural commodities.

References

Abadie, A., and G.W. Imbens. 2006. "Large Sample Properties of Matching Estimators for Average Treatment Effects." *Econometrica* 74(1): 235–267.

Arumugam, N., F.M. Arshad, E. Chiew, and Z. Mohamed. 2011. "Determinants of Fresh Fruits and Vegetables (FFV) Farmers' Participation in Contract Farming in Peninsular Malaysia." *International Journal of Agricultural Management and Development* 1(2): 65–71.

BBS (Bangladesh Bureau of Statistics). 2019. *Gross Domestic Product of Bangladesh (2015–16 to 2018–19)*. Ministry of Planning, Government of Bangladesh. Available at www.bbs.gov.bd/site/page/dc2bc6ce-7080-48b3-9a04-73cec782d0df/Gross-Domestic-Product-(GDP).

BBS (Bangladesh Bureau of Statistics). 2020. *Yearbook of Agricultural Statistics-2019*, May 2020. Ministry of Planning, Government of Bangladesh.

Baumann, P. 2000. *Equity and Efficiency in Contract Farming Schemes: The Experience of Agricultural Tree Crops*. Working Paper 139. London: Overseas Development Institute.

Bellemare, M.F. 2012. "As You Sow, So Shall You Reap: The Welfare Impacts of Contract Farming"? *World Development* 40 (7): 1418–1434.

Birthal, P.S., P.K. Joshi, and A. Gulati. 2005. *Vertical Coordination in High Value Food Commodities: Implication for Small Holders*. MTID Discussion Paper No 85. Washington, DC: International Food Policy Research Institute.

Fischer, E., and M. Qaim. 2012. "Linking Smallholders to Markets: Determinants and Impacts of Farmer Collective Action in Kenya." *World Development* 40(6): 1255–1268.

Ghosh, J. (2003). *Corporate Agriculture: The Implications for Indian Farmers*. Mimeo. Available at www.macroscan.org/fet/dec03/pdf/Corp_Agri.pdf.

Glover, D. 1984. "Contract Farming and Smallholders Out Grower Schemes in Less-Developed Countries." *World Development* 12 (11/12): 1143–1157.

Glover, D., and K. Kusterer. 1990. *Small Farmers, Big Business—Contract Farming and Rural Development*. London: Macmillan.

Goldsmith, A. 1985. "The Private Sector and Rural Development: Can Agribusiness Help the Small Farmer." *World Development* 13 (10/11): 1125–1138.

Guo H., R.W. Jolly, and J. Zhu. 2005. "Contract farming in China: Supply Chain or Ball and Chain." Proceeding of the Minnesota International Economic Development Conference (MIDC05), University of Minnesota, Minneapolis, MN, April 29−30.

Gupta, Kanupriya, and Devesh Roy. 2012. "Gains from Coordination in Milkfed Dairy in Punjab." *Journal of Agribusiness in Developing and Emerging Economies* 2(2): 92–114.

Hu, W. 2012. "Effect of Contract Farming on the Farmers' Average Return: The Case of the Grain Industry in the USA." Paper presented at the Agricultural and Applied Economics Association 2012 Annual Meeting, August 12–14, 2012, Seattle, Washington, US. No. 124659.

Ito J., Z. Bao, and Q. Sun. 2012. "Distributional Effects of Agricultural Cooperatives in China: Exclusion of Smallholders and Potential Gains in Participation." *Food Policy* 37(6): 700–709.

Kalamkar, S.S. 2012. "Inputs and Services Delivery System under Contract Farming: A Case of Broiler Farming." *Agricultural Economics Research Review* 25(1): 515–521.

Katchova A.L., and M.J. Miranda. 2004. "Two-step Econometric Estimation of Farm Characteristics Affecting Marketing Contract Decisions." *American Journal of Agricultural Economics* 86(1): 88–102.

Key, N., and D. Rusten 1999. "Contract Farming Smallholders, and Rural Development in Latin America: The Organisation of Agro-processing Firms and the Scale of Out Grower Production." *World Development* 27(2): 381–401.

Kumar, Anjani, D. Roy, G. Tripathi, P.K. Joshi, and R.P. Adhikari. 2016. *Can Contract Farming Increase Farmers' Income and Enhance Adoption of Food Safety Practices? Evidence from Remote Areas of Nepal*. IFPRI Discussion Paper 01524. Washington, DC: International Food Policy Research Institute.

Kumar, Anjani, P. Shinoj, and Shiv Jee. 2013. "Do Dairy Co-operatives Enhance Milk Production, Productivity and Quality? Evidences from the Indo-Gangetic Plain of India." *Indian Journal of Agricultural Economics* 68(3): 457–468.

Little, P.D., and M. Watts. 1994. *Living Under Contract: Contract Farming and Agrarian Transformation in Sub-Saharan Africa*. Wisconsin: The University of Wisconsin Press.

Masakure, O., and S. Henson. 2005. "Why Do Small-scale Producers Choose to Produce Under Contract? Lessons From Nontraditional Vegetable Exports From Zimbabwe." *World Development* 33(10): 1721–1733.

Michelson, H.C. 2013. "Small Farmers, NGOs, and a Walmart World: Welfare Effects of Supermarkets Operating in Nicaragua." *American Journal of Agricultural Economics* 95(3): 628–649.

Miyata, S., N. Minot, and D. Hu. 2007. *Impact of Contract Farming on Income: Linking Small Farmers, Packers, and Supermarkets in China*. IFPRI Discussion Paper 00742. Washington, DC: International Food Policy Research Institute.

Miyata, S., N. Minot, and D. Hu. 2009. "Impact of Contract Farming on Income: Linking Small Farmers, Packers, and Supermarkets in China." *World Development* 37(11): 1728–1741.

Morvaridi, B. 1995. "Contract Farming and Environment Risk: The Case of Cyprus." *The Journal of Peasant Studies* 23(1): 30–45.

Narrod, C., D. Roy, J. Okello, B. Avendao, K. Rich, and A. Thorat. 2009. "Public-private Partnerships and Collective Action in High Value Fruit and Vegetable Supply Chains." *Food Policy* 34: 8–15.

Opondo, M.M. 2000. "The Socio-economic and Ecological Impacts of the Agro-Industrial Food Chain on the Rural Economy in Kenya." *Ambio* 29 (1): 35–41.

Pomareda, C. 2006. *Contract Agriculture: Lessons from experiences in Costa Rica*. Santiago de Chile: RIMISP.

Porter, G., and K. Phillips-Howard. 1997. "Comparing Contacts: An Evolution of Contract Farming Schemes in Africa." *World Development* 25(2): 227–238.

Ramaswami, B., P.K. Joshi, and P.S. Birthal. 2006. *Efficiency and Distribution in Contract Farming: The Case of Indian Poultry Growers*. MTID Discussion Paper No. 91. Washington, DC: International Food Policy Research Institute.

Roy, D., and A. Thorat. 2008. "Success in High—Value Horticultural Export Markets for the Small Farmers: The Case of Mahagrapes in India." *World Development* 36(10): 1874–1890.

Setboonsarng, S., P. Leung, and A. Stefan. 2008. *Rice Contract Farming in Lao PDR: Moving from Subsistence to Commercial Agriculture*. ADBI Discussion Paper 90. Tokyo: Asian Development Bank Institute.

Simmons, P., P. Winters, and I. Patrick. 2005. "An Analysis of Contract Farming in East Java, Bali, and Lombok, Indonesia." *Agricultural Economics* 33(S3): 513–525.

Singh, S. 2002. "Contracting Out Solutions: Political Economy of Contract Farming in the Indian Punjab." *World Development* 30(9): 1621–1638.

Sivramkrishna, S., and A. Jyotishi. 2008. "Monopsonistic Exploitation in Contract Farming: Articulating a Strategy for Grower Cooperation." *Journal of International Development* 20(2): 280–296.

Tripathi R.S., R. Singh, and S. Singh. 2005. "Contract Farming in Potato Production: An Alternative for Managing Risk and Uncertainty." *Agricultural Economics. Research Review* 18(December): 47–60.

Wainaina, P.W., J.J. Okello, and J. Nzuma. 2012. "Impact of Contract Farming on Smallholder Poultry Farmers' Income in Kenya." Contributed Paper Presented at the 2012 Triennial Conference of International Association of Agricultural Economists, Foz do Iguacu, Brazil, August 18–24, 2012. No. 126196.

Wang, H.H., H. Yu, and B. Li. 2013. "Is Dairy Complex a Solution to Food Safety for Raw Milk? A Comparison of Farmers' Perceived and Realized Safety Effects." CAER-IFPRI Annual International Conference on Transforming China's Agricultural and Rural Sector: Challenges and Solutions, Wuhan, China, October 17–18.

Wang H.H., Y. Zhang, and L. Wu. 2011. "Is Contract Farming a Risk Management Instrument for Chinese Farmers? Evidence from a Survey of Vegetable Farmers in Shandong." *China Agricultural Economic Review* 3(4): 489–505.

Warning, M., and N. Key. 2002. "The Social Performance and Distributional Consequences of Contract Farming: An Equilibrium Analysis of the Arachide de Bouche Program in Senegal." *World Development* 30(2): 255–263.

Xu, J., and X. Wang. 2009. "An Empirical Analysis of the Impact of Contract Farming and its Organization Models on Farmers' Income." *Chinese Rural Economy* 2009(4): 39–47. (In Chinese).

Zhu, H. 2007. "An Assessment of the Effects of Adopting Contract Farming Structure in the Tomato Industry in Xinjiang." *Journal of Agrotechnical Economics* 3: 89–95. (In Chinese).

Zhu, H., and X. Wang. 2007. "An Analysis on the Influencing Factors of Tomato Growers' Participation in Contract Farming in Xinjiang Autonomous Region." *Chinese Rural Economy* 7: 67–75. (In Chinese).

Appendix

Table 11A.1 Status of adoption of food safety practices in brinjal cultivation in Bangladesh

Farm size class	*Food Safety Adoption Index*				
	All	*Contract*	*Independent*	*Difference*	*t-test value*
Marginal (<0.4 ha)	45.1 (19.6)	51.2 (18.4)	39.9 (19.2)	11.3***	3.2505
Small (0.4–1 ha)	42.6 (20.4)	48.6 (20.7)	38.3 (19.3)	10.2***	2.7294
Medium and large (≥1.0–4.0 ha)	39.1 (19.2)	32.9 (23.6)	41.2 (17.7)	−8.3	0.9197
All	43.4 (19.9)	49.0 (19.9)	39.3 (18.9)	9.7***	3.9587

Source: Authors' analysis based on field survey (2016).

Note: ***, ** and * represent significance at 1%, 5% and 10% levels, respectively. Figures in parentheses represent standard deviation.

Table 11A.2 Distribution of farmers by level of adoption of food safety practices in cultivation of brinjal in Bangladesh

FSI	*% of farmers*		
	All	*Contract*	*Independent*
<30 (low)	28.6	22.0	33.3
30–60 (medium-sized)	44.4	41.3	46.7
≥60 (high)	27.0	36.7	20.0

Source: Authors' analysis based on field survey (2016).

Table 11A.3 Status of adoption of different components of food safety practices

Dimensions	*Food Safety Adoption Index*				
	All	*Contract*	*Non-contract*	*Difference*	*t-test value*
Record keeping and site Management	36.2 (17.9)	38.1 (14.3)	34.8 (20.0)	−3.2	1.4424
Propagation Material	47.9 (21.9)	50.5 (21.3)	46.1 (22.2)	4.3	1.5511
Plant nutrition Management	40.5 (19.5)	44.9 (19.4)	37.2 (19.0)	7.7***	3.1957
Water management	39.8 (30.9)	44.0 (34.5)	36.7 (27.8)	7.4*	1.9019
Plant protection	40.9 (21.7)	49.1 (20.8)	35.0 (20.4)	14.2***	5.4718
Post-harvest Management	34.2 (25.4)	39.1 (26.8)	30.7 (23.9)	8.5***	2.6776

Source: Field survey (2016).

Note: ***, ** and * represent significance at 1%, 5% and 10% levels, respectively.

Table 11A.4 Sargan's test for overidentification of instrumental variables in the 2SLS regression

(1) Dependent variable: Profit (Taka/kg)

Instrumental variables: (i) range of price in last two years; (ii) prefers taking risk; (iii) information intensity of farmer organization; (iv) information intensity parent neighbor

Tests of overidentifying restrictions:

Sargan (score) $chi^2(3) = 2.16395$ ($p = 0.5391$)

Basmann $chi^2(3) = 1.96313$ ($p = 0.5801$)

(2) Dependent variable: FSI

Instrumental variables: (i) range of price in last two years; (ii) prefers taking risk; (iii) information intensity of farmer organization; (iv) information intensity parent neighbor

Tests of overidentifying restrictions:

Sargan (score) $chi^2(3) = 6.0244$ ($p = 0.1104$)

Basmann $chi^2(3) = 5.57251$ ($p = 0.1344$)

12 Value chains in aquaculture and fisheries in Bangladesh

Madan M. Dey and Prasanna Surathkal

Introduction

The importance of fish[1] in the Bangladeshi culture is captured by the adage 'māchey bhātey Bangāli'—that is, 'fish and rice make a Bengali.' The typical daily diet in Bangladesh consists of rice, some vegetables, small quantities of pulses and fish, depending on the availability (Bhattacharjee, Saha and Nandi, 2007). Fish is the most frequently consumed animal-sourced food in Bangladesh.[2] Fish consumption contributes to positive human outcomes by supplying macronutrients such as proteins, lipids and micronutrients, such as vitamins, minerals, essential fatty acids and amino acids. For example, Dasgupta et al. (2017) show that the risk of child mortality in Bangladesh is lower for children born during peak fishing season and to mothers who prefer to eat fish than for those born outside of peak fishing season and to mothers who do not prefer fish. Consumption of fish, including those sourced from capture fisheries, improves nutritional and dietary diversity in Bangladesh, a country with inadequate diversity of dietary items. Given the multiple roles fish play in the Bangladeshi diet, changes in the consumption and supply patterns of fish have wider implications for food and nutritional security in the country.

According to Needham and Funge-Smith (2014), per capita fish consumption in Bangladesh stands at 11.9 kg per year, and fish constitutes 11.1% of total protein consumption in the country. The statistics on per capita fish consumption and on fish's share of animal protein consumption reported by Needham and Funge-Smith (2014) for Bangladesh are considerably smaller than those in other studies. For example, Dey et al. (2005) and Dey, Alam and Paraguas (2011), both using data collected in 1998–1999, find average per capita fish consumption in Bangladesh was 22.2 kg per year. Dey et al. (2005) estimated that fish protein consumption constitutes more than 50% of total animal protein consumption. This finding is supported by other studies such as Dey, Bose and Alam (2008), FAO (2014) and Reardon et al. (2014). Dey et al. (2005) report Bangladesh residents in the lowest income quartile consume 13.05 kg of fish per capita annually and those in the highest income quartile consume 33.64 kg per capita. Toufique and Belton (2014) use the Household Income and Expenditure Survey (HIES) conducted by the Bangladesh Bureau of Statistics

(BBS) in 2000, 2005 and 2010. National average per capita fish consumption in 2000 was 14.1 kg, which grew to 15.4 kg in 2005 and to 18.1 kg in 2010. This discrepancy in per capita consumption statistics in different studies could be due to differences in the characteristics of data used for the analyses. As noted by Dey et al. (2005), BBS databases do not cover consumption of fish sourced through informal trade from neighboring countries. Nor do official statistics in Bangladesh include the consumption of many small and non-commercial fish species obtained from artisanal and subsistence fisheries, though 'assorted small fish' are one of the largest fish groups in terms of consumption, with a 20%–27% share of total consumption expenditures on fish (Dey, Alam and Paraguas, 2011).

Despite these differences in numbers attributable to the characteristics of databases, irrefutable evidence supports a substantial positive trend in per capita fish consumption over time in Bangladesh. Dey et al. (2005) find a consistent increase in per capita fish consumption during the 1981–2000 period, with the later years showing faster growth in consumption. Toufique and Belton (2014) show that fish consumption in urban and rural areas increased between 2000 and 2010, with urban areas showing stronger increases. Belton, van Asseldonk and Thilsted (2014) use survey data collected in 1996–1997 and 2006–2007 on the poverty impacts of development initiatives to analyze changes in fish consumption patterns across income quartiles. Per capita fish consumption increased between the two time periods, increasing strongly for higher income quartiles. Per capita consumption of fish from non-aquaculture sources declined, with stronger declines for lower-income quartiles. However, this decline was compensated for by increases in consumption of farmed fish, with lower-income groups showing stronger increases. Al Hasan et al. (2019) use the FAOSTAT Food Balance Sheets data to find fish consumption increased 2.25 times between 1961 and 2013. Substantial increases in per capita fish consumption in Bangladesh are impressive when seen in the context of the population's rapid growth, the country's small geographical area and the negative impacts of anthropogenic pressures on resources and other ever increasing constraints on production.

Apart from supplying macronutrients such as protein and lipids, fish is an important source of micronutrients such as vitamins and minerals. Small indigenous fishes, mostly sourced from inland and marine capture fisheries, play a significant role as a source of micronutrients. These fish do not grow more than 25 cm in length (Roos, Islam and Thilsted, 2003). About 140 species of 260 freshwater fish species in Bangladesh can be considered small indigenous fishes (Thilsted and Wahab, 2014). Seasonal and spatial dispersion in the composition of catches of this large number of species indirectly promotes dietary diversity. On average, fish consumers receive significantly higher intakes of energy content and fats from farmed fish, but small fish are significantly better sources of essential micronutrients such as iron, zinc, calcium and vitamins A and B_{12} than farmed fish (Bogard et al., 2017). Small fish usually are consumed whole (eyes, head, bones and/or viscera) and hence contribute to nutritional diversity.

However, the falling amounts of catches and rising prices of small indigenous fish are hindering their potential to contribute to food and nutritional security in Bangladesh.

Fish consumption in Bangladesh is highly responsive to prices and income (Dey, Alam and Bose, 2010; Toufique, 2015). Lower-income groups respond more strongly (i.e., more elastically) to changes in fish prices. Therefore, compared to affluent households, poorer households benefit more from falling prices (for example, from increased supply), but they also are harmed more by increasing prices (say, from falling catches). Belton, van Asseldonk and Thilsted (2014) found that poorer households showed greater declines in their consumption of captured fish and stronger increases in their consumption of farmed fish in 2006–2007 compared to 1996–1997. This period was characterized by a transition from capture fisheries to aquaculture as the major source of fish production in Bangladesh. Trade-offs in the types of fish consumed has implications in the context of the second Sustainable Development Goal, which is to achieve food security and improve nutrition while promoting sustainable agriculture. Bangladesh's economy, as measured by its gross domestic product (GDP), has grown impressively at an average rate of 6% per year since the year 2000, helping reduce the poverty level from 44.2% in 1991 to 13.8% in 2016–2017 (World Bank, 2018). However, given the poor dietary diversity and the low elasticity of nutrient intake with respect to income in developing countries such as Bangladesh, malnutrition has not been controlled effectively. Therefore, besides producing enough fish, value chains in aquaculture and fisheries need to be made more 'nutrition-sensitive' to achieve Sustainable Development Goals.

Structural transformations in fish value chain in Bangladesh

Fish production comes from two sources: aquaculture and capture fisheries. Aquaculture is the farming of aquatic organisms including fish, mollusks and crustaceans. Capture fishery production is the quantity of wild (non-fed) fish harvested from undomesticated ecosystems for all commercial, industrial, recreational and subsistence purposes. Seafood and fish are among the few food items in modern food systems for which harvests from the wild (as opposed to farmed or domesticated food) still play an important role in value chains. However, wild-harvested fish's share of total fish production has been shrinking continuously worldwide. Bangladesh is no exception to this, with aquaculture expanding rapidly and production from capture fisheries shrinking. Activities related to aquaculture and fisheries in Bangladesh can be classified broadly into three main subsectors: aquaculture (56% of total production), inland capture fisheries (28%) and marine and coastal capture fisheries (16%), with the total production estimated at 4,276,641 metric tons (MT) in 2017–2018 (Department of Fisheries Bangladesh, 2018).

Though the terms 'value chain' and 'supply chain' often are used interchangeably, there are some basic differences (Dey, Bjorndal and Lem, 2015; Nguyen et al., 2019). Value chains add incremental value to the product in the nodes of a chain by either adding or creating value. Seafood and fish value chain activities include value-adding or value-creating activities at each node in the supply chain to meet consumers' demand for the product. The smooth functioning of seafood/fish value chains requires not only factors of production and technology but also of efficient transport, market information systems, governance and management. Fish value chains in Bangladesh are generally long and complex, with many intermediaries between producers and final consumers of fish products in the country. Fish production/landing points are scattered all over the country, and many are quite distant from the final consuming markets. The four main types of domestic fish markets are: primary markets, located near the source of production; secondary markets, usually located in the subdistrict (upazila) headquarters; higher secondary markets, located in big cities; and terminal markets.

Four major changes can be observed in the fish value chain in Bangladesh over the recent decades: the emergence of aquaculture, specifically inland aquaculture, as the main source of fish supply, replacing inland capture fisheries; the impressive growth of entrepreneurial/intensive aquaculture, as opposed to homestead and semi-intensive aquaculture; the diversification of species for aquaculture; and the proliferation of value chain actors. These changes imply that in Bangladesh, aquaculture has emerged as the major source of fish production even as the aquaculture sector itself has undergone remarkable transformation. In fact, the transformation of the aquaculture sector from mostly homestead or semi-intensive production systems to entrepreneurial and commercial production has been a major factor responsible for aquaculture's rising position in overall fish production. Bangladesh is now the world's fifth-largest producer of farmed fish (FAO, 2018).

Shift from capture fisheries to aquaculture

Traditionally, the major source of Bangladesh's fish supply was inland capture fisheries. Unlike most other countries with substantial marine and coastal resources, production from inland capture fisheries in Bangladesh has been substantially larger than production from marine and coastal capture fisheries. In fact, Bangladesh is the only country with a larger share of inland capture fisheries (64%) than marine capture fisheries (36%) among the eight South Asian and Southeast Asian countries analyzed by Fernandes (2019). This is because the whole country can be considered a floodplain of the Ganga–Brahmaputra–Meghna river system. This is the second-largest river system in the world and drains into the Bay of Bengal via Bangladesh. This river system has endowed the country with a vast resource of inland and coastal water bodies that support a multitude of ecosystem services, including the third-greatest fish biodiversity in Asia. Water bodies in Bangladesh total 44,080 km^2, of which 91.8% are open water bodies and 8.2% are closed water bodies (Bangladesh Delta Plan 2001, 2018). Flooded lands (64.3% of the total area of water bodies), rivers and estuaries (23.4%), ponds (4.9%), coastal lowlands (3.2%), beels and haors (2.6%), Kaptai lake (1.5%) and baors (0.1%) are the major types of water bodies constituting the wetlands of Bangladesh. The Ganga–Brahmaputra–Meghna river system is the source of many of the 230 riverine tributaries and distributaries that traverse the length and breadth of the country (FAO AQUASTAT, 2014).[3] The riverine floodplains are inundated during monsoons, leading to rich fish harvests that sustain the livelihoods of landless and marginalized fisherfolk (Craig et al., 2004).

However, open water bodies that support rich fishery are under threat, leading to losses of fishery habitats and declines in fish catches (Bangladesh Delta Plan 2001, 2018). The amount of permanent wetlands has been depleted alarmingly, especially in Dhaka and the surrounding areas (Rai et al., 2017), leading to severe habitat loss. Satellite image analysis shows that the total dry period wetland area in the northwest region of Bangladesh decreased from 1,208.72 km^2 in 1989 to 903.54 km^2 in 2000 and to 867.18 km^2 in 2010 (Shopan et al., 2013). Interventions in riverine systems for flood control, drainage and irrigation systems also have been observed, obstructing the lateral migrations of rheophilic whitefish species and the passive drift of larvae from the main channel to the modified floodplains (Craig et al., 2004). Full flood control is the most obstructive in terms of its negative impacts on fish catches, fish movements and fish breeding. The impact levels of controlled flooding and partial flood control vary, but catch composition becomes less diverse after flood controls are implemented (Bangladesh Delta Plan 2001, 2018). Some other major causes of declining fish catches are industrial pollution, infrastructure building, encroachment of resources, agricultural intensification and runoffs and industrial pollution (Dey, Bose and Alam, 2008; Belton et al., 2011).

Figure 12.1 shows the *area plot* of contributions of different sources of fish production in Bangladesh from 1950 to 2017. The plot shows that until the mid-1970s, production from inland capture fisheries constituted about 70% to 75% of total fish production. From then on, the share of inland capture has declined continuously and appears to have settled at about 25% for the last few years. On the other hand, inland aquaculture had about a 10%–20% share of total fish production until the mid-1980s, before showing explosive growth in subsequent years. There can be two inflection points in the inland aquaculture production trend—one around 1995 and another around 2009. Around these time periods, the share of inland aquaculture increased substantially and irreversibly. The other two sources of fish production—marine/coastal capture and aquaculture—have contributed steadily to fish production. Marine/coastal capture fisheries' share of fish production has remained about 15%–20% over the last two decades, and marine/coastal aquaculture contributes about 5% of total fish production. Therefore, the rapid and sustained increase in inland aquaculture more than compensated for the decline in production from inland capture fisheries.

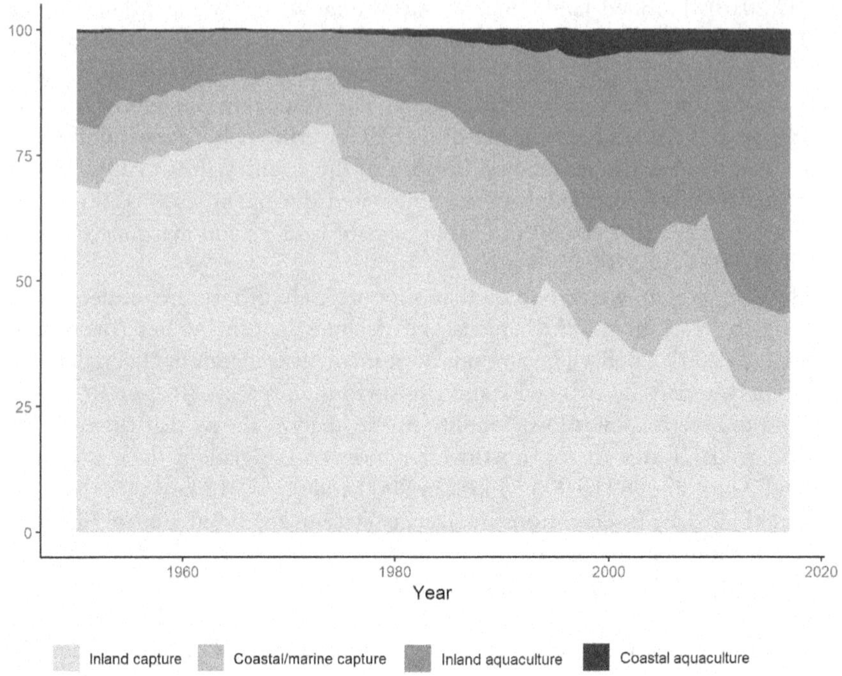

Figure 12.1 Share contribution to total fish production in Bangladesh by source of production, 1950–2017

Sources: FAO, 2019.

Figure 12.2 shows the decadal growth rates of fish production for the four sources of production in 10-year moving periods from 1950–1959 to 2008–2017. These growth rates have been estimated using the regression model,

$$\ln(Y_t) = \beta_0 + \beta_1 T + \epsilon_t$$

in 10-year rolling windows, where $\ln$ is the natural logarithm function, Y_t is the quantity of production from each source, β_0 is the intercept, β_1 is the coefficient on T the linear time trend thus representing estimated decadal growth rate, and ϵ_t is the residual term. Inland capture fisheries production grew about 5%–9% from 1950–1959 to 1966–1975, and then the growth rate decreased with negative growth (decreased production) in many periods, especially until the late 1990s. Growth rates of inland aquaculture remained steady at just over 2% until around the 1971–1980 period, then increased to about 8% until 1983–1992. Its fastest growth (rates of more than 10%) occurred between the 1988–1997 and 1995–2004 periods, with the highest growth rate

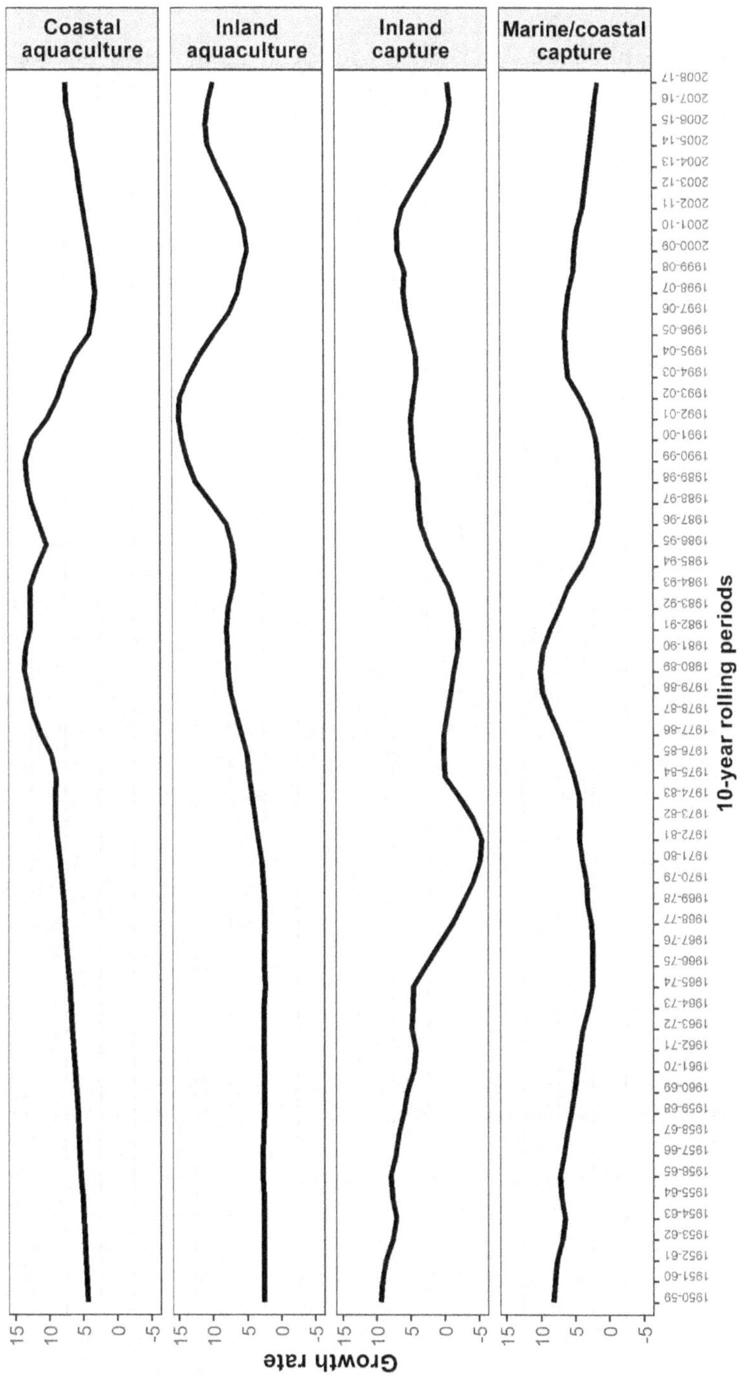

Figure 12.2 Growth rates in fish production, by sources of fish production, over 10-year moving windows.

Source: FAO, 2019.

of 14.97% achieved in the 1992–2001 period. After 1995–2004, growth has been more moderate, with rates of about 7%–9%.

Inland capture fish production shows growth in recent years, but some authors (e.g., Belton et al., 2011) are skeptical of these growth numbers. Given the widely reported severe problems affecting inland capture fisheries, statistics indicating consistent growth during recent years may not be reliable. At the same time, Belton et al. (2011) contend that aquaculture production statistics, especially those of tilapia and pangasius from inland aquaculture, are underestimated mainly due to the inadequacy of the official statistical procedures. This only reinforces the belief in substantial growth in inland aquaculture in Bangladesh in recent years.

Rise of entrepreneurial aquaculture

Aquaculture in ponds (as opposed to production in floodplains, modified rice fields, cages and lakes) comprises more than 85% of total aquaculture production. The vast and consistent increase in inland aquaculture production in Bangladesh over the last decades can be attributed to impressive growth in pond aquaculture. Specifically, pond aquaculture has been transformed by the increasingly important role of entrepreneurial, intensive and commercial aquaculture. For example, Belton et al. (2011) classify pond production into three distinct sources: homestead and extensive farming (producing 399,000 tons from 265,000 ha); commercial semi-intensive carp farming (390,000 tons from 110,000 ha); and commercial intensive and entrepreneurial farming by small and medium-sized enterprises (SMEs) of Nile tilapia and pangasius (and to some extent the climbing perch or koi), with a combined production of 395,000 tons from just 15,000 ha.

Although aquaculture in ponds always has been a major source of fish production, it was dominated by carp. Consumers readily accept Indian Major Carps (catla, rohu and mrigal) and indigenous carps. Chinese carps (silver carp and grass carp) also are important in aquaculture production. These carps were introduced in the 1960s from Hong Kong (Dey, Bose and Alam, 2008). Using survey data from 1998–1999, Dey et al. (2005) found that about 73% of rural Bangladesh's population practice polyculture of Indian and Chinese carps, along with a few other exotic species in ponds. The average pond size was 0.20 ha, and Indian carps and silver carp constituted 78% of total pond production. The study found that only 52% of the total sampled ponds were stocked with fingerlings and used limited inputs. Monoculture of pangasius and tilapia was in only the initial stages of adoption. Recent statistics show a dramatic change in species composition in aquaculture production. Table 12.1 shows the share of 20 major aquaculture species in Bangladesh's total aquaculture production from 2009 to 2017, ranked by their share in 2017. Carps are still important, but their combined share plummeted from about 75% in 2009 to about 45% in 2017. During the same time, the combined share of striped catfish and tilapias increased, from about 7% in 2009 to about 36% in 2017. Striped catfish and

Table 12.1 Share of major aquaculture species in the total aquaculture production in Bangladesh, 2009–2017

Fish/Group	*2009*	*2010*	*2011*	*2012*	*2013*	*2014*	*2015*	*2016*	*2017*
Striped catfish*	5.6	9.6	10.3	15.0	15.0	18.5	19.3	22.5	21.4
Tilapias NEI**	1.5	1.9	6.9	7.2	11.3	14.5	15.7	15.5	14.3
Rohu	21.3	19.4	18.2	17.1	14.3	12.0	12.6	11.9	12.3
Silver carp	16.2	14.9	9.1	10.5	12.6	10.3	9.0	8.2	8.9
Mrigal	12.5	11.4	10.4	9.4	9.4	8.4	8.3	7.7	7.7
Catla	16.8	15.0	14.1	12.9	10.8	8.9	8.1	7.2	7.6
Marine fishes NEI‡	4.5	5.6	4.0	3.7	3.9	4.8	4.7	5.1	5.0
Common carp	3.8	3.5	4.0	3.8	4.6	3.8	3.7	3.4	3.7
Giant tiger prawn‡	4.7	3.3	3.7	3.3	3.7	3.7	3.7	3.1	2.9
Freshwater fishes NEI	1.4	2.2	4.6	2.7	1.6	2.1	2.1	2.0	2.5
Giant river prawn	2.5	2.3	2.6	2.6	2.4	2.3	2.0	2.1	2.1
Grass carp	2.1	2.1	1.4	1.0	2.0	2.3	1.9	1.8	2.0
Cyprinids NEI	1.1	0.9	0.8	2.3	1.2	1.4	1.8	1.7	1.9
Climbing perch	0.2	0.5	0.9	1.8	2.1	1.8	2.7	2.6	1.8
Silver barb	0.7	0.9	3.1	2.5	1.7	2.1	1.7	1.9	1.8
Orangefin labeo	0.8	3.0	2.4	0.9	0.8	1.4	0.8	0.7	1.1
Orange mud crab‡	—	—	—	—	—	—	—	0.6	0.6
Freshwater prawns, shrimps NEI	0.5	0.5	0.2	0.3	0.3	0.2	0.3	0.3	0.4
Stinging catfish***	0.3	0.6	0.2	0.2	0.3	0.3	0.3	0.3	0.4
Philippine catfish****	0.2	0.5	0.3	0.3	0.3	0.3	0.3	0.3	0.4

Source: Department of Fisheries, Ministry of Fisheries and Livestock, Government of Bangladesh, Dhaka (various issues).

* *Pangasionodon hypophthalmus.*

** NEI: not elsewhere included.

*** *Heteropneustes fossilis.*

**** *Clarias batrachus.*

‡ Farmed in brakish water areas.

tilapias were the top-ranked species in terms of share of aquaculture production in 2017. Their impressive growth shines despite the contention that production of these species is underrepresented in official statistics.

Striped catfish was imported from Thailand into Bangladesh in 1990, and different species of tilapia have been introduced since 1954. Genetically improved farmed tilapia (GIFT), a faster-growing strain of Nile tilapia (*Oreochromis niloticus*), was imported in 1994 from the Philippines. The two species are more robust in a range of water qualities and are better suited than carp for commercial farming strategies such as higher stocking densities and manufactured feeds.

These species gained popularity among farmers as candidates for intensive aquaculture and became alternatives to extensive carp production in ponds that faced constraints such as inadequate water resources and financial limitations (Hussain, 2009). In contrast to extensive and semi-intensive types of aquaculture, small and medium-sized enterprises devote significant capital investment and operating costs to pond aquaculture, characterized by intensive management practices such as employing hired labor and the use of pelleted feed. Fish yields can be 40–70 tons of pangasius per hectare per year and 10 tons of tilapia per hectare per year.[4] The average culture period of pangasius is about seven to eight months and for tilapia, about three to four months. Farmers therefore often produce two crops of tilapia a year. Besides contributing substantially to fish production, these enterprises generate two permanent jobs per hectare, whereas homestead farming does not generate direct employment (Belton, Haque and Little, 2012).

Diversification of aquaculture

The intensification of aquaculture is one aspect of successful aquaculture ventures in Bangladesh, but the other equally impressive aspect is the trend toward diversification. Dey, Bose and Alam (2008) provide a timeline of exotic species introduced into Bangladesh for aquaculture purposes. As shown in Table 12.1, many of the introduced species such as pangasius (striped catfish) and tilapia now play significant roles in total production. Diversification began with a shift from farming of traditionally important native carps to the farming of exotic and introduced species, mainly tilapia, pangasius, silver carp and grass carp. The Department of Fisheries Bangladesh (2018) notes that farming of native species koi (climbing perch, *Anabas testudineus*) has expanded massively in recent times. Farming of other native species such as shing (stinging catfish, *Heteropneustes fossilis*), magur (walking catfish, *Clarias batrachus*), padba (butter catfish, *Ompok pabda*), gulsha (Gangetic mystus, *Mystus cavasius*), mola (*Amblypharyngodon mola*) and miscellaneous carps also is gaining popularity. This new wave of aquaculture diversification is induced by the high market demand for indigenous species (Department of Fisheries Bangladesh, 2018). Bangladesh is thus witnessing market-led diversification (product differentiation) following the intensification and commodification of aquaculture. Small indigenous fish species can be brought into this aquaculture diversification and intensification to achieve nutrition-sensitive fish value chains. To harness greater benefits from aquaculture development, subsequent efforts must ensure that aquaculture production of diversified products are intensified. This requires innovations along the value chain for the promising species—from technology of seed production and supply of other inputs to harvesting, post-harvest technology and marketing.

Proliferation of value chain actors

Hatcheries, fish feed mills, feed dealers and other non-farm enterprises have developed rapidly and proliferated throughout Bangladesh's fish value chain

(Bush et al., 2019; Hernandez et al., 2018; Uddin et al., 2019). These enterprises, many of them small and of medium scale, provide essential inputs, logistics, marketing and other services to fish farmers (Hernandez et al., 2018).

Aquaculture practices in Bangladesh started with seed collection from rivers, which now has been replaced almost entirely by hatchery-produced seeds. Private hatcheries supply most of these fingerlings (Department of Fisheries Bangladesh, 2018). A survey conducted by Hernandez et al. (2018) shows that hatcheries increased about 207% from 2004 to 2014. This growth in fish hatcheries has been accompanied by rapid expansions of nurseries, which buy hatchlings or fry from hatcheries and raise them to fingerling size for sale to farmers.

Fish feed production and its use in Bangladesh aquaculture have increased dramatically over the last decade or so. Feeding fish with formulated pelleted diets is common in many species, including shrimp, pangasius, koi, Nile tilapia and major carps. Most of these pelleted feeds are made by medium- and large-scale commercial mills. Pelleted feed is the largest cost component, accounting for 82% of the total cost of pangasius production in Bangladesh (Belton et al., 2011). Trade credit is a common practice in transactions involving feed in Bangladesh, whereby input suppliers provide farmers with short-term financing or deferred payment options under specified and agreed-upon terms and conditions. The availability of trade credit provides credit-constrained buyers with access to sufficient quality and quantity of feeds, thus facilitating the functioning of aquaculture product markets. Farmers start buying feed on credit from their supplier at the beginning of the crop and pay back their credit at the time of harvest (Ahmed, 2015). Suppliers incur risk when they grant trade credits, so they indulge in practices such as screening buyers carefully and charging higher prices on feed when farmers buy it on trade credit terms. Charging higher prices should not lead to situations of market power. Governments need to investigate whether local suppliers have sufficient capital to meet the requirements of larger small and medium-sized enterprises (SMEs). The government could also assess whether the SMEs have the capacity to absorb higher risks and longer exposure times.

Implications of transformation in fish value chains

The rapid growth and transformation of fish value chains in Bangladesh need to be analyzed in greater detail to better understand the implications of these changes and the possibilities for improvement. In this sense, the fish value chain in Bangladesh presents tremendous opportunities for research into the production, distribution and socio-economics of changes in food value chains. Some aspects of this transformation, such as consumption patterns, production agglomeration, clustering and welfare, have received attention, but several other aspects deserve to be better analyzed. Here we identify some promising research prospects and related suggestions in the context of Bangladesh's fish value chain.

The modern aquaculture sector in Bangladesh provides an excellent setting for the analysis of entrepreneurship and its determinants in a developing country's food value chain from macroeconomic and microeconomic frameworks. There is a growing body of evidence on the relationship between entrepreneurship and economic growth (Lundström and Stevenson, 2006). Entrepreneurship research is concerned with why, when and how individuals identify and exploit opportunities (Shane and Venkataraman, 2000). The sector or industry on which entrepreneurs choose to focus—and the problems, conditions and possibilities in the sector or industry—are important research settings in entrepreneurship analysis. However, such research has focused mostly on the digital world, and agricultural and food industries have not yet been analyzed (Alsos, Carter and Ljunggren, 2011; Pindado and Sánchez, 2017; Fitz-Koch et al., 2018; Kuckertz, Hinderer and Röhm, 2019). Moreover, even within agricultural and related sectors, most of the studies have focused on developed countries; developing countries, where agriculture and related activities play larger roles in the society and the economy, have been mostly ignored (Dias, Rodrigues and Ferreira, 2018). Entrepreneurship in the context of developing countries is seen as a major tool to eradicate poverty and help countries meet their development goals (Lundström and Stevenson, 2006). Hence, national and regional governments seek to support entrepreneurs through tax breaks, subsidies and other incentives (Rupasingha and Goetz, 2013). Given the importance of fish as food in Bangladesh and the role of entrepreneurial aquaculture in employment generation and food production, entrepreneurship in fish value chains in Bangladesh needs to be analyzed in a rigorous and contextualized framework to better understand factors influencing entrepreneurs' entry (and exit) decisions, the drivers of entrepreneurial investment at regional and national levels and approaches to improving rural economic opportunities.

Another important issue is gaining better knowledge of the nutritional impacts of structural transformations in fish production. On a positive note, much of the aquaculture production in Bangladesh is destined for domestic consumption, and only a small share is exported. The aquaculture revolution has brought about better market availability of a limited number of species, whereas capture fisheries produces a diverse fish harvest with spatiotemporal variations. Both urban and rural households are relying more on the market than on their own production for food consumption. Increasingly, more aquaculture takes place in public water bodies such as floodplains, which poor households used earlier for capture fisheries. And many of the wild-caught fisheries are under stress. Newton et al. (2007) show that poorer societies rely more on ecosystem services for subsistence and cash generation. Therefore, declines in Bangladesh's coastal and inland wild fishery resources would impact, in particular, the livelihoods and food security of poorer households. Using disaggregated data on species- or group-level fish prices and quantities, studies need to be performed on how different population segments' patterns of fish supply and dietary substitution respond to price fluctuations. Microeconomic theory-based analytical models relating nutritional outcomes of value chain interventions are absent (Allen and de Brauw, 2018). The basic model derived by Allen and de Brauw (2018) can be extended to understand the interplay between aquaculture intensification and diversification in terms of nutritional impacts. Their model shows that focusing on improving yields of only major crops will lead to stagnation in the yields of nutritious food crops.

Commercialization of aquaculture in Bangladesh has been accompanied by regional agglomeration and clustering of production to achieve lower transaction costs and facilitate co-innovation along the value chain (Hu et al., 2019). Lower transaction costs are expected to lead to better integration of spatial markets. The drivers and linkages of such clustering need to be better understood for identifying future sources of growth in entrepreneurial aquaculture. Implications of production clustering for product market integration need to be investigated. A higher degree of market integration reduces price volatility, and food price volatility is an important determinant of food security (Kalkuhl, 2016).

Procedures (sampling schemes, questionnaire structure) used in the collection of official databases such as the Household Income and Expenditure Survey data of the Bangladesh Bureau of Statistics and the 'Fisheries Statistics of Bangladesh' published by the Department of Fisheries need to be improved to understand the real contributions of the fisheries and aquaculture sectors. The HIES data can be improved with respect to fisheries and aquaculture sectors by seeking information on small indigenous fish consumption, at least as aggregate groups of fish. The Fisheries Statistics of Bangladesh survey sampling design needs to be improved to reflect the changes in fish production characteristics of Bangladesh. Another important publicly available database is the 'Commodity-wise Report' on prices, published by the Department of Agricultural Marketing. Although this database is a good source of information on wholesale- and retail-level prices, its coverage of producer-level prices needs much improvement. Real-time availability of information on market prices can help improve producers' marketing decision making, thereby augmenting their income.

In general, integrated Information and Communication Technology (ICT) facilities need to better meet producer's information needs. Better information flow through the optimal use of ICTs can improve consumer welfare (lower prices, reduced waste, efficient supply–demand matching), improve adoption of smarter farming technologies and incentivize producers through higher incomes (World Bank, 2017). Such an ICT facility could answer producers' questions on sources of improved seed and feeds, land availability, better market prices, credit facilities available, risk management, best aquaculture practices and extension and other public service provisions. Such ICT facilities would better serve their purposes if they are customized to different regional requirements. With the rapid penetration of mobile phones, wireless and Internet services into rural areas, such ICT platforms hold immense promise for solving problems related to information flow in supply chains.

Notes

1 The term 'fish' is used in this chapter in the broadest sense to include all aquatic animals, including finfish (both fed and non-fed), crustaceans (e.g., shrimp, prawns, crabs), molluscs (e.g., oysters, mussels, snails) and other aquatic invertebrates.
2 Belton, van Asseldonk and Thilsted (2014) find that almost all households consumed fish at least once in the 14-day period over which consumption was recorded.
3 Bangladesh Delta Plan 2100 (2018) reports the total number of rivers in Bangladesh to be 405.
4 While these yields are impressive, substantially higher yields have been achieved in Vietnamese pangasius aquaculture where it is common to produce 300 tons per hectare per crop (Phan et al. 2009).

References

Ahmed, N. (2015). Field survey report on technical, economic and social constraints to aquafeed production and management in Bangladesh. In M.R. Hasan & J.R. Arthur (Eds.), *Aquaculture seed and feed production and management in Bangladesh—Status, issues and constraints* (pp. 57–78). Rome: FAO.

Al Hasan, S.M., Saulam, J., Kanda, K., & Hirao, T. (2019). Temporal trends in apparent food consumption in Bangladesh: A join point regression analysis of FAO's food balance sheet data from 1961 to 2013. *Nutrients, 11*(8), 1864.

Allen, S., & de Brauw, A. (2018). Nutrition sensitive value chains: Theory, progress, and open questions. *Global Food Security, 16*, 22–28.

Alsos, G.A., Carter, S., & Ljunggren, E. (Eds.). (2011). *The handbook of research on entrepreneurship in agriculture and rural development.* Cheltenham, UK: Edward Elgar Publishing.

Bangladesh Delta Plan 2100. (2018). Baseline studies. Planning commission, government of the people's republic of Bangladesh. www.plancomm.gov.bd/site/files/0adcee77-2db8-41bf-b36b-657b5ee1efb9/Bangladesh-Delta-Plan-2100.

Belton, B., Haque, M.M., & Little, D.C. (2012). Does size matter? Reassessing the relationship between aquaculture and poverty in Bangladesh. *Journal of Development Studies, 48*(7), 904–922.

Belton, B., Karim, M., Thilsted, S., Jahan, K.M., Collis, W., & Phillips, M. (2011). Review of aquaculture and fish consumption in Bangladesh. Studies and Reviews 2011–53. The World Fish Center, Penang, p. 76.

Belton, B., van Asseldonk, I.J.M., & Thilsted, S.H. (2014). Faltering fisheries and ascendant aquaculture: Implications for food and nutrition security in Bangladesh. *Food Policy, 44*, 77–87.

Bhattacharjee, L., Saha, S.K., & Nandi, B.K. (2007). Food-based nutrition strategies in Bangladesh: Experience of integrated horticulture and nutrition development. Department of Agricultural Extension, Ministry of Agriculture, People's Republic of Bangladesh, Dhaka and Food and Agriculture Organization of the United Nations, Regional Office for Asia and the Pacific Bangkok, 2007. www.fao.org/3/ag126e/AG126E00.htm#Contents.

Bogard, J.R., Marks, G.C., Mamun, A., & Thilsted, S.H. (2017). Non-farmed fish contribute to greater micronutrient intakes than farmed fish: Results from an intra-household survey in rural Bangladesh. *Public Health Nutrition, 20*(4), 702–711.

Bush, S.R., Belton, B., Little, D.C., & Islam, M.S. (2019). Emerging trends in aquaculture value chain research. *Aquaculture, 498*, 428–434.

Craig, J.F., Halls, A.S., Barr, J.J.F., & Bean, C.W. (2004). The Bangladesh floodplain fisheries. *Fisheries Research, 66*(2–3), 271–286.

Dasgupta, S., Mustafa, M.G., Paul, T., & Wheeler, D. (2017). *The socioeconomics of fish consumption and child health in Bangladesh*. The World Bank Policy Research Working Papers. https://doi.org/10.1596/1813-9450-8217.

Department of Fisheries Bangladesh. (2018). *Yearbook of fisheries statistics of Bangladesh: 2017–18*. Vol. 35. Tejgaon, Dhaka: Bangladesh Govt. Printing Press (BG Press).

Dey, M.M., Alam, M.F., & Bose, M.L. (2010). Demand for aquaculture development: Perspectives from Bangladesh for improved planning. *Reviews in Aquaculture, 2*(1), 16–32.

Dey, M.M., Alam, M.F., & Paraguas, F.J. (2011). A multistage budgeting approach to the analysis of demand for fish: An application to inland areas of Bangladesh. *Marine Resource Economics, 26*(1), 35–58.

Dey, M.M., Bjørndal, T., & Lem, A. (2015). Guest editors' introduction: Value chain dynamics in aquaculture and fisheries. *Aquaculture Economics & Management, 19*(1), 3–7.

Dey, M.M., Bose, M.L., & Alam, M.F. (2008). Recommendation domains for pond aquaculture. Country case study: Development and status of freshwater aquaculture in Bangladesh. WorldFish Center Studies and Reviews No. 1872. The WorldFish Center, Penang, Malaysia. 73p.

Dey, M.M., Rab, M.A., Paraguas, F.J., Piumsombun, S., Bhatta, R., Alam, F.M., & Ahmed, M. (2005). Fish consumption and food security: A disaggregated analysis by types of fish and classes of consumers in selected Asian countries. *Aquaculture Economics & Management, 9*(1–2), 89–111.

Dias, C.S., Rodrigues, R.G., & Ferreira, J.J. (2018). What's new in the research on agricultural entrepreneurship? *Journal of Rural Studies, 65*, 99–115.

FAO. (2014). Fishery and aquaculture country profiles. The People's Republic of Bangladesh. www.fao.org/fishery/facp/BGD/en.

FAO. (2018). *The state of world fisheries and aquaculture 2018 - Meeting the sustainable development goals*. Rome. www.fao.org/3/i9540en/i9540en.pdf.

FAO AQUASTAT. (2014). Bangladesh country profile. www.fao.org/nr/water/aquastat/countries_regions/BGD/index.stm.

FAO FISHSTATJ. (2019). Fishery and aquaculture statistics. Global aquaculture production 1950–2017 (FishstatJ). In *FAO fisheries and aquaculture department* [online]. Rome. Updated 2019. www.fao.org/fishery/statistics/software/fishstatj/en.

Fernandes, J.A. (2019). Climate change impacts, vulnerabilities and adaptations: Southern Asian fisheries in the Arabian Sea, Bay of Bengal and East Indian Ocean. In *Impacts of climate change on fisheries and aquaculture* (p. 281). FAO Fisheries and Aquaculture Technical Paper 627. Rome: Food and Agricultural Organization of the United Nations, 2018.

Fitz-Koch, S., Nordqvist, M., Carter, S., & Hunter, E. (2018). Entrepreneurship in the agricultural sector: A literature review and future research opportunities. *Entrepreneurship Theory and Practice, 42*(1), 129–166.

Hernandez, R., Belton, B., Reardon, T., Hu, C., Zhang, X., & Ahmed, A. (2018). The "quiet revolution" in the aquaculture value chain in Bangladesh. *Aquaculture, 493*, 456–468.

Hu, C., Zhang, X., Reardon, T., & Hernandez, R. (2019). Value-chain clusters and aquaculture innovation in Bangladesh. *Food Policy, 83*, 310–326.

Hussain, M.G. (2009). A future for the tilapia in Bangladesh. *AQUA Culture Asia Pacific Magazine, 5*(4), 38–40.

Kalkuhl, M. (2016). How strong do global commodity prices influence domestic food prices in developing countries? A global price transmission and vulnerability mapping analysis. In M. Kalkuhl, J. Braun, & M. Torero (Eds.), *Food price volatility and its implications for food security and policy* (pp. 269–301). Springer. https://doi.org/10.1007/978-3-319-28201-5.

Kuckertz, A., Hinderer, S., & Röhm, P. (2019). Entrepreneurship and entrepreneurial opportunities in the food value chain. *NPJ (Nature Partner Journals) Science of Food, 3*(1), 6.

Lundström, A., & Stevenson, L.A. (2006). *Entrepreneurship policy: Theory and practice*. Series: International Studies in Entrepreneurship, Vol. 9. Boston, MA: Springer.

Needham, S., & Funge-Smith, S.J. (2014). The consumption of fish and fish products in the Asia-Pacific region based on household surveys. FAO Regional Office for Asia and the Pacific, Bangkok, Thailand. RAP Publication, 12. www.fao.org/3/a-i5151e.pdf

Newton, K., Cote, I.M., Pilling, G.M., Jennings, S., & Dulvy, N.K. (2007). Current and future sustainability of island coral reef fisheries. *Current Biology, 17*(7), 655–658.

Nguyen, T.A.T., Nguyen, K.A.T., Truong, H.C., & Jolly, C.M. (2109). Collective action governance and benefits distribution in the sturgeon value chain in Lâm Đồng province, Vietnam. *Aquaculture*. https://doi.org/10.1016/j.aquaculture.2019.734765.

Phan, L.T., Bui, T.M., Nguyen, T.T., Gooley, G.J., Ingram, B.A., Nguyen, H.V., . . . De Silva, S.S. (2009). Current status of farming practices of striped catfish, Pangasianodon Hypophthalmus in the Mekong delta, Vietnam. *Aquaculture, 296*(3–4), 227–236.

Pindado, E., & Sánchez, M. (2017). Researching the entrepreneurial behaviour of new and existing ventures in European agriculture. *Small Business Economics, 49*(2), 421–444.

Rai, R., Zhang, Y., Paudel, B., Li, S., & Khanal, N.R. (2017). A synthesis of studies on land use and land cover dynamics during 1930–2015 in Bangladesh. *Sustainability, 9*(10), 1866.

Reardon, T., Tschirley, D., Dolislager, M., Snyder, J., Hu, C., & White, S. (2014). *Urbanization, diet change, and transformation of food supply chains in Asia*. Michigan: Global Center for Food Systems Innovation. www.fao.org/fileadmin/templates/ags/docs/MUFN/DOCUMENTS/MUS_Reardon_2014.pdf.

Roos, N., Islam, M.M., & Thilsted, S.H. (2003). Small indigenous fish species in Bangladesh: contribution to vitamin A, calcium and iron intakes. *The Journal of Nutrition, 133*(11), 4021S–4026S.

Rupasingha, A., & Goetz, S.J. (2013). Self-employment and local economic performance: Evidence from US counties. *Papers in Regional Science, 92*(1), 141–161.

Shane, S., & Venkataraman, S. (2000). The promise of entrepreneurship as a field of research. *Academy of Management Review, 25*(1), 217–226.

Shopan, A.A., Islam, A.K.M.S., Dey, N.C., & Bala, S.K. (2013). Estimation of the changes of wetlands in the northwest region of Bangladesh using Landsat images. In 4th International Conference on Water & Flood Management (ICWFM-2013), 9–11 March 2013, Dhaka, Bangladesh.

Thilsted, S.H., & Wahab, M.A. (2014). Production and conservation of nutrient-rich small fish (SIS) in ponds and wetlands for nutrition security and livelihoods in South Asia. WorldFish.

Toufique, K.A. (2015). Analysis of fish consumption and poverty in Bangladesh. BIDS-REF Study Series No.15–01. https://think-asia.org/bitstream/handle/11540/6502/REF_15_01_ Full.pdf?sequence=1.

Toufique, K.A., & Belton, B. (2014). Is aquaculture pro-poor? Empirical evidence of impacts on fish consumption in Bangladesh. *World Development, 64*, 609–620.

Uddin, M.T., Goswami, A., Rahman, M.S., & Dhar, A.R. (2019). How can governance improve efficiency and effectiveness of value chains? An analysis of pangas and tilapia stakeholders in Bangladesh. *Aquaculture, 510*, 206–215.

World Bank. (2017). *ICT in agriculture: Connecting smallholders to knowledge, networks, and institutions*. World Bank Group. https://openknowledge.worldbank.org/handle/10986/27526.

World Bank. (2018). *Bangladesh: Reducing poverty and sharing prosperity*. www.worldbank.org/en/results/2018/11/15/bangladesh-reducing-poverty-and-sharing-prosperity.

13 Mango value chains in India

Madhuri Saripalle and Elumalai Kannan

Introduction

India's agricultural economy is highly diverse, constituting different agro-climatic conditions, soils and a wide variety of crops. Horticultural crops, particularly vegetables and fruits, occupy a prominent position in the cropping pattern and contribute significantly to farm household income, employment and nutrition (Joshi et al., 2004; Ali, 2003). Vegetables comprise 60% of India's total production of horticultural crops, and fruits comprise 30%, although the area devoted to each is about 40% and 25%, respectively (Government of India, 2018). Each crop has a unique supply chain based on the product's attributes, seasonality and market access. Crops such as cereals and pulses are essential commodities for which a price support system exists, and a standard mechanism of price discovery has been enabled by government-regulated markets and by a few private markets like *e-choupal*, making the farmers more aware of prices and more competitive (Goyal, 2010). In the case of horticultural crops like flowers, the high degree of perishability creates different markets at different times of the day—early-morning blooms are for exports; midday blooms are for garlands; and post-midday blooms are for the perfume market (Saripalle, 2016). For other crops like vegetables and fruits, informal markets play a greater role in mediating transactions, and market yards established by the state government serve as a minor platform for price discovery.

Despite these features, huge transportation, storage and transaction costs still exist in the sale of fruits and vegetables, which make farmers rely primarily on intermediaries such as wholesale traders and commission agents who serve as market aggregators. Within the value chain of farmer–wholesale agent–processor–retailer–consumer, there are several variations in contract or governance modes from which farmers choose to minimize their transaction costs and increase their revenues. For example, not all farmers choose to sell to an intermediary, and farmers who choose to use an intermediary contractor can choose to sell the crop at the flowering stage or the post-flowering stage. This chapter discusses some of value chain models prevalent in mango production in India and analyzes the factors determining farmers' choice of contract modes. The study uses primary data from a survey of 131 farmers in Srinivasapura, Kolar

District in Karnataka and key farmers in Chittoor District in Andhra Pradesh conducted during 2014 and 2019, respectively. Most of the farmers in the area were small and medium-sized farmers who sold their produce locally or to processing companies through agents. Some farmers also export their mangoes to other states in India for direct consumption or processing. To obtain a list of farmers who sent their mangoes to other states or other countries, information was collected from wholesale agents and key informants who could identify some of the farmers following good farming practices.

This chapter is organized as follows. The first section discusses broad trends in mango production in India. The second section presents the state of mango production and the profile of sample farmers in the study area. The third section provides a typology of mango value chains and discusses some of the factors influencing farmers' contract choice. The fourth section presents a model of determinants of the farmers' choice among modes of contracts. The fifth section provides conclusions and broad policy implications.

India is the world's largest producer of mango, with 40% of total production, followed by China and Thailand. Although India is the top producer, its productivity of mango remains relatively low (Government of India, 2018). Within India, major mango-producing states are Uttar Pradesh (24%), Andhra Pradesh (24%) and Karnataka (10%). The mango sector faces many challenges, of which post-harvest losses, poor infrastructure, weak market linkages and small orchard sizes, among other challenges, affect the sector's growth potential (Banerjee, 2011). Mango's share of total fruit area and the quantities of mangoes exported have been declining for the past decade (Tables 13.1 and 13.2). Although the area devoted to mangoes has fallen in relative terms, the area and production of mangoes have shown an increasing trend in absolute terms. The share of India's mangoes that is exported or processed mango products is comparatively low, and India ranks fifth globally in the export of mangoes. The quantity of fresh mangoes that India exports has declined and volatility in the quantities exported has increased. However, India's exports of mango pulp were almost three times its exports of fresh mangoes (Government of India, 2016).

A major reason for the decline of India's fresh mango exports since 2011–2012 is the presence of pesticide residue and fruit fly infestation, which resulted in Indian mangoes being banned from the U.S., European and Japanese markets (Jha, 2016; Goyal et al., 2017). Japan placed an embargo on the import of mangoes from India in 1986, and the ban was lifted only in 2003 once vapor heat treatment (VHT) facilities to sterilize the fruit were in place (*Business Standard*, 2013). The related infrastructure for washing, drying, pallet, precooling and cold storage facilities are available only in Mumbai and have been sponsored by the Maharashtra State Agricultural Marketing Board. Another reason behind the low demand for mango varieties such as Alphonso is that it does not compare well in color and appearance with mangoes from Israel and Latin America (Hegde, 2006). Nevertheless, demand for Indian mangoes continues to rise in global markets, particularly in the Gulf countries. Given

Table 13.1 Mango production in India

Year	*Area (1,000 ha)*	*% of total fruit area*	*Production (1,000 MT)*	*% of total fruit production*	*Productivity (MT/ha)*
2002–2003	1,623	42.9	12,733	28.2	7.8
2003–2004	1,907	39.8	11,490	25.2	6.0
2004–2005	1,970	39.7	11,830	24.0	6.0
2005–2006	2,081	39.1	12,663	22.9	6.1
2006–2007	2,154	39.1	13,734	23.1	6.4
2007–2008	2,201	37.6	13,997	21.3	6.4
2008–2009	2,309	37.8	12,750	18.6	5.5
2009–2010	2,312	36.5	15,027	21.0	6.5
2010–2011	2,297	36.0	15,188	20.3	6.6
2011–2012	2,378	35.3	16,196	21.2	6.8
2012–2013	2,500	35.8	18,002	22.1	7.2
2013–2014	2,516	34.3	18,431	20.7	7.3
2014–2015	2,163	34.7	18,527	20.7	8.5
2015–2016	2,209	35.1	18,643	20.7	8.4
2016–2017	2,212	34.7	19,506	20.9	8.8
2017–2018	2,258	34.7	21,822	22.4	9.6
2018–2019*	2,313	35.4	22,353	23.1	9.6

Source: Indian Horticulture Database 2009, Handbook on Horticulture Statistics 2014, Horticulture Statistics at a Glance 2017.

Note: *Advance Estimates, 2019; Government of India.

Table 13.2 Export of fresh mangoes from India

	Quantity (MT)	*Value (₹ Lakhs)*
2010–2011	58,863	16,484
2011–2012	63,441	20,974
2012–2013	55,585	26,472
2013–2014	41,280	28,543
2014–2015	42,998	30,254
2015–2016	36,329	31,710
2016–2017	52,760	44,366
2017–2018	49,180	38,234
2018–2019	46,510	40,650

Source: Government of India, Department of Commercial Intelligence and Statistics (DGCIS), Annual report, various years; http://agriexchange.apeda.gov.in/product_profile/exp_f_india.aspx?categorycode=0204.

the seasonal nature of production and the short marketing period, a complex value chain operates to supply mangoes to both domestic and international markets. This chapter maps the complexity of value chains and analyzes factors influencing the bargaining power of producers (mango growers) within different contract systems.

State of mango cultivation and profile of sample farmers

The Kolar District has the highest share of mango production in the Indian state of Karnataka (Table 13.3). Within the Kolar District, Srinivasapura taluk has the highest share of mango production (50%) and is known statewide for its mangoes (Government of Karnataka, 2013). In terms of exports to the United States and Europe, Indian states such as Uttar Pradesh, Maharashtra and Andhra Pradesh have relatively higher shares than Karnataka, which supplies mangoes mostly to the fruit-processing industry. The Kolar area is classified as a dry region among agro-climatic zones (Central Research Institute for Dryland Agriculture, 2012),[1] and application of irrigation water and inputs are very limited.

Mango harvesting starts in the first week of May and lasts until the end of June or the first week of July. During the first week of May, Alphonso mangoes are harvested and sold mostly to juice- and pulp-manufacturing companies. From May 25 on, more popular varieties like Banganapalli come into the market and are exported to all states in India. Mangoes also are sold to agents from other states in India and from markets in West Asia. In the first week of June, Totapuri and Neelam varieties are harvested, and together they comprise about 70% of all mangoes produced in Karnataka. The green varieties are sold to pulp-manufacturing units, and the more ripened varieties are sold across India for direct consumption. Many local varieties are sold in domestic markets within the state. The largest proportion of farmers was found to be growing Totapuri, followed by Neelam and Badami/Alphonso. Badami mangoes fetch the highest price, followed by Banganapalli and Mallika (Table 13.4).

Table 13.3 Mango statistics in Kolar, Karnataka

	Kolar District			*Karnataka State*		
Year	*Area (has)*	*Production (MT)*	*Productivity (MT/ha)*	*Area (has)*	*Production (MT)*	*Productivity (MT/ha)*
2005–2006	45,587	168,034	3.7	1181,58	450,688	3.8
2006–2007	41,868	168,519	4.0	116,780	609,383	5.2
2007–2008	32,280	58,556	1.8	108,774	358,560	3.3
2008–2009	32,831	109,360	3.3	114,972	485,384	4.2
2009–2010	33,131	136,135	4.1	120,018	510,407	4.3
2010–2011	40,769	181,218	4.4	137,197	665,012	4.8
2011–2012	41,570	219,032	5.3	142,546	798,290	5.6
2012–2013	41,882	170,753	4.1	144,753	761,893	5.3
2013–2014	37,609	131,782	3.5	139,316	735,696	5.3
2014–2015	39,299	145,210	3.7	143,549	676,358	4.7
2015–2016	40,550	82,357	2	143,831	560,229	3.8

Source: Department of Economics and Statistics, Karnataka; https://des.kar.nic.in/docs/reports/2014-15%20F%20&%20V%20%20Report.pdf

Table 13.4 Type of mango varieties grown and average price

Mango variety	*Number of farmers growing these varieties*	*Price (Rs/q)*
Mallika	27	2,500
Badami/Alphonso	76	3,000
Banisha	67	2,000
Totapuri	117	1,300
Nelam	92	1,300
Rasapuri	6	2,000
Rajgira	47	900
Khurdoos	5	900
Banganapalli	3	2,500
Mulgova	6	1,200
Others	4	500–800

Source: Field survey.

Mango-producing farmers face four markets in general: the government-facilitated Agricultural Produce Market Committee (APMC) yard, the village market, fruit-processing companies and the city market. At the harvesting stage, farmers can go to the market yard themselves or to the agents, who organize transportation and collection of the fruits. The farmers prefer the latter method because there are informal barriers to entry in the market yards. Farmers in developing economies generally depend on intermediaries and prefer not to go beyond the nearest market. However, factors such as age and distance play important roles in influencing the choice and awareness of markets (Saripalle, 2019).

We found that of the 131 farmers interviewed, 37% preferred not to sell to any contractor, and the other 63% sold to an intermediary contractor. Within the contracting farmers, the majority (83%) sold the crop at the pre-flowering stage, and the rest sold it at the post-flowering stage, as discussed in detail in the next section. We try to examine the reasons farmers choose a contractor and choose the flowering stage at which they sell the crop. Farms traditionally are contracted out during the pre-flowering or the post-flowering stage. According to rough estimates based on interviews in Kolar, most farms used to be leased to contractors at the post-flowering stage because farmers were owners and had the financial and agricultural know-how to grow the orchards. More recently, most owners lease out their farms to a third party at the pre-flowering stage because the owners lack either the financial resources to maintain the orchards or the interest in maintaining them.[2]

Age profile and type of contract arrangement

The sample farmers' average age was 50. Among farmers who did not go with any contractor, it was found that 38% were younger than 40 and that

48% were age 40 to 60 (Table 13.5). This indicates that younger farmers were more inclined to access markets directly instead of relying on intermediaries. However, elderly farmers are more risk-averse and tended to prefer the pre-flowering contract system of mango production.

Education and type of contract system

Analysis revealed that 35% of the sample farmers were either illiterate or had attended only primary school, 46% were educated to the secondary level, and the remaining 19% had a college degree. In terms of choice of contract, farmers who attended school were less likely to go with the pre-harvest contracts than were farmers who did not attend school. A higher proportion of mango farmers with no formal literacy opted for a pre-flowering contract, which is more informal in nature than a post-flowering contract. Interestingly, the percentage of farmers with a graduate in the family was much higher under the no-contract system than among farmers who sold to contractors (Tables 13.6 and 13.7).

Table 13.5 Distribution of sample farmers by age profile (%)

Age	*Pre-flowering*	*Post-flowering*	*No contract*
<40	27	25	38
40–60	43	55	48
>60	30	21	15
Overall	100	100	100

Source: Field survey.

Table 13.6 Choice of contract by education level of sample farmers (%)

Particulars	*Pre-flowering*	*Post-flowering*	*No contract*
Illiterate	37	9	8
Primary	7	25	27
SSLC	37	49	46
Graduate and above	20	17	19

Source: Field survey.

Table 13.7 Choice of contract by the highest education of family members (%)

Family	*Pre-flowering*	*Post-flowering*	*No contract*
Below SSLC	43	55	38
Graduate and above	57	45	63
Overall	100	100	100

Source: Field survey.

We found that small and marginal farmers comprised 51% of our sample (Table 13.8) and that this majority of farmers had fewer than 5 acres of mango orchards. The average productivity of small and medium-sized farmers was found to be higher than that of large farmers. Given the large variety of mangoes farmers grow to minimize risk and increase total revenue, we computed Simpson's Diversity Index and found that it was highest for large farmers.

Although revenue from the crop depended on the variety of mango grown (ranging from three to nine varieties), farming practices, growing of vegetables and the choice of market, farmers' overall profitability depended on the fixed and variable costs they incurred and on the costs they incurred during the gestation period. Table 13.9 shows that variable costs declined and that profit and average price per quintal increased as farm size increased. In the next section, we try to analyze in depth whether the farmers' choice of contract is related to factors such as age, education, annual income, distance to market and profitability per season.

Reported income and profits

In the survey, farmers were asked to state their annual income from all sources. It ranged from Rs10,000 to 40 lakhs. We also calculated their profits based on

Table 13.8 Average size of mango orchard and yield

Farm size	*% share*	*Average size of mango orchard (acre)*	*Average productivity (q/acre)*	*Variability in mango yield*	*Simpson index of diversity*
Marginal farmers	9.92	2.04	28.75	0.36	0.42
Small farmers	41.22	4.46	26.17	0.54	0.50
Medium-sized farmers	25.95	6.86	22.01	0.58	0.52
Large farmers	22.90	22.29	16.56	0.62	0.59
All	100.00	8.93	23.15	0.55	0.52

Source: Field survey.

Table 13.9 Average cost, price and profit

Farm size	*Average variable cost (Rs/acre)*	*Average Profit (Rs/acre)*	*Average Price (Rs/q)*
Marginal farmers	11,463	19,031	1,410
Small farmers	10,171	19,772	1,572
Medium-sized farmers	8,273	26,260	1,868
Large farmers	5,563	23,508	1,855
All	8,751	22,238	1,698

Source: Field survey.

Table 13.10 Reported income from mango orchard (% farmers)

Income (Rs)	*Pre-flowering*	*Post-flowering*	*No contract*
<1 lakh	33	34	31
1–5 lakh	57	45	48
>5 lakh	10	21	21

Source: Field survey.

Table 13.11 Estimated profits from mango production (% farmers)

Profit (Rs/acre)	*Pre-flowering*	*Post- flowering*	*No contract*
<0	20	19	13
0–10,000	17	17	27
>10,000–20,000	27	21	23
>20,000	36	43	37
Total	100	100	100
Average profit (Rs)	25,000	20,000	23,000

Source: Field survey.

mango sales and the costs incurred. We calculated average profit per acre as the total revenue per acre less variable cost per acre and fixed costs per acre, where fixed costs are apportioned over the age of the crop, assuming a discount rate of 10% to reflect the opportunity cost of capital. Since it takes up to six years for a mango plant to yield fruits, the variable-cost components were collected for the gestation period. Details on variable costs during the reference period also were collected. Fixed costs included seedling costs, field preparation, support material used, irrigation costs (investment in borewell) and any other costs. Appendix Table 13A.1 shows the cost components across all farmers' age groups.

Though there was wide divergence, in general we expect all farmers to underreport their income relative to their profits (Tables 13.10 and 13.11). In general, it was found that the average profit per acre was highest for farmers who chose pre-flowering contracts (Rs 25,000) and lowest for farmers who chose post-flowering contracts (Rs 20,000), and it was Rs 23,000 per acre for those who chose not to use a contractor.

Mango value chain channels

A value chain comprises a range of interrelated activities required to bring a product from the production stage to consumption. The product attains value as it moves from one actor to another along the value chain until it is finally delivered to consumers. Actors who create value in the chain may include farmers, traders, processors, retailers and final consumers. In countries such as India, most farmers are small and have fragmented land holdings, and agriculture suffers from a lack of adequate capital investment and from missing linkages to markets. The value chains are complex and may include more than one channel, with various actors and their corresponding functions affecting the value chain's performance (Kumar and Sharma, 2016). Among agricultural products, the value chain for mango is unique and has some special features, as this section describes. However, the number of actors and their functions in value chains vary, compounding the analysis of value chain development. Large numbers of actors are concentrated both at the downstream end (farmers and wholesale traders) and at the upstream end of the value chain (retailers and consumers). A few actors with greater levels of specialization (processors and exporters) also are present at the upstream end. The value chain for fresh mango is shown in Figure 13.1. Four different value chains for mango are observed, and they are explained here.

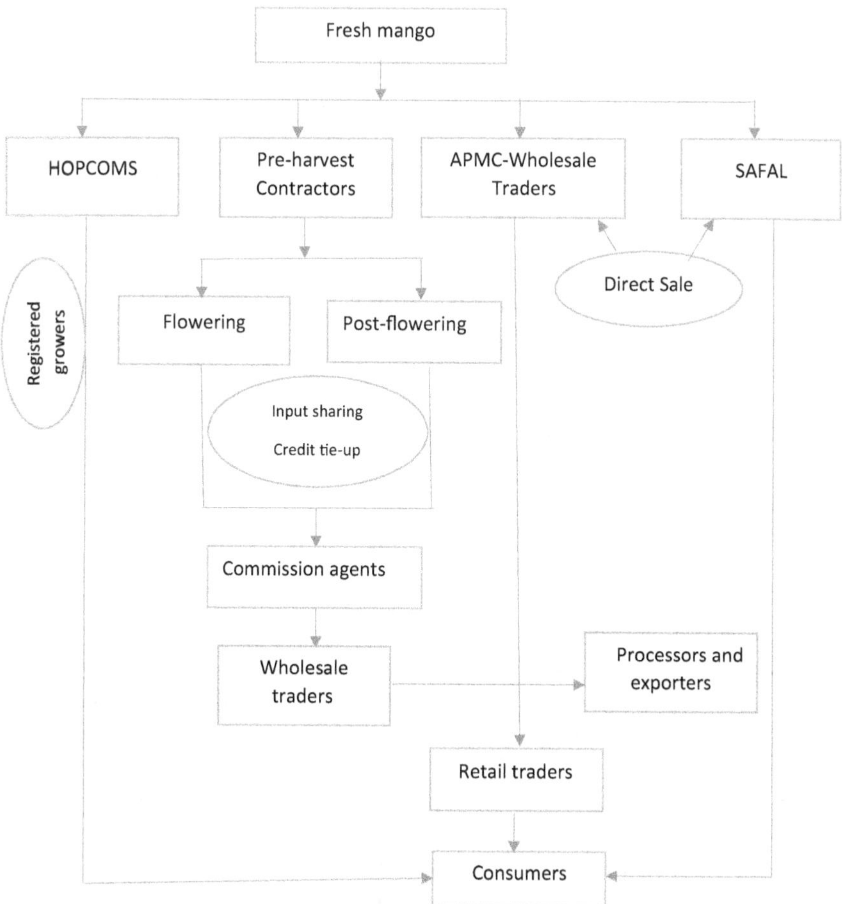

Figure 13.1 Mango value chain

Source: Developed by authors.

HOPCOMS-led value chain

The Horticultural Producers Cooperative Marketing and Processing Society Limited (HOPCOMS) is a Karnataka State–controlled cooperative society that buys horticultural products directly from farmers and sells them directly to consumers. HOPCOMS sells fresh mangoes, among other products, through its own outlets, largely in the Bangalore metropolitan region. The sale outlets have limited geographical coverage, so the quantity of fresh mangoes HOPSCOMS procures from farmers is relatively small. Only registered farmer-members[3] can sell mangoes directly to HOPCOMS' procurement centers. The products thus procured are consolidated centrally and sold through outlets to consumers.

HOPCOMS enforces certain quality standards when procuring mangoes from farmers. They include uniform fruit size, ripened to a yellow color and the absence of dots or patches on the fruit's surface. Farmers who are willing to sell mangoes to HOPCOMS enroll as members and have to declare the quantity to be supplied in a purchase order form in advance. The sample farmers reported certain advantages to selling mangoes to HOPCOMS. They receive Rs 3.0/kg more than they would receive if they sell at Agricultural Produce Market Committee (APMC) yards. Since the farmers sell their mangoes directly to procurement centers, problems of middlemen's involvement and charges paid for market transactions do not exist in this chain. Further, HOPCOMS organizes annual mango fairs at Bangalore city, where member-farmers are provided with stalls to sell mangoes directly to consumers. Despite these advantages, the field evidence shows that farmers' level of participation in this chain and mango quantities sold through this chain are low. HOPCOMS procures only a limited quantity of about 5–8 tons per day during the harvesting period. This limit restricts farmers from participating effectively in the chain. Since HOPCOMS accepts only good-quality mangoes, farmers must depend on private traders to sell the inferior-quality or rejected mangoes. This results in low price margins for the farmers. However, farmers with adequate capital and infrastructure facilities such as pack houses and ripening chambers actively participate in the HOPCOMS-led value chain.

Pre-harvest contract value chain

The value chain creates value in agricultural produce at each transaction stage and helps spread risk among actors in the chain. Contractual arrangements between farmers and commission agents or traders, particularly at the downstream end of the mango value chain, serve multiple purposes. These arrangements tend to reduce the risks of market price volatility, ensure secured supply of mangoes, decide input use, determine time of harvesting and provide for watching over the mango orchards. Here, both farmers and commission agents try to maximize their expected returns from mango orchards through contracts. Once the mangoes are harvested, the commission agents transport them to the APMC yard where the products are sold to wholesale traders. The wholesale traders then sell the mangoes to pulp processors and exporters at the APMC yard. The wholesale traders also supply to local retail traders and other cities in the state. From the retail traders, mangoes ultimately reach consumers in this chain.

Two types of contracts were observed between the mango growers and the commission agents/traders: leasehold contracts and pre-harvest contracts (which can be pre-flowering-stage contracts or post-flowering- or fruiting-stage contracts). These contractual arrangements in mango production and marketing are unique and mostly used to share risk between producers and traders. It is useful to discuss here the nature of these contracts, their enforcement and who bears risks and who gains in the transactions.

The leasehold contract generally is entered into between mango growers and agro-business firms. In this contract, the lessees (the firms) take ownership of the trees for an agreed-upon period. The firms temporarily own the trees, but the farmers retain title to the land. In this type of arrangement, the firms completely bear production risks, including the input use decisions and output marketing risks. In the Kolar area, some mango processing companies have adopted 10 to 15 GlobalG.A.P.-certified farms.[4] The companies conduct an audit once a year and inspect the farms at the post-flowering stage. After inspection, the farmers are required to follow a package of practices that consists of spraying chemicals according to fixed schedules. After harvesting, the farmers sell the mangoes at a price marginally (Rs 1) higher than the daily market price. Field evidence shows that leasehold contracts are not widely practiced in the study area. Only one firm engaged in leasehold contracts with a few farms, but the farmers reported an unsatisfactory experience. Farmers cited a breach of trust between themselves and the agro-business firms on the maintenance of orchards, application of inputs and sharing of outputs.

Pre-harvest contracts, comprising both pre-flowering and post-flowering contracts, are widely accepted among the farmers. A relatively high proportion of sample farmers prefer the pre-flowering contract (flowering initiation stage) to the post-flowering contract. The factors influencing the choice of contracts are econometrically tested in the next section. Discussions with farmers reveal that large farmers with adequate capital, education, risk-bearing ability, proximity to markets and better networks with traders enter post-flowering contracts. Farmers lease out their orchards to commission agents/traders for fixed cash payments of rent for a specific harvesting period. Farmers and traders do not share inputs in this arrangement. Traders own the entire harvest, implying that the lessee bears the production risk as well as the market risk. However, controlling for these factors, whether the net return from mango trees affects the farmers' choice of contract is an empirical question.

Pre-flowering-stage contracts have many important facets, including mechanisms to share market risk, arrange credit and share inputs. In general, contracting at the pre-flowering stage takes place in March, when the flowering initiation stage begins. In this arrangement to share market risk, the contracting process is highly informal, agreed upon orally and based on fixed cash payments of rent. This type of arrangement works purely on mutual trust between farmers and commission agents/traders (pre-harvest contractors). However, a few farmers also have executed written contracts with traders on the government-approved stamp paper.[5] The advantage of written contractual arrangements is that they are enforceable by both parties, and hence the probability of breach of contract is very low. Since the full payment is made when a contract is signed, the entire production risk is transferred to the traders. A pre-harvest contractor (PHC) may have multiple contracts with mango tree owners in the same village, and the contractor starts to gain the confidence among the farmers. In this way, contractors influence their contract farmers to persuade the other farmers in the village to lease the mango trees to a particular contractor. Contract negotiations generally focus on determining the cash rent, which is largely determined by the number of trees, type of varieties, input costs, flowering density, among other things. Once the contract is finalized with farmers, the contractor appoints a watch guard to look after the orchards until harvesting is complete.

In the pre-flowering contract system (oral and written), farmers have incentive to maintain the mango orchard well and to apply inputs such as irrigation and manure in order to get a better deal at the time of the next contract negotiation. Contractors also strive to maximize their return from the contract, so they apply certain yield-enhancing inputs during the post-contract period. For instance, the field evidence shows that contractors apply micronutrient spray at the flowering stage to improve the mango yield and the quality of the fruit's appearance. However, it is important to analyze who bears the production and market risks in oral contracts. Production risk might arise due to unseasonal rains, high temperatures during the fruiting period and pest outbreaks, leading to crop loss. Market risks are due to volatility in prices, leading to low expected returns. In the oral contracting system, contractors agree to pay cash rent in two to three installments normally spread over the harvesting period. In our field survey, farmers reported that contractors find some reasons to breach the agreement and renege on their payments to farmers.

However, farmers also reported that contractors were prompt in making the first installment (advance payment), amounting to 30% of the total contract. This generally accepted practice tends to gain the farmers' confidence in contractors and, more importantly, asserts contractors' stake in the mango orchards. But the field evidence shows that the subsequent installment payments to farmers sometimes run into trouble. Traders say they could not fully honor subsequent payments due to lower-than-expected crop output and lower-than-expected market prices. On the other hand, farmers say contractors deliberately stop harvesting the fruit toward the end of the marketing season. This leads to overripening and waste of fruit, and local villagers and trespassers take the opportunity to stealthily collect fruit. All these factors result in reduced mango output. Other issues are the costs involved in protecting trees. These situations can lead to disputes between the farmers and contractors. According to the farmers, disputes arising out of such informal oral contracts between farmers and contractors often are settled by the intervention of the village president or other influential persons in the village, but in most cases, the dispute resolution goes against the farmers, who end up bearing a significant proportion of loss.

Despite the known risks of pre-flowering contracts, many farmers still prefer this arrangement for various reasons. They include high labor costs for plucking and loading, lack of transportation facilities, smaller outputs, lack of pack houses, delayed payments at the APMC yard, uncertain prices, high rejection rates and unruly behavior of traders in the market. Perhaps farmers give more weight to these reasons than the cost of a breach in the oral contract. It was observed that most farmers change contractors every year to overcome the problem of contract violations. However, information asymmetry about contractors' behavior and market conditions continues to prevail. Collective action by farmers is difficult because every farmer has different irrigation and farming practices, resulting in different ripening times for the fruit. For example, a farmer with better irrigation can delay the harvest until the fruit reaches its ripening stage, but for a farmer without good irrigation, the fruit dries up faster and needs to be harvested before it reaches its ripening stage. These are some of the disadvantages of fragmented land ownership and uneven irrigation practices.

Another important factor responsible for entering pre-flowering-stage contracts is the credit relations between the farmers and traders. Credit relations are informal and, in oral contracts, work on the condition that the farmers lease out the mango orchard at the flowering stage to the traders, who also act as money lenders. Resource-poor small farmers who need capital borrow money at any time of year with a promise to lease out their mango trees. The field evidence shows that some farmers get trapped in such arrangements for periods of up to five years. This is due either to repeated borrowing each season for production and consumption requirements or to the loan amount remaining unadjusted after the harvesting period. However, it is important to understand that such a regressive contractual relation is an outcome of the imperfect rural credit markets. The unequal contractual relations can be easily understood from the desperate words of some farmers that 'our land is with the banks, while mango trees are with the traders as security for loans.' Despite these problems, most farmers engage in the pre-harvest contract chain.

APMC-led value chain

The Agricultural Produce Market Committee (APMC) yard is an important nodal point in the transfer of mangoes from farmers to consumers along the value chain. APMC facilitates the direct sale of mangoes from farmers to licensed traders in the market yard. In fact, wholesale traders are the key actors in this chain, influencing quantity, quality and price. After buying mangoes from the farmers, wholesale traders sell to mango pulp processors and exporters. The transactions between farmers and traders, processors and traders, and exporters and traders take place at the APMC yard. The wholesale traders also sell mangoes to retailers, through whom the mangoes reach consumers.

Various studies have shown problems in the APMC's functioning and in how traders manipulate grain transactions in the market yard, affecting the ability of actors in the chain, particularly farmers, to discover prices and hence lowering the prices they realize (Banerji and Meenakshi, 2002; Chand, 2003; Acharya, 2004). Mango trade in the APMC yard is certainly no exception. The field evidence shows that large farmers who have adequate capital, transportation facilities and pack houses/ripening chambers sell mangoes directly to traders at the APMC yard. In this chain, farmers tend to gain if market forces (demand and supply factors) operate freely in determining the price. But this rarely happens, due to imperfections in mango trading practices that traders have adopted to appropriate maximum returns. Since the mango marketing season lasts for only three months, from May to July, many large traders specializing in the mango trade try to make profits quickly. Field observations show that the traders rule the mango market in fixing prices and that the farmers simply supply mangoes with little understanding of actual market conditions. The farmers bear the market price risk and the market's incidental charges.

Discussions with APMC officials reveal that ideally, the price of different varieties of mango should be determined based on the demand for direct consumption, demand by the pulp-making industry and the quantity of mangoes arriving in the market. With this information, prices should be determined through an open auction system. However, some of the sample farmers reported that the traders' lobby is so strong that they do not allow the auction to be conducted. The sample farmers mentioned that mango prices vary almost daily, and predicting the next day's prices is difficult. Farmers can bring mangoes to the market yard between 10 a.m. and 10 p.m. every day. The wholesale traders then meet at midnight at the APMC yard and decide the purchase price of mangoes for the next day. The mango growers have no role in determining the price. After arriving at the market, they unload the mangoes at the traders' designated shops and return home. Farmers learn the price at which their mangoes sold when they visit the traders to collect the bills at least four days after delivery. Farmers say that traders do not like the farmers asking for details of their trade practices, prevailing market prices and methods of setting prices. They warn the farmers who ask for details that mangoes should not be brought to their shop next time. In this way, wholesale traders control the mango market and command the price not only for the farmers but also for other actors in the APMC-led chain.

SAFAL-led value chain

SAFAL is the fruit and vegetable wing of Mother Dairy, promoted by the National Dairy Development Board (NDDB). SAFAL sells fruits and vegetables directly to consumers through its outlets in Bangalore city. To procure mangoes directly from the farmers, SAFAL has set up a collection center near the APMC yard. Since the collection center procures only a limited quantity, some farmers carry mangoes to the SAFAL auction market in Bangalore.

Field evidence shows that large farmers who have transportation facilities, pack houses and adequate labor tend to participate in the SAFAL-led value chain. Although only a few farmers in the sample have participated in the SAFAL-led mango value chain, they reported certain advantages of dealing with SAFAL, including better prices, transparency in transactions, proper weighing and timely payments. More importantly, farmers reported knowing the price of mango at the time of selling, and it is slightly higher by Rs 4/kg than the price fixed at the APMC yard. With a proper pricing system and an assurance of quality, both producers and consumers benefit in this value chain.

The preceding discussion has clearly brought out the economic dimensions of four different value chains for mango. The government-run cooperatives—the HOPCOMS-led and SAFAL-led value chains—offer important marketing services to farmers and create value at each transaction stage. However, the scale of their operations is limited. Transportation bottlenecks and lack of infrastructure on farms constrain the mango growers from participating in these two value chains. The APMC-led value chain is highly dominated by the traders, and it is riddled with inefficiency in the price discovery mechanism. Direct participation by farmers in the APMC yard is very selective. Most farmers prefer the pre-harvest contract chain even though they face unequal contractual relations. Within the pre-harvest contract chain, some prefer pre-flowering-stage contracts and others enter post-flowering-stage contracts. The factors explaining the choice of contract are discussed in detail in the next section.

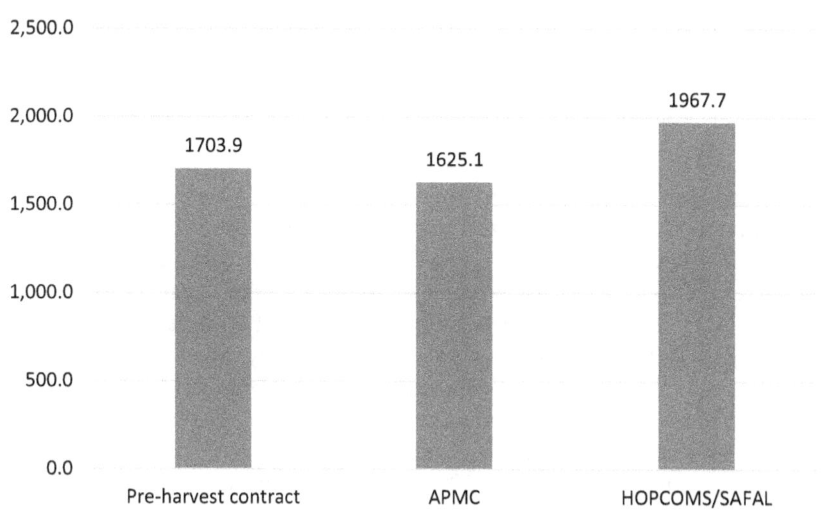

Figure 13.2 Average price received through different mode of sale of mango

Source: Field survey.

Model of contract choice

The study analyzes the determinants of contract choice as a function of farmer profile and profitability per acre. The following contract choices are observed: (1) no contract, (2) pre-flowering contract, or (3) post-flowering contract. The farmers' choice of contract could be random, or it could depend on some observable characteristics influencing the profitability of contract choice. We thus assume that profitability is an endogenous variable, dependent on factors such as farming practices and the availability of cheap labor. Hence, contract choice is modeled as a function of profitability, which in turn depends on factors such as farming practices and input availability. The standard OLS (ordinary least squares) estimation cannot capture the endogeneity of the profit variable, and this technique will result in omitted variable bias. To address the endogeneity of the explanatory variable, one can use selection models or an instrumental variable model. Heckman-type corrections typically are used when you have a truncated variable. Instrumental Variable Least Square (IVLS) regression is used in case of endogeneity but only when we have observations for all variables and outcomes. In the case of a binary dependent variable with an endogenous explanatory variable, we employ a probit model with endogenous regressors (IVProbit). It is assumed that instruments of the endogenous variable are not correlated with the stochastic error term of the contract choice equation. We estimate the equation for whether a farmer selects a contract. Then, for the farmers who chose to sell their produce to a contractor, we estimate the factors influencing the choice between a pre-flowering contract and a post-flowering contract.

The model is:

$$y^\star_{1i} = y_{2i}\beta + x_{1i}\gamma + ui$$
$$y_{2i} = x_{1i}\Pi_1 + x_{2i}\,\Pi_2 + vi$$

where $i = 1, \ldots, N$, y_{2i} is a $1\times p$ vector of endogenous variables, x_{1i} is a $1\times k_1$ vector of exogenous variables, x_{2i} is a $1 \times k_2$ vector of additional instruments, and the equation for y_{2i} is written in reduced form. By assumption, (ui, vi) ~ N(0, Σ), where σ_{11} is normalized to one to identify the model. β and γ are vectors of structural parameters, and Π_1 and Π_2 are matrices of reduced-form parameters. This is a recursive model: y_{2i} appears in the equation for $y^\star_{1i}$, but $y^\star_{1i}$ does not appear in the equation for y_{2i}. We do not observe $y^\star_{1i}$; instead, we observe $y_{1i} = 0$ if $y^\star_{1i} < 0$ and 1 if $y^\star_{1i} > 0$. Empirically, we estimate the choice of contract as a function of age, education, distance from market and profitability, where profitability is assumed to be endogenous and dependent on farming practices such as the application of pesticides and manure and the availability of irrigation and labor. Table 13.12 shows the descriptive statistics of the variables used in the model. As shown in the table, there is a huge variation in profitability among farmers, which is dependent upon various sorio-economic characteristics of the farmers and farming practices followed by them. The

Table 13.12 Important characteristics of sample households

Variable	*Observation*	*Mean*	*Std. Dev.*	*Min*	*Max*
Profit per acre	131	222,381	29090	−25,606	215,097
Age in years	131	50	14	24	86
Distance to market in km	131	6	11	0	70
Income reported (lakhs)	131	2	1	1	3
Family size (number of members)	131	7	5	4	42
Years of experience	130	22	13	5	70
Persons engaged in farming	130	3	3	1	30
Irrigation per month	131	2	5	0	40
Pesticide application per month	131	2	3	0	15

Source: Field survey.

Table 13.13 Factors influencing the choice of mango contract

	No contract	*Pre-flowering*
log profits per acre	0.23** (0.03)	0.22*** (0.04)
log age	−0.6 (0.4)	−0.4 (0.4)
log area_mango	0.09 (0.1)	−0.21 (0.2)
Simpson Index of Variability	−0.6 (0.5)	0.15 (0.7)
log years of Schooling	−0.08 (0.1)	−0.4*** (0.5)
log distance to market	0.4*** (0.1)	0.3*** (0.1)
Family_education	−0.003 (0.2)	0.1 (0.3)
Constant	0.01 (1.6)	0.3 (1.7)
N	130	130
Wald test of exogeneity Prob > chi²	0.00	0.006
Instrumented: lprofit_new		
Instruments: lage lnarea_mango simpson_index_var lnedu_years_new ldist fam_edu lpa_n lm_n ldap lirr lfam_engaged 2.village_D 3.village_D 4.village_D 5.village_D 6.village_D 7.village_D 8.village_D 9.village_D 10.village_D 11.village_D		

Source: Generated by the author using data collected from the field survey.

average family size was seven members, and most of the male members were involved in mango cultivation. Their years of experience in mango cultivation ranged from five to 70, the latter indicating the involvement of previous generations of family members. Table 13.13 reports the results from the estimation of the model. Results of the profitability estimation are reported in Appendix Table 13A.2.

Decision to sell to a contractor

Some interesting relationships emerge from the estimated results. Regarding the first equation on the decision to sell mangoes directly (with no contract) to markets, profitability and distance to market have positive impacts on the contract choice. The higher the profits, the less likely farmers are to sell to a contractor. Similarly, the greater the distance to market, the less likely farmers are to sell to a contractor. Farmers who have adequate capital and transportation infrastructure tend to participate directly in spot market transactions. Farmers who sell to the city market usually prefer to sell their produce independently. Age and education have a negative impact on the decision to sell to contractors but are not statistically significant.

Choice between types of contracts

Regarding the equation determining the choice between types of contracts, the higher the farmers' education is, the less likely they are to select a pre-flowering contract. Farmers who are more educated are more likely to go with a post-flowering contract, since they are more capable of managing the farm and more aware of farming practices than farmers with fewer years of education. Profits and distance have a positive impact on the decision to go with a pre-flowering contract compared to a post-flowering contract. The greater the distance, the more likely farmers are to select a pre-flowering contract instead of a post-flowering contract. This may be because the contractor bears the responsibility for transportation in pre-flowering contracts.

Conclusions

This chapter analyzed the typology of mango value chains and discussed the relative economic positions of various actors, particularly mango growers, in the chains. Factors influencing the choice of contract in mango production and marketing also were examined. Analysis shows that younger farmers were more inclined to access mango markets directly, but elderly farmers were more risk-averse and tended to prefer pre-flowering contract arrangements. Depending upon the risk-taking ability, access to capital and transportation infrastructure, farmers' participation in different value chains varies. Although the government-run cooperative value chains provide better prices and market linkages, their limited scale of operations and stringent quality requirements constrain resource-poor farmers from participating and from investing in quality-enhancing activities. Field evidence shows that most farmers preferred the pre-harvest contract system to share market risks. Within pre-harvest contracts, most farmers entered pre-flowering contracts, which in most cases were highly informal and oral. Regarding the choice of contract, profitability and distance to market have positive effects on farmers' decisions to sell mangoes directly to the market (with no contract). Within the pre-harvest contract system, highly educated farmers are more likely to enter post-flowering contracts than pre-flowering contracts. These results have broader implications for enhancing investment in improving market infrastructure, providing enabling environments for growers' participation in profitable value chains and framing appropriate policies for regulating agricultural contracting systems.

Notes

1 According to the erstwhile Planning Commission, Kolar falls under agro-climactic zone 10, which covers the Southern Plateau and Hills region. In the finer classification of the National Agricultural Research Project (NARP), Kolar falls under Eastern Dry Zone KA-5.
2 In Chittoor District, some well-to-do farmers have sold their land to a Special Economic Zone. Farmers in the nearby region have leased the land from the government to grow mango orchards.
3 A farmer can become a member of HOPCOMS by paying a life membership fee of Rs 250.
4 GlobalG.A.P. is a scheme for good agricultural practices at the farm level, developed by EUREP, an association of European fresh produce retailers and importers. It originally was started by retailers belonging to the Euro-Retailer Produce Working Group and was renamed GlobalG.A.P. in 2007.
5 The written contract contains, among other things, the names of buyer and seller, the survey number of the land, the total contract amount, the duration of contract and the conditions under which fruits should be supplied to the traders.

References

Acharya, S. S. 2004. *Agricultural Marketing, State of the Indian Farmer A Millennium Study. Volume 14*. Academic Foundation, New Delhi.

Ali, M. 2003. "Developing Sustainable Horticulture Production Systems for Economic and Nutritional Development". In *Impacts of Agriculture on Human Health and Nutrition, from Encyclopedia of Life Support Systems (EOLSS)*. UNESCO, EOLSS Publishers, Oxford. www.eolss.net.

Banerjee, G. D. 2011. "Economics of Mango Cultivation". NABARD Occasional Paper No 58. Department of economic analysis, National Bank for Agriculture and Rural Development, Mumbai.

Banerji, A. and J. V. Meenakshi. 2002. "Buyer Collusion and Efficiency of Government Intervention in Wheat Markets in Northern India: A Symmetric Structural Auction Analysis". Working Paper No. 104. Centre for Development Economics, Delhi School of Economics, Delhi.

Business Standard. 2013. "Japan Lifts 20 Year Ban on Mango Imports". www.business-standard.com/article/economy-policy/japan-lifts-20-year-ban-on-indian-mango-imports-106062300042_1.html.

Central Research Institute for Dryland Agriculture. 2012. "Agriculture Contingency Plan for District: KOLAR". Accessed on December 2016. www.crida.in/CP-2012/statewiseplans/Karnataka%20(Pdf)/GKVK,%20Bangalore/KAR15-KOLAR%2031.03.2011.pdf.

Chand, R. 2003. "Government Intervention in Foodgrain Markets in the New Context". Policy Paper 19. National Centre for Agricultural Economics and Policy Research, New Delhi.

Government of India. 2016–2018. "Horticulture Statistics at a Glance 2017". Horticulture Statistics Division, Department of Agriculture, Cooperation and Farmers Welfare; Ministry of Agriculture & Farmers Welfare.

Government of India. Various years. "Annual Report". Department of Commercial Intelligence and Statistics, Ministry of Commerce and Industry, New Delhi, India. http://agriexchange.apeda.gov.in/product_profile/exp_f_india.aspx?categorycode=0204.

Government of Karnataka. 2013. "District and Taluk-wise Statistics of Major Horticultural Crops in Karnataka State 2011–12". Directorate of Economics & Statistics, Bangalore. www.horticulture.kar.nic.in/Design_final/A&P%20%20Final%202015-16.pdf.

Goyal, Aparajita. 2010. "Information, Direct Access to Farmers and Rural Market Performance in Central India". *Applied Economics* **2** (3), 22–45.

Goyal, M. Tanu, Arpita Mukherjee and Avantika Kapoor. 2017. "India's Export of Food Products: Food Safety and Related Issues". ICRIER Working Paper No 345. Indian Council for Research on International Economic Relations, New Delhi.

Hegde, R. N. 2006. "Prospects for Export of Indian Fresh Alphonso Mangoes". *CAB Calling*, January–March, 40–42.

Jha, Dilip Kumar. 2016., "UAE Issues Warning to India's Mango, Rice Producers". *Business Standard.* Accessed on June 2016. https://www.business-standard.com/article/markets/uae-issues-warning-to-india-s-mango-vegetable-exporters-116052300160_1.html.

Joshi, P. K., Ashok Gulati, Pratap S. Birthal and Laxmi Tewari. 2004. "Agriculture Diversification in South Asia: Patterns, Determinants and Policy Implications". *Economic and Political Weekly* **39** (24), 2457–2467.

Saripalle, Madhuri. 2016. "Jasmine Cultivation in Tamil Nadu: Market Structure and Pricing". *World Development Perspectives* **1**, 12–14.

Saripalle, Madhuri. 2019. "Market Awareness and Profitability: Case Study of Mango Production in Karnataka, India". *Economic and Political Weekly* **LIV** (4), 52–59.

Saurabh, Kumar and Aparna Sharma. 2016. "Agricultural Value Chains in India: Prospects and Challenges". Discussion Paper, CUTS International. Accessed on August 2019. www.cuts-citee.org/pdf/Agricultural_Value_Chains_in_India_Prospects_and_Challenges.pdf.

Appendix

Table 13A.1 Cost distribution by age group

	<9 years	9 to <12 years	12 to <20 years	20 to <30 years	≥30 years
Variable costs per acre (including material and labor costs) (Rs)	7,406	12,044	12,186	9,099	8,244
Tillage	2,607	2,247	1,956	2,457	2,150
Manure	2,495	3,346	2,274	2,209	1,599
Fertilizer	13	46	641	133	183
Transplantation	581	751	4489	1201	947
Irrigation	676	2204	542	533	615
Weeding	429	1,127	925	1,118	795
Pesticides	419	409	831	703	1,164
Topping	26	361	76	165	168
Harvesting	145	474	330	464	298
Grading	0	7	121	118	325
Storing	15	1071	0	0	0
Fixed costs per acre (Rs)	2,279	3,453	4,741	2,486	11,124
Planting (including seedling cost)	1,465	1,653	1,210	1,538	6,857
Field preparation	562	759	882	464	620
Support	183	661	696	413	158
Irrigation	0	318	179	68	3125

Source: Generated by the author using data collected from the field survey.

14 Moving toward sustainability

An evaluation of Indian coffee in the global food value chain

Parmod Kumar, Manjunatha, A. V., and Devika, C. M.

All activities through which agricultural production passes to reach the final consumer—packaging, processing, trading and distribution—are called the food value chain. This chain enables agricultural produce to obtain higher value, which increases profits for each stakeholder from production to consumption. A global value chain highlights the global scale and structure of commodity chains as a result of the internationalization of production (Gereffi et al., 2005). It also points to the fact that consumption of commodities often is distanced from various stages of production (Princen, 2001). Like many tropical agro-commodities, coffee is characterized by southern production and northern consumption and thus constitutes a link between less developed countries and more advanced global markets. Coffee is a highly traded commodity, second in the world to oil, and demand for it continues to grow steadily in the world market. Over the years, the pattern in global coffee chains has been changing rapidly: market liberalization, expansions in east Asia, corporate consolidation, deregulation of trading, new consumption patterns, quality control practices, and, above all, volatile prices have constantly influenced world trade in this commodity. Increasing consumer awareness about quality, taste, health, safety and the environment has created a growing demand for specialty and eco-labelled coffee that complies with sustainable agricultural practices (Potts et al., 2014). As India exports nearly 70% of its coffee, the sector needs to improve the quality and diversity of its product offerings and improve the livelihood of small coffee producers, who are the majority producers of coffee in India.

This chapter on coffee value chains looks at the dominant trends in Indian coffee production and markets, the emergence of specialty and sustainably certified value chains and the key actors involved. In the first part of the chapter, we briefly review theoretical literature on the FAO's global value chain framework. The subsequent section analyzes sustainability standards prevalent in global value chains, with particular reference to the coffee industry. The last section focuses on the coffee value chain in the context of India, supplemented by a primary comparative analysis at the micro-level evaluating the sustainability of Indian coffee's value chains from the perspective of the producing country.

Embedding sustainability in value chains

Across the ambit of innovation in value chains, embedding sustainability has been at the forefront and gaining traction, as value chains are the biggest lever for change toward a sustainable future. Embedding sustainability requires more than independent, isolated efforts by individual actors for transformation—it needs value chain actors performing in an aligned, collaborative manner toward a common sustainable strategy (Lassale-de Salins et al., 2014; Soosay and Hyland, 2015). The FAO (2014) proposed a guiding approach to incorporate and analyze sustainability in food value chains and to develop strategies to improve sustainability across value chain activities. The approach is similar to the principles of the shared-value concept (Porter and Kramer, 2011), combining an analysis of the actors' needs and expectations with practices to achieve greater sustainable results.

The concept of sustainable food value chains is a market-oriented, dynamic approach to measure, analyze and improve the performance of food value chains in ways that help ensure their economic, social and environmental sustainability. The framework identifies incentives, bottlenecks and constraints in production and various activities along the value chain. The FAO defines a sustainable and inclusive food value chain as quoted here:

> [T]he full range of farms and firms and their successive coordinated value-adding activities that produce particular raw agricultural materials and transform them into particular food products that are sold to final consumers and disposed of after use, in a manner that is profitable throughout, has broad-based benefits for society, and does not permanently deplete natural resources.

A value chain is considered sustainable economically if each actor's activities are competitive and commercially viable. In the social dimension, sustainability refers to socially and culturally acceptable outcomes in terms of the distribution of benefits and costs associated with increased value creation. In the environmental dimension, sustainability is determined by value chain actors' ability to generate positive or neutral environmental externalities from their activities (FAO, 2014). For example, a product's greener brand image may represent a higher value to consumers and differentiate the product positively in the market.

Value chain actors' activities relate to production, aggregation, processing and distribution. These actors are linked horizontally at a particular stage of the chain, such as producers organizing themselves into cooperatives, and they are linked vertically within the overall chain, such as producers contracting their produce to companies (Figure 14.1). The sustainable food value chain focuses on principles that identify the interlinkage issues prevalent among value chain actors. These principles are grouped into three phases of the development cycle (measuring, understanding and improving performance) to cater to the gaps between actual and potential performance. Using these guiding principles in the development approach, consequent multilateral partnerships and interventions, such as greater vertical coordination and innovation within the value chain, would improve value creation and achieve greater efficiency. Therefore, development of the value chain requires institutional, organizational and technological upgrading throughout the value chain, such as product and process upgrading, certification and standards, good agricultural practices, contracts, cold chains, information and communication technology etc.

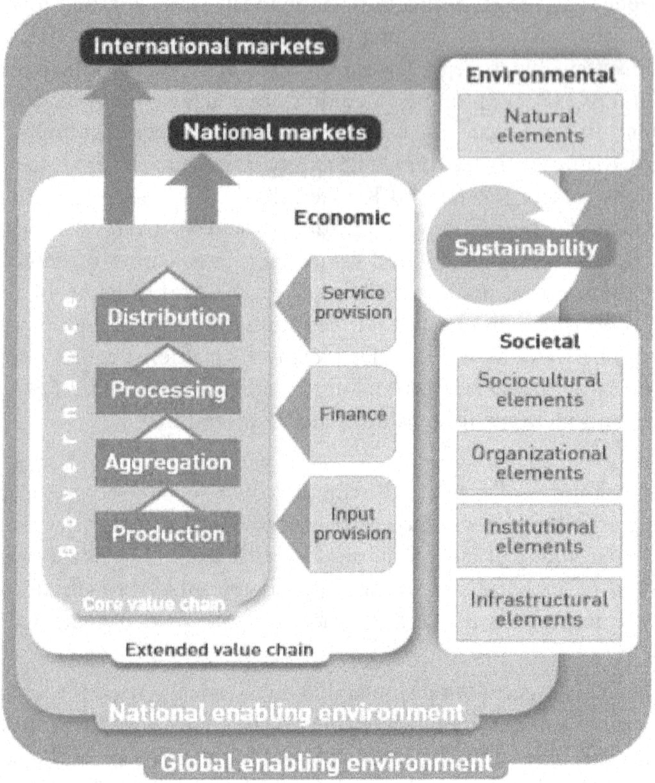

Figure 14.1 Sustainable food value chain framework

Source: FAO, 2014.

Coffee value chain

Our analysis of the coffee value chain focuses on the global coffee economy, which is comprised of a wide array of coffee value chains that connect producers with consumers and have an impact on livelihoods at multiple spatial scales. The coffee value chain can be characterized as a buyer-driven chain with a small number of large roasters who generate the highest margins in the value chain, compared to numerous smallholder coffee producers with no direct connection to and little knowledge of the world market for which they grow their product. As such, the mass segment of the coffee chain is characterized by the market transactions between roasters/traders and growers/processors that are illustrated Figures 14.2(a) and 14.2(b). Our focus is on the producing country of India and how it has addressed concerns of sustainability in the global coffee value chain.

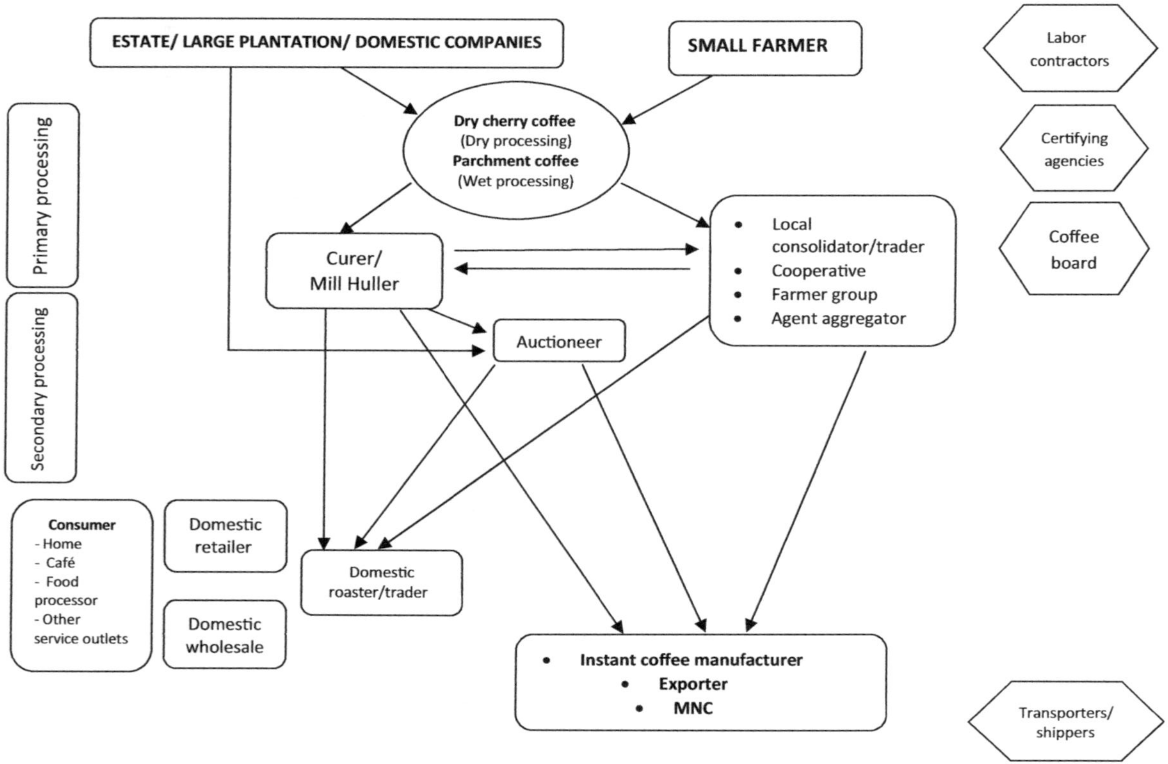

(a)

Figure 14.2 Generic structure of the global coffee value chain: (a) producing country—India; (b) consuming country

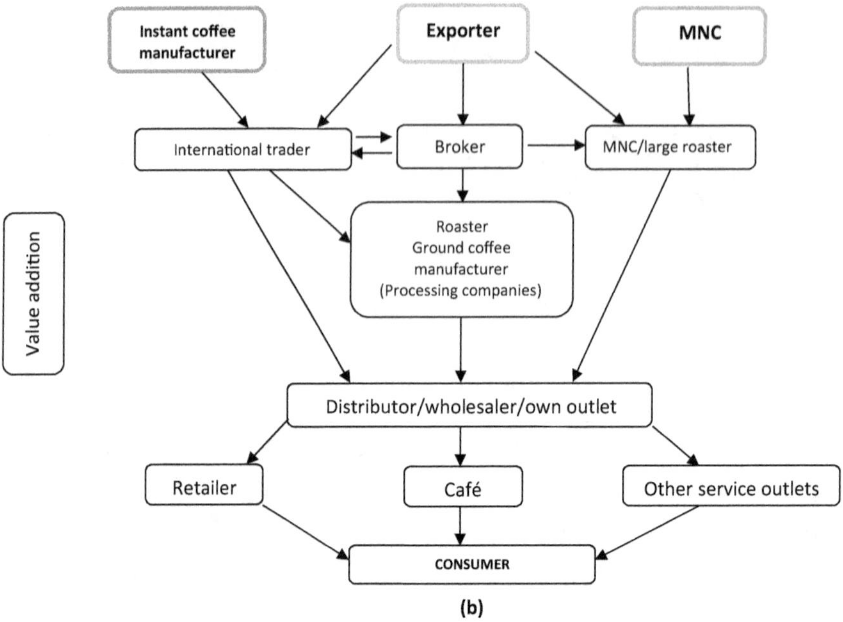

Figure 14.2 (Continued)

Sustainable coffee value chain

Economic reforms, liberalization and cost pressures have plagued the coffee sector recently. As a result, a number of private and multi-stakeholder initiatives have been launched to promote more socially responsible and environmentally friendly practices in coffee production (Petkova, 2006). These initiatives resulted in the development of sustainability standards that coffee roasters and farmers' cooperatives, such as Fairtrade International, Utz Kapeh and 4C, are increasingly adopting. These initiatives have induced a move toward a governance mode that is closer to producer-driven chain structures because it could improve the producers' position compared to that of roasters and/or traders (Muradian and Pelupessy, 2005). As such, coffee producers' voluntary adoption of sustainability standards rapidly is becoming a *sine qua non* for access to specialty coffee markets. Table 14.1 provides the prevailing international voluntary regulation systems in the coffee industry that rely on different strategies for enhancing sustainable production and/or responsible trade. Since these standards were developed initially in particular national contexts by stakeholders located and operating in these contexts, they have become an important source of standards variation and continue to influence the coevolution of standards.

Table 14.1 Voluntary sustainable regulation systems in the coffee industry

	First party	*Second party*	*Third party*				*Fourth party*
	Starbucks code	*SAI[a] code*	*Fairtrade International*	*Organic*	*Rainforest Alliance*	*Utz Kapeh*	*4C[b]*
Distance between standards and 'common' practices (Stringency)	Short	Short	Large	Large	Short	Short	Short
Importance of 'extra-standards' information (Specificity)	High	Low	High	Low	Low	Low	Low
Monitoring	Third-party (paid by farmers)	Third-party (probably paid by farmers)	Third-party (paid by farmers)	Third-party (paid by farmers)	Third-party (paid by farmers)	Third-party (paid by farmers)	Third-party (probably paid by farmers)
Overall entry barrier	High	Low	Low to be registered. High to actually participate	High, becoming low	Low	Low	Low
Expected impact on price premium to farmers	Medium Flexible (decided by Starbucks)	Very low Flexible (market)	High Fixed	Medium, becoming low Flexible (market)	Low Flexible (market)	Low Flexible (market)	Very low Flexible (market)
Target groups (growers)	Growers of high-quality coffee	Any kind	Small landholders in cooperatives	Any kind	Large estates	In practice large estates	Any kind
Upgrading constraints for growers	Control by Starbucks	It tends to become a 'market requirement'	Limits to the number of farmers the system may reach	Increasing competition (price premium erosion)	Reduced consuming market	It tends to become a 'market requirement'	It tends to become a 'market requirement'
Coordination type (between traders/roasters and farmers)	Strong coordination	Very weak coordination (near to market transactions)	Strong coordination	Weak coordination, becoming closer to market transactions	Very weak coordination (near to market transactions)	Very weak coordination (near to market transactions)	Very weak coordination (near to market transactions)

Source: Muradian and Pelupessy, 2005.

Notes:
[a]SAI: Sustainable Agriculture Initiative.
[b]4C: Common Code for Coffee Community.

Review of literature

Global private regulation of externally authored ethical and environmental standards was found to have several implications for value chain structures and institutions in the smallholder coffee systems of Indonesia. Neilson (2008) observed that the sustainable coffee agenda has resulted in structural changes in the modes of farmer organization and in trader–farmer relationships and has increased the presence of multinational trading companies. A retail-led reorganization of value chains has enhanced product traceability, and corporate definitions of sustainable production have challenged local and national institutional structures. These corporate self-regulating norms also impose requirements without offering developmental support, which ultimately questions the effectiveness of such schemes that initially were developed to deliver development benefits to disparate communities in developing countries.

Based on a matched panel analysis of 218 coffee-growing farm households belonging to three cooperatives in central Kenya, Van Rijsbergen et al. (2016) found that Fairtrade and Utz-certified coffee production improved coffee returns and that Fairtrade was more effective than Utz in coffee processing, while Utz contributed to productivity. Under stagnating coffee prices, Fairtrade farmers increased their coffee specialization, whereas Utz farmers reduced their coffee area but increased yield. In Colombia, a program led by a multinational firm induced suppliers to upgrade their coffee farms while planting trees and incorporating more efficient and sustainable practices. Nearly 80,000 farmers and 1,000 villages benefited from the program. The quality of coffee improved, and farmers' profits increased 15% (World Bank, 2020).

Further, Bolwig et al. (2009) used a Heckman selection model to identify certification's effect on revenue and the adoption of organic farming techniques and concluded that the largest effects were due to engagement in coffee processing. Mendez et al. (2010) demonstrated that Fairtrade-certified farmers received better prices and higher coffee revenues to non-certified farmers, but sales to certified markets were far too limited to achieve sustainable livelihoods. A similar result was found in Weber's (2011) analysis of coffee-growing households in southern Mexico who participated in Fairtrade organic markets through grower cooperatives. Although these coffee growers received an average premium of 12.8 cents per pound, which led to a 5% gain in the total household gross income, the price premiums had limited potential to increase household returns. In Peru, Ruben and Fort (2012) observed that certification had modest direct income and production effects but substantial changes in the organization, input use, wealth and assets and risk attitudes among small coffee producers.

An analysis of the value distribution of Fairtrade coffee in Nicaragua and Guatemala revealed that consumer countries acquire a large share of the economic income because large multinationals control the supply chain and Fairtrade is positioned within the conventional market. The certified producer cooperatives face increasing pressure from these multinationals, and the premiums they receive are only modest (Johannessen and Wilhite, 2010). Minten et al. (2017) analyzed various developments in Ethiopia's coffee sector from the adoption of improved production, harvest practices and post-harvest practices. The authors show that improvements in marketing and large investments in processing capacities positively impacted coffee productivity and prices. These changes are linked to multiple factors such as local market reforms, greater presence of public extension agents, high international prices and a push for certification by international buyers. However, widespread uptake of improved practices has not materialized due to a combination of production and institutional issues, revealing the complexity of transforming settings at the farm level. Minten et al. (2018) also found that the quality premiums on coffee are small and that less than one-third of this premium is passed on to the producer. Some studies find that certification has brought limited changes in the relations among actors throughout the value chain (Muradian and Pelupessy, 2005; Raynolds, 2009; Valkila et al., 2010). Snider et al. (2017) stated that although financial incentives were weak, certification offered non-financial benefits to farmers and cooperatives, including better management and more resilient cooperatives.

A study of the social effects of Fairtrade certification on Rwandan small coffee producers was conducted by using a logistic regression model to measure farmer trust and participation. The results showed a negative association between Fairtrade and farmer trust in cooperative leadership and a positive association between Fairtrade and a perceived higher level of participation of women. Social capital was linked most significantly to farmers' interaction with their neighbors (Elder et al., 2012). In addition, as a result of reforms in the coffee global value chain, approximately 50,000 rural households saw their incomes from coffee production more than double, and nearly 2,000 jobs were created in coffee-washing stations in Rwanda (Karuretwa, 2016). A gender analysis in Uganda to assess whether involvement in certified coffee production and marketing helped women improve their status in society and daily well-being found a greater need to integrate gender into all stages of the coffee value chains because women were positioned at the bottom of the value chain (Kasente, 2012).

In India, Chengappa et al. (2014) found that value chains for coffee are diffused, with limited coordination in terms of quality and specifications in the conventional chain. Coordination is stronger in certified and organic chains, but incentives and motivation for upgrading largely stem from individual efforts to add value rather than from chain-level efforts. This suggests that integrating conservation principles in a branding strategy could be difficult at the chain level without institutional support or the entry of chain champions, though individual farmers could adopt such a strategy. The authors identified three distinct types of production systems for coffee—conventional, certified and organic—in the largest coffee-growing district, Kodagu, Karnataka in India. These three coffee value chains were mapped by following the Value-Links methodology in which differentiation between processes in the chain was denoted by block arrows, actors associated with the different processes were denoted by rectangles and various institutional supporters were denoted by trapezoids. The maps showed that certified and organic chains have significantly fewer actors, particularly intermediaries. Certified producers have direct contact with buyers, which improved communication about desired supplies and demand. In the organic chain, producers were found to undertake multiple roles simultaneously (processing, local trading and exports), augmenting the investment and consequent risk in that value chain.

Kundu and Chopra (2009) mapped the Indian coffee value chain for the fair-tracing project by illustrating the traditional coffee value chain and inputs from the traceable value chain. The project used digital tracing technologies in value chains to provide consumers and producers with enhanced information and thereby differentiated the product. Rich et al. (2017) survey results revealed a strong positive association with the environment by coffee producers, especially among certified and organic producers in India. However, price premiums for certified and organic coffee were relatively small. The authors suggested that although the potential of conservation-oriented certification for coffee in the study region (Coorg) might be relatively limited outside of a few individual-level niches, branding Coorg more generally as a conservation-oriented region would be viable as a differentiated product offering.

Methodology

In India's coffee scenario, Chengappa et al. (2014) highlighted the problems of lengthy supply chains and disproportionate market power, resulting in lower overall prices and lack of transparency between buyers and coffee growers leading to lower prices for producers. Therefore, assessing India's coffee value chain is an important area of inquiry, leveraging particular areas where sustainable production can be encouraged. This chapter's analytical focus is to study opportunities for coffee producers in a sustainable value chain. Toward this end, primary data were collected in July 2018 using a questionnaire administered to coffee growers, operators/owners of processing units and workers employed in these activities for the agricultural period of July 2017 to June 2018. The sample included 20 certified growers, 26 conventional growers, 10 workers from plantation/farms, 10 workers from processing units, nine local agents, six curers and one roaster. The analysis uses a standardized methodology that entails understanding the adoption of attributes from the FAO's sustainable food value chain development to cover various dimensions of the value chain that can foster sustainability through value creation using inductive reasoning. Analysis of the data involved computing simple descriptive statistics to estimate costs of production, marketing and processing. This chapter contributes to the literature on the ways coffee growers can upgrade as sustainability-oriented markets expand in the global coffee value chain.

Study region

In India, coffee is cultivated in the hilly terrains under agro-forestry systems. There are nearly 334,000 coffee land holdings, of which about 331,000 (99%)

are small growers (up to 10 ha) and only 1% are large growers with holdings of more than 10 ha. The most common intercrops in these agro-forestry systems are pepper, orange, banana, cardamom, jackfruit, vanilla and, seasonally, ginger, vegetables, pineapple and medicinal plants.

Coffee is traded in large quantities and comes in many different qualities, varieties and forms. These include arabica and robusta, roasted or green, as well as instant and solubles. Approximately 60% of the world's coffee production is the arabica variety, and the other 40% is robusta. The former generally is considered of superior quality and fetches much higher prices. Until 2013, prices of arabica were declining, primarily due to the increased availability of the cheaper robusta beans in world markets. Between 2013 and 2014, however, prices of both types rose (International Coffee Organization, historical data). Although Indian coffee is a plantation crop, because of its export-oriented production (70% being exported) and commercial importance, it has been brought under the Ministry of Commerce rather than the Ministry of Agriculture. India's share of world coffee exports was 2.78% in 2016–2017 (ICO), and there has been a positive trend in the compound annual growth rates of the quantity and value of coffee exports over the last two decades of study, with robusta cherry accounting for the bulk of exports (Figure 14.3).

As of 2017–2018, India produced 316,000 metric tons (MT) of coffee, of which 70% was from the robusta variety and 30% from arabica. Production has increased over the last two decades by 1.45% per year, and the bearing area has grown 1.82% per year. The positive growth in overall production of coffee occurred despite the fact that there was a slight negative growth in production while yield declined by −2.0% per annum in arabica coffee due to biotic factors such as high infestation of white stem borer and abiotic factors as a result of erratic weather patterns in India's arabica-growing regions. Nonetheless,

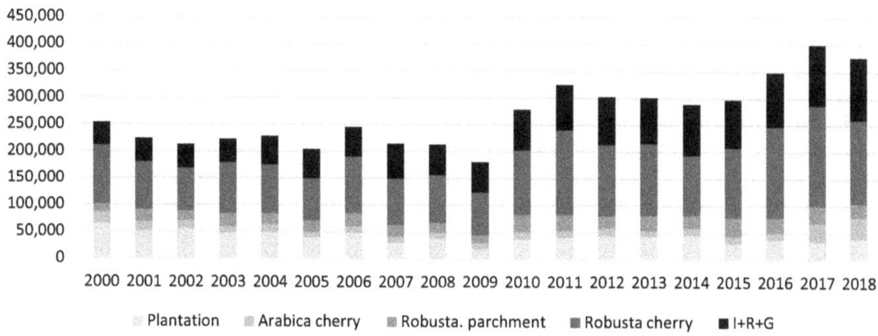

Figure 14.3 Exports by type of coffee (MT)

Source: *Coffee Statistics* (various issues), Coffee Board of India.

Note: *I+R+G*—Instant, Roasted, Ground Coffees

the overall coffee yield has improved in the last decade, with a positive 0.45% compound annual growth rate.

India also exports a variety of specialty coffee, which has been increasing at 3% per year for the last seven years. Arabica cherry-AB and robusta cherry-AB are referred to as monsooned coffees, as their flavor comes from the moisture the beans absorb. Nuggets are a new addition introduced in 1992 in which washed arabica beans go through tighter grading and sorting. Robusta Kaapi Royale is robusta variety's equivalent of arabica's Mysore Nuggets introduced in 1993 and is commonly included in espresso blends (Table 14.2). Among them, the average annual growth rate was highest for Monsooned Robusta Triage, followed by Mysore Nuggets EB. India also produces single-estate or single-cultivar plantation-A coffees that have distinct characteristics, such as coffees from the Attikan estate, Yellikodige estate and Watapi estate, among others.

Because the State of Karnataka is India's leading coffee producer, a value chain assessment of a few specific coffee growers in Karnataka has been conducted to identify potential entry points for value creation and to identify constraints on a sustainability-oriented strategy for upgrading or scaling up coffee exports. Of particular focus is Kodagu, the state's largest coffee-growing district. The district contributes 38% to India's total coffee production, largely from smallholding coffee farms numbering 41,590 (98.9%),[1] and is located in the Western Ghats biodiversity hotspot. These factors highlight the role ecologically based coffee production in Kodagu can have in the global coffee value chain.

Table 14.2 Export of specialty coffees from India (MT)

Specialty coffee	*2010–2011*	*2011–2012*	*2012–2013*	*2013–2014*	*2014–2015*	*2015–2016*	*2016–2017*	*2017–2018*	*AAGR (%)*
Mysore Nuggets EB	929	1,145	1,601	2,166	1,607	1,699	1,624	2,306	16.55
Monsooned Malabar AA	3,315	2,894	3,580	4,230	5,105	5,260	6,169	7,046	12.05
Monsooned Robusta AA	1,044	1,302	1,151	926	812	890	777	1,328	7.01
Monsooned Arabica Triage	126	175	233	209	90	49	185	205	35.37
Monsooned Robusta Triage	—	12	37	10	14	10	41	52	69.09
Monsooned Basabally	528	316	387	375	207	245	429	652	11.41
Robusta Kapi Royale	9,071	7,778	5,678	7,121	4,805	7,888	6,840	8,088	2.97
Total	**15,013**	**13,622**	**12,666**	**15,036**	**12,657**	**16,085**	**16,670**	**19,678**	5.05

Source: Coffee Board of India, 2019.

Results and discussion

Production: coffee grower

At the base of the coffee value chain are its producers, who can be classified based on their subscription to a voluntary sustainability certification. In this comparative analysis, the total sample covered 20 certified and 26 conventional coffee growers (henceforth referred to as non-certified growers). The certified and non-certified growers reported an average coffee holding size of 7.22 ha and 6.56 ha, respectively. This included irrigated medium-sized plantations (<10 ha) and large (>10 ha) plantations. Most of the growers were in the age group of 25–35 years, and 30 of them held a graduate degree. Half of the coffee growers surveyed had close to 15 years' experience and had knowledge passed down from their elders, as most lived with extended families. Of the 46 growers surveyed, 42 had five to ten family members in a household (Tables 14.3 and 14.4).

Table 14.3 Socio-economic characteristics of coffee growers

Characteristics of growers	*Certified (number)*	*Non-certified (number)*	*Total*	*Average*
Age of grower (years)				(years)
25–35	13 (65)	10 (38)	23 (50)	
>50	4 (20)	7 (27)	11 (23.9)	
35–50	3 (15)	9 (35)	12 (26.1)	
Total	20 (100)	26 (100)	46 (100)	42.9
Educational qualification				
High school	5 (25)	0	5 (11)	
PUC	2 (10)	9 (35)	11 (24)	
Graduate	13 (65)	13 (50)	26 (57)	
Postgraduate and above	0	4 (15)	4 (9)	
Total	20 (100)	26 (100)	46 (100)	
Family size (number of members)				(no)
Less than 5	1 (5)	3 (12)	4 (9)	
5 to 10	19 (95)	23 (88)	42 (91)	
Total	20 (100)	26 (100)	46 (100)	04
Experience as coffee grower				(years)
>15	8 (40)	15 (58)	23 (50)	
15–30	9 (45)	8 (31)	17 (37)	
>45	1 (5)	0	1 (2)	
30–45	2 (10)	3 (11)	5 (11)	
Total	20 (100)	26 (100)	46 (100)	19
Size of coffee holdings				(in ha)
Number of large holdings (>10 ha)	14 (70)	23 (88)	37 (80)	33
Number of medium-sized holdings (<10 ha)	6 (30)	3 (12)	9 (20)	8
Total	20 (100)	26 (100)	46 (100)	

Source: Primary data; percentage in parentheses.

Table 14.4 Coffee crop details

Crop Type	*Certified*		*Non-certified*
	Arabica parchment	*Robusta cherry*	*Arabica parchment*
Area in ha (average)	5.38	9.07	6.56
Productivity (q/ha)	24.09	31.04	13.71
Cost of cultivation /ha	144,938	126,886	76,760
Price (INR/q)	14,675	6,200	12,911.54
Gross returns (INR/ha)	353,520	192,448	177,017
Net returns (INR/ha)	208,582	65,562	100,257

Source: Primary Data (2017–2018), calculated by the authors.

In terms of institutional credit, our survey showed that four of the 20 certified growers borrowed an average working capital of Indian Rupees[2] (INR) 0.5 million per household, and eight of the 26 non-certified growers borrowed INR 0.75 million per household. The certified coffee growers have, on average, 295 trees per hectare compared to only 170 trees per hectare in non-certified plantations. These coffee plantations also have a common intercrop, i.e., pepper. Although the cost of cultivation per hectare for pepper was lower on non-certified plantations (INR 8,249) than on certified plantations (INR 38,408), the yield and value of pepper output was higher: 2.79 q/ha and INR 42,298 per hectare on certified plantations compared to 1.68 q/ha and INR 25,069 per hectare on non-certified plantations, respectively. However, the cultivation costs and the productivity of certified coffee were higher for certified varieties of arabica and robusta (Tables 14.4 and 14.5) than for non-certified coffee. Certified arabica gained the highest net returns per hectare. Coffee quality norms also were higher for certified holdings with respect to moisture content and an out-turn[3] of 20%. This reveals that in the sustainable food value chain, certified coffee plantations are able to maintain both environmental sustainability with a rich agro-forestry system and economic sustainability by earning higher returns from quality produce.

In this study, a majority of the growers used wet processing techniques, in which fresh berries are pulped and then sun-dried to obtain 'parchment' coffee. Both certified and non-certified growers of arabica processed it into parchment, while robusta cherries were sun-dried by spreading the harvested coffee fruits over the drying yard or floor (mud, cement, or tile). The survey revealed that a majority of the certified growers did not store the harvested coffee, and the same is true of non-certified growers. However, a few stored their coffee for up to six months to speculate on obtaining higher prices. Growers of arabica certified coffee sold mostly to curers or exporters, depending on the price. While a majority of growers of non-certified coffee sold to local traders/agents, who aggregated the produce of multiple coffee growers in the

Table 14.5 Cost of cultivation (in INR)

Sl. number	*Particulars*	*Certified*			*Non-certified*
		Arabica	*Robusta*	*Arabica and Robusta*	*Arabica*
1	Fertilizers	12,603.1	12,892.9	1,2791.7	8,560.9
2	Pesticides	2,733.8	929.6	478.5	3,447.2
3	Weed management	8,723.6	6,372.3	6,741.6	1,775.4
4	Irrigation	496.7	485.7	490.0	500.0
5	Trenching				3,000.0
6	Harvesting	9213.9	7,500.0	10,694.4	3,785.9
7	Gleaning				2,135.0
8	Pruning of coffee	11,093.3	11,013.5	10,746.7	2,515.4
9	Pruning of shade trees	9,272.6	7,841.9	7057.7	4,617.5
10	Post-harvest operations	1,518.8	1,314.3	1,366.7	726.9
11	Transport and Marketing	3,000.0	3,000.0	3,000.0	
	Total (per acre)	58,655.7	51,350.2	53,367.3	31,064.2
	Total (per ha)	**144,938**	**126,886**	**131,871**	**76,760**

Source: Primary data (2017–2018), calculated by the authors.

area (Table 14.6). Small growers prefer to deal with local traders because they provide gunny bags, weighing facilities, transportation from the grower's doorstep and immediate cash payment. These local, village-level consolidators or traders sell the coffee to large traders, hullers, curing works, facilitators/agents of multinational corporations and exporters.

Perceptions of coffee growers

For arabica coffee, coffee certification is secured from the international agency Rainforest Alliance (RFA) and organic certification from the International Federation of Organic Agriculture Movements; for robusta coffee, certification comes from the RFA. Across both varieties, a majority of the growers said they chose to certify their coffee for environmental concerns and to earn a higher income from exports of such coffee. However, an equal proportion of them found these programs expensive (Table 14.7). The prime reasons non-certified growers gave for non-adoption were lack of awareness and difficulty in adopting and maintaining the standards and requirements set by the certification bodies. Other reasons included expensive procedures, the small size of coffee holdings and disinterest in certification. These reasons deter growers from participating in certification programs. As such, although these certification programs are important initiators of change, they have not been significantly influential in extensively turning the coffee chain into a sustainable chain.

Table 14.6 Marketing of coffee by coffee growers

Marketing	*Certified coffee*			*Non-certified coffee*		
	Quantity(q)	*Price (INR/q)*	*Farmers*	*Quantity (q)*	*Price (INR/q)*	*Farmers*
Agents	1,973	6,500	5	1,711	12,988	21
Curers	198.5	15,000	4	557	12,600	5
Exporters	2,103	14,527	11	—	—	—

Source: Primary data (2017–2018), calculated by the authors.

Table 14.7 Views of certified growers

	Disagree	*Neutral*	*Agree*	*Moderately agree*	*Strongly agree*	*Total*
Meeting requirement for certification is easy.	—	—	8 (40)	12 (60)	—	20 (100)
Certification has led to increase in income.	—	—	—	—	20 (100)	20 (100)
Certification rules are transparent.	—	—	6 (30)	10 (50)	4 (20)	20 (100)
Certification is expensive.	6 (30)	4 (20)	5 (25)	5 (25)	—	20 (100)
Maintenance of certification is easy.	—	—	8 (40)	7 (35)	5 (25)	20 (100)
Certification has led to increase in demand for coffee growers.	—	5 (25)	5 (25)	7 (35)	3 (15)	20 (100)

Source: Primary data (2017–2018), calculated by the authors

Note: Percentages in parentheses.

Although the non-certified growers said they were aware of the environmental and social impacts of coffee production, including the factors that affect the product's quality, they hesitated to adopt international certification standards. Instead, these growers said they try to practice good environmental practices without a certification tag. However, they did not fully adhere to social principles of sustainability, such as facilities for the workforce, because they cannot provide all the necessary labor requirements that certified growers can provide to their labor. The limited capital investment in labor is mainly due to the uncertainty in growers' annual net income, owing to the high volatility of world coffee prices. Therefore, the non-certified growers' most frequent suggestion was to fix a support price for coffee similar to the minimum support price provided for other agricultural commodities in India.

Aggregation: local trader/agent

Local traders are the primary procurers of harvested coffee from non-certified growers. They procured mostly arabica cherry and robusta cherry, as shown in Table 14.8, during 2017–2018. The parameters inspected during procurement are moisture content, outturn percentage, black and bits and any foreign matter.[4] Moisture content and out-turn are the two major criteria buyers use in purchasing coffees. A 12% moisture content and a 52% outturn are the standard norms for robusta cherry coffee. If growers fail to maintain these parameters, traders make *pro rata* deductions from the final price. Similarly, if the quality parameters are above the stipulated standard, traders pay premiums. Local agents face growers' constant demand for prices higher than the market price. Among the local traders interviewed, eight procured no certified coffee during the study period; one trader procured certified coffee at a price similar to that of non-certified coffee with no separate arrangements. This occurs because growers tend to deviate from the expected course of sale to exporters when the price for non-certified coffee is higher than the price for certified coffee. All the local traders interviewed also hulled coffee at INR 400/tonnes to obtain higher margins in the value chain, and they stored procured coffee for up to six months to insure themselves against volatile prices.

Processing: curing and roasting

The curer stands at the secondary processing stage of the harvested coffee in the production value chain. Of the six curers interviewed, four were private enterprises, and two were proprietary entities. In 2018–2019, the interviewed curers procured coffee mostly from growers directly, followed by local traders. The price the curers paid to growers was higher (INR 12,766/q) than the price they paid to local traders (INR 11,500/q). Roasters procured their coffee entirely from the curer at INR 14,700/q. Exporters were the largest buyers of

Table 14.8 Procurement of coffees

Coffee type	*Total quantity purchased (q)*	*Purchase price (INR/q)*	*Sales price (INR/q)*
Arabica parchment	2,000 (0.10)	14,400	15,000
Arabica cherry	1,954,000 (95.6)	7,100	7,470
Robusta parchment	1,000 (0.05)	13,600	14,100
Robusta cherry	87,000 (4.25)	5,911	6,038

Source: Primary data (2017–2018), calculated by the authors.

Note: Percentages in parentheses.

cured coffee, followed by roasters, who mostly supplied it to the international market for blends. The fixed and variable costs for curers and roasters are presented in Table 14.9, which indicates labor and power/electricity were the major components of expenditures. The Food Safety and Standards Authority of India and Coffee Board of India govern the curing and roasting process to ensure food safety practices are maintained. The waste generated during these processes is either used as fuel or sold as husk for the production of organic manures. Roasters blend different varieties and grades of coffee beans before undertaking roasting. Many roasters held long-term contracts with curers and with a few larger producers, although most of the procurement occurs through commission agents and curers. There were two kinds of roasters: the first is both a roaster and a retailer, grinding and selling roasted beans in local coffee shops, and the second includes large operators or wholesalers, who distribute roasted beans to retailers locally, regionally or nationally. Roasters follow stringent quality parameters because they have direct links with consumers and obtain the highest margins in the value chain. It is evident that power and returns are intensely concentrated in the hands of roasters. which affects the value addition and income distribution along the chain.

Labor (plantation and processing units)

A number of sustainability initiatives such as certifications seek to halt the unfavorable working conditions laborers face and seek to bring fair trade. The various sustainability certification standards spearheaded the use of socially responsible voluntary regulations in international agro-food networks, which work to foster fairness principles in terms of equity and empowerment. However, as evident in agriculture across developing countries, most employment is informal, and facilities provided to labor are limited. The workers interviewed in both the farm and processing plants were mostly men in the 35–50 age group, with an average age of 38. However, in recent years, women have been providing substantial labor in harvesting and coffee pruning. Most have a high school education and come from nuclear families. Those working in the coffee plantations live in *Katcha* houses, and those working in the processing activities (curing and roasting) live in *Pucca* houses. Laborers in both categories have worked for more than a decade in these plantations or processing units (15–30 years). The wages the coffee growers pay their workforce depend on the type of activity undertaken (e.g., fertilizer and pesticides application, INR 240; weed management, INR 220; irrigation, INR 500; harvesting, INR 240; pruning coffee plants, INR 350; and canopy management, INR 660). Workers in the processing units are paid a fixed wage of INR 340 per day on a weekly basis. The workforce is mostly temporary and employed intermittently during the year, which compels them to move from one plantation to another in search of employment at either the plantation or processing units. At times, the temporary workforce also undertakes work related to government-sponsored jobs under Mahatma Gandhi National Rural Employment Guarantee Act or construction activities in the area. Another aspect to be noted is that housing, medical care, insurance and education are provided to the permanent workforce, which makes up a minority of the workforce irrespective of certification adoption. However, both categories of workers are dissatisfied with the current wage rate and suggest their wages be increased because the cost of essential commodities has escalated recently.

Workers on the farms face the hazards of eye irritation and insect bites, and they are provided gloves and gumboots. Workers interviewed at the processing plants, however, did not have any immediate concerns about work hazards. The workforce suggested that their employers, be it the coffee grower, curer or roaster, provide them with housing, medical care and education, as well as ensured year-round employment, which will discourage their migration in search of employment in the off season. Until recently, coffee companies did not give due acknowledgement to this social sustainability dimension of the value chain described in the FAO's framework.

Challenges in the global coffee value chain

Having increased coffee production, India's next step would be to move to a higher value-added position in the global food value chain. Sustainability standards provide scope for higher earnings among coffee growers, as shown in the case study. However, all aspects of sustainability measures, specifically the environmental and socially responsible aspects, need further promotion to shed

Table 14.9 Curer and roaster costs (Rs)

Sl. Number	*Particulars*	*Cost of Curing*	*%*	*Cost of Roasting*	*%*
Fixed cost					
1	Cost of machinery	5,416,667	58.8	1,500,000	23.1
2	Building cost	3,800,000	41.2	5,000,000	76.9
3	Storages	0	0	0	0
	Total	9,216,667	100	6,500,000	100
Variable cost					
4	Labor	1,173,333	17.6	350,000	47.9
5	Fuel	150000	2.3	0	0
6	Electricity	3,772,000	56.6	160,000	21.9
7	Packaging	0	0	100,000	13.7
8	Transportation	616,667	9.3	100,000	13.7
9	Rent	600,000	9	0	0
10	Machine maintenance	266,667	4	20,000	2.7
11	Miscellaneous charge	80,000	1.2	0	0
	Total	6,658,667	100	730,000	100

Source: Primary data (2017–2018), calculated by the authors.

light on the transformative potential of new governance and coordination practices along a sustainability-oriented global coffee value chain. Challenges and obstacles in sustainable value chains vary widely across sectors and geographies, and those related specifically to coffee across the world are as follows:

- Lengthy supply chains result in lower prices for producers and a lack of transparency between buyers and producers (Akarsha, 2009; Bhavya, 2011).
- Chattopadhayay and John (2007) observed that disproportionate market power among downstream actors has resulted in small farmers selling at prices lower than their cost of production, while traders and multinational corporations make huge profits.
- Muradian and Pelupessy (2005) observed that the economic rewards accruing to coffee farmers investing in quality improvement may be less than expected.
- Different certification schemes have multiple and overlapping standards.
- Price premiums associated with social or environmental labeling initiatives are not always substantial.
- Low market demand for certified coffee, weak price incentives and high auditing and management costs encourage cooperatives to certify only a portion of their members. This strategy rewards compliant farmers rather than inducing all members to make widespread changes in their farming practices (Snider et al., 2017).
- Giovannucci and Ponte (2005) also questioned whether sustainability standards in the coffee sector were likely to benefit actors in developing countries due to insufficient transparency and clarity of standards, inadequate participation of actors in producing countries in procedures for setting standards and the system's inability to compensate growers for improving performance.
- Although the Fairtrade Label Organization has challenged inequality by directly entering the value chain (Venkatechalam, 2005; Tallontire and Vorley, 2005), global commodity chains remain tilted toward multinational corporations and their subsidiaries in consuming markets (developed countries), leaving the other end of the value chain in producing countries with little market control and no means of value addition (Kaplinsky, 2004).

Conclusions

In the face of climate change escalating to a climate crisis, current coffee production areas are projected to experience temperatures gradually increasing to more extreme ranges as well as periods of drought and heavy rainfall. Indian growers will become increasingly vulnerable to a series of climate risks—droughts, storms, strong winds, intensive rainfall and flooding—which the case study district has faced in the last two years.[5] Coffee growers' precarious revenue situation is further intensified by high short-term price volatility. However, an optimistic outlook is that Indian coffee production is based on agro-forestry systems that are more resilient than sun-grown coffee or unshaded plantations. However, agro-forestry and management practices are crucial to ensure that plantations are well adapted to future climatic conditions and extreme climatic events. Indian coffee growers still have significant leeway to make their coffee farms resilient while sustainably intensifying their production and mitigating their farms' greenhouse-gas emissions. One-hectare shade-grown coffee plantations with large forest trees can sequester an estimated 70–80 MT of carbon per hectare, which is almost equivalent to the carbon stored in an equal area of forest (Kumar et al., 2019). As such, this strategy has been recognised as a viable afforestation and reforestation strategy under the Clean Development Mechanism of the Kyoto Protocol (Schmitt-Harsh et al., 2012).

Other interventions for upgrading are more skilled farming techniques, better use of technologies and higher productivity. At the institutional level, producers' cooperative organizations could access specialty certifications that offer higher-priced markets, extension information and other benefits. However, certifications have had limited benefits for producers, particularly where administered through cooperatives. On the other hand, the Indian Coffee Board has taken the initiative in technological innovations by launching a blockchain-based market app that creates a digital platform linking all stakeholders, including growers, processors, exporters and importers. This helps create a brand image for Indian coffee through traceability and reduces growers' dependence on intermediaries to find suppliers and exporters.

Notes

1 The Indian Coffee Board classifies small producers as those with coffee holdings below 10 ha.

2 Exchange rate 1 US$ = 75.32 INR (on July 15, 2020).

3 Out-turn is the quantity of total produce obtained after processing or the rate of conversion of cherry/parchment to clean coffee. For example, 50 kg of cherry coffee should yield 26.5 kg bean, leaving behind the husk.

4 Standards for moisture content, 13%; out-turn percentage, 26%; black and bits, 10%; and foreign matter, 1%.

5 https://india.mongabay.com/2019/08/extreme-rainfall-devastates-kodagu-yet-again/ (accessed on September 14, 2019); www.downtoearth.org.in/news/climate-change/drought-to-deluge-kodagu-was-parched-3-months-ago-now-receives-extreme-rainfall-66109 (accessed on September 14, 2019).

References

Akarsha, B. M. (2009). *Farm labour in the Indian coffee sector: Emerging challenges for factor intensive systems in Karnataka*. Master's thesis, Humboldt University of Berlin, Berlin.

Bhavya, K. V. (2011). *Value chain analysis for coffee in Karnataka, India*. Master's thesis, Ghent University, Ghent.

Bolwig, S., Gibbon, P., & Jones, S. (2009). The economics of smallholder organic contract farming in tropical Africa. *World Development*, *37*(6), 1094–1104.

Chattopadhayay, S., & John, P. (2007). *Bitter beans: An analysis of coffee crisis in India, partners in change*. First edition. www.picindia.org.

Chengappa, P. G., Rich, K. M., Rich, M., Muniyappa, A., Yadava, C. G., & Pradeepa, B. B. (2014). *Promoting conservation in India by greening coffee: A value chain approach*. NUPI Working Paper 831. nupi.brage.unit.no.

Elder, S. D., Zerriffi, H., & Le Billon, P. (2012). Effects of fair-trade certification on social capital: The case of Rwandan coffee producers. *World Development, 40*(11), 2355–2367.

FAO. (2014). *Developing sustainable food value chains—Guiding principles*. FAO, Rome.

Gereffi, G., Humphrey, J., & Sturgeon, T. (2005). The governance of global value chains. *Review of International Political Economy, 12*(1), 78–104.

Giovannucci, D., & Ponte, S. (2005). Standards as a new form of social contract? Sustainability initiatives in the coffee industry. *Food Policy, 30*(3), 284–301.

Johannessen, S., & Wilhite, H. (2010). Who really benefits from Fairtrade? An analysis of value distribution in Fairtrade coffee. *Globalizations*, 7(4), 525–544.

Kaplinsky, R. (2004). Spreading the gains from globalization: What can be learned from value-chain analysis? *Problems of Economic Transition, 47*(2), 74–115.

Karuretwa, Kaliza. (2016). *Case 14: Rwanda coffee sector*. Case Studies on the Future of Manufacturing, World Economic Forum Global Agenda Council on the Future of Manufacturing, World Economic Forum, Geneva.

Kasente, D. (2012). Fair trade and organic certification in value chains: Lessons from a gender analysis from coffee exporting in Uganda. *Gender & Development, 20*(1), 111–127.

Kumar, N.P.A., Khan, A.I.K.S., & Balakrishnan, V. (2019). Coffee, climate and biodiversity: Understanding the carbon stocks of the shade coffee production system of India. In W. Leal Filho, J. Barbir, R. Preziosi, *Handbook of Climate Change and Biodiversity* (pp. 113–134). Springer, Cham.

Kundu, A., & Chopra, A. (2009). The fair tracing project: Mapping a traceable value chain for Indian coffee. *Contemporary South Asia, 17*(2), 213–223.

Lassale-de Salins, M., Bertoluci, G., & Chapdaniel, A. (2014). *Managing sustainability in supply chains: The sustainable demand-supply chain approach, a proposal for a pragmatic approach in the food sector*. http://tinyurl.com/ldqef3j.

Méndez, V. E., Bacon, C. M., Olson, M., Petchers, S., Herrador, D., Carranza, C., . . . Mendoza, A. (2010). Effects of fair trade and organic certifications on small-scale coffee farmer households in central America and Mexico. *Renewable Agriculture and Food Systems, 25*(3), 236–251.

Minten, B., Dereje, M., Engida, E., & Kuma, T. (2017). Coffee value chains on the move: Evidence in Ethiopia. *Food Policy, 83*, 370–383.

Minten, B., Dereje, M., Engida, E., & Tamru, S. (2018). Tracking the quality premium of certified coffee: Evidence from Ethiopia. *World Development, 101*, 119–132.

Muradian, R., & Pelupessy, W. (2005). Governing the coffee chain: The role of voluntary regulatory systems. *World Development, 33*(12), 2029–2044.

Neilson, J. (2008). Global private regulation and value-chain restructuring in Indonesian smallholder coffee systems. *World Development, 36*(9), 1607–1622.

Petkova, I. (2006). Shifting regimes of governance in the coffee market: From secular crisis to a new equilibrium? *Review of International Political Economy, 13*(2), 313–339.

Porter, M. E., & Kramer, M. R. (2011). Creating shared value: Redefining capitalism and the role of the corporation in society. *Harvard Business Review, 89*(1/2), 62–77.

Potts, J., Lynch, M., Wilkings, A., Huppe, G., Cunningham, M., & Voora, V. (2014). *The state of sustainability initiatives review 2014*. International Institute for Sustainable Development, International Institute for Environment and Development, Winnipeg, Canada; London.

Princen, T. (2001). Consumption and its externalities: Where economy meets ecology. *Global Environmental Politics*, *1*(3), 11–30.

Raynolds, L. T. (2009). Mainstreaming fair trade coffee: From partnership to traceability. *World Development*, *37*(6), 1083–1093.

Rich, K. M., Muniyappa, A., Yadava, C. G., Manjyapura, G. S., PradeepaBabu, B. N., Shubha, Y. C., & Rich, M. (2017). Coffee certification in India: Awareness, practices, and sustainability perception of growers. *Agroecology and Sustainable Food Systems*, 1–27.

Ruben, R., & Fort, R. (2012). The impact of fair-trade certification for coffee farmers in Peru. *World Development*, *40*(3), 570–582.

Schmitt-Harsh, M., Evans, T. P., Castellanos, E., & Randolph, J. C. (2012). Carbon stocks in coffee agroforests and mixed dry tropical forests in the western highlands of Guatemala. *Agroforestry Systems*, *86*(2), 141–157.

Snider, A., Gallegos, A. A., Gutiérrez, I., & Sibelet, N. (2017). Social capital and sustainable coffee certifications in Costa Rica. *Human Ecology*, *45*(2), 235–249.

Soosay, C. A., & Hyland, P. (2015). A decade of supply chain collaboration and directions for future research. *Supply Chain Management: An International Journal*, *20*(6), 613–630.

Tallontire, A., & Vorley, B. (2005). *Achieving fairness in trading between supermarkets and their agrifood supply chains*. London: UK Food Group Briefing.

Valkila, J., Haaparanta, P., & Niemi, N. (2010). Empowering coffee traders? The coffee value chain from Nicaraguan fair-trade farmers to Finnish consumers. *Journal of Business Ethics*, *97*(2), 257–270.

Van Rijsbergen, B., Elbers, W., Ruben, R., & Njuguna, S. N. (2016). The ambivalent impact of coffee certification on farmers' welfare: A matched panel approach for cooperatives in Central Kenya. *World Development*, *77*, 277–292.

Venkatachalam, L. (2005, September). Perspectives on sustainability and globalization and the challenges for the coffee sector. In *Proceedings of the 2nd world coffee conference* (pp. 23–25). http://www.ico.org/event_pdfs/wcc2/presentations/venkatachalam.pdf.

Weber, J. G. (2011). How much more do growers receive for Fair Trade-organic coffee? *Food Policy*, *36*(5), 678–685.

World Bank. (2020). *World development report 2020: Trading for development in the age of global value chains*. Washington, DC: World Bank. doi:10.1596/978-1-4648-1457-0. License: Creative Commons Attribution CC BY 3.0 IGO.

Part III

Contract farming, storage and technical efficiency

15 Indian agriculture and agro-processing in the global value chains

Seema Bathla and Abhishek Jha

Trade in agricultural commodities is a sensitive matter for most economies across the globe. The post-Uruguay round of negotiations on the Agreement on Agriculture (AoA) was a historic attempt to include the agricultural sector under multilateral trade negotiations. It compelled both developed and developing countries to halt continuing protective regimes on agricultural exports to gain from multilateral trade (Aksoy and Beghin, 2005). Member countries were asked to implement three broad stipulations of the AoA under the aegis of the World Trade Organization (WTO). These were market access, domestic support and export subsidies, each having different requirements for the developed and developing countries to follow while integrating with world markets. The key measures that member countries agreed on were a reduction in applied tariffs as per the WTO prescribed bound rates on imports; conversion of non-tariff barriers into their tariff equivalents; cuts in export subsidies within a stipulated period; classification of domestic support (i.e., subsidies) under the amber, blue and green boxes;[1] and reduction support in a phased manner to lessen distortions in trade.

Over the years, the degree of protectionism accorded to agriculture has decreased, and trade has proliferated. Developing countries, however, resort to protection on the pretext of agriculture's sensitivity to the vagaries of nature, price volatility, and other market risks, maintaining that food security and a reasonable level of income are necessary for small and poor farmers (Sharma and Gulati, 2003; Sharma, 2016). In contrast, developed countries impose stringent non-tariff barriers on developing countries' exports to ensure food safety and food standards (Bosworth, 1999). The extent to which this protective regime has affected a country's agricultural trade is not known with certainty. However, it has significant implications for developing countries that possess considerable comparative advantages in agricultural exports. Barriers to and controls on accessing developed nations' markets also may be daunting. In addition, both domestic and world agricultural trade have been transforming rapidly due to a competitive business environment evolving through agribusiness, also called production networks or value chains, thus limiting gains to developing economies.

We take India as a case study to examine its position in production and exports of primary agriculture, allied activities (mining, fishery, forestry) and processed food and beverages from domestic and foreign value addition—that is, their integration in global value chains (GVCs).

India's agricultural and food industries are growing steadily, and so are exports from these sectors. India's involvement in global value chains may not have grown much. Still, it has considerable potential to participate through exports of those products, which constitute a high share (more than 70%) of global exports.[2] Banga (2016) opined that by increasing exports of manufactured products through global value chains, India can become more competitive, upgrade workers' skills and generate employment. However, in the case of agro-processing, India and other developing countries confront several eclectic challenges to becoming attractive partners in global value chains. The biggest challenge is that, by and large, their processed food products lack price competitiveness compared to their primary (raw) agricultural commodities (Bathla and Kannan, 2021). It may imply that food enterprises have to cut costs and have a lower protective regime. Other key challenges include information asymmetries, the predominance of small and medium farms, inadequate technical know-how, logistics and infrastructure, high global food safety standards, large-volume supply and reliability of delivery, customization through processing and packaging and strategies for product differentiation, in particular for traditional exports involving certification and regulatory clearances (Raju, 2014; Levchenko, 2007).

We use a Leontief input–output framework to analyze the magnitude of integration of primary and processed agricultural exports as inputs (for value addition) into and as final consumption in global value chains from 2000 to 2014. The data are given in the World Input–Output Table (WIOT) and is sourced from the World Input–Output Table database (WIOD) (Timmer, 2012).[3] The WIOD also provides a National Input–Output Table (NIOT) at the country level to identify and estimate the inter-sectoral (agricultural and industry) production linkages and between primary and processed agricultural products.

The rest of this chapter is structured as follows. The second section briefly explains the functioning of global value chains and outlines the methodology used to estimate exports' integration into global value chains. The third section presents trends in agricultural exports, bifurcated into primary categories (raw products that undergo minimal processing) and secondary categories (products that undergo value addition in the industry) from 2001 to 2017. The fourth section follows with empirical estimates on the production (output) linkages between primary and processed agricultural products and on the integration of exports from the agricultural, processed food and beverage and allied sectors into global value chains. The last section draws conclusions and implications.

Functioning of global value chains and approach to measure integration

A global value chain is composed of a set of interrelated activities in the productive cycle, from research and development to design, manufacturing and distribution, involving value creation across a range of activities. Traditionally, companies made products primarily in one country, from the first stage to the finished stage of exports. With the evolution of global value chains, a single finished product often results from manufacturing and assembling in multiple countries, with each step adding value to the end product and to the exchange of know-how. Imports of goods and services matter as much as exports to successful global value chains. To illustrate, country A exports some product worth US$ 2, which will be an intermediary good for country B. Country B adds value worth US$ 24 and exports to country C, which further adds value worth US$ 46. Finally, the product is consumed in country D (Figure 15.1). The global value chains integrate the know-how of lead firms and suppliers of key components at each stage of production and in multiple offshore locations. The international, inter-firm flow of knowledge is the key distinguishing feature of global value chains.

Literature indicates that global value chains, be they in agricultural, manufacturing or services sectors, provide impetus to export competitiveness, maintain quality standards and enable higher incomes (Lodefalk, 2015; Nag, 2019). According to the United Nations Industrial Development Organisation (UNIDO) (2009), a major hypothesis of the global value chains' approach is that

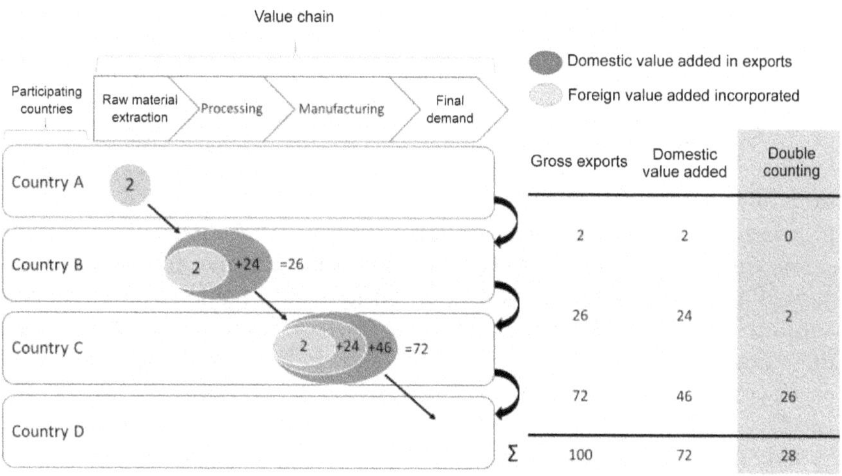

Figure 15.1 Global value chain (GVC) schematic map

Source: Organisation for Economic Co-operation and Development (OECD, 2013).

national development requires linking with the most significant lead firms in an industry. These lead firms are not necessarily traditional vertically integrated manufacturers, nor are they necessarily involved in making the finished products. Because most developing countries are agriculture-based, global value chains make it strategic and convenient for them to move away from exports reliant on primary products and toward manufacturing and services. In this process, the ratio of domestic value-added to gross export value falls (Banga, 2014). Developing countries often place themselves at the end of the value chains (downstream participation), with a labor-intensive assembly of parts produced elsewhere. Gross exports from a country can be substantial, but its value-added contribution may be much smaller.

Nevertheless, aspiring to increase foreign value-added contribution to exports has to be approached cautiously. It may seem like simple math that a higher share of value added domestically means higher total value-added to exports and hence more income. However, it ignores the reality that imported goods and services are key support for a country's competitiveness. If a country artificially replaces key inputs with inferior domestic versions, the result is likely to be a decrease in both gross exports and total value-added exports. Thus the value-added exports require decoding within the framework of domestic and foreign inputs. If an economy simply concentrates on escalating domestic value addition, it may lose global integration and hence find it difficult to increase participation in the upstream ladder of global value chains.

This situation may describe the competitiveness of a country and its industries by looking specifically at the production of value-added goods and the level of integration into global value chains. The new trade patterns under these chains suggest a revision of strategies that aim to foster competitiveness, trade and development policies at large (Cattaneo et al., 2013). International trade is facilitated by improvements in transportation, information and telecommunications and by widespread liberalization of investment. Fragmentation of production processes and the associated increase in vertical specialization in specific stages of the chain have implications. They indicate that firms in developing countries now can participate in international trade without having to create a full range of capabilities across the value chain, essentially 'compressing' the development experience and making non-linear catch-up possible.[4] By opening access to new and often higher-value markets, participation in global value chains offers these firms an opportunity to add more value in their local industries, drive employment and raise incomes (Organisaton for Economic Cooperation and Development [OECD], 2012).

Several developing countries and even some of the least developed ones have responded positively to these opportunities (United Nations Conference on Trade and Development -UNCTAD, 2013). The growth rate of exports of intermediate goods from developing countries entering different stages of global value chains has outpaced the growth rate of those from developed economies (IDE-JETRO/WTO [Institute of Developing Economies–Japan External Trade Organization/World Trade Organization], 2011). As participation in global value chains becomes synonymous with economic development, developing countries are trying to design policies to reinforce the emergence and local presence of firms linked to these chains, as well as to attract foreign firms and improve border procedures to facilitate trade flows. Acknowledging the significance of imports to domestic production processes, both developed and developing countries, also mandated by WTO, have called to reduce import tariffs to lower costs and facilitate access to world-class inputs (Cattaneo et al., 2013; OECD, 2012).

Sustained participation in these competitive chains, however, is challenging. Today's global value chains are highly dynamic, place high demands on the participating firms and are increasingly consolidated around a small number of durable global suppliers. Further, addressing gaps in the measurement of global value chains is essential, both for advancing understanding of the workings of the modern global economy and for addressing policy questions. According to the World Development Report 2020, global value chains influence trade's response to frictions and may amplify gains from trade. The chains also change the nature of macro spillovers across countries. At the micro-level, offshoring (one manifestation of participation in global value chains) is central to explaining the firm's performance and labor market outcomes. The report also highlighted that from a normative perspective, these chains alter government incentives to impose trade protections and have implications for optimal monetary policies in an open economy.

Methodology and database to measure integration into global value chains

Figure 15.2 explains a two-country international input–output (IIO) table for the estimation of inter-sectoral linkages within a domestic economy and foreign value-added (through exports) under global value chains.

Explanation of matrix calculation

$$X = \mathrm{A}X + F$$

where X is the $GN\times$ vector of gross output, consisting of stacked vectors of gross output for each country. The $N\times1$ vector X_i denotes the gross output of country $N\times1$ in each sector:

$$X = \begin{bmatrix} X1 & \cdots & \\ \vdots & \ddots & \vdots \\ & \cdots & XG \end{bmatrix}$$

A two-country IIO table Intermediate use				Final use			Total use
			Country 1	Country 2	Country 1	Country 2	
			$1 \cdots N$		$1 \cdots N$		
Supply	Country 1	$1{:}N$	1's use of its own inputs	2's use of inputs from 1	1's use of its own final goods	2's use of final goods from 1	1's total output
	Country 2	$1{:}N$	1's use of inputs from 2	2's use of its own inputs	1's use of final goods from 2	2's use of its own final goods	2's total output
Value added			1's value added	2's value added			
Total supply			1's total output	2's total output			

Figure 15.2 Tabular form of input–output

Source: Timmer, 2012; OECD, 2012.

The $GN \times GN$ matrix A provides the direct intermediate input-output coefficients, where A_{ij} denotes the $N \times N$ matrix giving direct use of inputs supplied by each sector of country i in each sector of country j.

$$A = \begin{bmatrix} A11 & \cdots & A1G \\ \vdots & \ddots & \vdots \\ AG1 & \cdots & AGG \end{bmatrix}$$

Final demand is given by the $GN \times 1$ matrix F, which gives world demand for final goods. The $N \times 1$ vector F_1 denotes the value of final goods produced in country i.

$$= \begin{matrix} F1 \\ \vdots \\ FG \end{matrix}$$

where $F_i = \sum iFij$ and $F_{ij} = D_{ij} + E_{ij}$:

$$\begin{bmatrix} F11 & \cdots & F1G \\ \vdots & \ddots & \vdots \\ FG1 & \cdots & FGG \end{bmatrix} = \begin{bmatrix} D11 & \cdots & 0 \\ \vdots & \ddots & \vdots \\ 0 & \cdots & DGG \end{bmatrix} + \begin{bmatrix} 0 & \cdots & E1G \\ \vdots & \ddots & \vdots \\ EG1 & \cdots & 0 \end{bmatrix}$$

where D_{ii} is the $N\times1$ vector of final goods and services produced and consumed domestically, and E_{ij} denotes the $N\times1$ vector of final goods and services produced in i and exported to (and consumed in) country j.

$$X = (I-A)^{-1} F=BF$$

where B is the $GN\times GN$ Leontief inverse matrix. Elements of this matrix express the total output, used both directly and indirectly, that is required to produce $1 of final goods and services. As with the direct coefficient matrix A, the Leontief inverse matrix B is composed of $N\times N$ submatrices B_{ij} that denote the value of output used in each sector of country i to produce final goods in each sector of country j. Using the World Input–Output Database, the gross output produced by a country r must be used as an intermediate good or a final good at home or abroad (following exports), which can be expressed using the following equation:

$$X_{rr} = A_{rr}X_r + A_{rs}X_S + Y_{rs} + Y_{rr}$$

where X_r is $N\times1$ gross output vector of a country r, Y_{rs} is the $N\times1$ final demand vector that gives demand in country s for final goods produced in country r, and A_{rs} is the $N\times N$ input–output coefficient matrix, giving intermediate use in s of goods produced in r. Following is the decomposition of exports:

$$E_{rs} = Y_{rs} + A_{rs}.\,X_s$$
$$E_{rs} = Y_{rs} + A_{rs}X_{ss} + \Sigma_{r,s}A_{rs}X_{st} + A_{rs}X_{sr}$$

The last equation has four terms. The first term indicates final goods exported to country s, the second term refers to intermediate goods absorbed in s, the third term is for goods processed and exported to another country t, and the last term is for goods processed and exported back to r, where r is the home country (Hummels et al., 2001). Based on the National Input Output Table and the World Input Output Table, estimations are worked out at three points in time—2000, 2007 and 2014. A case of the United States is taken separately to see India's foreign value-added agricultural exports, since the United States is the largest destination for India's agricultural exports.

Composition and temporal trends in agricultural exports and imports

This section analyses the composition of India's agricultural exports and imports and delineates their temporal trends at the four-digit level, along with their key destinations. The Indian Trade Clarification based on Harmonised System of Coding (ITC HS) classifies agricultural exports and imports from chapters 1 to 24. We have taken the value of exports and imports at the four-digit level and categorized them into four groups as per the United National Conference on Trade and Development (UNCTAD) classification:

1 Category I, live animals and animal products: ITC chapters 1–6
2 Category II, vegetable products and cereals: ITC chapters 7–14
3 Category III, animal or vegetable fats and oils and their cleavage products, prepared edible fats and animal or vegetable waxes: HS chapter 15
4 Category IV, prepared foodstuffs; beverages, spirits and vinegar; tobacco and manufactured tobacco substitutes: HS chapters 16–24

A finer disaggregation of products in each chapter helps understand the composition of trade and elicits broader trends in raw, intermediate and finished value-added products. In some ways, this categorization reflects the level of processing that agricultural commodities generally undergo. Commodities in Categories I and II (ITC HS chapters 1–6 and 7–14, respectively) can be termed primary due to lower requirements for processing—mainly cleaning, sorting, freezing and sometimes transforming raw produce into fine products such as flour. In contrast, commodities in Categories III and IV undergo value addition with the use of sophisticated technology and skills. These products may be exported directly by the agro- and food-processing industry or through distributors/exporters.

India possesses a comparative advantage in several primary agricultural commodities, such as basmati rice, spices, groundnut seed, soybean seed and meals. These commodities continue to have a dominant share in total agricultural exports, though the commodity basket changed rapidly from 2001 to 2017. We find that throughout 2001 to 2017, primary agricultural exports' (categories I and II, chapters 1–14) share of India's total agriculture exports is much higher at 75%. The primary agricultural exports' share in total global agricultural exports, is almost 50%. In value terms, agricultural exports from India increased from \$6.3 billion in 2001 to \$35.7 billion in 2017. In terms of India's share of world agricultural exports, this was largely insignificant, increasing from 1.4% in 2001 to 2.3% in 2017. India's agricultural exports share in total exports reveal large year-to-year variations, with a high of 14.4% in 2001 to less than 2% share in 2017. Similarly, total agricultural imports increased from \$2.67 billion to \$25.2 billion during the same period. India's share of world agricultural imports is minimal, at 1.6%, and the country's total imports (agricultural and non-agricultural) were consistently close to 5.5% during the 2001–2017 period.

A category-wise share of exports depicted in Figure 15.3 reveals that almost 50% of exports are from Category II, vegetable products, which fell slightly to 46.8% by 2017. The share of exports from Category I, live animals, increased from 26.5% to 32.4% over the 2001–2017 period. The share of these two groups (termed primary) increased four percentage points by 2017, implying that almost 76% of exports are primary and the remaining 24% are from the

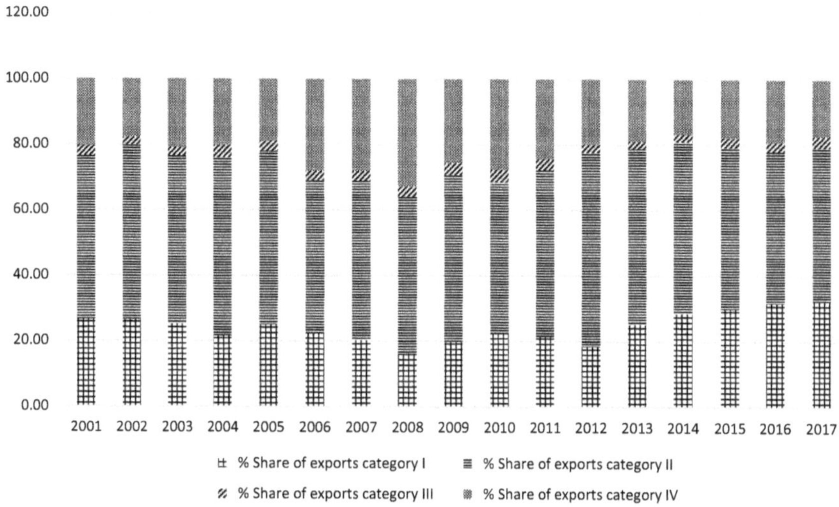

Figure 15.3 Share of categorical agriculture exports as a percentage of total agriculture exports in India

Source: UN COMTRADE (United Nations International Trade Statistics Database).

other two categories, which are highly processed products such as edible oils, prepared food, spirits and tobacco.

The scenario for agricultural imports depicted in Figure 15.4 reveals that India depends relatively more on processed commodities from categories III and IV, as their combined share of total imports remained high, at 62.73% in 2001, decreasing nearly four percentage points to 58.92% in 2017. Comparing these two categories, agricultural imports from Category III, animal and vegetable fats and oils, are much higher, at 47% in 2017, than imports from Category IV, prepared food products and tobacco. A low share of imports of primary commodities may indicate that India has a comparative advantage in these commodities and depends on foreign markets mainly for value-added commodities. In other words, India's processed food industry is not fully equipped and competitive enough to produce highly processed items. India also depends little on imports and fulfills its raw-material requirements mainly through domestic markets, due to either cost or high tariffs. During the 2001–2017 period, imports mainly comprised raw and intermediate goods, such as cocoa, that are not produced domestically.

A closer look into a disaggregate analysis of exports and imports at the four-digit level shows that Category I, live animals, chapters 1–6, had a very high share of total agricultural exports, increasing from 25.97% during the triennium ending (TE) 2003 to 31.34% during TE 2017 at the rate of 15.16% per

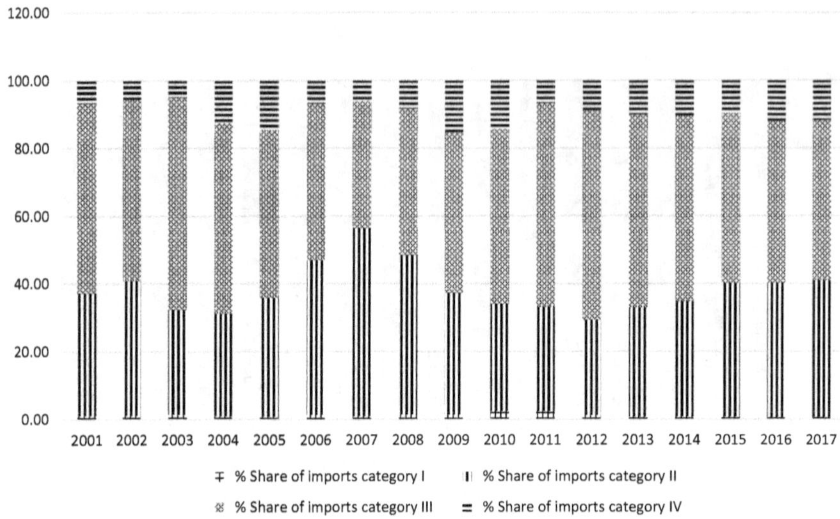

Figure 15.4 Share of categorical agriculture imports as a percentage of total agriculture imports by India

Source: UN COMTRADE (United Nations International Trade Statistics Database).

year. Bovine animals' meat as a share of total agricultural exports increased from 3.87% to 11.92%, crustaceans' share decreased slightly from 14.3% to 11.8%, and frozen fish's share fell from 3.6% to 2%. The export value of raw products has improved considerably since 2001. Edible offal of bovine animals and meat of bovine animals are the two products with the greatest increases in their share of total agriculture exports, at nearly 12%. However, a decline in exports of goods under category I is visible over the period, with an unchanged share in exports since 2001.

Like Category I products, products in Category II also are considered primary. The share of coconut, brazil nuts and cashew nuts, tea, coffee, other oil seeds and oleaginous fruits and dried leguminous vegetables in total exports has decreased over the years. Products in this category have much higher value than those in Category I, increasing almost five times from US$ 3.49 billion during the triennium ending 2003 to US$ 15.45 billion during the triennium ending 2017 for an annual growth rate of 13.38%. Among various products, rice, groundnut, grapes and dates, figs, pineapples, avocados, guavas, mangoes and tea showed exceptional increases in their export values. During the triennium ending 2017, the highest shares of total agricultural exports were of rice (19.2%), coconut (2.8%), vegetable saps and extracts (2.7%), pepper (2.7%) and tea (2.2%).

In the case of processed agricultural products in Category III, their share of total agricultural exports remained stagnant at almost 3% over the years. Major exportables included fixed vegetable fats and oils. The value of these exports was way below that of Categories I and II exports, growing from US$ 174 million to US$ 1.014 billion at an annual rate of 13.5%. Among major exportables—boiled, oxidized and dehydrated animal oil, oils and oil's fractions of fish—are the products whose exported value increased the most, with annual rates varying from 10% to 30%.

Export Category IV comprises highly processed products such as prepared foodstuffs; beverages, spirits and vinegar; unprocessed tobacco; and manufactured tobacco substitutes. Similar to products in Category III, products in Category IV make up a smaller share of total agricultural exports, at 18.2%, with cane/beet sugar having the highest share of Category IV products at 3.7%. Cane's share and raw unmanufactured tobacco's share of agricultural exports have decreased over time, and oilcake and other solid residues also have experienced major setbacks in their share of total agricultural exports. We find a sizeable increase in export value of category IV products, from US$ 1.32 billion in TE 2003 to US$ 7.64 billion during TE 2013, followed by a decline to US$ 5.92 billion during TE 2017. The annual growth rate is estimated to be close to 13%, or nearly the same as in the other two product categories. Products in Category IV have much higher export values than those in Category III. Increases in demand are visible for cane/beet sugar, crustaceans, mollusks, food preparations and unmanufactured tobacco. Under food preparations, the value of bread, pastry, cakes and biscuits has increased significantly.

Compared to the composition of agricultural exports, the composition of agricultural imports differs. The value of imports in Category I increased from US$ 41.2 million in the triennium ending 2003 to US$ 185 million during TE 2017. A major increase came in animal products, from US$ 4.34 million to US$ 22.95 million, and in whey, fish fillets and crustaceans by more than 12% per year. Though growing at 13% per year, primary commodity imports constituted a very low share (less than 0.10%) of total agricultural imports over the years. The value of primary imports in Category II were much higher than the value of those in Category I. Growing at an annual rate of 15%, their value jumped from 1.145 billion to US$ 9.045 billion over the selected period. Among primary importables, dried leguminous vegetables, coconut and other nuts had the highest shares, at 16.9%, 5.9% and 4.44%, respectively. Most of the other products, such as apples and other fruits, oilseeds, coffee and lac, had less than a 1% share of total agricultural imports. Wheat imports were not consistent as their share rose to 9.48%, fell to 1.22% in the subsequent period and then rose to 2.56% by 2017. It is clear that India imports wheat only when needed, compared to many other primary products whose share of total imports remained unchanged over the period. Products that experienced reduced imports were milk and cream, falling from US$ 5.79 million to US$ 3.22 million.

The value of imports in Category III was the highest among the four categories considered. It increased from US$ 1.88 billion to US$ 10.949 billion over the period, with a major share of the value coming from palm oil and edible oils, mainly soybean and sunflower oils. Soybeans' share of total agricultural imports increased from 1.73% in 2001 to 6.59%, and soybean oil's and palm oil's shares decreased from 16.1% to 12.4% and 36.4% to 26.8%, respectively, during the triennium ending 2017. Most of the importable items in Categories I, II and III are for direct consumption and show high growth rates, above 14% per year. The value of processed products in Category IV increased from US$ 0.184 billion to US$ 2.562 billion but is way below the value of imports in Categories II and III. A steady increase in imports of Categories III and IV is observed, along with a growth rate above 20%, which is much higher than that of commodities imported in the first two categories. Of all the agricultural imports, cane or beet sugar showed the largest increase in the value of imports, from US$ 6.67 million in 2001 to US$ 825.76 million in 2017, growing at a rate of 40.78% per year. Its share of total agricultural imports increased from 0.20% to 3.63% during the period. For other major imports, the share of total agricultural imports increased for animal feed preparations; undenatured ethyl alcohol of an alcoholic strength; spirits, water, chocolate and other food preparations; cocoa beans, cocoa butter and other sugars. Most of these products have less than a 1% share of agricultural imports, but their value increased more than two to four times over the period. Furthermore, products such as cocoa and other food preparations are used as intermediate products in manufacturing final consumables in the industry, signaling India's self-dependency on these products. Overall, importable products in Category IV are either raw or used for intermediate consumption by the industry.

Regarding the direction of agricultural trade, India exports mainly to the United States, Vietnam, United Arab Emirates, Saudi Arabia, Iran and China. Among these, the United States and Vietnam receive exports worth US$ 4.61 billion and US$ 3.85 billion, respectively. As previously discussed, India's exports mainly constitute primary products such as rice, meat, tea, marine products and spices, which are generally consumed as finished products. Basmati rice is exported mainly to the Middle East. Tables 15.1 and 15.2 list major

Table 15.1 Key destination of India's exports of agricultural products (US$ billion)

	2014	*2015*	*2016*	*2017*	*2018*
World	38.96	31.58	30.49	35.64	35.30
United States	4.62	3.53	3.53	4.64	4.61
Vietnam	4.35	3.45	3.89	5.15	3.85
UAE	2.04	2.00	2.19	2.11	2.04
Saudi Arabia	2.24	1.91	1.47	1.49	1.61
Iran	2.07	1.08	0.81	1.16	1.57
China	0.79	0.70	0.64	0.77	1.23
Bangladesh	1.44	0.77	0.43	0.89	0.94
Nepal	0.64	0.55	0.72	0.82	0.89
Malaysia	1.07	1.04	0.89	0.88	0.86
Indonesia	0.85	0.40	0.60	0.54	0.84

Source: UN COMTRADE (United Nations International Trade Statistics Database).

Table 15.2 Key destination of India's imports of agricultural products (US$ billion)

	2014	*2015*	*2016*	*2017*	*2018*
World	19.420	20.923	22.093	25.211	19.736
Indonesia	4.289	3.968	3.947	5.472	4.076
Ukraine	1.559	1.333	1.641	2.483	1.910
Argentina	1.578	2.025	2.477	2.344	1.647
Malaysia	2.620	2.439	2.044	1.584	1.434
United States	0.956	1.098	1.172	1.364	1.423
Brazil	0.955	1.122	1.501	1.494	1.176
Singapore	0.082	0.066	0.068	0.075	0.485
Afghanistan	0.241	0.316	0.282	0.413	0.419
Malaysia	0.195	0.128	0.115	0.250	0.405
Indonesia	0.190	0.121	0.102	0.189	0.290

Source: UN COMTRADE (United Nations International Trade Statistics Database).

export and import destinations of Indian agricultural products. The United States, Vietnam and the United Arab Emirates are the top three export destinations, and Indonesia, Ukraine and Argentina are three economies from which India imports agricultural products. The world totals show clearly that India has been a net agriculture-exporting economy.

Integration of agriculture, allied and food-processing exports into global value chains

The magnitude of the integration of primary and processed agricultural exports from India into global value chains is estimated using an input–output analysis. As discussed, Leontief introduced this economic tool on an assumption of a fixed-coefficient linear production function, relating inputs used by an industry along each column to its output flow. The fixed-coefficient linear production function indicates that for one unit of an industry's output, a fixed amount of each kind of input is required. The matrix of technical coefficients A describes an economic sector's relation to other sectors. The matrix of technical coefficients is a matrix such that each column vector represents a different industry, and each corresponding row vector represents what that industry's inputs as a commodity into the column industry. The demand vector is represented by **F**, the amount of product consumers will need. Total production vector **X** represents the total production needed to meet the demand vector **F**. The total production vector **X** is explained as follows.

At the outset, we calculated India's technological matrix for the years 2000, 2007 and 2014 based on the National Input Output Database to decipher the domestic value addition of agriculture commodities. Of the 56 sectors in the database, we filtered five sectors that pertain to agriculture and allied activities. As shown in Table 15.3, these five sectors juxtapose broadly with HS ITC chapters 1–24 on trade in agriculture and food products. All the

Table 15.3 India's technology matrix as per NIOD, 2000 and 2014

Row/Column	*Primary agriculture activities*	*Forestry and logging*	*Fishing and aquaculture*	*Mining and quarrying*	*Manufacture of processed food and beverages*
Primary agricultural activities: 2000	0.1685	0.00010	0.00005	0.00002	0.3892
Forestry and logging: 2000	0.00004	0.00341	0.00	0.00	0.00185
Fishing and aquaculture: 2000	0.00	0.00	0.00919	0.00	0.01711
Mining and quarrying: 2000	0.00	0.00	0.00000	0.00180	0.00019
Manufacture of processed food and beverages: 2000	0.00609	0.00003	0.00172	0.00040	0.10907
Primary agricultural activities: 2014	0.12974	0.0003	0.0013	0.0000	0.3195
Forestry and logging: 2014	0	0.00119	0	0	0.00132
Fishing and aquaculture:2014	0	0	0.00352	0	0.01624
Mining and quarrying:2014	0	0	0	0.00219	0.00024
Manufacture of processed food and beverages: 2014	0.00726	0	0.00083	0.00043	0.1313

Source: National Input Output Database (NIOD) from the World Input–Output Database (WIOD).

processed (high-value) products are grouped into the fifth sector. According to the technological matrix, the intra-sectoral contribution (i.e., within the primary agricultural sector) is minimal and mostly work in isolation. During the 2000s, primary agriculture's contribution as an input into its own output was 16.85%. Agriculture's contribution to processed food and beverages was higher, at 38.92%, due to consumption of agricultural products as intermediate products for value addition. This indicates the food industry's backward production linkage with agriculture. The intra-industry linkage—the food industry using its own processed products for further value addition, or secondary processing—was again modest, at 10.9%.

Estimates for 2014 show some change in the technology matrix's structure. Primary agriculture's contribution as an input into its own output fell to 12.9% in 2014 from 16.8% in 2000. Agriculture's contribution to processed food and beverages also fell, to 31.9%. The only improvement was in processed food and beverages' contribution to its own output, increasing from 10.9% in 2000 to 13.13% in 2014. We also find no significant linkages between primary economic agricultural activities and allied activities, namely forestry, fishing and mining. The backward production linkage of the food and beverage industry with agriculture has been modest, and the magnitude of intra-industry linkage has increased, which may be explained by the stagnating growth rate of agriculture and allied activities of 3% to 4% per year, compared to the relatively higher and increasing growth rate in the processed food industry.

We now turn to gauge India's Leontief inverse coefficients within agriculture and allied sectors. The Leontief inverse matrix $(I–A)^{-1}$ provides a set of disaggregated multipliers that are recognized as more precise and sensitive than Keynesian multipliers for studies of detailed economic impacts. The Leontief inverse matrix—a multiplier matrix—takes into account that the total effect on output will vary, depending on which sectors are affected by changes in final demand. The total output multiplier for a sector measures the sum of direct and indirect inputs needed from all sectors to fulfill a given sector's final demand requirements. Therefore, once the initial change in final demand is known, the values of all inputs and outputs needed to fulfill it can be determined.

As shown in Table 15.4, during 2000 and 2014, the output multipliers of direct input required were moderate for primary agriculture, at 1.21 and 1.155 and, for processed food and beverages, at 1.129 and 1.158. The output multipliers of indirect requirements were nearly zero for almost all the sectors within agriculture, except for the output multiplier in processed food provided by primary agriculture. We find hardly any structural change in the output multipliers during this period. In fact, the size of direct output multipliers decreased in all four sectors under the primary activities. The only exception was in processed food and beverages, where values increased marginally, from 1.1288 to

Table 15.4 Leontief inverse coefficient, 2000 and 2014

Row/column	*Primary agricultural activities*	*Forestry and logging*	*Fishing and aquaculture*	*Mining and quarrying*	*Manufacture of processed food and beverages*
Primary agricultural activities: 2000	1.2101	0.0034	0.0033	0.0045	0.5344
Forestry and logging: 2000	0.0007	1.0038	0.0002	0.0015	0.0062
Fishing and aquaculture: 2000	0.0001	0.0000	1.0093	0.0000	0.0195
Mining and quarrying: 2000	0.0059	0.0025	0.0019	1.0117	0.0115
Manufacture of processed food and beverages: 2000	0.0099	0.0011	0.0022	0.0022	1.1288
Primary agricultural activities: 2014	1.1552	0.00162	0.00115	0.00383	0.43047
Forestry and logging: 2014	0.00052	1.00137	6.49E-05	0.00119	0.00494
Fishing and aquaculture: 2014	0.00021	2.25E-05	1.00355	6.73E-05	0.01892
Mining and quarrying:2014	0.00314	0.00073	0.00040	1.00804	0.00675
Manufacture of processed food and beverages: 2014	0.01135	0.00079	0.00108	0.00262	1.15811

Source: Author's calculations based on the World Input–Output Database (WIOD).

1.1581. This implies that the additional effect of the multiplier resulting from direct input will be 0.03. The values closer to zero multipliers indicate a minimal possibility of establishing domestic value chains. This also means that the domestic primary activities are not strongly linked in terms of creating domestic value addition for final consumption. The size of the output multiplier of indirect agriculture inputs provided to the processed food and beverage sector declined by 20% between 2000 and 2014. This is a positive signal explaining why the composition of the value addition to processed food and beverage increased and the weighting of primary commodities decreased relatively, albeit at a slow pace.

These findings validate Ghosh (2014) and Bathla and Gautam (2018) on an increasing yet low (less than 15%) magnitude of the processing of agriculture produce in the food and beverage industry. The backward production linkages and the intra-industry linkages, though increasing, are also on the lower side. Further, services related to crop production make minimal contributions to the allied activities of forestry and logging, fishing and mining. The services' contribution to processed food products is also negligible. Allied activities tend to work in isolation, indicating the absence of value addition—that is, little movement of a product into other sectors. This could be one reason behind processed products' low share of total agricultural exports, as analyzed earlier. The implication is clear that India's growing food and beverage industry is fulfilling the domestic demand adequately.

Table 15.5 presents estimates of domestic value addition and integration of India's primary agricultural activities, allied activities and processed agricultural exports into global value chains during 2000 and 2014. A surge in domestic value addition is visible in every sector except fishing and aquaculture. For instance, during 2014, the domestic value addition of primary agricultural

Table 15.5 Domestic value addition of India's agriculture exports and integration into GVCs, 2000 and 2014

Sectors	*Domestic value addition US$, in 2000 (US$ million)*	*Domestic value addition US$, in 2014 (US$ million)*	*CAGR in domestic value addition from 2000 to 2014 (%)*
Primary agriculture activities	109,496 (7.1%)	132,288 (5.1%)	1.36
Forestry and logging	7,106 (0.51%)	11,800 (0.4%)	3.69
Fishing and aquaculture	4,238 (0.9%)	3,124 (1.3%)	−2.16
Mining and quarrying	6,887 (1.1%)	30,088 (3.3%)	11.11
Manufacture of processed food and beverages	35,514 (1.1%)	42,691 (1.6%)	1.32

Source: Author's calculation using the World Input–Output Database (WIOD); figures in brackets indicate integration of the respective sector into GVCs.

products was much higher, at US$ 132.28 billion, than that of processed/value-added products, at US$ 42.69 billion. Clearly, India's position in processed products is low under global value chains. For fishing and aquaculture, domestic value addition is just over US$ 3 billion. Primary agricultural exports, estimated at US$ 132.28 billion, are being used as end products and hardly go through value chains.

The integration of primary agriculture into global value chains was estimated at 5.1% in 2014, down 2 percentage points from 7.1% in 2000.

A decline in agriculture's contribution to global value chain can be explained by the fact that the non-agricultural sector (manufacturing and services) is growing at a significantly higher rate than agriculture, thus making the denominator component (the growth rate of overall GDP) higher than the numerator. The linkage of processed food and beverages with global value chains is less than 2%. Similarly, for the other three segments—mining, forestry, fishing—the estimates are low and varied, at 3.3%, 0.4% and 1.3%, respectively. Another observation is that domestic value addition in primary agriculture and in processed food exports grew marginally, at 1.3% per year, in the final demand generated. The highest growth rate in domestic value addition is observed in mining and quarrying, at 11%. These estimates differ slightly from those obtained in TiVA (Trade in Value-Added, 2018), perhaps due to different time periods and databases used.

Recognizing that the United States is India's largest agricultural trade partner, we illustrate whether there is any foreign value addition of agriculture and processed exports. From Leontief, inverse figures furnished in Tables 15.6 and 15.7, we find no processing or value addition, as the diagonal values in

Table 15.6 Leontief inverse coefficient of India's agriculture and allied exports to the United States, 2014

Row/column	*Primary agriculture activities*	*Forestry and logging*	*Fishing and aquaculture*	*Mining and quarrying*	*Manufacture of processed food-beverages*
Primary agriculture activities	1.0001	0.0000	0.0000	0.0000	0.0002
Forestry and logging	0.0002	1.0004	0.0004	0.0000	0.0000
Fishing and aquaculture	0.0001	0.0002	1.0000	0.0000	0.0000
Mining and quarrying	0.0000	0.0000	0.0000	1.0000	0.0000
Manufacture of processed food and beverages	0.0001	0.0000	0.0000	0.0000	1.0003

Source: Author's calculation using the World Input–Output Database (WIOD).

Table 15.7 Value addition of India's agriculture inputs in United States, 2014

Sectors	*India's agriculture value addition in United State's final demand (US$ million)*
Primary agriculture	421.10
Forestry and logging	32.55
Fishing and aquaculture	1.26
Mining and quarrying	27.53
Manufacture of processed food-beverages	915.43

Source: Author's calculation using the World Input–Output Database (WIOD).

the matrix are either 1 or just over 1 and the non-diagonal values are close to zero. In other words, agricultural products that India exports to the United States are used for final consumption, signaling a negligible foreign value addition component. Similarly, the Leontief inverse of India's agricultural inputs exported to the United States suggests a zero-output multiplier for indirect input required, which simply indicates their negligible value addition in the United States.

Conclusions and implications

Integrating economic sectors in value chains can accelerate economic growth and exports and generate employment. This chapter estimated India's integration of agriculture, allied activities (mining, fishery and forestry) and processed food and beverages into final domestic consumption and exports during 2000 and 2014. Using data from the UN COMTRADE (United Nations International Trade Statistics Database), the analysis reveals a steady increase in agricultural exports from India, with the share of primary agricultural products being much higher than the share of high value-added (processed) agricultural products. India has been a net exporter of agriculture products, and the structure and composition of its exports and imports have changed little. The input–output analysis based on the WIOD database shows that domestic value addition of agricultural commodities for final demand remains low and stagnant. That is, the processing industry's backward production linkages with agriculture are modest, at around 31.9%, whereas intra-industry linkages have grown steadily. Domestic value addition of primary agriculture for domestic consumption moved at a snail's pace (1.32%) annually from 2000 to 2014.

As of now, there is little integration of India's agriculture, allied sectors and processed food exports into global value chains. The integration of primary agricultural exports into global value chains is estimated at 5.1%, and that of processed food and beverages is a little less than 2%. From the Leontief inverse matrix, we found little structural change in the output multipliers. The estimated values are closer to zero multipliers, indicating a minimal possibility of establishing domestic value chains. In the context of agricultural exports to the United States, India's main export destination, the value of multipliers in foreign value addition are almost zero, signaling that India's agricultural products are used for final consumption and not for value addition in the United States. This is not an encouraging signal as it may prevent India from participating in the upstream activities of agriculture.

These findings have implications for the growth of India's agriculture and processed food and beverage enterprises. The government should accelerate the pace of reforms in agriculture, including public investment to provide impetus to private investment and to gain from the growing world trade in agriculture. Lessening a protectionist structure and improving transportation, marketing and communication infrastructures can address the disadvantage of a remote location. Similarly, the processed food industry, though on a high growth path, has to be globally competitive. Liberalizing domestic markets, negotiating trade in the global markets and participating in deep integration agreements, including technical and financial assistance, can help firms compete. Attracting foreign direct investment can overcome the scarcity of capital and technology in this industry. Finally, greater emphasis has to be put on a wide range of specific activities within the processing segment to gain from the value chain. These include developing and disseminating plant and animal genetic material; improving technologies in production, post-harvest handling, cooling, storing, packing, grading criteria and facilities; and upgrading food quality and standards.

Notes

1 As per the Uruguy Round Agreement on Agriculture, subsidies under the amber box includes measures to support prices directly related to production quantities, subject to *de minimis* (generally 5% of agriculture production for developed countries and 10% for the developing countries). Member countries qualify for green box subsidies if not trade distorting or at most cause minimal distortion. They have to be government funded (not by charging consumers higher prices) and must not involve price support. The blue box subsidies are linked to one product but do not increase according to the production levels. This includes aid that is linked to production limitation programmes and calculated according to the fixed production data from an earlier period.

2 India's foreign value-added content in exports of primary agriculture, processed food and textiles remained sluggish at 3.7%, 7.8% and 17%, respectively, from 2005 to 2015 (TiVA, 2018). As such, TiVA addresses double-counting implicit in the current gross trade data by measuring flows in terms of value added by a country in production of goods and services. The process of estimating TiVA consists of two stages; the first stage is to construct an international/regional input–output table (IOT), which in itself requires several steps, significant amounts of data and making some assumptions.

3 The use of WIOD has an advantage. The series is available from 1995 for 43 countries and 56 economic sectors. It uses supply-use tables (SUT) from individual countries' national accounts as the starting point to integrate with bilateral trade statistics and derive a final symmetric world I-O table (WIOT), covering 27 EU members and 16 other major economies (Timmer et al., 2012). Intuitively, this approach links trade statistics (which are product-based) with product statistics on one hand and value-added/employment data

(which are industry-based) with industry statistics on the other hand. It also avoids errors inherent in the assumptions imposed when transferring SUTs to symmetric I-O tables before the reconciliation process even starts.

4 See among others, Gereffi and Fernandez-Stark (2011), Koopman et al. (2011), Timmer et al. (2014), Baldwin (2012). A few highlighted that the pace of increment is exponential and not linear or constant.

References

Aksoy, M.A., and J.C. Beghin. 2005. *Global agricultural trade and developing countries*. Washington, DC, The World Bank.

Baldwin, R. 2012. "Global supply chains: Why they emerged, why they matter, and where they are going?" CEPR Discussion Paper No. 9103, August.

Banga, K. 2016. "Impact of global value chains on employment in India." *Journal of Economic Integration* 31(3): 631–673.

Banga, R. 2014 "Linking into global value chains is not sufficient: Do you export domestic value-added contents?" *Journal of Economic Integration*: 267–297.

Bathla, S., and M. Gautam. 2018. "Size and nature of post-harvest food management and agribusiness sectors in India." Report submitted to the World Bank.

Bathla, S., and E. Kannan (ed.). 2021. *Agro and food processing industry in India: Inter-sectoral linkages, employment, productivity and competitiveness*. Singapore, Springer Nature.

Bosworth, M. 1999. "Non-tariff measures as trade barriers – yesterday's problem or what?" Paper presented at the OECD Workshop with Non-member Economies on Barriers to Trade in Goods and Services in the Post-Uruguay Round Context, Paris, 27–28 September 1999.

Cattaneo, O., G. Gereffi, S. Miroudot, and D. Taglioni. 2013. *Joining, upgrading and being competitive in global value chains: A strategic framework*. World Bank Policy Research Working Paper 6406. Washington, DC, The World Bank.

Gereffi, G., and K. Fernandez-Stark. 2011. *Global value chain analysis: A primer center on globalization, governance & competitiveness (CGGC)*. North Carolina, NC, Duke University.

Ghosh, N. 2014. "An assessment of the extent of food processing in various food sub-sectors." Report submitted to the Ministry of Agriculture and Farmers Welfare, GOI.

Hummels, D., J. Ishii, and K.-M. Yi. 2001. "The nature and growth of vertical specialization in world trade." *Journal of International Economics* 54(1), 75–96.

Koopman, Robert, William Powers, Zhi Wang, and Shang-Jin Wei. 2011. "Giving credit where credit is due: Tracing value added in global production chains." NBER working paper number 16426, Revised. www.nber.org/papers/w16426.

Levchenko, Andrei A. 2007. "Institutional quality and international trade." *The Review of Economic Studies* 74(3), July, 791–819.

Lodefalk, M. 2015. "Servicification of manufacturing firms makes divides in trade policy-making antiquated." Örbero University Working Paper 1/2015.

Nag, B. 2019. "Saon Ray and Smita Miglani: Global value chains and the missing links: Cases from Indian industry". *Indian Economic Review*, 54, 367–370. https://doi.org/10.1007/s41775-019-00058-1.

OECD. 2013. *Interconnected economies: Benefiting from global value chains*. Paris: OECD Publishing. http://dx.doi.org/10.1787/9789264189560-en.

OECD-WTO. 2012. "Trade in value-added: Concept, methodologies and challenges." Joint OCED-WTO note. www.oecd.org/sti/ind/49894138.pdf.

Raju, S. 2014. *Global value chains and Indian food sector: A preliminary analysis of issues and options*, W.P. No: EC-14–23. New Delhi: Indian Institute of Foreign Trade, July.

Sharma, Vijay Paul, and Ashok Gulati. 2003. "Trade liberalization, market reforms and competitiveness of the Indian dairy sector." MTID Discussion Paper No. 61, Markets, Trade and Institutions Division, International Food Policy Research Institute, Washington, DC. April 2003.

Sharma, S.K. 2016. *The WTO and food security: Implications for developing countries*. New Yok: Springer Publication.

Timmer, Marcel P. (ed.). 2012. "The world input–output database (WIOD): Contents, sources and methods." WIOD working paper number 10. www.wiod.org/publications/source_docs/WIOD_sources.pdf.

Timmer, Marcel P., Abdul Azeez Erumban, Bart Los, Robert Stehrer, and Gaaitzen J. de Vries. 2014. "Slicing up global value chains." *Journal of Economic Perspectives*, 28(2), 99–118.

Timmer, Marcel P., Bart Los, Robert Stehrer, and Gaaitzen de Vries. 2012. "Fragmentation, incomes, and jobs: An analysis of European competitiveness." WIOD Working Paper No. 9. www.wiod.org/publications/papers/wiod9.pdf

Trade in Value Added (TiVA). 2018. *The changing nature of international production: Insights from trade in value added and related indicators*. Paris, OECD.

United Nations Conference on Trade and Development (UNCTAD). 2013. *Global value chains and development*. New York and Geneva, United Nations. https://unctad.org/system/files/official-document/diae2013d1_en.pdf.

UNIDO. 2009. "Agro-value chain analysis and development: The approach." A staff Working Paper, 2009. www.unido.org/sites/default/files/2010-02/Agro_value_chain_analysis_and_development_0.pdf.

16 Harvesting the booming potential

The case of the maize value chain in Pakistan

Akhter Ali and Muhammad Umer Afzal

Agriculture, industry and commerce are the crucial sector for any country's economy—the progress of one sector affects growth in another sector. Pakistan is an agricultural country, and agricultural gains are important to feeding people, providing raw materials for industry and forming a base for foreign trade. In Pakistan, maize contributes 2.4% to value-added in agriculture and 0.5% to overall GDP. Maize is one of Pakistan's major crops, along with wheat, cotton, rice and sugar cane, and is gaining an important position because of its higher yield potential and short growth duration. In Pakistan, about 50% of the maize varieties have originated from International Maize and Wheat Improvement Center (CIMMYT) germplasm.

Maize is the third-largest crop grown in Pakistan, after wheat and rice, and has a variety of uses. Maize grain is a rich source of starch, vitamins, proteins and minerals. One hundred grams of fresh maize grains deliver 361 calories of energy, 9.4 g of protein, 74.4 g of carbohydrates, a small amount of fiber, 140 vitamins, calcium, phosphorus and traces of iron. In its green state, maize can be dried, baked, roasted, boiled or steamed on the cob. Maize flour has a very mild flavor and is used for making bread and as a thickening agent in foods such as custards and jellies. Popcorn is kernels of a particular maize that burst when heated, forming fluffy pieces that are eaten as a snack.

Pakistan's maize industry faces significant challenges: weak extension services, enormous post-harvest losses, inadequate infrastructure and a lack of private-sector quality controls. The rising global demand for maize as a raw material for feed milling or as a finished product for animal feed offers Pakistan a good opportunity to export to regional markets. Development of Pakistan's agricultural sector in general and its maize industry in particular will require significant reforms in the purchasing regime and the deployment of best practices at all points along the value chain. Demand for locally produced maize is expected to increase, due in part to feed mills supplying the poultry and other livestock industries.

Most of Pakistan's commercial maize is irrigated, but the industry's production is inferior to that of Asian competitors such as Thailand, whose yields are consistently more than 13 tons/ha. Pakistan's national yield has averaged 4.7

tons/ha for the last five years, but it is increasing because of higher-yielding hybrid seed. Yields are higher in Punjab province, followed by Khyber Pakhtunkhwa (KP) and other provinces. In Pakistan, 99% of the maize is produced in two provinces: Punjab and Khyber Pakhtunkhwa. Over the last few years, the area and production of maize are increasing in Punjab province but are decreasing in KP province. Sindh and Baluchistan provinces are virgin lands for maize production and hence offer a lot of promise.

This chapter's primary purpose is to assess the role of actors in Pakistan's maize value chain and how these actors can contribute to enhancing and strengthening the value chain business. The value chain is a set of linked activities that create and build value at every step. In Pakistan, the key actors in the maize value chain include producers, consumers and intermediaries, or the brokers who act as a connecting element between producers and maize processors. These actors can be categorized into three groups: production, marketing and processing. The production group comprises seed companies and farmers. International seed companies import hybrid seed, and the farmers prefer their seed as compared to locally produced seeds. However, local seed companies are trying to produce local maize hybrid seed, and they are succeeding in capturing the market to some extent. Still, locally producing maize hybrids in Pakistan will take time.

The marketing group consists of brokers, intermediaries, grain dealers, seed dealers, wholesalers and so on. The processing group consists of poultry feed mills, processors of maize-derived products, general grit mills (which produce maize flour) and silage producers. The government's role in the maize value chain is negligible compared to its role in the wheat value chain, where the government is involved as a trader, storage operator, supplier to flour mills and decision maker on support prices Grant et al. (2012); Kapuya et al. (2010); Sharan (2013); Tchale and Keyser (2010); Kausar and Alam (2016); Rashid et al. (2010); Wilson and Lewis (2015).

The maize value chain in Pakistan is not complicated, as direct consumption of maize is minimal in Pakistan. The maize value chain consists mainly of the following actors: seed companies, dealers, producers, maize processors and consumers. This chapter documents various stakeholders' roles in the maize value chain and how it can be strengthened.

Methodology

This study uses cross-sectional data. A detailed questionnaire was designed for each stakeholder. The data were collected from the seven maize-producing districts of Pakistan, which included 126 respondents from areas of mixed-cropping zones. The survey instrument underwent a pilot test to ensure that questions captured the study's core elements. Based on results of the pilot test, the survey instruments were refined. Details regarding data collection are presented in Table 16.1.

Table 16.1 Sampling details of various stakeholders

Stakeholder	*Sample size*
Dealers	16
Producers	52
Consumers	41
Poultry feed mill	2
Silage	3
Maize oil	1
Miller/*chakki*	3
Seed companies	8

Source: Authors' calculations.

Empirical results

The prices of maize hybrids in Pakistan are among the highest in the world, at $7 to $8 US$/kg. Multinational seed companies import mostly hybrid seed, and production of local hybrids is limited. The costly hybrids are mostly unaffordable to small farmers, and this is a major impediment to increasing maize yield. Local production of maize hybrid seed will lower seed prices and the overall cost of production for farmers. In Pakistan, during the past 20 years, maize research programs have been strengthened at the provincial and federal levels. The research infrastructure at the provincial maize experiment stations has improved greatly. Today, a viable maize research institute is in place in Yousafwala (Sahiwal District), Pirsabak (Nowshera) and National Agricultural Research Center (NARC) (Islamabad). Partial research activities also are carried out when and where needed, as in Ayub Agricultural Research Institute (AARI) (Faisalabad District), Azad Jammu and Kashmir (AJK) and Bhalwal (Sargodha District).

Maize producers

Maize farmers in Pakistan have mostly less education levels and lack information about the latest technology. Maize producers can be categorized into two categories: those who sell products in the local market and those who sell to their local maize industry. A team of well trained enumerators collected data from 52 maize farmers. About 79% of the farmers were producing the maize hybrids, and 21% were producing the open pollinated varieties (OPV) varieties. The data were collected from seven maize-producing districts, including Sahiwal, Pakpatan, Chinniot, Multan, Faisalabad, Sargodha and Toba Tek Singh.

The respondents' mean age was 42, their mean education was seven years of schooling, and their mean experience in farming was 17 years. About 44% of the farmers were owners, and the rest were tenants and owner cum tenants. The farmers owned an average of 19.3 acres of land. The farmers obtained seed for OPV varieties mostly from fellow farmers, dealers and their own seed, and they

Table 16.2 Maize production and sale (mean at household level, kg)

Mean value in kg	*OPV*	*Hybrids*
Total production	7,104	68,532
Domestic consumption	124	28
Seed	344	0.00
Sold in market	6,736	63,380
Animal feed	88	120

Source: Authors' calculations.

purchased hybrid seed mainly from dealers and seed companies. Prices of OPV and hybrid seeds differ greatly. The OPV seed is mostly broadcasted, and the hybrid seed is sown by hand. Table 16.2 presents details about maize production and the sale of OPV varieties and hybrids. It shows there is a huge difference in the total maize production and domestic consumption of OPV varieties.

In the study area, some farmers also sold maize as silage. Cultivating maize as a silage crop is helpful for farmers who want to reduce costs and save time. For silage, making the harvesting time is shifted to the maize milking stage, and the whole crop is harvested by machine and packed in bags. It saves threshing costs and enables the farmers to produce three crops in a year. The total cost of production for silage was calculated as 35,082 Pakistani Rupees (PKR) per acre. The total revenue was 63,000 PKR/acre, and the total profit was 27,918 PKR/acre. Figure 16.1 compares profits and revenue of different hybrid crops. The data show that, among hybrid maize cultivation, silage maize generates the least profit (27,918 PKR/acre). Profits increase for summer hybrids, to 327,030 PKR/acre. Maize grown in the spring generates a profit of 52,476 PKR/acre, which is almost double the profit generated by maize grown as silage.

Seed companies

In Pakistan, many local and multinational seed companies deal with hybrid maize seed. During the early 1990s, a few multinational seed companies started to produce hybrid maize seed, but due to a lack of intellectual property rights protection in Pakistan for their inbred lines, the companies could not develop their seed production locally. As a result, Pakistan must import more than 80% of its maize seed from other countries. Pioneer, Syngenta, Monsanto, ICI and a few more seed companies import and sell their seed in Pakistan. The seed companies sampled had operated in Pakistan for a mean of 15 years. Half of the seed companies have business networks across the country. The main crops with which the seed companies deal include wheat, cotton, rice, maize and sorghum. The seed companies were asked about maize seed as a share of their seed business. Wheat accounted for the largest share of the seed business, at 38%; cotton, 25%; maize, 19%; rice, slightly more than 10%; and sorghum, 7%, as presented in Figure 16.2.

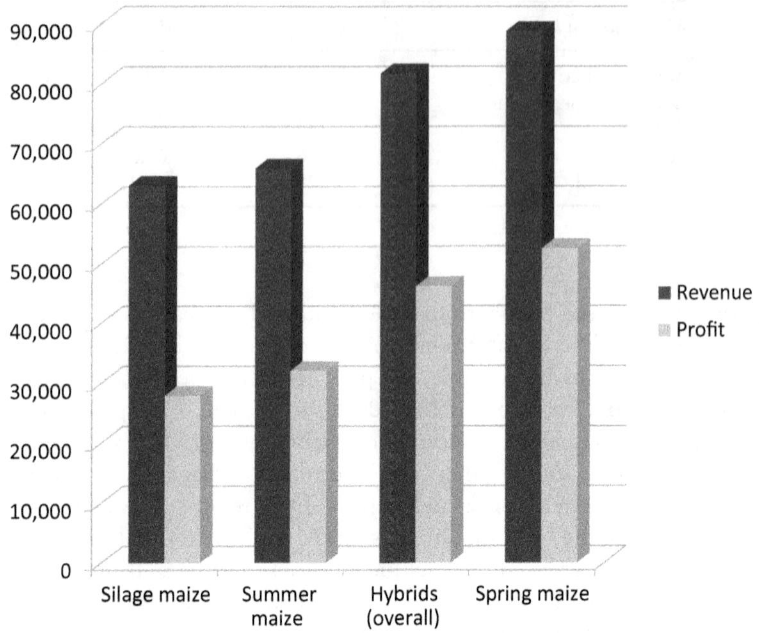

Figure 16.1 Comparison of the profits of the maize hybrids

Source: Authors' calculations.

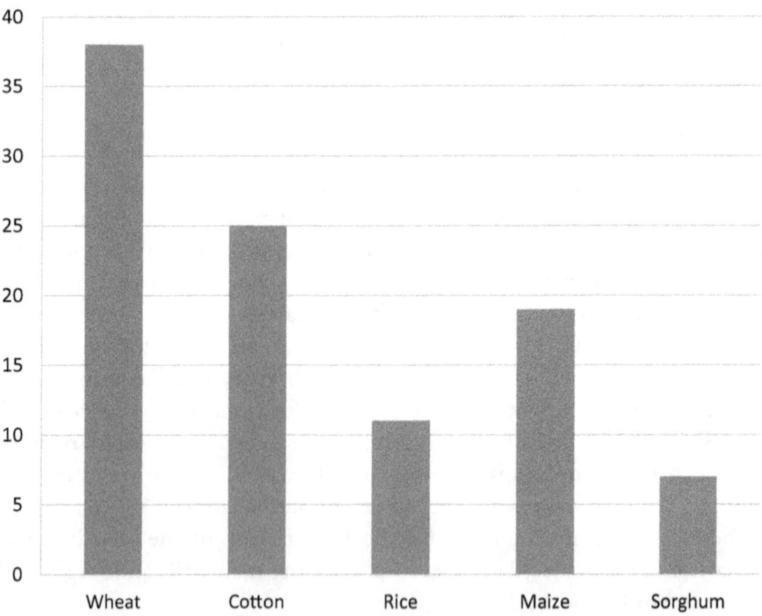

Figure 16.2 Percentage share of crops in company's seed business.

Source: Authors' calculations.

Respondents also were asked about maize crop seeds as a share of their overall seed business. One of the eight seed companies surveyed reported maize crops accounted for up to 30% of its business. However, five of seed companies confirmed that the maize crop's share of their seed business was 30% to 60%. Over time, hybrid maize seed is becoming more popular. According to the data, four of the seed companies produced only hybrid maize seed, and three seed companies produced both OPV and hybrid maize seed. Only one seed company produced and marketed OPV maize seed. About six of the seed companies reported an increasing trend in the maize seed business, and two seed companies reported a decreasing trend. About 6% of the seed was lost during maize seed processing, and minimizing these losses would mean that a considerable portion of the maize seed can be saved.

Seed and grain dealers

There are mostly three types of dealers: maize seed dealers, maize grain dealers and those who deal in both maize grain and seed. Seed dealers are the intermediaries who procure hybrid maize seed from seed companies and sell it to growers. These dealers also purchase OPV maize seed from seed companies, progressive farmers and fellow dealers, depending upon the demand for and supply of maize seed in the market. Whatever the type of seed procured, after taking their commission, the dealer sells it to maize producers. Maize grain dealers usually purchase the grain from producers at low prices just after harvest, store it for some time and then sell it to processors and feed millers after taking their profit. Information was collected from 16 dealers from different districts (Sahiwal, Sargodha, Khanewal, Pakpatan, Okara and Toba Tek Singh). Seven of the dealers were wholesalers, and the rest were retailers, commission agents etc. The dealers mainly dealt with various types of crop seeds and grains. Six of the dealers said maize's share of their business ranges from 25% to 50%, and another six reported maize's shares at 50% to 75%.

The seed dealers marketed both certified and uncertified maize seeds, with seven seed dealers reporting that they sold certified maize seed. According to seed dealers over the years, the trend for the maize seed dealers is increasing, mainly due to an increase in area devoted to maize. The dealers perform a series of activities (grading, sorting, cleaning, packaging, storage and transportation) to improve seed and grain quality. Dealers reported that they must face delays of 10 to 15 days in the payment from the farmers. The dealers were found purchasing maize grains from farmers at their farm-gate level, and there is a difference in prices offered by the dealers. Almost 40% of maize grains dealers were buying maize from farm-gate. According to 70% of the dealers, they provided a lower price for maize grains buying from farm-gate level as compared to market. All the seed dealers have storage facilities, and they store the maize seeds on a scientific standard. About 15 dealers reported having storage facilities for maize grains, and about 12 seed grain dealers store maize grains on a scientific basis. Eight of the dealers who deal with both maize grains and maize seeds keep their maize storage facilities on an experimental basis.

The dealers store maize seeds and grains for six months to obtain higher profits. Maize seed dealers noted their storage capacity was an average of 9.3 tons, and maize grain dealers had much higher storage capacity, at 33.9 tons. Sales and purchase of maize grains and maize seeds require dealers to provide several facilities to the farmers, including transporting maize from the farms to the market, providing credit and providing input for cultivation. Four dealers extend loans to the farmers, and six dealers provide agricultural input to the farmers to cultivate the crops.

The provision of such facilities is not free. Dealers charged 9.3 PKR per 40 kg for transportation. Similarly, the premium on loans was reported as 11.3%, and the premium on agricultural input was reported at 8.5%. The role of the market committee is vital for a better business environment; all the seed dealers said they were satisfied with the committee's role. The 12 grain dealers (80%) were also satisfied. Most of the seed dealers said the government needs to encourage a better business environment to the dealers, including lower taxes, design and implementation of supportive agricultural policy, maize support prices and regulating the produce cutting by feed mills.

Almost four grain dealers reported problems of high moisture levels and fungus issues in maize seeds, and mixed dealers reported the small size of maize grains as a problem. About three seed dealers said they pay high transportation costs for maize. One grain dealer complained about the farmers' low rate of production. Late payments were an issue reported by two seed dealers and two grain dealers, respectively. Only two seed dealers said that farmers have a low level of awareness about maize cultivation. Five mixed dealers complained about maize quality at the time of purchase, and five dealers faced complaints from farmers regarding seed germination. Two seed and grain dealers have to face the issue of labor shortage and laborers' monopoly. Three seed dealers complained about seed companies marketing inferior maize seeds at lower prices, which also affects maize production in Pakistan.

Maize processors

Figure 16.3 reveals four types of maize processors in the maize value chain: poultry feed mills, silage, bakery products and corn oil. The survey team collected information from all these processors.

Poultry feed mills

The poultry industry uses about 70% of Pakistan's maize. The country has about 25,000 poultry farms, and the industry has a present turnover of about 700 billion PKR. The poultry industry is one of the most organized branches of Pakistan's agro-based sector and consumes more than 7 million metric tons of residues produced by the agricultural sector. Poultry meat accounts for 31% of the country's total meat production. Poultry contributed 1.4% of Pakistan's GDP in 2016–2017 and contributed 162.8 billion PKR, or 7.1%, in

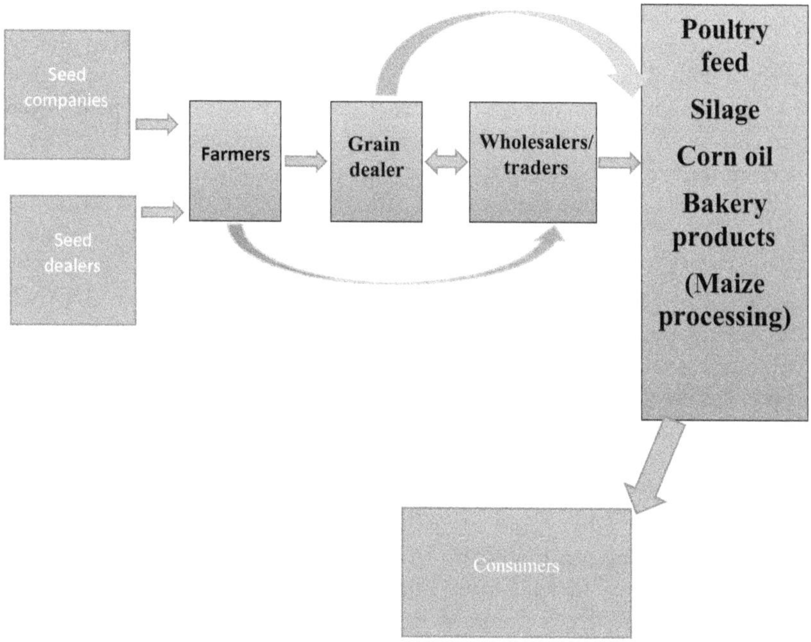

Figure 16.3 Maize value chain in Pakistan

Source: Authors.

agricultural value-added, compared to livestock's contribution of 12.2%. Its growth rate is 10%–12% annually. Pakistan produces 17.083 billion table eggs and 1.276 million kg of chicken meat annually. Pakistanis consume only 7 kg of meat and 60 eggs per capita per year, whereas people in the developed world consume 25–28 kg of meat and more than 300 eggs per capita per year. The poultry feed millers reported that only a few of their mills were working at optimum production levels. The mills' mean production capacity was 135 tons per day, but most were operating at a capacity of 95 tons per day. The main reasons for the underproduction of poultry feed were load shedding, the high prices of maize grains and non-supportive policies. The feed millers purchased almost 67% of their maize grains from wholesalers and the rest from farmers.

The feed millers have problems procuring maize from either farmers or wholesalers due to higher maize prices in the market. One feed miller said that the timely availability of maize grains was a general problem. One also reported that the transportation and storage of maize was a problem. The feed millers mentioned many problems in purchasing maize grains. High moisture content at the time of harvesting was the main problem, followed by mixed grains marketed by farmers and wholesalers. Both feed millers said the supply of maize grains was highly influenced by the season, with supply increasing in the spring and decreasing in the summer. Both also reported that OPV and hybrid maize produced the same quality of feeds. However, feed mills generally preferred hybrid maize for feed making, reporting that they had no preference for a specific maize variety and that they required only good-quality maize grains for better feed production. Regarding maize quality, both said they did not compromise on the quality of maize grains, selecting only those maize lots that fulfill their standard requirement. Aflatoxin is a considerable problem for the feed millers because it damaged the quality of the poultry feed produced. They said the acceptable level of Aflatoxin in maize stocks selected for purchase was up to 1.5%, and the ideal level of moisture in maize grains was 11.5%. One feed miller reported that there was no remedy to control Aflatoxin, and they have to reject maize lots having traces of it.

Feed millers said the maize crop is the main ingredient in the feed-making procedure. However, the percentage of maize grains used varies for different types of feeds. The feed millers also were asked about the main nutrients they incorporated for feed quality. One respondent reported that maize was incorporated, and other main ingredients included cereals, wheat bran, rice bran, oil cakes, bone meal, different minerals and enzymes in the ratio of 5.7% of each ingredient. The mills stored poultry feed for up to two weeks before marketing it, where it was stored by following scientific standards. The millers reported their storage capacity for feed averaged 825 tons. Poultry feed usually was marketed to four types of actors: wholesalers, small poultry farmers, large poultry farmers and retail shops. Feed millers said they marketed 33% of their poultry feed to wholesalers and 17% to small poultry farm owners or retailers. The poultry feed millers were asked about the seasonal impact on feed demand. One of the respondents said demand for poultry feed was influenced by season, and both feed millers reported that the demand for poultry feed was increasing with time. Asked whether they used alternate power sources, both millers said they used generators as an alternative source of power. Similarly, all of the respondents reported load shedding had severely affected their feed mills' efficiency. One feed miller reported that the load-shedding issue had changed the business.

Silage processors

In the silage making process, green feed or fodder is fermented using a type of bacteria that can survive without oxygen. The resulting feed is rendered tasty and easily digestible for animals. It is then packed airtight to preserve good quality. Silage depends on the timely harvesting of fodder, the quantity of air in it at the time of packing and the method of preservation. In this process, a useful bacterium converts soluble starches into lactic acid. It decreases its acidic quality (pH) to 3.0–4.0, which stops the growth of harmful germs and which makes the fodder safe for animal consumption. If the moisture content of hay is high, wheat straw or crushed maize cobs can be added to make silage. Steps for making silage involve selecting good-quality fodder (maize, oats, sorghum etc. usually are considered best), checking moisture, harvesting, chopping, pressing and storing.

On average the silage processors reported processing on 65 acres. The minimum processed acres were 40 and maximum processed acres were 80. The silage producers said they purchased maize from contract growers and open markets. The producers said that they bought 67% of their maize from general farmers and the rest 33% from contract growers. According to the data, slightly higher amounts (170 PKR/40 kg) are paid to contract growers than to general farmers (158 PKR/40 kg) for their product. The silage processors complained about damages due to insects and pests during storage and fungi infestation. One silage processor faced insect pests or fungal problems during storage. However, two silage processors faced the challenge of Aflatoxin.

Farmers using silage to feed their cows reported a considerable increase in milk production, but the timing of results varied. Two silage processors said their customers reported that their animals responded rapidly to the use of their silage, increasing the quantity of milk produced. One processor said its customers reported animals had a delayed response to the use of its silage. Animals also took some time to switch from fodder to silage—up to 15 days, according to the data. The silage processors sold their product mostly to dairy farms and wholesalers. Two silage processors market their produce to dairy farms, and one sells it to wholesalers. Of the silage sold to dairy farms, 67% goes to big dairies rather than to small dairy farms. According to the silage processors, the business is profitable, demand for silage is continuously increasing, and autumn is the best season for silage processing and marketing. Two silage processors were not satisfied with government policies, as the government provided no facilities or subsidies to promote silage production, which ultimately would increase milk production in Pakistan.

Maize-grinding mills

The milling portion of the maize processing industry might include business such as grinding mills, flour mills, feed mills and bakery product manufacturers or similar who use maize as an ingredient. The main activity in maize processing is grinding it into a maize meal. Milling can take place at small hammer mills, which process individuals' daily or weekly household maize needs, or at large rolling mills, which produce vast quantities of maize meal for commercial sale. This chapter includes details gathered from maize grinding mills operating at the village or neighborhood level and usually grinding maize for a service fee. Inhabitants of Punjab province occasionally consume maize flour. However, in Azad Jammu and Kashmir (AJK) and Gilgit Baltistan provinces, maize flour is the proper part of the inhabitant's diet. The maize millers were asked about the sources of their maize purchases. The price of maize ranged from 850 to 1,000 PKR during harvest season. The maximum amount was reported as 1,000 PKR per 40 kg.

The maize processors reported that they have no difficulty purchasing maize from farmers or wholesalers. However, two-thirds (67%) of maize processors said maize supplies vary with the season, increasing during the spring. Purchasing good-quality maize grains is necessary for better-quality maize flour. According to 43% maize processors, they properly checked the stock before buying, whereas 29% of them were either paying a high price for maize or buying fresh maize stock every month. The main maize products include maize flour, maize bran, maize porridge and Vanda (animal feed). The increased rate and prolonged duration of load shedding were affecting the business activities of maize millers. The maximum damage caused by the load shedding was reported up to 35%, and the average cost reported was 28%.

Oil extractor

During the survey, the team was able to interview only one maize oil extractor. In Pakistan maize oil is gaining popularity, but still majority of the population is using canola, sunflower and olive oil for cooking purposes. Maize oil extractors face a number of challenges including the entrance into the market. However, keeping the increasing demand in view, the opportunities are also many. The public sector needs to facilitate the maize oil sector to increase the local oil production to cut the import bill.

Consumers

In Pakistan, maize is not considered a crop for direct consumption. Only in the northern mountainous area, Azad Jammu and Kashmir (AJK) and Gilgit Baltistan (GB) is maize flour used as a staple food. Data were collected from 41 consumers in the Attock, Rawalpindi, Faisalabad, Mandi Bauhdin, Okara, Pakpatan, Sahiwal, Sargodha and Toba Tek Sindh Districts. Asked about the maize products they most consumed, consumers listed roasted maize grains, maize flour, maize porridge, maize bakery products, corn oil and other maize products in the form of canned maize or baby corn. Figure 16.4 shows the details of the amount of each product consumed. On average, the households consumed 2 kg of roasted maize grains, 2.6 kg of maize flour, 2.8 kg of maize porridge, 1.4 servings of bakery products, 3.5 L of corn oil and 1 kg of other processed maize products every month.

Asked about their average monthly expenditures on the different maize products, most consumers reported spending 224 PKR (1 US$ = 168 PKR) on roasted maize grains, 211 PKR on maize flour, 200 PKR on maize porridge, 513 PKR on maize bakery products and 114 PKR on other products or on maize in the form of canned maize or baby corn. The highest amount, 1,271 PKR per month, was reported spent on corn oil. The consumers were asked about the presence of small milling units in their area, and most reported having two to four small milling units in their area. They also reported that the cost of grinding maize was 96.3 PKR per 40 kg but that some milling units charged

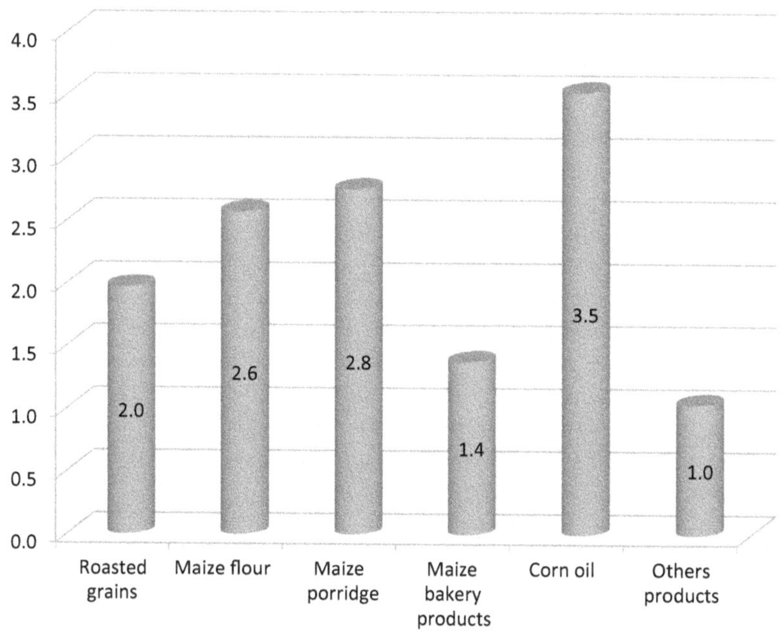

Figure 16.4 Average quantity of maize consumed (kg/month)

Source: Authors' calculations.

80 PKR per 40 kg. The exciting thing to be noted was that wheat milling units grind maize and sell it in the form of maize flour. Normally the wheat mills do not grind maize. Consumers were more concerned with the quality of processed maize products, including biscuits and flavored canned maize. Consumers said they face difficulties purchasing baby corn and canned maize products, as these products were not very common until recently and prices are high. Consumers also were concerned about the high price of corn oil compared to the price of other cooking oils and said the government should subsidize maize oil to make it accessible, as they considered it essential for human health.

Conclusions

The maize value chain actors are not well connected. The analysis of various scenarios indicates that cultivating maize as a silage crop is helpful for the farmers who want to save both production costs and time. Farmers prefer to buy maize seeds directly from seed companies, but the general farmer finds access to the seed company complicated and finds buying seeds in bulk quantity difficult. If this channel is developed, farmers will incur lower costs for quality seed. The revenue and profits for hybrid maize are double those of open pollinated maize due to better yield and resistance to diseases. However, due to higher prices of maize hybrids in Pakistan, the majority of the farmers are not able to buy costly hybrid seed. The local production of the maize hybrid can help to lower the hybrid prices. There can be up to 6% losses during seed processing. However, if these losses are minimized, then a considerable portion of maize seed can be saved. This would contribute to increased supplies of maize seed and eventually reduce the prices of hybrid maize seed in the local market. Most local seed companies are earning 350 PKR/ kg on hybrid maize seed, indicating much higher profit margins as compared to other businesses. The dealers perform several activities to improve seed and grain quality, such as grading, sorting, cleaning, packaging, storage and transportation. However, dealers acknowledge paying farmers lower prices. Though silage is a good business, two of the silage processors were not satisfied with government policies, as the government provided no facilities or subsidies to promote silage production and ultimately to increase milk production in Pakistan. The local production of hybrid maize seed also needs to be improved through an enabling business environment.

References

Grant, W., Wolfaardt, A. and Louw, A., 2012. *Technical Report: Maize Value Chain in the SADC Region*. USAID Southern Africa, Gaborone.

Kapuya, T., Saruchera, D., Jongwe, A., Mucheri, T., Mujeyi, K., Traub, L.N. and Meyer, F., 2010. *The Grain Industry Value Chain in Zimbabwe*. All Africa Commodities Programme, FAO, Rome, Italy.

Kausar, A.G. and Alam, M.J., 2016. Marketing Efficiency of Maize in Bangladesh. *Asian Journal of Agricultural Extension, Economics & Sociology* 11(2): 1–12.

Sharan, S., 2013. The India Maize Summit 2013, Agricultural Marketing Policy Roadmap. http://tvi.com.pk/new-high-yielding-maize-varieties-introduced-in-Pakistan/ Nov2015\www.dawn.com/news/236949.

Tchale, H. and Keyser, J., 2010. *Quantitative Value Chain Analysis: An Application to Malawi*. Policy Research Working Paper.

Rashid, S., Getnet, K. and Lemma, S., 2010. *Maize Value Chain Potential in Ethiopia: Constraints and Opportunities for Enhancing the System*. International Food Policy Research Institute Working Paper.

Wilson, R.T. and Lewis, J., 2015. *The Maize Value Chain in Tanzania, a Report from the Southern Highlands Food Systems Program*. Food and Agriculture Organization of the United Nations, Rome, Italy.

17 Storage and structural factors determining the commercialization of Indian agriculture

A. Ganesh-Kumar and Varun Kumar Das

Commercialization of agriculture, in which farmers produce and sell their output in the market, is expected to improve farmers' income and welfare. Commercialization of agriculture acquires importance in the context of the Government of India's policy of Doubling of Farmers' Income by the Year 2022. The Committee on Doubling Farmers' Income (Dalwai Committee Report—DCR, 2018) emphasizes the commercialization of agriculture for higher returns. It argues that commercialization provides signals on emerging trends in the demand for different agricultural products, helps in value addition for farm produce and thus ensures that both producers' and consumers' interests are satisfied. The report notes that market-linked farming and market expansion would help raise farmers' incomes. Policies such as recent Agricultural Produce Market Committee (APMC) Act amendments, National Agriculture Market (eNAM), public procurement through minimum support prices (MSP), market infrastructure development, direct purchase of agricultural produce from farmers, participatory market management, encouraging contract farming and so on are steps toward providing better marketing avenues for farmers (Singh, 2019).

Yet the fact is that a significant proportion of farmers in India do not participate in output markets and essentially operate as subsistence farmers, producing for their own consumption needs. Even when farmers decide to participate in output markets, their degree of market participation—the extent to which they are commercialized—varies substantially. The degree of farmers' market participation and the extent of their commercialization can be assessed in at least three dimensions: the number of products they offer for sale, the number of market transactions they undertake and the diversity of agencies (marketing channels) with which they transact. Regarding the first dimension of market participation, many farmers in India grow one or more primary crop(s) for sale in the market and at the same time cultivate another subsidiary crop(s) exclusively for household consumption. A measure of this dimension is the ratio of the number of crops sold to the number of crops cultivated. The closer this ratio is to 1, the greater the extent of the farmer's commercialization.

Regarding the second dimension of market participation, farmers rarely sell their produce in a single transaction; instead, they engage in multiple or staggered sales. For example, a farmer may sell half the crop at harvest time and save the rest to sell later. As such, the number of market transactions that farmers in India undertake in a particular product is another indicator of the extent to which they are commercialized. The higher this number, the greater the extent of the farmer's commercialization. This number could depend on several factors, including the nature of marketing institutions and infrastructure, prevailing market conditions and the farmer's ability to hold on to stocks and not be forced into a distress sale.

The third dimension of market participation is the diversity of agency or marketing channels through which farmers can sell their produce. Farmers in India have the option of selling their products through several agencies, such as local private traders, *mandis*, a market place where sellers and buyers meet, input dealers, co-operative/government agencies and processors. In principle, a farmer can engage in transactions with one or more of these agencies. Nevertheless, farmers often use only one or a few of these agencies for their sale transactions. It is argued that farmers in India are often at a disadvantage due to interlinked input and output markets (Bardhan, 1980; Basu, 1986; Bell and Srinivasan, 1989). That is, the farmers' choice of output marketing channels or agencies is contractually predetermined in their transactions in other markets, such as input or credit markets. Having diversified options for sales to different agencies would imply greater bargaining power for farmers in the market, which in turn is likely to reap them higher returns on produce than concentrated sales arising out of tied contracts. What determines farmers' decisions to participate in output markets, and to what extent? This chapter examines (1) farmers' decisions to participate in an output market, (2) their degree of participation in output markets in terms of the number of products sold, (3) the number of output market transactions that they undertake and (4) the diversity of marketing agencies through which they sell their produce.

Several factors are likely to influence farmers' commercial decisions. One may expect that farm- and household-level factors are likely to determine these decisions. Such factors could be farm size, access to credit, irrigation, household demography etc. However, farm households operate not in isolation but under a larger structural environment. Several studies have highlighted the importance of providing better rural infrastructure such as roads, transport services, storage and marketing facilities to facilitate farmers' physical access to output markets as a prerequisite for commercialization (Umali-Deininger and Deininger, 2001; Acharya, 2004; Banerji and Meenakshi, 2004; Fafchamps and Hill, 2005; Fafchamps et al., 2006, 2008; Shilpi and Umali-Deininger, 2008; Vaidyanathan, 2010; Chamberlin and Jayne, 2011; Takeshima and Nagarajan, 2012; Asher and Novosad, 2016; Aggarwal, 2018).

Rural infrastructure is only one such structural factor, albeit an important one. Several other region-specific characteristics spanning social, demographic, economic, agro-ecological and government policy dimensions are also part of the structural environment in which farmers operate and over which they have no control. Recently, Das (2018) and Das and Ganesh-Kumar (2019) demonstrated structural factors' importance in influencing farmers' on-farm and off-farm diversification choices, respectively. Similarly, Das and Ganesh-Kumar (forthcoming) showed that several of these structural factors are significant determinants of farmers' income. Given these, it is conceivable that these structural factors also could influence farmers' commercialization decisions.

Against this background, this chapter provides an integrated study of farmers' commercialization decisions by combining structural conditions with farm- and household-level factors. The chapter uses nationally representative data from the 70th round of the National Sample Survey (NSS) of agricultural households for the year 2012–2013 and combines it with information on various structural variables from the census and other sources (described later in this chapter).

Among the various factors that could influence farmers' sale decisions and marketing practices, access to a storage facility is perhaps one of the most important. The availability of storage is a precursor to improved post-harvest management and marketing practices. Lack of access to storage facilities often leads to distress sales or to selling at lower-than-market-clearing rates, resulting in suboptimal outcomes.

Access to storage facilities, on the other hand, offers the farmer the flexibility to postpone a sale to a later date when market conditions are more favorable and to choose the agency with which to enter into a sale transaction. Indeed, farmers who undertake more than one sale transaction point to the benefits of access to storage facilities. These are *ex ante* theoretical explanations of the possible channels through which storage can help farmers, but there is a dearth of empirical understanding of storage facilities' influence on farmers' marketing decisions. A possible reason for this dearth of studies on storage is the lack of nationwide comprehensive data on the availability of and access to storage facilities. A few studies have relied on primary surveys whose scope was limited to select commodities or regions to explore this issue. For example, Minten et al. (2010) analyze cold storage's benefits for potato marketing in the state of Bihar in India. They find that access to cold storage mostly benefits large farmers, and small farmers benefited indirectly through higher potato prices in the market.

To overcome this data limitation, this chapter proposes a novel approach to indirectly identify farm households that might have access to storage facilities. Specifically, the information contained in the 70th round of the National Sample Survey is used. This survey provides information on the number and quantity of crop sales and the quantity of crop output at the household level. Using this information, the ratio of sales quantity to output quantity can be generated. By observing cases in which this ratio exceeds 1 or cases in which this ratio is undefined due to positive sales with zero output, one can develop an indicator of households that are likely to have access to a storage facility, either self-owned or procured from the market. The analysis demonstrates that this indeed is a significant determinant of farmers' decisions to participate in output markets and their extent of commercialization.

The rest of the chapter is arranged as follows. The next section discusses the data used in this study. Indicators of commercialization, storage and various explanatory variables considered in the analysis are defined, and some summary statistics are provided. The study methodology is then discussed, and a discussion of the results follows. The chapter concludes with policy implications from the study.

Data description

Measuring the extent of commercialization

As mentioned, this chapter is based primarily on agricultural household-level data from the 70th National Sample Survey Situation Assessment Survey (Schedule 33). The 70th round of the National Sample Survey defines an agricultural household as one (1) receiving produce equal to or greater than Rs 3,000 in value from agricultural activities (cultivation of crops, animal husbandry, poultry, fishing etc.) during the last 365 days and (2) having at least one household member self-employed in agriculture, either in a principal or subsidiary status. The National Sample Survey (NSS) survey is canvassed for the agricultural year July 2012 to June 2013 in two visits. The first visit (Visit 1) was for *Kharif* season from July to December 2012, and the second visit (Visit 2) canvassed for the *Rabi* season from January to June 2013. It surveyed 34,907 agricultural households across both visits. Among the 34,907 agricultural households, further scrutiny leaves only 28,917 households with complete information of all the explanatory variables. Of these, only 19,976 households reported growing crops. Hence, the analysis is restricted to those 19,976 households. The National Sample Survey provides information on various farm- and household-level characteristics. To bring in information on structural variables, the survey data are combined with Census 2011 and other statistical sources (discussed later in this section).

The National Sample Survey records up to five different crops grown by each household during each visit (Table 17.1). A total of 4,790 farm households reported growing only one crop in each visit. Some 2,903 households grew one crop during Visit 1 but grew two types of crops in Visit 2. Similarly, 2,292 households grew two crops during Visit 1 and one crop during Visit 2. Only 69 households reported growing five different types of crops in each season.

For each crop-growing household, the National Sample Survey recorded the sale of at most four crops. If a household grew a crop for subsistence purposes, the survey recorded the cultivation of that crop but not its sale. If a household reported sales of a crop, the survey recorded up to four sales transactions, or three major sales and one ‘other’ sale. Thus, a household can report a maximum of 16 transactions across four different crops. The highest recorded number of sale transactions was 12 during Visit 1 (Table 17.2) and 14 during Visit 2. Some 3,834 subsistence farmer households reported growing crops but not

Table 17.1 Number of crop types grown in Visit 1 and Visit 2

	Number of crop types grown in Visit 2					
Number of crop types grown in Visit 1	*1*	*2*	*3*	*4*	*5*	*Total*
1	4,790	2,903	1,300	641	911	10,545
2	2,292	1,474	680	259	415	5,120
3	1,057	659	317	119	192	2,344
4	496	261	128	37	69	991
5	474	266	124	43	69	976
Total	9,109	5,563	2,549	1,099	1,656	19,976

Source: Authors' calculation based on NSS 70th round.

Table 17.2 Sale transition matrix for number of crop sales in Visit 1 and Visit 2

	Number of sales in Visit 2												
Number of sales in Visit 1	*0*	*1*	*2*	*3*	*4*	*5*	*6*	*7*	*8*	*11*	*13*	*14*	*Total*
0	3,834	353	124	35	9	1	3	1	1	0	0	0	4,361
1	1,630	4,527	2,117	642	356	47	27	11	6	1	1	0	9,365
2	646	1,914	890	321	137	17	14	5	0	0	1	1	3,946
3	249	709	329	125	55	12	9	3	0	0	0	0	1,491
4	94	282	140	40	27	1	2	2	0	0	0	0	588
5	12	45	21	8	3	1	0	0	0	0	0	0	90
6	8	41	14	11	7	0	0	0	0	0	0	0	81
7	2	15	4	4	3	0	1	0	0	0	0	0	29
8	1	10	4	0	4	1	0	0	0	0	0	0	20
9	1	0	0	1	0	0	0	0	0	0	0	0	2
10	0	1	0	0	0	0	0	0	0	0	0	0	1
11	0	1	0	0	0	0	0	0	0	0	0	0	1
12	0	1	0	0	0	0	0	0	0	0	0	0	1
Total	6,477	7,899	3,643	1,187	601	80	56	22	7	1	2	1	19,976

Source: Authors' calculation based on NSS 70th round.

making a sale (i.e., 0 sale records) during both seasons. Some 4,527 households reported making at least one market transaction in both seasons. More than 2,117 households made one sale in Visit 1 and two sales in Visit 2. Similarly, 1,914 households engaged in two market transactions in Visit 1 and one in Visit 2. The number of farm households reporting that higher numbers of market transactions declined sharply in both seasons.

The National Sample Survey also records the agency of sale for each sale transaction. In all, six different agencies are recorded: local private, *mandis*, input dealers, cooperative/government agencies, processors and others. Crop cultivation and sale transactions varied drastically across the two visits. The agencies with which these sale transactions were made also varied significantly across the two visits. The most market transactions were made with the local private trader, followed by transactions at *mandis*, in both visits (Table 17.3). Quite a few sale transactions were made with agencies, input dealers and processors in both visits.

Based on the preceding information from the National Sample Survey, one can measure four different aspects of the commercialization of agriculture as follows:

1 *Decision to participate in market*: Captured through a binary variable. It takes a value of 1 if the farmer has transacted at least once in the market, 0 otherwise.
2 *Degree of market participation*: The ratio of the number of crops sold to the number of crops cultivated can be considered an indicator of the farmer's degree of market participation. This ratio can range between 0 (indicating subsistence farming) and 1 (full commercialization).
3 *Number of market transactions*: A count of the number of market transactions indicates how frequently the farmer transacts in the market. A farmer transacting more than once is likely to be better integrated with the market than a farmer with no transactions or only one transaction. Since far fewer farmers reported more than two transactions, this aspect is measured as a categorical variable, taking the value 0 if there is no transaction, 1 if transacted once and 2 if there are two or more transactions.
4 *Diversity of agency of sale*: This indicates the farmer's ability to transact with multiple agencies, suggesting the farmer may not be subject to interlinked or tied-markets problems. This aspect is measured using a Simpson index of agency diversification, which ranges between 0 (complete concentration) and 1 (complete diversification).

Table 17.3 Number of sales by agency

Number of transactions	*Local private*	*Mandi*	*Input dealer*	*Coop-government*	*Processors*	*Others*
Visit 1						
0	10,547	15,454	18,639	18,639	19,568	19,143
1	6,438	3,086	1,020	1,231	393	644
2	2,032	1,003	247	90	14	128
3	732	349	58	15	1	46
4	227	84	12	1	0	15
Visit 2						
0	11,736	16,165	18,783	19,139	19,675	19,552
1	5,220	2,488	880	796	294	341
2	2,057	920	246	39	5	59
3	691	296	53	2	1	16
4	272	107	14	0	1	8

Source: Authors' calculation based on NSS 70th round.

Measuring storage

As mentioned, there is no comprehensive nationwide data on availability and access to storage facilities, either privately or publicly provided. Therefore, using data on the quantity of crops sold and produced, as contained in the 70th round of the National Sample Survey, we applied an indirect approach to capture farm households that are likely to have access to a storage facility (either self-owned or market-sourced). The ratio of crop sales quantity to produced quantity (SR) can indicate available storage facilities. The SR thus generated revealed some patterns. Three scenarios are possible: (1) SR > 1; (2) SR is undefined, which occurs when a farmer reports a sale transaction of a crop during a particular season during a survey visit but did not produce that crop during that season; or (3) 0 ≤ SR ≤ 1. Situation 1 can arise only when the amount of sales in a season exceeds the output in that season, meaning the excess amount had been produced and stored in the previous cropping season. Similarly, in situation 2, the entire quantity sold that season must have been produced and stored in the previous cropping season. Thus, both situations 1 and 2 indirectly indicate that the farmer likely had access to storage—either self-owned or hired. Situation 3 is uninformative about whether the farmer had access to storage.[1]

Analysis of the data shows that more than 48% and nearly 43% of households belonged to situations 1 and 2 in Visit 1 and Visit 2, respectively (Table 17.4). Thus, using SR, a dummy variable is constructed to indicate whether the farm household is likely to have access to a storage facility. This dummy variable takes the value 1 for farm households belonging to situations 1 and 2, 0 otherwise. This indicator variable of a farm household's likely access to a storage facility is used in this study.

Table 17.4 Sales ratio frequency

Types	*Frequency*	%
Visit 1		
SR less than or equal to 1	18,077	51.65
SR greater than 1	15,936	45.53
SR undefined	989	2.83
Total	35,002	100
Visit 2		
SR less than or equal to 1	22,498	57.76
SR greater than 1	15,814	40.6
SR undefined	640	1.64
Total	38,952	100

Source: Authors' calculation based on NSS 70th round.

Note: SR refers to sales ratio defined as quantity of crop sold to quantity of crop output.

Other factors likely to affect the extent of commercialization

Various farm- and household-level variables affect a farmer's marketing decisions. These are available from the National Sample Survey data. At the farm level, the average number of crops cultivated during both visits was 2 (Table 17.5). The average farm size was 1.6 ha. On average, 60% and 50% of farmland was under irrigation during Visit 1 and Visit 2, respectively. About 10% of households had crop insurance in Visit 1, and this fell to only 4% during Visit 2. Some 73% of households had an institutional outstanding credit. At the household level, the average household size was about 6, and 93% households were male headed. The average household age was 31. The average male/female ratio was 0.52. The average monthly per capita consumption expenditure was Rs 1,397.4 during Visit 1 and Rs 1,705.6 during Visit 2. At the village neighborhood level, the off-farm labor market may impact household marketing decisions. Using National Sample Survey data, the proportion of households in a village engaged in any form of non-farm activity was calculated for each farm household (except that particular household). About 44% of households in a village were engaged in off-farm work in Visit 1 and 48% during Visit 2.

Information regarding the structural feature of the economy is available at the district level. As village codes are not the same for the National Sample Survey, the census and other sources, we measured most of the district-level variables in terms of proportion. The proportion of Scheduled Castes (SC) and Scheduled Tribes (ST) households in a district denotes the social composition of the district. On average, 20% of the district's population is SC, and 8% are ST population. To control for access to infrastructure, the proportion of villages with public transport averaged 98%, and the proportion of villages with towns within 5 km averaged 23%. On average, 39% of a district's credit was agricultural credit. Some 66% of districts had villages with self-help groups (SHGs), and 32% of villages in districts had access to financial services. The average power available for agricultural use in a district, weighted by net sown area was 7 hours per day during the summer and 6.3 hours per day during the winter. Farm households' marketing decisions are influenced significantly by urbanization. This study considers urban centers classified by population sizes. On average, districts have either a Class 1 city or a Class 2 city.

To account for state-level policy variables that could influence a farm household's marketing practice, this study controls for the amount of capital expenditure and total expenditure in agriculture and for per capita state Gross State Domestic Product (GSDP). On average, Rs 590.3 million/ha was spent on capital expenditure in agriculture, and Rs 31.08 billion/ha was spent on total agriculture. The average per capita state GSDP for 2012–2013 was about Rs 81,833.

Table 17.5 Summary statistics

Variable	*Description*	*Mean*	*Std. dev.*
(I) FARM and HOUSEHOLD (Source: NSS 70th round)			
(i) Commercialization			
Dummy participate in market transaction (Visit 1)	Dummy = 1 if sold any crop in Visit 1	0.78	0.41
Dummy participate in market transaction (Visit 1)	Dummy = 1 if sold any crop in Visit 2	0.68	0.47
Sale ratio of number of crops sold to crops cultivated (Visit 1)	Ratio of number of crops sold to number of crops cultivated in Visit 1	0.62	0.41
Sale ratio of number of crops sold to crops cultivated (Visit 2)	Ratio of number of crops sold to number of crops cultivated in Visit 2	0.52	0.43
Number of market transactions (0, 1, or ≥ 2) (Visit 1)	Categorical variable of number of market transactions 0, 1 or ≥ 2 in Visit 1	1.09	0.72
Number of market transactions (0, 1, or ≥ 2) (Visit 2)	Categorical variable of number of market transactions 0, 1 or ≥ 2 in Visit 2	0.96	0.78
Simpsons index (Visit 1)	Simpsons index for diversity of agency sale in Visit 1	0.20	0.27
Simpsons index (Visit 2)	Simpsons index for diversity of agency sale in Visit 2	0.16	0.26
(ii) Storage			
Dummy LTHS (likely to have storage)	Dummy = 1 if sale quantity > produced quantity	0.85	0.36
(iii) Other farm and household level variables			
Number of crops cultivated (Visit 1)	Total number of crop types cultivated in Visit 1	1.80	1.10
Number of crops cultivated (Visit 2)	Total number of crop types cultivated in Visit 2	2.00	1.20
Total land	Total land possessed (in has)	1.60	2.00
Proportion of irrigation (Visit 1)	Share of irrigated land in Visit 1	0.60	0.50
Proportion of irrigation (Visit 2)	Share of irrigated land in Visit 2	0.50	0.50
Dummy insurance (Visit 1)	Dummy = 1 if any crop insured in Visit 1	0.10	0.20
Dummy insurance (Visit 2)	Dummy = 1 if any crop insured in Visit 2	0.04	0.20

(*Continued*)

Table 17.5 (Continued)

Variable	*Description*	*Mean*	*Std. dev.*
Dummy credit	Dummy = 1 if any outstanding credit	0.73	0.45
Dummy head male (Visit 1)	Dummy = 1 if head is male, 0 otherwise in Visit 1	0.93	0.25
Dummy head male (Visit 2)	Dummy = 1 if head is male, 0 otherwise in Visit 2	0.92	0.27
Dummy head illiterate (Visit 1)	Dummy = 1 if head is illiterate, 0 otherwise in Visit 1	0.37	0.48
Dummy head illiterate (Visit 2)	Dummy = 1 if head is illiterate, 0 otherwise in Visit 2	0.37	0.48
Household size	Household size	5.60	2.90
Dummy SC/ST household	Dummy = 1 if household ST/SC	0.30	0.40
Average household age	Average age of the household members	31.20	11.50
Proportion of dependents	Proportion of dependents in the household	0.49	0.24
Male female ratio	Ratio of male to female members in the household	0.52	0.16
Graduates and above	Proportion of household members graduate and above	0.05	0.05
Monthly per capita consumption (Visit 1)	Monthly per capita consumption in Visit 1	1397.4	1441.5
Monthly per capita consumption (Visit 2)	Monthly per capita consumption in Visit 2	1705.6	2387.3
(II) VILLAGE (*Source*: NSS 70th round)			
Village proportion of non-farm workers (Visit 1)	Proportion of households engaged in non-farm activities in the village (except itself) in Visit 1	0.44	0.35
Village proportion of non-farm workers (Visit 2)	Proportion of households engaged in non-farm activities in the village (except itself) in Visit 2	0.48	0.34
(III) DISTRICT (*Source*: Census, RBI, GOI, IMD)			
Proportion of SC	Proportion of SC population in the district	0.20	0.09
Proportion of ST	Proportion of ST population in the district	0.08	0.13

Variable	*Description*	*Mean*	*Std. dev.*
Proportion with public transport	Proportion of villages in the district with access to public transport	0.98	0.10
Proportion with towns within 5 km	Proportion of villages in the district with town < 5 km	0.23	0.22
Proportion of agri-credit to total credit	Proportion of agricultural credit to total credit	0.39	0.19
Proportion of agri-markets	Proportion of villages in the district with agricultural markets	0.50	0.31
Proportion of SHG	Proportion of villages in the district with self-help groups	0.66	0.28
Proportion of financial services	Proportion of villages with access to financial services	0.32	0.25
Average power for agri use (hr/day) Summer	Average power available for agricultural use during summer	7.00	4.91
Average power for agri use (hr/day) Winter	Average power available for agricultural use during winters	6.30	4.65
District rainfall deviation (Visit 1)	Rainfall deviation from normal (Visit 1)	–22.7	43.2
District rainfall deviation (Visit 2)	Rainfall deviation from normal (Visit 2)	69.7	491.7
Class 1 cities	Number of urban centers with population 100,000 or above	1.20	1.00
Class 2 cities	Number of urban centers with population 50,000–99,999	1.10	1.30
Class 3, 4, 5, 6 cities	Number of urban centers with population 20,000–49,999, 10,000–19,999, 5,000–9,999, below 500	320.9	1,161.8
Ratio of class 1 and 2 cities	Ratio of class 1 and 2 urban centers	0.20	0.20
(IV) STATE (Source: RBI, EPWRF)			
Capital expenditure in agriculture (Rs million/ha)	Capital expenditure in agriculture in the state	590.3	1,116.7
Total agri expenditure (Rs million/ha)	Total capital and revenue expenditure in agriculture	3,108.1	2,178.9
Size of the state economy	Per capita state GDP	8,1832.9	43,434.6

Source: Authors.

Methodology

As previously described, the variable of interest in this study—commercialization—has been defined in four ways: (1) Decision to participate in the market, defined as a binary variable taking the value 1 if the farmer transacted at least once in the market, 0 otherwise; (2) degree of market participation, defined as the ratio of the number of crops sold to the number of crops cultivated, which can range between 0 and 1; (3) number of market transactions, measured as a categorical variable taking values of 0 if no transaction, 1 if transacted once and 2 for two or more transactions; and (4) the Simpson index of diversity of agency of sale, which ranges between 0 (complete concentration) and 1 (complete diversification). As is evident, the four variables capturing different aspects of commercialization vary in nature. Accordingly, different econometric models are specified for each, and appropriate estimation methods are applied. These are now described.

Decision to participate in the market

The following binary probit model is considered in order to understand the factors affecting a farmer's decision to sell a crop or to produce it for household consumption (subsistence). The model includes two main agricultural seasons in India, $t = 1, 2$, where 1 represents *Kharif* season and 2 represents *Rabi* season:

$$P^{*}_{ivdst} = \alpha_0 + \alpha_1 FARM_{ivdst} + \alpha_2 HHLDCH_{ivdst} + \alpha_3 VILLCH_{vdst} + \alpha_4 DISTCH_{ds} + \alpha_5 STATEPOL_s + \epsilon_{ivdst} \tag{17.1}$$

In Equation (17.1), P^{*}_{ivdst} is a latent variable representing a farmer's decision to sell in the market or to produce only for household consumption for i^{th} household, in v^{th} village, in d^{th} district, in s^{th} state, in seasons $t = 1,2$. Since the latent variable P^{*}_{ivdst} is not observed, the response variable that is observed is P_{ivdst}, for both $t = 1, 2$, where:

$$P_{ivdst} = \begin{cases} 1\, if\ there\, is\, at\, least\, one\, market\, sale \\ 0\, if\ there\, is\, no\, market\, sale\, at\, all \end{cases} \tag{17.2}$$

$FARMCH_{ivdst}$ are the individual farm-level characteristics such as farm size, number of crops cultivated, land under irrigation, credit, crop insurance etc. $HHLDCH_{ivdst}$ are household socio-economic and demographic characteristics such as social group, household size, average age, education, gender composition etc. $VILLCH_{vdst}$ could be village characteristics such as labor market conditions. $DISTCH_{ds}$ represents district-level structural features, such as storage facilities, social composition, physical and financial infrastructure and urbanization. $STATEPOL_s$ represents state-level policy variables such as agricultural expenditure and per capita state GDP. The error term is denoted by $\epsilon_{ivdst} \sim N(0,\sigma^2)$. The binary variable on market participation, P_{ivdst}, and farm-, household- and village-level explanatory variables are available for the two agricultural seasons, t = 1, 2. However, variables at the district and state levels are only available annually. Hence the preceding binary probit models in Equation (17.1) for the two seasons are estimated under a Seemingly Unrelated Regression (SUR) system as in Das (2018).

Degree of market participation

The following linear model is specified to understand the determinants of the farmer's degree of market participation:

$$SR_{ivdst} = \beta_0 + \beta_1 FARM_{ivdst} + \beta_2 HHLDCH_{ivdst} + \beta_3 VILLCH_{vdst} + \beta_4 DISTCH_{ds} + \beta_5 STATEPOL_s + u_{ivdst} \quad (17.3)$$

SR_{ivdst} is the sales ratio of number of crops sold to the number of crops produced for a particular farmer-producer, $0 \le SR_{ivdst} < 1$. The explanatory variables $FARMCH_{ivdst}$, $HHLDCH_{ivdst}$, $VILLCH_{vdst}$, $DISTCH_{ds}$ and $SATEPOL_s$ have the same interpretations as in the former estimation in Equation (17.2). The error term is $u_{ivdst} \sim N(\mu,\sigma^2)$. Similarly, since most of the district- and state-level explanatory variables are annual, Equation (17.3) is estimated as ordinary least squares (OLS) under an SUR set-up.

Number of market transactions

Farm households could engage in several market transactions. The following ordered probit model is estimated to identify the factors affecting a farmer's decision on the number of times the farmer engages in selling produce to the market:

$$y^*_{ivdst} = \gamma_0 + \gamma_1 FARM_{ivdst} + \gamma_2 HHLDCH_{ivdst} + \gamma_3 VILLCH_{vdst} + \gamma_4 DISTCH_{ds} + \gamma_5 STATEPOL_s + v_{ivdst} \quad (17.4)$$

y^*_{ivdst} is a latent variable denoting the total number of market transactions that a farmer-producer makes to sell all the types of crops produced. The observed variable y_{ivdst} represents the following:

$$y_{ivdst} = \begin{cases} 0\, if\ no\ sale transaction \\ 1\, if\ only\, 1\, sale\, transaction \\ 2\, if\ 2\, or > 2\, sale\, transactions \end{cases} \quad (17.5)$$

The explanatory variables $FARMCH_{ivdst}$, $HHLDCH_{ivdst}$, $VILLCH_{vdst}$, $DISTCH_{ds}$ and $SATEPOL_s$ have the same interpretations as previously stated, and the error term is $v_{ivdst} \sim N(0,\sigma^2)$. In Equation (17.5), since most of the district- and state-level explanatory variables are annual, Equation (17.3) is estimated as ordinary least squares (OLS) under an SUR set-up.

Diversity of agency

Finally, the following linear model is specified to understand the factors affecting the diversity of agency of sales:

$$SDIV_{ivdst} = \delta_0 + \delta_1 FARM_{ivdst} + \delta_2 HHLDCH_{ivdst} + \delta_3 VILLCH_{vdst} + \delta_4 DISTCH_{ds} + \delta_5 STATEPOL_s + \omega_{ivdst} \quad (17.6)$$

$SDIV_{ivdst}$ is a Simpson index measure of sale agency diversity calculated as:

$$SDIV_{ivdst} = 1 - \sum_a AP_a$$

AP_a is agency proportion sale to an agency $a = 1, 2, \ldots, 6$, where:

$$AP_a = \frac{\text{Number of sale to agency } a}{\text{Total sales}}$$

As the Simpson index is related to the diversity of agency sale, Equation (17.6) is estimated only for farm households that made at least two transactions in both seasons.[2] Therefore, the agency diversity index, $0 \leq SDIV_{ivdst} \leq 1$. 0 denotes least diversified (i.e., most concentrated) and 1 is most diversified (i.e., least concentrated). It is conceivable that the number of sale transactions could affect $SDIV_{ivdst}$. But the number of sale transactions (Sale_{ivdst}) could itself be affected by many of the explanatory variables as follows:

$$\text{Sale}_{ivdst} = \theta_0 + \theta_1 FARM_{ivdst} + \theta_2 HHLDCH_{ivdst} + \theta_3 VILLCH_{vdst} + \theta_4 DISTCH_{ds} + \theta_5 STATEPOL_s + \tau_{ivdst} \quad (17.7)$$

Hence Equations (17.6) and (17.7) are jointly estimated as a recursive system of a simultaneous equation model (SEM).

Results and discussion

The factors affecting farm households' decisions to sell their products are estimated using four different models. Model (17.1) is a binary probit for any sale in Visit 1 and Visit 2 estimated as an SUR system. Model (17.2) is a linear OLS estimation of the sale ratio of the number of crops sold to total crops grown for both visits under an SUR system. Model (17.3) is an ordered probit estimation for understanding the frequency of market sale for both visits in an SUR set-up. Finally, using an OLS estimate under SUR, Model (17.4) identifies the factors determining the diversity of agency sale. Results are presented in Table 17.6.

Table 17.6 Results for market participation

	Model 1		*Model 2*		*Model 3*		*Model 4*	
	Binary probit		*Sale ratio*		*Ordered probit*		*Simpson's index*	
	Visit 1	*Visit 2*	*Visit 1*	*Visit 2*	*Visit 1*	*Visit 2*	*Visit 1*	*Visit 2*
(I) FARM & HOUSEHOLD LEVELS								
Dummy LTHS	0.245	0.278***	0.093***	0.108***	0.497***	0.284***	−0.040	0.036
	(0.97)	(2.71)	(10.18)	(5.99)	(4.07)	(3.28)	(−0.47)	(0.42)
Number of sales transactions							0.008	−0.014
							(0.56)	(−0.84)
Number of crops cultivated	0.158	0.052	−0.342**	−0.322***	0.073*	0.021	0.005	0.051**
	(0.94)	(1.27)	(−66.33)	(−39.27)	(1.70)	(0.63)	(0.23)	(2.52)
Sq number of crops cultivated	−0.004	−0.020***	0.0366***	0.0363***	−0.002	−0.011*	−0.001	−0.009**
	(−0.13)	(−2.68)	(38.22)	(24.86)	(−0.28)	(−1.95)	(−0.14)	(−2.16)
Total land	0.017	0.001	−0.002	−1.17e−04	−0.016*	−0.005	0.008	0.006
	(0.53)	(0.10)	(−1.63)	(−0.07)	(−1.69)	(−0.77)	(1.15)	(0.88)
Sq total land	−4.77e−04	−5.78e-06	4.25e-05	− 1.45e-05	− 2.05e-05	2.05e-04	−0.001	−0.001*
	(−0.35)	(−0.01)	(1.12)	(−0.23)	(−0.05)	(0.68)	(−0.78)	(−1.88)
Prop of irrigation	0.163	0.187***	0.001	0.016	−0.0561	0.148***	0.0691**	0.031
	(0.66)	(2.62)	(0.11)	(1.12)	(−0.87)	(2.71)	(2.41)	(1.01)
Dummy insurance	−0.662	0.053	−0.011	0.004	−0.382**	0.019	0.117*	0.098
	(−1.62)	(0.35)	(−0.69)	(0.13)	(−2.53)	(0.17)	(1.77)	(1.02)
Dummy credit	5.430***	1.678***	0.628***	0.377***	3.173***	1.470***	−0.204**	0.078
	(15.95)	(18.98)	(66.99)	(23.83)	(25.31)	(19.05)	(−2.28)	(0.89)

(*Continued*)

Table 17.6 (Continued)

	Model 1		*Model 2*		*Model 3*		*Model 4*	
	Binary probit		*Sale ratio*		*Ordered probit*		*Simpson's index*	
	Visit 1	*Visit 2*	*Visit 1*	*Visit 2*	*Visit 1*	*Visit 2*	*Visit 1*	*Visit 2*
Dummy LTHS* Dummy credit	−0.252	−0.201**	−0.112***	−0.106***	-0.562***	−0.221***	0.0625	− 0.0483
	(−0.94)	(−2.34)	(−12.46)	(−7.00)	(−4.59)	(−2.94)	(0.74)	(−0.58)
Dummy LTHS* Prop of irrigation	0.114	−0.039	0.014*	−0.007	0.051	−0.053	−0.050	−0.009
	(0.43)	(−0.51)	(1.71)	(−0.49)	(0.74)	(−0.92)	(−1.62)	(−0.28)
Dummy LTHS* Dummy insurance	0.461	−0.015	0.002	−0.001	0.380**	0.048	−0.068	−0.027
	(1.01)	(−0.10)	(0.12)	(−0.03)	(2.37)	(0.38)	(−0.95)	(−0.26)
Dummy head male	−0.408*	−0.028	−0.009	−0.010	−0.054	−0.067**	0.013	−0.015
	(−1.87)	(−0.68)	(−1.63)	(−1.25)	(−1.15)	(−2.04)	(0.60)	(−0.75)
Dummy head illiterate	−0.054	-0.045*	8.29e-05	−0.005	0.017	−0.023	−0.011	−0.028**
	(−0.57)	(−1.86)	(0.03)	(−1.05)	(0.70)	(−1.19)	(−0.89)	(−2.27)
Household size	−0.029*	−0.001	−0.001**	−2.52e-04	0.001	−6.64e-04	0.002	−0.001
	(−1.87)	(−0.24)	(−2.45)	(−0.28)	(0.37)	(−0.19)	(0.72)	(−0.26)
Dummy SC/ ST household	0.042	−0.036	−0.006**	−0.002	0.051*	−0.028	0.024*	0.002
	(0.37)	(−1.30)	(−1.97)	(−0.33)	(1.85)	(−1.33)	(1.81)	(0.14)
Avg household age	0.005	0.001	0.001***	0.001***	0.004***	0.002**	3.88e-04	0.001
	(1.07)	(1.29)	(3.69)	(3.19)	(3.18)	(2.08)	(0.67)	(1.06)
Prop of dependents	0.172	−0.026	0.029***	−0.015	0.110*	−0.005	0.032	0.028
	(0.75)	(−0.53)	(4.38)	(−1.59)	(1.95)	(−0.14)	(1.15)	(1.23)

Male female ratio	−0.394	−0.069	−0.004	−0.025*	−0.036	−0.085	−0.088**	−0.026
	(−1.35)	(−0.98)	(−0.46)	(−1.84)	(−0.50)	(−1.55)	(−2.51)	(−0.82)
Graduates and above	−0.290	0.023	−0.026***	0.018	−0.098	0.080	−0.006	−0.030
	(−1.09)	(0.31)	(−2.91)	(1.17)	(−1.30)	(1.37)	(−0.15)	(−0.87)
Monthly per capita consumption	−1.07e-05	7.31e-06*	3.26e-06	1.00e-06	−7.65e-07	4.27e-06	8.16e-06	−2.76e-06
	(-0.44)	(1.75)	(0.34)	(1.00)	(−0.09)	(1.07)	(1.26)	(−0.65)
(II) Village level								
Village prop of non−farm workers	−0.051	−0.241***	0.004	−0.031***	−0.008	−0.143***	0.033*	0.013
	(−0.35)	(−6.63)	(0.96)	(−4.33)	(−0.24)	(−5.07)	(1.93)	(0.75)
(III) District level								
Prop of SC	2.698***	0.759***	0.154***	0.185***	0.122	1.158***	−0.0547	−0.138
	(3.51)	(4.48)	(7.52)	(5.30)	(0.70)	(8.55)	(−0.57)	(−1.45)
Prop of ST	0.524	−0.814***	−0.073***	−0.059**	−0.551***	−0.483***	−0.184***	0.075
	(0.93)	(−6.01)	(−5.32)	(−2.53)	(−4.45)	(−4.75)	(−2.88)	(1.19)
Prop with public transport	1.217	−0.585	0.035	−0.081	0.538	−0.649*	−0.174	0.201
	(0.40)	(−1.25)	(0.68)	(−0.92)	(1.30)	(−1.95)	(−0.88)	(1.03)
Prop with towns within 5 km	3.255	0.873	0.064	0.279	1.158	0.649	0.062	0.530
	(0.49)	(0.97)	(0.64)	(1.64)	(1.47)	(1.02)	(0.16)	(1.41)
Public transport* towns 5 km	−4.025	−0.069	−0.128	−0.137	−1.793**	0.202	0.039	−0.497
	(−0.60)	(−0.08)	(−1.27)	(−0.80)	(−2.26)	(0.31)	(0.10)	(−1.31)

(Continued)

Table 17.6 (Continued)

	Model 1		*Model 2*		*Model 3*		*Model 4*	
	Binary probit		*Sale ratio*		*Ordered probit*		*Simpson's index*	
	Visit 1	*Visit 2*	*Visit 1*	*Visit 2*	*Visit 1*	*Visit 2*	*Visit 1*	*Visit 2*
Prop of agri credit to total credit	−0.493	−0.364***	−0.079***	−0.037	−0.050	−0.408***	−0.072	−0.114*
	(−1.18)	(−2.68)	(−5.35)	(−1.48)	(−0.38)	(−3.85)	(−1.10)	(−1.74)
Prop of agri markets	−0.006	−0.231**	0.0232**	−0.031	0.266***	−0.302***	0.009	0.107**
	(−0.01)	(−2.32)	(2.01)	(−1.58)	(2.77)	(−3.92)	(0.19)	(2.26)
Agri credit* agri markets	0.466	1.070***	0.141***	0.175***	0.357	1.163***	−0.055	−0.129
	(0.46)	(4.74)	(5.38)	(3.96)	(1.63)	(6.58)	(−0.49)	(−1.16)
Proportion of SHG	−1.115*	0.052	0.007	1.12e-04	0.230**	0.008	0.120*	0.099
	(−1.81)	(0.46)	(0.53)	(0.01)	(2.00)	(0.09)	(1.78)	(1.49)
Proportion of finservices	0.811	−0.892***	−0.0767***	−0.161***	−0.306	−0.792***	0.120	0.339**
	(0.92)	(−4.91)	(−4.48)	(−5.56)	(−1.51)	(−5.15)	(0.78)	(2.21)
SHG* finservices	−0.572	1.008***	0.145***	0.250***	0.416*	1.082***	−0.173	−0.322*
	(−0.57)	(4.35)	(6.20)	(6.35)	(1.68)	(5.69)	(−0.99)	(−1.88)
Avg power for agri use	−0.344***	−0.105***	−0.021***	−0.017***	−0.121***	−0.080***	0.012**	−0.017***
	(−6.45)	(−11.08)	(−20.24)	(−9.51)	(−11.70)	(−10.90)	(2.25)	(−3.25)
Sq avg power for agri use	0.019***	0.005***	0.001***	0.001***	0.006***	0.004***	−0.001**	0.001***
	(5.99)	(9.20)	(13.63)	(9.34)	(8.69)	(9.01)	(−2.04)	(3.91)
Class 1 cities	0.128	0.085***	−2.14e-04	0.015**	−0.019	0.063**	−0.037**	0.023

	(0.85)	(2.58)	(−0.06)	(2.33)	(−0.59)	(2.49)	(−2.37)	(1.46)
Sq class 1 cities	−0.028	−0.003	3.62e-05	−0.001	0.009	−0.004	0.003	−0.002
	(−1.28)	(−0.49)	(0.52)	(−0.90)	(1.55)	(−1.04)	(1.28)	(−0.89)
Class 2 cities	−0.172	0.028	0.002	0.0065	0.053**	0.021	−0.030**	0.021*
	(−1.05)	(1.15)	(0.58)	(1.31)	(2.15)	(1.10)	(−2.39)	(1.68)
Sq class 2 cities	0.068	−0.011***	−4.80e-04	−0.002***	−0.012***	−0.010***	0.007***	−0.002
	(1.53)	(−2.77)	(−0.94)	(−2.58)	(−2.80)	(−2.96)	(3.05)	(−0.92)
Class 3, 4, 5, 6 cities	0.046**	0.010***	0.004***	0.003***	0.019***	0.013***	0.001	−0.009***
	(2.14)	(2.68)	(7.81)	(3.26)	(4.91)	(4.25)	(0.74)	(−4.86)
Sq class 3, 4, 5, 6 cities	−4.06e-04**	−1.09e-04***	−3.02e-05***	−2.67e-05***	−1.63e-04***	-1.17e-04***	−2.29e-05	7.80e-05***
	(−1.98)	(−2.95)	(−6.68)	(−3.48)	(−4.40)	(−3.99)	(−1.27)	(4.37)
Ratio of class 1 and 2 cities	0.796	0.193	0.055***	0.044*	0.001	0.238**	−0.002	−0.125**
	(1.03)	(1.52)	(3.75)	(1.80)	(0.01)	(2.50)	(−0.03)	(−2.18)
District rainfall deviation	0.001	7.77e-05***	2.73e-04***	1.36e-5***	4.70e-04	7.45e-05***	5.00e-06	9.01e-06
	(1.20)	(3.06)	(6.29)	(2.79)	(1.33)	(4.05)	(0.25)	(0.07)
(IV) STATE								
Capital exp in agri	−0.001***	−0.001***	−1.38e-04***	−2.41e-04***	−5.53e-04***	−8.87e-04***	−9.63e-05**	1.76e-04***
	(−4.63)	(−17.95)	(−16.45)	(−17.16)	(−6.91)	(−15.34)	(−2.09)	(3.87)
Sq capital exp in agri	4.81e-07***	1.87e-07***	2.60e-08***	3.43e-08***	1.61e-07***	1.31e-07***	8.01e-09	−1.68e-08**
	(6.37)	(18.88)	(25.06)	(19.15)	(13.98)	(17.06)	(1.19)	(−2.46)
Total agri exp	0.002***	1.97e-04***	6.53e-06	3.75e-05***	3.01e-04***	2.37e-04***	−2.63e-05	5.83 e-05**
	(4.28)	(4.50)	(1.31)	(4.57)	(5.88)	(6.96)	(−0.90)	(2.08)
Sq total agri exp	−2.28e-07***	−1.46e-08***	−6.95e-10	−3.14e-09***	−4.57e-08***	−1.89e-08***	3.13e-09	−6.61e-09*
	(−4.29)	(−2.78)	(−1.24)	(−3.36)	(−6.76)	(−4.56)	(0.79)	(−1.72)
Per capita state GDP	−1.29e-04***	−3.67e-05***	−7.90e-06***	−6.70 e-06***	−3.51 e-05***	−2.12e-05***	5.13 e-06**	9.01 e-06***

(Continued)

Table 17.6 (Continued)

	Model 1		*Model 2*		*Model 3*		*Model 4*	
	Binary probit		*Sale ratio*		*Ordered probit*		*Simpson's index*	
	Visit 1	*Visit 2*	*Visit 1*	*Visit 2*	*Visit 1*	*Visit 2*	*Visit 1*	*Visit 2*
	(−8.22)	(−10.33)	(−19.49)	(−10.24)	(−9.92)	(−7.82)	(2.57)	(4.73)
Sq per capita state GDP	5.72e-10***	2.30e-10***	4.05e-11***	4.03e-11***	1.65e-10***	1.39e-10***	−2.36e-11**	−5.14e-11***
	(6.78)	(11.61)	(18.02)	(11.07)	(8.20)	(9.16)	(−2.10)	(−4.81)
Cropcodes(jt)	+++	+++	+++	+++	+++	+++	+++	+++
Log likelihood	−8,519.777				−24,341.161			
LR test of rho = 0	61.908				149.170			
Prob > chi^2	0.000		0.000	0.000	0.000		0.000	0.000
RMSE			0.186	0.314			0.253	0.250
R^2			0.796	0.472			0.108	0.103
Chi^2			76,142.37	17,640.28			234.5	250.85
N	19,976	19,976	19,976	19,976	19,976	19,976	2,218	2,218

Notes: Authors' calculation based on NSS 70th round. Cropcodes (jt) are controls for each crop j = 1; 2; 3; 4 in visit t = 1, 2. +++ denote that all the four Cropcodes (jt) are positive and significant at 1% level. t and Z statistics reported in parentheses for models 1 and 3 and for models 2 and 4, respectively.

*** $p < 0.001$.

** $p < 0.05$.

* $p < 0.1$.

Decision to participate in market—binary probit

Estimation results under Model (1) show that the possibility of having a storage facility (Dummy LTHS) has a positive and significant effect on the farm household's decision to participate in a market transaction during Visit 2. Under other farm variables, the number of crops cultivated does not determine a farmer-producer's decision regarding market participation. However, the squared term of the number of crops cultivated has a negative and significant effect on market participation only in Visit 2. Access to irrigated land has a positive and considerable influence on the probability of market sale only during Visit 2. The dummy variable on outstanding credit has a significant positive effect on market sale decisions during both seasons. The interaction of Dummy LTHS and Dummy outstanding credit has a negative impact on sale decisions only in Visit 2. Under village neighborhood impact, the analysis shows that the proportion of households with non-farm work has a negative effect on market participation only during Visit 2.

At the district level, having a higher proportion of SC population in a district increases the probability that farmers will participate in the market. The results show that access to public transport and the proportion of villages with towns within 5 km do not impact sale decisions. Agricultural credit and agricultural market density have a significant negative impact on sale decisions only during Visit 2. However, the interaction term between agricultural credit and market density has a positive effect on sale decisions. Similarly, only the interaction term between the proportion of villages in a district with self-help groups (SHGs) and the proportion of villages with access to financial services has a significant positive effect on sale decisions during Visit 2. Average power availability for agricultural use has a U-shaped relationship with sale decisions in both visits. This implies that at a lower level, agricultural power availability has a negative impact on sale decisions. But at a higher level (squared term), agricultural power availability has a positive impact on sale decisions. The presence of Class 1 cities has a positive influence on the probability of sale decisions during Visit 2, whereas the presence of Class 3, 4, 5 and 6 cities has a significant positive effect on sale decisions during both visits. However, the squared term of the presence of Class 3, 4, 5 and 6 cities has a negative and significant effect on sale decisions. This implies that though the presence of small urban centers helps in market participation, at a higher level, it may have a negative effect on sale decisions, showing an inverted U-shaped relationship with the probability of sale decisions. At the state level, state capital expenditure in agriculture has a U-shaped relationship with sale decisions during both visits, and total agricultural expenditure has an inverted U-shaped relationship with sale decisions. The size of the state economy, measured by per capita state GDP, has a positive and significant effect on market participation only at a higher level (squared term).

Degree of market participation—share of commodities sold—OLS

Model 2 shows that Dummy LTHS has a positive and significant effect on the sale ratio of the number of crops sold in the market to the number of crops cultivated. This implies that the possibility of using storage facilities significantly improves a farm household's sales ratio, signifying the farmer is more commercialized. The number of crops cultivated increases the sales ratio of the crop in a U-shaped fashion, implying that only at a higher level (squared term) does the number of crops cultivated raise the sales ratio. An outstanding credit is associated positively with SR, implying that having an outstanding loan leads a farmer to sell a greater number of crops and hence be more commercialized. However, the interaction between Dummy LTHS and having an outstanding loan has a significant negative effect on the sales ratio. The average age of the household has a positive and significant effect on the sale ratio during both visits. Village neighborhood proportion of households having non-farm work negatively affected the sales ratio during Visit 2.

At the district level, having a higher proportion of SC population in the district is positively associated with the sales ratio in both visits, but having a higher proportion of ST population has a negative and significant effect. Interaction between agricultural credit and agricultural market has a significant positive effect on the sales ratio in both seasons. Similarly, the interaction of the proportion of villages with self-help groups and the proportion of villages with access to financial services has a significant positive impact on the sales ratio in both visits. The availability of power for agricultural use has a U-shaped relation with the sales ratio. That is, the squared term of power availability for agricultural use has a positive and significant effect on sales ratio. The presence of cities in Classes 3, 4, 5 and 6 has an inverted U-shaped relationship with sales ratio. The presence of number of Class 1 and 2 cities has a positive effect on sales ratio. At the state level, state capital expenditure in agriculture has a significant negative impact on sales ratio; however, its squared term has a positive effect, signifying a U-shaped relationship. This implies that capital expenditure has a significant positive role in raising sales ratio but only at a higher level. Total agricultural spending has an inverted U-shaped relationship with sales ratio only during Visit 2. Per capita state GDP has a U-shaped relationship with sales ratio.

Number of market transactions—ordered probit

The determinants of farmers' decisions on the frequency of their market transactions are identified in Model 3. The results show that the possibility of having access to a storage facility has a positive and significant effect on the number of market transactions. Having outstanding institutional credit also has a positive and significant effect on the number of market transactions. However, the interaction between the possibility of having access to storage and having an outstanding loan has a significant negative effect on the number of market transactions. Among household variables, the average age of the household has a positive and significant effect on the number of market transactions. Village neighborhood proportion of households having non-farm work negatively affects market transactions during Visit 2.

At the district level, having a higher proportion of SC population in the district is positively associated with the number of market transactions in Visit 2, but having a higher proportion of ST population has a negative and significant effect in both visits. Interaction between agricultural credit and agricultural markets has a significant positive impact only during Visit 2. The interaction term between self-help groups and access to financial services has a significant positive effect on the number of market transactions in both visits. Agricultural power availability has a U-shaped relationship with the number of market transactions. Among urban centers, the presence of Class 3, 4, 5 and 6 cities has an inverted U-shaped relationship with the number of transactions. The higher the proportion of Class 1 and Class 2 cities, the higher the market transactions during Visit 2. At the state level, state capital expenditure in agriculture has a U-shaped relationship with the number of sales in both visits, but total expenditure on agriculture has an inverted U-shaped association with the number of sales. Per capita state GDP has a U-shaped relationship with the number of sales.

Diversity of agency—Simpson index—SEM

As mentioned, the National Sample Survey records six different types of agencies to whom farmers sell their produce. A higher diversity in sales agencies signifies more options for crop sales and higher bargaining power for farmers. In Model 4, the Simpson index of diversity in agency sale is estimated. Since there is an endogeneity issue with the total number of market transactions, a simultaneous recursive system is estimated with the total number of market transactions as a dependent variable.

Results show that the possibility of having access to storage facilities does not significantly affect the diversity of agency sale. The number of crops cultivated has a positive relationship only during Visit 2, but the squared term of the number of crops cultivated has a negative relationship with the diversity of agency sales. The proportion of irrigated land shows a positive and significant impact on diversity only during Visit 1. Insurance coverage increases the diversity of sale only in Visit 1. Having outstanding credit negatively affects the diversity of sale only during Visit 1. Dummy of SC/ST household raises the diversity of agency sale only during Visit 1. The village neighborhood proportion of households having non-farm work positively affects market transactions during Visit 1. At the district level, access to power for agricultural use has an inverted U-shaped relationship with diversity in sale in Visit 1 but has a U-shaped relationship during Visit 2. The presence of Class 1 and Class 2 cities has a varied impact on the diversity of agency sales in Visit 1 and Visit 2.

At the state level, state capital expenditure and total agricultural expenditure have an inverted U-shaped association with the diversity of agency sale only in Visit 2. Per capita state GDP has an inverted U-shaped relationship with the diversity of sale in both visits. The analysis also reveals that state policy variables such as state-level capital and total agricultural expenditure can significantly affect selling decisions, the sale ratio of crops and the number or frequency of crop sales. This may imply that policymakers can significantly affect a farmer's marketing behavior through economic policy changes. Access to power for agricultural use also can significantly affect a farmer's marketing decision. Smaller urban centers (Class 3, 4, 5 and 6) have a more significant role than bigger urban centers in affecting selling decisions. Providing higher agricultural credit and market access leads to a higher sale ratio. Having a greater number of self-help groups and access to financial services in a district is found to significantly affect a farmer's sales ratio and number of market transactions.

In all four models, crop types are controlled for using exact crop codes recorded in the National Sample Survey. In general, the crop codes are arranged in an increasing manner with regard to a crop's value (that is, a more highly valued crop has a higher value). Sale information is reported for four crops in each visit, thus there are eight crop codes in total in the regressions. In all four types of regressions, the crop codes have a significant impact on the dependent variables under consideration. This implies that the higher the crop's value is, the higher the probability of market sale of crops in Model 1, the higher the sale ratio in Model (2), the higher the number of sales in Model 3, and the higher the sale diversity in Model 4.

Conclusions

This chapter analyzes the factors affecting a farmer-producer's decisions on market participation, or commercialization. Various farm- and household-level factors affect sale decisions. In particular, access to or availability of storage facilities could significantly influence the farmer's marketing decisions. Especially in developing countries where farmers do not have proper marketing facilities, access to storage facilities would allow farmers to store their produce to delay their sale and sell their produce at a better price. This study's objective is to consider various forms of farmers' commercialization decisions to understand the farm, household and structural variables affecting farmers' selling decisions.

The 70th round of the National Sample Survey's farm household-level data from India are analyzed to understand this phenomenon. These data are combined with various structural-level variables from census and other government statistical sources. Four different models of farm commercial behavior are analyzed. The first model is a binary probit model of farmers' selling decisions. The second is a linear model of the sale ratio of the number of crops sold to the number of crops cultivated. In the third model, the number or frequency of market transactions is analyzed using an ordered probit set-up. In the last model, the diversity of agency sales is analyzed by considering agency diversity index in a linear model.

The analysis shows that access to a storage facility could significantly influence farmers' commercialization decisions. Results from this study revealed that farm households with access to a storage facility are more likely than households without such access to take part in a market transaction. They are likely to sell a greater number of crops and are more likely than farmers without storage access to have higher number of market transactions. These findings substantiate DCR (2018)'s policy emphasis on improving farmers' access to storage facilities to increase agricultural commercialization in India.

The results also show that, apart from farm- and household-level factors, many structural or location-specific variables that are beyond the farm household's control affect the farmer's marketing decisions. Having outstanding credit affects a farmer's decision to participate in the market and thus a farmer's sale ratio. Higher agricultural credit, together with market access, influences market sales ratio. Agricultural power availability shows a U-shaped relationship with a farmer's selling decision, sales ratio and number of sales. The presence of smaller urban centers (Class 3, 4, 5 and 6 cities) has an inverted U-shaped relationship with a farmer's selling decision, sale ratio and number of sales. State-level capital and total expenditures in agriculture significantly affect a farmer's market participation. This may imply that policymakers can influence the farmer's marketing behavior by making effective structural changes. Due to the lack of information on storage facilities at the household level, this study used an indirect method of measuring access to storage facilities. Without direct or actual measures of farmers' access to storage facilities, the findings are limited to the likelihood or possibility of a farm household having access to such facilities.

Notes

1 There are at least three possibilities in such cases. (1) The farmer does not have access to storage facilities and has kept aside only a part of the output for self-consumption; (2) the farmer has access to storage facilities, has sold only a part of the output and has kept the rest in storage; and (3) the farmer has access to storage facilities, has kept one part of the output in storage and another part for self-consumption and has sold only the remaining part.

2 The number of farm households is restricted to only 2,218, unlike the 19,976 households in the previous three commercialization specifications.

References

Acharya, S. S. (2004). "Agricultural marketing in India", in *State of the Indian farmer: A millennium study*, New Delhi: Academic Foundation.

Aggarwal, S. (2018). "Do rural roads create pathways out of poverty? Evidence from India", *Journal of Development Economics* **133**, 375–395.

Asher, S. and Novosad, P. (2016). "Market access and structural transformation: Evidence from rural roads in India", Unpublished Manuscript, Department of Economics, Oxford.

Banerji, A. and Meenakshi, J. V. (2004). "Buyer collusion and efficiency of government intervention in wheat markets in northern India: An asymmetrical structural auction analysis", *American Journal of Agricultural Economics* **86 (1)**, 236–253.

Bardhan, P. K. (1980). "Interlocking factor markets and agrarian development: A review of issues", *Oxford Economic Papers* **32(1)**, 82–98.

Basu, K. (1986). "One kind of power", *Oxford Economic Papers* **38(2)**, 259–282.

Bell, C. and Srinivasan, T. N. (1989). "Interlinked transactions in rural markets: An empirical study of Andhra Pradesh, Bihar and Punjab", *Oxford Bulletin of Economics and Statistics* **51(1)**, 73–83.

Chamberlin, J. and Jayne, T. S. (2011). "Unpacking the meaning of 'market access': Evidence from rural Kenya", *World Development* **41**, 245–264.

Das, V. K. (2018). "Looking beyond the farm and household: Determinants of on-farm diversification in India", IGIDR Working Paper No. WP-2018–23.

Das, V. K. and Ganesh-Kumar, A. (2019). "Off-the-farm Livelihood choice of farm households in India", IGIDR Working Paper No. WP-2019–032.

Das, V. K. and Ganesh-Kumar, A. (forthcoming). "Commercialisation, diversification, and structural determinants of farmers' income in India", in Dev S. M. (ed.) *India Development Report-2020*, New Delhi: Oxford University Press.

DCR. (2018). "Report of the committee on doubling farmers' income. Vol. I to XIV, committee on doubling farmers' income", Ministry of Agriculture, Cooperation and Farmers Welfare, Government of India.

Fafchamps, M. and Hill, R. (2005). "Selling at the farmgate or traveling to market", *American Journal of Agricultural Economics* **87(3)**, 717–734.

Fafchamps, M., Hill, R. and Minten, B. (2006). *The Marketing of Non-Staple Crops in India*, Washington, DC: Mimeo, World Bank.

Fafchamps, M., Hill, R. and Minten, B. (2008). "Quality control in nonstaple food markets: Evidence from India", *Agricultural Economics* **38**, 251–266.

Minten, B., Reardon, T., Singh, K.M. and Sutradhar, R. (2010). "The benefit of cold storages: Evidence from Bihar", MPRA Paper No. 54345.

Shilpi, F. and Umali-Deininger, D. (2008). "Market facilities and agricultural marketing: Evidence from Tamil Nadu, India", *Agricultural Economics* **39**, 281–294.

Singh, S. (2019). "Re-organising agricultural markets for doubling farmer incomes in India: Relevance, mechanisms and role of policy", *Indian Journal of Agricultural Economics* **74(3)**, 390–407.

Takeshima, H. and Nagarajan, L. (2012). "Minor millets in Tamil Nadu, India: Local market participation, on-farm diversity and farmer welfare", *Environment and Development Economics* **17(5)**, 603–632.

Umali-Deininger, D. and Deininger, K. (2001). "Towards greater food security for India's poor: Balancing government intervention and private competition", *Agricultural Economics* **25**, 321–335.

Vaidyanathan, A. (2010). *Agricultural Growth in India: Role of Technology, Incentives and Institutions*, New Delhi. Oxford University Press.

18 Agri-commodity futures and value chains

Tirtha Chatterjee, Raghav Raghunathan and Ashok Gulati

It is well recognized that agricultural value chains are long, fragmented and inefficient in India. Prices vary massively, and farmers get a meager share of the rupees that consumers spend on a commodity (Acharya, 2004; Ghosh, 2013; Chand, 2016a, 2016b; Chatterjee and Kapur, 2017). Although value chains are commodity specific, a typical value chain (Figure 18.1) broadly involves farmers, aggregators, commission agents, traders, wholesalers, retailers and, finally, consumers. Each player at every stage charges fees for his or her services, thereby increasing the difference between the prices consumers pay and the prices farmers receive. The longer the channel, the more inefficient and rent-seeking it potentially can be.

One direct implication of these lengthy and fragmented value chains is the lack of a transparent process for discovering prices. The lack of scientific and efficient price discovery leads to a vicious cycle of glut and low prices one year, followed by scarcity and steep prices the next. Acreage-related decisions are based on past prices rather than on their future, expected values. This is where agricultural futures, or agri-futures, potentially can come to aid. Agri-futures are financial contracts requiring the buyer to purchase or the seller to sell a standardized physical agricultural commodity at a predetermined future date and price. Trading in the futures market ensures that both buyer and seller are guaranteed a fixed price at a future date. The role of agri-futures is critical, given that these futures not only aid in price discovery but also mitigate price risk by ensuring a predetermined price.

Despite being more than a century old, the agri-futures market lacks depth and liquidity in India (Gulati et al., 2017). Farmers' association with the futures market is limited. Several factors could be behind this, ranging from farmers' lack of understanding of how futures markets work to constraints emerging from lack of liquidity or even difficulties fulfilling regulatory requirements. Linking farmers to futures markets might mutually benefit both markets and farmers. Such linkages can help farmers better discover prices, hedge their price risk, base their planting decisions on future prices and provide more liquidity that can deepen markets.

With this idea in mind, this chapter aims to identify constraints in farmers' and farmer groups' participation in futures markets and to identify how best to

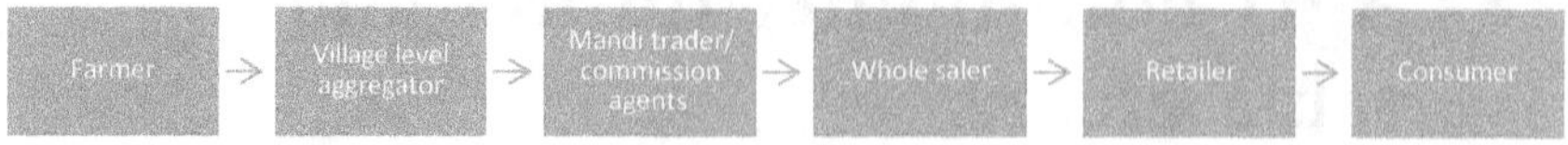

Figure 18.1 Typical marketing channel

Source: Author's compilation.

resolve the constraints. It also looks at selected case studies in India and experiences in another smallholder economy, China, to learn best practices. Because farmers in India are small, they often cannot meet the commodity exchange's lot size and quality standards and thus are not eligible to trade directly in the futures market. Farmer producer organizations (FPOs) or any form of farmer cooperatives can come to rescue by procuring and aggregating produce from the farmers and ensuring it meets the exchange's standards. Therefore, in this chapter, we look at linking futures to value chains through two interim steps: linking farmers to farmer-producer organizations and linking those organizations to futures markets.

The chapter is organized as follows. We discuss the present state of participation in the futures market in India in the second section. Some successful cases in which farmer-producer organizations have used futures markets are discussed in the third section. We identify the constraints in linking futures to value chains, especially for farmers in India, in the fourth section. Some lessons are drawn from experiences in China in the fifth section, and policy recommendations are made in the final section.

Farmer-producer organizations' participation in India's futures market

The National Commodity Derivative Exchange (NCDEX) is India's largest futures exchange for agricultural commodities, with 81% of the country's overall agri-futures trade.[1] The total value of agricultural futures trade at the exchange (Figure 18.2) was Rs 706 billion in April 2016 and came down to Rs 417 billion in May 2018.[2] The roller coaster nature of the plot reflects uncertainty in India's overall agricultural futures trade. Figure 18.2 shows that the value of futures trade by farmer-producer organizations at the exchange was insignificant compared to the value of the overall trade.

The value of agricultural futures trade by farmer-producer organizations was Rs 2.4 million in April 2016 (Figure 18.3). It increased to Rs 104.8 million and Rs 101.7 million in August and September 2017, respectively. Since then, it again has been significantly lower. The spike in the value of futures trade in August and September 2017 was due to the high value of trade by farmer-producer organizations in Bihar state.

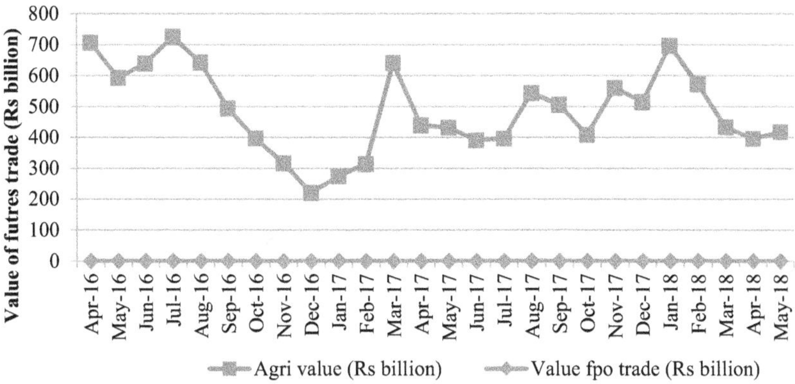

Figure 18.2 Value of overall futures trade in NCDEX and by FPOs in India

Source: Authors' compilation based on NCDEX data.

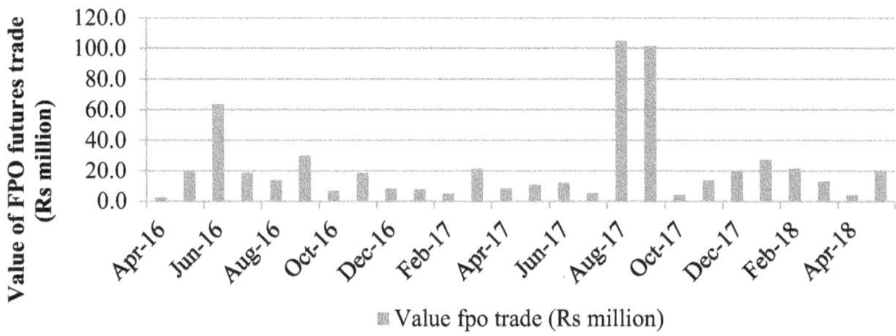

Figure 18.3 Value of futures trading by FPOs, April 2016–May 2018

Source: Authors' compilation based on NCDEX data.

Trade is highly skewed for the commodities traded by farmer-producer organizations. Soybean complex and maize together formed 87% of the organizations' total futures trade between April 2016 and May 2018 (Figure 18.4).

Bihar alone accounted for 64% of the overall futures trade recorded by farmer-producer organizations. The distribution of futures trade across states, along with the number of organizations in each state, is given in Figure 18.5.

Several government initiatives through the National Board of Agriculture and Rural Development (NABARD) and the Small Farmers Agribusiness Consortium (SFAC) have been taken to encourage the formation of farmer-producer organizations across India. The agricultural development board NABARD has dedicated two funds—the Producers Organization Development Fund (PODF) since 2011 and the Producers' Organization Development

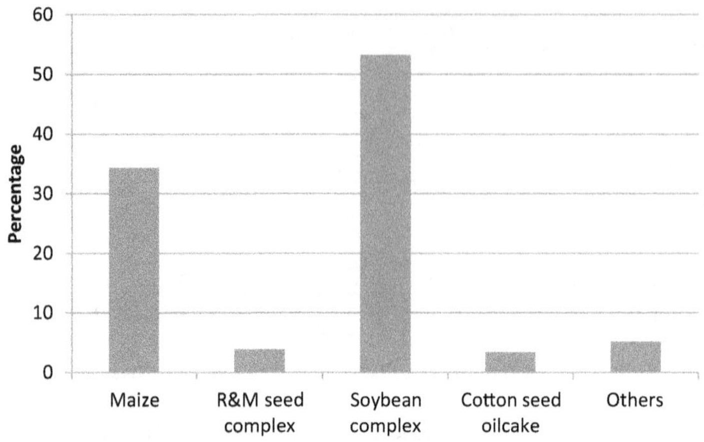

Figure 18.4 Share of commodities in total FPOs futures trade

Source: Authors' compilation based on NCDEX data.

Note: Others include turmeric, barley, cotton, guar complex, pepper, jeera, chah, castor, wheat. Total FPO futures trade of Rs 508 million between April 2016 and May 2018.

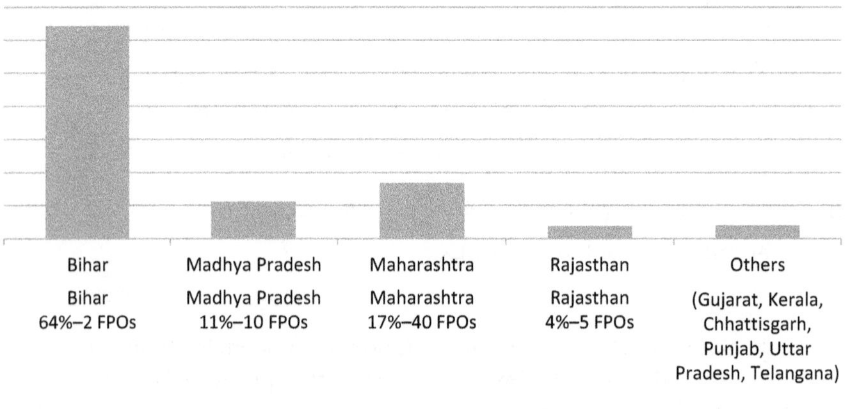

Figure 18.5 Share of states in total FPOs futures trade, April 2016–May 2018

Source: Authors' compilation based on NCDEX data.

Note: Total FPO futures trade of Rs 508 million between April 2016 and May 2018.

and Upliftment Corpus Fund (PRODUCE fund) since 2014—to support farmer-producer organizations with credit support, capacity building and market linkage.

Data retrieved from the farmer-producer organizations portal on NABARD's website shows there are now 2,064 such organizations supported by the

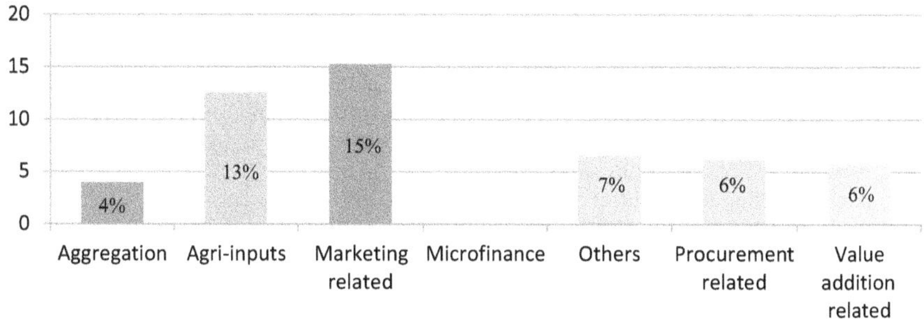

Figure 18.6 Distribution of NABARD FPOs on the basis of business activity

Source: Compiled by the authors based on NABARD and NCDEX data.

Note: The % share is computed out of a total of 1039 FPOs that have specified business activities (accessed in June 2018).

development board NABARD FPOs.[3] Of those, we find that 1,025 have no specified business activities. Figure 18.6 gives a distribution of the organizations based on their business activities. Of the 2,064 NABARD farmer-producer organizations across India, the number of those trading at the futures market is extremely low. According to data retrieved from the National Commodity Derivative Exchange, only 20 of the 2,064 farmer-producer organizations have traded in the market. These small numbers reflect the lack of penetration of NABARD farmer-producer organizations in terms of futures trade in India. It is plausible that the organizations' slow mobilization is due to the natural time they require to attain maturity. It takes time to change from being an aggregator and dealing with marketing activities to trading in futures markets. However, to ensure that futures markets are deepened, the government must give these farmer-producer organizations the necessary support to facilitate their transition from simple aggregation-related activities to participation in the market.

Case studies on farmer participation

As discussed, Bihar is the most significant player in the overall futures trade by farmer-producer organizations in India. Aranyak Agri Producer Co. (AAPCL), located in Purnea, Bihar, is a good example of an organization trading in the futures platform. Aranyak's participation is due to a collaboration of the World Bank; JEEViKA, a Bihar government initiative; technical partner Technoserve. Aranyak has established a farmer-centric model of aggregation and marketing in winter maize. World Bank research[4] documents how the company has linked with the National Commodity Derivative Exchange and benefitted by realizing higher prices. Its extraordinary growth can be gauged by growth rates of nearly 1,000% in both the number of women farmers and in the quintals of maize aggregated (Table 18.1).

Table 18.1 Futures trade in Aranyak Agri Producer Company

	Some metrics	*2015–2016*	*2016–2017*	*2017–2018*
1	Number of women farmers participated	299	818	3,479
2	Maize aggregated (quintal)	10,140	30,640	1,39,442
3	Average procurement price (INR/quintal)	1,000	1,141	1,155
4	Average cost of operations (INR/quintal)	175	245	255
5	Average selling price (INR/quintal)	1,265	1,531	?

Source: Aranyak Agri Producer Company.

Note: Average selling price is not known since all produce was not sold during that time.

Aranyak's model involved procuring produce from farmers and exploring different channels to market it, including open market sales, futures and spot exchange such as NeML that facilitates FPOs in buying and selling of the farmers' produce. The open market gives Aranyak greater flexibility in the quality of produce it sells, and the futures market gives it price certainty. In discussions with several stakeholders at the company, we found that one factor crucial to the project's rapid scaling was accessibility to Gulabagh, the delivery center for *Rabi* (winter season) maize. This center is located within a 30-km radius of villages where Aranyak is based.

However, sources confirmed that in 2017–2018 the model had a setback because of significant losses in inventory of 90,000 quintals maize. The losses purportedly were due to issues in decision making and coordination between the buying, storing and selling operations. Market prices did not rise to the extent of costs (logistics and storage), resulting in losses. One reason that might have contributed to such losses could have been the organization's strategy of using warehouse receipts to fulfill working-capital requirements. This incentivized the organization to accumulate inventory rather than sell it quickly. More flexible working capital that allows collateral-free loans for buying and selling operations—as opposed to buying, storing and then selling—would grant farmer-producer organizations more operational freedom.

In this section, we discuss three other cases in which farmer-producer organizations successfully used the futures market to hedge their price risk. They are Ram Rahim Pragati Producer Co. in Madhya Pradesh, Nari Shakti Cluster Level Federation in Rajasthan and Samruddhi Mahila Crop Producer Co. Ltd., also in Rajasthan. Ram Rahim was the first farmer-producer organization to trade in the futures market. Nari Shakti involved a combination of state government and resource institutions and started as pilot projects. Samruddhi Mahila shows how well managed producer companies, with an empowered group of shareholders with proactive leadership, can trade successfully in the futures market.

Ram Rahim, Madhya Pradesh

Based in the tribal block of Bagli, in the Dewas District of Madhya Pradesh, more than 3,000 women members belonging to 162 self-help groups with

Table 18.2 Ram Rahim futures trade

	2015–2016	*2016–2017*	*2017–2018*
Number of farmers	205	0	0
Total soybean aggregated (q)	178.72	0	0
Quantity sold to *mandi* (q)	0	156.31	0
To National Commodity Derivative Exchange (q)	7,800	4,800	0

Source: Samaj Pragati Sahayog.

Note: Quantity sold to NCDEX is more than that procured as this reflects a mix of active hedging and carefully managed speculation, including using Soya as a proxy hedging tool for other crops.

the support of Samaj Pragati Sahayog, an organization focused on water and livelihoods, started this enterprise in 2012. The objective was to aggregate and market the members' farm produce, which included soybean, chana, maize and wheat. Previously, the value chain was such that farmers were trapped in a vicious cycle in which they took loans from and sold their produce to informal moneylenders who also happened to be traders. However, after the Ram Rahim organization started procuring the produce, the intermediaries' role became limited. The organization began trading in the futures market in 2014 after it incurred losses marketing Bengal gram the previous *Kharif* (summer season). It was able to mitigate price risk by hedging on the national commodity exchange in 2014. Since then, the enterprise evolved this mechanism to use the contracts to sell soya that it would purchase in October (before the harvest) and lock in prices, if favorable. Table 18.2 shows no trade in 2016–2017 or 2017–2018 because the organization's focus shifted over the years toward crops that had been neglected earlier, like maize and pulses. The organization stopped aggregating soybean and moved toward pulses and maize as a step toward agricultural diversification. Sources from the field identified a few reasons for the lack of trade in these crops, including a lack of delivery centers and a lack of contracts for some essential pulses such as green gram and red gram. Constraints that the pilot program faced included stiff competition from traditional value chain players, a limited number of delivery centers and warehouses, large farmers who were averse to pre-harvest hedging and a lack of futures contracts for the commodities produced.

Nari Shakti, Rajasthan

Rajasthan Grameen Aajeevika Vikas Parishad, Government of Rajasthan (RGAVP/Rajeevika[5]); the LetzDream Foundation[6] (LDF), a non-profit grant-making foundation; and the Cluster Level Federations (CLFs) together ensured futures trading in Nari Shakti, Rajasthan. To date, there are 352 cluster-level federations in 157 blocks of Rajasthan, catering to 100,000 women. LetzDream Foundation professionals deployed in four cluster-level federations in Sangod Block and developed a model in which farmers could sell their produce at the

National Commodity Derivative Exchange platform. The exchange's platform was chosen as an alternative after considering its expected benefits compared to those of the traditional marketing channel, in which farmers sold produce to middlemen. After comparing prices at the futures market and at agricultural *mandis*—open markets where producers and wholesalers meet—a contract account was opened through the commodity broker Religare. In March 2017, after a pilot project of securing soybean the previous season, four cluster-level federations in the Sangod Block of the Kota District kick-started a program to procure mustard. Of the four clusters, Nari Shakti Cluster Level Federation was used as the nodal agency for procurement. The procurement chain started with purchases from farmers at the household level. Quality checks and rate finalization were done per local *mandi* prices, and farmers were paid accordingly. The produce was transferred to warehouses at Kota, where the Kota *mandi* operated, or to institutional buyers or traders through the national exchange, NCDEX. Table 18.3 gives the details regarding procurement and quantities sold on the exchange in 2016–2017. Some of the pilot project's major bottlenecks were the timely availability of warehouses, making self-help group members understand and move away from the traditional intermediaries of *mandis*, value addition at the cluster-level federation level and high rejection rates because of failure to meet quality and quantity specifications.

Samruddhi Mahila Crop Producer Co. Ltd. is one of the largest producer companies in Rajasthan, with a shareholder base of more than 2,500 women members. Farmers grow urad and soya bean in the *Kharif* season and mustard and wheat in the *Rabi* season. The producer company initially focused on selling improved seed varieties and on crop productivity, but farmers also began to demand better markets to sell their surplus. The company entered a partnership with Bunge Ltd., an American agribusiness multinational headquartered in New York, to supply soya beans at fair and fixed prices. In September 2016, Samruddhi Mahila experimented with futures by taking up a short/sell position on soya for 10 metric tons (MT), or one lot. The enterprise thus became the first producer company to undertake a hedging-based futures trade in Rajasthan. As prices fell during the subsequent period, the enterprise sold or

Table 18.3 Nari Shakti futures trade

	2016–2017
Number of farmers in each CLF	3,740
Number of farmer sold at NCDEX	139
Total quantity of soybean sold at NCDEX	77.1 q
Total quantity of mustard sold at NCDEX	974 q
Additional profit earned by farmers	Rs 200/q
Profit earned by each cluster-level foundation	Rs 42,324

Source: LetzDream Foundation, Samruddhi Mahila Crop Producer Co. Ltd., Rajasthan.

squared off the position and used the trading profits to give bonuses to a few farmers who had offered to sell on the platform. The experiment's success generated a lot of interest among other farmers. The organization was backed by a strong management team and by Self-Reliant Initiatives through Joint Action (SRIJAN), which had a history of promoting and nurturing grass roots organizations. SRIJAN, the management, the producer company's board and the farmers worked together to ensure that there were no slippages in documentation, in the logistics of finding warehouse spaces, in booking the warehouse and finally in using the national exchange to deliver at the contracted rate.

Encouraged by these results, another farmer-producer organization promoted by SRIJAN, the Jaisingh Nagar Soya Samruddhi Producer Co., based in Sagar District in Madhya Pradesh, ventured to take part a year later, using soya futures. In January and February 2018, Jaisingh Nagar Soya Samruddhi used soya futures to offload 40 MT of soya using the national exchange at prices of about Rs 3,350 and Rs 3,391/q. It is interesting to note that this was the year that the Bhavantar Bhugtan Yojna, a scheme of government of Madhya Pradesh that pays farmers the difference between official minimum support price (MSP) and the farmer's crop selling price, was in operation. A few months earlier, spot prices below Rs 2,600/q had prevailed, and futures were at a premium. Farmers were able to receive prices nearly 30% higher than those in the local market and 10% higher than the minimum support price announced for soya that year or than the ceiling price for Bhavantar Yojna.

Some lessons

These case studies show how well managed producer companies, along with an empowered group of shareholders and proactive leadership, can help in adopting and sustaining the practice of using futures, both as a hedging tool and as an alternative marketplace. They show the graduation of producer companies from being single-commodity players to multi-commodity and multi-season participants in the exchange. A key finding from these case studies is that farmer-producer organizations have no one reason for trading in the futures market. They can enter the market because of prior losses due to market volatility, a new pathway for market access or better price discovery, among other reasons. For example, Ram Rahim began trading in the futures market to avoid holding losses and then started using futures primarily as a hedging technique. For Samruddhi Mahila, the futures market evolved as an instrument to offer support against uncertainty when the organization used it before harvest. Nari Shakti used the futures market in discovering an alternative pathway to existing market channels for primary produce when selling through or at the *mandis* did not materialize.

These farmer-producer organizations have pursued different strategies while participating in the futures platform (Table 18.4). Ram Rahim pursued both pre- and post-harvest hedging. Pre-harvest hedging is a medium-risk option, as prices might increase post-harvest. Post-harvest hedging has the maximum

Table 18.4 Showing different strategies pursued by different producer companies

	Producer companies/ strategies employed	*Post-harvest hedging*	*Post-harvest hedging + Delivery on the exchange*	*Pre-harvest hedging*	*Pre-harvest hedging + delivery*
1	RamRahim	Yes		Yes	
2	Nari Shakti		Yes		
3	Samruddhi Mahila			Yes	Yes

Source: Authors' compilation.

risk, as the farmer-producer organization lies completely exposed to markets for as long as it remains unhedged or for the extent of its holding time. The exact strategy for hedging—whether pre-harvest, during harvest or post-harvest after a certain amount of holding—can be quantified as a model based on risk preferences. Nari Shakti's strategy was a combination of post-harvest hedging and delivery at the exchange, since produce bought from the farmers was sold at the exchange. We found that Samruddhi Mahila undertook pre-harvest hedging for *Kharif* soybeans in 2016 and pre-harvest hedging plus delivery for *Rabi* mustard in 2017.

Reasons for low participation

Since most farmers are small and marginal in India and unable to meet the national commodity exchange's quality and quantity specifications, we look at farmer participation as an outcome of two steps: linking farmers to farmer-producer organizations and linking the organizations to the exchange. Farmer-producer organizations or any other farmer groups can procure and aggregate produce from the farmers who maintain the required quality and quantity restrictions required and can trade at the exchange. Here, we look at the bottlenecks in these two steps.

Step 1: Linking farmers to farmer-producer organizations

1 A network of traders and intermediaries controls agricultural value chains. The intensity of the relationships facilitates strong networks of reciprocity and manifests as a power relationship, binding smallholder farmers to these traders in many ways. Given the financial constraints that the farmers face, they have to resort to traditional buyers and traders for loans and therefore often are obliged to sell them their produce. Consequently, farmers are unable and often unwilling to let go of their relationship with these traders. Farmer-producer organizations, being relatively new, have not been able to displace such networks.

2 Financial constraints prove to be one of the most critical bottlenecks for farmer-producer organizations. They have to depend on farmer members or shareholders for access to capital in the form of equity. Access to debt capital or working capital in the form of bank loans also is constrained. Discussions at the field level show that local banks, regional rural cooperatives and mainstream banks are reluctant to lend to farmer-producer organizations. It was only in fiscal 2017–2018 that the Reserve Bank of India formally categorized farmer-producer organizations as a priority sector in the Reserve Bank's lending mandates for public-sector and private-sector banks. All these conditions make for a high barrier for access to capital.

3 Financials constraints have an impact on the kind of activity a farmer-producer organization performs. Most of the organizations engage in the business activities of aggregating and selling inputs as opposed to aggregating and selling produce. This is because the risk involved in procurement and output-related activities is higher than the risk on the input side of the market. When dealing with output-related risks, farmer-producer organizations have to manage price risks, storage and interest costs.

4 Farmer-producer organizations face the classic issue of the principal–agent problem, in which decisions affecting the principal, the farmers and the shareholders of the enterprise are being made by the agents or the managers of the producer company. Most of them are staff members on the payroll of the parent non-governmental organization. If shareholders' interests are not aligned with management's interests, achieving robust and enduring models of producer companies will be difficult (Singh and Singh, 2012).

Step 2: Linking farmer-producer organizations to the futures market

Some reasons for organizations' low participation in the futures market are as follows:

1 *Lack of trust in and understanding of the futures market*: The futures market is seen as a black box, even among policymakers in India. Therefore, farmers are confused about it and do not trust the platform as much as they could. It is thought to be similar to gambling, and most farmers choose to stay away from it. In several instances, farmers have been subject to huge losses because of some miscreants. The activities of these miscreants have raised further negative beliefs about futures markets.

2 *No grading and sorting facilities at the farm level*: The quality of the produce that the farmer-producer organizations procure does not always match the standards required by the national exchange. This often leads to high rejection rates, which discourage farmer-producer organizations from participating in the futures market. Instead, the organizations favor selling produce in the *mandis*, despite the traders' high margins and the lower price realizations.

3 *The reluctance in pre-harvest hedging*: Farmer-producer organizations are generally risk averse, and they believe that holding stock would give them greater bargaining power. They are reluctant to lock in prices before the harvest, which often leads to huge losses because prices are likely to fall post-harvest and, given the limited shelf life of produce, all the procured quantity has to be sold at lower prices. This increases the organizations' inventory and squeezes their margins.
4 *The location of national exchange's delivery centers far from farmer-producer organizations*: Given that crop varieties differ from one plot to a neighboring plot, or even within different plots of the same farmer, closer delivery centers would help in the price discovery process.
5 *Tedious documentation and entry barriers*: First, farmers have to be part of registered farmer-producer organizations, and in turn, these organizations have to become clients of brokering entities that are members of the national exchange. This entails a three-step process since direct membership of farmer-producer organizations in the exchange is not feasible,[7] and the organizations have to rely on brokers to access the exchange. These brokers, which are based predominantly in urban areas, often lack incentives to address the needs of farmer-producer organizations. For brokers, revenue earned by catering to organizations that might not be regular clients is not worth the investment of time, money and effort. At the broker level, more than 20 documents are mandated, including know your customer (KYC) details of directors of the producer companies, some of which are unavailable.
6 *Different objectives or producer collectives of resource institutions, which are often at different stages of maturity*: Producer organizations have various objectives, such as dealing with inputs, microfinance and others. They are also at different stages of maturity, and it is plausible that they might not have felt the need to deal with procurement and selling at the futures market platform.

Mismatch between production centers, delivery centers and futures trade

The lack of delivery centers close to production centers was identified as a major bottleneck in all three case studies explored in this chapter. Several factors could influence the feasibility of a place becoming a delivery center for futures-trading activities, such as whether the region is a production center, whether the region has significant trade flow and whether the area's infrastructural and logistical facilities, such as roads and warehouses, are conducive for futures trading. Among these factors, we focus here on how well linked production centers are to delivery centers and therefore to the futures market. We find a considerable gap between producing and trading centers across India. Using data for 2014–2015, which was the latest data available for all the commodities, we identified the following producing districts:

1 States with 80% of the total production of the commodity
2 Districts that cover 80% of the area under production

Table 18.5 Production districts and trading districts

	Particulars	*Soybean complex*	*R&M complex*	*Maize*	*Cotton and cottonseed oilcake*	*Chana*	*Barley*
1	All three districts	3	1	1	1	0	1
2	Only production center	9	21	68	25	46	21
3	Only futures trade	16	3	4	6	0	3
4	Only delivery center	2	1	2	0	1	0
5	Futures trade and delivery center	4	1	1	1	0	0
6	Production center and delivery center	2	3	1	2	3	1
7	Production center and futures trade	4	2	1	0	2	0

Source: Based on data from NCDEX and Ministry of Agriculture.

The intersection of delivery and producing centers can be the first focus of districts seeking to encourage and pilot futures trade. Delivery centers have to be built first in regions that are both producing and trading centers. This will boost trade and encourage further participation in the futures market. Table 18.5 gives the number of production centers, futures trading centers and delivery centers and the intersections of the three sets for some other crops. The numbers in the first row, which show the intersection of producing centers, futures trade and delivery centers, highlight the lack of mapping among the three.

For soybean, only three districts are producing centers, have delivery centers and trade in the futures market. For chana, no districts have an intersection of all three. These low numbers show that much has to be done in terms of linking production centers with the futures market. The liquidity and depth of the futures market can be raised only when major production centers are linked to the market. Developing more delivery centers in the producing districts, in addition to encouraging participation by all stakeholders, could aid in more farmer participation.

Lessons from China

Lessons from China's experience are particularly impressive given that, as in India, small and marginal farmers dominate the country's agriculture. Despite the similarity to Indian agriculture, however, the stark difference between the two economies in terms of the deepening of futures markets is striking. In this section, we review the initiatives that the commodity exchanges in China and the Government of China have taken to encourage farmers' participation in the futures market. Despite starting as late as 1993, China is the world's most significant player in the futures market in terms of the number of contracts traded. As documented by studies such as Peck (2001), the genesis of Chinese futures was a deliberate and cautious attempt and was based extensively on pilot projects and experimentation.

China started encouraging farmers' participation in the futures market as early as 2005. Some of the initiatives by the Dalian Commodity Exchange (DCE) and the Government of China to promote farmers' participation are given here.

1 The United Nations Conference on Trade and Development (UNCTAD) Report (2006)[8] documents that the Dalian Commodity Exchange conducted a broad-based farmer education program beginning in 2005 called 1,000 Villages, 10,000 Farmers. This exchange is the largest exchange in China that deals with futures trading in agricultural commodities. The program was launched in the major grain production regions in northeast China, including Heilongjiang Province. Farmers were trained to use futures-market-related information to form more accurate expectations about future price developments across two crops, improving their planting, harvesting and selling decisions as a result.
2 In 2007, the Dalian exchange launched the program to serve rural households. This involved training and educating farmers, commodity enterprise executives and cadres in rural communities about futures trading. They were trained in hedging their risks and adjusting plantation structures according to price changes in the futures market.
3 The Dalian exchange signed an agreement with the cities of Wuhan and Chongqing in 2007 in which the governments expressed their support for using their local advantages to help the exchange introduce new products.
4 The Dalian exchange signed strategic cooperation agreements with the provinces of Sichuan, Hubei and Chongqing to jointly foster the development of live hog contracts in 2007.
5 The Rural Communities and Families Service Project, the Dalian Commodity Exchange and the Heilongjiang Province Agricultural Committee co-sponsored the Heilongjiang Province Initial Farmer Cooperative Leader Futures Training Program. At the end of September 2009, there were 7,702 registered farmers' cooperatives in Heilongjiang Province, with 57% of them focused on planting corn and soybeans. The establishment of these specialized cooperatives has improved the level of organization of agricultural production.
6 The National Development and Reform Commission (NDRC) and the Ministry of Agriculture published 'Guidelines for Accelerating the Transformation of Northeast China's Agricultural Development and Constructing Modern Agriculture,' which recommended the timely launching of new futures products focused on Northeastern agriculture at the Dalian Commodity Exchange in 2010.
7 The exchange and the Heilongjiang Provincial Agriculture Commission in 2012 signed the Strategic Development and Cooperation Agreement of

Services for Agriculture, Farmer and Rural Area to train farmer marketing teams and to add content about futures to the training programs for the farmer marketing teams.

8 The 'No.1 Document of Communist Party of China Central Committee for 2016' considers the futures market crucial for the economy and sets out requirements to create and design agricultural futures products, to carry out a pilot for agricultural options and to steadily expand the 'insurance plus futures' pilot programs.

In 2016, the Central No. 1 Document recommended the launch of this scheme to offer subsidies to insurance companies to provide agricultural insurance policies based on futures prices (Kenderdine, 2018). The futures companies have been required to provide the service to protect households, family farms and rural cooperatives against price risks through the 'insurance plus futures' projects. The price data related to the insurance contracts are based on the corresponding Dalian Commodity Exchange futures data (Figure 18.7). As of 2017, there had been 32 pilot projects in corn and soybean in the provinces of Heilongjiang, Jilin, Liaoning, Inner Mongolia, Hebei, Anhui and Chongqing, and 678,300 tons of spot corns and 114,000 tons of spot soybeans had been traded under the scheme (Dalian Commodity Exchange).

It must be noted that the futures market cannot exist and function efficiently in isolation. It can function efficiently only when it gets support from all three stakeholders—the government, the regulator and the exchange. Lower levels of market intervention will reduce distortion, and futures markets will be able to discover prices more efficiently and achieve their objective. More efficient price discovery will increase trust in the futures markets' functioning and encourage participation. In this regard, the Chinese government's evolution

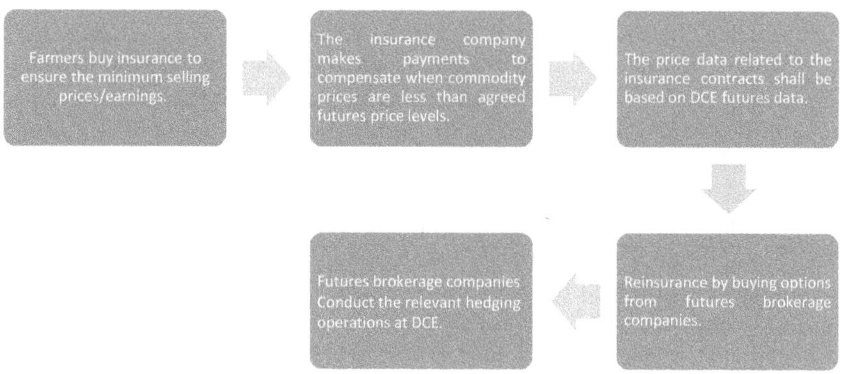

Figure 18.7 Steps in the futures + insurance model

Source: Dalian Commodity Exchange.

away from minimum support and procurement-based policies and toward more market-oriented support is noteworthy.

Policy recommendations

Farmers' participation in futures trade is meager in India. Some of the following suggestions can help farmer-producer organizations participate further in futures trading.

1 Identify production centers for crops and focus initiatives on encouraging futures trading in these areas. The focus has to be put on areas located in districts producing the commodities. The next focus has to be on building delivery centers around producing districts. Since this may not be feasible for all cases, more location-based contracts should be offered. This is where India's National Commodity Derivative Exchange can lead the way.
2 Resource institutions are another vital link in encouraging farmer participation. These ground-level organizations are involved with the workings of farmer-producer organizations and have to be trained, educated and made comfortable with concepts related to futures markets and pre-harvest hedging. Given the ground presence of these resource institutions, their role is crucial in the linking process.
3 Government initiatives like those in Bihar and Rajasthan need rigorous assessments. If found useful, they can make a case for increasing such pilots in other states. Such initiatives show how farmer-owned institutions, in the presence of government support, can successfully make use of market mechanisms.
4 Government bodies like National Agricultural Cooperative Marketing Federation of India, the National Board of Agriculture and Rural Development, the Small Farmers Agribusiness Coalition and Primary Agricultural Credit Society all can play a part by providing training, participating or both in the market. The presence of government bodies will build trust and encourage farmers to participate in the market and can have a role in clearing the market's negative image. Government- and exchange-aided training is done in other countries, such as China. The first bottleneck to futures trade is a lack of trust in and understanding of the workings of the futures market, and government participation in the process can significantly correct this.
5 India's futures market can learn lessons from China's in terms of the support that the state provides to the futures market, not only by directly participating in the model but by encouraging farmers and creating a suitable policy environment for the futures market.
6 Other market-based instruments, such as options and forwards, can be more appropriate for farmers than open market. The case studies discussed earlier show that farmer-producer organizations prefer forwards-like arrangements over futures as a price risk instrument. All these together could enrich the possibility of free and possibly fair trade of produce between buyers and sellers.

Notes

1 SEBI Annual Report (2019).
2 The time frame considered is constrained because of data availability on farmer participation.
3 Accessed in June 2018 at https://nabfpo.in/images/staticFPO.html.
4 Source: http://documents.worldbank.org/curated/en/298391515516507115/122290272_20180012014525/additional/122548-WP-P090764-PUBLIC-India-BRLP-Booklet-p.pdf.
5 It is a flagship rural development program. A range of livelihood promotion activities is driven through a cluster-based approach.
6 LetzDream Foundation (LDF), a non-profit grant-making foundation, has partnered with RGAVP since July 2016 to assist the work of CLFs.
7 Regulatory requirement that stipulates a minimum net worth of Rs 1 crore for membership and deposits of up to Rs 50 lakhs (for trading and clearing members) is a huge entry barrier for producer companies. www.ncdex.com/Membership/TypeofMembership.aspx
8 http://unctad.org/en/Docs/ditccom20084_en.pdf.

References

Acharya, S. (2004). Agricultural Marketing in India. In *State of the Indian Farmer: A Millennium Study*, Vol. 17. New Delhi: Academic Foundation and Department of Agriculture and Cooperation, Ministry of Agriculture, Government of India.

Chand, R. (2016a). e-Platform for National Agricultural Market. *Economic & Political Weekly EPW*, II(28).

Chand, R. (2016b). Regional Agricultural and Trade Policies: Indian Perspective. In *2016 Conference (60th)*, February 2–5, 2016, Canberra, Australia (No. 235263), Australian Agricultural and Resource Economics Society.

Chatterjee, S., & Kapur, D. (2017, August). Six puzzles in Indian agriculture. *India Policy Forum 2016*, 17, 13.

Ghosh, N. (2013). *India's Agricultural Marketing*. Market Reforms and Emergence of New Channels, Springer, New Delhi, India.

Gulati, A., Chatterjee, T., & Hussain, S. (2017). *Agricultural Commodity Futures: Searching for Potential Winners*. ICRIER Working Paper No-349.

Kenderdine, T. (2018). Insurance Plus Futures: Agricultural Commodity Price Reform in China. *Asia & the Pacific Policy Studies*, 5(2), 331–346.

NCDEX Group, Report on Connecting Farmers to Markets.

Peck, A. E. (2001). The Development of Commodity Exchanges in the Former Soviet Union, Eastern Europe, and China. *Australian Economic Papers*, 40(4), 437–460.

Singh, S., & Singh, T. (2012). *Producer Companies in India: A Study of Organization and Performance*. Draft report, Ministry of Agriculture, Government of India, IEG, New Delhi.

19 Contract farming and its impact on fertilizer usage

Evidence from India

Ashok K. Mishra, Anjani Kumar and Alwin Dsouza

The Green Revolution increased food production and food security in India, leading to higher incomes for farm families and rural households (Hazell, 2009). Farm families in the northwestern states, including Punjab and Haryana, enjoyed significant prosperity in income and in farmland holdings. However, after five decades of overusing water, electricity, subsidized fertilizer and pesticides, farmers in the northwestern states face significant declines in agricultural productivity. For example, agricultural productivity growth rates declined from 5.1% in 1981–1982 to 2.4% in 2013–2014 in Punjab and from about 4% in 1981–1982 to 2.5% in 2013–2014 in Haryana. Binswanger and D'Souza (2015) note that agricultural growth rates were significantly lower for Punjab and Haryana than for a majority of other states. The declining growth rates have been attributed to limited expansion of cropped areas and lower productivity of major crops (Chand et al., 2007). Feola and Binder (2010) note that unsustainable practices are causing water shortages, soil erosion, higher levels of soil salinity and significant damage to the ecosystem in most marginal areas of the developing world.

The Green Revolution introduced hybrid varieties of wheat, rice and maize, and it introduced modern agricultural technologies, including irrigation and heavy doses of chemical fertilizer (Binswanger et al., 1993; Saifi and Drake, 2008). In India, farmers in major grain-producing states, including Punjab and Haryana, adopted rice-wheat crop rotation. Because these crops require large amounts of water and fertilizers, rice-wheat crop rotation led to overexploitation of groundwater and heavy use of chemical fertilizers, leading to a decline in the water table and an increase in soil salinity (Singh and Sidhu, 2004; Ladha et al., 2008; Singh and Sidhu, 2004). For instance, during the 1973–2003 period, the groundwater table fell significantly, about 24 cm/year, in both Punjab and Haryana (Bhalla, 2007). Significant amounts of nutrients (nitrogen (N), phosphorus (P) and potassium (K), also known as NPK) have been removed from agricultural soil—from about 2.6 million tons removed in 1960–1961 to about 135 million tons removed in 1998–1999—and rice-wheat crop rotation alone removed about 83% of the major nutrients (Singh and Sidhu, 2004; Sidhu, 2002). Removal of nutrients has adversely impacted yields of both rice and wheat, with rice productivity falling from 75% in 1970–1971 to 9% in 2010–2011 and wheat productivity falling from 80% to a negative 1% (Government of Punjab, 2012). Chemical fertilizers may lead to surface and groundwater pollution (e.g., through run-off and leaching), and the discharge of saline water into rivers and watersheds could lead to salinization of farmland and destruction of crops (Sharpley et al., 2001).

A continuous rice-wheat cropping system leads to several problems: natural resource degradation, water scarcity and low farm profitability. This makes maize an alternative crop for enterprise diversification and livelihood security (Gulati et al., 2017; Bhatt et al., 2016). Switching to other enterprises also may help increase the sustainability and productivity of both land and water. Maize, the so-called Queen of Cereals, has multiple benefits, including as a staple food, as starch in industrial uses for starch and in breweries and as feed for poultry and cattle (Murdia et al., 2016). Maize is a versatile crop that can adapt to different agro-climatic conditions (Parihar et al., 2011). It also provides opportunities for farm mechanization and conservation agriculture, resulting in greater farming efficiency, reduced soil erosion, improved soil health, reduced costs of cultivation and increased farm profitability.

An interesting recent development is that of growing maize for vegetable purposes (Dass et al., 2008). Adding value to the traditional maize, specialty corn has been popularized and cultivated by large numbers of farmers (Parihar et al., 2011). The National Food Security Act 2013 also may boost demand for maize grain, particularly of specialty corn. In the context of peri-urban agriculture, specialty corns such as baby corn and sweet corn hold great promise for ensuring livelihood security. Many common sweet corn and field corn cultivars can be used for baby corn production.[1] Baby corn is rich in proteins, vitamins and iron and is one of the richest sources of phosphorus. It is a good source of fibrous protein and is easy to digest. In our study, we focus on baby corn, a niche crop that has tremendous potential for improving the income and livelihood of smallholders in India, especially in regions facing environmental degradation. Baby corn provides income within two months of sowing, and it provides income from good-quality fodder during the lean season (Chaudhary et al., 2012). Additionally, green fodder, a by-product of baby corn, can be used by cattle, perhaps boosting India's dairy industry (Mahajan et al., 2007). In a recent study, Sharma and Banik (2013) found that intercropping[2] of baby corn and legumes can lead to better soil health and reduce the use of weedicide. Finally, as noted by Lamichhane et al. (2015), the sustainable production of minor crops, like baby corn, is vital for human health, nutritional food supplies and food security as well as for national economies.

Baby corn is becoming popular in domestic and foreign markets and has enormous processing and export potential. Joshi et al. (2005) conclude that with changing food preferences, demand for quality protein maize like baby corn will increase rapidly and that producers and consumers would benefit from the development of institutional arrangements to strengthen production-marketing-processing linkages. Finally, policy reforms of the Government of India are aimed at promoting the growth of the private sector in agribusiness through contract farming (CF). Contract farming is a contractual agreement, either written or oral, between a company and smallholders. It accelerates technology transfer and provides assured output markets, capital flows and a consistent quality of output (Eaton and Shepherd, 2001). Contract farming plays a crucial role in farming practices, benefiting farmers when selling their products, since they have risk assurances in price, marketing and other production factors, which leads to stable incomes (Bauman, 2000). Development and acceptance of innovative institutional arrangements like contract farming to strengthen production-marketing-processing linkages would benefit producers, consumers and the emerging baby corn industry. Additionally, self-sustaining, low-input and energy-efficient agricultural systems in the context of sustainable agriculture[3] have always been at the center of attention of many smallholders, researchers and policymakers in India.

This chapter's objective is to assess contract farming's impact on the productivity, irrigation costs and fertilizer costs of baby corn. We also investigate contract farming's impact on the use of the chemical fertilizers urea and DAP. Unlike previous studies, we use propensity scores[4] as weights (PSW) to match and evaluate the treatment effect of contract farming on outcome variables. PSW matching is preferred for small sample sizes and control groups. Among the many estimators, we use the doubly robust marginal mean weighting through stratification (DR-MMWS), as it overcomes mis-specification of the functional form when propensity score and outcome models are wrongly specified. We use data from a farm-level survey of smallholders in two states of India, namely Punjab and Haryana, which are considered on the forefront of the Green Revolution but now face significant productivity, soil and environmental problems.

This study contributes to the literature on several fronts. Besides investigating contract farming's effects on outcome variables, this study assesses its impact on fertilizer use. Fertilizer usage is directly linked to groundwater contamination and soil degradation. If private market intervention, like contract farming, can increase yield, decrease irrigation costs and lower fertilizer usage, it bodes well for both farmers and policymakers and provides environmental benefits for society at large.[5] We also use propensity score weighting matching to account for all observations and to match control and treatment groups. This method overcomes the problems of a lack of common support and of the large sample required in the propensity score method.

The rest of this chapter is organized into five sections. The second section covers background information on the crisis in northwestern Indian agriculture and charts the advantages of maize cultivation and maize-wheat cropping patterns. The third section describes the methodology, and the fourth section describes survey data. The fifth section covers the evaluation approach used for the study, results and discussion. The final section provides the study's key findings and discusses policy recommendations.

Background

High-yielding seed varieties, irrigation water and the use of chemical fertilizers significantly increased India's output of rice and wheat and have made India a food-secure nation (Singh and Sidhu, 2004). The increased output resulted in higher incomes for Indian farmers who specialized in rice-wheat cropping systems, especially in Punjab and Haryana—the epicenter of the Green Revolution (Binswanger and D'Souza, 2015). Conventionally, rice-wheat cropping systems have been water, capital and energy intensive and as a result have adversely affected natural resources. Recent data reveal that yield growth[6] has declined by about 2.7% per year and that rice-wheat cropping systems have become unsustainable due to yield stagnation, declining underground water tables, soil degradation and atmospheric pollution (Bhatt et al., 2016). Decreasing groundwater tables and increased soil salinity caused by excessive use of chemical fertilizer have plagued Indian farmers in recent decades. The successful use of high-yielding-variety seeds lies in the availability of water at the right time and in the right quantity. For example, Bhatt et al. (2016) found that states practicing rice-wheat cropping systems consume about 11,650 m^3/ha of water, 65% of which is consumed by the rice crop alone. During the last two decades, the groundwater table level has declined by about 24 cm/year (Ladha et al., 2008). The rice-wheat cropping system poses a serious threat of groundwater depletion due to over-exploitation when the rate of groundwater withdrawal is higher than the rate of replenishment.

Another issue facing Indian farmers is the excessive use of chemical fertilizers. One-third of farmers in areas dominated by rice-wheat cropping systems apply an average of 180 kg/ha of nitrogen fertilizer to the rice and wheat crops combined, compared to the recommended dosage of about 120 kg/ha (Ladha et al., 2008). These actions have led to increased soil salinity and to nitrates leaching into the groundwater, reducing water quality and compromising the usability of water for irrigation or drinking (Bhatt et al., 2016; Singh et al., 2010). Rice cultivation also leads to subsurface compaction due to repeated puddling of coarse- and medium-textured soils. Additionally, seed bed preparation leads to the exposure of hidden organic matter, resulting in the oxidation of organic matter. Seed bed preparation adversely impacts the quality of the soil (Kukal and Aggarwal, 2003a, 2003b). Finally, burning crop residues, specifically from rice, results in nutrient loss. Almost 82% of the rice straw is burned in Punjab and Haryana (Ladha et al., 2008). Once farmers know that straws are not fit for fodder, they tend to further increase fertilizer usage (Bhatt et al., 2016). These problems have encouraged farmers to move to a more sustainable cropping pattern that reduces usage of water and fertilizer without compromising yields and incomes of smallholders.

In contrast, maize-wheat cropping systems are sustainable and maintain or improve the economic well-being of Indian farmers (Gulati et al., 2017; Bhatt et al., 2016), particularly in the epicenter of the Green Revolution. In an earlier study, Jalota and Arora (2002) found that irrigation requirements to meet evapotranspiration and losses due to drainage were lower in the maize-wheat cropping system (144.7 cm) than in the rice-wheat cropping system (190.3 cm). They also found that water loss due to deep drainage was about 2.4 times greater in rice than in maize. In another study, Humphreys et al. (2010) compared irrigation water savings in two cropping systems: rice-wheat and wheat-maize. The authors found that a wheat-maize cropping system reduces irrigation water requirements by 450–500 mm and reduces deep drainage irrigation and evapotranspiration by 50–70 mm, compared to a rice-wheat cropping system. In sum, the wheat-maize cropping system provides greater environmental benefits than the rice-wheat cropping system, even under scenarios of lower irrigation requirements. Another advantage of the wheat-maize cropping system is the reduction in the loss of soil organic matter. Kukal et al. (2014) found that, compared to rice-wheat cropping systems, the expected loss in soil organic matter for wheat-maize cropping systems was small, when no fertilizer was applied. A wheat-maize cropping system has higher infiltration and profile recharge than a rice-wheat cropping system. Recently, Bhatt et al. (2016) found that 8 to 10 years of a rice-wheat cropping system would lead to selenium toxicity, but not with the wheat-maize cropping system. Given the benefits of the wheat-maize cropping system and maize as a possible substitution for rice, the wheat-maize cropping system should prove beneficial in sustainable agriculture.

Maize—especially baby corn—has economic benefits as well. For instance, Dass et al. (2008) found that farmers in India earned about Rs 50,000–60,000/year with the cultivation of two to three crops of baby corn. A baby corn crop also afforded farmers about 100 quintals/acre per crop of nutritious fodder (Dass et al., 2008). Additionally, the authors note that a by-product of baby corn, green fodder, has the potential to enhance milk production by about 15%–20%. Finally, increased demand for baby corn from peri-urban areas, changing food habits and improved economic status (Kumar et al., 2012) give baby corn producers the potential to earn higher profits. The preceding presentation describes multiple benefits, both economic and environmental,[7] for baby corn production in India, but the literature falls short in quantifying the reduction in irrigation and fertilizer costs and the exact reduction in chemical fertilizer use. This study intends to fill this gap in the literature.

Contract farming benefits smallholders in reducing production risks through the provision of inputs, access to credit and technical assistance. Through contract farming, contractors or corporations can overcome land size constraints and achieve reliability and consistency in production (Eaton and Shepherd, 2001). In a study of baby corn producers in the state of Karnataka, India, Nagaraj et al. (2008) found that better seed quality, fertilizer and technical advice reduced farmers' working capital needs and significantly reduced transaction costs. The authors found that contract producers of baby corn had higher productivity, about 23 q/acre, compared to 16 q/acre for independent growers. A similar trend was observed with respect to income. Contract farmers of baby corn earned (net returns) Rs 8,050, more than twice the Rs 3,035 earned by independent producers. However, this study failed to assess the costs (irrigation and fertilizer) and the environmental benefits (lower usage of fertilizer) of participation in contract farming.

Empirical framework

Observational data are being used increasingly for causal inferences, as in comparative effectiveness studies where the goal is to estimate the causal effects of treatment. Random control trials are necessary to evaluate programs and policies. However, it is difficult to conduct random control trials; instead, researchers use quasi-experimental data and ensure that both control and treatment groups are comparable to a significant extent (Linden, 2014). Therefore, various adjustment approaches such as matching, stratification and weighting (Stuart, 2010; Austin, 2007; Sturmer et al., 2006) are used in evaluating impacts. Applied economics often has used propensity score matching (PSM) with unstructured data. However, PSM suffers from the 'curse of dimensionality,' meaning that finding matches is difficult unless the data set is considerably large. The matching method also suffers from lack of common support, which may bias results (Linden and Samuels, 2013).

In other words, the PSM technique requires matching individuals in both treatment and control groups. This is defined as the common support or overlap condition (Caliendo and Kopeinig, 2008). However, this requires large sample sizes, since a significant amount of data may be wasted due to non-matching. This problem becomes important when the sample size is small. If significant numbers of treated subjects are excluded, it may lead to biased results due to incomplete matching (Austin, 2013). Moreover, internal consistency and generalizability of the treatment effect may be compromised if individuals are dropped from the treatment group, particularly when the sample size is small. This issue could be resolved by using the PSW technique. In the PSW technique, no individual is excluded from the analysis, and this is done without compromising the statistical power to detect the treatment effect (Stone and Tang, 2013).

Two weighting techniques are widely used: the inverse probability treatment weighting (IPTW[8]) and the marginal mean weighting stratification (MMWS). The MMWS combines the stratification and weighting methods and received attention in health policy studies, epidemiology and medical care. The MMWS method includes the investigative sample that is stratified into quantiles of propensity scores and that then assigns everyone a weight corresponding to each stratum and treatment assignment (Linden, 2014, 2017). The MMWS method is preferred over IPTW because it is more flexible and can be applied to a broad range of experimental conditions, including binary, ordinal and nominal treatments (Hong, 2010, 2012). The IPTW method tends to introduce additional bias when only a portion of the population provides support for causal inference (Hong, 2010). This problem is avoided in MMWS. MMWS tends to provide more robustness than IPTW because of its non-parametric approach, which usually provides a better approximation of non-linear relationships between treatment assignment and pre-treatment covariates (Hong, 2010).

Therefore, it is preferred to compare the estimates of IPTW with MMWS in order to eliminate the possible problem of mis-specification of the functional form in the propensity score model (Hong, 2010). Recently, a doubly robust marginal mean weighting through the stratification (DR-MMWS) method has been used in the impact evaluation literature. The DR-MMWS method is a combination of MMWS and regression adjustment (RA)[9] methods. According to Linden (2017), DR-MMWS performs better than regression-based treatment effects when either the propensity score or the outcome model is wrongly specified or when both are wrongly specified. Therefore, with the drawbacks of the PSM method and a small treatment group, in this study we assess and compare the estimates of DR-MMWS with RA, IPTW and MMWS.

We assume that K units are drawn from a large population. For each $i = 1, \ldots, K$ in the sample, there exists an outcome variable (Y_i), a treatment variable (T_i), which takes integer values between 0 and 1 in binary treatment case, and (X_i), which is the set of pre-treatment covariates. According to Imben (2000), if pre-treatment differences are adjusted, the issue of deriving causal inferences could be solved. This is overcome by the following formulation of unconfoundedness. Let $D_{it}(T_{it})$ represents the event of receiving the treatment t:

$$D_{it}(T_{it}) = \begin{cases} 1, if\ T_i = 1 \\ 0, otherwise \end{cases} \tag{19.1}$$

The potential outcome set is represented by (Y_{i0}, Y_{i1}) for each individual. The potential outcome for each individual i is represented by Y_{it} for which $T_i = t, t \in T = \{0,1\}$. Though there are two possibilities, only one is observed, depending on the status of the treatment (Linden et al., 2016). The observed outcome Y_i could be defined as a result of both treatment event and potential outcome Y_{it} :

$$Y_i = D_{i0}(T_{i0})Y_{i0} + D_{i1}(T_{i1})Y_{i1} \tag{19.2}$$

Therefore, the individual-level treatment effects of treatment level m versus 1 could be represented by $Y_{im} - Y_{il}$ or the differences of potential outcomes. Hence, the population average treatment effect is obtained by taking differences of the means of these two potential outcomes (Linden et al., 2016):

$$\Delta_{ml} = E[Y_{im} - Y_{il}] = \mu_m - \mu_l \cdot \tag{19.3}$$

An additional conditioning is required, $_{ml}$, in a quasi-experimental setting. In other words, we assume that the treatment assignment is a random like that of a randomized experimental design. Note that Imben (2000) termed this weak unconfoundedness. Another assumption is that there is a complete overlap in the distribution of covariates between treatment groups. Given these two assumptions and the conditional expectation of the potential outcome for treatment, t is identified by the conditional expectation of the observed outcome of and individual receiving the treatment (Imben and Wooldridge, 2009).

$$E\left[Y_{it}|X_{it}\right] = E[Y_{it}|D_{it}(T_i) = 1, X_i] = E\left[Y_i|D_{it}(T_i) = 1, X_i\right] = [$$
$$[Y_i \mid T_i = t, X_i] \tag{19.4}$$

Averages of these conditional means then are calculated to derive the average outcome (Imben, 2000). In the binary treatment case, according to Rosenbaum and Rubin (1983), it is adequate to adjust the propensity scores ($e(t,x)$) instead of pre-treatment covariates where:

$$e(t,x) \equiv \Pr[T_i = 1 |X_i = x] = E\left[D_{it}(T_i) = 1 \mid X_i = x\right] \tag{19.5}$$

Furthermore, the weighting of observed outcomes by conditional probability of receiving the treatment results in the mean of potential outcomes.

$$E\left(\frac{Y_i D_{it}(T_i)}{e(t, X_i)}\right) = E\left[Y_{it}\right] \tag{19.6}$$

This can be used to estimate the average causal effect $E\left[(Y_{i1}) - (Y_{i0})\right]$. The MMWS weights are computed for individuals using the following formula:

$$MMWS = \frac{n_{s1} * Pr(T = t)}{n_{T=t,s_t}} \tag{19.7}$$

$Pr(T = t)$ represents the estimated probability of assignment to the treatment group, t; n_{s1} is the number of individuals in s_1 constructed in the estimated probability treatment level t; and $n_{T=t,s_t}$ is the total number of individuals in stratum s_1 who were assigned to treatment group, t (Linden et al., 2016). These weights are used in the regression with different outcomes for each treatment group. Then treatment-specific predicted outcomes are estimated (Linden, 2017). Valid standard errors could be obtained using the differences in the averages of these means. According to Linden (2017), DR-MMWS performs better than other regression-based treatment effects estimators when a misspecification exists in both propensity scores and outcome model, whereas the estimator performs comparatively similarly to the DR-MMWS estimator when only the propensity score is mis-specified.

Data

This study is based on a primary survey of smallholder households. The survey was conducted during March and April of 2016 in the states of Punjab and Haryana of India's subcontinent. We surveyed 76 contract baby corn farmers and 84 independent baby corn farmers. All the contract farmers had formal contracts with three different agribusiness firms. The contract was a marketing contract; in other words, farmers were assured of selling the produce but at spot prices. Contracts were renewed every year. Independent baby corn growers were chosen randomly from eight villages in four blocks belonging to the districts of Jalandhar and Shaheed Bhagat Singh Nagar in Punjab and the District of Sonipat in Haryana. The survey data collected include farm characteristics (farm size, asset ownership); household and farmer characteristics (e.g., age of the operator, household size, education and caste); cropping patterns; economics of cultivation (inputs, costs, yield and output price); marketing channels; risk behavior; and information on distances to key infrastructures. The contract farmers were assured their produce would be purchased at a minimum price of Rs 50/kg. The contract price of baby corn was based on the spot price of baby corn in the Azadpur Fruit and Vegetable Market in Delhi, not far from the village. The contracting firm exported the fresh baby corn produce to the United Kingdom and sold the processed baby corn in India to the hotel and restaurant industry and to corporations like Del Monte, Holyland Group and Birla foods.

Comparison of contract and independent baby corn farmers

Table 19.1 represents the differences between the contract and independent baby corn farmers. There seems to be no statistical difference in age, education or caste status and no significant difference in household size, access to credit, number of extension visits, cost of labor, cost of pesticides and weedicides or distances to roads and cooperatives. However, there are differences in farming experience, total land size cultivated, percentage membership in a cooperative, cost of seed, availability of irrigation facility and risk preferences.

Contract baby corn farmers on an average had 20 years of farming experience, and independent baby corn farmers had 23 years of experience—a difference statistically significant at the 10% level of significance. Contract baby corn farmers cultivated an average of about 21 acres, and independent baby corn farmers cultivated an average of about 15 acres—a difference statistically significant at the 10% level of significance. Almost 28% of contract baby corn farmers had cooperative membership, compared to 14% for independent baby corn farmers—a difference significant at the 5% level of significance. Contract baby corn farmers also spent significantly less on seed than independent baby corn farmers (1% level of significance). Almost 95% of contract baby corn farmers had irrigation available for the last five years, compared to 84% for independent baby corn farmers, suggesting that having irrigation might be

Table 19.1 Descriptive statistics, all baby corn farmers with and without contracts, India

Variable	*Total sample*	*Smallholders with contract farming*	*Smallholders without contract farming*
	Mean (std. dev.)	*Mean (std. dev.)*	*Mean (std. dev.)*
Dependent variables			
Yield (kg/acre)	1,330.06	1,598.58***	1,084.19
	(73.07)	(142.46)	(34.24)
Cost of fertilizer (Rs/acre)	4,516.19	4,281.74	4,728.32
	(282.66)	(345.88)	(438.86)
Irrigation cost (Rs/acre)	2,590.86	2,659.38	2,623.41
	(115.10)	(116.85)	(81.83)
Urea[a] usage (kg/acre)	177.46	164.19***	189.47
	(4.43)	(51.7)	(6.79)
DAP[b] usage (kg/acre)	51.81	49.17*	54.19
	(1.47)	(1.91)	(2.18)
Explanatory variables			
Age, household head (HH) (years)	50.33	50.64	50.06
	(0.94)	(1.37)	(1.31)
Education, HH (years)	10.11	10.05	10.16
	(0.27)	(0.41)	(0.37)
Scheduled caste, Scheduled tribes[c] (%)	96.25	97.36	95.23
	(1.50)	(1.80)	(2.33)
General & other backward caste[d] (%)	3.75	2.63	4.76
	(1.50)	(1.84)	(2.33)
Farming experience, HH (years)	21.36	19.61*	22.94
	(0.96)	(1.25)	(1.42)
Total land cultivated (acres)	17.66	21.09*	14.56
	(1.78)	(3.31)	(1.53)
Households size (number)	6.94	6.56	7.28
	(0.28)	(0.39)	(0.41)
Access to credit in last five years (%)	11.25	13.15	9.52
	(2.50)	(3.90)	(3.22)
Member of a cooperative (%)	20.62	27.63**	14.28
	(3.20)	(5.16)	(3.84)
Extension visits, govt. agents (number)	71.87	77.63	66.67
	(6.93)	(11.78)	(7.82)
Cost of labor (Rs/acre)	7,786.67	7,709.55	7,856.46
	(411.54)	(463.12)	(665.23)
Cost of seed (Rs/acre)	4,746.57	4,578.19***	4,898.92
	(83.54)	(144.37)	(88.53)
Cost of pesticide (Rs/acre)	793.64	727.37	853.59
	(55.37)	(62.36)	(88.99)
Cost of weedicide (Rs/acre)	623.50	532.95	705.43
	(88.23)	(51.39)	(161.48)
Irrigation available for last five years (%)	89.37	94.73**	84.52
	(2.44)	(2.57)	(3.96)
Risk averse (%)	52.50	57.89	47.61
	(3.96)	(5.70)	(5.48)

(*Continued*)

Table 19.1 (Continued)

Variable	*Total sample*	*Smallholders with contract farming*	*Smallholders without contract farming*
	Mean (std. dev.)	*Mean (std. dev.)*	*Mean (std. dev.)*
Risk neutral (%)	30.00 (3.63)	30.26 (5.30)	29.76 (5.01)
Risk loving (%)	17.50 (3.01)	11.84* (3.73)	22.61 (4.59)
Distance of road (km)	0.47 (0.06)	0.40 (0.07)	0.54 (0.09)
Distance to cooperative (km)	1.57 (0.20)	1.77 (0.41)	1.38 (0.13)
Sample Size	**160**	**76**	**84**

Source: IFPRI-India survey.

Notes:
Indian rupee; exchange rate was US$ 1 = 65 INR at the time of the survey.
[a] Urea, a white crystalline solid containing 46% nitrogen, is widely used in the agricultural industry as an animal feed additive and fertilizer.
[b] DAP = diammonium phosphate.
[c] Includes designated groups of historically disadvantaged indigenous people in India. The terms are recognized in the Constitution of India, and the various groups are designated in one or other of the categories. Since independence, the Scheduled Castes and Scheduled Tribes were given Reservation status, guaranteeing political representation.
[d] Includes castes that are socially and educationally disadvantaged.
* Significant at the 10%.
** significant at the 5%.
*** significant at the 1% level.

an important criterion for being under contract. Finally, a significantly lower proportion (about 12%) of contract baby corn farmers were risk lovers compared to about 23% of independent baby corn farmers—a difference statistically significant at 10%, suggesting that contract baby corn farmers are more risk averse. Though almost 58% of contract baby corn farmers showed risk-averse behavior, the proportion was insignificantly lower for independent baby corn farmers (48%).

Results and discussion

In this section, we will discuss the evaluation approach, pre-intervention and post-intervention, and then discuss results from the treatment effects model. Tables 19.2 and 19.3 show the unadjusted and adjusted pre-intervention characteristics of the contract and independent baby corn producers. Following Linden and Samuels (2013), we use the absolute standard mean difference to assess the balancing of the covariates. In Table 19.2, the absolute standard difference (Column 4) is greater than zero, and seven of the 18 covariates have

Table 19.2 Unadjusted pre-intervention characteristics of beneficiaries and control groups

Variables	*Treatment* (N = 76)	*Control* (N = 84)	*Absolute standardized difference*
	Mean	*Mean*	
Ln_age, HH (years)	3.90	3.88	0.044
Ln_education, HH (years)	1.84	2.16	0.195
Farming experience, HH (years)	19.62	23.10	2.89
Ln_household size (numbers)	1.77	1.89	0.261
Scheduled Caste, Scheduled Tribes	0.97	0.96	0.115
Ln_land, cultivated (acres)	2.38	2.33	0.030
Irrigation available for last five years	0.95	0.86	0.310
Access to credit in last five years	0.13	0.10	0.110
Member of cooperatives	0.28	0.14	0.325
Extension visits, govt. agents (numbers)	0.78	0.66	0.128
Ln_cost of pesticide (Rs/acre)	5.91	6.45	0.270
Ln_cost of weedicide (Rs/acre)	3.82	4.66	0.178
Ln_cost of seed (Rs/acre)	8.35	8.46	0.248
Ln_cost of labor (Rs/acre)	8.35	7.08	0.319
Risk loving (=1 if operator likes taking risk; 0 otherwise)	0.12	0.23	0.293
Risk averse (= 1 if operator dislikes risk; 0 otherwise)	0.58	0.47	0.218
Distance to cooperative (km)	1.78	1.40	0.142
Distance of road (km)	0.40	0.55	0.197

Source: Authors' estimation.

Table 19.3 Weighted pre-intervention characteristics of beneficiaries and control groups

	Mean	*Mean*	
Ln_age HH (years)	3.90	3.87	0.089
Ln_education, HH (years)	1.84	2.09	0.153
Farming experience, HH (years)	19.62	19.19	0.036
Ln_household size (numbers)	1.77	1.75	0.028
Scheduled Caste and Scheduled Tribes	0.97	0.93	0.190
Ln_land, cultivated (acres)	2.41	2.27	0.082
Irrigation available in last five years	0.95	0.94	0.022
Access to credit in last five years	0.13	0.11	0.059
Member of a cooperative	0.28	0.25	0.074
Extension visits, govt. agents (numbers)	0.78	0.65	0.140
Ln_cost of pesticide (Rs/acre)	5.91	6.38	0.023
Ln_cost of weedicide (Rs/acre)	3.82	3.82	0.001
Ln_cost of seed (Rs/acre)	8.35	8.34	0.031
Ln_cost of labor (Rs/acre)	8.35	8.13	0.057
Risk loving (= 1 if operator likes taking risk; 0 otherwise)	0.12	0.17	0.137
Risk averse (= 1 if operator dislikes risk; 0 otherwise)	0.58	0.60	0.051
Distance to cooperative (km)	1.78	1.08	0.021
Distance of road (km)	0.40	0.40	0.002

Source: Authors' estimation.

values greater than the 0.25 cut-off limit proposed by Rubin (2001). Table 19.3 reports the weighted pre-intervention characteristics, for both treatment and control groups, and all the values are less than the 0.25 cut-off limit; in many cases, they are close to zero.

These findings show that the two groups (contract farmers and independent baby corn farmers) with the listed covariates are comparable. Using these covariates, a logistic regression was performed with outcome variables of interest, such as yield (kg/acre), irrigation cost (Rs/acre), fertilizer cost (Rs/acre), urea usage (kg/acre) and DAP usage (kg/acre), for a binary treatment variable of contract-farming adoption in baby corn farming. Following Linden (2016) implementation of DR-MMWS, based on the estimated propensity scores, the study sample was divided into five strata. For each estimator, potential outcome means were calculated for the respective treatment group (contract baby corn growers) and the control group (independent baby corn growers). To arrive at the treatment effect, pair-wise testing was performed. Finally, to assess the robustness of our findings, we also report and compare the estimates of the outcome variables using RA, IPTW and MMWS estimators.

Table 19.4 provides the estimates of the treatment effects for respective outcome variables by each estimator. Column 1 of the table reports estimates of treatment effects, and Columns 2, 3 and 4 report the estimates of yield, irrigation costs and fertilizer costs. Results in Column 2 of the table show that contract baby corn producers have significantly higher yield than independent baby corn producers. Specifically, under the DR-MMWS robust estimator, contract baby corn producers had higher yields, by about 508 kg/acre, than did independent baby corn producers. Findings suggest that the contract baby corn growers produce more, almost 508 kg/acre, than the independent baby corn growers. Indeed, contract farming in baby corn production can increase yield, and similar findings have been reported in the literature (Otsuka et al., 2016). Our findings are consistent with Nagaraj et al. (2008); however, the estimates are about one-fourth (5 q/acre versus 23 q/acre) of those reported by Nagaraj et al. (2008). The DR-MMSW estimate is the highest of the estimators, with yield impact ranging from about 461 kg/acre in the RA estimator to about 508 kg/acre in the DR-MMWS estimator. Interestingly, all estimates are significant at the 5% level of significance.

Turning our attention to irrigation and fertilizer costs, we found that contract baby corn growers had significantly lower irrigation and fertilizer costs than independent baby corn producers had. For instance, under the DR-MMWS robust estimator estimates in Table 19.4, Column 3, irrigation costs were significantly lower, by about Rs 320/acre, for contract baby corn farmers than for independent baby corn producers. Note that the impact of irrigation cost ranges from about Rs 274/acre in the RA estimator to about Rs 336/acre in the IPTW estimator. Interestingly, all estimates are significant at the 10% or higher level of significance. Since this is a cross-sectional study and assuming that both types of farmers face the same input prices, one can conclude that water usage is significantly lower under contract farming than

Table 19.4 Estimated average treatment effects by estimator on: yield, irrigation cost, fertilizer cost, urea and DAP usage

Estimator	*Yield (kg/acre)*	*Irrigation cost (Rs/acre)*	*Fertilizer cost (Rs/acre)*	*Urea usage[1] (kg/acre)*	*DAP[2] usage (kg/acre)*
	ATE (std. dev.)	*ATE (std. dev.)*	*ATE (std. dev.)*	*ATE (std. dev.)*	*ATE (std. dev.)*
RA[3]	461.40***	–274.46**	–12,739.82**	–31.02***	–5.34*
	(153.47)	(184.11)	(5,335.73)	(8.97)	(2.96)
IPTW[4]	488.44***	–336.26**	–14,827.29**	–37.97***	–6.39*
	(147.84)	(170.85)	(5,721.81)	(11.61)	(3.44)
MMW[5]	484.26***	–312.40*	–13,666.58**	–40.90***	–7.78*
	(146.26)	(167.06)	(5,983.38)	(13.76)	(4.09)
DR-MMWS[6]	508.19***	–319.74*	-112,218.64*	-127.79***	-15.90*
	(166.37)	(138.34)	(5,988.88)	(11.47)	(3.50)

Source: Authors' estimation.

Notes:

1 Urea, a white crystalline solid containing 46% nitrogen, is widely used in the agricultural industry as an animal feed additive and fertilizer.

2 DAP = diammonium phosphate is the world's most widely used phosphorus fertilizer. It is relatively high in nutrient content, and its excellent physical properties make it a popular choice in farming and other industries.

3 Regression adjustment.

4 Inverse probability of treatment weighting.

5 Marginal mean weighting.

6 Doubly robust marginal mean weighting.

* Significant at the 10%.

** Significant at the 5%.

*** Significant at the 1% level.

under independent baby corn production. Our findings are consistent with field experiments (Humphreys et al., 2010; Jalota and Arora, 2002; Sur et al., 1980; Bhatt et al., 2016; Vanernon, 2002) in the maize-wheat cropping system that calls for lower water requirements. Perhaps the production of baby corn could be more sustainable than the rice-wheat cropping system. Column 4 of Table 19.4 reports contract farming's impact in baby corn and its impact on fertilizer costs. Results suggest that contract baby corn farmers have significantly lower fertilizer costs than independent baby corn producers have. For instance, the DR-MMWS robust estimator estimates in Table 19.4, Column 4, show that fertilizer cost was significantly lower, by about Rs 12,219/acre, for contract baby corn farmers than for independent baby corn producers. The estimates were significant at the 10% level of significance. Again, the reduction in fertilizer costs could range from a low of Rs 12,219/acre in DR-MMWS to a high of Rs 14,827/acre in the IPTW method.

We also considered contract farming's impact on fertilizer usage. Columns 5 and 6 of Table 19.4 report contract farming's impact on the physical quantities of chemical fertilizer used in baby corn production (urea and diammonium phosphate, or DAP). Our finding suggests that contract baby corn producers use about 28 kg/acre less urea than independent baby corn producers use. Note that the urea usage impact ranges from about 28 kg/acre in the DR-MMWS estimator to about 41 kg/acre in the MMWS estimator; all estimates are significant at the 1% level of significance. Similarly, Column 6 of Table 19.4 shows contract farming's impact in baby corn and usage of DAP. Note that the DAP usage impact ranges from about 5 kg/acre in the RA estimator to about 8 kg/acre in the MMWS estimator; all estimates are significant at the 10% level of significance. Our finding suggests that contract baby corn producers use about 6 kg/acre less DAP than independent baby corn producers use. Findings here reinforce the above cost reduction in fertilizer applications for contract farming in baby corn production. Such findings also suggest that contract farming can be used to incentivize farmers to reduce their usage of chemical fertilizers. Reducing the application of urea and DAP could benefit the environment and soil health and reduce groundwater contamination.

Conclusions and policy implications

Once the champion of the Green Revolution, India has been experiencing falling productivity in rice and wheat, overexploitation of natural resources and lower incomes for smallholders (Sidhu and Byerlee, 1992). During the last two decades, groundwater tables have declined at an alarming rate of about 23 cm/year in the Indian states of Punjab and Haryana, the epicenter of the Green Revolution. Overusage of fertilizer due to the new agricultural strategy and a favorable pricing structure have considerably reduced soil health and increased groundwater contamination. Aldy et al. (1998) argue that market failure could constrain the development of more sustainable practices.

A maize-wheat cropping system requires significantly less irrigation water than a rice-wheat cropping system and has negligible negative impact on soil health. Baby corn, a specialty corn, has potential in domestic and international markets given its high value for nutrition, industrial use and cattle fodder. In this study, we investigate contract farming's impact on the productivity, irrigation costs and fertilizer costs of baby corn farmers. We also assess contract farming's impact on the usage of the chemical fertilizers urea and DAP. We used farm-level data from the states of Punjab and Haryana in India and newer propensity score weighting (PSW) matching to evaluate the treatment effect of contract farming on outcome variables. We used the doubly robust marginal mean weighting through stratification (DR-MMWS) matching method.

Findings from this study reveal that contract farmers of the specialty crop baby corn have higher yield, by about 508 kg/acre, than do independent baby corn farmers. Contract baby corn growers also spend less on irrigation and fertilizer than independent baby corn growers spend. Irrigation costs and fertilizer costs were comparatively lower for contract baby corn farmers, by about Rs 320/acre for irrigation costs and by about Rs 12,281/acre for fertilizer costs, than for independent baby corn farmers. Since this is a cross-sectional study, and if baby corn farmers face the same input prices, one can conclude that contract farming in baby corn leads to reductions in the irrigation water required and in the quantity of chemical fertilizers used. Our study finds that, compared to independent baby corn producers, contract baby corn producers use significantly lower amounts of urea, by about 28 kg/acre, and of DAP, by about 6 kg/acre. Reducing the usage of irrigation water and chemical fertilizers is environmentally beneficial for farmers, the soil and the well-being of the public at large.

We conclude that baby corn contract farmers have higher yield, spend less on fertilizer and irrigation and use less chemical fertilizer such as urea and DAP than do independent baby corn farmers. Therefore, using contract farming in baby corn could be an initiative that could replace rice cultivation in high-stress areas like Punjab and Haryana. Further effects of cultivating baby corn are that it reduces the stress on groundwater and reduces soil and environmental degradation without compromising yield. The reduction in the use of chemical fertilizers and irrigated water could be attributed to the extensive monitoring by extension staff members working for the contractor and to the need for maintaining quality standards. Extension staff members ensure that farmers adhere to requirements concerning the application of inputs such as seeds, fertilizer, pesticides and water. The produce also has to conform to international market standards, like those of the United States and United Kingdom, if farmers expect higher profits from international markets.

Findings from this study show that markets can be used to ensure the benefit of more sustainable agricultural practices (e.g., lower usage of fertilizers and pesticides) and environmental outcomes (reduced use of groundwater). The findings are particularly relevant to policymakers in designing incentives for the effective adoption of contract farming in baby corn production with potential impacts on productivity, irrigation and fertilizer costs and chemical fertilizer usage. Public policies, especially in a developing country like India, can play a major role in helping smallholders adopt contract farming. Contract farming can provide smallholders with the latest technology, credit and good extension service, and it can link them to international markets. It has the potential to augment revenues and increase environmental benefits. This research identifies the extent to which smallholders, including those involved in contract farming, are taking a serious approach to implementing sustainable farming. Smallholders with contract farming are better positioned to more seriously address the issue of agricultural sustainability because contract farming is a novel farming trend in the agricultural sector of many developing and emerging economies and has the potential to open international markets. Contract farming also has the potential to benefit the sustainability of land and water management, increase agricultural productivity and improve the marketing and management of agricultural products.

Notes

1 Baby corn is a short-duration crop of 50–70 days during the *Kharif* growing season. Two crops of baby corn can be cultivated in a year after wheat, adding to the income of smallholders and providing a better substitute for rice in the rice-wheat cropping system, thus maintaining good soil health.
2 Intercropping is a way to increase diversity in an agricultural ecosystem. Intercropping enhances productivity and provides security against the potential risk of monoculture (Lithourgidis et al., 2011).
3 According to Flora (1992), sustainable agriculture encompasses a set of dynamic practices with the use of technology that brings minimum damage to the environment (e.g., contamination of water, water table issues, soil salinity) and at the same time provides income to farmers.
4 A potential drawback of the propensity scores when used for matching is that a very large number of subjects may be needed, especially in the control group.
5 Aldy et al. (1998) and Ruttan (1994) point out market failure constraints in the development of more sustainable practices. Society underinvests in more sustainable agricultural practices.
6 Declining ecological diversity, resulting from an overuse of natural and ecological resources, is one reason for the deceleration in agricultural growth (Singh and Sidhu, 2004).
7 Reduction in usage of water and chemical fertilizer, compared to water-intensive rice crop (Sharma and Banik, 2013).
8 Inverse probability treatment weighting (IPTW) weighs the treated individuals inverse to the estimated propensity score, while the untreated individuals are weighted equal to the inverse of 1 less than the estimated propensity score. It is a way of standardizing the treatment group (Rubin, 2001; Rosenbaum, 1987).
9 In regression adjustment (RA), first for each treatment level, the outcome variable is regressed on a set of covariates separately, and then the outcome for each subject and treatment level is estimated using data from each individual who was assigned treatments (Linden, 2016, 2017).

References

Aldy, J., Hrubovcak, J. and Vasavada, U., 1998. The role of technology in sustaining agriculture and the environment. *Ecological Economics*. 26, 81–96.

Austin, P. C., 2007. Propensity-score matching in the cardiovascular surgery literature from 2004 to 2006: A systematic review and suggestions for improvement. *Journal of Thoracic Cardiovascular Surgery*. 134, 128–1135.

Austin, P.C., 2013. A comparison of 12 algorithms for matching on the propensity score. *Statistics in Medicine*. 33(6), 1057–1069.

Bauman, P., 2000. *Equity and Efficiency in Contract Farming Schemes: The Experience of Agricultural Tree Crops*. London: Overseas Development Institute.

Bhalla, P., 2007. Impact of declining groundwater levels on acreage allocation in Haryana. *Economic and Political Weekly*. 42(26), 2701–2707.

Bhatt, R., Kukal, S.S., Busari, M.A., Arora, S. and Yadav, M., 2016. Sustainability issues on rice-wheat cropping system. *International Soil and Water Conservation Research*. 4, 64–74.

Binswanger-Mkhize, H.P. and D'souza, A., 2015. Structural change and agricultural performance at the state level in India: 1980–2010. *Agricultural Economic Research Review*. 28(1), 27–38.

Binswanger-Mkhize, H.P., Khandker, S.R. and Rosenzweig, M.R., 1993. How infrastructure and financial institutions affect agricultural output and investment in India. *Journal of Development Economics*. 41(2), 337–366.

Caliendo, M. and Kopeinig, S., 2008. Some practical guidance for the implementation of propensity score matching. *Journal of Economic Surveys*. 22(1), 31–72.

Chand, R., Raju, S.S. and Pandey, L.M., 2007. Growth crisis in agriculture: Severity and options at national state levels. *Economic and Political Weekly*. 42(26), 2528–2533.

Chaudhary, D.P., Kumar, A., Mandhania, S.S., Srivastava, P. and Kumar, R.S., 2012. *Maize as Fodder—An Alternative Approach*. New Delhi: Directorate of Maize Research.

Dass, S., Yadav, V.K., Kwatra, A., Jat, M.L., Rakshit, S., Kaul, J., Parkash, O., Singh, I., Singh, K.P. and Sekhar, J.C., 2008. Baby corn in India. *Technical Bulletin, Directorate of Maize Research, Pusa Campus, New Delhi*. 6, 1–45.

Eaton, C. and Shepherd, A.W., 2001. *Contract Farming Partnership for Growth*. FAO Agricultural Services Bulletin, 145, FAO, Rome.

Feola, G. and Binder, C.R., 2010. Towards an improved understanding of farmers' behaviour: The integrative agent-centred (IAC) framework. *Ecological Economics*. 69, 2323–2333.

Flora, C.B., 1992. Building sustainable agriculture: A new application of farming system research and extension. *Journal of Sustainable Agriculture*. 2, 37–49.

Government of Punjab., 2012. Statistical abstract of Punjab. *Economic and Statistical Organization*. 944.

Gulati, A., Roy, R. and Hussain, S., 2017. *Getting Punjab Agriculture Back on High Growth Path: Sources, Drivers and Policy Lessons*. New Delhi: ICRIER.

Hazell, P.B.R., 2009. *The Asian Green Revolution*. IFPRI discussion paper 00911, pp. 1–25.

Hong, G., 2010. Marginal mean weighting through stratification: Adjustment for selection bias in multilevel data. *Journal of Educational and Behavioral Statistics*. 35, 499–531.

Hong, G., 2012. Marginal mean weighting through stratification: A generalized method for evaluating multi-valued and multiple treatments with non-experimental data. *Psychological Methods*. 17, 44–60.

Humphreys, E., Kukal, S.S., Christen, E. W., Hira, G.S., Singh, B., Yadav, S. and Sharma, R.K. 2010. Halting the groundwater decline in North-West India—which crop technologies will be the winners? *Advances in Agronomy*. 109, 155–217.

Imben, G.W., 2000. The role of the propensity score in estimating does-response functions. *Biometrika*. 87(3), 706–710.

Imbens, G.W. and Wooldridge, J.M., 2009. Recent developments in the econometrics of program evaluation. *Journal of Economic Literature*. 47(1), 5–86.

Jalota, S.K. and Arora, V.K., 2002. Model based assessment of water balance components under different cropping systems in north-west India. *Agricultural Water Management*. 57, 75–87.

Joshi, P.K., Singh, N.P., Singh, N., Gerpacio, R.V. and Pingali, P.L., 2005. *Maize in India: Production Systems, Constraints, and Research Priorities*. Mexico: CIMMYT.

Kukal, S.S. and Aggarwal, G.C., 2003a. Puddling depth and intensity effects in rice—wheat system on a sandy loam soil I. Water use and crop performance. *Soil and Tillage Research*. 72, 1–8.

Kukal, S.S. and Aggarwal, G.C., 2003b. Puddling depth and intensity effects in rice—wheat system on a sandy loam soil II. Water use and crop performance. *Soil and Tillage Research*. 74, 37–45.

Kukal, S.S., Singh, Y., Jat, M.L. and Sidhu, H.S., 2014. Improving water productivity of wheat-based cropping systems in South Asia for sustained productivity. *Advances in Agronomy*. 127, 159–230.

Kumar, R.S., Kumar, B., Kaul, J., Karjagi, C., Jat, S.L., Parihar, C.M. and Kumar, A., 2012. Maize research in India—historical prospective and future challenges. *Maize Journal*. 1(1), 1–6.

Ladha, J.K., Pathak, H. and Gupta, R.K., 2008. Sustainability of the rice-wheat cropping system-issues, constraints, and remedial options. *Journal of Crop Improvement*. 19(1–2), 125–136.

Lamichhane, J.R., Arendse, W., Dachbrodt-Saaydeh, S., Kudsk, P., Roman, J.C., van Bijsterveldt-Gels, J.E.M., Wick, M. and Messéan, A., 2015. Challenges and opportunities for integrated pest management in Europe: A telling example of minor uses. *Crop Protection*. 74, 42–47.

Linden, A., 2014. Combining propensity score-based stratification and weighting to improve casual inference in the evaluation of health care interventions. *Journal of Evaluation in Clinical practice*. 20, 1065–1071.

Linden, A., 2017. Improving causal inference with a doubly robust estimator that combines propensity score stratification and weighting. *Journal of Evaluation in Clinical Practice*. 23(4), 697–702.

Linden, A. and Samuels, S.J., 2013. Using balance statistics to determine the optimal number of controls in matching studies. *Journal of Evaluation in Clinical Practice*. 20, 968–975.

Linden, A., Uysal, S.D., Ryan, A. and Adams, J.L., 2016 Estimating causal effects for multivalued treatments: A comparison of approaches. *Statistics in Medicine*. 35(4), 534–552.

Lithourgidis, A.S., Dordas, C.A., Damalas, C.A. and Vlachostergios, D.N., 2011. Annual intercrops: An alternative pathway for sustainable agriculture. *Australian Journal of Crop Science*. 5, 396–410.

Mahajan, G., Sharda, R., Kumar, A. and Singh K.G., 2007. Effect of plastic mulch on economizing irrigation water and weed control in baby corn sown by different methods. *African Journal of Agricultural Research*. 2(1), 19–26.

Murdia, L.K., Wadhwani, R., Wadhawan, N., Bajpai, P. and Shekhawat, S., 2016. Maize utilization in India: An overview. *American Journal of Food and Nutrition*. 4(6), 167–176.

Nagaraj, N., Chandrakanth, M.G., Chengappa, P.G., Roopa, H.S. and Chandakavate, P.M., 2008. Contract farming and its implications for input−supply linkages between markets and farmers in Karnataka. *Agricultural Economic Research Review*. 21, 307–316.

Otsuka, K., Nakano, Y. and Kazushi, T. 2016. Contract farming in developed and developing countries. *Annual Review of Resource Economics*. 8(1), 353–376.

Parihar, C.M., Jat, S.L., Singh, A.K., Kumar, R.S., Hooda, K.S., Chikkappa, G.K. and Singh, D.K., 2011. Maize production technologies in India. *DMR Technical Bulletin, Directorate of Maize Research, Pusa Campus, New Delhi*. 110012, 1–30.

Rosenbaum, P.R., 1987. Model based direct adjustment. *Journal of the American Statistical Association*. 79, 516–524.

Rosenbaum, P.R. and Rubin, D.B., 1983. The central role of propensity score in observational studies for casual effects. *Biometrika*. 70, 41–55.

Rubin, D., 2001. Using propensity scores to help design observational studies: Application to the tobacco litigation. *Health Services and Outcomes Research Methodology*. 2(3–4), 169–188.

Ruttan, V., 1994. Constraints on the design of sustainable systems of agricultural production. *Ecological Economics*. 10, 209–219.

Saifi, B. and Drake, L., 2008. Swedish agriculture during the twentieth century in relation to sustainability. *Ecological Economics*. 68, 370–380.

Sharma, R.C. and Banik, P., 2013. Baby corn-legumes intercropping system: II weed dynamics and community service. NJAS-Wageningen. *Journal of Life Sciences*. 67, 11–18.

Sharpley, A., McDowell, R. and Kleinman, P., 2001. Phosphorus loss from land to water: Integrating agricultural and environmental management. *Plant and Soil*. 237(2), 287–307.

Sidhu, D.S. and Byerlee, D., 1992. *Technical Change and Wheat Productivity in the Indian Punjab in the Post-Green Revolution Period*. CIMMYT Economics Working Paper 92–02. Mexico: CIMMYT.

Sidhu, H.S., 2002. Crisis in agrarian economy in Punjab. *Economic and Political Weekly*. 37(30), 3132–3138.

Singh, A., Krause, P., Panda, S.N. and Flugel, W., 2010. Rising water table: A threat to sustainable agriculture in an irrigated semiarid region of Haryana, India. *Agricultural Water Management*. 97(10), 1443–1451.

Singh, J. and Sidhu, R.S., 2004. Factors in declining crop diversification: case study of Punjab. *Economic and Political Weekly*. 39(52), 5607–5610.

Stone, C.A. and Tang, Y., 2013. Comparing propensity score methods in balancing covariates and recovering impact in small sample educational program evaluations. *Practical Assessment, Research & Evaluation*. 18(13), 1–12.

Stuart, E.A., 2010. Matching methods for causal inference: A review and a look forward. *Statistical Science*. 25, 1–21.

Sturmer, T., Joshi, M., Glynn, R.J., Avorn, J., Rothman, K.J. and Schneeweiss, S., 2006. A review of the application of propensity score methods yielded increasing use, advantages in specific settings, but not substantially different estimates compared with conventional multivariable methods. *Journal of Clinical Epidemiology*. 59, 437–447.

Sur, H.S., Parihar, S.S. and Jalota, S.K., 1980. Effects of rice-wheat and maize-wheat rotations on water transmissions and wheat root development in a sandy loam of the Punjab, India. *Soil and Tillage Research*. 1, 361–371.

Vanernon, I., 2002. Economic appraisal of profitability and sustainability of peri-urban agriculture in Bangkok. *Ecological Economics*. 61, 516–529.

20 Assessing and explaining the technical efficiency of contract and non-contract farms in India

Manjunatha A. V., Parmod Kumar and Suman Kumar Sourav

Technology's role in enhancing farm output and income and as a significant economic development tool is well acknowledged in the literature (Schultz, 1964; Kuznets, 1966; Hayami and Ruttan, 1985). Farm output and income depend not only on the kind of technology used but also on the efficiency with which the given resources are used (Nishimizu and Page, 1982). Several studies have measured farm efficiency as a means of increasing production. For example, studies by Saini (1969), Sahota (1968) and Hopper (1965) evaluated and recommended appropriate production techniques that result in more efficient use of resources. Similarly, other studies covered input–output relations and variations of output in different climatic and ecological regions.

Data envelopment analysis (DEA) has been applied to agricultural crop production in several studies internationally. However, measuring the efficiency of farms with contract versus non-contract using this type of analysis in the context of India is limited. An institution in the form of contract farming has evolved recently and addresses the problems involving dissemination of information, provision of on-farm extension, reduction of price risk, provision of credit and providing alternatives to missing markets. Several studies have shown contract farming's positive effect on productivity and farmers' income (Tadesse and Krishnamoorthy, 1997; Saigenji and Zeller, 2009; Miyata et al., 2009; Bellemare, 2010). However, very few studies (Swain, 2007; Mishra et al., 2018) addresses the efficiency issue in contract farming. This study uses DEA technique to measure the efficiency of farms in contract versus non-contract situations. The first part of the analysis in this chapter estimates the farms' efficiency, and the second part assesses the determinants of efficiency measures using Tobit regression. This study provides valuable information on efficiency in contract and non-contract farms and on factors affecting the farms' efficiency. The findings show the difference between the efficiency of contract farms and that of non-contract farms producing barley, wheat, potato, mustard, tomato, green chili and baby corn. The paper also has substantial policy implications for improving farm efficiency, whether by bringing farms under contract or simply adjusting their input resources or extension services.

The rest of this chapter is structured as follows. The second section presents the study's data and methodology, along with descriptive statistics of households. The section also describes the data envelopment analysis model used by specifying the sample size of each set of crop data collected from the field. The third section presents efficiency scores of all farms in each crop and their determinants. The fourth section presents the conclusions and policy recommendations.

Data and methodology

Data and field survey

The study is based primarily on field data collected from contract and non-contract farmers for the crop reference year 2015–2016. Seven crops have been selected: barley, wheat, potato, mustard, tomato, green chili and baby corn. Wheat and mustard are grown for seeds in India's Punjab and Haryana states. Barley is grown mainly for malting purposes in Punjab and Haryana, where a company has contracted with farmers to procure barley at an agreed-upon price and processes the barley into beer. Potato farmers in Punjab and Haryana are engaged with companies producing chips and other salty snacks. Baby corn, tomato and green chili contract farming is done in Karnataka for pre-agreed prices. For this study, a list of contract farmers was obtained, and a simple stratified random sampling was done to select contract and non-contract farmers in the region. The study region includes Hisar, Kaithal, Karnal, Kurukshetra and Sirsa Districts in Haryana; Fatehgarh, Ludhiana, Mansa, Patiala and Sangrur Districts in Punjab; and Ramnagar and Kolar Districts in Karnataka. The non-contract farmers were selected from the village periphery, which had the same cropping pattern as the contract farmers.

The analysis of this study is based on 255 farm households (170 contract and 85 non-contract) of barley, 238 farm households (109 contract and 129 non-contract) of wheat, 232 farm households (165 contract and 67 non-contract) of potato, 77 farm households (32 contract and 45 non-contract) of mustard, 61 farm households (35 contract and 26 non-contract) of green chili, 60 farm households (35 contract and 25 non-contract) of tomato and 256 farm households (206 contract and 50 non-contract) of baby corn.

Descriptive statistics of sample households

Nguyen et al. (2015) reviewed 23 studies, of which 11 were on contract farming's impact on productivity and 12 were on contract farming's effect on farmers' income. The majority of the reviewed studies were conducted in developing countries and involved different crops such as paddy, soybean, tea, dairy, poultry, hog and vegetables. These studies argue that agricultural productivity can be increased through contract farming. Two of the 11 studies on productivity show a significant increase in productivity, four showed moderate levels of increase in productivity, and five saw a slight increase in productivity. This study also finds some significant increase in productivity (in the range of 1–19 quintals (q)/acre) in the case of barley, wheat, tomato and mustard under contract farming. The other crops—baby corn, green chili and potato—show a positive difference in the productivity of contract and non-contract farms, but the difference is not significant. Tables 20.1 and 20.2 and Appendix Tables 20A.1 to 20.A5 show the descriptive statistics of the farm households for each crop by

Table 20.1 Descriptive statistics of barley farmers in Punjab and Haryana

Farm type	*Contract (n = 170)*	*Non-contract (n = 85)*	*Contract (n = 170)*	*Non-contract (n = 85)*	*p-value*
Variable	*Mean*		*Std. dev.*		
Crop acres	3.0	2.4	3.8	2.2	0.140
Main output (q/acre)	16.7	14.8	4.2	4.4	0.001***
Main output price per quintal	1,289	1,282	211	300	0.822
Main output value per acre	21,550	18,841	6,405	5,934	0.001***
By-product value per acre	534	875	1,587	2,432	0.180
Net return per acre	12,640	11,518	7,599	6,115	0.238
Land preparation cost per acre	1,476	1,527	783	631	0.600
Total seed cost per acre	1,008	793	1,181	297	0.100
Farm yard manure cost per acre	169	40	692	230	0.096*
Fertilizer cost per acre	1,794	1,671	430	426	0.031**
Plant protection cost per acre	641	525	601	414	0.110
Other material cost per acre	3,134	2,784	2,001	1,341	0.146
Total material cost per acre	6,780	5,776	2,601	1,639	0.001***
Hired labor cost per acre	2,657	2,421	1,313	969	0.143
Family worker-days per acre	11.2	11.8	9.6	8.0	0.619
hired worker-days per acre	2.0	1.0	3.0	1.5	0.002***
Age of the respondents	42	43	12	13	0.980
Education of the respondents	7.6	6.9	4.5	4.5	0.242
Family size	6.6	6.0	2.6	2.8	0.094*
Percentage of adult family members involved in agriculture	43.1	44.2	18.0	19.2	0.664

Source: Primary data (2015–2016), calculated by authors.

Note: ***, **, * = significant at 1%, 5%, 10% level.

Table 20.2 Descriptive statistics of baby corn farmers in Karnataka

Farm type	*Contract (n = 206)*	*Non-contract (n = 50)*	*Contract (n = 206)*	*Non-contract (n = 50)*	*p-value*
Variable	*Mean*		*Std. dev.*		
Crop acres	2.0	1.8	1.1	1.1	0.239
Main output produced (q/acre)	39.2	38.7	8.6	10.4	0.699
Main output price per quintal	603	607	35.3	31.9	0.522
Main output value per acre	23,727	23,406	5,692	6,212	0.724
By-product value per acre	11,411	12,416	4,048	4,716	0.129
Net return per acre	17,052	17,931	7,116	7,565	0.439
Land preparation cost per acre	2,818	2,904	808	853	0.506
Total seed cost per acre	2,335	2,579	336	600	0.000***
Farm yard manure cost per acre	2,553	2,421	2,044	1,444	0.667
Fertilizer cost per acre	3,943	4,519	1,659	2,341	0.044**
Plant protection cost per acre	216	153	325	275	0.203
Other material cost per acre	3,863	3,829	1,318	1,408	0.870
Total material cost per acre	12,884	13,481	3,449	4,325	0.298
Hired labor cost per acre	5,201	4,410	2,754	1,790	0.054*
Family worker-days per acre	28	33	15	19	0.056*
hired worker-days per acre	26	22	12	9	0.025**
Age of the respondents	48.51	41.46	11.14	11.66	0.000***
Education of the respondents	6.1	5.7	5.2	5.5	0.668
Family size	5.2	4.8	2.3	1.8	0.210
Percentage of adult family members involved in agriculture	69.91	71.64	24.20	23.81	0.650

Source: Primary data (2015–2016), calculated by authors.

Note: ***, **, * = significant at 1%, 5%, 10% level.

state. The cultivated acreage of each crop did not differ significantly between contract and non-contract farms except in the cases of wheat and tomato. In wheat, contract farmers averaged 19.4 acres/household, and non-contract farmers averaged 9.8 acres/household. In tomato, contract farmers cultivated an average of 1.4 acres per household, and non-contract farmers cultivated an average of 1.8 acres per household.

Some contract farmers, such as those producing tomato, mustard, potato and wheat, received prices that were Rs 51/q to Rs 172/q higher than the prices that non-contract farmers received. The combined effect of higher productivity and higher prices per quintal significantly increases gross income per acre in the case of all six crops under contract farming. The net income per acre for five of the crops also came out significantly higher in the case of contract farming; only barley and baby corn showed no significant difference in their per acre net income. The difference in net income varied from about Rs 1,100/acre to about

Rs 27,500/acre, depending on the crop. The greatest difference in net income was found in the case of green chili, followed by tomato, potato, mustard, wheat and barley. Only baby corn contract farmers had lower net returns than non-contract farmers had, but the difference was not significant. The increase in the contract farms' net income occurred despite higher material and labor costs in most crops.

Crops such as barley, potato, green chili and tomato had significantly higher material costs under contract farming than under non-contract farming. The increase in costs ranged from about Rs 1,000/acre to about Rs 10,000/acre. These contract crops also required greater hired labor costs to carry out the field operations. On the other hand, wheat contract farmers significantly reduced their total material and labor costs by more than Rs 1,400/acre. This occurred because the average acreage of wheat under contract farming was almost double the average acreage under non-contract farming, and economies of scale reduced the average cost of materials and labor for contract wheat farmers. Other socio-economic factors did not differ significantly between contract and non-contract wheat farms. However, younger farmers were found to participate more in contract farming than in non-contract farming, and years spent on education were considerably higher for contract farmers of some crops, such as wheat, mustard, green chili and tomato, than non-contract farmers of those crops.

Methodology

Efficiency is a widely used concept in economics. Economic efficiency (EE) has two components: technical efficiency (TE) and allocative efficiency (AE). Technical efficiency ensures that input costs are minimized at a given level of output or that output is maximized at a given level of input(s). Allocative efficiency measures the ability of a decision-making unit (DMU) to use input resources optimally, given input prices. A decision-making unit is an individual or a group of individuals of a sample population participating in a buyer decision process. Economic efficiency is the product of technical efficiency and allocative efficiency and captures a decision-making unit's efficiency in both measures.

Researchers apply several methods to measure technical efficiency and allocative efficiency in different research areas. Two methods are commonly used to measure the efficiency of a decision-making unit: the non-parametric data envelopment analysis and the parametric stochastic frontier analysis (SFA) (Begum et al., 2012). Comparative studies between these two methods are done by Fecher et al. (1993), Lovell (1993), Hjalmarsson et al. (1996) and Sharma et al. (1997). Lampe and Hilgers (2014) performed a literature survey from 1978 to 2012 and found that data envelopment analysis is a standard technique in operation research, whereas stochastic frontier analysis is applied mainly in economic research. The choice between these two methods depends primarily on the study's objective, the type of decision-making unit and the availability of data.

Using data envelopment analysis to measure efficiency in this study has some advantages over other econometric approaches. First, the technique is non-parametric and does not require any assumptions of the functional form for the frontier technology. Second, this technique constructs an envelope/surface over the data, which helps compare the performance of one production method with the others in terms of their relative efficiency. Hence, this technique provides a straightforward approach to calculate efficiency gaps between best-performing and relatively underperforming decision-making units by accessing actual observations of the decision-making units' inputs and outputs (Haji, 2006; Reig-Martinez and Picazo-Tadeo, 2004; Malano et al., 2004; Wadud and White, 2000). The calculation of efficiencies in data envelopment analysis is either input oriented or output oriented. In input-oriented calculations, the objective is to reduce the number of inputs to produce the same level of output(s). In contrast, output-oriented calculations try to use the same level of inputs to produce more output(s) (Cooper et al., 2000, 2004).

This study applied the input-oriented efficiency calculation of the farms to decrease the number of inputs that are scarce or hazardous to the environment. The model applied in this study uses data of K inputs and M outputs for each of the N farms. Each farm can make its individual decision on inputs and outputs. The $K \times N$ input matrix X and the $M \times N$ output matrix Y comprise all the data of all the farms. This study is limited to the calculation of technical efficiency. The estimates of technical efficiency under constant return to scale (CRS) and variable return to scale (VRS) are calculated using DEAP V2.1 software. In this model, the ratio of outputs to inputs is used to measure the efficiency of each decision-making unit relative to that of all other decision-making units. The CRS model is reduced from a multiple-output/multiple-input situation (for each decision-making unit) to a single 'virtual' output and 'virtual' input. The ratio of this single virtual output and virtual input gives a measure of efficiency that is a function of the multipliers. In a mathematical programming language, the objective function for a particular decision-making unit is to maximize this ratio. Mathematically, it can be represented as:

$$\text{Max}_{v,u}\ Z = u \ldots \tag{20.1}$$
$$\text{subject to: } vx_j = 1;\ -vX + uY \leq 0;\ v \geq 0,\ u \geq 0;\ u_j$$

where a set of observed decision-making units (DMU_j; $j = 1, \ldots, n$); x_j, y_j are input and output vectors; row vector u, v are output and input multipliers; and X, Y are input and output matrices. In practice, most of the available programs for data envelopment analysis use the dual forms of linear programming as expressed in Equation (20.2), which lower the calculation burden and are virtually the same as Equation (20.1) (Ji and Lee, 2010). Mathematically, this can be expressed as:

$$\text{Min}_{\theta\lambda}\theta \ \ldots \tag{20.2}$$

$$\text{Subject to: } \theta x_j - X\lambda \geq 0;\ Y\lambda \geq y_j;\ \lambda \geq 0$$

where λ is a semi-positive vector in R^k, and θ is a real variable. A computational procedure for Equation (20.2) is performed in two steps, which are expressed in Equations (20.3) and (20.4):

$$\text{Min}_{\theta}\theta \ \ldots \tag{20.3}$$

$$\text{Min}_{\lambda,s^+,s^- \sum s^+ - s^-} \ldots \tag{20.4}$$

$$\text{subject to: } \theta x_j - X\lambda - s^- = 0;\ Y\lambda - s^+ = y_j;\ \lambda \geq 0$$

where s^+(output slack), s^-(input slack) and λ are semi-positive vectors in R^k, and θ is a real variable. The efficiency calculated under the single-stage data envelopment analysis model solves Equation (20.3), and the two-stage model solves Equations (20.3) and (20.4) consecutively. This study applied the two-stage input-oriented model through DEAP V2.1. Once each decision-making unit's efficiency scores (under constant and variable returns to scale) are calculated, the efficiency scores are regressed over possible influential variables using Tobit regression. Tobit regression is used because the efficiency scores are censored at the maximum value, i.e., 1. The Tobit regression used in the model finds the determinants of efficiency gaps between the best-performing and the relatively underperforming decision-making units.

After computing the efficiency of different farms, the efficiency scores were converted into percentages and regressed for different influential factors using the Tobit model in STATA 11 software. The model can be written in the following way (Equation [20.5]):

$$TE = a_0 + a_1CONT + a_2PDVTY + a_3PPQ + a_4BPVPA + a_5LPCPA + a_6TSCPA + a_7FYMCPA + a_8FCPA + a_9PPCPA + a_{10}ICPA + a_{11}HLCPA + a_{12}FMDPA + a_{13}AGE + a_{14}EDU + a_{15}OCP + a_{16}FS + a_{17}PFMIA + e \tag{20.5}$$

where CONT is a dummy variable of participation in contract farming (1 = participated, 0 = did not participate); PDVTY is the productivity of an acre of land (in q/acre); PPQ is the price per quintal of produce (in Rs); BPVPA is the by-product value per acre (in Rs/acre); LPCPA is the land preparation cost per acre (in Rs/acre); TSCPA is the total seed cost per acre (in Rs/acre); FYM-CPA is the farm yard manure (FYM) cost per acre (in Rs/acre); FCPA is the fertilizer cost per acre (in Rs/acre); PPCPA is the plant protection cost per acre (in Rs/acre); ICPA is the irrigation cost per acre (in Rs/acre); HLCPA is the hired labor cost per acre (in Rs/acre); FMDPA is the family worker-days per acre; AGE is the age of respondents in years; EDU is the education of respondents in years; OCP is the main occupation of the household (1 = agriculture, 0 = other); FS is the family size of a household; and PFMIA is the percentage of adult family members involved in agriculture in a household.

The technical efficiency computed under conditions of constant and variable returns to scale is regressed separately, and the results are presented in Tables 20.5 and 20.6 and Appendix Tables 20A.6 to 20A.10. A post-regression goodness-of-fit test was done using the 'fitstat' function in STATA. McFadden's R^2 value has been tabulated with each regression result. The value of McFadden's R^2 lies between 0 and 1. The better the goodness of fit in a model, the higher the McFadden's R^2 value. To explain factors influencing the efficiency of farms, our analysis focuses on Tobit results with variable returns to scale because it gives a more realistic view of the results.

Results and discussion

Measuring the farms' efficiency

The cost of inputs in the selected crops includes seed cost, farm yard manure and fertilizer cost, total plant protection cost and hired labor cost. These costs cover 82%–97% of the average total material and labor costs of the farms selected for this study. Usually, in some cases contracting companies provide seeds, plant protection chemicals, extension services and fertilizer. The cost of seeds, plant protection and fertilizer is deducted from the payment the companies make to the farmers after the farm produce is delivered. Table 20.3 shows that only three crops—wheat, potato and mustard—displayed a significant difference in average efficiency between contract and non-contract farms. Mustard farms showed no significant difference in average efficiency under the condition of variable returns to scale. In the previous section, it was found that five crops had a significant difference in per acre net income. Still, in the present case, only three crops showed a significant difference in the farms' average efficiency. The difference in average efficiency varied from only 4% to 12%. This indicates that contract farming does little to enable farmers to achieve higher efficiency (Table 20.3).

In terms of constant return to scale (CRS), the optimal farm percentage varies from 17% to 37%, whereas the suboptimal farm (increasing return to scale) percentage ranges from 30% to 68% across different crops. The super-optimal (decreasing return to scale) farms show a higher variance among the three categories of return to scale, with the percentage of these farms varying from 1.6% to 50%. Table 20.4 shows the number and percentage distribution

Table 20.3 Average technical efficiency of contract and non-contract farmers

Crops	*CRS*			*VRS*		
	Contract	*Non-contract*	*P-value*	*Contract*	*Non-contract*	*P-value*
Barley	71.68	67.72	0.1818	78.46	76.42	0.4276
Wheat	82.43	77.77	0.0124	85.52	81.8	0.0547
Potato	77.18	63.43	0.0001	83.27	71.37	0.0001
Mustard	83.08	74.09	0.0591	86.71	79.46	0.1069
Green Chili	83.62	79.58	0.4178	90.04	90.46	0.9024
Tomato	90.04	90.46	0.9024	86.48	88.9	0.4624
Baby-corn	79.42	82.07	0.2872	83.59	87.25	0.1359

Source: Primary data (2015–2016), calculated by authors.

of different returns to scale farms, along with their mean output value per acre and their range of output values per acre. The below-frequency distribution of farms, with returns to scale, indicates that a greater number of farms lie in the suboptimal category, which shows they have scope for improving their productivity by efficiently utilizing inputs. In other words, if all farms use the same technology and management that optimal farms use, suboptimal farms could be expected to increase their productivity and superoptimal farms would reduce their productivity.

The mean output per acre shows a consistent trend in each crop except for wheat. The optimal farms have the highest output value per acre, followed by superoptimal farms and suboptimal farms. In the case of wheat farms, the superoptimal farms have a higher output value per acre than optimal farms have. The reason is that 50% of wheat farms lie in the superoptimal category, which captures a large number of output values, and so the average is a little higher, by Rs 200 per acre. The superoptimal wheat farms also have a higher range of values than the optimal wheat farms.

Factors affecting the farms' efficiency

After the efficiency of different farms was computed, their efficiency scores were regressed on different influential factors. The factors influencing the farms' efficiency consist of major input costs, such as land preparation cost, seed cost, fertilizer cost, plant protection cost and labor cost; return obtained from main products and by-products; dummy; and socio-economic factors such as age, education, occupation, family size and percentage of adult family members involved in agriculture.

Tables 20.5 and 20.6 and Appendix Tables 20A.6 to 20A.10 present the factors influencing technical efficiency of the farm households for each of the crops by states. The Tobit results of different crop farms show that participation in contract farming does not significantly improve the farms' efficiency. Only

Table 20.4 Optimal, suboptimal and superoptimal per acre total output value (including by-products) of different farms

Crops	*Optimal*			*Suboptimal*			*Superoptimal*		
	Per acre output value range (Rs)	*Mean output value per acre*	*Number of farms (%)*	*Per acre output value range (Rs)*	*Mean output value per acre*	*Number of farms (%)*	*Per acre output value range (Rs)*	*Mean output value per acre*	*Number of farms (%)*
Barley	44 (17.32)	24,930	9,600–35,000	172 (67.72)	19,016	2,080–31,050	38 (14.96)	23,126	13,000–29,700
Wheat	46 (19.33)	2,9478	15,400–40,770	73 (30.67)	27,333	2,272–38,640	119 (50.00)	29,686	16,944–42,826
Potato	56 (24.14)	76,758	25,000–120,000	149 (64.22)	66,120	19,200–105,000	27 (11.64)	68,856	40,000–93,750
Mustard	21 (27.27)	28,337	9,571–40,000	30 (38.96)	21,172	7,800–37,200	26 (33.77)	21609	12,000–36,450
Chili	23 (37.70)	189,373	90,000–324,000	35 (57.38)	137,945	50,000–216,000	3 (4.92)	176,000	135,000–198,000
Tomato	21 (35.00)	123,893	60,000–195,428	38 (63.33)	90,897	27,500–160,000	1 (1.67)	100,000	100,000–100,000
Baby corn	57 (22.27)	27,331	12,000–48,000	114 (44.53)	21,823	1,800–34,800	85 (33.20)	23,676	12,000–33,000

Source: Primary data (2015–2016), calculated by authors.

Note: Figures in the parenthesis indicates percentage.

Table 20.5 Tobit regression estimates of the factors influencing technical efficiency of barley farmers in Haryana and Punjab

Factors	*Constant return to scale (CRS)*	*Variable return to scale (VRS)*
Constant	−12.120	11.702
Contracting	0.598	−0.128
Productivity	4.091***	3.083***
Price per quintal	0.049***	0.041***
By product value per acre	0.003***	0.003***
Land preparation cost per acre	−0.004***	−0.003**
Total seed cost per acre	−0.001	0.000
Farm yard manure cost per acre	0.001	0.001
Fertilizer cost per acre	−0.010***	−0.009***
Plant protection cost per acre	−0.006***	−0.004*
Irrigation cost per acre	−0.001	−0.002*
Hired labor cost per acre	−0.003***	−0.003***
Family worker-days per acre	−0.184**	0.257**
Age of the respondents	0.115*	0.112
Education of the respondents	−0.079	0.253
Occupation	−9.050**	−12.200**
Family size	−0.739***	−0.293
Percentage of adult family members involved in agriculture	−0.011	0.049
Sigma (δ)	10.666	15.807
Log-likelihood	−855.905	−859.848
LR (χ^2)	398.990	182.080
$p > \chi^2$	0.000	0.000
Number of observation	255	255
McFadden's R^2	0.189	0.096
McFadden's Adj R^2	0.171	0.076

Source: Primary data (2015–2016), calculated by authors.

Note: ***, **, * = significant at 1%, 5%, 10% level.

two crop farms—potato and mustard—showed that contracting had a significant positive impact on efficiency. Overall, productivity, price per quintal of produce, irrigation cost per acre, family worker-days per acre, fertilizer cost per acre and plant protection cost per acre were vital factors that influenced farm efficiency. Socio-economic factors such as age, education, family size, members involved in agriculture and occupation were not found to be very influential in affecting farms' efficiency. Farmers' education usually receives more attention in the efficiency literature, but in this study, farmers' years of formal education was found insignificant in all crops, except for green chili, under conditional and variable returns to scale. Several other studies also found insignificant relationships between farmers' education and farm efficiency (Phillips and Marble, 1986; Kalirajan, 1991; Bravo-Ureta and Evenson, 1994; Begum et al., 2012).

Table 20.6 Tobit regression estimates of the factors influencing technical efficiency of baby corn farmers in Karnataka

Factors	*Constant return to scale (CRS)*	*Variable return to scale (VRS)*
Constant	−40.158**	−10.677
Contracting	−2.028	−3.646
Productivity	1.278***	1.242
Price per quintal	0.160***	0.118
By product value per acre	0.002***	0.002
Land preparation cost per acre	−0.006***	−0.007
Total seed cost per acre	−0.006***	−0.002
Farm yard manure cost per acre	−0.002***	−0.002
Fertilizer cost per acre	−0.001***	−0.002
Plant protection cost per acre	−0.013***	−0.019
Irrigation cost per acre	−0.002***	−0.002
Hired labor cost per acre	−0.002***	−0.001
Family worker-days per acre	0.070	0.145
Age of the respondents	0.116**	0.122
Education of the respondents	−0.093	−0.268
Occupation	−0.817	−3.354
Family size	0.452	0.755
Percentage of adult family members involved in agriculture	0.055**	0.021
Sigma (δ)	8.771	8.771
Log-likelihood	−778.760	−778.760
LR (χ^2)	354.580	354.580
$p > \chi^2$	0.000	0.000
Number of observation	256	256
McFadden's R^2	0.185	0.133
McFadden's Adj R^2	0.166	0.111

Source: Primary data (2015–2016), calculated by authors.

Note: ***, **, * = significant at 1%, 5%, 10% level.

Conclusion and policy recommendation

This study considered a broad spectrum of contract farming in seven crops—barley, wheat, potato, mustard, tomato, green chili and baby corn—from northern to southern India. Descriptive statistics of contract and non-contract farms were done by using an independent sample *t*-test. The study found significantly greater productivity under contract farming that non-contracting farming in the cases of four crops—barley, wheat, tomato and mustard. Other crops also showed positive differences in productivity between contract and non-contract farms, but the differences ranging from 1 to 19 quintals per acre were not significant. Contract farmers also were found to receive higher prices than non-contract farmers received in the cases of tomato, mustard and wheat, obtaining Rs 50/q to Rs 172/q more than non-contract farmers obtained.

The combined effect of productivity and price made significant differences between contract and non-contract farmers in the per acre net income for five crops, varying from about Rs 1,100/acre to about Rs 27,500/acre. Only baby corn and barley did not show significant differences between contract and non-contract farmers in net income per acre.

The average technical efficiency computed for different farms varied from 60% to 90%, but only three contract crops—wheat, potato and mustard—showed higher average efficiency than non-contract crops. Mustard showed higher efficiency for contract farms than for non-contract farms under conditional return to scale but not under variable return to scale. Although in descriptive statistics, there is significant difference between contract and non-contract farms in per acre net income for five crops, but only three crops (mustard partially showing a difference) showed positive significant difference between contract and non-contract farms' average efficiency. In addition, a majority of farms (30%–64%) fell into the suboptimal category of farms, in which inputs are not utilized to their full potential. In general, some factors significantly influence farm efficiency. Those factors include productivity, price per quintal of produce, irrigation cost per acre, family worker-days per acre, fertilizer cost per acre and plant protection. Socio-economic factors such as age and education of the respondents, family size, members involved in agriculture and their occupation did not play much of a significant role in affecting the farms' efficiency. From these findings, we can conclude that contract farming in India creates significant differences in farmers' income but does not improve efficiency of the farms.

Socio-economic factors do not play any major role in enhancing the farms' efficiency. Also, the majority of farms are unable to utilize the full potential of inputs to optimize their production. Therefore, needs some technological advancement in crop production and higher remuneration for harvested crops and in shortening supply chain that could bring them higher remuneration for harvested crops. Policymakers should consider promoting contract farming in India by reducing some inefficiency factors and strengthening some efficiency-enhancing factors. Companies mostly are engaged in procuring raw material from farmers, but they should strengthen their extension systems and integrate with other extension agencies (government or non-governmental organizations). The public extension system is the dominant extension agency in India, and the Government can act as a facilitating agency in integrating its extension system with those of private companies. The Government also should adopt information and communication technology (ICT) in disseminating prices of different commodities to farmers, making them aware of current price in their local markets and enabling them to deal accordingly with contracting agencies.

References

Begum, I. A., Alam, M. J., Buysse, J., Frija, A. and Huylenbroeck, G. V. (2012). Contract farmer and poultry farm efficiency in Bangladesh: A data envelopment analysis. *Applied Economics*, 44(28), 3737–3747.

Bellemare, M. F. (2010). *As You Sow, So Shall You Reap: The Welfare Impacts of Contract Farming*. Working Paper, Duke University.

Bravo-Ureta, B. E. and Evenson, R. E. (1994). Efficiency in agricultural production: The case of peasant farmers in eastern Paraguay. *Agricultural Economics*, 10, 23–37.

Cooper, W. W., Seiford, L. M. and Tone, K. (2000). Data envelopment analysis. *Handbook on Data Envelopment Analysis*, 1–40.

Cooper, W. W., Seiford, L. M. and Zhu, J. (2004). Data envelopment analysis. *International Series in Operations Research & Management Science*, 71, 1–39.

Fecher, F., Kessler, D., Perelman, S. and Pestieau, P. (1993). Productive performance of the French insurance industry. *Journal of Productivity Analysis*, 4, 77–93.

Haji, J., (2006). Production efficiency of smallholders' vegetable-dominated mixed farming system in Eastern Ethiopia: A non-parametric approach. *Journal of African Economies*, 16(1), 1–27.

Hayami, Y., and Ruttan, V. (1985). *Agricultural Development: An International Perspective*. Baltimore: The Johns Hopkins University Press.

Hjalmarsson, L., Kumbhakar, S. C. and Heshmati, A. (1996). DEA, DFA and SFA: A comparison. *Journal of Productivity Analysis*, 7, 303–328.

Hopper, W. D. (1965). Allocation efficiency in a traditional Indian agriculture. *Journal of Farm Economics*, 47(3), 611–624.

Ji, Yong-bae and Lee, Choonjoo. (2010). Data envelopment analysis. *Stata Journal*, 10(2), 267–280.

Kalirajan, K. (1991). The importance of efficient use in the adoption of technology: A micro panel data analysis. *Journal of Productivity Analysis*, 2, 113–126.

Kuznets, S. (1966). *Modern Economic Growth: Rate, Structure, and Spread*. New Haven: New Haven Yale University Press.

Lampe, H. W. and Hilgers, D. (2014). Trajectories of efficiency measurement: A bibliometric analysis of DEA and SFA. *European Journal of Operational Research*, 240(1), 1–21.

Lovell, C. A. K. (1993). Production frontiers and productive efficiency. In *The Measurement of Productive Efficiency* (Eds.) H. O. Fried, C. A. K. Lovell and S. S. Schmidt. New York: Oxford University Press, pp. 3–91.

Malano, H., Burton, M. and Makin, I. (2004). Benchmarking performance in the irrigation and drainage sector: A tool for change. *Irrigation and Drainage*, 53, 119–133.

Mishra, A. K., Shaik, S., Khanal, A. and Bairagi, S. (2018). Contract farming and technical efficiency: Evidence from low-value and high-value crops in Nepal. *Agribusiness: An International Journal*, 34, 426–440.

Miyata, S., Minot, N. and Hu, D. (2009). Impact of contract farming on income: Linking small farmers, packets, and supermarkets in China. *World Development*, 37(11), 1728–1741.

Nguyen, A. T., Dzator, J. and Nadolny, A. (2015). Does contract farming improve productivity and income of farmers? A review of theory and evidence. *The Journal of Developing Areas*, 49(6), 531–538.

Nishimizu, M. and Page, J. M. Jr. (1982). Total factor productivity growth, technological progress and technical efficiency change: Dimensions of productivity change in Yugoslavia, 1965–78. *The Economic Journal*, 92, 920–936.

Phillips, J. M. and Marble, R. P. (1986). Farmer education and efficiency: A frontier production function approach. *Economics of Education Review*, 5, 257–264.

Reig-Martinez, E. and Picazo-Tadeo, A. J. (2004). Analysing farming systems with data envelopment analysis: citrus farming in Spain. *Agricultural Systems*, 82, 17–30.

Sahota, G. S. (1968). Efficiency of resource allocation in Indian agriculture. *American Journal of Agricultural Economics*, 50, 584–605.

Saigenji, Y. and Zeller, M. (2009). *Effect of Contract Farming on Productivity and Income of Small Holders: The Case of Tea Production in North-Western Vietnam*. Contributed Paper prepared for presentation at the International Association of Agricultural Economists Conference, 16–22 August, Beijing, China.

Saini, G. R. (1969). *Farm Size, Resource Use Efficiency and Income Distribution*. New Delhi: Allied Publishers Pvt.

Schultz, T. W. (1964). *Transforming Traditional Agriculture*. New Haven: Yale University Press.

Sharma, K. R., Leung, P. and Zaleski, H. M. (1997). Productive efficiency of the swine industry in Hawaii: Stochastic frontier versus data envelopment analysis. *Journal of Productivity Analysis*, 8, 447–459.

Swain, B. B. (2007). *An Analysis of Impact of Contract Farming on Farm Productivity and Efficiency- the Case of Hybrid Paddy Seed Cultivation in South India*. New Delhi, India: International Livestock Research Institute (ILRI).

Tadesse, B. and Krishnamoorthy, S. (1997). Technical efficiency in paddy farms of Tamil Nadu: An analysis based on farm size and ecological zone. *Agricultural Economics*, 16, 185–192.

Wadud, A. and White, B. (2000). Farm household efficiency in Bangladesh: A comparison of stochastic frontier and DEA methods. *Applied Economics*, 32, 1665–1673.

Appendix

Table 20A.1 Descriptive statistics of wheat farmers in Punjab and Haryana

Farm type	*Contract (n = 109)*	*Non-contract (n = 129)*	*Contract (n = 109)*	*Non-contract (n = 129)*	*p-value*
Variable	*Mean*		*Std. dev.*		
Crop acres	19.4	9.8	27.2	16.7	0.001***
Main output produced (q/acre)	19.5	18.4	2.8	2.6	0.003***
Main output price per quintal	1,553	1,502	165	66	0.001***
Main output value per acre	30,347	27,721	5,057	3,923	0.000***
By-product value per acre	2,987	3,354	1,847	2,544	0.211
Net return per acre	23,101	19,362	5,787	5,716	0.000***
Land preparation cost per acre	1,727	1,761	568	805	0.707
Total seed cost per acre	1,154	1,376	783	772	0.029
Farm yard manure cost per acre	112	114	520	653	0.978
Fertilizer cost per acre	2,383	2,386	801	638	0.972
Plant protection cost per acre	1,187	1,329	1,033	1,070	0.300
Other material cost per acre	2,640	3,006	1,019	1,355	0.021**
Total material cost per acre	7,388	8,096	2,355	2,488	0.026**
Hired labor cost per acre	2,853	3,615	1,132	1,903	0.000***
Family worker-days per acre	3.3	8.9	3.3	7.8	0.000***
Hired worker-days per acre	2.1	2.5	2.5	4.5	0.483
Age of the respondents	47.7	49.0	10.7	13.4	0.410
Education of the respondents	8.8	6.6	4.6	4.9	0.000***
Family size	6.7	6.5	2.9	2.9	0.470
Percentage of adult family members involved in agriculture	38.9	40.4	18.4	19.0	0.537

Source: Primary data (2015–2016), calculated by authors.

Note: ***, **, * = significant at 1%, 5%, 10% level.

Table 20A.2 Descriptive statistics of potato farmers in Punjab and Haryana

Farm type	*Contract (n = 165)*	*Non- contract (n = 67)*	*Contract (n = 165)*	*Non- contract (n = 67)*	*p-value*
Variable	*Mean*		*Std. dev.*		
Crop acres	8.6	6.8	12.5	6.3	0.245
Main output produced (q/acre)	105.4	106.6	24.3	26.8	0.748
Main output price per quintal	717	545	131	190	0.000***
Main output value per acre	74,446	55,610	17,575	17,049	0.000***
By-product value per acre	40	0	394	0	0.403
Net return per acre	32,995	20,557	17,215	17,076	0.000***
Land preparation cost per acre	3,237	2,828	1,861	1,533	0.112
Total seed cost per acre	18,036	13,874	7,416	5,841	0.000***
Farm yard manure cost per acre	447	455	1,090	2,492	0.974
Fertilizer cost per acre	5,845	5,484	2,008	2,447	0.246
Plant protection cost per acre	2,670	2,578	1,670	1,740	0.708
Other material cost per acre	4,474	3,949	2,481	1,980	0.124
Total material cost per acre	31,156	26,089	8,723	8,086	0.000***
Hired labor cost per acre	10,349	8,970	4,092	3,222	0.014**
Family worker-days per acre	7.1	10.1	7.2	8.8	0.008***
Hired worker-days per acre	13.0	12.0	12.7	12.4	0.602
Age of the respondents	42	44	11	14	0.163
Education of the respondents	10.5	10.6	3.5	2.6	0.900
Family size	7.6	8.1	4.0	3.3	0.384
Percentage of adult family members involved in agriculture	40.5	40.1	15.1	16.0	0.858

Source: Primary data (2015–2016), calculated by authors.

Note: ***, **, * = significant at 1%, 5%, 10% level.

Table 20A.3 Descriptive statistics of mustard farmers in Punjab and Haryana

Farm type	*Contract (n = 32)*	*Non-contract (n = 45)*	*Contract (n = 32)*	*Non-contract (n = 45)*	*p-value*
Variable	*Mean*		*Std. dev.*		
Crop acres	4.5	3.7	3.5	2.9	0.279
Main output produced (q/acre)	7.3	6.4	1.8	1.8	0.032**
Main output price per quintal	3,484	3,321	323	411	0.065*
Main output value per acre	25,886	21,416	7,560	6,733	0.007***
By-product value per acre	716	310	1,233	1,148	0.142
Net return per acre	18,642	14,600	7,650	6,741	0.016**
Land preparation cost per acre	1,579	1,552	914	512	0.865
Total seed cost per acre	333	406	266	207	0.183
Farm yard manure cost per acre	205	0	784	0	0.081*
Fertilizer cost per acre	1,796	1,811	520	570	0.907
Plant protection cost per acre	413	433	387	457	0.846
Other material cost per acre	3,147	2,544	1,484	793	0.023**
Total material cost per acre	5,756	5,101	2,411	1,223	0.122
Hired labor cost per acre	2,205	2,014	942	619	0.286
Family worker-days per acre	6.6	10.3	4.7	7.3	0.015
Hired worker-days per acre	2.1	2.2	2.5	5.1	0.977
Age of the respondents	44.5	45.7	13.1	11.7	0.691
Education of the respondents	8.4	6.6	5.0	4.6	0.097*
Family size	6.7	6.2	3.7	2.7	0.509
Percentage of adult family members involved in agriculture	44.4	53.3	18.9	24.4	0.086*

Source: Primary data (2015–2016), calculated by authors.

Note: ***, **, * = *significant at 1%, 5%, 10% level.*

Table 20A.4 Descriptive statistics of green chili farmers in Karnataka

Farm type	*Contract (n = 35)*	*Non-contract (n = 26)*	*Contract (n = 35)*	*Non-contract (n = 26)*	*p-value*
Variable	*Mean*		*Std. dev.*		
Crop acres	1.6	1.4	1.1	0.7	0.287
Main output produced (q/acre)	98.2	84.5	28.8	35.7	0.103
Main output price per quintal	1,782	1,769	87.3	457.6	0.870
Main output value per acre	174,931	138,042	52,022	43,080	0.004***
By-product value per acre	—	—	—	—	—
Net return per acre	89,738	62,196	48,903	38,693	0.021**
Land preparation cost per acre	6,526	4,346	2,125	1,104	0.000***
Total seed cost per acre	5,188	4,991	2,453	2,572	0.761
Farm yard manure cost per acre	12,809	9,064	6,868	4,438	0.018**
Fertilizer cost per acre	23,733	15,792	10,860	5,914	0.001***
Plant protection cost per acre	13,757	13,179	5,421	5,056	0.673
Other material cost per acre	22,461	19,033	10,963	6,283	0.158
Total material cost per acre	64,466	54,579	20,534	8,893	0.025**
Hired labor cost per acre	20,726	17,744	7,749	5,941	0.107
Family worker-days per acre	78	73	51	35	0.673
Hired worker-days per acre	108	88	42	24	0.041**
Age of the respondents	41.6	47.7	11.8	9.1	0.032**
Education of the respondents	8.0	4.3	4.7	4.2	0.002***
Family size	6.4	5.6	3.2	1.6	0.234
Percentage of adult family members involved in agriculture	80.3	69.8	23.7	21.3	0.080*

Source: Primary data (2015–2016), calculated by authors.

Note: ***, **, * = significant at 1%, 5%, 10% level.

Table 20A.5 Descriptive statistics of tomato farmers in Karnataka

Farm type	*Contract (n = 35)*	*Non-contract (n = 25)*	*Contract (n = 35)*	*Non-contract (n = 25)*	*p-value*
Variable	*Mean*		*Std. dev.*		
Crop acres	1.4	1.8	0.7	1	0.080*
Main output produced (q/acre)	106.3	87.3	28.6	30.3	0.016**
Main output price per quintal	1,091	980	154	287	0.057*
Main output value per acre	114,991	85,246	31,511	36,576	0.001***
By product value per acre	—	—	—	—	—
Net return per acre	49,526	34,300	27,000	26,848	0.035**
Land preparation cost per acre	4,129	4,148	705	696	0.920
Total seed cost per acre	6,704	6,351	872	1093	0.169
Farm yard manure cost per acre	8,213	4,716	4,300	2,398	0.000***
Fertilizer cost per acre	17,424	9,491	7,596	5,940	0.000***
Plant protection cost per acre	7,385	6,042	3,003	2,512	0.073*
Other material cost per acre	16,646	13,110	7,083	6,588	0.054*
Total material cost per acre	46,078	35,848	9,585	8,739	0.000***
Hired labor cost per acre	19,385	12,879	5,643	4,693	0.000***
Family worker-days per acre	66.8	64.5	37.7	37.7	0.821
Hired worker-days per acre	94.3	63.6	26.6	20.9	0.000***
Age of the respondents	47.6	47.3	10.5	12.7	0.921
Education of the respondents	4.5	7.4	4.5	4.9	0.021**
Family size	5.3	6	2.8	3.2	0.392
Percentage of adult family members involved in agriculture	75.8	74.3	24.4	23.6	0.820

Source: Primary data (2015–2016), calculated by authors.

Note: ***, **, * = *significant at 1%, 5%, 10% level.*

Table 20A.6 Tobit regression estimates of the factors influencing technical efficiency of wheat farmers in Haryana and Punjab

Factors	*Constant return to scale (CRS)*	*Variable return to scale (VRS)*
Constant	11.580	23.995*
Contracting	−0.062	0.176
Productivity	2.732***	2.965***
Price per quintal	0.027***	0.024***
By product value per acre	0.002***	0.002***
Land preparation cost per acre	−0.010***	−0.012***
Total seed cost per acre	0.000	0.000
Farm yard manure cost per acre	0.000	−0.001
Fertilizer cost per acre	−0.003***	−0.003**
Plant protection cost per acre	0.001*	0.001
Irrigation cost per acre	−0.005***	−0.007***
Hired labor cost per acre	0.000	-0.001
Family worker-days per acre	0.156	0.674***
Age of the respondents	0.088	0.059
Education of the respondents	0.041	0.180
Occupation	−6.658***	−9.406***
Family size	−0.185	−0.091
Percentage of adult family members involved in agriculture	−0.013	−0.051
Sigma (δ)	9.950	12.751
Log-likelihood	−788.304	−730.281
LR (χ^2)	214.740	170.430
$p > \chi^2$	0.000	0.000
Number of observation	238	238
McFadden's R^2	0.120	0.104
McFadden's Adj R^2	0.099	0.081

Source: Primary data (2015–2016), calculated by authors.

Note: ***, **, * = significant at 1%, 5%, 10% level.

Table 20A.7 Tobit regression estimates of the factors influencing technical efficiency of potato farmers in Haryana and Punjab

Factors	*Constant return to scale (CRS)*	*Variable return to scale (VRS)*
Constant	1.343	52.783***
Contracting	11.228***	15.758***
Productivity	0.681***	0.466***

Factors	*Constant return to scale (CRS)*	*Variable return to scale (VRS)*
Price per quintal	0.069***	0.044***
By product value per acre	−0.005	0.047
Land preparation cost per acre	−0.002***	−0.002**
Total seed cost per acre	−0.001***	−0.001***
Farm yard manure cost per acre	0.000	0.000
Fertilizer cost per acre	−0.003***	−0.002***
Plant protection cost per acre	−0.001	−0.002**
Irrigation cost per acre	−0.004***	−0.006***
Hired labor cost per acre	0.000*	−0.001
Family worker-days per acre	0.294**	1.296***
Age of the respondents	−0.035	−0.059
Education of the respondents	−0.089	−0.158
Occupation	−5.450	−11.758**
Family size	0.163	−0.050
Percentage of adult family members involved in agriculture	0.007	−0.048
Sigma (δ)	11.805	16.502
Log-likelihood	−765.879	−734.819
LR (χ^2)	277.660	160.920
$p > \chi^2$	0.000	0.000
Number of observation	232	232
McFadden's R^2	0.153	0.099
McFadden's Adj R^2	0.132	0.077

Source: Primary data (2015–2016), calculated by authors.

Note: ***, **, * = significant at 1%, 5%, 10% level.

Table 20A.8 Tobit regression estimates of the factors influencing technical efficiency of mustard farmers in Haryana and Punjab

Factors	*Constant return to scale (CRS)*	*Variable return to scale (VRS)*
Constant	−9.278	2.176
Contracting	8.994**	10.834
Productivity	9.046***	9.643
Price per quintal	0.020***	0.017
By product value per acre	0.005**	0.006
Land preparation cost per acre	−0.006**	−0.004
Total seed cost per acre	−0.028***	−0.033
Farm yard manure cost per acre	−0.008**	−0.011
Fertilizer cost per acre	0.001	0.001
Plant protection cost per acre	−0.015***	−0.020
Irrigation cost per acre	−0.020***	−0.023
Hired labor cost per acre	−0.003	−0.004

(*Continued*)

Table 20A.8 (Continued)

Factors	*Constant return to scale (CRS)*	*Variable return to scale (VRS)*
Family worker-days per acre	0.555**	0.996
Age of the respondents	−0.063	0.008
Education of the respondents	0.164	0.146
Occupation	—	—
Family size	0.325	0.239
Percentage of adult family members involved in agriculture	0.023	0.036
Sigma (δ)	12.360	15.547
Log-likelihood	−235.431	−212.756
LR (χ^2)	101.930	80.210
$p > \chi^2$	0.000	0.000
Number of observation	77	77
McFadden's R^2	0.178	0.159
McFadden's Adj R^2	0.115	0.087

Source: Primary data (2015–2016), calculated by authors.

Note: ***, **, * = significant at 1%, 5%, 10% level.

Table 20A.9 Tobit regression estimates of the factors influencing technical efficiency of green chili farmers in Karnataka

Factors	*Constant return to scale (CRS)*	*Variable return to scale (VRS)*
Constant	25.783	−37.261
Contracting	7.677	−1.779
Productivity	0.715***	0.716***
Price per quintal	0.016	0.069***
By product value per acre	—	—
Land preparation cost per acre	−0.001	0.001
Total seed cost per acre	−0.001	0.000
Farm yard manure cost per acre	−0.001***	−0.001**
Fertilizer cost per acre	−0.001**	0.000
Plant protection cost per acre	−0.001	0.000
Irrigation cost per acre	−0.005***	−0.003**
Hired labor cost per acre	0.000	0.000
Family worker-days per acre	0.046	0.126
Age of the respondents	0.057	-0.409
Education of the respondents	−0.176	−1.145*
Occupation	—	—
Family size	1.281	−0.800
Percentage of adult family members involved in agriculture	0.130	0.051

Factors	Constant return to scale (CRS)	Variable return to scale (VRS)
Sigma (δ)	12.628	11.906
Log-likelihood	−162.122	−119.032
LR (χ^2)	75.630	58.410
$p > \chi^2$	0.000	0.000
Number of observations	61	61
McFadden's R^2	0.189	0.197
McFadden's Adj R^2	0.104	0.082

Source: Primary data (2015–2016), calculated by authors.

Note: ***, **, * = significant at 1%, 5%, 10% level.

Table 20A.10 Tobit regression estimates of the factors influencing technical efficiency of tomato farmers in Karnataka

Factors	Constant return to scale (CRS)	Variable return to scale (VRS)
Constant	35.796	81.759***
Contracting	5.864	4.329
Productivity	0.786***	0.675***
Price per quintal	0.051***	0.026**
By product value per acre	—	—
Land preparation cost per acre	−0.004*	−0.002
Total seed cost per acre	−0.005**	−0.007***
Farm yard manure cost per acre	−0.001***	−0.001*
Fertilizer cost per acre	−0.001***	−0.001***
Plant protection cost per acre	−0.001	−0.001
Irrigation cost per acre	−0.004**	−0.003
Hired labor cost per acre	0.000	−0.001
Family worker-days per acre	0.054	0.140*
Age of the respondents	0.149	0.160
Education of the respondents	0.548	0.521
Occupation	—	—
Family size	−0.153	−0.158
Percentage of adult family members involved in agriculture	0.034	−0.035
Sigma (δ)	10.055	12.210
Log-likelihood	−164.744	−160.833
LR (χ^2)	78.570	44.500
$p > \chi^2$	0.000	0.000
Number of observation	60	60
McFadden's R^2	0.193	0.122
McFadden's Adj R^2	0.109	0.029

Source: Primary data (2015–2016), calculated by authors.

Note: ***, **, * = *significant at 1%, 5%, 10% level.*

21 Who quits and who sustains participation in a supermarket supply chain?

An insight from the Aditya Birla More supply chain

D. Suganthi, S. Mahendra Dev and Vijay Laxmi Pandey[1]

The supply relationship between an agro-processing firm or a supermarket-led supply chain and farmers is considered one of the promising policy interventions that enable markets to work for poor farmers in developing countries. Firms tailor the firm–farm relationships to promote private investment in agribusiness, and enabling policies are a prerequisite. In the same spirit, India has initiated many policy measures to attract corporate investment in agriculture. One such measure is the 2003 amendment to the Agricultural Produce Market Committee (APMC) Act, under which agribusiness firms could procure produce directly from farmers. The act was intended to reduce transaction costs through disintermediation (shortening the supply chain) and, by creating quality standards for traceability, to address concerns related to food safety and quality (DIPP, 2010, 2015). To further promote firm-farm relationships, the Model Agricultural Produce and Livestock Contract Farming and Services Act was approved in 2018, in which farmer-producer organizations (FPOs) would have a significant role in encouraging contract farming. Recognizing the large-scale post-harvest waste of perishable crops in the supply chain, the government is liberalizing foreign direct investment (FDI) for both wholesale and retail trade. The expectation is that domestic and multinational supermarkets and agribusiness firms would use FDI in their back-end operations. Formal or informal firm–farm relationships are not a recent phenomenon, but the supermarkets' entry into direct procurement is new. In the context of the organized food retailing and multi-brand retail segment in India, there is a renewed focus on the liberalization of FDI (Reardon et al., 2009).

Empirical narratives on transactional relationships argue that these relationships can render multiple forms of production support. For instance, such relationships can provide credit, technical advice, inputs and price insurance; introduce new technology; and bring certainty in transactions to resource-poor rural farmers (Minot, 1986, 2008; Da Silva, 2005; Eaton and Shepherd, 2001). The literature also points out that small farmers can be connected with the dynamic firm–farm relationships because they have self-supervising family labor, which is pertinent for producing labor-intensive and perishable high-value commodities seems redundant (Key and Runsten, 1999). While recognizing the benefits of the transactional relationships, the literature so far has focused on 'social performance' (Warning and Key, 2002) or the inclusiveness of transactional relationships. The inclusion of small farmers in transactional relationships is essential, but it is not sufficient when they drop out involuntarily because of their inability to meet quality parameters (Narayanan, 2013). The involuntary exit of resource-constrained small farmers is a serious concern since Indian agriculture is predominantly a smallholder economy. As FDI in multi-brand retail has increased, small farmers might have to face powerful and resourceful multinational retailers of both domestic and foreign origin.

Evidence on the social performance of firm–farm relationships is mixed. Many studies show that firms willingly work with small farmers (Glover and Kusterer, 1990; Wang et al., 2009). However, another strand of the literature shows evidence that firms exclude resource-constrained small farmers (Zamora, 2004). In other cases, stringent quality standards hinder these farmers from sustained relationships (Boselie et al., 2003). Neven et al. (2009) found that a threshold resource requirement prevented small and rain-fed farmers from entering the supermarket supply chain in rural Kenya. The dominance of large farmers also has been highlighted in the literature (Guo and Jolly, 2008; Runsten and Key, 1996; Singh, 2002) since transaction costs are lower when agribusiness firms and large farmers are involved in a contract. Moreover, large farmers possess abundant resources to comply with the agribusiness firms' volume and quality requirements. A few other studies report firms working with both small and large farmers (Bivings and Runsten, 1992). Therefore, the type of growers participating in firm–farm relationships varies over time. Firms shift from large farmers to small farmers and vice versa as they experiment and learn from their experiences (Minot, 1986, 2008; Key and Runsten, 1999; Narayanan, 2013; Barrett et al., 2011; Michelson, 2013; Miyata et al., 2009).

Furthermore, recent literature argues that although farm size might be one of the elements affecting inclusiveness in dynamic firm–farm relationships but that it is inadequate when, to explore inclusiveness, farmers selection into dynamic firm–farm relationships is of a sequential (Barrett et al., 2011) or layered nature (Narayanan, 2014). These studies articulate that farm size might conceal other key factors driving participation, for instance, farmers' inclination and commitment to quality (Runsten and Key, 1996) and their access to irrigation and roads (Hernandez et al., 2007; Miyata et al., 2009). Also, firms often identify by reputation and reliability with the help of lead farmers, traders or village heads or through existing participants in the supply chains (Warning and Key, 2002; Rao and Dev, 2005; Miyata et al., 2009). Further, Narayanan (2014) argues that farmers could be excluded from relationships with firms for various reasons at different spatial levels. For instance, an agribusiness firm's choice of a particular region excludes farmers from other areas, or the firm's selection of specific blocks within the chosen region excludes other blocks. The firm's choice of certain villages within selected regions and blocks excludes farmers from other villages. Hence considering only producer-level characteristics may not completely reveal the actual process of exclusion. Therefore, to assess the reach of firm–farm relationships, factoring in the selection of geography is necessary to avoid results that give a sketchy picture.

Against this backdrop, the central goal of this chapter is to examine the drivers of initial inclusion and retention of farmers in the Aditya Birla More Collection Center (ABM CC) supply chain, conditional on spatial characteristics. The chapter also examines the dynamic elements of the transactional relationship and how farmers' perception of risk in supplying to ABM's CC, as opposed to supplying to traditional markets, shapes the transactional relationship. The chapter also probes factors influencing the firm's choice of this particular region for procurement. A total of ten villages were chosen randomly for the study: eight villages from the supermarket data, two non-participant villages and thus five from each block. A total of 543 households were surveyed. Even though the analysis is based on cross-sectional data, the experiences of suppliers who discontinued their relationship with ABM's CC provide insight into the dynamic aspect of the transactional relationship between farmers and the ABM supply chain.

The rest of this chapter is arranged as follows. The next section describes the study area and the nature of the supply relationship between farmers and ABM's CC. We then elaborate on the need to study spatial selection and the dynamic elements of modern supply chains. A section on the perception of risk in the ABM chain and descriptive statistics follows. The subsequent sections discuss the empirical framework and the results. The final section gives the conclusion and policy implications.

Study area and ABM collection center supply relationship

For the empirical analysis, this paper focuses on the Junnar and Ambegaon blocks of the Pune District of Maharashtra, primarily because of its history of cultivating horticulture crops and because it has become the destination for supermarket procurement operations. Supermarkets such as Aditya Birla More (ABM), Spencers and Reliance Fresh procure directly from farmers through their collection center, and Bharti-Walmart, Food Bazaar, Godrej Adhaar and Metro procure through dedicated traders. ABM's collection center was established in 2006 close to the highway between Pune and Nashik, instead in interior clusters, and hence was easily accessible by farmers. These cluster of villages have access to canal irrigation through the network of rivers and dams. The center initially was established within the tomato market yard of Narayangaon town. Later, the collection center was relocated to the adjacent Ambegaon block but still near the highway and within 10 km of its initial location. The collection center's new site is near a regulated market, Manchaar, giving the center the advantage of procuring produce from the regulated market in the case of shortfalls. The center also is readily accessible by farmers visiting the regulated spot market. The survey data was collected when ABM CC used to procure for its 'More' outlets in Mumbai before it ceased its operations.

The ABM collection center's daily intake was about 12 to 15 tonnes for all commodities, and the center procured only a portion of a farmer's harvest (an average 25% of farmers' produce)—and that the portion of premier quality. However, the center's daily demand for certain commodities, such as cauliflower, cabbage, bottle gourd, eggplant and tomato, was slightly more than a tonne, which was relatively higher than the demand for other commodities. The supermarket manager is informed about the required amounts a day before and communicates the requirements to the farmers over the phone the same night. Having a cell phone therefore is a necessary factor for participation in the ABM supply chain. ABM's procurement price is 70% of the regulated market price in Pune. ABM follows product-specific quality standards, defined by color, size, freshness and volume. For instance, cauliflower and cabbage weighing more than 450 g and crooked vegetables were weeded out at the time of procurement. The suppliers to ABM's collection center sell the premium-quality portion of their produce to the center and the rest to alternative markets. Hence the alternative channels play an important role in marketing the majority of the farmers' produce. Most often, pickup truck operators collect the farmers' produce in the evening to market it in the Pune and Mumbai regulated markets. In the case of the Manchaar market, farmers visit the market around noon.

Initially, ABM's collection center identified potential farmers with the help of Bayer Crop Science (BCS) field officials. BCS is an input supplier company, which introduced the Food Chain Partnership (FCP) program in 2006 as a marketing program to coordinate between farmers and retailers. The program was designed to upgrade the farmers' ability to meet retailers' and processors' stringent quality standards. The program also aimed to reduce the information gap facing retailers and processors, who often lacked network and geographical information, which prevented them from entering into direct procurement practices. Thus BCS acted as a networking partner and shared its database of progressive and reliable farmers with retailers and processors. The company used its network of sales representatives to launch the program and appointed field officers, who guide the farmers throughout the growing season and help maintain the health and quality of the crops. Even though the company says it empowers farmers, it seems to have a vested interest in promoting its products to capture a significant share of the demand for inputs of high-value crops (HVC), driven by the organized retail and processing industries. In a way, poor state extension services have helped BCS sustain its activities (Trebbin and Franz, 2010). With the support of BCS field officials, the ABM CC manager reviewed the number of farmers available for future procurement of particular crops. The manager deals daily with 40 to 50 farmers on a diverse range of crops. The relationship is quite flexible for the farmers, as they bargain bilaterally over prices, and the collection center is situated within the production area. When prices in the Manchaar regulated market are higher than the ABM CC prices, farmers negotiate to match the spot market prices. The ABM CC manager stated that often the center falls short of the required quantities because of the farmers' habit of selling on the side, and, to compensate, the center procured from the Manchaar regulated market.

Spatial selection and farmers' participation

Empirical evidence on the process of establishing supply relationships between farmers and agro-processing or supermarket-led supply chains reveals that the selection of geography precedes the selection of farmers (Barrett et al., 2011; Michelson, 2013; Narayanan, 2014). Agro-processing firms select procurement regions based on the feasibility of growing the necessary commodity. Unlike commodity-specific agro-processing companies, supermarkets need various high-value crops throughout the year. Detailed interviews with the supermarket procurement manager in the study area suggest that there is a systematic process for selecting regions and farmers. The ABM CC manager said the company chose these two blocks in Pune District as a procurement basin based on agro-climatic factors such as the availability of water for irrigation throughout the year and an altitude conducive to cultivating horticulture crops. The chosen location is about 2,250 feet above sea level and is near major dams, the Western Ghats and the Sahyadri mountain range. It has five major dams: the Yedgaon dam on the river Kukadi, the Wadaj dam on the river Meena, the Pimpalgaon Joge dam on the river Pushpavati, the Manikodh dam on the river Kukadi and the Chilewadi dam on the river Mandavi.

The collection center manager said the company chose Pune as the procurement basin instead of Nasik, a well known horticulture zone in Maharashtra, because commodities from the Nasik region are of premium quality, mostly serving the export market, and their prices and procurement costs are higher than those of the Pune District, which caters only to the domestic market. In addition, ABM's distribution center is located in the Pune city, serving outlets in Pune and Mumbai. Hence the proximity to the distribution center and the need to minimize the transaction costs of procurement and the perishability of commodities drove the company to choose the Pune District.

The ABM manager also stated that the company targets progressive farmers because they often come with a diverse social network. The social networks influence adherence to transactional terms. A list of potential farmers who meet the firm's informal eligibility criteria, such as irrigation facility, willingness to supply small quantities of only first-grade produce and ability to follow the quality standards, was identified. Although ABM identified initial adopters, late adopters entered the market through the initial adopters' social network. Interviews with farmers reveal that their perception of future benefits and risks associated with supplying to ABM's CC influenced their decision to accept or reject the transactional relationship. Initial suppliers perceived that they would save on transaction costs, as these costs are relatively lower in the ABM CC supply chain. Moreover, these suppliers anticipated that the ABM center would offer higher prices than the spot markets since it procures only first-grade produce. However, after the farmers entered the supply chain, high rates of rejection discouraged many of them from continuing the relationship. High rejection rates increase their transaction costs, as the farmers have to take the rejected produce to the spot market, and going to two markets instead of one makes it unprofitable for the farmers to sustain their relationship with AMB's collection center. This empirical account makes a case for understanding the dynamic effects of firm–farm relationships, for understanding the reasons that trigger farmers to drop out and for suggesting policies to make firm–farm relationships fruitful and sustainable.

Risk factors associated with ABM collection center's supply chain

Several empirical studies suggest that firm–farm relationships bring new problems but simultaneously reduce risks in other aspects (Bellemare, 2012; Narayanan, 2012). Some of the often cited issues that farmers face are firms reneging on their commitment to buy produce, rejection based on arbitrary quality standards, poor quality of technical services and delay or deliberate default of payments (Echanove and Steffen, 2005; Mannon, 2005; Ramaswami et al., 2005; Glover, 1987).

We found a similar set of risk factors associated with the supply relationship between farmers and the ABM CC. This information was obtained through focus group discussions with farmers and traders and from the primary survey. The discussions and survey revealed that the collection center often bid for more than its required quantity of produce to reduce the risk of farmer default and that it often reneged on its promise to buy the produce, increasing the farmers' transportation costs. Another significant risk associated with the supply relationship was in the quantity being rejected. In many instances, the quantities were small, so farmers used them for home consumption. When the quantities were large and were of low quality, rather than a mix of all grades, farmers perceived that finding a buyer in the open market was challenging. The quality standards became incomprehensibly stringent when open market prices crashed. Farmers also observed that, when the center contracts for more than it requires of a particular commodity and if the local market for that commodity happens to be fragile, the center bought only the required quantity that day. However, with the farmer's consent, the center retained the remaining produce without refrigeration and assured the farmers that it would buy the leftover produce the next day. Farmers then bear the risk of reduction in weight due to moisture loss. These observations reveal that even though the firm–farm relationship between the ABM CC and the producers reduces transaction costs, it creates a new set of risks and forces farmers to exit the relationship. The farmers who discontinued the relationship and the non-suppliers were dissatisfied with the center's quality standards, procurement of small quantities and rejection rates. There is no commitment between suppliers and the ABM collection center, and instances of both farmers and the center reneging on their transactional terms have been reported. These instances show that the perception of risks associated with supplying to the ABM collection center would be a key factor driving non-participation or attrition.

Qualitative evidence and descriptive statistics

Almost all the suppliers to ABM's CC revealed that low packaging costs, the absence of participation fees, reliable weighing machines and often low transportation costs were some of the ABM supply chain's attractive features. Farmers were unhappy about rejection rates in the collection center's initial years of operation but eventually learned its requirements. Accordingly, they sort and supply only superior-quality products, which saves their transaction costs. Table 21.1 presents mean comparisons by supplier status for the variables included in the regression analysis and the *t*-test of difference in means for each variable. The average household size of continuous suppliers and late entrants in the sample is 6.1. Two-thirds of the household members of continuous suppliers and of late entrants are adults, significantly higher than the share of adults in the households of non-suppliers. Some 4% of the discontinued suppliers belong to Scheduled Castes (SC) and Scheduled Tribes (ST), social groups significantly different from the social group of non-suppliers. The heads of continuous-supplier households and of late-entrant households completed an average of 9.5 years and 9 years of education, respectively—considerably greater than the years of education for heads of non-supplier households. The average farming experience is highest among late entrants (31 years), followed by discontinued suppliers (29 years) and continuous suppliers (24 years), all of which are significantly lower than the average farming experience of non-suppliers. The heads of continuous-supplier households tend to have, on average, significantly more years of schooling and fewer years of farming experience than non-suppliers have. About 24% of the heads of continuous-supplier households are members of one or more voluntary organizations, compared to 7% of late entrants and 8% of discontinued suppliers, shares that are significantly higher than that of non-suppliers. The percentage of all supplier categories growing exotic crops is lower than the percentage of non-suppliers growing these crops. However, they cannot reject the mean equivalence except for late entrants.

Regarding pre-participation wealth (2005–2006), continuous suppliers rank higher on the household asset index and are more likely to have to access to drip irrigation than the other categories of suppliers, and the differences compared to non-suppliers are significant. All the supplier categories ranked significantly higher on the farm asset index than non-suppliers. The majority of continuous suppliers (84%) had access to cell phones in 2005–2006, which

Table 21.1 Descriptive statistics by supplier status

Category	*Continuous suppliers*		*Late entrants*		*Discontinued suppliers*		*Non-suppliers*	
	Mean	*Standard deviation*	*Mean*	*Standard deviation*	*Mean*	*Standard deviation*	*Mean*	*Standard deviation*
Landholdings 2005 (acres)	6.911*	0.815	5.253*	0.448	5.202*	0.545	.185	0.225
Age of the head of the household (years)	46	1.590	46.7	0.745	45	1.147	46.903	0.585
Household size	6.4*	0.354	6.1	0.287	5.4	0.223	6.2	0.151
Number of adult members	4.289*	0.219	4.046*	0.176	3.706	0.160	3.755	0.080
Number of dependents	2.178	0.279	2.000	0.181	1.912	0.212	1.819	0.118
Household belonging to SC/ST (D)	3.889	NA	3.719	NA	4.000*	NA	3.841	NA
Farming experience (years)	24.044*	1.792	31.052*	1.000	29.235*	1.538	33.386	0.668
Education of the household head (years)	9.578*	0.486	9.248*	0.291	8.779	0.381	7.986	0.228
Member of a voluntary organization (D)	0.244*	NA	0.072*	NA	0.088*	NA	0.036	NA
Grow exotic vegetables (D)	0.311	NA	0.281*	NA	0.309	NA	0.357	NA
Household asset index (2005)	0.517*	0.228	—0.157	0.135	0.014	0.202	0.068	0.103
Farm asset index (2005)	1.180*	0.269	0.031*	0.087	0.157*	0.102	—0.242	0.072
Relationship with a trader (years)	20.067*	1.305	22.830	0.725	23.618	1.135	23.069	0.523
Drip irrigation 2005 (D)	0.356*	NA	0.105	NA	0.118	NA	0.165	NA
Mean well depth (m)	45.224	1.019	48.494*	0.404	45.754*	0.745	46.795	0.997
Distance to highway (km)	3.911*	0.678	5.086*	0.486	3.256*	0.564	4.958	0.518
Distance to market (km)	14.407*	0.491	12.904*	0.342	12.131	0.528	11.719	0.363

(*Continued*)

Table 21.1 (Continued)

Category	*Continuous suppliers*		*Late entrants*		*Discontinued suppliers*		*Non-suppliers*	
	Mean	*Standard deviation*	*Mean*	*Standard deviation*	*Mean*	*Standard deviation*	*Mean*	*Standard deviation*
Distance to ABM CC (km)	11.244*	0.546	9.744*	0.362	8.468*	0.549	16.542	0.664
Non-farm employment (D)	0.133	NA	0.072	NA	0.103	NA	0.079	NA
Possess cell phone (D)	0.844*	NA	0.784	NA	0.779	NA	0.769	NA
Perception of price difference between CC and spot market	3.411*	0.531	2.999*	0.262	—0.054*	0.377	—0.476	0.155
Perception of percentage of produce rejected (%)	9.644*	0.737	9.425*	0.431	10.765	0.817	10.679	0.233
Percentage of produce supplied to CC	56.765*	3.338	47.505*	1.837	43.456*	3.074		
Percentage change in the area allocated to vegetable area	0.373*	0.103	0.292	0.045	0.278	0.063	0.310	0.048

Source: Primary field survey in the Pune District, 2011–2012.

Note: * Statistically significant at least up to the 10% level in comparison with non-suppliers.

was significantly higher than non-suppliers and discontinued suppliers. As far as pre-participation landholdings (2005–2006) are concerned, the continuous suppliers, late entrants and discontinued suppliers had significantly higher landholdings than non-suppliers had. The average years of relationship with traders are lower for the continuous suppliers and late entrants than for the non-suppliers and are substantially different from the non-suppliers' years of relationships.

All the spatial characteristics related to accessibility and potential for horticulture crop production show that suppliers differ significantly from non-suppliers. One interesting fact is that the continuous suppliers and late entrants were significantly farther from the spot market than non-suppliers were. Other geographical characteristics such as well depth are significantly higher for late entrants and lower for discontinued suppliers; distance to ABM's CC is significantly lower for all three categories of suppliers; distance to the highway is significantly lower for continuous and discontinued suppliers but significantly higher for late entrants. On average, continuous suppliers, late enterants and discontinued suppliers perceived that the ABM CC paid higher prices than the spot market, a perception that was significant compared to non-suppliers. All the categories of suppliers observed high rates of rejection, at 9.4% and higher. The average percentage of produce supplied to ABM's CC and the percentage change in the area allocated to vegetable was highest for the continuous suppliers, at 57% and 37%, respectively, compared to the other categories. In the case of the previously mentioned factors, the continuous suppliers, late entrants and discontinued suppliers were significantly different from non-suppliers.

Estimation methodology

The literature on supply relationships between farmers and supermarket-led supply chain notes that it is hard to disentangle the effect of firms choosing farmers or farmers wanting to participate (Barrett et al., 2011). Even though the ABM CC initially chose farmers, the supplier portfolio was modified over time according to the center's experience and lessons learned from previous periods. Here, the drivers of participation underlying the model are both the farmers self-selecting into the supply chain and the firms choosing farmers.

Several farmers had been supplying produce to the ABM CC since its inception and continued (at least until the year of the survey). These early adopters were introduced by BCS fieldworkers and had participated in the monthly extension service meetings conducted in the first two years of the center's operation. Hence, the farmers know the center's requirements regarding quality and quantity. In 2008, the center moved to the adjacent block, and the majority of farmers from villages near its initial location exited the supply chain due to the distance and the ABM supply chain's low daily requirement (1–2 tonnes per day). There also were late entrants (farmers who entered the ABM supply chain from villages near the new location) and discontinued suppliers (farmers from villages near both locations who, for various reasons, entered and exited the supply chain between 2006 and 2011).

A multinomial logit regression framework was used to model the drivers of participation since all the regressors are case specific. Farmers were asked for their ex-ante impressions of the percentage of income they gained by participating in ABM's collection center. Another variable was constructed by obtaining the knowledge of the percentage of produce that farmers expected to be rejected at the center's gate (before they supplied to the center and the spot market for the year 2010–2011). Since farmers supply a diversity of crops to the center, a common crop was identified. Tomato is popular in the study area, and most of the farmers grow it. For households that did not cultivate tomato for the reference period, it was replaced by cabbage or bottle gourd, as these crops are procured more in quantity than others by the ABM CC. Respondents were asked the following questions and offered the following choice of answers:

> Did you expect to obtain higher net income from ABM CC than the regulated market when you decided to supply to ABM CC? (More, less and same)
> Do you (non-suppliers) expect to obtain higher net income from ABM CC than the regulated market if you had decided to supply to ABM CC? (More, less and same)
> What do you think the percentage of rejection would have been for your produce if you were to sell to CC (for 10 kg)?

A dummy variable was created to capture the perception of the income increase. A farmer perceiving the net gain from the ABM collection center to be at least as much as or more than the net gain from the spot market was given a value of 1 and 0 otherwise.

Estimation results

Table 21.2 presents the estimation results of multinomial logistic regression for drivers of participation. The dependent variable has four categories based on supplier status: continuous suppliers, late entrants, discontinued suppliers and non-suppliers. The base group is non-suppliers; hence, the results are in comparison to them. The regression estimates of factors driving continuous participation in the ABM CC, compared to non-participation, suggest that the participation is scale neutral. According to conventional knowledge, large farmers are the main participants in the supermarket supply chains; however, the results show that small farmers do participate. Even though the firm identified the initial participants, there seems to be no discrimination against small farmers' participation in the ABM supply chain. However, farmers were more likely to continue to participate if they had access to pre-participation assets and irrigation facilities (such as farm equipment, drip irrigation, cell phones and canal irrigation). These findings are consistent with the case studies on Ghana, India and Nicaragua discussed in Barrett et al. (2011), which found that, contrary to the general notion, landholdings do not influence inclusion in the supply chain. This shows that resources are essential for producing good-quality produce and that the lack of such resources prevents farmers from sustaining their participation in the ABM CC. At the same time, continuous suppliers, late entrants and discontinued suppliers were more likely than non-suppliers to have ex-ante perceptions about income gains, and continuous suppliers were more likely to have fewer years of relationships with a reliable trader or commission agent than non-suppliers. This result is more relevant as FDI has been

Table 21.2 Multinomial logit regression results for participation in ABM supply chain

Variables	*Continuous suppliers*		*Late entrants*		*Discontinued suppliers*	
	Coefficients	*Robust standard errors*	*Coefficients*	*Robust standard errors*	*Coefficients*	*Robust standard errors*
Landholdings in 2005 (acres)	−0.01	0.057	0.039	0.053	0.014	0.055
Age of the head of the household (years)	−0.011	0.022	0.004	0.015	−0.045**	0.02
Household size	−0.062	0.077	0.064	0.051	−0.128*	0.072
Social group (D)	0.297	0.366	−0.315*	0.188	3.866***	0.718
Farm asset index (2006)	0.536**	0.225	−0.014	0.147	0.162	0.164
Household asset index (2006)	0.329	0.222	0.044	0.075	0.128	0.097
Education of household head completed (years)	−0.218	0.414	0.169	0.295	−0.529	0.392
Member of a voluntary organization (D)	0.427	0.702	−0.133	0.562	0.387	0.689
Drip irrigation in 2006 (D)	1.470**	0.569	−0.242	0.452	0.113	0.61
Perception about income increase (D)	17.822***	1.153	17.308***	0.24	17.450***	0.333
Percentage of produce rejected (%)	−0.051	0.042	−0.091***	0.028	0.049*	0.029
Possession of cell phone in 2006 (D)	1.247**	0.521	0.629**	0.304	0.915**	0.405
Relationship with a trader (years)	−0.804*	0.467	−0.279	0.328	0.377	0.464
Mean well depth (log m)	−3.081**	1.509	−1.881**	0.762	−5.945***	1.952
Distance to supermarket CC in 2011 (log km)	−0.647	0.628	−1.437**	0.577	−0.464	0.352
Distance to supermarket CC in 2007 (log km)	−0.009	0.264	0.13	0.193	−0.425*	0.23
Distance to highway (log km)	−0.253	0.197	−0.424***	0.144	−0.079	0.185
Distance to market (log km)	2.227**	1.019	2.780***	0.95	−0.388	0.526
Access to canal irrigation in 2006 (D)	0.896*	0.521	1.192***	0.352	1.269***	0.424
Constant	−13.96***	4.666	−14.878***	2.79	−14.838***	3.998
Wald chi^2	8688.63					
p-value	0.00					
R^2	0.352					

liberalized in the retail sector. Even though the study area has experienced a mushrooming of firm–farm relationships and collection centers of various other supermarkets, it seems that the organized retailers cannot easily break the bond between farmers and traders or commission agents. Since supermarkets procure only a fraction of farmers' produce and procure only produce of first-grade quality, farmers still depend on traders and commission agents to market the rest of their produce in the regulated markets. Factors such as mean well depth, which is a proxy for the underground water table and the distance of a farmer's field from the regulated market are significant predictors of a particular community being included in the supply chain, similar to the findings of Michelson (2013).

Factors such as ex-ante possession of cell phones and canal irrigation influence the late entrants positively. Positive ex-ante perception about income gains and lower rejection rates are associated with new entrants. Interestingly, farmers belonging to a disadvantaged social group (SC/ST) are more likely to enter the supply chain late. This reveals that social group has a bearing on participation in the supply chain in the given context. All community characteristics are predictors of a community's inclusion in the procurement basin of ABM's supply chain. Distance to the supermarket collection center in 2011 is significant; this shows that farmers near the ABM CC new location are more likely to be late entrants than farmers farther from the new location.

The regression estimates of drivers of quitting the ABM CC supply chain indicate that young farmers with small families have a high propensity to drop out. Farmers belonging to a disadvantaged social group (SC or ST) are more likely than farmers in other social groups to discontinue their supply relationship with the collection center. More interestingly, conditional on ex-ante assets and social group, farmers who perceive the center's quality standards as strict and its rejection rates as high are more likely than those who do not share those perceptions to exit the supply chain. Farmers located away from the center's new location are more likely than those located closer to the new location to discontinue their relationship.

These results reflect the qualitative evidence, presented in Table 21.3, that the majority of the farmers involuntarily exited their relationship with the ABM's CC because of their inability to comply with quality standards. Nearly 80% of the discontinued suppliers in this study were smallholders, who dropped out because of high rejection rates. Almost 43% reported that higher rejection rates pushed them to quit the ABM center's supply chain. Others complained that the ABM center arbitrarily rejected more produce when the spot market prices crashed. Medium-sized landholders and large landholders said they discontinued their participation due to the low quantity of procurement. Other factors were distance, high labor costs due to the labor shortage and delays in weekly payments. These findings are consistent with Narayanan (2013), Ashraf et al. (2009) and Fold and Gough (2008). These results have implications for public policy, as the supply chain's inclusion of small farmers may not guarantee their sustained participation.

Table 21.3 Self-reported reasons to exit the ABM supply chain

Reasons for discontinuing	*Percentage*
High rate of rejection	42.65
Loss of income	18.4
Distance to CC	8.59
Low quantity of procurement	8.31
Weekly payments	7.35
Labour shortage hence high labour cost	7.35
Firm refused to contract me	5.88
Stopped growing horticulture crop	1.47

Source: Primary field survey in the Pune District, 2011–2012.

Conclusion and policy implications

There are sufficient reasons to regard the ABM CC supply chain as inclusive of small farmers. However, the center seems to have obscure features that determine who can sustain the relationship. Even though there is no discrimination of farmers based on land size, the lack of other productive resources including access to pre-participation assets—cell phone, irrigation and farm assets—forces small farmers to involuntarily discontinue their participation. These results are similar to the findings of other studies (Narayanan, 2013; Bellemare, 2012). Further, farmers' perception of rejection rates shows that non-suppliers are oriented against supplying to the ABM center, and discontinued suppliers tend to associate supplying to the center with increased risk factors and eventually dropout. Another interesting finding is that farmers' strong interpersonal relationships with traditional traders have an adverse influence on sustaining a supplier relationship with the ABM center, as farmers depend on the traders to market a significant share of their produce. Hence dynamic elements of supply relationships need to be identified and understood for effective policymaking.

Saving on transactions costs is one of the critical drivers of farmers' choice of a marketing channel for their produce. In their current form, APMC spot markets are fraught with inefficiencies due to numerous intermediaries, which increases farmers' transaction costs. Historically, producers were denied their choice of marketing channel, but the availability of multiple markets in the production regions would increase diversity in the marketing channels, which would encourage agribusiness firms and supermarkets to offer farmers competitive prices. However, side selling is widely present, and sustaining such arrangements is often questionable. Like Sulaiman et al. (2010), this paper considers that when informal procurement operations grow, formal contracts and the state's proactive involvement in dispute resolution are imperative. Investment in infrastructure development to reduce transportation costs, by introducing subsidized means of transport in the production centers, would be particularly useful. State extension services also need to be restructured to upgrade poor farmers' capacity. The farmers should be informed about post-harvest handling and sorting to realize remunerative prices in both traditional and supermarket channels. These can help prevent farmers from involuntarily dropping out of the modern supply chains.

Another significant finding is that the firms chose a procurement region based on their preference for geographies with desirable spatial characteristics that can minimize their transaction cost. Establishing food parks, food cluster developments and agricultural export zones within production regions might deepen the trends in farmers' participation in collection centers and promote a competitive environment, limiting any room for farmer exploitation. These initiatives would encourage farmers to grow the right varieties for food processing. There is a dire need for a more focused policy to develop infrastructure and improve the food supply chain. As in India, the food supply chain has been adversely affected by the lockdowns and other restrictions due to the outbreak of COVID-19. Maintaining efficient supply chain operations is crucial to food and nutritional security. Thus there is a need to provide farmers with continued market access at all times and, more specifically, at a time of crisis like the COVID-19 pandemic. This can be done through a mix of private markets and government procurement, and APMCs.

Note

1 The views and opinions expressed in this chapter are those of the authors and do not necessarily represent the views of the Reserve Bank of India or any other institutions with which the authors may be affiliated. The institution to which they belong is not accountable for the views or use of information in this paper.

References

Ashraf, N., Gine, X. and Karlan, D. S. (2009). "Finding missing markets (and a disturbing epilogue): Evidence from an export crop adoption and marketing intervention in Kenya," *American Journal of Agricultural Economics*, 91(4), 973–990.

Barrett, C. B., Bachke, M. E., Bellemare, M. F., Michelson, H. C., Narayanan, S. and Walker, T. F. (2011). "Smallholder participation in contract farming: Comparative evidence from five countries," *World Development*, 52(4), 64–71.

Bellemare, M. (2012). "As you sow, so shall you reap: The welfare impacts of contract farming," *World Development*, 40(7), 1418–1434.

Bivings, L. and Runsten, D. (1992). "Potential competitiveness of the Mexican processed vegetable and strawberry industries," Report prepared for the Ministry of Agriculture, Fisheries and Food, British Columbia, Canada.

Boselie, D., Henson, S. and Weatherspoon, D. (2003). "Supermarket procurement practices in developing countries: Redefining the roles of the public and private sectors," *American Journal of Agricultural Economics*, 85(5), 1155–1161.

Da Silva, C. (2005). "The growing role of contract farming in agri-food systems development: Drivers, theory and practice," Agricultural Management, Marketing and Finance Service, Food and Agriculture Organisation, Rome.

DIPP (2010). "Discussion paper on FDI in multi-brand retail trading," Department of Industrial Policy and Promotion, Ministry of Commerce, Government of India. Available at http://www.dipp.nic.in accessed on 10 November 2012.

DIPP (2015). "Consolidated FDI policy circular of 2015," Department of Industrial Policy and Promotion, Ministry of Commerce, Government of India. Available at http://www.dipp.nic.in.

Eaton, C. and Shepherd, A. (2001). "Contract farming: Partnerships for growth," Agricultural Services Bulletin, Food and Agriculture Organization of the United Nations, Rome.

Echanove, F. and Steffen, C. (2005). "Agribusiness and farmers in Mexico: The importance of contractual relations," *The Geographical Journal*, 171, 166–177.

Fold, N. and Gough, K. V. (2008). "From smallholders to trans-nationals: The impact of changing consumer preferences in the EU on Ghana's pineapple sector," *Geoforum*, 39, 1687–1697.

Glover, D. J. (1987). "Increasing the benefits to smallholders from contract farming: Problems for farmers' organizations and policy makers," *World Development*, 15(4), 441–448.

Glover, D. and Kusterer, K. (1990). *Small Farmers, Big Business: Contract Farming and Rural Development*. International Political Economy Series. St. Martin's Press, New York.

Guo, H. and Jolly, R. W. (2008). "Contractual arrangements and enforcement in transition agriculture: Theory and evidence from China," *Food Policy*, 33(6), 570–575.

Hernandez, R., Reardon, T. and Berdegue, J. (2007). "Supermarkets, wholesalers, and tomato growers in Guatemala," *Agricultural Economics*, 36, 281–290.

Key, N. and Runsten, D. (1999). "Contract farming, smallholders, and rural development in Latin America: The organization of agroprocessing firms and the scale of outgrower production," *World Development*, 27, 381–401.

Mannon, S. E. (2005). "Risk takers, risk makers: Small farmers and non-traditional agro-exports in Kenya and Costa Rica," *Human Organization*, 64, 16–27.

Michelson, H. (2013). "Small farmers, NGOs, and a Walmart world: Welfare effects of supermarkets operating in Nicaragua," *American Journal of Agricultural Economics*, 95(3), 628–649.

Minot, N. (1986). "Contract farming and its effect on small farmers in less developed countries," *Food Security International Development Working Papers 54740*, Michigan State University, Department of Agricultural, Food, and Resource Economics. Available at https://ideas.repec.org/p/ags/midiwp/54740.html accessed on 6 April 2020.

Minot, N. (2008). "Contract farming in developing countries: Patterns, impact, and policy implications," In Pinstrup-Andersen, P. and Cheng, F. (eds.), *Food Policy for Developing Countries: Case Studies*, 13 pp., Cornell University Press, Ithaca, NY.

Miyata, S., Minot, N. and Hu, D. (2009). "Impact of contract farming on income: Linking small farmers, packers, and supermarkets in China," *World Development*, 37, 1781–1790.

Narayanan, S. (2012). "Safe gambles? Farmer perceptions of transactional certainty and risk-return trade-offs in contract farming schemes in Southern India," *Working paper No. 2012–021*, Indira Gandhi Institute of Development Research, Mumbai. Available at www.igidr.ac.in/pdf/publication/WP-2012-021.pdf accessed on 6 April 2020.

Narayanan, S. (2013). "Smallholder attrition in contract farming schemes in India: Extent, causes and concerns," *Food Chain*, 3(3), 155–170.

Narayanan, S. (2014). "Geography matters: Evidence and implications of spatial selection in contract farming schemes in Southern India," World Scientific Book Chapters, In Christy, Ralph D., da Silva, Carlos A., Mhlanga, Nomathemba and Mabaya, Edward (eds.), *Innovative Institutions, Public Policies, and Private Strategies for Agro-Enterprise Development*, chapter 4, pp. 87–111, World Scientific Publishing Co. Pte. Ltd, Singapore.

Neven, D., Odera, M. M., Reardon, T. and Wang, H. (2009). "Kenyan supermarkets, emerging middle-class horticultural farmers, and employment impacts on the rural poor," *World Development*, 37, 1802–1811.

Ramaswami, B., Birthal, P. S. and Joshi, P. K. (2005). "Efficiency and distribution in contract farming: The case of Indian poultry growers," Discussion Papers, Indian Statistical Institute, Planning Unit, New Delhi.

Rao, C. and Dev, S. M. (2005). "Food processing and contract farming in Andhra Pradesh: A small farmer perspective," Review of agriculture, *Economic and Political Weekly*, 40(26), 2705–2713.

Reardon, T., Barrett, C. B., Berdegue, J. A. and Swinnen, J. F. M. (2009). "Agrifood industry transformation and small farmers in developing countries," *World Development*, 37, 1717–1727.

Runsten, D. and Key, N. (1996). "Contract farming in developing countries: Theoretical aspects and analysis of some Mexican cases," Report prepared for the United Nations Economic Commission for Latin America and the Caribbean, Santiago, Chile.

Singh, S. (2002). "Contracting out solutions: Political economy of contract farming in the Indian Punjab," *World Development*, 30(9), 1621–1638.

Sulaiman, V. R., Kalaivani, N. J. and Handoo, J. (2010). "Organised retailing of fresh fruits and vegetables: Is it really helping producers?" *Working Paper: 2010–01*, Centre for Research on Innovation and Science Policy (CRISP), Hyderabad.

Trebbin, A. and Franz, M. (2010). "Exclusivity of private governance structures in agrofood networks: Bayer and the food retailing and processing sector in India," *Environment and Planning*, 42, 2043–2057.

Wang, H., Dong, X., Rozelle, S., Huang, J. and Reardon, T. (2009). "Producing and procuring horticultural crops with Chinese characteristics: The case of Northern China," *World Development*, 37, 1791–1801.

Warning, M. and Key, N. (2002). "The social performance and distributional consequences of contract farming: An equilibrium analysis of the Arachide de Bouche program in Senegal," *World Development*, 30, 255–263.

Zamora, M. (2004). *The Rapid Expansion of Supermarkets in Ecuador and Its Effects on Dairy and Potato Production Chains*, Mimeo.

Index

Note: Page numbers in italic indicate a figure and page numbers in bold indicate a table on the corresponding page.

For Product Safety Concerns and Information please contact our EU
representative GPSR@taylorandfrancis.com
Taylor & Francis Verlag GmbH, Kaufingerstraße 24, 80331 München, Germany

www.ingramcontent.com/pod-product-compliance
Lightning Source LLC
LaVergne TN
LVHW021115300926
849160LV00010B/749

* 9 7 8 0 3 6 7 6 9 6 3 3 7 *